# A HISTORY
OF
# THE AMERICAN BAR

# A HISTORY

OF

# THE AMERICAN BAR

BY

CHARLES WARREN

"All men at all times and in all places do stand in need of Justice, and of Law, which is the rule of Justice, and of the interpreters and Ministers of the Law, which give life and motion unto Justice."

*Preface Dedicatory* to Sir John Davies' *Reports* (1615).

NEW YORK

Howard Fertig

1966

HOWARD FERTIG, INC. EDITION 1966
Published by arrangement with Little, Brown
and Company (Inc.).



Library of Congress Catalog Card Number: 66-24357

PRINTED IN THE UNITED STATES OF AMERICA
BY NOBLE OFFSET PRINTERS, INC.

# PREFACE

THIS book is not a law book for those who wish to study law. It is an historical sketch for those who wish to know something about the men who have composed the American Bar of the past, and about the influences which produced the great American lawyers.

Part of the material in this book has been previously published in a work which had a limited circulation among subscribers interested in the history of a particular law school. I have now revised, corrected and amplified this material, in order to present it in such form as may be of interest and of value to American lawyers in general.

So far as I know, no effort has ever hitherto been made to bring together from the innumerable scattered sources the scanty information existing in relation to the early Colonial Bars in this country. Part One of this book, therefore, is an attempt to show the legal conditions in each of the various American Colonies during the Seventeenth and Eighteenth Centuries and prior to the Revolutionary War. In each, the status of the Common Law as applied by the courts is described; the methods of appointment and composition of the courts are set forth; and an account of the leading lawyers, together with brief biographical data, is given. The legislation regarding the legal profession in each Colony is stated in some detail. A chapter is devoted to a thorough description of the materials for, and methods of, a lawyer's education in those early days; and another chapter gives an account of the Colonial Bar Associations and of the

Colonial lawyers who received their education or who became barristers in the Inns of Court in London.

In order to correlate the progress of the legal profession in England and America, two chapters are concerned with a description of the state of the law, the law books and reports, the lawyers and the courts of England in the Seventeenth and Eighteenth Centuries, — thus bringing into view contemporaneous legal conditions in the two countries.

Part Two of this book portrays the growth of the American Bar from the foundation of the United States Supreme Court to the opening of the Civil War. One chapter describes the curious and interesting widespread prejudice against lawyers as a class and against the Common Law as a relic of English dominion, which existed from 1786 until after 1800. Three chapters are devoted to the composition of the Bar of the United States Supreme Court during the three eras between 1789 and 1860, — the first era ending with the close of the War of 1812 in 1815; the second ending with the zenith year of the reign of Chief Justice Marshall in 1830; and the third covering Chief Justice Taney's career and ending with the year 1860. In these chapters, the leading cases argued before the Court from year to year are taken up and described, not as mere cases deciding points of law, but as striking events in legal history. Particular attention is given to the great lawyers who acted as counsel in the various cases, to the manner of the argument, and to the effect produced by the decisions upon the surrounding conditions of the times, economic, social and legal.

Much resort has been had to contemporary letters and newspapers in depicting the actual part that each case played in its own time, and the actual weight which the eminent counsel had upon the decisions of the Court.

Care has been taken to give in foot-notes the date of birth of all the lawyers of distinction, together with a few other data, such as their college graduation, admittance to practise and appointment to legal official positions, so that the book in this way may serve as a handy reference for short legal biography.[1]

A chapter is devoted to the history of all the early law professorships and law schools from 1784 to 1830.

The rise and development of American law books is shown in two chapters giving practically complete lists of all the most important legal works of this country between 1785 and 1860, with the date of their appearance.

And in order to make plain the influences which developed the American Bar from the small group of men of which it consisted at the beginning of the Nineteenth Century, to the vast and influential body which composed it at the end of the succeeding half century, three chapters have been devoted to the four great factors in the development of the Bar, — the rise and growth of corporation and of railroad law between 1830 and 1860, the expansion of the Common Law to meet the new economic and social conditions arising between 1815 and 1860, and the weighty movement for codification between 1820 and 1860. These three chapters are written from a purely historical point of view, and do not attempt to state legal doctrines as they may be found in law books, but to describe rapidly and graphically the progress of American law as a highly important factor in American history.

CHARLES WARREN.

[1] My authorities for dates are chiefly *Appleton's Cyclopedia of American Biography* (1898); *Biographical Annals of the Civil Government of the United States*, by Charles Lanman (1876); and the various biographies cited in the notes *infra*.

# THE FIRST AMERICAN ADDRESS TO LAWYERS

## By COTTON MATHER, 1710

"It was a Passage in a Speech of an Envoy from His Brittanick Majesty to the Duke of Brandenburgh, twenty years ago: 'A Capacity to Do Good not only gives a Title to it, but also makes the doing of it a Duty.' Ink was too vile a Liquor to Write that Passage; Letters of Gold were too Mean to be the Preservers of it. . . .

"Gentlemen: Your Opportunities to Do Good are such, and so Liberal and Gentlemanly is your Education . . . that Proposals of what you may do cannot but promise themselves an Obliging Reception with you. 'Tis not come to so sad a pass that an Honest Lawyer may, as of old the Honest Publican, require a Statue merely on the Score of Rarity. . . .

"A Lawyer should be a Scholar, but, Sirs, when you are called upon to be wise, the main Intention is that you may be wise to do Good. . . . A Lawyer that is a Knave deserves Death, more than a Band of Robbers; for he profanes the Sanctuary of the Distressed and Betrayes the Liberties of the People. To ward off such a Censure, a Lawyer must shun all those Indirect Ways of making Hast to be Rich, in which a man cannot be Innocent; such ways as provoked the Father of Sir Matthew Hale to give over the Practice of the Law, because of the Extreme Difficulty to preserve a Good Conscience in it.

"Sirs, be prevailed withal to keep constantly a Court of Chancery in your own Breast. . . . This Piety must Operate very particularly in the Pleading of Causes. You will abhor, Sir, to appear in a Dirty Cause. If you discern that your Client has an Unjust Cause, you will faithfully advise him of it. You will be Sincerely desirous that Truth and Justice may take place. You will speak nothing which shall be to the Prejudice of Either. You will abominate the use of all unfair Arts to Confound Evidence, to Browbeat Testimonies, to Suppress what may give Light in the Case. . . .

"There has been an old Complaint, That a Good Lawyer seldom is a Good Neighbor. You know how to Confute it, Gentlemen, by making your Skill in the Law, a Blessing to your Neighborhood. You may, Gentlemen, if you please, be a vast Accession to the Felicity of your Countreys. . . . Perhaps you may discover many things yet wanting in the Law; Mischiefs in the Execution and Application of the Laws, which ought to be better provided against; Mischiefs annoying of Mankind, against which no Laws are yet provided. The Reformation of the Law, and more Law for the Reformation of the World is what is mightily called for."

[*Bonifacius — An Essay upon the Good that is to be Devised and Designed by those who Desire to Answer the Great End of Life and to Do Good while they Live. A Book offered first in General unto all Christians in a Personal Capacity, or in a Relative; then more particularly unto Magistrates, unto Ministers, unto Physicians, unto Lawyers, unto Scholemasters, unto Wealthy Gentlemen, unto several Sorts of Officers, unto Churches, and unto all Societies of a Religious Character and Intention, with Humble Proposals, of Unexceptionable Methods to Do Good in the World. — By Cotton Mather* (*Boston, 1710*).]

# CONTENTS

## PART I

### COLONIAL BAR

PAGE

PREFACE . . . . . . . . . . . . . . . . . . v

THE FIRST AMERICAN ADDRESS TO LAWYERS . . . . . ix

INTRODUCTORY

LAW WITHOUT LAWYERS . . . . . . . . . . 3

CHAPTER

I ENGLISH LAW, LAW BOOKS AND LAWYERS IN THE SEVENTEENTH CENTURY . . . . . . . . . 19

II THE COLONIAL BAR OF VIRGINIA AND MARYLAND . . 39

Virginia . . . . . . . . . . . . . . . . 39

Maryland . . . . . . . . . . . . . . . . 49

III COLONIAL MASSACHUSETTS BAR . . . . . . . . 59

IV COLONIAL NEW YORK, PENNSYLVANIA AND NEW JERSEY BAR . . . . . . . . . . . . . . . . 90

New York . . . . . . . . . . . . . . . 90

Pennsylvania . . . . . . . . . . . . . . 101

New Jersey . . . . . . . . . . . . . . 111

V THE COLONIAL SOUTHERN BAR . . . . . . . . . 118

South Carolina . . . . . . . . . . . . 118

North Carolina . . . . . . . . . . . . 122

Georgia . . . . . . . . . . . . . . . 125

VI NEW ENGLAND COLONIAL BAR . . . . . . . . . 128

Connecticut . . . . . . . . . . . . . . 128

New Hampshire . . . . . . . . . . . . . 134

Maine . . . . . . . . . . . . . . . . . 139

Rhode Island . . . . . . . . . . . . . . 140

CHAPTER | PAGE

VII The Law and Lawyers in England in the Eighteenth Century . . . . . . . . . . 146

VIII A Colonial Lawyer's Education . . . . . . 157

IX Early American Barristers, and Bar Associations 188

## PART II

### FEDERAL BAR

X Prejudices Against Law and Lawyers . . . . 211

XI The Federal Bar and Law, 1789–1815 . . . . 240

XII Early State Bars of New York and New England 292
New York . . . . . . . . . . . . . . . 292
Massachusetts . . . . . . . . . . . . 304
New Hampshire . . . . . . . . . . . . 319
Vermont . . . . . . . . . . . . . . 321
Connecticut . . . . . . . . . . . . 322

XIII Early American Law Books . . . . . . . . 325

XIV Early Law Professorships and Schools . . . 341

XV The Federal Bar and the Law, 1815–1830 . . 366

XVI The Federal Bar and Law, 1830–1860 . . . . 408

XVII The Progress of the Law, 1830–1860 . . . . 446

XVIII The Rise of Railroad and Corporation Law . . 475

XIX The Era of Codes, 1820–1860 . . . . . . . 508

XX American Law Books, 1815–1910 . . . . . . 540

Appendix . . . . . . . . . . . . . . . 563

Index . . . . . . . . . . . . . . . . 567

# A HISTORY
OF
# THE AMERICAN BAR

# PART ONE

## COLONIAL BAR

# A HISTORY OF THE AMERICAN BAR

## INTRODUCTORY

### LAW WITHOUT LAWYERS

NOTWITHSTANDING the various American Colonies were founded separately, each in its own peculiar mode, and were maintained as separate governments, having slight connection with each other in administration and little intercommunication in trade or otherwise until the early years of the Eighteenth Century, their usages and their institutions developed on closely parallel lines. In nothing is this more marked than in the history of their judicial organizations and of the constitution of their legal Bars.

In all the Colonies, the General Assembly or Legislature at first constituted the sole court of law; later, the Governor and his Deputies or Assistants; and in many Colonies it was not until half a century after settlement that separate and independent courts were instituted. In all the Colonies, the courts were composed of laymen, with the possible exception of the Chief Justice. It was not until the era of the War of the Revolution that it was deemed necessary or even advisable to have judges learned in the law. In most of the Colonies, the Chief Justice, and through him the courts, were subject in a great degree to the control of the

Royal Governors. In none of the Colonies were there any published reports of decided cases, prior to the Revolution.

In all of the Colonies, the question of whether the Common Law was to be accepted as the basis of the Colonial Law was a live issue. Some Colonial Legislatures and courts very early accepted the Common Law as binding. In others, the right of the Colony to institute or adopt the Common Law, or such parts of it as they saw fit, was earnestly maintained; and it cannot be said that it was generally accepted as binding until many years after the close of the Seventeenth Century. Nothing, however, in the early legal history of the Colonies is more striking than the uniformly low position held in the community by the members of the legal profession, and the slight part which they played in the development of the country until nearly the middle of the Eighteenth Century. In every one of the Colonies, practically throughout the Seventeenth Century, a lawyer or attorney was a character of disrepute and of suspicion, of whose standing or power in the community the ruling class, whether it was the clergy as in New England, or the merchants as in New York, Maryland and Virginia, or the Quakers as in Pennsylvania, was extremely jealous. In many of the Colonies, persons acting as attorneys were forbidden to receive any fee; in some, all paid attorneys were barred from the courts; in all, they were subjected to the most rigid restrictions as to fees and procedure.[1]

It is perhaps fair, however, in reviewing the constant legislation against attorneys, to bear in mind that the word "attorney," as used in early records of Colonial cases and statutes, did not imply necessarily a man bred to the law or who made its practise an exclusive employment. These

[1] For a work treating of lawyers in the various Colonies, see *The Lawyers' Official Oath and Office*, by Josiah H. Benton (1909).

"attorneys" were very largely traders, factors, land speculators and laymen of clever penmanship and easy volubility, whom parties employed to appear and talk for them in the courts. The few persons who acted as professional attorneys were at first mostly pettifoggers, or minor court officers such as deputy sheriffs, clerks and justices, who stirred up litigation for the sake of the petty court fees. This latter practise became such an evil that in most of the Colonies statutes were passed prohibiting such persons acting as attorneys.

Nevertheless, after making due allowance for the differences in the use of the word "attorney," the fact remains that the development of the law as a profession and of lawyers as an influential class in the community was a matter of remarkably slow growth in the American Colonies. The responsibility for this condition may be attributed to seven different factors, varying in weight of influence in each Colony, all of which will be clearly shown, as the history of each Colonial Bar is separately described in this book. These factors may be summed up as follows.

In the first place, law as a science was in so rigid a condition that it failed to touch the popular life. The Common Law was still feudal and tyrannical. The people felt the restrictions it imposed, and knew little of the liberties it guaranteed. As has been well said:

"It is not altogether strange that our law at that time should seem to a plain Puritan to be a dark and knavish business; for it was still heavily encumbered with the formalism of the Middle Ages. It was, indeed, already, like Milton's lion, 'pawing to get free its hinder parts;' and there was a sort of truth in Coke's dithyrambic praise of it, then but recently published, that 'reason is the life of the law — nay, the common law itself is nothing else but reason;' but it was the truth of prophecy, and not the truth of fact. The law also was then mainly hidden away from laymen and wrapped in a foreign tongue; and it was taught at the Inns of Court in the rudest way — '*hanc rigidam Minervam*,' said Sir Henry Spelman, a contemporary of our founders, '*ferreis amplexibus coercendam*.' 'My mother,' said Spelman, 'sent me to London to begin upon our law' (1570), '*Cujus vestibulum salutassem reperissemque linguam peregrinam, dialectum barbarum, methodum inconcinnam, molem non ingentem solum sed perpetuis humeris sustinendam, excidit mihi (fateor) animus*.' "[1]

In the second place, lawyers, as the instruments through which the subtleties and iniquities of the Common Law were enforced, were highly unpopular as a class in England. John Milton expressed the general low opinion of the aims of the profession thus:

"Most men are allured to the trade of law, grounding their purposes not on the prudent and heavenly contemplation of justice and equity which was never taught them, but on the promising and pleasing thoughts of litigious terms, fat contentions and flowing fees."

The following sentiments expressed in an anonymous book published in England in 1677, entitled *A Discourse on The Rise and Power of Parliament*, were echoed in the Colonies:

There was Law before Lawyers; there was a time when the Common Customs of the land were sufficient to secure Meum and Tuum. What has made it since so difficult? Nothing but the Comments of Lawyers confounding the Text and writhing the Laws, like a Nose of Wax, to what Figure best serves their purpose.

And the lawyer's reputation in London may be estimated to some extent by the titles of numerous tracts printed in the Seventeenth Century, such as the following: *The Downfall*

[1] Speech of James B. Thayer at the 250th Commemoration of Harvard College, Nov. 5, 1886.

*of Unjust Lawyers; Doomsday Drawing Near with Thunder and Lightning for Lawyers* (1645); *A Rod for Lawyers Who are Hereby declared Robbers and Deceivers of the Nation; Essay Wherein is Described the Lawyers, Smugglers and Officers Frauds* (1659). In the minds of many Englishmen, moreover, the lawyer was synonymous with the cringing Attorneys-General and Solicitors-General of the Crown and the arbitrary Justices of the King's Court, all bent on the conviction of those who opposed the King's prerogatives, and twisting the law to secure convictions.

The third impediment in a lawyer's path was the scanty materials at hand in the Colonies for the study of law, the scarcity of printed law books and reports, and the lack of schools of law. Even in England at the end of the Seventeenth Century, hardly more than seventy law books had been published, of which not more than ten or fifteen were known in the Colonies, and less than one hundred volumes of law reports, of which not over thirty were in use in the Colonies.

In the fourth place, lawyers were obliged to face the hostility of religious elements in the community. In Pennsylvania, the Quakers were opposed to anything of a litigious tendency. In New England, the clergy for a long time maintained a complete supremacy in the magistracy and in the courts. "During the period from 1620 to 1692," said a writer in the *North American Review*, in 1829, "no trace can be found of law as a science or profession. The clergy possessed, as in England, much of the legal knowledge of the community."[1] It was to their clergymen that the colonists looked to guide their new governments, and in their clergymen, they believed, lay all that was necessary and proper for their lawful and righteous govern-

[1] See review of *American Jurist*, Vol. I, in *North American Review*, Vol. XXIX (Oct. 1829).

ment. It followed, therefore, that the "Word of God" played a greater part in the progress and practise of the law than the words of Bracton, Littleton or Coke. Where such was the condition, there was more need of clever clergymen than of trained lawyers.

Fifth, in New York, Maryland and Virginia, there was extreme jealousy felt by the merchants and wealthy landowners and planters at the exercise of power by any other class in the community.

Sixth, the participation and interference of the Royal Governors in the judicial system of the Colonies nullified the influence of a trained Bar. As early as 1747, Dr. W. Douglass, in his *Summary of the Present State of the British Settlements in North America*, wrote that "it is said that a Governor and such of the council as he thinks proper to consult with, dispense with such provincial laws as are troublesome or stand in their way of procedure of their court of equity so called." In New York, a Royal Governor found it necessary to remove a Chief Justice who failed to decide in his favor, in order "to discourage advocates of Boston principles." In Maryland, the Bar was at constant war with the Governor in order to preserve the legal rights of the Colony from the arbitrary dictates and proclamations of the executive. In South Carolina, the lawyers were forced to petition the proprietary in complaint of the Governor holding all the judicial offices.[1]

Lastly, such was the ignorance and lack of legal education of the judges themselves that their courts offered little opportunity for the development of a trained and able Bar.

In 1764, Thomas Pownall, "late Gov. Capt. Gen. Commander in Chief and Vice-Admiral of His Majesty's Prov-

[1] See especially *The Provincial Governor*, Chap. VII, by Evarts B. Greene (1898).

inces, Massachusetts Bay and South Carolina, and then Governor of New Jersey," wrote:[1]

"I cannot in one view better describe the defects of the provincial courts in these infant governments than by that very description which my Lord Chief Justice Hale gives of our County Courts in the infancy of our own government; wherein he mentions, First, the ignorance of the judges, who were the freeholders of the county. Secondly, that these various courts bred variety of law, especially in the several counties; for, the decisions or judgments being made by divers courts and several independent judges and judiciaries who had no common interest amongst them in their several judicatories, thereby in process of time every several county would have several laws, customs, rules and forms of proceedings. Upon the first article of this parallel it would be no dishonour to many gentlemen sitting on the benches of the courts of law in the Colonies to say that they are not and cannot be expected to be lawyers or learned in the law."

And Henry W. DeSaussure, the great lawyer and Chancellor of South Carolina, in the preface to his *Chancery Reports*, in 1817, described the early Colonial judges as follows:

"The emigrants brought with them a deep abhorrence of the intolerance and tyranny of those princes [Charles I, Charles II, James II]; and especially of the great abuses prevailing in the courts of justice. And they partook of the general joy in the prodigious securities obtained in the subsequent reigns for civil and political liberty; among which, the establishment of the independence of the judges formed a principal feature. Their attachment to these principles was further increased by the mischiefs resulting from the incautious appointments made by the British government, in many instances, of very inferior men to preside in the courts of justice of the Colonies, who did no

[1] *The Administration of the British Colonies*, by Thomas Pownall (1764).

honour to the mother country, and whose irregularities and improper conduct contributed in a considerable degree to weaken the attachment of the Colonies to the government of Great Britain."

The development of the American lawyer was thus retarded by the influence of all these factors which, however, varied in degree of effect in each separate Colony. In New England, however, the lack of educated lawyers in the Seventeenth Century is especially attributable to still another cause — the absence of any respect for, or binding authority of, the English Common Law.[1] Although it has so frequently been announced in judicial decisions that,

"Our ancestors when they came into this new world claimed the Common Law as their birthright and brought it with them, except such parts as were judged inapplicable to their new state and condition — the Common Law of their native country as it was amended or altered by English statutes in force at the time of their immigration,"[2]

it was never historically true that either in Massachusetts, Connecticut or Rhode Island did the colonists recognize the English Common Law as binding *ipso facto*. So far from being proud of it "as their birthright," they were, in fact, decidedly anxious to escape from it and from the ideas connected with it in their mind.

The Common Law was neither popular nor a source of pride at this time, even in England.[3] It was a period when

[1] See especially *English Common Law in The Early American Colonies*, by Paul F. Reinsch (1899).

[2] Parsons, C. J., in *Commonwealth* v. *Knowlton*, 2 Mass. p. 354 (1807). See Shaw, C. J., in *Young* v. *Emery*, 16 Pick. p. 110 (1833). And see Judge Story in his *Commentaries on the Constitution*, and in *Van Ness* v. *Pacard*, 2 Peters, 144 (1829).

[3] Signs of the dissatisfaction with the state of the law in England may be seen from the flood of pamphlets demanding its reform, such as: *Reformation Proceedings at Law*, by Thomas Felds in 1645; *Survey of the English Laws, their Unsoundness and Corruption Discovered*, by F. W. in 1652; *Eng-*

Sir Edward Coke had been removed as Chief Justice of King's Bench by James I, in 1616. The judges held office only at the King's pleasure. The Star Chamber Court had flourished under Charles I. The Chancellors were endeavoring to mitigate some of the harshness and irrationality and technicality of the Common Law courts. The old feudal tenures were extant, with all their follies and burdens.

The fact is, that the English Common Law, from 1620 to 1700, was in force in New England only so far as it was specifically adopted by statute — or so far as the colonists, by custom, had assented to its binding force.

Thus, in a case in Massachusetts, as late as 1687, the defendant pleaded that the Magna Charta of England and the statute law, "secure the subjects' properties and estates .... To which was replied by one of the Judges, the rest by silence assenting, 'We must not think the laws of England follow us to the ends of the earth or whither we went.' "[1]

Chief Justice Atwood, who visited Boston in 1700, in his report to the Lords of Trade, states that he had "publicly exposed the argument of one of the Boston clergy that they were not bound in conscience to obey the laws of England;"[2] and he notes that the methods of the courts were "abhorent from the Laws of England and all other nations."

John Adams in his *Novanglus* said, even in 1774:

"How then do we New Englanders derive our laws. I say not from Parliament, not from the Common Law; but

*land's Balme, or Proposals by way of Grievance and Remedy towards the Regulation of Law and Better Administration of Justice*, by William Sheppard in 1657; *Certain Proposals for Regulating the Law*, by John Shepheard in 1651; *Perspicuous Compendium of Several Irregularities and Abuses in Present Practice of Common Laws of England*, by D. W., in 1656; Warr's *The Corruption and Deficiency of the Laws of England;* Jones' *An Experimental Essay touching the Reformation of the Laws of England.*

[1] *Judicial History of Massachusetts*, by Emory Washburn, p. 106.

[2] *Documents relative to Colonial History of New York*, Vol. IV, p. 929.

from the law of nature and the compact made with the King in our charter, our ancestors were entitled to the Common Law of England when they emigrated; that is to say to as much of it as they pleased to adopt and no more. They were not bound or obliged to submit to it unless they chose." [1]

Connecticut was extremely independent of the Common Law; and as Robert Quary reported to the Board of Trade in England: "The people are of a very turbulent, factious and uneasy temper. I cannot give their character better than by telling your Lordships that they have made a body of laws for their government which are printed; the first of which is that no law of England shall be in force in their government till made so by act of their own." [2] In the famous case of *Winthrop* v. *Lechmere*, in 1728, the Colony's agent in London was instructed to argue that English Common Law could be binding beyond the sea, only in case it had been accepted by the colonists' own choice. "The Common Law always hath its limits environ'd by the sea." [3]

In fact, Connecticut never adopted the Common Law, even by statute. Its recognition grew up through usage and

[1] *Adams' Life and Works*, Vol. IV, p. 122.

Thomas Jefferson said in a letter to Attorney-General Rodney Sept. 25, 1810, speaking of Levi Lincoln of Massachusetts as a possible successor to Cushing as Chief Justice of the United States Supreme Court: "He is not thought to be an able common lawyer, but there is not and never was an able one in the New England States. Their system is *sui generis*, in which the common law is little attended to."

See *Jefferson's Complete Works*, Vol. V, p. 546. As to Common Law in Massachusetts Colony, see *Tucker's Blackstone*, Appendix, Vol. I, p. 397 *et seq.*

[2] Quoted in *The Connecticut Intestacy Law*, by Charles M. Andrews, *Yale Law Journal*, Vol. III, 189.

[3] *Governor Talcott Papers*, Vol. II, Appendix. These instructions were drawn up by John Read, afterwards the leader of the Bar in Boston, in the early Eighteenth Century.

custom only, and was coincident with the first professional education of lawyers and judges. As the Bar grew to be composed of men familiar with the law of England and its reported cases and commentaries, the legal character of the bench improved, and the rules of Common Law gradually became, by judicial application, the law of Connecticut. But Judge Jesse Root, in the preface to the first volume of his *Reports*, as late as 1798, denied that English Law had ever been applicable, *per se:*

"Our ancestors who emigrated from England to America were possessed of the knowledge of the laws and jurisprudence of that country; but were free from any obligations of subjection to them. The laws of England had no authority over them to bind their persons, nor were they in any measure applicable to their condition and circumstances here. . . . In every respect their laws were inapplicable to an infant country or state, where the government was in the people, and which had virtue for its principle and the public good for its object and end; where the tenure of land was free and absolute, the objects of trade few, and the commission of crimes rare."[1]

In Rhode Island, it was not until 1770 that by statute the Common Law was formally adopted, as follows:

"In all actions, matters, causes and things whatsoever where no particular law of the Colony is made to decide and determine the same, then in all such cases the Law of England shall be put in force to issue, determine and decide the same, any usage, custom or law to the contrary notwithstanding."

The real fact is, that during these years, 1620–1700, the colonists were making a Common Law for themselves; and their usages and customs, and the expedients to which they were forced, in order to adapt their rules of life to the

[1] See Zephaniah Swift's *System of Laws of Connecticut;* Peter's *History of Connecticut.*

surroundings and the time, gradually hardened into positive rules of law.[1]

An interesting commentary on this growth of an American Common Law is to be found in the Diary of Ezra Stiles, President of Yale College:[2]

"Jan. 6, 1773 — Dined with Judge (Peter) Oliver (Chief Justice of Massachusetts) and spent the afternoon together. We discoursed on the extending of the English Law to America, whether Statute or Common. He said all the English statutes before the Colonies had Existence were to be extended here — (a singular opinion) — all made since with extending clauses reached us — those made without, etc., did not extend here. This I see is Court Law. He considered the Descent of Inheritance in Massachusetts as being neither according to England in general or Co. of Kent, but Mosaic. He said by Common Law the Estates of Felons went to the King, in Kent to the children, in New England to the children; so that the Common

[1] See Parsons, C. J., in *Com.* v. *Knowlton*, 2 Mass. p. 534 (1805).

Shaw, C. J., in *Com.* v. *Chapman*, 13 Metc. p. 68 (1847).

In England, in 1600, Lord Coke was deriving Common Law from usages and precedents three, four and five hundred years old; but in Massachusetts in 1810, customs only one hundred and fifty years old had crystallized into a part of its Common Law.

For example, a practise of the court in early days, of proceeding with the suit against one debtor, when the other lived out of the Colony — "a practise originated from necessity" in the early Seventeenth Century, was held in 1809 a Common Law rule. (*Tappan* v. *Bruen*, 15 Mass. 19.)

In *Campbell* v. *Johnson*, 11 Mass. p. 187 (1814), it was held that: "Immemorial usage [i. e. usage since 1620] has a force equally binding as statutes;" and see Parker, C. J., in *Potter* v. *Hall*, 3 Pick. p. 373 (1825). So "the immemorial usage of Massachusetts, founded on necessity," of a wife conveying her dower by joining in the deed, had become Common Law in Massachusetts early in the Eighteenth Century. "The celebrated Mr. Read, the first lawyer in his time, resolved this usage into New England Common Law," said Parsons, C. J., in *Fowler* v. *Shearer*, 7 Mass. 21.

So the statute as to low-water mark ownership of Massachusetts Bay Colony, being a usage and practise all over Massachusetts, had become a Common Law rule in 1832; see Shaw, C. J., in *Barker* v. *Bates*, 13 Pick. 258.

[2] *Literary Diary of Ezra Stiles*, Vol. I, p. 331 (1901).

Law he said would not apply to New England in this Case. In England and Massachusetts no Quaker evidence by affirmation can convict capitally — Judge (Frederick) Smyth (Chief Justice of New Jersey) told Judge Oliver that when he came to Jersies he objected this but they all cried out their usage to admit Quaker Testimony in capital cases and that he was obliged to give way to it, tho' different from the Laws of England. We also discussed on Slavery of Negroes in Virginia, etc.; that of necessity the American Public Law must differ and vary from the Public Law of England."

And the exact status of American law was strikingly expressed by Chief Justice William Tilghman of Pennsylvania, in 1813, in *Poor* v. *Greene* (5 Binney, 554):

"Every country has its Common Law. Ours is composed partly of the Common Law of England and partly of our own usages. When our ancestors emigrated from England, they took with them such of the English principles as were convenient for the situation in which they were about to place themselves. It required time and experience to ascertain how much of the English law would be suitable to this country. By degrees, as circumstances demanded, we adopted the English usages, or substituted others better suited to our wants, till at length before the time of the Revolution we had formed a system of our own."

And by Judge John Bannister Gibson in *Lyle* v. *Richards* (9 Serg. & Rawle, 322) in 1823:

"To a greater or less extent there necessarily exists in every country a species of legislation by the people themselves, which in England and in this country is the foundation of the Common Law itself, or in other words general custom obtaining by common consent. . . . In the infancy of this Colony it produced not only a modification of some of the rules of the Common Law, but a total rejection of many of the rest."

The absence of lawyers in the Seventeenth Century is,

therefore, easily understood, when once the conditions described above are appreciated. When English precedents were not followed or used as a guide in the courts, and the courts were composed of clergymen and merchants, of Governors and their Deputies or Assistants, of politicians appointed or elected, rather than of trained lawyers, there was no real need or scope for men trained in English law; and no real lawyers appeared until the call arose for them.

With the beginning of the Eighteenth Century, however, a new set of factors began to work to produce the American Bar, which soon counteracted the old retarding influences.

After the passing of the troublous times of James II and the revocation of most of the Colonial charters, and after the Treaty of Utrecht, when peace was established on two continents, the American Colonies rapidly grew in wealth and influence.

Means of education increased. William and Mary College was founded in Virginia, in 1692, Yale College, in 1700, Kings College (Columbia), in New York, in 1754, College of New Jersey (Princeton), at Newark, in 1746, Brown at Providence, in 1764. The first public library was established in New York in 1729, consisting of 1600 volumes. While the first printing-press had been brought into Massachusetts in 1629 and set up at Cambridge, being owned partially by Henry Dunster, President of Harvard College, there were nine printers in Massachusetts prior to 1692; and the first paper in all the Colonies was published in 1704, the *Boston News Letter*.

In January, 1673, the first monthly postman began his trip between New York and Boston. In 1693, the first act was passed, encouraging "A general Letter Office in Boston." In 1704, the office of "Deputy Postmaster General for the Colonies," located in New York, was established by

Act of Parliament. In 1753, Benjamin Franklin, then filling this office, established a penny post.

There was, at the same time, a very rapid extension of commerce, of export trade, of shipbuilding, fisheries and slavetrading. A class of rich merchants began to control in the community. Questions as to business contracts and business paper began to arise. Land grew more valuable, and the legal determination and stability of landed rights became more necessary. Though less encumbered with elaborate trusts and settlements than in England, wills grew more complicated. Important questions arose between the government of the various Colonies. The political liberties guaranteed by the principles of the English Common Law became increasingly more vital to the colonists, as the Royal Governors attempted to enlarge their own powers, and the King and Parliament began to trespass on what the Colonies regarded as their own prerogatives.

The practise of the law became more extended and disciplined. The many new contingencies, unprovided for by statute or local custom, forced the judges to go to the Common Law for rules of decision. The precedents springing from local customs themselves became numerous and complicated, requiring a trained body of men to interpret them. And so arose the need for lawyers versed in law as a science.

This need was supplied at first by barristers imported from England. Soon, however, men of family and men of a collegiate education in the Colonies began to enter upon the career of a lawyer, producing a marked change in the character of the profession; and though law schools were lacking and law books were scarce, they developed to a considerable extent into masters of the Common Law.

The rise of Bar Associati ns, designed to dignify the

profession, in excluding from practise the pettifoggers and sharpers, also added to the confidence reposed in the profession by the community.

Another leading influence in changing the standard of ability and character among members of the Bar, and in spurring the development of adequate modes of legal instruction in the Colonies, was the growth of a class of Colonial lawyers who received their education in the English Inns of Courts. This growth was particularly marked in Maryland, Pennsylvania, Virginia and South Carolina, from which Colonies nearly one hundred and fifty lawyers were educated in the Inner and Middle Temple Inns in London between 1750 and 1775. In fact, it may be said without exaggeration that the American lawyer of the late Eighteenth Century was the product either of the English Inns of Court or of the American Colleges — Harvard, Yale, Princeton, Brown and the College of William and Mary. And it was this superior education and training which fitted the lawyer of the Eighteenth Century to become the spokesman, the writer and the orator of the people when the people were forced to look for champions against the pretensions of the Royal Governors and judges and of the British Parliament. So that when the War of the Revolution broke out, the lawyer, from being an object of contempt to restrain whom restrictive legislation was yearly necessary during the Seventeenth Century, had become the leading man in every town in the country, taking rank with the parish clergyman and the family doctor.

# CHAPTER I

## ENGLISH LAW, LAW BOOKS AND LAWYERS IN THE SEVENTEENTH CENTURY

THE slow development of the American lawyer during the Seventeenth Century can hardly be understood, unless the contemporaneous state of the law and of lawyers and of legal education in England is borne in mind.

One of the first American-born lawyers to study law in England was Benjamin Lynde of Massachusetts, who was admitted to the Middle Temple Inn, in 1692.

At that time, the Common Law as a system to be studied from reported decisions was only about a century old. Those cases which to the modern student are almost his earliest landmarks, were then to be found in reports published only a few years before the Pilgrims landed at Plymouth. Thus, *Shelley's case* (1 Coke 93) had been decided in 1579–1581; *Thorogood's case* (2 Coke 9), on fraud in the execution of a deed, in 1582; *Spencer's case* (5 Coke 16), in 1583; *Calye's case* (8 Coke 32), on the liability of innkeepers, in 1584; *Slade's case* (4 Coke 91), which established the use of the action on the case upon assumpsit in place of debt, in 1603; *Twyne's case* (3 Coke 80), on gifts in fraud of creditors, had been decided in 1601; *Dumpor's case* (4 Coke 119), on waiver of forfeiture, in 1603; *Lopus* v. *Chandelor* (Cro. Jac. 1), the Bezoar Stone case on warranties, in 1604; *Semayne's case* (5 Coke 91), on sheriff's liability, in 1605; the Six Carpenters case, or *Vaux* v. *Newman* (8 Coke 146), on trespass ab initio, in 1611; the *Sutton Hospital case* (10 Coke 1), on corporations, in 1612;

*Lampleigh* v. *Braithwait* (Hobart 105), on consideration in assumpsit, in 1616; *Manby* v. *Scott* (1 Lev. 4), on a wife's contract, in 1659.

While the Common Law on its civil side had begun, by 1620, to provide fairly complete and even-handed justice as between one private citizen and another,[1] on its criminal side it was a source of horror to lovers of liberty and right, throughout the Seventeenth Century. Great judges, as a rule, were hardly possible under the arbitrary rule of the Stuarts or of Cromwell. The State Trials were trials only in name.

In 1637, about the time when Connecticut was being settled, and when the first lawyer of record appeared in Maryland, John Hampden was being tried in England for refusing to pay ship money.

In 1641, the year when Massachusetts adopted its *Body of Liberties*, occurred the trial for treason of the Earl of Strafford; and two years later, the trial of William Laud, Archbishop of Canterbury. In 1649, Chief Justice Rolle refusing to preside, King Charles I was tried before Lord President Bradshaw at a Special High Court of Justice, his line of defense having been laid out by Sir Matthew Hale. This was three years after the passage of the statute in Virginia forbidding attorneys to practise for pay.

In 1660, the regicides were tried for treason at Old Bailey before Sir Orlando Bridgman, Chief Baron of the Court of Exchequer.

In 1670, William Penn was tried for "tumultuous assembly." In 1683 came the trial for treason of Lord Russell (the Ryehouse Plot Case) before Sir Francis Pemberton, Chief Justice of Common Pleas, and of Algernon Sydney before the infamous Lord Chief Justice Jeffreys. This was the year when a writ of *quo warranto* was issued to

[1] *The Five Ages of the Bench and Bar of England*, by John M. Zane.

forfeit the charter of Massachusetts, and when William Penn's government in Pennsylvania began.

In 1685, Lady Alice Lisle had been tried and executed by Jeffreys; and Titus Oates had been tried for perjury and pilloried. In 1688 occurred the trial of the Seven Bishops for libel, before Lord Chief Justice Wright; this was four years before the witchcraft trials in Massachusetts, and twenty-one years before the first attorney was formally licensed to practise in New York.

In the midst of these dark times of the law in England, however, two clear lights had shone out in the persons of the great Lord Chief Justices — Sir Edward Coke and Sir Matthew Hale. The former had been deposed by James I, in 1616, before the settlement of New England. The latter had been head of the Court of King's Bench from 1671 to 1676. He presided in 1665 as Chief Baron of the Exchequer at the witch trials in Suffolk, which were the prototype of those occurring twenty-seven years later in Salem, Massachusetts.[1] In 1676, he presided over the trial of John Bunyan, the tinker, to the long sentence imposed on whom the world owes *Pilgrim's Progress*. It was not, however, the historical association with these cases to which Hale owes his fame in the development of the law. He was the first to conceive the opinion that the law of England was capable of being reduced to a system and created scientifically.[2] Since the reign of Edward I, there

[1] Chandler in his *American Criminal Trials* says that "the account of the trial of witches in Suffolk was published in 1684. All these books were in New England, and the conformity between the behaviour of Goodwin's children and most of the supposed bewitched at Salem and the behaviour of those in England, is so exact as to leave no room to doubt the stories had been read by the New England persons themselves or had been told to them by others who had read them."

[2] See Lecture on *The System of Law*, in *Life of Nathaniel Chipman*, by Daniel Chipman (1846).

had been slight change in the laws or in the mode of administering justice in England, and they had become quite unsuited to the altered circumstances of the country; but in 1653 Hale was made chairman of a committee on law reform of which Cromwell, Sir Algernon Sydney and Sir Anthony Ashley Cooper were members. He drew up a plan for many legal reforms, including a scheme for the recording of deeds; but England was not ready for most of these innovations; and though the public registry of deeds had already been adopted in most of the American Colonies, this, with many of Hale's other suggestions, failed in the more conservative country. To Hale, however, was largely due the action of Parliament, in 1649, in requiring the use of the English language in law books and proceedings — a reform which lasted until the Restoration of Charles II, and which was put permanently in force in 1731 (4 Geo. II, c. 26).[1]

A new era for the Common Law and a revolution in its methods was initiated when the Bill of Rights was granted in 1688, under which the judges were no longer to hold office at the King's pleasure, but *quam diu se bene gesserint*. From that date it was no longer possible for the King to say, as did James II: "I am determined to have twelve lawyers for judges who will be all of my mind as to this matter;" bringing forth the reply of Chief Justice Jones of the Common Pleas: "Your Majesty may find twelve *judges* of your mind, but hardly twelve lawyers." [2]

[1] Campbell's *Lives of the Chief Justices*, Vol. II, p. 185. As early as 1609, King James had said in a speech when the *Revised Version of the Bible* was nearly ready for publication, "I wish the law written in one vulgar language; for now it is an old mixt and corrupt language only understood by lawyers."

It may be noted that a statute as early as 1360 required pleas to be made in the English language, though judgments were still to be enrolled in Latin.

[2] Campbell's *Lives of the Chief Justices*, Vol. II, p. 337.

For two hundred years after the Norman Conquest legal proceedings were almost entirely in the hands of the clergy as the only class versed in reading and in knowledge of civil and canon law.

The first learned lay lawyers appeared in the reign of King John; and finally, in Henry III's reign, the Pope forbade his clergy to study temporal law or to sit in lay courts.[1] Lawyers as a separate class in the community were a gradual development. It was not until 1235 that parties to a suit were formally permitted by statute to appear by attorney; and for many years no attorney could appear for a party except by special license of the King. In 1275, the First Statute of Westminster recognized and extended appearance by attorney; and in 1283, a statute allowed attorneys made by written warrant to appear in the absence of the parties.[2] By 1290, there appears to have been a well-recognized class of pleaders, termed serjeants, who alone pleaded the cases in court. The serjeants, therefore, are the most ancient order of the profession. They had the exclusive practise in the Court of Common Pleas, and from their ranks the judges were always chosen. In 1292, Edward I ordered that the justices of the Court of Common Pleas should provide and ordain from every county certain attorneys and apprentices "of the best and most apt for their learning and skill who might do service to his court and people;" and that those so chosen only, and no other, should attend his court and transact the affairs therein. The King considered one hundred and forty to be sufficient for that employment; but it was left to the discretion of the justices to add to that number or diminish as they should

[1] *Legal Profession in England,* — *American Law Review,* Vol. XIX, 677. It is curious to find this history reproduced in the early days of Massachusetts when the clergy again were the preponderating factor in the law.

[2] See *The Golden Age of the Common Law,* by John M. Zane, *Illinois Law Rev.* (1907).

see fit.[1] This establishment of a limit for the number of attorneys, however, does not seem to have been intended to interfere with the established pleaders; and a distinction seems to have existed even then between the two classes of lawyers.[2]

The ethics of legal practise were early fixed on a high plane; and in the *Miroir des Justices* (written by Andrew Horne about 1307, in the reign of Edward II) it was laid down:

> "Every pleader is to be charged by oath that he will not maintain nor defend what is wrong or false to his knowledge, but will fight for his client to the utmost of his ability; thirdly, he to put on before the Court no false delays; nor false evidence, nor move nor offer any corruptions, deceits, tricks or false lies, nor consent to any such, but truly maintain the right of his client, so that it fail not through any folly, negligence or default in him."

It is interesting to note that the first statute in England on the subject of conspiracy, enacted in 1305, referred to conspiracies to maintain lawsuits. It defined conspirators as "they that do confeder or bind themselves together by oath, covenant, or other alliance," either to indict or maintain lawsuits; and "such as maintain men in the countrie with liveries or fees for to maintain their malicious enterprises,—and this extends as well to the takers as to the givers." In the fear of the evil practises which this statute shows must have been prevalent at that early time, there may be seen the prototype of conditions which gave rise to so much legislation against fee-taking lawyers in the American Colonies during the Seventeenth Century.

[1] Pollock and Maitland's *History of English Law*, Vol. I.
*The Constitutional Power of the Court over Admission to the Bar*,—*Harv. Law Rev.*, Vol. XIII.

[2] *A History of the English Law*, by W. S. Holdsworth, Vol. II (1909).

The fact that the English Parliament was at this time, in reality, "The High Court of Parliament" — a law-declaring, as well as a law-making, body — is notably shown by a statute, in 1362, prohibiting lawyers from sitting in that body, because of their interest and activity in stirring up lawsuits over which they might later be in a position to act.[1] This same legislation was enacted for the same reason in the Colonies of Massachusetts and Rhode Island, three hundred years later.[1]

In 1404, lawyers were forbidden election to Parliament by the King, Henry IV, who, without the sanction of that body, issued his writ of summons expressly excluding choice of any lawyer. The effect of this exclusion, and the consequent terming of this body the "Lack-learning" or "Dunce's" Parliament, is quaintly described by an old law-writer, Sir Bulstrode Whitelock, in his *Notes upon the King's Writt:*

"The King being in great want of money, and fearing that if the lawyers were parliament men they would oppose his excessive demaunds and hinder his illegall purposes (according to their knowledge and learning in the lawes and publique affayres); to prevent this the King issued forth writs of summons with a clause of 'nolumus' to this effect: 'We will not that you or any other sherife of our kingdome or any other man of lawe by any means be chosen.' This parliament was held 6 Hen. 4, and was called the lacke-learning parliament, either (saith our historian) for the unlearnedness of the persons or for their malice to learned men. It is stiled by Sir Thomas Walsingham in his *Margent* 'the parliament of unlearned men,' and from them, thus packed, the king (saith our author) obtained a graunt of an unusual taxe and to the people 'full of trouble and very grievous.' . . . They who will have a 'nolumus' of learned senators must be contented with a 'volumus' of

[1] See *The High Court of Parliament*, by C. H. McIlwain, esp. pp. 214–216 (1910).

uncouth lawes which I hope will never be the fate of England."

In 1376, Parliament forbade women to practise law or "sue in court by way of maintenance or reward," especially naming one Alice Ferrars (the unpopular mistress of Edward III).

The profession was very early placed under the control of the courts; and in 1403, in the reign of Henry IV, the attorneys having increased to two thousand in number, an act was passed requiring that all attorneys be examined and none admitted but such as were "virtuous, learned and sworn to do their duty;" and a form of oath was framed, on which most of the forms of oaths prescribed later in the American Colonies were founded. In 1413, the under-sheriffs, clerks, receivers and bailiffs had been excluded from practising as attorneys, because "the King's liege people dare not pursue or complain of the extortions and of the oppressions to them done by the officers or sheriffs."

It is interesting to note that legislation of precisely similar character was found necessary three hundred years later in most of the American Colonies from 1700 to 1750.

Lawyers as a class, however, incurred to a considerable extent a popular odium, as shown in the outcry against them in Wat Tyler's Rebellion in 1381, and in Jack Cade's Rebellion in 1450, an example of which is seen in Cade's proclamation: "The law serveth as naught else in these days but for to do wrong, for nothing is sped but false matters by color of the law for mede, drede and favor."[1]

[1] See also Shakespeare's *Henry VI*, Part II, Act IV, Scene 2. "Dick the Butcher — The first thing we do, let 's kill all the lawyers.

"Cade — Nay, that I mean to do. Is not this a lamentable thing, that of the skin of an innocent lamb should be made parchment? That parchment being scribbled o'er, should undo a man. Some say: the bee stings; but I say 't is the bee's wax, for I did but seal once to a thing, and I was never mine own man since."

It is probable that this unpopularity was due in large part to the fact that the practise of the profession of the law was confined to the upper classes. Fortescue wrote in the Fifteenth Century, it cost twenty marks a year to maintain a student in one of the Inns of Court, "and thus it falleth out that there is scant any man founde within the Realme skilfull and cunning in the lawes, except he be a gentleman borne, and come of a noble stock."

With the rise of professional attorneys, controlled by the courts, and the enlarged powers of appointing attorneys given to litigants, it might well have happened that the distinction between pleader and attorney would have been obliterated.[1] The distinction was revived, however, by the action of the judges, later confirmed by statute, in granting to those bodies known as the Inns of Court the sole power of calling lawyers to the Bar, i. e. giving them the right to plead in court under the designation of barristers.

The growth of this power in the Inns of Court is a peculiar and interesting development in English legal history. As gradually from the time of King John to Edward I, the courts became localized at Westminster Hall in London, the lawyers gathered in that city from all parts of the kingdom, and formed there a kind of university of their own in certain buildings called "Inns," where instruction was given in the principles of English Common Law and Statute law exclusively. Gradually, "Inns of Court" came to signify the four Honourable Societies of Lincoln's Inn, Gray's Inn, The Inner Temple and The Middle Temple.[2]

This popular antagonism to lawyers was also reproduced in America four hundred years later, as seen in the Shays' Rebellion in Massachusetts, in 1787.

[1] *A History of the English Law*, by W. S. Holdsworth, Vol. II (1909).

[2] The term "Inn" or "Inne" was the Saxon equivalent for the French "hostel," signifying, not a public place of entertainment, but the private city or town mansion of a person of rank or wealth; thus, "Lincoln's Inn"

The exact origin of these Inns of Court is unknown; but they probably existed in their present form in the reign of Edward III in 1327. Henry III had taken them under his special protection, and in 1235 prohibited the study of law in any other place in London than the Inns of Court. Little satisfactory information, however, is to be had about them until the time of Henry VI (1422–1461), when Sir John Fortescue, the Chancellor, sketched them in detail in his *De Laudibus Legum Angliae.*

He described them as composed of four large Inns of about two hundred students each, and ten lesser Inns of Chancery having about one hundred students each. The students were chiefly young men of birth. In 1586, the number of students in the various Inns of Court and Chancery was 1,703.

The term "barrister" did not become a usual name until the Sixteenth Century; and the severance between the two branches of the profession dates probably from an order of Lincoln's Inn in 1556, as follows: "From henceforth no man that shall exercise the office of Attorneyship shall be admitted into the fellowship of this House without consent of six of the Bench." And in 1557, the judges made a similar order that attorneys should be excluded from the Inns of Court.

was the hostel of the Earl of Lincoln and leased to lawyers and students of law, and the Inner and Middle Temple was the home of the Knights Templar.

See especially *Laws and Jurisprudence of England and America,* by John F. Dillon, Chapters II, III and IV, for much information about the Inns of Court; and *Antiquities of the Inns of Court and Chancery,* by W. Herbert (1802).

See also *Education for the English Bar in the Inns of Court,* — *Green Bag,* Vol. XV; and for an elaborate account see *Introductory Lecture,* by David Hoffman (1823).

Even as early as the reign of Henry VIII, when Erasmus visited England, he described the English lawyer as "a most learned species of profoundly ignorant man." See *Green Bag,* Vol. I, p. 341.

In 1606, by statute, none were to be admitted as attorneys in the courts except those brought up in the Inns "well practised and skilled and of an honest disposition." The only persons, therefore, henceforth entitled and admitted to practise in the courts were those who had been "called" as barristers by the "benchers" or officers of one of the four Inns of Court. Attorneys (officers of the Common Law Courts) and solicitors (officers of the Courts of Chancery) could only draw writs and papers, and instruct the barristers as to the matter in litigation; and they were generally graduates of the Inns of Chancery.

The principal methods of instruction in the Inns of Court in the Seventeenth Century were the exercises of reading, bolting and mooting of cases. There were, however, no prescribed attendance, no lectures and no regular course of study, a student being simply obliged to eat three dinners (six, in case of a non-University man) in the Hall of the Inn, in each of the four terms, Hilary, Easter, Trinity and Michaelmas; and after "keeping" a certain number of terms (at different periods, seven, ten and five years) he was called by the "benchers" as a barrister. The mooting of cases consisted of arguments by barristers who had been called to the Bar, or by students who had become expert "bolters," — generally at meal-time in the Hall in the presence of the students. Bolting consisted of conversational discussions upon cases put to the student by a bencher or two barristers, sitting as judges in private chambers. The readings were performed by two Readers appointed yearly from among the oldest and most distinguished barristers. The Reader generally chose as his topic some statute, and for three weeks elaborated on it with much form and solemnity, giving out cases to be argued by the barristers in his presence; thus, Littleton's was on the Statute De Donis, Bacon's was on the Statute of Uses, Dyer's was upon the Statute of Wills, and Coke's upon the Statute of Fines. As it was a high honor to be selected as Reader, the expense of the feasts given by him in return became very great; and finally the high festival into which the reading developed quite overbalanced the serious portion of the exercises.[1]

By the beginning of the Eighteenth Century, even the very moderate amount of instruction given through the readings and moots had been gradually discontinued, or had failed, because of inattendance by the barristers and students; and the legal education received became almost nominal. The student could, if he chose, carry on independent study; but no assistance was given to him, and no examination required. In fact, the Inns were legal societies or clubs, rather than Law Schools.

In spite of the poor facilities for acquiring a knowledge of the law, it is interesting to note what course of reading a law student of the Seventeenth Century was expected to pursue. Thus Rolle, in his *Abridgment* in 1668, gives the following advice to students:

"Spend two or three years in the diligent reading of *Littleton*, *Perkins*, *Doctor and Student*, Fitzherbert's *Natura Brevium*, and especially my Lord Coke's *Commentaries*, and possibly his *Reports*. . . . After two or three years so spent, let him have a large commonplace book, afterwards it might be fit to read the *Year Book;* because many of the elder *Year Books* are filled with law not so much in use, he may single out for his constant reading such as are most useful, as the last part of *Edward III*, the *Book of Assizes*,

[1] See *The Five Ages of the Bench and Bar of England*, by John M. Zane. Pepys in his *Diary*, March 3, 1664–65 writes: "To see Mrs. Turner, who takes it mighty ill I did not come to dine with the Reader in Law, her husband, which, she says, was the greatest feast that ever was yet kept by a Reader, and I believe it was well. But I am glad I did not go, which confirms her in an opinion that I am grown proud."

the second part of *Henry VI*, *Edward IV*, *Henry VII*, and so come down in order and succession of time to the latter law, viz.: *Plowden*, *Dyer*, *Coke's Reports*, the Second *Term*, and those other *Reports* lately printed."

And Lord Coke in the third volume of his *Reports* says :

"Right profitable are the ancient books of the common law yet extant, as *Glanville*, *Bracton*, *Britton*, *Fleta*, *Ingham* and *Novae Narrationes;* and those also of later times, as the *Old Tenures*, *Old Natura Brevium*, *Littleton*, *Doctor and Student*, *Perkins*, *Fitzherbert*, *Natura Brevium* and *Stamford*. If the Reader, after the diligent reading of the case shall observe how the case is abridged in these two great Abridgments of Justice Fitzherbert and Sir Robert Brooke, it will both illustrate the case and delight the Reader; and yet neither that of Statham nor that of the Book of Assizes is to be rejected; and for pleading, the great Book of Entries is of similar use and utility. To the former Reports, you may add the exquisite and elaborate commentaries at large of Master Plowden . . . and the summary and fruitful observations of . . . Sir James Dyer . . . and mine own simple labours; then have you fifteen books or treatises and as many volumes of the Reports besides the abridgments of the common law."

It is interesting also to note that, as early as 1600, a book of instructions to law students had been published — William Fulbeck's *Direction Preparative to the Study of the Lawe;* and in 1667, William Phillips published a second edition of his *Studii Legalis Ratio, or Directions for the Study of the Law.*

The absence of a legal profession in America at this time can be better understood, perhaps, if one bears in mind the extremely limited resources on which the student and the practitioner of law in England had at this time to depend.

In the year 1692, at the time of the establishment of the first system of separate courts in Massachusetts, the first printed law book in England was only about two hundred years old — Littleton's *Tenures*, printed in 1481 in the reign of Henry VI, only a few years after the introduction of the printing-press into England.

Before the beginning of the Seventeenth Century, there were comparatively few law books in existence, even in manuscript, and of these, hardly more than thirty had been printed.[1]

The following are the most important of the works on law which were at the disposal of lawyers at that time:

Ranulf de Glanville's *Treatise on the Laws and Customs of England*, 1187–1189, printed about 1554–1557.
Richard Fitz-Neale's *Dialogus de Scaccario*, written about 1178.
Henry Bracton's *Laws and Customs of England*, 1262, printed 1569.
John Britton's *Abridgment*, about 1290, printed 1540.
*Old Tenures*, written in reign of Edward III, printed in 1525.
*Old Natura Brevium*, 1328–1376, printed 1524.
*Novae Narrationes* — 1448, printed about 1515.
Littleton's *Tenures*, 1472, printed 1481.
Nicholas Statham's *Abridgment*, about 1476, printed about 1495.
*Nova Statuta*, printed 1497.
Anthony Fitzherbert's *Grand Abridgment of the Law*, 1514–1516.
J. Rastell's *Expositions of the Terms of the Laws of England*, 1567.
W. Rastell's *Register Original*, 1531.
Phaer's *Book of Presidents*, 1576.
*Boke for a Justice of the Peace, and Returna Brevium* (1538).
*Diversity of the Courts*, 1561
Saint Germain's *Doctor and Student*, 1518–1522.
Rastell's *Entries*, 1566.

[1] See Dugdale's *Origines Juridiciales* (1666) as to law books of this period, also Reeves' *History of the English Law;* also *Law and Lawyers*, by W. L. Willis, in *American Quarterly Review*, Vols. XIII–XIV; *The Common Law*, by Charles P. Daly (1894); *The Sources of English Law*, by H. Brunner; *Materials for the History of English Law*, by F. W. Maitland, *Pol. Sci. Qu.*, Vol. IV (1889).

The dates given for the law books in the text are in general stated as given in *A History of English Law*, by W. S. Holdsworth (1909).

John Perkins' *Profitable Book of Conveyancing*, 1532.
William Staunford's *Pleas of the Crown*, 1557.
Brooke's *Grand Abridgment of the Law*, 1568.
Lombard's *Archaiomea*, 1568.
Pulton's *Abstract of the Penal Statutes*, 1577.
Theloal's *Digest of Original Writs*, 1579.
Kitchen's *Courts*, 1579.
Lombard's *Eisenachia*, 1581.
*Vetera Statuta*, 1588.
Manwood's *Forest Law*, 1598.
Fleta's *Commentary*, about 1290, printed 1647.
Ralph de Hengham's *Register of Writs*, 1300, printed 1616.
Andrew Horne's *Miroir des Justices*, about 1307, printed 1642.
Fortescue's *De Laudibus Legum Angliae*, about 1460.

Until the decree of Parliament of 1649, requiring all reports to be in English, almost all law books had been in Norman French or Latin, for the reason, as Coke says in the Preface to the third volume of his *Reports*,

"It was not thought fit nor convenient to publish either those or any of the statutes enacted in these days in the vulgar tongue lest the unlearned by bare reading without understanding might suck out errors and trusting to their own conceit might endanger themselves and some times fall into destruction."

During the Seventeenth Century, the law books of chief importance had been the following: West's *Symboleography* was printed about 1601. In 1605, Cowell's *Institutes* had appeared; in 1606, Cowell's *Interpreter*, and in 1607, Cowell's *Dictionary*;[1] Swinborne on *Wills and Testaments*, in 1611; Dalton's *Justice of the Peace*, in 1612; Finch's *Common Law of England*, in 1613;[2] Spelman's *Glossary* in

[1] These three books were largely used by law students and passed into many editions down to as late as 1727. Cowell's *Institutes* received the compliment of being translated into English by direction of order of Parliament in 1651.

[2] Regarded as the best elementary book for students until the publication of *Blackstone*, in 1765.

1626. Lord Bacon's great work (though small in size), on *Elements of the Common Laws of England*, was published in 1630.[1] And just about the same time, Lord Coke put forth his famous *Institutes* — the first volume, *Commentary on Littleton*, in 1628. His *Exposition of Magna Charta* was published in 1642, after his death; *Pleas of the Crown*, in 1644, and *Jurisdiction of Courts*, in 1644. In 1631 came Doddridge's *English Lawyer;* in 1646–1648 March's *Slander;* in 1653, Brownlow's *Declarations and Pleadings.*

In 1641 was published Sheppard's *Touchstone of Common Assurance;* in 1655, Wingate's *Body of the Common Law of England;* in 1656, William Sheppard wrote his *Abridgment;* in 1656 appeared Booth's *Examen Legum Angliae;* and in 1659 the first English law book on Corporations, entitled *Of Corporations, Fraternities and Guilds.*[2]

In 1666, Sir William Dugdale wrote his famous *Origines Juridiciales*, the mine from which comes a large part of our information as to English laws, writs, judges, attorneys and serjeants. In 1668 appeared Chief Justice Rolle's *Abridgment.*[3] In 1678 appeared Hale's *Pleas of the Crown.* In 1680 and 1689 appeared two books, much used by the American colonists later, Sir John Hawle's *The Englishman's Right* and Henry Care's *English Liberties.*

The earliest reports of cases had been, of course, the *Year Books*, which first began to be printed about 1481, and

[1] The full title of this famous book is of interest: "*The Elements of the Common Lawes of England branched into a Double Tract: the one contayning a Collection of some principall Rules and Maxims of the Common Law, etc.; the other the Use of the Common Law for Preservation of our Persons, Goods, and Good Names, according to the Lawes and Customes of the Land.*"

[2] See especially as to this *The First Book in English on the Law of Corporations*, by Amasa M. Eaton, — *Yale Law Journal*, Vol. XIV (1903).

[3] There were also a few books on the law merchant and admiralty law, such as Malynes' *Lex Mercatoria or Ancient Law Merchant* (1622); Davies on *Impositions* (1656); Godolphus' *View of Admiralty* (1686); Prynne's *Animadversions* (1669); Zouch's *Jurisdiction of the Admiralty* (1686).

covered cases from about 1280 in Edward I's reign to 1537 in Henry VIII's.[1]

During the next one hundred years down to the time of the Commonwealth there had only been a few volumes of reports — those of *Plowden*, *Dyer*, *Keilway*, *Benlow*, *Dalison*, *Davies*, *Hobart*, *Bellewe* and *Coke*, about fifteen in all.[2]

These few reports, together with a small number of authoritative reports published in the reign of Charles II, such as *Croke* (1657), *Leonard* (1658), *Yelverton* (1661), *Rolle* (1675), *W. Jones* (1675), *Vaughan* (1677) and *Saunders* (1686), were practically the only reports known in the American Colonies, and substantially the only ones having any weight in England as law.

Nevertheless, during the time of the Commonwealth and the later Stuarts (1649–1689) a flood of other reports had burst from the press, — nearly fifty volumes.[3]

[1] For full account of these, see *Year Book Bibliography* — *Harvard Law Review*, Vol. XIV.

[2] The first volume of *The Commentaries or Reports of Edward Plowden of the Inner Temple, An Apprentice of the Common Law*, had been published in 1571; the volumes covering roughly the times of Edward III to Elizabeth (1350–1580), and their value consisting largely in the fact that while many of the early reports and year books contained the off-hand opinions of the judges upon motions, all of Plowden's cases were "upon points of law tried and debated."

Sir James Dyer's *Notes* (Chief Justice of Common Pleas) had been the next cases printed as *Reports*, a posthumous work, in 1585; and Keilway and Bellewe had also come out in Elizabeth's reign. Lord Coke's *Reports* (which were really Commentaries), had been published from 1601 to 1616, when he was Attorney-General and Chief Justice of the Common Pleas and of the King's Bench, and covered nearly completely the law of the reigns of Elizabeth and James I; each case generally containing the full pleadings and often a treatise on the point at issue. Of them Lord Bacon had said, "Had it not been for Sir Edward Coke's *Reports* . . . the law by this time had been almost like a ship without ballast for that the cases of modern experience are fled from those that are adjudged and ruled in former time."

[3] See Wallace's *The Reporters* (1845); *The English Law Reporters*, — *Harvard Law Review*, Vol. XV.

Of this raking up of old cases and precedents Wallace in his book on the *Reporters* says:

"It was the mistake of Charles I, that for nearly the whole of his arbitrary measures he endeavoured to obtain the sanction of the common law. Noy, his Attorney-General, had found in the recesses of his recondite lore some precedents which relieved the King of most of his difficulties . . . for they gave to the Crown the powers of the people . . . and Charles . . . assumed them as authority. This brought the law into unnatural prominence."

Most of these reports were worthless as law, and in general it may be said that they completely disregarded Bulstrode's advice, given in the preface of his second volume: "That as the laws are the anchor of the Republic, so the Judicial Reports are as anchors of the laws and therefore ought to be well weighed before put out." [1]

Few, if any, of these reports were known in the American Colonies.

As to the Chancery reports at this time (1692), scarcely any existed. In fact, the decrees of Lord Ellesmere, who had been Lord Chancellor from 1596 to 1617, were practically the first to be recorded to any extent. The decrees of

In 1662 the act was passed requiring the licensing of printed publications; and under this, until 1692, all law books were required to bear the imprimatur of the Lord Chancellor, the Lord Chief Justice or the Lord Chief Baron.

[1] Most of the reports were well described in 1657 by Sir Harbottle Grimstone (later Master of the Rolls), "a multitude of flying reports, whose authors were as uncertain as the times when taken, have of late surreptitiously crept forth. We have been entertained with barren and unwarranted products which not only tends to the depriving of the first grounds and reasoning of the young practitioner, who by such false lights is misled, but also to the contempt of divers of our former grave and learned justices."

Chief Justice Holt in later days also complained bitterly of his reporters, saying that the "skimblescamble stuff which they published would make posterity think ill of his understanding."

the early chancellors — politicians and ecclesiastics as they were — as well as the decrees of the later lawyer chancellors, headed by Sir Thomas More, had been, as Blackstone said, "rather in the nature of awards formed on the sudden . . . with more probity of intention than knowledge of the subject, founded on no settled principles, as being never designed, and therefore never used for precedents." And as Whitelock said: "A keeper of the seal has nothing but his own conscience to direct him, and that is sometimes deceitful." This was the "Roguish Equity," of which Selden spoke in his *Table Talk*, "which varied with the length of the Chancellor's foot." [1]

There was therefore no scope or reason for reports of their decisions; and the only Chancery reports covering this time were hardly more than brief notes on procedure, "reports shadowy, obscure and flickering," as Judge Story called them.[2]

Such was the meagre list of Common Law and Chancery reports, less than one hundred in all, from which English students and lawyers of the Seventeenth Century were obliged to extract the law, and out of which English judges had built and were building the fabric of the Common Law of England.

Yet to such an extent had this Century increased the roll of law books as compared with the previous Sixteenth

[1] Wallace says: "Though the binding nature of precedent in equity is said to have been acknowledged a good while ago by Bridgman (1 Mod. 307) and Lord C. J. Treby (3 Chanc. Cas. 95), it is yet true as a general thing at any rate that until the time of Lord Hardwicke equity was administered pretty much according to what appeared to be good conscience applied to the case."

[2] *Carey* (1557–1604), *Choyce Cases in Chancery* (1557–1606), *Tothill* (1559–1646), *Reports in Chancery* (1616–1710), *Nelson* (1625–1693), *Cases in Chancery* (1660–1690), *Freeman* (1676–1706), *Finch* (1673–1680), *Swanston*, *Vernon* (1681–1720). See *Vidal* v. *City of Philadelphia* (2 Howard 193).

Century, that the writer of the preface of 5 *Modern* (1711), describing eighty volumes of the Common Law, said:

"Thus I have given an historical account of our reports which a country lawyer (who was afterwards advanced to a seat of justice) told the Bar were too voluminous, for when he was a student he could carry a complete library of books in a wheelbarrow, but they were so wonderfully increased in a few years they could not then be drawn in a waggon."

## CHAPTER II

### THE COLONIAL BAR OF VIRGINIA AND MARYLAND

THE history of lawyers in Virginia is a peculiar one, for in no Colony was the early prejudice against the profession stronger, and in none did a more eminent Bar develop.

The binding force of the Common Law was early recognized; and in the preamble to the revision of the statute laws made in 1660–1661 it was stated: "We have endeavored in all things (as near as the capacity and constitution of this country would admit) to adhere to these excellent and often refined laws of England to which we profess and acknowledge all our obedience and reverence." Hugh Jones, in his *Present State of Virginia*, wrote, in 1724, that Virginia was

"ruled by the laws, customs, and constitution of Great Britain which it strictly observes, only where the circumstance and occasion of the country by an absolute necessity requires some small alteration, which nevertheless must not be contrary (though different from and subservient) to the Laws of England."

And Judge Story in his *Commentaries on the Constitution* remarks that:

"The laws of Virginia during its colonial state do not exhibit as many marked deviations in the general structure of its institutions and civil polity from those of the parent country as those in the northern colonies. The Common Law was recognized as the general basis of its jurisprudence — and expressly provided for in all the charters . . . and was . . . in its leading features very acceptable to the colonists."

In the earliest days of the Colony, the Governor was the sole fountain of justice; and in the instructions laid down for Sir Thomas Gates, Governor in 1609 under the Proprietary Charter of 1606, it was enjoined that:

"In all matters of Civill Justice you shall find it properest and usefullest for your government to proceede rather as a Chancellor than as a Judge, rather uppon the naturall right and equity than uppon the niceness and lettre of the lawe which perplexeth in this tender body rather than dispatcheth all causes; so that a summary and arbitrary way of Justice discreetly mingled with those gravities and fourmes of magistracy as shall in your discrecon seeme aptest for you and that place, will be of most use both for expedition and example."

In the same year, a civil code was prepared entitled "Lawes and Orders Divine Politique and Martiall for the Colony of Virginia." In 1618, provision was made for two judicial bodies, the Governor and Council, and the Assembly. This latter body, composed of twenty-two elected burgesses and the Governor and Council, convened at Jamestown, July 30, 1619, the first English legislative body in America; and on the second day of its sitting constituted itself a Court to try one Thomas Garret for indecent behavior, and later in the session it heard a civil case. In 1643, a judicial system was established, much resembling that of Massachusetts, consisting of County Courts (begun in 1623–1624) composed of local wealthy planters, with an appeal to the Quarter Courts (or General Court as they were termed after 1662), composed of the Governor and his Councillors (thirteen in number at first, later nineteen, and still later sixteen). There was also an appeal in some matters to the General Assembly. As early as 1661–1662, an act was passed, regulating very precisely the procedure of the courts and requiring all declarations, answers and evidence to be preserved.

Notwithstanding the early acceptance of the English Common Law as the basis for its own law, Virginia produced no trained Bar for nearly one hundred years. This condition was undoubtedly due to the fact that its governing class was practically a landed aristocracy, conservative and extremely jealous of any other power. The Colony, however, seems to have been troubled from an early date with the lower class of petty attorneys; and the problem of how to control these attorneys appears to have perplexed Virginia more than any other Colony.

As early as 1642–1643, under an act "for the better regulating of attorneys and the great fees exacted by them," fees were confined to twenty pounds of tobacco in the County Court and forty pounds in the Quarter Court: attorneys were forbidden to plead without obtaining license from the court; they could not plead in more than the "Quarter Court and one County Court;" and they could not refuse to be "entertayned in any cause" under heavy fines to be paid in tobacco. This act, however, did not apply to "such who shall be made speciall attorneys within the collony or to such who shall have letters of procuration out of England."

In 1645, it was provided that "whereas many troublesom suits are multiplied by the unskilfulness and covetousness of attorneys who have more intended their own profit and their inordinate lucre than the good and benefit of their clients, be it therefore enacted that all mercenary attorneys[1] be wholly expelled from such office." In 1647, the courts, if they perceived that either party was like to lose his cause "by his weakness," were themselves to "open the cause" or to "appoint some fitt man out of the people to plead the cause . . . and not to allow any other attorneys in

[1] The word "mercenary" here meant only "serving for pay or fees." It did not have the opprobrious definition later given to the word.

private causes betwixt man and man in the country;" and attorneys were forbidden to "take any recompence either directly or indirectly." This Mercenary Attorney Act was repealed in 1656; and provision was made for licensing attorneys. The next year, however, trouble apparently having again arisen, all fees were taken away from attorneys; and "whereas there doth much charge and trouble arise by the admittance of attorneys and lawyers through pleading of causes thereby to maintain suites in lawes to the great prejudice and charge of the inhabitants of this collony," they were forbidden to plead in any court "or give counsel in any cause or controversie, for any kind of reward or profitt," on penalty of five thousand pounds of tobacco, and were required to swear, when they appeared in any cause, that they had not violated this Act, "because the breakers thereof through their subtillity cannot easily bee discerned."

In 1680, however, a law was passed again, allowing attorneys to practise under rigid restrictions and after license by the Governor.

The following reason for this reversal of policy was given in the preamble to the statute:

"Whereas all courts in the country are many tymes hindered and troubled in their judiciall proceedings by the impertinent discourses of many busy and ignorant men who will pretend to assist their friend in his business and to cleare the matter more plainly to the court, although never desired nor requested thereunto by the person whom they pretended to assist and many tymes to the destruction of his cause and the greate trouble and hindrance of the court."

This act, being found "inconvenient," was repealed after two years; but the repealing act was itself annulled by royal proclamation. As late as 1705, Beverly wrote in his *History and Present State of Virginia:*

"Every one that pleases may plead his own cause, or else his friends for him, there being no restraint in that case, nor any licensed Practitioners in the law."

In 1732, however, another statute was passed declaring that "the number of unskilled attorneys practising at the County Courts is become a great grievance to the country in respect to their neglect and mismanagement of their clients' causes and other foul practices," and providing for licenses for the admission of lawyers, upon the taking of an oath (the form of oath being practically that in use in the New England Colonies). There appears to have been a distinction, however, at this time, between that class of men who practised only in the County Courts and those who appeared in the General Court; for this statute of 1732 provided that it should not be construed to extend "to any attorney who at the time of passing thereof is a practitioner in the General Court or to any counsellor or barrister at law whatsoever." This reference to the distinction between attorneys and barristers is one of the earliest in all American Colonial legislation or court rules.

Finally, in 1748, a general statute provided for licensing of all lawyers and also a form of oath to be taken by them.

All this early legislation was directed probably not so much against the legal profession itself, as against the character of the men who composed it. Most of the attorneys were mere charlatans, men of no character or influence. As Judge Minor said in his *Institutes*,[1] "for fully a century, the lawyer seems to fortune and to fame unknown," not one of them having attained a notoriety or distinction worthy of a biographer. John Fiske says that "they were frequently recruited by white freedmen, whose career of rascality as attorneys in England had

[1] Minor's *Institutes*, Vol. IV, p. 168 (1875).

suddenly ended in penal servitude." Although this statement is unqualifiedly denied by a Virginia lawyer, claiming that there are no records to sustain it,[1] there is record in 1736 of one, Henry Justice, an English barrister of the Middle Temple, who was convicted of stealing a Bible and other books from Trinity College Library in Cambridge and sentenced to transportation to Virginia.[2]

The fact undoubtedly is that the litigation in the courts was so simple, and so exclusively confined to commercial matters (actions of debt and on bonds), that it was largely entrusted to the prominent officials and wealthy merchants and planters.[3] The business was not lucrative enough to attract educated English lawyers; and above all, the ruling class in Virginia were the landowners, who eyed with suspicion the rise of any other class to positions of influence in the community. Moreover, the courts themselves were composed almost exclusively of these landed gentry, who had no trained knowledge of law, and in practising before whom such knowledge was of little avail. Thomas Jefferson well described the condition of practise as late as the middle of the Eighteenth Century as follows:

"When I was at the Bar of the General Court, there were in the possession of John Randolph, Attorney General, three volumes of MSS. reports of cases determined in that

[1] *Lawyers of the Seventeenth Century, — William and Mary College Quarterly*, Vol. VIII.

[2] *Old Virginia*, Vol. II, by John Fiske.

[3] Thus in York County Records, of the names of thirteen men who appeared on the docket as attorneys between 1640 and 1675, with the exception of William Sherwood (who was a trained lawyer) and John Holdcraft and William Swinnerton, all were either planters or merchants prominent in the community; Francis Willis, James Bray, Thomas Bullard, John Page and Daniel Parke becoming members of the Virginia Council; William Hockaday, Thomas Bushrod, Dr. Robert Ellyson, Gideon Macon being at different times members of the House of Burgesses and Karbry Kiggars. (See *William and Mary College Quarterly*, Vol. VIII.)

Court, the one taken by his father, Sir John Randolph, a second by Mr. Barradall, and a third by Hopkins. These were the most eminent of the counsel at the Bar and give us the measure of its talent at that day. All, I believe, had studied law at the Temple in England, and had taken the degree of Barrister there. The volumes comprehended decisions of the General Court from 1730 to 1740, as well on cases of English law as on those peculiar to our own country. The former were of little value because the Judges of that Court consisting of the King's Privy Counsellors only, chosen from among the gentlemen of the country, for their wealth and standing, without any regard to legal knowledge, their decisions could never be quoted, either as adding to, or detracting from the weight of those of the English courts on the same points. Whereas on our peculiar laws, their judgments, whether formed on correct principles of law or not, were of conclusive authority. As precedents, they established conclusively the construction of our own enactments and gave them the shape and meaning under which our property has been ever since transmitted and is regulated and held to this day."[1]

In 1680, there were thirty-three lawyers in the Colony; but with the exception of the Royal Attorneys-General, and Benjamin Harrison, and William Fitzhugh, who was born in 1651 and educated as a lawyer in England, no lawyers of any note appear to have been in practise in the Seventeenth Century.[2]

In the early Eighteenth Century, most of the Virginia lawyers had received an Inns of Court education in England. Prominent among them were William Byrd of Westover, who, born in 1674, studied law in the Middle Temple, collected the finest library in the American Colonies, and died in 1743; John Clayton, who, born in 1665, studied

[1] Preface to *Reports of Cases Determined in the General Court of Virginia from 1730 to 1740*, by Thomas Jefferson (1829).

[2] See *Virginia Magazine*, Vol. I.

law in the Inner Temple, was made Attorney-General of Virginia in 1714 and died in 1737; Edward Barradale, who, born in 1704, was Attorney-General and Judge of Admiralty, and died in 1743; William Hopkins, a well-educated lawyer who practised in Virginia for twelve years prior to 1734; Sir John Randolph, who, born in 1693, graduated at the College of William and Mary, studied law at Gray's Inn and the Temple in London, and ranked at his death, in 1737, as one of the great practitioners in America; Stevens Thomson, one of the early Attorneys-General, and John Ambler, who practised between 1735 and 1766, both of whom had studied in the Middle Temple.

The lawyer of largest general reputation, prior to his death in 1734, was probably John Holloway, who had been an attorney of the Marshalsea Court in London. Though described by Sir John Randolph as relying more on learning and the subtle artifices of an attorney than the solid reasoning of a lawyer, his opinions were looked upon as authoritative, and his fees were exorbitant. Between the years 1750 and 1775, there was a marked growth in the size and ability of the Virginia Bar; and there arose a group of lawyers, most of whom were educated either at Princeton, William and Mary, or in the English Universities or Inns of Court, and whose political and legal talents placed Virginia in the forefront of the American Colonies. Among these were Peyton Randolph,[1] John Randolph,[2] Edmund Pendleton,[3]

[1] Born in 1721, a graduate of William and Mary College, of Oxford, of the Inner Temple, King's Attorney-General in Virginia in 1748, President of the first Congress in 1774.

[2] Brother of Peyton, born in 1727, educated at William and Mary and the Inner Temple, Attorney-General in 1766, "One of the most splendid monuments of the Bar," says Wirt, "a polite scholar as well as a profound lawyer," and who left Virginia in 1775 as a Tory refugee.

[3] Born in 1721, examined and licensed to practise law "by the eminent lawyer Barradale" in 1744, Chief Justice of Virginia Court of Appeals in 1779.

John Blair,[1] John Lewis,[2] George Wythe,[3] Robert Carter Nicholas,[4] Thomas Jefferson,[5] John Tyler,[6] Dabney Carr,[7] Peter Lyons, George Johnson, Paul Carrington, George Mason,[8] Richard Henry Lee,[9] and Patrick Henry.[10]

[1] Born in 1732, graduate of William and Mary College, a student in the Temple, in 1779 Chief Justice of Virginia Court of Appeals, in 1789 Judge of the United States Supreme Court.

[2] In whose office the eminent George Wythe studied.

[3] Born in 1726, admitted to the Bar in 1756, Professor of Law in 1780 in the College of William and Mary, sole chancellor of the Court of Equity in 1788, the legal teacher of Jefferson, who called him "my faithful and beloved mentor in youth and my most affectionate friend through life," instructor also of Marshall, Madison and Monroe, of whom Wythe once remarked that "all three would at least become 'Minent.' "

[4] Born in 1715, graduate of William and Mary College, and in 1779 judge of High Court of Chancery and of Court of Appeals.

[5] Born in 1743, admitted to the Bar in 1767, after nearly five years' study and preparation in the office of George Wythe and others.

[6] Born in 1747, studied law in office of R. C. Nicholas, Judge of the General Court 1788–1808, Governor, 1808–1811, United States District Judge 1811–1813.

[7] Born in 1744.

[8] Born in 1725, the author in 1776 of the Virginia Constitution, the first written constitution of a free commonwealth, pronounced by Madison in the debates on the Federal Constitution, "the ablest man in debate he had ever seen."

[9] Born in 1732, a student in the Temple, returned to Virginia in 1752, never actively practised.

[10] Born in 1736, admitted to practise in 1760, sprang into instant fame by his argument of the "Parsons Case" in 1763. This case is interesting as an illustration of the fact that practically all the cases in which American lawyers in the Eighteenth Century gained distinction were of a political nature. The facts were, that as far back as 1696, each minister of a parish had been provided with an annual stipend of 16,000 pounds of tobacco, at ten shillings eight pence per 100 pounds. In 1755, the tobacco crop fell short; and the Legislature passed an act, to continue for ten months, allowing persons from whom any tobacco was due, to pay in tobacco or in money at the rate of sixteen shillings eight pence per 100 pounds, at the option of the debtor. Rich planters benefited by paying their debts at this rate and getting from fifty to sixty shillings for their tobacco.

In 1758, on a surmise of a short crop, a similar act was passed. The price rose to fifty shillings. The King in Council denounced the act as

This Virginia Bar before the Revolution was thus interestingly summed up by St. George Tucker in a letter to William Wirt in 1813:

"Literary characters may leave their works behind them, as memorials of what they were; soldiers may obtain a niche in the temple of Fame, by some brilliant exploit; orators, whose speeches have been preserved, will be remembered through that medium; judges, whose opinions have been reported, may possibly be known to future judges, and members of the bar; but the world cares little about them; and if they leave no reports, or meet with no reporter to record their opinions, etc., they sink into immediate oblivion. I very much doubt if a single speech of Richard H. Lee's can be produced at this day. Nevertheless, he was the most mellifluous orator that ever I listened to. Who knows any thing of Peyton Randolph, once the most popular man in Virginia, Speaker of the House of Burgesses, and President of Congress, from its first assembling, to the day of his death? Who remembers Thompson Mason, — esteemed the first lawyer at the bar? Or his brother, George Mason, of whom I have heard Mr. Madison, (the present President), say, that he possessed the greatest talents for debate of any man he had ever seen, or heard speak. What is known of Dabney Carr, but that he made the motion for appointing committees of correspondence in 1773? Virginia has produced few men of finer talents, as I have repeatedly heard. I might name a number of others, highly respected and influential men in their day. The Delegates to the first Congress, in 1774, were Peyton Randolph, Edmund Pendleton, Patrick Henry, George Washington, Richard H. Lee, Richard Bland and Benjamin Harrison. Jefferson, Wythe and Madison did not come in till afterwards. This alone may show what estimation the former were held in: yet, how little is known of one-

a usurpation. The Clergy resolved to test the question, and suit was begun by Rev. James Maury against the Collector of the County, in 1762, with Peter Lyons for the plaintiff and the able and widely known John Lewis for the defendant. The first trial resulted in a victory for the plaintiff; the second was won by Patrick Henry for the defendant.

half of them at this day? The truth is, that Socrates himself would pass unnoticed and forgotten in Virginia, if he were not a public character, and some of his speeches preserved in a newspaper: the latter might keep his memory alive for a year or two, but not much longer."[1]

## Maryland

From the foundation of Maryland in 1634, its colonists claimed to be governed by the Common Law, notwithstanding the opposition of the Proprietor, who asserted that this was an interference with his absolute right to govern under the charter granted to him. In 1642, however, the Colonial Assembly or Legislature so far prevailed as to adopt the following "Act for Rule of Judicature:"

"Right and just in all civil causes shall be determined according to the law or most general usage of the Province since its plantation or former presid'ts of the same or like nature to be determined by the judge. And in defect of such law, usage or president, then right and just shall be determined according to equity and good conscience, not neglecting, — so far as the judge or judges shall be informed thereof and shall find no inconvenience in the application to this Province, — the rules by which right and just useth and ought to be determined in England in the same or the like case. And all crimes and offences shall be judged and determined according to the law of the Province, or in defect of certain law then they may be determined according to the best discretion of the judge or judges, judging as near as conveniently may be to the laudable law of usage of England in the same or like offences."

As early as 1662, an act was passed declaring that when the laws of the Province were silent, justice was to be administered according to the laws and statutes of England,

[1] *Memoirs of William Wirt*, by John P. Kennedy (1849).

and that "all courts shall judge of the right pleading and of the inconsistency of the said laws with the good of the Province according to the best of their judgment."

In 1732, the controversy between the colonists and the Proprietor was settled by an act providing that "when the acts and usages of the Province are silent, the rule of judicature is to be according to the law and statutes and reasonable customs of England, as used and practised within the Province." It is to be noticed, however, that even here the colonists claimed their right to adopt the Common Law, or not, as they saw fit.[1] From the beginning of its history, Maryland had a more complete system of courts than any other Colony, based largely on the English judiciary — Courts of Pupowder (Pypowdry) or Market Courts, Courts Baron and Leet incident to the landed estates, County Courts, the Provincial Court, and a Court of Appeal. Although in 1638 the General Assembly tried many cases, the Provincial Court gradually absorbed all superior jurisdiction. It consisted of the Governor and his Council, appointed by the Proprietor or his deputy, and therefore "dependent on the mere breath of his nostrils." [2] Its members also composed the Upper House of the General Assembly. In 1692, when Maryland became a Royal, instead of a proprietary Province, a Provincial Court was organized apart from the Council, and the Governor ceased to be Chief Justice. The Governor and Council were constituted, however, the Court of Appeals.

Few lawyers of learning or distinction were to be found among the judges of these courts; and as late as 1767, the eminent leader of the Bar, Daniel Dulany, made this

[1] See especially *State* v. *Buchanan*, 5 H. & J. 356 (1821).

[2] See *Calvert* v. *Eden*, 2 Harris & McHenry 345, 360.

For a history of the courts in Maryland, see dissenting opinion of Taney, C. J., in *Kendall* v. *U. S.*, 12 Peters, p. 631.

comment on the courts in a formal opinion rendered by him:

"On perusing the record, I am strongly of the opinion that the judgment of the Provincial Court ought to be reversed; but what may be the opinion of the Court of Appeals I should be more confident in predicting, if the judges were lawyers by profession, than I am on the consideration that they are not."[1]

The records of the proceedings of the Provincial Court are extant in the first two volumes of Maryland Archives up to 1657, and in cases to be found in volumes one and four of *Harris and McHenry's Reports,* covering cases from 1658 to 1776.

The early recognition of the Common Law and the high organization of the judicial system were undoubtedly the chief factors in developing a trained Bar in Maryland at an earlier date than in any other Colony. For in no Colony did attorneys appear in such numbers, or of so high a character, or under such early statutory recognition.

The first lawyer of record, and "father of the Maryland Bar," was John Lewger, Attorney for the Lord Proprietary, who landed in 1637, three years after the settlement of the Province, and whose name appears as counsel in a case that same year. The next attorney of record was James Cauther, in 1637, who appeared in a confession of debt. Like many "attorneys" of this time, he was also a planter. In 1638, Cyprian Thoroughgood appeared as attorney in a suit for damages for refusal to furnish lumber under a contract. Cuthbert Fenwick (termed in the writ for the General Assembly in 1640, "Gent. Attorney") appeared, in 1644, to collect a claim for tobacco for a Virginian client;

[1] See Opinion of Daniel Dulany on the judgment of the Provincial Court in *West* v. *Stegar,* 1 H. & McH. 247 (1767).

and between the years 1634 and 1660, the names of many other attorneys appear of record.[1]

At this time, there appeared the first American woman lawyer, Mrs. Margaret Brent, who not only pleaded in court, but even insisted on her right to take part in the General Assembly, as appears from the following quaint record of that body:

"Jan. 21, 1647–8 — came Mrs. Margaret Brent in the house for herselfe and voyce also, for that att the last court 3rd Jan. it was ordered that Mrs. Brent was to be looked uppon and received as his Lps. [Lordship's] attorney. The Gov'r denyed that the sd. Mrs. Brent should have any vote in the howse. And the sd. Mrs. Brent protested agst all proceedings in this first Assembly unless shee may be pst and have vote as aforesaid."

In 1659, the presence of attorneys was recognized by a statute which provided that "the attorneys on both sides speak distinctly to one error first before they proceed to the next, without disturbing each other." By the year 1669, the attorneys had so increased as to occasion a report by a Committee of the Lower House of the Assembly "that the privileged attorneys are one of the great grievances of the country." Charges of impeachment were preferred against one John Morecraft for having taken fees on both sides of a case, and also for "that he is retayned as attorney for some, with unreasonable fees, for a whole year's space, so that by that means it causes several suits to the utter ruin of people." The Upper House, however, dismissed the charges, expressing its wonder that "attorneys of ability and sworn to be diligent and faithful in their places and offices" should be "called a grievance, nay the grand grievance of the country."

[1] Thomas Gerrard, Thomas Notley (later Governor), Peter Draper, Thomas Mathews, William Harditch, John Weyville, George Manners and, most distinguished of all, Giles Brent (later Attorney-General).

In 1671, an act was passed forbidding sheriffs, commissioners, clerks, and deputy sheriffs, and officers of the court, from practising as attorneys in their respective courts. In 1674, an act was passed declaring "the abuse of several persons in this Province practising as Attorneys, Councellors and Solicitors at Law by taking and exacting excessive fees of their Clyents whereby many of the good people of this Province are much burthened and their causes much delayed, and by the great number of attorneys, whereby many unnecessary and troublesome suits are raysed and fomented;" and providing that thereafter only a "certain number of honest and able attorneys be admitted, nominated and sworn" by the Captain-General to be attorneys and counsellors, and all others to be forbidden to practise. Fees were regulated, and heavy fines and the penalty of disbarment were imposed for demanding or receiving more than the legal fees. County Courts attorneys should practise only after appointment by the Commissioners or Justices of the County Courts. Another act regulating the fees and conduct of attorneys was passed in 1714; and in 1715 a comprehensive act was passed "for rectifying the ill practices of attorneys of this province and ascertaining fees," providing that no person should practise law without being admitted thereto by the justices of the court, establishing rates of fees, and providing against neglect of duty. At the same time, court rules required gowns to be worn by both lawyers and judges. In 1721 and 1722, laws were passed to punish attorneys who by neglect of their duties caused loss to their clients.

The natural jealousy against lawyers, entertained by all agricultural communities, culminated in 1725, in an act regulating lawyers' fees with extreme strictness, and giving an option to the planter to pay in tobacco or in currency at a fixed rate. Against this act, a petition was presented in the Upper House by Daniel Dulany, Senior, Thomas Bordley, Joshua George and Michael Howard, "late practitioners of the law," alleging the act to be destructive of their privileges as British subjects.

This petition is of vital interest as being one of the first of the series of struggles by the colonists to maintain their rights under the English laws and constitution; it was followed by the publication by Dulany, in 1728, at Annapolis, of his famous pamphlet, *The Right of the Inhabitants of Maryland to the Benefit of the English Laws*.

In 1729, when the act was extended for three years, the lawyers petitioned the Proprietor in London against it, employing John Sharpe, a barrister of Lincoln's Inn, as their counsel. The Proprietor gave his dissent, on the ground that such a law "was not agreeable to any known law here," and to his dissent was appended the opinion of the then Attorney-General of Great Britain, Philip Yorke (later the great Lord Chancellor Hardwicke).

Of the Bar of the early Eighteenth Century, this Daniel Dulany, the elder, stood at the head. He was born about 1680, educated at the University of Dublin, admitted to the Bar of the Provincial Court in 1710, barrister of Gray's Inn in 1716, later Attorney-General of the Province.

Others of prominence were Charles Carroll, born in 1660, educated at the University of Douai in France and in the Inner Temple in London, who came to Maryland in 1688, as Attorney-General vigorously resisted the attempt to overthrow Lord Baltimore's Government, was arrested for high misdemeanor by the Royal Governor, and died in 1720; Thomas Bordley; Robert Ridgely; Col. Henry Jowles, a barrister, and Chancellor of the Province in 1697; Griffith Jones and Stephen Bordley.[1]

[1] In 1692, it is recorded that on the assembling of the Provincial Court after the Protestant Revolution, George Plates, Griffith Jones, William

By the year 1765, conditions had arisen in Maryland which had produced a Bar of great ability and of trained men educated in the law. The increase of wealthy landed proprietors had given rise to extremely complicated land laws, with a highly technical mass of court decisions. The broad development of commerce in the Province gave rise to much contract and maritime litigation. In no Province was there greater excitement over the Stamp Act or greater struggle against the assertion of arbitrary legislative powers by the Royal Governors. To deal with these conditions, the pre-Revolutionary Bar was brilliantly fitted. At its head was Daniel Dulany, the younger, who was born in 1721, educated in the Temple, and admitted to the Bar in 1747. So extended became his reputation that he was consulted on questions of jurisprudence by eminent lawyers in England; and cases were frequently withdrawn from Maryland courts, and on one occasion even from the Chancellor of England, to submit to him and abide by his award. His opinions, like those of his father, were deemed of such weight that many of them were included with reports of decided cases, when law reports were first printed in Maryland, in 1809.[1]

At the time of the Stamp Act agitation, he was hailed as the William Pitt of Maryland, because of his remarkable pamphlet on *Considerations on the Propriety of imposing*

Dent, Samuel Watkins and Philip Clark took the new test oath, and on motion the court limited the number of attorneys to be allowed to practise.

[1] Samuel Tyler in his *Memoirs of Roger Brooke Taney* (1872) says: "The opinions of Daniel Dulany had almost as much weight in court in Maryland, and hardly less with the court lawyers of England, than the opinions of the great Roman jurists that were made authority by edict of the Emperor, had in Roman court. This was due, on some degree, to the fact that there were no reports of Maryland decisions until 1809. . . . The high reputation of this great lawyer stimulated the ambition of the Maryland Bar, while his opinions were models of legal discussion for their imitation."

*taxes on the British Colonies for the purpose of raising a revenue by Act of Parliament*, published at Annapolis in 1765.

Contemporary with Dulany were Thomas Johnson, who, born in 1732, became Chief Justice of the General Court of the State in 1790 and Judge of the United States Supreme Court in 1791; Charles Carroll, who, born in 1737, studied in the Temple in London in 1757, returned to Maryland in 1765, and was one of the Signers of the Declaration of Independence; William Paca, born in 1740, a graduate of the College of Philadelphia in 1759 and of the Middle Temple in London, was Chief Justice of the State in 1778, Governor in 1782, and Judge of the United States District Court in 1789, also one of the Signers; Samuel Chase, the "torch that lighted up the Revolutionary flame" in Maryland, born in 1741, Signer of the Declaration, Chief Justice of the State in 1791, Judge of the United States Supreme Court in 1796; Thomas Stone, born in 1743, one of the Signers; Charles Gordon; John Hammond; and George Chalmers, a Scotch lawyer, who came to Baltimore in 1763 and returned to England in 1775, a noted writer, his *Opinions of Eminent Lawyers on various points of English jurisprudence concerning the Colonies, Fisheries and Commerce of Great Britain* being of especial interest to students of Colonial law.

## NOTE

### To Virginia Text

For authorities in general see:

*History of the Colony and Ancient Dominion of Virginia*, by Charles Campbell (1860).

*History of Virginia*, by R. R. Howison (1846).

*History of Virginia Codification, — Virginia Law Register*, Vol. XI.

*The American Colonies in the Seventeenth Century*, by Herbert L. Osgood (1904).

Hildreth's *History of the United States*, Vols. I and II.

*Court and Bar of Colonial Virginia*, — *Green Bag*, Vol. X.

*Old Virginia*, by John Fiske, Vol. II (1897).

*Great American Lawyers*, Vols. I–III(1908).

*Lawyers in Virginia between 1704 and 1737*, — *Virg. Law Reg.*, Vol. I (1877).

*Virginia Historical Register*, Vol. I, p. 119 *et seq.*

*Speech of Charles M. Blackford*, in *Proceedings of Virginia Bar Association*, Vol. VII (1898).

*Glance at Our Colonial Bar*, — *Green Bag*, Vol. XIII.

*Thomas Jefferson as a Lawyer*, — *Green Bag*, Vol. XV.

*Patrick Henry as a Lawyer*, — *Green Bag*, Vol. XVI.

*Virginia Lawyers*, — *Green Bag*, Vol. X, Nos. 1, 2, 3.

*Sketches of the Life and Character of Patrick Henry*, by William Wirt (1817).

*Edmund Randolph*, by Moncure D. Conway (1888).

*John Randolph of Roanoke*, by Hugh A. Garland (1851).

*Henry Clay as a Lawyer*, — *Law Reporter*, Vol. XV (1852).

*Local Institutions of Virginia*, — *Johns Hopkins University Studies in Historical and Political Science*, 3d series (1885).

*Our Judicial System*, by Benjamin Watkins Leigh. *Proc. Virginia Bar Association*, Vol. I (1889).

*County Courts in Virginia*, — *Proc. Virginia Bar Association*, Vol. VI (1894).

*The General Court of Virginia*, — *Proc. Virginia Bar Association*, Vol. VII (1895).

*Life of Chancellor Wythe*, in *Wythe's Cases in Chancery* (1852 edition).

*Letters and Times of the Tylers*, by Lyon G. Tyler (1884).

*Discourse on the Life and Character of Hon. Littleton Waller Tazewell*, by Hugh Blair Grigsby (1860).

Preface to *Virginia Statutes*, by William Waller Hening (1809).

*Virginia Colonial Decisions*, Vol. I, edited by R. T. Barton (1909).

*Virginia Magazine*, Vol. I, 260.

## To Maryland Text

For authorities in general see:

*Glance at our Colonial Bar,* — *Green Bag,* Vol. XI.

*Adoption of English Law in Maryland,* — *Yale Law Journal,* Vol. VIII.

*Bar of Early Maryland,* — *Green Bag,* Vol. XII.

*Studies in the Civil, Social and Ecclesiastical History of Early Maryland,* by Theodore C. Gambrall (1893).

*Historical View of the Government of Maryland,* by John Van L. McMahon (1831).

*Maryland Jurisprudence,* — *American Jurist,* Vol. XV.

*Maryland Archives, Proceedings and Acts of the General Assembly.*

*Some Characteristics of the Provincial Judiciary,* by Charles E. Phelps, *Maryland Bar Association Report,* Vol. II (1897).

*The Founders of the Bar of Maryland,* by Elihu S. Riley, *Maryland Bar Ass. Report,* Vol. II (1897).

*The Courts and Bench of Colonial Maryland,* — *Maryland Bar Ass. Report,* Vol. III (1898).

*Development of the Legal Profession,* 1669–1715, by Elihu S. Riley, *Maryland Bar Ass. Report,* Vol. IV (1899).

*Economics and Politics in Maryland,* 1720–1750, *and Public Service of Daniel Dulany the Elder,* by St. George Leakin Sioussat, in *Johns Hopkins Univ. Studies in Historical and Political Science Series,* Vol. XXI (1903).

*Beginnings of Maryland,* by Bernard A. Steiner, in *Johns Hopkins Univ. Studies in Historical and Political Science Series,* Vol. XXI (1903).

*The English Statutes in Maryland,* in *Johns Hopkins Univ. Studies in Historical and Political Science Series,* Vol. XXI (1903).

*Life of George Chalmers,* in *Loyalists of American Revolution,* by Lorenzo Sabine (1864).

*Life of Charles Carroll of Carrollton,* by Kate Mason Rowland (1898).

# CHAPTER III

## COLONIAL MASSACHUSETTS BAR

THE history of the legal profession in Massachusetts deserves, perhaps, a fuller statement than that of any other Colony, for two reasons — first, because of the richness of materials at hand in the shape of documents, records, contemporary letters, diaries and histories; and second, because of the fact that this Colony developed a larger and better organized Bar than any other in pre-Revolutionary days. Moreover, the extreme spirit of independence in its colonists on the one hand, the preponderating influence of the clergy among them on the other, and the existence within its borders of the largest college in the country, had an effect upon the course of its law and the growth of its Bar that differentiated its history in some respects from that of the others. Nevertheless, even Massachusetts, like the other Colonies, started its career lawyerless.

Of the sixty-five men who landed at Plymouth in 1620 and founded the Plymouth Colony, no one was a lawyer; and among the founders of the Massachusetts Bay Colony (1628–1634) there was not an actual practising lawyer. Although John Winthrop, its Governor, and Emanuel Downing had been admitted to the Inner Temple in London, and Richard Bellingham, Simon Bradstreet, Herbert Pelham, John Humphreys, and Thomas Dudley and a few others had doubtless been students of law or university men, they were not engaged in the practise of the profession.[1]

[1] *Proc. Mass. Hist. Soc.* (1878), p. 3.

The early provisions for a judiciary were also elementary. At the foundation of the Plymouth Colony the whole community acted as the Court. Thus, in the first recorded offence against the law, in March, 1621, "John Billington is convented before the whole company for the contempt of the captain's lawful commands with opprobrious speeches; for which he is adjudged to have his neck and heels tied together." The second offence was, as Governor Bradford informs us, the first duel fought in New England upon a challenge at single combat with sword and dagger, between Edward Doty and Edward Lester, servants of Mr. Hopkins. "They are adjudged by the whole company to have their heads and feet tied together and so to lie for twenty-four hours, without meat or drink."

It was not until 1623 that there is record of the passage of any order concerning judicial administration; in that year trial by jury was introduced. In 1632, the records show that there were sessions of the General Court, a body which acted both as Legislature and Court, and of the Court of Magistrates or Assistants, presided over by the Governor. In 1685, County Courts were established, and the Court of Assistants exercised an appeal and admiralty jurisdiction.

The law administered by the courts was the Colony's own law, and not the Common Law, except so far as it was expressly adopted. Thus, in 1636, the Colony recognized among what it termed its "General Fundamentals" "the good and equitable laws of our nation suitable for us in matters which are of civil nature (as by the Court has been accustomed), wherein we have no particular law of our own." And, in 1671, the *General Laws and Liberties of New Plymouth Colony* provided that "no person shall be endamaged in respect of Life, Limb, Liberty, Good name or Estate under colour of Law or countenance of authority, but by virtue or equity of some express Law of the General

Court of this Colony, the known law of God, or the good and equitable laws of our Nation, suitable for us."

In Massachusetts Bay Colony, the Governor, Deputy Governor and eighteen Assistants constituted the Court, as well as the Legislature, from 1629 to 1635. They acted both as judges, magistrates and legislators.[1] At their first meeting at Charlestown, in August, 1630, as a "Court of Assistants," they established rules of proceedings in civil matters and powers for punishing criminals. In 1634, the General Court, consisting of a House of Deputies or Representatives of the "free men" of the Colony, and sitting with the Governor and Assistants, was established by a law declaring that:

"The General Court . . . is the chief civil power of this Commonwealth . . . and may act in all affairs of this Commonwealth according to such power, both in matters of counsel, making of lawes and matters of judicature by impeaching and sentencing any person or persons according to law and by receiving and hearing any complaints orderly presented against any person or court.

The General Court from 1635 to 1684, therefore, acted both as a Legislature and as a judicial Court of Appeals; but the Court of Assistants sat also as a separate court, holding four sessions yearly, known as the Quarter Courts.

In 1638, the town magistrates were given jurisdiction to hear petty causes; and in 1639, County Courts were established, consisting of five magistrates and associates chosen by the General Court.

In 1642, the first attempt was made to distinguish by law

[1] The records of the proceedings of the Court of Assistants are found in the same book and intermixed with the records of the proceedings of the General Court. See Preface by John Noble to *Records of the Courts of Assistants* (1901).

*Early Court Files of Suffolk County*, by John Noble, — *Publications of the Colonial Society of Massachusetts*, Vol. III (1895–1897).

between the sphere of the General Court and the Court of Assistants sitting as a separate judicial body; and it was provided that owing to the amount of time consumed in hearing civil cases, all such cases should be first heard in the lower courts, and only when relief could not be obtained there, should the General Court be appealed to.[1] In 1660, the Court of Assistants became an absolutely separate judicial body, as a Superior Court, with powers and terms of sitting prescribed in detail by statute.

In modes of procedure, the magistrates and the courts followed somewhat the general proceedings of English law; but in their decisions they were practically uncontrolled by any system of law. They were inclined to believe, as Winthrop said, that "such laws would be fittest for us which should arise *pro re nata* upon occasions."

This was quite in accordance with the desires of the clergy, who then formed the prevailing power in the Colonies; for, as Thomas Lechford said in 1642:[2]

"The ministers advise in making of laws, especially ecclesiasticall, and are present in courts and advise in some special causes annual and in framing of Fundamental Lawes. Matters of debt, trespass and upon the case, equity, yea and of heresy also are tryed by a jury."

Another contemporary wrote:[3]

"The preachers by their power with the people made all the magistrates, and kept them so entirely under obedience that they durst not act without them. Soe that whenever

[1] For an early case appealed from the Court of Assistants to the General Court in 1648, see *Saltonstall & D. Yale* v. *Abraham Shurt.* — *Col. Rec.*, Vol. II, p. 231.

[2] *Plaine Dealing or News from New England*, by Thomas Lechford (1642).

[3] *An Account of the Colonies* in *Lambeth MSS.*, *Perry's Historical Collection*, Vol. III, 48.

anything strange or unusual was brought before them, they would not determine the matter without consulting their preachers."

But while so much power lay in the discretion of the magistrates, the people felt themselves unsafe. As John Winthrop wrote:[1]

"The deputies having conceived great danger to our State in regard that our magistrates for want of positive law in many cases might proceed according to their discretion, it was agreed that some men should be appointed to frame a body of grounds of law, in resemblance to a Magna Charta, which being allowed by some of the ministers and the General Court, should be received for fundamental laws."

Accordingly, "At the General Court, May 25, 1636, it was ordered that the Governor (Henry Vane), the Deputy Governor (John) Cotton, Mr. (Hugh) Peters and Mr. Shepherd are entreated to make a draught of laws agreeable to the word of God which may be the Fundamentals of this Commonwealth and to present the same to the next General Court."

In the meantime, the magistrates were ordered to hear and determine causes according to law; but where there was no law, "then as near the Law of God as they can." It was natural and characteristic of the times, that this matter of framing a code should have been entrusted by the magistrates to two clergymen, each of whom framed a separate model. Rev. John Cotton, a Fellow of Emmanuel College, Cambridge, England, prepared a code called by Governor Winthrop "A copy of Moses, his judicials, compiled in an exact method."[2] It was founded on the Scripture throughout, with references thereto, and established a pure theoc-

[1] *History of New England*, by John Winthrop, Vol. I, p. 194.

[2] See Cotton's *Moses, His Judicials*, in *Mass. Hist. Soc. Proc.* (2d Series), Vol. XVI (1902).

racy. The other was compiled by Rev. Nathaniel Ward, a minister at Ipswich, and the author of a curious book entitled *The Simple Cobbler of Agawam.* He had been a barrister of Lincoln's Inn, in England, in 1615,[1] had entered the ministry in 1618 and been suspended for puritanism in 1633 by Archbishop Laud. This great work of his, called *The Body of Liberties*, consisting of one hundred fundamental laws, is entitled to the fame of being the first American law book.[2] It was accepted by the people in 1641, as better suited to the times than Cotton's Code.[3] Still, even in Ward's Code it is to be noted that in cases not therein provided for it was the "word of God" which was to guide the courts, and not the English Common Law. Thus Liberty Number I provided:

> "1. No man's life shall be taken away, no man's honour or good name shall be stayned, no man's person shall be arrested, restrayned, banished, dismembered, nor any wayes punished, no man shall be deprived of his wife or children, no man's goods or estates shall be taken away from him nor any way indamaged under colour of law or Countenance of Authority, unless it be by virtue or equitie of some expresse law of the Country warranting the same stablished by a generall court and sufficiently published, or in case of the defect of a law in any particular case by the word of God. And in Capitall cases, or in cases concerning dismembering or banishment, according to that word to be judged by the Generall Court."

Many of their enactments at this time differed greatly

[1] See Gray, C. G., in *Jackson* v. *Phillips*, 14 Allen (Mass.), p. 599 (1867).

[2] No copy of this was discovered until 1843, when Mr. Francis C. Gray found it in the Boston Athenaeum. See *Mass. Hist. Soc. Coll.*, Vol. VIII (3d Series), p. 196.

See also *Colonial Laws of Massachusetts*, by W. H. Whitmore (1890).

[3] In 1641 there was published in London *An Abstract of the Lawes of New England As they are now Established*, which is probably Cotton's Code. See *Mass. Hist. Soc. Proc.* (2d Series), Vol. XVI (1902).

from the English Common Law of the day, as, for instance, that there should be no monopolies "except such as were profitable to the country, and those for a short time only;" that all deeds of conveyance, whether absolute or conditional, should be recorded; and that instead of the right of primogeniture, the elder son should have a double portion of his parent's real and personal estate.

This *Body of Liberties* was probably not printed in full or published at the time; but in 1649 a revision of all the laws then in existence was published, known as the *Laws and Liberties*, and a similar revision was made in 1660 (the earliest of which any copy is extant), and another revision was made in 1672.[1]

In 1644, the General Court requested the opinion of the elders as to whether the magistrates should be guided by the word of God in cases not covered by statute, and the elders replied in the following terms: [2]

"We do not find that by the patent they are expressly directed to proceed according to the word of God: but we understand that by a law or liberty of the country, they may act in cases wherein as yet there is no express law, so that in such acts they proceed according to the word of God."

In 1646 the General Court itself stated:[3]

[1] See *The Body of Liberties of 1641*, by H. H. Edes, *Publications of the Massachusetts Colonial Society*, Vol. VII (1900–1902).

[2] *Col. Rec.*, Vol. II, p. 93.

[3] See Winthrop's *History of New England*, Vol. II. The foundation of the law upon the Word of God was even at this time a familiar doctrine even in Common Law England.

Thus as late as 1650, Lord Chief Justice Keble said in 5 *How. St. Trials* that the law of England was "the very consequence of the very decalogue itself — as really and truly the law of God as any Scriptural phrase. . . . Whatever was not consonant to the law of God in Scripture . . . was not the law of England but the error of the party which did pronounce it."

So John Milton in his *Defence of the People of England* in 1651 appealed

"The laws of the colony are not diametrically opposed to the laws of England for then they must be contrary to the laws of God on which the common law, so far as it is law, is also founded. Anything that is otherwise established is not law but an error."

It seems to be a fact, therefore, that the Common Law was regarded as binding, only so far as it was expressive of the Law of God, or of a particular statute of the Colony. The early court records themselves show the constant citation of scriptural authority. "The reasons of appeal and the answers make much use of quotations from Scripture — a pertinent quotation seemed sometimes decisive in settling a disputed point. Possibly there was sometimes a readier acquiescence in an opinion of Moses than in one of the Lord High Chancellor."[1] It is evident that with such a basis for the decisions of the courts, there was little need of lawyers learned in the English Common Law. "When the holy Scriptures were considered as a proper guide in all cases of doubt, and the parties spoke for themselves, there was no place for an order of lawyers."[2] There can be little wonder therefore that "for more than the ten

"to that fundamental maxim in our law by which nothing is to be counted as law that is contrary to the law of God or of reason."

In a book entitled *Quaternio or a Fourfold way to a Happy Life. Set forth in a Discourse between a Countryman and a citizen, a divine and a lawyer, wherein the Commodities of the Countrey and the Citie; together with the excellency of Divinitie and the Law are set forth*, published in 1636 by Thomas Nash of the Inner Temple, it is said: "Now because it is a hard thing, yea indeede impossible almost, for a man to observe these lawes which he knoweth not; therefore I did desire to know the Lawes of the Kingdome wherein I lived and thereby as a rule to frame and fashion all my actions by . . . I had often heard and upon Inquiry I have found it to be true that all Lawes politicall are meere derivatives out of the primitive Law of God and Nature."

[1] *Early Court Files of Suffolk County*, by John Noble, *Publications of the Massachusetts Colonial Society*, Vol. III (1895–1897).

[2] *Address before the Suffolk Bar on Origin and History of the Legal Profession in Massachusetts*, by William Sullivan, in 1825.

first years," as Hutchinson says, "the parties spake for themselves for the most part; sometimes, when it was thought the cause required it, they were assisted by a patron, or man of superior abilities without fee or reward."[1] And though Ward, in a sermon preached at the annual election in 1641, had declared that the magistrates "ought not to give private advice and take knowledge of any main cause before it came to public hearing," his proposition was rejected on the ground that its adoption would render it necessary to provide lawyers to direct men in their causes.

Probably the first lawyer in the Colonies was Thomas Morton, described by Governor Bradford as "a kind of pettie-fogger of Furnewells Inne," although set forth by himself on the title-page of his book, *The New British Canaan* (1637), as "of Clifford's Inn Gent."[2] Governor Dudley spoke of him as "a proud, insolent man," who had been "an attorney in the West Countries while he lived in England." He came to Massachusetts in 1624 or 1625 with Captain Wollaston and settled in what is now Quincy. At his place named Merry Mount he opened, as the old chronicler says,

> "a school of atheisme, set up a maypole and did quaff strong waters and act as they had anew revived and celebrated the feast of ye Roman Goddess Flora or the beastly products of ye madd Bacchanalians."

[1] *History of Massachusetts Bay Colony*, by Thomas Hutchinson, Vol. I.

[2] Clifford's Inn and Furnewell's Inn were Inns of Chancery. The Inns of Chancery were so called, "probably because they were appropriated to such clerks as chiefly studied the forming of writs which was the province of the cursitors who were officers of Chancery, such as belong to the Courts of Common Pleas and King's Bench, and in Stowe's time were chiefly filled with attorneys, solicitors and clerks." They were inferior in rank to the Inns of Court, at which only those who were studying to be called as barristers were admitted. See Chapter I, *supra*.

The patience of the rulers being exhausted, he was imprisoned and then shipped out of the Colony.

The first educated lawyer who practised in the Colony appeared on the horizon in 1637 or 1638, when Thomas Lechford, "of Clement's Inn in the County of Middlesex, Gentleman,"[1] landed in Boston. For three years he was, so Washburn calls him, "the Embodied Bar of Massachusetts Bay."[2] Under the conditions prevalent, he found the practise of law in Boston far from lucrative; and he described himself as being supported largely as a scrivener "in writing petty things." Little is known of him; but it is certain that his legal knowledge was of value in the Colony, for it was at his suggestion that a law was passed in 1639, by which it was ordered, that in order that the records should "bee of good use for president to posterity . . . every judgment with all the evidence bee recorded in a book, to bee kept to posterity."[3]

In 1639, his habits brought him into such trouble with the authorities, that at a Quarter Court in September it was ordered, that "Mr. Thomas Lechford for going to the Jewry and pleading with them out of court is debarred from pleading any main cause hereafter unless his own and admonished not to presume to meddle beyond what he shall be called to by the court." In 1640, he was "convented" before the Quarter Court, and, according to the record, "acknowledged he had overshot himself, and was sorry for it, promised

[1] Mr. Justice Shallow — "By yea or nay, sir, I dare say my cousin William is become a good scholar. He is at Oxford, still, is he not?"

Silence — "Indeed, sir, to my cost."

Shallow — "He must then to the inns of court shortly. I was once of Clement's Inn, where, I think, they will talk of mad Shallow yet." — *King Henry IV*, Part II, Act III, Scene 2 (Printed in 1600).

[2] *Judicial History of Massachusetts*, by Emory Washburn (1840).

[3] *Mass. Colony Records*, Vol. I, p. 275. To him therefore is owed the *Records of the Court of Assistants* (published first in print in Massachusetts in 1901).

to attend to his calling, and not to meddle with controversies, and was dismissed." In 1642, after his return to England, he published his *Plaine Dealing or News from New England*, from which it appears that his trouble with the courts was due to the fact that he tried to set up the Common Law, while the Puritan courts cared nothing at all for the Common Law, but were trying to set up, especially in criminal matters, the Mosaic Law.[1] The foreman, he wrote, gave the charge to the grand juries, "under the heads of the ten commandments," and this was his warning:

"I fear it is not a little degree of pride and dangerous improvidence to slight all former laws of the church and state, cases of experience and precedents, to hammer out new, according to several exigencies, upon pretence that the Word of God is sufficient to rule us."

It has been said that it was because of their experience with Lechford that the colonists adopted Article No. 26 of the *Body of Liberties*, providing that: "Every man that findeth himself unfit to plead his own cause in any Court shall have Liberty to employ any man against whom the Court doth not except to help him, *provided he give him no fee or reward for his pains*." This statute remained in force, however, only a few years.

Forty years passed on after Lechford's disgusted return to London, and still no educated lawyer appeared in Massachusetts. There were, however, attorneys of some kind, as they are mentioned in the records of the General Court in 1649 and elsewhere. Little, however, is known of them, and they were doubtless what Governor Winthrop would call "mean men," of but little or no legal education.

[1] *The First Lawyer in Boston*, — *Amer. Law Rev.*, Vol. XIX. See also *Mass. Col. Rec.*, Vol. I, p. 270.

They appeared, probably by special powers, and by judicial requisition.[1]

In 1663, an act was passed prohibiting every person who was a "usual or common attorney in any Inferior Court" from sitting as a Deputy in the General Court;[2] and in 1656 an act was passed, providing that:

"This court taking into consideration the great charge resting upon the colony by reason of the many and tedious discourses and pleadings in court, both of plaintiff and defendant, as also the readiness of many to prosecute suits

[1] See *Address to Worcester County Bar, October 2, 1829*, by Joseph Willard. Thus in 1652, in Middlesex, Mr. Coggan appeared as attorney to Stephen Day, the first printer: in 1654, in the case of Ridgway against Jordan, the defendant appeared by his attorney, Amos Richardson: and in 1656, in the case of John Glover against Henry Dunster, who had been president of Harvard College, Edmund Goffe and Thomas Danforth appeared for the plaintiff. This Amos Richardson was a tailor, and Coggan (John) was in the mercantile business and kept the first shop in Boston. Goffe, then an old man, was for several years the representative from Cambridge, and Danforth also; and the latter, besides, filled the office of assistant and deputy governor; but neither of them was of the legal profession.

[2] The date of this is sometimes given as 1654, but Willard considers 1663 as the more accurate. This provision of law is strangely suggestive of the famous "Dunces' Parliament" held in 1404 at the order of Henry IV, and described by Sir Edward Coke as follows: "At a parliament holden at Coventry Anno 6 H 4 the parliament was summoned by writ and by colour of the said ordinance it was forbidden that no lawyer should be chosen knight, citizen, or burgess, by reason whereof this parliament was fruitless and never a good law made thereat, and therefore called indoctum parliamentum or lack learning parliament, and seeing these writs were against law, lawyers ever since (for the great and good service of the Commonwealth) have been eligible; for as it hath been said the writs of parliament cannot be altered without an act of parliament; and albeit the prohibitory clause had been inserted in the writ, yet being against law, lawyers were of right eligible and might have been elected knights, citizens, or burgesses in that parliament of 6 H 4."

See *New York Bar Ass. Proc.*, Vol. XIII.

James I issued a proclamation to voters for members of Parliament directing them "not to choose curious and wrangling lawyers who seek reputation by stirring needless questions." See *Green Bag*, Vol. V (1893).

in law for small matters: it is therefore ordered by this court and the authority thereof that when any plaintiff or defendant shall plead by himself or his attorney for a longer time than one hour, the party that is sentenced or condemned shall pay twenty shillings for every hour so pleading more than the common fees appointed by the court for the entrance of actions, to be added to the execution for the use of the country."

It was not until 1647 that any English law books were to be found in the Colony, when the Governor and Assistants ordered the importation of two copies each of Sir Edward Coke on *Littleton;* the *Book of Entries;* Sir Edward Coke on *Magna Charta;* the *New Terms of Law;* Dalton's *Justices of the Peace;* and Sir Edward Coke's *Reports*, "to the end that we may have better light for making and proceeding about laws." And in 1650, it was ordered that "whereas this Commonwealth is much defective for want of laws for maritime affairs and for as much as there are already many good laws made and published by our own land and the French Nation and other kingdoms and commonwealths . . . the said laws printed and published in a book called *Lex Mercatoria* shall be perused and duly considered and such of them as are approved by this court shall be declared and published to be in force in this jurisdiction."

Throughout the Seventeenth Century, the forms of judicial proceedings were exceedingly simple. The writs were concise and the proceedings summary. Testimony was given in open court and written down by the clerk in the form of depositions and became a part of the record of the case. The questioning of witnesses was principally by the court. "Little regard, was paid to forms of action. They had actions of replevin, debt and trespass, and sometimes adopted a proper form of process to recover possession of real estate. But the most common form of action, as well to recover lands as damages for direct and immediate injuries, was that of case."[1]

"The records which have survived indicate that the administration of justice was regular and systematic. . . . The magistrates maintained a somewhat patriarchal attitude, and in the justice which they administered there was a large element of equity. . . . The impression gained from the records is that, on the whole, the declaration contained in the first clauses of the Body of Liberties, guaranteeing the resident against arbitrary judicial action was made good in practise. The spirit of justice was there, although by no means all its modern safeguards, such as elaborate judicial formalities and rules of evidence, the activity of attorneys, and the presumption that the accused is innocent until he is proven guilty. But in cases where religious and governmental prejudices were concerned, defendants had little protection. The magistrates were judges, attorneys and accusers — all in one; the exaction of an oath from witnesses and the services of attorneys were denied to the defendants."[2]

In 1686, a new court, the Superior Court, was created under the new Governor, Sir Edmund Andros, composed of a majority of the Councillors. Three judges were appointed, no one of whom was a lawyer — William Stoughton, Chief Justice, John Richardson and Simon Lynde. Benjamin Bullivant, a physician and apothecary, was appointed Attorney-General — a man of "considerable eloquence and knowledge of laws."

At the same time, a table of attorneys' fees was established; and attorneys were obliged, upon admission to the Bar, to take oath. This was the earliest prescribed attor-

[1] *Judicial History of Massachusetts*, by Emory Washburn.

[2] *The American Colonies in the Seventeenth Century*, by H. L. Osgood (1904–1907).

neys' oath in all the Colonies, and followed, largely, the wording of the oath then established in England. Giles Masters, Capt. Nathaniel Thomas, Anthony Checkley, a merchant and military man, Christopher Webb, a merchant, and John Watson, a merchant, were admitted and sworn as attorneys.

There were still no trained lawyers in the Province, so that Edward Randolph, Secretary to Governor Andros, wrote to England in 1689:

"I have wrote you the want we have of two, or three, honest attorneys, (if any such thing in nature). We have but two; one is West's creature, — came with him from New York, and drives all before him. He also takes extravagant fees, and for want of more, the country cannot avoid coming to him so that we had better be quite without them than not to have more. I have wrote Mr. Blackthwaite the great necessity of judges from England."[1]

But the necessity of procuring judges and lawyers from England was soon to pass away. For in 1686 Benjamin Lynde graduated from Harvard College, and "was admitted," his Diary says,

"for the study of the law (as my father had advised) into the Honorable Society of the Middle Temple as by the admission of October 18, 1692."[2]

A new royal charter for Massachusetts was granted by King William in 1691; and with it began a new era for the law.

The courts became an institution, separate and distinct

[1] The two were probably James Graham, Attorney-General under Andros, and George Farwell, Clerk of the Court of Oyer and Terminer.

[2] Benjamin Lynde was made Judge of the Superior Court in Massachusetts in 1712 and Chief Justice in 1728.

On the occasion of publishing Judge Lynde's commission, Judge Sewall, in an address to the jury, remarked, "that they would hereafter have the benefit of Inns of Court education, superadded to that of Harvard College."

from the magistrates. The judges, however, held their commissions at the King's pleasure, and were chosen by the Royal Governors, still largely influenced by the clergy, who preferred men with no legal training.

In 1690, an act was passed, approved by the King in 1699, which established a Superior Court of Judicature and inferior courts; at the same time, forms of writs were directed, and the courts were empowered to make rules for the regulation of practise. No one of the judges appointed, however, was a lawyer.

A similar condition prevailed in that Court of Special Oyer and Terminer, appointed in 1692, to try the witchcraft cases. In this court, Chief Justice William Stoughton and Judge Samuel Sewall were educated for the ministry, Judges Nathaniel Saltonstall and Peter Sergeant were gentlemen without a profession, Judges Wait Winthrop and Jonathan Curwin, and Anthony Checkley, the Attorney-General, were merchants or military men.

It may be noted, however, that this absence of legal training was not confined to the Colonies, for several of the Lord Chief Justices of England in this Century were men of little education at the Bar; and of Sir John Kelynge, who was at the head of the King's Bench under Charles II, it was said, that "however fit he might have been to charge the Roundheads under Prince Rupert, he was very unfit to charge a jury in Westminster Hall." [1]

[1] While the witchcraft court has been criticised for its reckless disregard of rules of evidence, and also for condemning the defendants unheard, it is to be remembered that no defendant at this time, even in England, was allowed to have counsel to plead for him in a criminal trial for felony or treason. It was not until 1696 (7–8 William III, c. 3) that this privilege was granted to persons accused of treason, and not until 1836 (6–7 William IV, c. 114), in cases of felony.

An interesting defence of the legal ability of this court is made by Abner E. Goodell in a paper on *Witch Trials in Massachusetts*, — *Mass. Hist. Soc. Proc.*, Vol. XX (1883), in which he says: "The regret which some, in

Unlike the Colonies outside of New England, the Chief Justices in Massachusetts continued to be laymen in many instances, even down to the War of the Revolution. Thus the first, William Stoughton (Chief Justice 1692–1701), was a clergyman;[1] his successor, Waite Winthrop (Chief Justice 1701 and 1708–1717), was a physician;[2] Isaac Addington (1702–1703) was a physician;[3] Samuel Sewall (1718–1728) was a clergyman;[4] Benjamin Lynde (1728–1745) was a barrister of the Middle Temple;[5] his successor, Paul Dudley (1745–1751), was a barrister of the Inner Temple;[6] Stephen Sewall (1752–1760) was a tutor in Harvard College;[7] Thomas Hutchinson (1761–1769) was a wealthy merchant;[8] Benjamin Lynde, the younger (1769–1771), had a legal education in the Colony;[9] Peter Oliver (1772–1775) was a literary man.[10]

Of the twenty-three associate judges, Edmund Trowbridge, Chambers Russell[11] and William Cushing were the

consequence of the representations of late writers upon the witch trials, may have been led to feel, that those trials had not been conducted by lawyers, is not warranted by the disclosure of the records of the tribunals of England or her colonies if it springs from the belief that a more humane and rational course of procedure might, in that case, have been expected . . . Lawyers and laymen, as well as clergymen, were equally under the influence of the superstitious terrors of that day of darkness and delusion."

It is to be noted that as late as 1676 two women had been tried as witches before Sir Matthew Hale in England, and executed.

[1] Born in 1631, Harvard graduate of 1650.

[2] Born 1642, grandson of John Winthrop, Judge of Admiralty 1699.

[3] Born 1645.

[4] Born 1652, Harvard 1671, Judge of Probate 1715–1728.

[5] Born 1666, Harvard 1686, Advocate-General of the Court of Admiralty 1697.

[6] Born 1675, Harvard 1690, Attorney-General 1702.

[7] Born 1704, Harvard 1721.

[8] Born 1711, Harvard 1727, Judge of Probate 1752, Lieutenant-Governor 1758.

[9] Born 1700, Harvard 1718.

[10] Born 1713, Harvard 1730.

[11] Born 1713, Harvard 1731, Judge of Probate 1752.

only ones who had any regular legal education, the rest being laymen or men trained for the ministry. Roger Mompesson and Robert Auchmuty, Judges of Admiralty, had been English barristers. No other trained lawyers appeared on the Bench.[1]

Notwithstanding their lack of systematic legal training, however, many of these judges were men of great learning and some of them had read considerable law. Thus it has been said of William Stoughton that:[2]

"He had extraordinary attainments in legal learning. . . . It is true that he as well as Dudley and Sewall was bred a clergyman; but those who imagine that the study of divinity unfits the student for forensic, legislative or magisterial duties are to be reminded that the legal is but a lay branch of the clerical profession from which it sprung; and that the secularizing of jurisprudence is a work of modern times. . . . I think the three magistrates I have named, each of whom acceptably held the post, either in Massachusetts or New York, of Chief Justice of the highest judicial court will compare favorably in respect to all those acquirements necessary to the proper conduct of trials and the administering of forensic justice, with, at least, the average benchers of the Inns of Court in the days of William and Anne."

So, too, of Samuel Sewall, Washburn says:

"From a perusal of his journal it is apparent that he had a natural taste for legal science which he had cultivated by a very respectable course of study. . . . He must have been altogether better read in the principles of the Common Law than any other judge upon the bench."

Thomas Hutchinson, being a man of liberal culture, had

[1] It is a noticeable fact, however, that 20 out of 33 of the Superior Court Judges, though without legal training, were graduates of Harvard College. And even of the judges of the lower Courts of Common Pleas in Suffolk County, 12 out of 25 were graduates of Harvard; in Middlesex, 7 out of 20; in Essex, 12 out of 30; in Plymouth, 8 out of 19.

[2] See *Witch Trials in Massachusetts*, by Abner E. Goodell. *Mass. Hist. Soc. Proc.*, Vol. XX (1883).

devoted much time to the reading of law, though he had never practised; but, as he remarks in his Diary: "Though it was an eyesore to some of the Bar to have a person at the head of the law who had not been bred to it, he had reason to think the lawyers in general at no time desired his removal."[1]

That the lawyers were restive under the Chief Justice's lack of legal knowledge is shown, however, in a letter written by John Adams to William Tudor, regarding a controversy between the Governor and the General Court in which he had appeared as counsel:[2]

"Mr. Hutchinson had wholly misunderstood the legal doctrine of allegiance. . . . I had quoted largely from a law authority which no man in Massachusetts had ever read. Hutchinson and all his law counsels were in fault; . . . They dared not deny it lest the book should be produced to their confusion. It was humorous enough to see how Hutchinson wriggled to evade it. He found nothing better to say than that it was 'the artificial reasoning of Lord Coke.' The book was *Moore's Reports*. . . . It had been Mr. Gridley's."

It was not until 1701 that practise of the law became first dignified as a regular profession, through the requirement *by statute* of an oath for all attorneys admitted by the courts, as follows:

" You shall do no falsehood, nor consent to any to be done in the court, and if you know of any to be done you shall give knowledge thereof to the Justices of the Court, or some

[1] An interesting sidelight is thrown on this, by an entry in his diary under date of July 22, 1774, when he was in England visiting Sir Francis Bernard.

"Sir Francis mentioned among other things that he apologized to Lord Mansfield for appointing me Chief Justice, not having been bred to the law; adding that he had no cause to repent it. Lord Chief Justice Wilmot being by, broke out with an oath, "By ——, he did not make a worse chief for that!" See *Diary of Thomas Hutchinson*, p. 195.

[2] *Life of Thomas Hutchinson*, by James K. Hosmer (1896).

of them, that it may be reformed. You shall not wittingly and willingly promote, sue or procure to be sued any false or unlawful suit, nor give aid or consent to the same. You shall delay no man for lucre or malice, but you shall use yourself in the office of an attorney within the court according to the best of your learning and discretion, and with all good fidelity as well to the courts as to your clients."[1]

At the same time, the General Court established forms of writs, and authorized the courts to establish rules of practise. It was some time, however, before there were any strict legal forms or technical rules in use in the courts, and most of the early improvements in judicial procedure and much of the enhanced elevation of the character of the profession were due to the individual efforts of the two English barristers in the Colony — Paul Dudley, the first lawyer to sit on the bench, Judge of the Superior Court from 1718 to 1751, and Robert Auchmuty, who practised in Massachusetts as early as 1719.

The scarcity of lawyers and the fear that a party might be able to retain the whole Bar to the prejudice of his adversary are shown by the enactment of a statute in 1715, providing that "no person shall entertain more than two of the sworn allowed attorneys at law, that the adverse party may have liberty to retain others of them to assist him, upon his tender of the established fee, which they may not refuse."[2]

At first the native lawyers were, in general, men of little

[1] This oath followed almost exactly the form set forth in England in *The Book of Oaths* (1649); and see also *The Practick Part of the Law* (1676).

Practically this same form of oath was prescribed in Connecticut in 1708, in Pennsylvania in 1726, in Virginia in 1732.

[2] This provision appeared again in 1785; and as late as 1836 (*Rev. St.*, ch. 88, sect. 26) it was provided that, no more than two persons for each party should, without permission of the court, be allowed to manage any case.

distinction; although among those sworn in 1701, there were two of real ability — Thomas Newton and Joseph Hearne.

During the first half of the Eighteenth Century, New England was crippled by foolish financial management, through the unlimited issue of paper money, and from 1704 to 1741 the depreciation of the currency produced innumerable troubles. These conditions gave rise to much litigation; and William Shirley reported to the Board of Trade, in 1743, that:

"It was not infrequent for persons of some circumstances and character to suffer judgments to be given against them by default in open court for such debts, and to appeal from one court to another merely for delay; whereby lawsuits were scandalously multiplied and a litigious, trickish spirit promoted among the lower sort of people."[1]

In 1747, Dr. Douglass wrote in his *Summary:*

"Generally in all our colonies, particularly in New England, people are much addicted to quirks of the law. A very ordinary countryman in New England is almost qualified for a country attorney in England."[2]

John Adams, writing to William Cushing in 1756, expressed a low estimate of the legal profession:

"Let us look upon a lawyer. In the beginning of life we see him fumbling and raking amidst the rubbish of writs, indictments, pleas, ejectments, enfiefed, illatebration and one thousand other *lignum vitae* words which have neither harmony nor meaning. When he gets into business, he often foments more quarrels than he composes, and enriches himself at the expense of impoverishing others more honest and deserving than himself. Besides, the noise and fume of Courts and the labour of inquiring into and pleading dry

[1] *Life of Thomas Hutchinson*, by James K. Hosmer, p. 20 (1896).

[2] *A Summary, Historical and Political, of the First Planting, Progressive Improvements and Present State of the British Settlements in North America*, by William Douglass (London, 1747).

and difficult cases have very few charms in my eyes. The study of law is indeed an avenue to the more important offices of the State and the happiness of the human society is an object worth the pursuit of any man. But the acquisitions of these important offices depends upon many circumstances of birth and of fortune, not to mention capacity, which I have not, and I can have no hopes of being useful that way."[1]

And even as late as 1758, Adams, having finally decided to adopt the profession which he had thus condemned, stated that he

"found the practice of law was grasped into the hands of deputy sheriffs, pettifoggers, and even constables, who filled all the writs upon bonds, promissory notes and accounts, and received the fees established for lawyers, and stirred up many unnecessary suits."

Nevertheless, during the first forty years of the Eighteenth Century, a small Bar of native lawyers of really great ability was slowly being established; and to their learning and influence was due the gradual growth of forms, special pleading and general judicial development.

The Nestor of them was John Read, who, born in 1679, graduated from Harvard in 1697, studied in Connecticut and was admitted to the Bar in New Haven in 1708. Before his death in 1749, he acquired the reputation of being "the greatest common lawyer that ever lived in New England." Of him, Adams said later: "He had as great a genius and became as eminent as any man." To him is due many of the forms of writs, actions, declarations and conveyancing later in use. He was retained by the Colony of Connecticut, and also by Massachusetts, in important boundary dispute cases with New York, New Hampshire and Rhode Island; also for the town of Boston in many cases, one of par-

[1] Published in *Nantucket Gazette* (1817).

ticular importance involving the title to Dock square, tried for six years and appealed to the King in Council, where he won.[1]

After Read came Jeremiah Gridley, who, born in 1702, a Harvard graduate of 1725, studied first for the ministry and later became "the father of the Boston Bar," Attorney-General in 1742 and again in 1761, and the great legal scholar of the Century. His office was the training school for James Otis, Jr., and John Adams, of whom Gridley used to observe, that "he had reared two young eagles who were one day to peck out his eyes." Oxenbridge Thacher, Benjamin Pratt (later Chief Justice of New York), and William Cushing (later Chief Justice of the Supreme Court of Massachusetts and Justice and Chief Justice of the Supreme Court of the United States) were also his pupils.

Judge Edmund Trowbridge, born in 1709, a Harvard graduate of 1728, was the great "real estate" lawyer of the time, termed by Chief Justice Isaac Parker, in 1813, "perhaps the most profound common lawyer of New England before the Revolution." His opinions and his essay on the law of mortgages were considered of such value as to be annexed (after his death in 1792) to volume eight of *Massachusetts Reports;* and such was his learning and ability, that it is said by John Adams, that he had the entire command of the practise in Middlesex, Worcester and several other counties, and had the power to crush any young lawyer by a frown or nod. In his office in Cambridge studied Francis Dana and Theophilus Parsons (both of whom became Chief Justices of the Supreme Court of the State of Massachusetts), James Putnam, Royall Tyler (Chief Justice of Vermont), Rufus King, Christopher Gore and Harrison Gray Otis.

[1] *Life of John Read,* by George B. Read (1903).

Contemporary with Gridley were William Shirley, Robert Auchmuty and William Bollan, who were native English lawyers, Richard Dana,[1] Benjamin Kent,[2] James Otis, Sr.,[3] Timothy Ruggles[4] and Benjamin Pratt.[5]

It was of these men that John Adams wrote in his Diary, as a young law student, October 24, 1758:

"Went into the court house and sat down by Mr. Paine at the lawyers' table. I felt shy under awe and concern; for Mr. Gridley, Mr. Pratt, Mr. Otis, Mr. Kent and Mr. Thacher were all present and looked sour. I had no acquaintance with anybody but Paine and Quincy and they took but little notice."

About two decades later, another group of lawyers added distinction to the Bar — James Otis, Jr.,[6] Oxenbridge Thacher,[7] Samuel Adams,[8] Jonathan Sewall,[9] Robert Treat Paine,[10] John Worthington[11] and Joseph Hawley,[12] the two latter being the most prominent of the few lawyers practising in the western part of the Province.

About 1765, just prior to the Revolution, a third group of eminent young lawyers of considerable law learning began

[1] Born in 1700, Harvard graduate of 1718.

[2] Born about 1705, Harvard 1727, educated as a clergyman.

[3] Born in 1702, father of James Otis, Jr., Attorney-General 1748.

[4] Born in 1711, Harvard 1732.

[5] Born in 1710, Harvard 1737, Chief Justice of New York in 1761.

[6] Born in 1725, Harvard 1743, studied with J. Gridley.

[7] Born in 1720, Harvard 1738, studied for the ministry, later studied law with J. Gridley.

[8] Born in 1722, Harvard 1740.

[9] Born in 1728, Harvard 1748, a school teacher, later studied law with Judge Chambers Russell, admitted to practice 1758, Attorney-General 1767.

[10] Born in 1731, Harvard 1749, became a minister, later admitted to the Bar in 1759.

[11] Born in 1719, Yale 1740, studied law with Gen. Phineas Lyman.

[12] Born in 1724, Yale 1742, studied for the ministry, later studied law with General Lyman.

to distinguish themselves — John Adams,[1] Josiah Quincy, Jr.,[2] Samuel Quincy,[3] Sampson Salters Blowers,[4] Theophilus Bradbury,[5] William Cushing,[6] Daniel Leonard,[7] Theodore Sedgwick,[8] Caleb Strong[9] and Francis Dana.[10]

At first, no special qualifications and no definite term of study had been required for admission to the Bar. But, in reality, in order to master the profession, a student in the Colonies had to acquire far more knowledge than a student at the Inns of Court in London; for as Gridley said to Adams in 1758:[11]

"A lawyer in this country must study common law and civil law and natural law and admiralty law and must do the duty of a counsellor, a lawyer, an attorney, a solicitor and even of a scrivener; so that the difficulties of the profession are much greater here than in England."

As early as 1761, the Bar had formed a regular association; and had prescribed seven years of probation — three of

[1] Born in 1735, Harvard 1755, studied law with Judge James Putnam, admitted to the Bar in 1758, called as Barrister 1761.

[2] Born in 1744, Harvard 1763.

[3] Born in 1735, Harvard 1754, studied with Benjamin Pratt; Solicitor-General 1767.

[4] Born in 1742, Harvard 1763, studied law under Governor Hutchinson.

[5] Born in 1739, Harvard 1757, practised law in Maine 1761–1779, one of the earliest lawyers there.

[6] Born in 1732, Harvard 1751, studied law with J. Gridley, was the first regular educated lawyer to settle in Maine, 1755, Chief Justice of Massachusetts 1776.

[7] Born in 1740, Harvard 1760.

[8] Born in 1746, left Yale without graduating in 1765, studied for the ministry, admitted to the Bar in 1766.

[9] Born in 1745, Harvard 1764, admitted to the Bar in 1772.

[10] Born in 1743, Harvard 1762, Chief Justice of Massachusetts 1791–1806.

[11] *John Adams' Life and Works*, Vol. II, p. 46.

General Gage later denounced "this country where every man studies law;" and in 1768 the British Attorney-General said, "Look into the papers and see how well these Americans are versed in Crown Law."

preliminary study, two of practise as attorney in the Inferior Court, and two of practise as attorney in the Superior Court.[1] John Adams, noting in his Diary, July 28, 1766, the Bar meeting for the admission of three young gentlemen, Mr. Oliver, Mr. Quincy and Mr. Blowers, consoled himself for the "swarming and multiplying" of lawyers, by the reflection that four years must elapse before they could assume the gown. Adams describes as follows the admission to practise of himself and Samuel Quincy, in 1758, their sponsor before the Court being Gridley, the Attorney-General:

"I began to grow uneasy, expecting that Quincy would be sworn and I have no patron, when Mr. Gridley made his appearance, and, on sight of me, whispered to Mr. Pratt, Dana, Kent, Thacher, about me. Mr. Pratt said nobody knew me. 'Yes,' says Gridley, 'I have tried him and he is a very sensible fellow!' At last he rose up and bowed to his right hand and said, 'Mr. Quincy,' when Quincy rose up; then he bowed to me, 'Mr. Adams,' when I walked out.

" Mr. Gridley then presented the young candidates to the Court with the following remarks:

"'May it please your Honors, I have two young gentlemen, Mr. Quincy and Mr. Adams, to present for the oath of an attorney. Of Mr. Quincy it is sufficient to say that he has lived three years with Mr. Pratt; of Mr. Adams, as he is unknown to your Honors, it is necessary to say that he has lived between two and three years with Mr. Putnam of Worcester, has a good character from him, and all others who know him, and that he was with me the other day several hours, and I take it, he is qualified to study the law by his scholarship, and that he has made a very considerable, a very great proficiency in the principles of the law, and therefore, that the clients' interests may be safely entrusted in his hands, I therefore recommend him with the consent of the Bar to your Honors for the oath.'

[1] *Life and Works of John Adams*, Vol. II, p. 197, G. Dexter, *Mass. Hist. Soc. Coll.*, Vol. VI, p. 145.

"Then Mr. Pratt said two or three words and the clerk was ordered to swear us; after the oath, Mr. Gridley took me by the hand, wished me much joy, and recommended me to the Bar. I shook hands with the Bar and received their congratulations, and invited them over to Stone's to drink some punch, where most of us resorted, and had a very cheerful chat."

This genial relationship between the seniors and juniors of the Bar on days of admission was preserved for some time later. Thus, Prentiss Mellen (later Chief Justice of Maine), who studied with Shearjashub Bourne at Barnstable and was admitted to the Plymouth Bar, said that:

"According to the fashion of that day on the great occasion, I treated the judges and all the lawyers with about half a pail of punch, which treating aforesaid was commonly called the colt's tail."

In 1763, Adams writes in his Diary that the Bar had agreed "that nobody should answer to a suit but the plaintiff himself or some sworn attorney, and that a general power should not be admitted;" also that "no attorney should be allowed to practise in the Superior or Inferior Courts unless duly sworn."

About 1760, Chief Justice Hutchinson, by a rule of court, introduced the distinction between barristers and attorneys, and provided that none but barristers could argue in the Superior Court. This rule was not always enforced; for Josiah Quincy, Jr., who was refused to admission as a barrister, being obnoxious in his politics to the ruling powers, says in his *Reports* in August, 1769:

"At the last sitting of the Superior Court in Charlestown I argued (for the first time in this court) to the jury though not admitted to gown, the legality and propriety of which some have pretended to doubt; but as no scruples of that kind disturbed me, I proceeded (maugre any) at this court to manage all my own business, (for the first time in this country) though unsanctified and uninspired by the pomp and magic of the long robe."

By rule of court, three years of practise was required before admission as a barrister. This was later increased to seven years, with a regular grade of promotion — similar to the custom of England, where five years' residence in the Inns of Court was required, and three years, of a graduate of Oxford or Cambridge.

At the same time, Hutchinson also introduced a costume for the judges, consisting of a black silk gown, worn over a full black suit, white bands, and a silk bag for the hair. This was worn by the judges in civil causes and criminal trials, excepting those for capital offences, in which trials they wore scarlet robes,[1] with black velvet collars and cuffs to their large sleeves, and black velvet facings to their robes. Of such importance was this costume that Hutchinson deemed it worthy of record to note in his Diary, after describing the riot in Boston on the night of the 26th of August, 1765, when all his plate, family pictures, furniture, wearing apparel, and the books and manuscripts which he had been thirty years collecting, were destroyed by the mob, that:

"The Superior Court was to be held the next morning in Boston. The Chief Justice who was deprived of his robes and all other apparel, except an undress he was in when the mob came, appeared in that undress and an ordinary great coat over it which he borrowed."[2]

[1] The color of the robes may remind one of Cromwell's remark, "Well, if I cannot rule by red gowns, I will rule by redcoats." Campbell's *Lives of the Chief Justices*, Vol. II, p. 187.

[2] *Diary and Letters of Thomas Hutchinson*, pp. 67, 69. See also *Life of Thomas Hutchinson*, by James K. Hosmer, p. 95. "So strict was Lord Eldon (on matters of dress) that I remember Wetherell, when Attorney-General, having forgot the full bottom wig and appeared in a tie, Lord Eldon 'regretted that his Majesty's Attorney-General was not present at

Soon after the Revolution this costume was laid aside, it is supposed, because it was not suited to the simplicity of the form of government, and the last appearance of the judges in gowns was at the funeral of Governor Hancock in October, 1793, when they wore black silk.[1]

John Adams, writing to his pupil, William Tudor, says of these innovations:

"I pass over that scenery which he introduced so showy and so shallow, so theatrical and so ecclesiastical of scarlet and sable robes, of broad bands and enormous tie wigs more resembling fleeces of painted merino wool than anything natural to man and that could breathe with him. I pass over also the question whether he or his court had legal authority to establish a distinction between barristers and attorneys. Innovations, though often necessary, are always dangerous."[2]

It appears from the court records for the August term, 1762, that twenty-six gentlemen had been called by the court to be barristers at law, and that twelve of them had appeared in barristers' habits — black silk gown, bands and bag wigs.[3]

By 1768, the order of barristers was so well recognized that it is known that there were then twenty-five.[4] In 1770,

the bar, as the interests of the Crown were concerned.'" *Life of Lord Campbell*, Vol. I, p. 793.

[1] William Sullivan in his *Familiar Letters on Public Characters* (1847) says that "the judges had up to this time (1793) worn robes of scarlet faced with black velvet in winter, and black silk gowns in summer."

[2] *Adams' Life and Works*, Vol. X, p. 233, Vol. II, p. 133. G. Dexter, in *Mass. Hist. Soc. Proc.*, Vol. XIX, p. 144.

[3] See *Life of James Otis*, — *Amer. Law Rev.*, Vol. I, 541.

[4] Of these twenty-five, eleven were in Suffolk, Richard Dana, Benjamin Kent, James Otis, Jr., Samuel Fitch, William Read, Samuel Swift, Benjamin Gridley, Samuel Quincy, Robert Auchmuty and Andrew Cazneau, of Boston, and John Adams of Braintree; five were in Essex, Daniel Farnham and John Lowell, of Newburyport, William Pynchon, of Salem, John Chipman, of Marblehead, and Nathaniel Peaselee Sergeant, of Haver-

a new Bar Association was formed in Boston; and several of the other counties, notably Essex, had similar associations, of great ability.

## NOTE

For authorities in general, see:

*Courts of Justice in the Province of Massachusetts Bay*, 1630–1684 — *Amer. Law Rev.*, Vol. XXXIV, 1902.
*Judicial Action by the Provincial Legislature of Massachusetts Bay* — *Columbia Law Rev.*, Vol. II, 1902.
*Local Law in Massachusetts and Connecticut*, by W. C. Fowler.
*The Colonial Laws of Massachusetts*, by W. H. Whitmore (1889).
*Judicial History of Massachusetts*, by Emory Washburn (1840).
*Plymouth Colony Laws.*
*Massachusetts Colonial Records.*
*Records of the Courts of Assistants*, edited by John Noble (1901).
*Plaine Dealing, or News from New England*, by Thomas Lechford (1642).

hill; one was in Middlesex, Jonathan Sewall; two in Worcester, James Putnam, of Worcester, and Abel Willard, of Lancaster; three in Bristol, Samuel White and Robert Treat Paine, of Taunton, and Daniel Leonard, of Norton; in Hampshire, John Worthington, of Springfield; in Plymouth, James Hovey and Pelham Winslow.

After 1768, the following barristers were called: Joseph Hawley, of Northampton, David Sewall, of York, Moses Bliss, of Springfield, Zephaniah Leonard, of Taunton, Theophilus Bradbury, of Falmouth (Portland), David Wyer, of Falmouth, Mark Hopkins, of Great Barrington, Simeon Strong, of Amherst, John Sullivan, of Durham, Daniel Oliver, of Hardwick, Francis Dana, of Cambridge, Sampson Salter Blowers, of Boston, Daniel Bliss, of Concord, Samuel Porter, of Salem, Joshua Upham, of Brookfield, Shearjashub Bourne, of Barnstable, James Sullivan, of Biddeford, Jeremiah D. Rogers, of Littleton, Oaks Angier, of Bridgewater, John Sprague, of Lancaster, Caleb Strong, of Northampton, Elisha Porter, of Hadley, Theodore Sedgwick, of Sheffield, Benjamin Hichborn, of Boston, Theophilus Parsons, of Newburyport, Jonathan Bliss, of Springfield, William Tudor, Perez Morton and William Wetmore of Boston, and Levi Lincoln, of Worcester.

See, for particularly good account of the Hampshire and Hampshire and Hampden County Bars, Address of George Bliss, Sept. 26, 1826.

*Emancipation of Massachusetts*, by Brooks Adams (1887).
*History of New England*, by John Winthrop.
*History of New England*, by John G. Palfrey (1858).
*Address on Origin of the Legal Profession in Massachusetts*, by William Sullivan (1826).
*Three Episodes of Massachusetts History*, by C. F. Adams (1892).
*Judicial History of New England*, by Conrad Reno (1900).
*History of the Judiciary of Massachusetts*, by William T. Davis (1900).
*Address to Worcester County Bar*, Oct. 2, 1829, by Joseph Willard.
*Judicial History of Massachusetts*, by Albert Mason, in *The New England States* (1897).
*Attorneys and their Admission to the Bar in Massachusetts*, by Hollis R. Bailey (1907).
*Courts of Chancery in the American Colonies*, by Solon D. Wilson, *Amer. Law Rev.*, Vol. XVIII (1884.)

# CHAPTER IV

## COLONIAL NEW YORK, PENNSYLVANIA AND NEW JERSEY BAR

New York, like Virginia, adopted the Common Law of England as the basis of its law at a very early date; but as in Virginia also, this did not lead to the early development of any trained Bar. There were two very strong obstacles to success in the legal profession — the supremacy of the merchant and land-holding class, who deplored the rise of any other influential body of men; and the constant interference in, and control of, litigation by the Royal Governors.

When the Dutch Colony of New Amsterdam became "New Yorck," upon the English conquest in 1664, a code of law and practise, known as the Duke's Laws, was promulgated in 1665 as the basis of its government.[1] This code was largely prepared by Mathias Nichols, an English barrister of Lincoln's Inn, partly, it is said, from suggestions made by Lord Chancellor Clarendon, but chiefly from the Dutch Colonial law and the local laws in force in the New England Colonies. It gave to New York a more elaborate system of courts than was to be found in most of the other Colonies, and fixed with great detail their organization and administration.

[1] In 1673, the Dutch again conquered New York, and reverted at once to their old laws; but when Sir Edmund Andros returned in 1674 to reclaim the English rule, he, as Governor, restored to New York, by proclamation, the "known books of laws formerly establisht."

It is evident from many contemporary writings that the Common Law received very early recognition, and the best statement as to its status in New York is that made by Judge Horsmanden in the case of *Forsey* v. *Cunningham*, in 1765:

"The Supreme Court here proceeds in the main according to the practice of the courts at Westminster; and the Common Law of England, with the statutes affirming or altering it before a legislature was established, and those passed since such establishment expressly extended to us without legislative acts (which are not to be repugnant to the laws of England) constitute the law of this Colony."[1]

In 1683, a Charter of Liberties, containing many of the provisions of Magna Charta and of Habeas Corpus Act was framed expressly for the Colony by the Duke of York, and though never assented to by the King, was always claimed by the colonists to be operative for their protection.

The early courts were those of the small local justices of the peace, sitting in Courts of Sessions, and the Court of Assizes consisting of the Sessions Justices and the Governor and Council. This latter Court not only had full law and equity jurisdiction, but also exercised legislative powers.

In 1683, the first New York Legislature established distinct Courts of Sessions for each county, a Court of Oyer and Terminer together with other minor courts, and a Supreme Court consisting of the Governor and Council.

In 1691, the Supreme Court of Judicature was established, consisting of a Chief Justice and four associate judges, all appointed by the Royal Governors.[2]

The privilege of a Court Leet and Court Baron also was

[1] See reported case in *N. Y. Hist. Soc. Collections*.

[2] It is a curious fact that just at the time when Courts of Pypowdry (Market Courts) were dying out in England, they were revived in New York in 1692, and as late as 1773 were extended to the new counties.

attached to many of the old manor holding families, such as the Livingstones, Van Rensselaers, Courtlandts, Philips and Beekmans.

As in the other Colonies, few of the judges, other than the Chief Justices, were men of legal training. The first Chief Justice, Joseph Dudley, who four years previously had been Chief Justice of Massachusetts, had been educated as a clergyman, had then entered on a political career, and had no legal education. Two other early Chief Justices were men of little legal note — Stephen Van Cortlandt in 1700, and Abraham De Peyster in 1701. William Smith, Chief Justice from 1692 to 1700 and again in 1702, was on the other hand the leading lawyer of the Province.[1] William Atwood, Chief Justice in 1701, and John Bridges, in 1703, were English lawyers of distinction, as was Roger Mompesson, in 1704. Of Lewis Morris, who was Chief Justice from 1715 to 1733, it was said that "no man in the Colony equalled him in the knowledge of the law." His successor, Lieutenant-Governor James DeLancey, was a barrister of the Inner Temple, but of little profundity in legal acquirements.

From 1761 to 1763, the distinguished Massachusetts lawyer and Harvard graduate, Benjamin Pratt, was Chief Justice, of whom Lieutenant-Governor Colden wrote in 1762, after speaking of the insufficient salary paid to the judges:

"Sure I am, men of greater abilities may be found out of this Province than in it. . . .

"Mr. Pratt has come to this place with the best character as to his skill in the law and integrity. He was at the top of his profession at Boston. He has left a beneficial practice and now lives at the expense of his private fortune

[1] He came to New York about 1686, and is to be distinguished from William Smith, the leader of the Bar of a later period.

to show his regard to the honour His Majesty has done him in appointing him Chief Justice of this Province."[1]

From 1763 to 1778, Daniel Horsmanden, a very inferior lawyer, filled the position.

One of the chief obstacles to the maintenance of an adequate judiciary was the long struggle during the middle of the Eighteenth Century between the Royal Governors and the Assembly, the former insisting on their right to appoint judges "during His Majesty's pleasure," the Assembly insisting on appointments of judges "during good behaviour," and refusing to vote the judicial salaries until the Governor should acquiesce in this right. The result was great difficulty in finding men to fill positions on the bench.

Chief Justice Pratt complained to the Lords of Trade, May 24, 1762:

"All the Colonies are vested with legislative powers, by which the systems of their laws are gradually varying from the Common Law and so diminishing in that respect their connection with the Mother Country; and if the judgments of the Supreme Executive Courts are only vague and desultory decisions of ignorant judges it must augment the mischief; and this cannot be guarded against without some such establishment for the King's judge as to render the office worth a lawyer's acceptance."

Such was the Colonial antagonism towards the King's officers in New York that the position of Attorney-General was also filled by inferior men: and Colden wrote to England, January 25, 1762:

"The Attorney-General's office for upwards thirty years past, has been filled with men of no esteem as to their skill in the law. Formerly, and I believe everywhere else, when a gentleman came to the office of Attorney-General, it

[1] *Colonial Documents of New York,* Vol. VII, letter Jan. 11, 1762.

gave such reputation to his character, that he was thereby introduced into a great share of practise in suits between private persons; but for some time past we find no man entrusting his private affairs to the person with whom the King's rights in the Province are entrusted."

The first lawyer of New Amsterdam was Dirck Van Schelluyne, in 1653. He had obtained in Holland a license to practise, but, there being no other lawyers in the new city to fight, and consequently no suits, he performed the duties of notary, kept a grocery store, and finally, becoming discouraged, left the city.

In the early days of the English occupation, the estimation in which lawyers were held will appear from the following entry on the minutes of the Council, held at the Stadt Huys on May 16, 1677:

"Query? Whether attorneys are thought to be useful to plead in courts or not. Answer. It is thought not. Whereupon resolved and ordered, That pleading attorneys be no longer allowed to practise in ye Government, but for ye pending cases."

This was later modified, and the Court in 1677 made a rule that:

"No one be admitted to plead for any other person or as attorney in court without hee first have his admittance of the court or have a warrant of attorney for his so doing from his clyent."

It was many years, however, before there existed any trained Bar.

While the records of the Assize Court give the names of a number of "attorneys" appearing for the parties, it is not likely that they were men who made practise of the law an exclusive profession, but rather agents and men of business who were clever at writing and speaking, and so employed by others to represent them in the courts. It is certain, however, that there was no such great popular prejudice against lawyers in New York as in the other Colonies; although, in 1683, the same legislation was passed as elsewhere, forbidding sheriffs, constables, clerks and justices of the peace from acting as attorneys in their courts. A few English lawyers of distinction practised in the Colony between 1680 and 1700 — James Graham, John Palmer and Thomas Rudyard; but the scarcity of lawyers made it so easy for a party to a suit to monopolize the Bar, that, in 1695, a statute was passed which recited that, "whereas the number of attorneys at law that practise at the Bar in this Province are but few and that many persons retain most of them on one side to the great prejudice and discouragement of others that have or may have suits at law," and which provided that no person should retain more than two attorneys in any suit — this act to continue in force for two years.

In the account, published in 1744 by Daniel Horsmanden, of the famous Negro Plot case in 1741, it is stated that the whole Bar of the city, consisting of eight members only, Attorney-General Bradley and Messrs. Murray, Alexander, Smith, Chambers, Nichols, Lodge and Jameson, offered their services to the prosecution "as a matter affecting not only the city but the whole Province."

The chief lawyers of distinction in the early Eighteenth Century were James Alexander,[1] William Smith,[2] John Tudor and David Jamieson.

From an early date, the power of appointment of attorneys was exercised by the Governor; and the first license to an attorney bears date of 1709. W. Smith, Jr., in his con-

[1] Born about 1691, came to New York in 1715, studied law after his arrival, Attorney-General 1721–1723, and "though no speaker, was at the head of his profession; for sagacity and business penetration and in application to business no man could surpass him."

[2] Born in 1697, came to New York in 1715.

temporary history, laments that the Governors at times licensed all applicants, "however indifferently soever recommended," though sometimes they took advice of the Chief Justices. The smallness of the Colonial Bar is shown by the fact that in the sixty-eight years between 1709 and 1776 only one hundred and thirty-six had been licensed as attorneys by the Governor.[1]

Valentine, in his *History of the City of New York*, gives a list of only forty-one lawyers practising in the city between 1695 and 1769.[2]

[1] It is interesting to note that the last license in the *Book of Commissions*, signed by the Royal Governor Tryon, is under date of March 11, 1776, and that on the very next page the "People of the State of New York, by the Grace of God free and independent," make their first appointment of a Secretary of State. See *In the matter of Cooper*, 22 N. Y. 67.

[2] *History of the City of New York*, by David T. Valentine (1853), Clerk of Common Council.

Names of Attorneys practising in the City of New York between the year 1695 and the Revolutionary War.

1697 David Jamison, "Gentleman"
1698 James Emott, "Gent. and Atty at Law"
1701 Thomas Weaver Esq.
1702 John Bridges "LL.D. on suit of Gov. Cornbury"
Robert Milwood
1708 May Bickley
Jacob Regnier
Roger Mompesson
1718 Tobias Boel
1728 Joseph Murray
John Chambers
1730 Abraham Lodge
Richard Nicholls
James Alexander
William Smith
1740 Daniel Horsmanden
1743 Lancaster Graen
1745 Elisha Parker
John Burnet
Samuel Clowes
1746 William Searle

These few men, however, formed, as Chancellor Kent later said, "a constellation of learned and accomplished men."[1] Chief among them were William Livingston, who was born in 1723, a Yale graduate of 1741, studied law with James Alexander in 1745, later with William Smith, and in 1752 collected and published the first digest of Colony laws; and William Smith, Jr., from whose personal recollections most of New York's early history is now known, born in 1728, a Yale graduate of 1745. Among others were Whitehead Hicks,[2] John Tabor Kempe, the last Royal Attorney-General; Benjamin Kissam; Peter Van Schaack, Recorder of New York and editor of the revision of the statutes in 1774;[3] John Morin Scott;[4] Samuel Jones, Re-

1747 John McEvers Jr.
John Van Cortlandt
1748 Bartholomew Crannell
William Livingston
1749 John Alsop
1751 Augustus Van Cortlandt
Lambert Moore
1763 Whitehead Hicks
1768 Benjamin Kissam
Benjamin Helme
Rudolphus Ritzema
John McKesson
1769 Richard Harrison
Philip Livingston Jr.
Thomas Jones
Philip J. Livingston
John William Smith
John D. Crimshire
David Mathews
Samuel Jones

[1] See Address before the Law Association of the City of New York, by James Kent (1836).

[2] Born in 1728, Judge of Supreme Court 1776–1780.

[3] Born in 1747, a Columbia graduate of 1768, studied with W. Smith, Jr.

[4] Born in 1730, a Yale graduate of 1746.

corder; Benjamin Nicoll; George Clinton;[1] James Duane;[2] Robert Yates,[3] and John Jay.[4] Though small in numbers, the Bar of New York formed the earliest Bar Association in the Colonies, such an organization being in existence there as early as 1748. While professional practise was scanty, and as Sedgwick said, in his *Life of William Livingston*:

> "the great number of cases were collection of debts owed by English merchants and suits in ejectment — which does much to diminish any regret which may be felt for the want of colonial reports,"

yet the influence of the legal profession upon the development of New York's legal and political institutions was very great. Of this powerful status of the Colonial Bar during the fifteen years prior to the Revolution a very clear picture has been preserved in the letters of Lieutenant-Governor Colden, between whom and the united Bar a heated struggle had taken place from 1763 to 1765, over Colden's attempt to force the courts to allow an appeal to the Governor and Council on matters of fact as well as of law. This conflict ended in a victory for the Colonial contention against such an appeal, and this result confirmed Colden in his opinion of the great dangers to the Crown and to the Colony itself from this "domination of lawyers," and from the "dangerous influence of the proprietors of large tracts of land in the Colony," who combined with them to antagonize the Crown.

September 14, 1763, he wrote:

[1] Born in 1739, studied in office of W. Smith, Governor of New York 1777–1795, 1801; Vice-President 1804.

[2] Born in 1733, U. S. District Judge 1789.

[3] Born in 1738, studied with W. Livingston.

[4] Born in 1745, a Columbia graduate of 1764, studied with Benjamin Kissam, admitted to the Bar in 1766 — see *infra*.

"We have a set of lawyers in this Province as insolent and petulant and at the same time as well skilled in the chicaneries of the Law as perhaps are to be found anywhere else. This requires judges of ability and skill in the law to restrain them, who are not easily to be found in this place, and at the same time disinterested; for the distinguished families in so small a country as this are so united by inter-marriages and otherwise, that in few cases, a cause of any consequence, especially where the King's Rights are concerned, can be brought before a judge who is one of these families in which he can be supposed entirely disinterested, or free from connections with those interested either in that case or in other cases similar to it."

Again, on November 7, 1764, he wrote:

"In a young country like this, where few men have any acquired learning or knowledge, where the judges and principal lawyers are proprietors of extravagant grants of land or strongly connected with them in interest or family alliances, it is possible that a dangerous combination may subsist between the Bench and the Bar, not only greatly injurious to private property, but likewise dangerous to his Majesty's prerogative and authority and his Rights — in this Province, in case no appeals as to the merits of the cause be allowed to the King in his Privy Council."

On January 22, 1765, he wrote:

"If the profession of the law keep united as they are now, the abilities of an upright judge will not be sufficient to restrain the lawyers, without the security of an appeal to a court where they can have no undue influence. The lawyers influence every branch of our Government, a domination as destructive of Justice as the domination of Priests was of the Gospel; both of them founded on delusion."

And on February 22, 1765, he wrote to the Earl of Halifax:

"The dangerous influence which the Profession of the Law has obtained in this Province more than in any other part of his Majesty's Dominions is a principal cause of disputing appeals to the King, but as that influence likewise extends to every part of the administration, I humbly conceive that it is become a matter of State which may deserve your Lordship's particular attention.

"After Mr. DeLancey had, by cajoling Mr. Clinton, received the Commission of Chief Justice during good behaviour, the Profession of the Law entered into an Association the effects of which I believe your Lordship had formerly opportunity of observing some striking instances. They proposed nothing less to themselves than to obtain the direction of all the measures of Government by making themselves absolutely necessary to every Governor, in assisting him while he complied with their measures, and by distressing him when he did otherwise. For this purpose, every method was taken to aggrandize the power of the Assembly where the profession of the law must allwise have great influence over the members and to lessen the authority and influence of the Governor. In a country like this, where few men, except in the profession of the law, have any kind of literature, where the most opulent families in our own memory, have arisen from the lowest rank of the people, such an association must have more influence than can be easily imagined. By means of their profession they become generally acquainted with men's private affairs and necessities, every man who knows their influence in the courts of justice is desirous of their favor and affrayd of their resentment. Their power is greatly strengthened by inlarging the powers of the popular side of government and by depreciating the powers of the Crown.

"The Proprietors of the great tracts of land in this Province have united strongly with the lawyers as the surest support of their enormous and iniquitous claims and thereby this faction is become the more formidable and dangerous to good government. . . .

"All Associations are dangerous to good government, more so in distant dominions; and associations of lawyers the most dangerous of any, next to military.

"Were the people freed from the dread of this Domination of the Lawyers, I flatter myself with giving general joy to the people of the Province."

In spite of the attacks upon it by the Governor, the Association of the Bar continued to act with undiminished vigor, and in 1765 it was largely the originator and mainstay of the determined and successful resistance to the Stamp Act, in New York.[1] Shortly after this, the Association went out of existence as an organized body; but the individual lawyers of the day continued to be leaders in the struggle for the rights of the Colony which resulted in the Revolution.

## Pennsylvania

Until about the middle of the Eighteenth Century, the development of law in Pennsylvania was extremely rudimentary. Its settlers were active in their opposition to the introduction of the legal subtleties of the English Bar and the legal procedure and processes of the English Bench.

William Penn, the Proprietor, certainly had no reason to love the English courts, for English judges had cast aside all bounds of decency and legal principle in connection with Penn's trial on an indictment for "tumultuous assembly" in 1670. Penn's famous comment on the Common Law uttered in this case is well known; and the following colloquy between the presiding judge in the Old Bailey and the stout-hearted Quaker well illustrates the reason for the popular resentment towards the English law as administered in criminal cases in the Seventeenth Century:[2]

"Penn. I desire you would let me know by what law it is you prosecute me and upon what law you ground my indictment.

"Recorder. Upon the common-law.

[1] Sir William Johnson wrote to England from New York that the lawyers' opposition to the Stamp Act was for fear that "business must decrease from the duties on Law Proceedings."

[2] See 6 *Howell's State Trials*, 953 *et seq.*

"PENN. Where is that common-law?

"RECORDER. You must think that I am able to run up so many years and over so many adjudged cases which we call common-law, to answer your curiosity.

"PENN. This answer I am sure is very short of many questions, for if it be common, it should not be hard to produce. . . . Unless you shew me and the people the law you ground your indictment upon, I shall take it for granted your proceedings are merely arbitrary.

"RECORDER. The question is whether you are guilty of this indictment.

"PENN. The question is not whether I am guilty of this indictment, but whether this indictment be legal. It is too general and imperfect an answer to say it is the common law, unless we knew both where and what it is. For where there is no law, there is no transgression; and that law which is not in being is so far from being common, that it is no law at all.

"RECORDER. You are an impertinent fellow, will you teach the court what law is? It is 'Lex non scripta,' that which many have studied thirty or forty years to know; and would you have me to tell you in a moment?

"PENN. Certainly, if the common law be so hard to be understood, it is far from being very common; but if the Lord Coke in his Institute be of any consideration, he tells us that Common Law is common right, and that Common Right is the Great Charter Privileges."

The Quakers who sought in Pennsylvania relief from such tyranny of English judges were unlikely to welcome any efforts to establish the lawcraft in power in their new home. It is not strange, therefore, that for seventy years after the settlement, the courts of the Province were maintained with practically no lawyers present, either on the Bench or at the Bar.

Nevertheless the early founders and Penn himself were too able administrators to conceive that the new Province could exist without laws at all; and it was due largely to

Penn that Pennsylvania had from the beginning a very full and well settled code of written law, consisting of the "Frame of Law" agreed upon in England, in 1682, the "Great Law" or "Body of Law" enacted at Chester in the same year, the "Act of Settlement" passed in Philadelphia in 1683, and eight chapters of statutes enacted the same year, the "Frame of Government" in 1683 and 1696, and the laws of 1701. These codes embodied a complete system and rendered more elaborate legislation unnecessary for a long time.

The colonists, however, were extremely independent in their attitude towards the Common Law of England. While they claimed the advantage of all rights and privileges of Englishmen guaranteed by that law, and while Penn published at Philadelphia, as early as 1687, an edition of the *Magna Charta*, of the *Confirmation of the Charters*, and of the *Statute De Tallagio non Concedenda*, with an address to the reader "not to give away anything of Liberty and Property that at present they do . . . enjoy," the colonists felt themselves free to decide for themselves how much of the other doctrines of the Common Law they would adopt, and what portion they would reject. So that within a very few years, when the first Royal Governor, Benjamin Fletcher, was appointed, in 1682, he called the attention of the Assembly severely to several criminal statutes, laws as to inheritance of land, marriage and other matters, which he deemed repugnant to the laws of England, and therefore invalid.

The first courts in Pennsylvania were the County Courts, constituted under the Duke of York's Government in 1673, the records of at least one of which (Upland or Chester County) from 1676 to 1681 are still extant. They exercised legislative as well as judicial powers, hearing suits for debts, approving indentures of apprentices, imposing taxes and fines, punishing misdemeanors, granting lands, adjusting title disputes and directing uses of the revenue. The judges were for many years exclusively Swedes and of no legal training. No attorney was allowed to practise for pay before them.

In 1682–1683, the judicial power was exercised by the Governor and Council.

In 1684, under William Penn's charter, a Provincial or Supreme Court was constituted, composed of five judges, of which Nicholas More, a physician, was Chief Justice. Of the next six Chief Justices, only one was a trained lawyer —John Guest, an English barrister, who became Chief Justice in 1706. In the same year, Roger Mompesson, who had been an educated lawyer, and the Recorder of Southampton in England, was appointed Chief Justice, at the instance of Penn, who wrote to James Logan, advising "the people to lay hold of such an opportunity as no government in America ever had of procuring the services of an English lawyer."

After him, in 1715, came Joseph Growdon, a man of little legal note; then came David Lloyd, a noted English lawyer (1719–1731). James Logan, a man of great ability but of little legal training, followed (1731–1739); then Jeremiah Langhorne, a preacher (1739–1743). The records of the Court, April 5, 1743, throw light on the prevailing condition of the Bench. "His honour told the Council that as the place of Chief Justice was vacant by the death of Mr. Langhorne and it would be of very great advantage to the province that one of the profession of the law preside in the Supreme Court, he had made an offer of it to Mr. Kinsey." The succeeding Chief Justices, however, John Kinsey (1743–1750), William Allen (1751–1774) and Benjamin Chew (1774–1779) were all trained lawyers (the last two being English barristers).

With the above exceptions, it may be said without qualification that laymen, and usually merchants, filled all judicial positions, not only in the Supreme Court, but also in the Court of Common Pleas.

No records of the Supreme Court are extant; and David Lloyd says that in his time (the end of the Seventeenth Century) they were written "on a quire of paper." The slight attention paid to the judicial records may be seen from the record of a case in 1684 — *Johnson* v. *Hance*, tried before the Provincial Council, in which the following decree is extant: "The Governor and Council advised them to shake hands and to forgive one another, and ordered that they should enter into bonds for £50 a piece, for their good abearance, which accordingly they did. It was also ordered that the records of the Court concerning that business should be burnt."[1] A few of the decided cases, however, are reported in *Dallas' Reports;* and in 1892 a volume of Colonial cases, the earliest dating back to 1683 — seventy years before the earliest case reported in *Dallas* — was published by Judge Pennypacker.

As a substitute for a trained Bench, the Quakers had from a very early date constituted a system of settlement of disputes by laymen. In 1683, provision was made for the appointment of three "common peacemakers" in every precinct, whose arbitration was to be valid and final as a judgment. In 1705, an act was passed, providing that parties having accounts against each other might refer them to persons mutually chosen by them in open court, whose award should have the effect of a verdict by a jury. Immense numbers of contract disputes were settled by referees in this way. Later, the practise was extended to

[1] See *Provincial Minutes*, Vol. I, p. 52.

See also especially *The Forum*, by David Paul Brown, Vol. I, Chap. II (1856).

other forms of legal action, so that by 1766 there are records of elaborate decisions by referees resembling decrees in equity in real estate matters, and in 1790, Dallas in the preface to his *Reports* states that one of his motives in publishing was their "use in furnishing some hints for regulating the conduct of referees, to whom, according to the present practise, a very great share of the administration of justice is entrusted."

The existence of this referee system is probably accountable in large part for the very slow development of a Pennsylvania law. Merchants and land-owners alike were content with the laymen's judgment without the aid of lawyers. Moreover, for lawyers as a class, Penn and his Quakers had an instinctive antipathy, as being men of strife and of barratrous tendencies, and therefore opposed to the fundamental religious views of the new settlers.

Accordingly in the *Laws Agreed Upon* in England of 1682, it was provided: "that in all courts all persons of all persuasions may freely appear in their own way and according to their own manner and there personally plead their own case themselves and if unable, by their friends; that all pleadings, processes and records in court shall be short and in English and in an ordinary and plain character that they may be understood and justice speedily administered."

In 1686 and in 1690, the Provincial Council attempted, but without success, to pass a bill preventing any person pleading in any civil causes of another, before he "be solemnlye attested in open court that he neither directly nor indirectly hath in any wise taken or received or will take or receive to his use or benefit any reward whatsoever for his soe pleading."

The popular attitude towards lawyers is shown by the

quaint remark of Gabriel Thomas, who wrote, in 1690:[1] "Of Lawyers and Physicians I shall say nothing, because this country is very peacable and healthy: Long may it so continue and never have occasion for the tongue of the one nor the pen of the other — both equally destructive of men's estates and lives."

During the first twenty years, there were probably not more than three or four trained English lawyers in the whole Province, although there were twenty-three persons called attorneys whose names are extant. These were, however, almost entirely laymen, with no legal education.[2]

The paucity of lawyers was well illustrated by Penn in 1700, in replying to the charges made by Robert Quary, Judge of Admiralty, of failing to prosecute William Smith, Jr., for a heinous crime. In his answer Penn stated that the defendant had "subsequently married ye only material witness against him, which in the opinion of ye only two lawyers of the place (and one of them ye King's advocate of ye Admiralty and ye attorney general of the county) has rendered her incompetent to testify against him."

It has been said that, in 1706, the whole Bar of Philadelphia consisted of G. Lowther, David Lloyd, Robert Assheton and Thomas Clark.[3] At all events, it was so small that there are records of cases in which the plaintiff complained that the defendant had cornered all the lawyers in the Province. Thus in 1708, there was a petition to the Council from one complaining that he had been sued in trover by Joseph Growden and that the latter had retained all the lawyers in the county, wherefore he prayed the Council to assign him counsel. So, too, in 1709, one

[1] *An Historical and Geographical Account of the Province and Country of Pennsylvania and of West Jersey in America*, by Gabriel Thomas (London, 1698).

[2] *Bench and Bar of Philadelphia*, by John H. Martin (1883).

[3] *Discourse before the Law Academy*, by P. McCall (1838).

Francis D. Pastorius complained that one Spogell had got a writ of ejectment and had feed and retained the four known lawyers of the Province "in order to deprive the Petitioner of all advice in law," and the petitioner being too poor to "fetch lawyers from New York or remote places, prays that Spogell's proceedings may be enjoined."

Of this early Bar, possibly the most noted was David Lloyd, a Welsh jurist, who was sent out from England as Attorney-General in 1686 and held many offices of trust in the Province, being looked upon as the great advocate of the people's rights. He became Chief Justice in 1718, and was described by James Logan, his successor as Chief Justice in 1731, in a letter to Penn, as "a man very stiff in all his undertakings, of a sound judgment and a good lawyer, but extremely pertinaceous and somewhat revengeful."

Early in the Eighteenth Century other English lawyers came into the Province, — of whom William Assheton, John Moland and Andrew Hamilton may be especially named. The latter is probably entitled to the distinction of being the ablest and best known lawyer in the American Colonies. Born in Scotland in 1676, he had first settled in Maryland, but afterwards removed to Philadelphia.[1] He went to England in 1712, and was called to the Bar in Gray's Inn. Returning, he became successively Attorney-General, Recorder, Vice-Admiralty Judge and Speaker of the Assembly in Pennsylvania. His fame among American lawyers is chiefly due to his brilliant defense of the rights of free speech, and his attack on the old law of libel in the famous trial of John Peter Zenger for criminal libel in New York in 1735. In the *Colonial Records* in 1736 (Volume IV), it is said of Hamilton that he "was esteemed and

[1] Different dates are given for Hamilton's birth, but the date 1676 is that stated in *Great American Lawyers* (Vol. I), 1908.

allowed to be as able in that profession as any on the Continent of America."

The first statute as to the admission of lawyers was enacted in 1722, providing that "there may be a competent number of persons of an honest disposition and learned in the law admitted by the Justices . . . to practise as attorneys." A form of oath was prescribed in 1726.

The real Bar of Pennsylvania may, probably, be said to have begun about 1740, when Tench Francis, the brother of Richard Francis (the well-known author of *Maxims of Equity*), came from England. He is stated to have been "the most eminent . . . the first of the lawyers of that Province to master the technical difficulties of the profession;" and Secretary Peters wrote that, except Francis and Moland, all of the lawyers of that period "are persons of no knowledge and, I had almost said, no principle."

Horace Binney (the leader of the Philadelphia Bar in the early Nineteenth Century) thus sums up the conditions: "Of the primitive Bar of the Province of Pennsylvania we know nothing, and next to nothing of the men who appeared at it from time to time up to the termination of the Colonial Government.

"The statement of Chief Justice Tilghman in the Bush Hill case reveals to us all we know and all that probably we can ever know in regard to this subject; for as the grandson of Tench Francis who was Attorney-General in 1745, and connected by marriage association with the most eminent families of the Bar, he knew as much of the former Bar as any of his contemporaries, and they have all long since departed without adding anything to what he left. 'From what I have been able to learn,' said the Chief Justice, 'of the early history of Pennsylvania, it was a long time before she possessed lawyers of eminence.

There were never wanting men of strong minds very well able to conduct the business of the courts without much regard to form. Such in particular was Andrew Hamilton. . . . But Mr. Francis appears to have been the first of our lawyers who mastered the technical difficulties of the profession. His precedents of pleading have been handed down to the present day.' "[1]

Between the years 1742 and 1776, seventy-six lawyers were admitted to practise in the Supreme Court.

The twenty years before the War of the Revolution in Pennsylvania were remarkable for producing a group of lawyers of broad legal education and distinguished ability. No other Colony except South Carolina possessed a Bar having so many men who had received their training in the English Inns of Court. At its head may be placed Benjamin Chew, a Maryland lawyer, born in 1722, a barrister of the Middle Temple, who succeeded Tench Francis as Attorney-General in 1755, and became Chief Justice in 1774. Next in distinction was Thomas McKean, who was born in 1734, admitted to practise in 1757, became a barrister in the Middle Temple, and Chief Justice in 1777. Edward Shippen was born in 1729, admitted in 1748, a barrister of the Middle Temple in 1750, and Chief Justice in 1799. John Dickinson was born in Maryland in 1732, studied in the office of John Moland in Philadelphia, and became a barrister of the Middle Temple. Francis Hopkinson, who was born in 1737, was one of the Signers of the Declaration of Independence, and from 1779 to 1791 Judge of Admiralty, and of the United States District Court. George Read was born in Maryland in 1733, became a barrister of the Middle Temple, was one of the Signers, and later Chief Justice of Delaware.

[1] See *Lyle* v. *Richards*, 9 Sergeant & Rawle 322 (1823).

## New Jersey

In the *Judicial and Civil History of New Jersey*, by John Whitehead (1897), no names of any lawyers practising in the Seventeenth Century are given; and it is said "the Courts of New Jersey were not established upon any settled plan nor upon any perfected system, until about the beginning of the Eighteenth Century." [1]

This statement is only partially accurate, however, for in East New Jersey there is record of courts held in Monmouth County as early as 1667; and in 1675, the Legislature created small local courts and a Court of Assize for appeals. In 1682, by statute, a regular system of courts was established, consisting of local courts held monthly, Session or County Courts held annually, and a Court of Common Right having full law and equity jurisdiction and founded on Scotch models. In West New Jersey, statutes as early as 1681 provided for local courts; a Court of Appeals was created in 1693, consisting of the county justices of the peace and the Governor's Council; and this, in 1699, became the Provincial Court or Court of Appeals.

Until New Jersey became consolidated as a Royal Province in 1702, the courts were created by the people. In 1704, the Governor, Lord Cornbury, by ordinance

[1] In a letter to the Lords of Trade, in 1703, Lord Cornbury wrote: "The first thing we proceeded upon was to settle some courts, and in order to do it, I asked the gentlemen of the Council what courts they had under the proprietary government. They said that their courts were never very regularly settled, but such as they were, it was under this regulation: first they had a court for determining all causes under forty shillings. . . . The next court they had was a quarterly court where the justices of the peace determined all causes under £10, and they had a court which they called the Court of Common Right, where all causes, both criminal and civil, were heard. . . . This Court of Common Right consisted of the Governor and Council."

established a system of courts consisting of Justices of the Peace, a Court of Common Pleas, a Court of General Sessions of the Peace, and a Supreme Court of Judicature, with an appeal to the Governor and Council.

The Supreme Court records are extant from as early a period as 1702. The first Chief Justice was the English barrister, Roger Mompesson, who was also Chief Justice of New York and of Pennsylvania.

Out of eight of his successors down to the Revolution, three only, Thomas Gordon, in 1709, David Jamison, in 1710, and Robert Hunter Morris, 1738–1744, were educated lawyers. Of the latter it was said, that "he reduced the pleadings to precision and method and possessed the great perfection of his office, knowledge and integrity, in more perfection than has often been known before in the Colonies." Few of the other judges before the Revolution had legal training.

There was little early legislation as to lawyers. In 1682, the Legislature of East Jersey enacted that "in all courts, all persons of all persuasions may freely appear in their own way and according to their own manner, and there personally plead their own cause, and if unable, by their friends or attorneys."

The practise of the law was evidently engaged in chiefly by pettifoggers and by the court officers, for, as in the other Colonies, statutes were passed, in 1676 and 1694, forbidding justices of the peace, sheriffs, deputies, clerks and messengers from practising as attorneys.

In 1698, all attorneys who pleaded for fee or hire were required to be admitted to practise by license of the Governor.

In 1740, an act was passed regulating in detail the practise of law and establishing fees. In 1769–1770, a storm of attacks centred around lawyers, arising from the cost, abuses and multiplicity of suits. Charges were preferred in the Assembly against even the leaders of the Bar; and mobs attempted to prevent the lawyers from entering the court houses. With the passing, however, of the financial crises then prevailing, these attacks gradually died out.[1]

It is a well-known fact that in its administration of justice New Jersey has always, even to the present day, followed more closely the old English precedents than any other American State.

As an example, in 1755, the Supreme Court instituted the order of sergeants, in imitation of the ancient English degree of sergeant at law; and in 1763 it was ordered that "no person for the future shall practise as a sergeant in this court but those that are recommended by the Judges to the Governor for the time being and duly called up by writ and sworn agreeably to the practise in England."[2] Later, the number of sergeants was fixed at twelve; and they conducted examinations for admission to the Bar. They were not abolished until as late as 1839.

In 1767, a distinction was made (as in Massachusetts) between attorney and barrister (or counsellor as it was termed in New Jersey); and it was provided that no man should practise as counsellor until he had been an attorney for three years and duly examined in court for the advanced status.

By the time of the Revolution, an organized Bar had grown up; and there is a record of the call of a meeting of the State Bar, in September, 1765, to discuss the Stamp

[1] *The Provincial Court of New Jersey, with Sketches of the Bench and Bar*, by Richard F. Field, *N. J. Hist. Soc. Coll.*, Vol. III.

*Constitution and Government of New Jersey, with Reminiscences of the Bench and Bar*, by L. Q. C. Elmer (1872), *N. J. Hist. Soc. Coll.*, Vol. VII.

[2] *History of the Supreme Court of New Jersey*, by Francis B. Lee, Vol. I (1896).

Act, at which meeting it was unanimously resolved to use no stamps for any purpose.

Of lawyers of prominence, prior to the Revolution, two stand forth pre-eminent. David Ogden, born in 1707, a Yale graduate of 1728, judge of the Supreme Court in 1772, of whom it was said that as a lawyer he had no equal in New York or New Jersey; and his pupil, Richard Stockton, born in 1730, a Princeton graduate of 1748, who was admitted to the Bar in 1754, as counsellor in 1758, and as sergeant at law in 1763, in 1774 made Judge of the Supreme Court. Stockton's practise was very extensive, and his reputation was such that a legal education in New Jersey was hardly considered complete unless it included a course of study in his office, frequent applications being made besides from students of other States.[1]

## NOTE

### To New York Text

For authorities in general, see:

*Organization of the Supreme Court of Judicature of the Province of New York*, by Robert L. Fowler, *Albany Law Journal*, Vols. XIX, XX.

*Observations on the Particular Jurisprudence of New York*, by Robert L. Fowler, *Albany Law Journal*, Vols. XXI, XXII, XXIII.

*Influence of New York on American Jurisprudence* — *Mag. of American History* (April, 1879).

*Colonial Documents of New York.*

*Colonial Laws of New York from 1664 to the Revolution.*

*Documentary History of New York*, by E. B. O'Callaghan.

*Allegiance and Laws of Colonial New York* — *Harv. Law Rev.*, Vol. XV.

[1] Many of the prominent lawyers became Tories — Isaac Allen, William Taylor, Henry Waddell, Cortlandt Skinner the last Royal Attorney-General, Frederick Smyth the last Royal Chief Justice, William Franklin.

See Lives in *Loyalists of the American Revolution*, by Lorenzo Sabine.

*History of New York*, by William Dunlap (1840).
*History of New York*, by William Smith (Vol. I, pub. in London in 1757; Vol. II, in New York in 1826).
*History of New York*, by Ellis H. Roberts (1887).
*Lives and Times of the Chief Justices*, by Henry Flanders (1881).
*Dutch and Quaker Colonies in America*, by John Fiske (1899).
*Memoirs of the Life of William Livingston*, by Theodore Sedgwick, Jr. (1833).
*American Criminal Trials*, by Peleg W. Chandler (1841).
*The Bench and Bar of New York*, by David McAdams and others (1897).
*John Peter Zenger, his press, his trial and bibliography*, by Livingston Rutherford (1909).

## To Pennsylvania Text

*Dutch and Quaker Colonies*, by John Fiske (1899).
*A Glance at our Colonial Bar — Green Bag*, Vol. XI.
*Pennsylvania Colonial and Federal*, by Howard McJenkins (1903).
*English Common Law in the Early American Colonies*, by Paul S. Reinsch.
*Bench and Bar of Old Philadelphia*, by John H. Harris (1883).
*Discourse before the Law Academy*, Sept. 15, 1838, by P. McCall (1838).
*An Essay on Equity in Pennsylvania*, by Anthony Laussat (1825), in *Penn. Bar Ass. Rep.*, Vol. I (1895).
*Pennsylvania Jurisprudence*, by John W. Simonton, *Penn. Bar Ass.*, Vol. I.
*Bar of Pennsylvania and its Influence*, by J. Levering Jones, *Penn. Bar Ass.*, Vol. X.
*Courts of Pennsylvania in the Seventeenth Century*, by Lawrence Lewis, Jr. (1881), *Penn. Bar Ass.*, Vol. I.
*The Common Law of Pennsylvania*, by George Sharswood (1855), *Penn. Bar Ass.*, Vol. I.
*The District Court*, by James T. Mitchell, in *Penn. Bar Ass.*, Vol. V (1885).
*Joseph Galloway*, by Ernest H. Baldwin (1902).
Life of Joseph Galloway and Edward Shippen, in *Loyalists of The American Revolution*, by Lorenzo Sabine.

*Remarks to Bar on Death of Charles Chauncey and John Sergeant*, by Horace Binney (1853).
*The McKean Family*, by Roberdeau Buchanan (1890).
*William Tilghman*, by Horace Binney (1827).
*Life of Horace Binney*, by Charles C. Binney (1903).
*Horace Binney — Green Bag*, Vol. V.
*The Supreme Court of Pennsylvania*, by Judge F. Carroll Brewster, in *The Supreme Court of the States and Provinces*, Vol. I, Series 3 (1895).
*Life of Thomas McKean*, by Judge James T. Mitchell, in *The Supreme Court of the States and Provinces*, Vol. I, Series 3 (1895).
*Life and Times of John Dickinson*, by Charles J. Stillé (1891).
*Memoir of William Rawle*, by T. J. Wharton, *Penn. Hist. Ass. Proc.*, Vol. IV (1837).
*Memoir of William Bradford*, by Horace Binney Wallace (1856).
*The Republican Court, or American Society in the Days of Washington*, by Rufus W. Griswold (1855).
*Life of George Read*, by William T. Read (1870).
*Life of Charles Jared Ingersoll*, by William M. Meigs (1897).
Scharf and Westcott's *History of Philadelphia* (1884).
*The Supreme Court of Pennsylvania*, by Owen Wister — *Green Bag*, Vol. III.
*Life and Writings of Alexander James Dallas*, by George M. Dallas (1871).
*Pennsylvania Colonial Cases*, by Samuel W. Pennypacker (1892).
*The Law Association of Philadelphia, 1802–1902* (1906).
*The Courts of Pennsylvania Prior to the Revolution — Univ. of Penn. Law Rev.*, Vol. LVI (1908).
*Judicial Memoranda in the History of Pennsylvania*, in *The Journal of Jurisprudence*, Vol. I (1821).
*Great American Lawyers*, Vols. I, II (1908).
*The Forum*, by David Paul Brown, Vol. I (1856).

## To New Jersey Text

*Judicial and Civil History of New Jersey*, by John Whitehead (1897).
*The Courts of New Jersey, also Some Account of their Origin and*

*Jurisdiction*, by W. M. Clevenger and Edward R. Keasbey (1903).

*The Provincial Court of New Jersey, with Sketches of the Bench and Bar*, by Richard F. Field (1849), *N. J. Hist. Soc. Coll.*, Vol. III.

*Constitution and Government of New Jersey, with Reminiscences of the Bench and Bar*, by L. Q. C. Elmer (1872), *N. J. Hist. Soc. Coll.*, Vol. VII.

*Sources of Law in New Jersey* — *New Jersey Law Journal*, Vols. IV and V.

*General Sources of Historical Information in New Jersey*, by Francis B. Lee — *New Jersey Law Journal*, Vol. XXX (1907).

*New Jersey Archives*, 1637–1776 (ten volumes).

*An Outline Sketch of the Early West Jersey Courts* — *New Jersey Law Journal*, Vol. XIV (1891) Vol. XV (1892).

*Bibliography of the Colonial Law Books of New Jersey* — *New Jersey Law Journal*, Vol. XIV (1891).

*The Supreme Court of the States and Provinces of North America*, by C. Bell (1893).

## CHAPTER V

### THE COLONIAL SOUTHERN BAR

### South Carolina

In South Carolina, under its charter of 1663, a form of government and an institution of laws, courts and law procedure was initiated, which differed from anything in America. This was John Locke's celebrated but chimerical *Fundamental Constitutions of Carolina*, issued in 1669–1670 by the Proprietors. It provided for a most elaborate system of courts of eleven different kinds and jurisdictions; and it contained the following curious limitation on the courts:

"Since multiplicity of comments as well as of laws have great inconveniences, and serve only to obscure and perplex; all manner of comments and expositions on any part of these Fundamental Constitutions, or any part of the common or statute law of Carolina, are absolutely prohibited."

Owing to their impracticability, few of these *Constitutions* ever came into actual operation; and after being modified in 1682, they were substantially abrogated in 1698. For many years, there was much doubt as to how far the English law was applicable; and in 1692, the Assembly, in an address to Governor Ludwell, had complained because the court had "assumed to put in force such English laws as they deemed adapted to the Province; but the Assembly conceived that either such laws were valid of their own force or could only be made so by an act of the Assembly."

In 1712, by a special act, the Assembly adopted the English Common Law as a rule of adjudicature, and also such English statutes (126) as had been selected by Chief Justice Trott as applicable to the condition of the Colony.

No law passed prior to 1682 is to be found on record. The first authority for printing the laws was given in 1712; and the first compilation of the law, made by Chief Justice Trott, was published in 1736.

Up to 1683, all judicial business was done by the Governor and Council. In that year, a Provincial Court was established with a Chief Justice appointed by the Proprietor; but it was not until 1720 that any assistant judges were appointed. The Governor and Council became a Court of Appeals. There were few other statutes, if any, relating to courts or their jurisdiction prior to the wholesale adoption of English law, in 1712. There is no regular record of any judicial proceedings prior to 1703, nor any record entered in any bound books prior to 1710. Regular court records are extant from 1716. Practically nothing is known of any inferior courts. The expense of attending court and the delays in obtaining justice became so intolerable, however, that in 1769, circuit courts were established in the various counties. The amount of business transacted in the courts was not large; as it is said that in the seven years before the War of the Revolution the average number of judgments yearly in the whole Colony was only 236.[1]

The first Chief Justice of record was Edmund Bohun, in 1698, a man of no legal training; the next, in 1702, Nicholas Trott, an English lawyer of distinction. He remained in office for many years, finally becoming so arbitrary and so obnoxious that, in 1719, articles of complaint were brought

[1] *Lives of the Chief Justices*, by G. Van Santfoord.

by "Richard Allein, Richard Whittaker and other practitioners of law," alleging that he had "contrived many ways to increase and multiply his fees," that he gave advice in causes depending in his courts, and not only acted as counsellor in these cases, but had drawn deeds between party and party, and that the whole judicial power of the Province was lodged in his hands; he being, at the same time, sole judge of the Court of Common Pleas, King's Bench, Vice-Admiralty, also member of the Council and hence judge of the Court of Chancery. The Governor, Council and Assembly joined in an address to the Proprietary for his removal.

When South Carolina became a Royal Province in 1720, an act was passed providing for a Supreme Court consisting of a Chief Justice and four assistants. The Chief Justices were, as a rule, educated lawyers; but being appointed by the Royal Governors, were largely subservient to the Crown. Practically all of the thirty-four assistant judges, from 1720 to 1776, were laymen with no legal training.

Nevertheless as William Henry Drayton (later Chief Justice), writing about the time of the Revolution, said:

> "A few years ago the bench of justice in this Colony was filled with men of property, and if all of them were not learned in the law, there were some among them who taught their brethren to administer justice with public approbation; and one in particular (Rawlins Lowndes) had so well digested his reading, although he had never eat commons at the Temple, that he was without dispute, at least, equal to the law learning of the present bench."[1]

Of the early lawyers little is known; but the early prejudice against the legal profession is shown by the following clause in Locke's *Constitutions :*

[1] *Life and Times of William Lowndes*, by Mrs. St. J. Ravenel.

"It shall be a base and vile thing to plead for money or reward; nor shall anyone (except he be a near kinsman, not farther off than a cousin-german to the party concerned) be permitted to plead another man's cause, till, before the judge in open court, he hath taken an oath, that he doth not plead for money or reward, nor hath nor will receive nor directly nor indirectly bargained with the party, whose cause he is going to plead, for money or any other reward for pleading his cause."

That this provision was not enforced, however, appears from the enactment of a statute in 1694, prescribing tables of court fees, which included attorneys' fees.

Among the English statutes adopted as in force in 1712 was that of Henry IV (1402) as to admission and examination of attorneys by the courts; and in 1721, admission of attorneys was specifically provided in county courts in a statute which recited that "whereas divers unskilful persons do often undertake to manage and solicit business in the courts of law and equity, to the unspeakable damage of the clients occasioned by the ignorance of such solicitors who are no ways qualified for that purpose, tending to the promoting litigiousness and encouraging of vexatious suits," and enacted that no person should practise as attorney unless admitted and sworn by the Supreme Court.

In 1761, at the time when John Rutledge, the earliest of South Carolina's great lawyers, began to practise, the Bar consisted of probably not more than twenty, and prior to the Revolution no more than fifty-eight had been admitted to practise. But though small in numbers, it was more highly educated than any Bar in America, for a considerable proportion of its members had received their legal training in England.

Thus, William Wragg, one of the earliest lawyers, born in 1741, was an English barrister; Peter Manigault, born in 1731, was a barrister of the Inner Temple, and returned to practise in South Carolina in 1754. John Rutledge, born in 1739, studied in the office of James Parsons, at Charleston, and became a barrister of the Inner Temple in 1761; returning to Charleston, he at once took rank as the ablest lawyer of the Province, headed the Stamp Act opposition, was one of the Signers, and became Chief Justice of the State Court in 1791, and of the United States Supreme Court in 1795. William Henry Drayton, "the Sam Adams of the South," born in 1742, was educated at Oxford. Thomas Heyward, born in 1746, became a barrister of the Middle Temple, and was one of the Signers. Thomas Lynch, Jr., born in 1749, a barrister of the Middle Temple, was the third Signer from South Carolina.

Of the generation of lawyers who came into practise at the time of the Revolution, there were many of great education and distinction at the Bar. The following studied in the Inner Temple: John Laurens, born in 1755; John Julian Pringle, born in 1753; Edward Rutledge, born in 1749; Charles Cotesworth Pinckney, born in 1746; Thomas Pinckney, born in 1750; William H. Gibbes, born in 1754, and Hugh Rutledge, born in 1741. John F. Grimke, born in 1752, Theodore Gaillard and Arthur Middleton received their education in English universities; Aedanus Burke, born in 1743, was educated as a priest in the College of St. Omer in France; Richard Hutson, born in 1747, and Chancellor from 1784 to 1793, was a graduate of Princeton.

### North Carolina

In North Carolina, which became known as a separate Province about 1691 (although not formally made so until 1731), John Locke's *Constitutions* were theoretically the frame of government until their abrogation; but in 1715, an act was passed by the Provincial Legislature providing that the Common Law should be in force, "so far as shall be compatible with our way of living and trade," and certain specific English statutes were also adopted. No compilation of laws was made until 1732. A Commission was appointed to revise the laws in 1746, and again in 1776; and the first printed collection of laws was in 1751.

Until 1702, the Governor and Council acted as the Court. In that year a General Court, consisting of a Chief Justice and two assistant judges, was established. The earliest Chief Justice named in the records was the famous Anthony Ashley Cooper, Lord Shaftesbury, who exercised the duties of his post through a deputy. Only a few of the Chief Justices prior to 1746 were trained lawyers, and when such, they were English barristers sent from England, the first barrister, William Smith, coming in 1731; but in 1746, a Superior Court was constituted, the judges of which were required by statute to be lawyers.

The earliest record of County Courts is in 1693.

Of North Carolina lawyers, little is recorded; and the condition of education in the Colony was unfavorable to the development of native talent.

Early in the Eighteenth Century, however, they were allowed to practise; but the Court ordered that they must be licensed by the Chief Justice and judges; and that no sheriff, undersheriff or clerk should plead as attorney at law. The English statute, 3 James I, c. 7, as to admission and regulation of attorneys, was treated as in force in the Colony.

The only eminent members of the early Colonial Bar were Thomas Barker; Samuel Johnston, a Scotch lawyer; Henry Eustace McCulloch, a barrister of the Inner Temple, who practised in the Province from 1761 to 1767; Thomas Jones and Alexander Elmsly, both English lawyers; John Dawson, a Virginian; William Avery, born in Connecticut, a Princeton graduate, and Attorney-General in 1777; Jasper Charlton; William Cumming, and Robert Smith.

Undoubtedly the most prominent of all the later North Carolina Bar was James Iredell, who, born in England in 1750, came to the Province in 1768, where he studied law under Samuel Johnston, and in 1770, "with the approbation and recommendation of Chief Justice Howard, received from Governor Tryon a license to practise law in all the Inferior Courts." In 1771, he was licensed by the Governor to practise in the Superior Courts.

Of the conditions of the legal profession in North Carolina in his day, the following graphic account is given:[1]

"Upon horseback, often alone, through the dense forests and across the almost trackless Savannahs, the lawyer of that day travelled his weary circuit. Accommodations by the way were generally despicably vile; inns or taverns in the true sense had no existence. After the fatigue of a long day's journey the wayworn traveller was often content with a bench by the hearth of some primitive log cabin. . . . Books he had not, save a volume or two stuffed into his saddle-bags with a scanty supply of apparel. At this period, too, in what was then called the 'back country,' now the interior of North Carolina, the gentlemen of the Bar were objects of obloquy and denunciation to a generally poor and illiterate people, and frequently experienced at their hands the grossest outrages. . . . The people justly complained of the burden of their taxes — a burden augmented by the extortion of illegal fees by the officers of the courts; but with a blind prejudice, many of them only saw in the profession, those who defended their oppressors, and who prosecuted them when their opposition broke out into acts of violence. Uncultivated settlers who subdue the wilderness are apt to look with suspicion upon the proprietor of the soil when he demands rent for his land or its value; . . . and the attorneys employed to bring ejectments or sue for use, as the venal instruments of tyranny, bandits hired by gold to despoil them of the fruits of their honest industry."

[1] *Life and Correspondence of James Iredell*, by Griffith J. McRee (1857).

In 1777, Iredell became Judge of the Superior Court, resigning the next year, and in 1789 he was appointed Judge of the Supreme Court of the United States.

Contemporary with him, after the Revolution, were Abner Maurice Moore; Archibald McClaine; Alfred Moore, who, born in 1755, a student at Harvard but not a graduate, succeeded Iredell in the United States Supreme Court; William R. Davie, born in England in 1756, a Princeton graduate of 1776, admitted to practise in North Carolina in 1780, and of whom it was said, "if he had superiors in legal learning and close reasoning, he as an orator was inferior to none in the State;" John Haywood, who was born in 1753, became Attorney-General in 1791 and published his *Reports* in 1799.

Both of the Signers of the Declaration of Independence from North Carolina were lawyers. One, William Hooper, was born in Boston in 1742, a graduate of Harvard in 1760, and a student under James Otis in 1761, the same year in which Otis argued the Writs of Assistance. He came to North Carolina in 1767, and within six years became a leading member of the Bar. The other, John Penn, was born in Virginia in 1741, a student under Edmund Pendleton, and removed to North Carolina in 1774.

### Georgia

No laws were passed by the General Assembly of Georgia until 1755, the Colony having previously been under the arbitrary rule of the Proprietor.

The first court of Georgia, held at Savannah in 1733, was lawyerless; but when Georgia became a Crown Colony in 1752, the Chief Justice was required to be an English barrister. The three assistant judges were usually laymen of high standing in the community, and received no salaries.

In 1789, the Superior Court of the State was established.

The native Bar of the early Eighteenth Century was small; but a few English barristers practised in Savannah. George Walton, one of the Signers, who was born in Virginia in 1740, admitted to the Bar there in 1774 and removed to Georgia, where he became Chief Justice in 1783, and Abraham Baldwin, who was born in Connecticut in 1754 and a Yale graduate of 1772, are two of the few Colonial American lawyers of Georgia whose names survive. Admission to practise and the lawyer's oath were regulated by the English statute of 1729 (2 George II), which was treated as a force in Georgia after 1731.

## NOTE

### To South Carolina Text

For authorities in general, see:

*History of South Carolina*, by David Ramsay (1808).
*Sketch of History of South Carolina*, by W. J. Revers (1856).
*View of the Constitution of the British Colonies in North America and the West Indies*, by Anthony Stokes (1783).
*Glance at our Colonial Bar — Green Bag*, Vol. XI.
Willis on *Law and Lawyers — Amer. Quarterly Review*, Vol. XIV and Vol. XV.
*Bench and Bar of South Carolina*, by John B. O'Neall (1859).
*Old Virginia and her Neighbors*, by John Fiske (1897).
*Life and Times of William Lowndes*, by Mrs. St. J. Ravenel (1901).
*The History of South Carolina*, by Edward McCrady (1897).

### To North Carolina Text

*North Carolina Records.*
*History of North Carolina*, by F. K. Hawks (1889).
*English Common Law in the early American Colonies*, by Paul F. Reinsch.
Sanderson's *Lives of the Signers.*
*Life and Correspondence of James Iredell*, by Griffith J. McRee (1857).

*Address on the Life of William Hooper*, by Edward A. Alderman (1894).
*Life of William R. Davie*, in Sparks' *American Biography.*
*The Supreme Court of North Carolina*, by Walter Clark — *Green Bag*, Vol. IV.
*Alfred Moore* — *Green Bag*, Vol. XII.
*A Masterpiece of Constitutional Folly* — *Green Bag*, Vol. XII.

### To Georgia Text

*Bench and Bar of Georgia*, by Stephen F. Miller (1858).
*Glance at Our Colonial Bar* — *Green Bag*, Vol. XI.
*History of Georgia*, by Charles C. Jones (1883).
*History of Augusta*, by Salem Dutcher (1890).
*Georgia Law Books*, by Joseph R. Lamar, in *Georgia Bar Ass. Proc.*, Vol. XV.
*A Lawyerless Court*, by Walter G. Charlton, in *Georgia Bar Ass. Proc.*, Vol. XVIII.
*Georgia Lawyers Viewed by a Woman*, in *Georgia Bar Ass. Proc.*, Vol. XVIII.

# CHAPTER VI

## NEW ENGLAND COLONIAL BAR

### Connecticut

The development of the law and of the Bar in Connecticut followed exactly, step by step, that of Massachusetts.

Of the leaders in its settlement in 1636–1637, only three were men educated in the law, — Roger Ludlow, an Oxford graduate, a student in the Inner Temple in 1612, a member of the Court of Assistants in Massachusetts; Governor John Haynes, a man "very learned in the laws of England;" and Governor John Winthrop the younger, a barrister of the Inner Temple in 1624. With these exceptions, there are no records of the existence of any trained lawyers in Connecticut during the Century.

The first American written constitution, known as the "Fundamental Orders," was prepared by Ludlow in 1639; and in 1650 he drafted, at the request of the General Assembly, a *Body of Lawes* in seventy-seven sections, fourteen of which were taken from the Massachusetts *Body of Liberties*, the rest being the fruit of his own learning. This code, which showed great ability, originality and research, became the foundation of all law in Connecticut.

The general attitude towards the English law entertained by both the settlements which made up the Colony of Connecticut was much the same as that of Massachusetts; and may be expressed by the resolution framed by the freemen of the New Haven settlement, in 1639: "That the words of God shall be the onely rule to be attended unto in ordering the affayres of government in this plantation."

The sole court at first consisted of the General Court or Assembly, composed of the Governor, Deputy-Governors, the twelve Assistants (or Councillors), elected at large and constituting the higher branch of the Legislature, and the Representatives or lower branch. After the Royal charter of 1662, the Governor, Deputy-Governor and at least six of the twelve Assistants exercised all the judicial powers of the General Court, and were called the Court of Assistants. It was not until 1710 that a separate Superior Court was constituted, with a Chief Justice and four justices (usually elected from the Assistants). The General Assembly, however, still continued as a final Court of Appeal.

As a result of the elective system in choosing the judges, they were seldom trained lawyers; and even when they had received any legal education, they had frequently been first brought up in some other trade or profession. Thus, Roger Wolcott, who was Chief Justice in 1741, was originally a weaver; Jonathan Trumbull, a most distinguished Chief Justice from 1766 to 1769, was first a minister, and later a merchant, only incidentally studying law.[1] This condition of affairs prevailed even after the War of the Revolution; for Oliver Ellsworth, who was a judge of the Superior Court in 1784 and who became Chief Justice of the Supreme Court of the United States in 1796, studied first for the ministry,[2] as did Jesse Root, who was Chief Justice in 1796.

With a court constituted largely of laymen, it was natural that there should be little pleading of any kind in

[1] Born in 1710, a graduate of Harvard in 1727. So great was his sagacity and ability, that during his long Governorship of the State (1769–1784), Washington's constant reliance on his advice, taking the form of "we must consult Brother Jonathan," became the foundation of that nickname for the United States.

[2] Born in 1745, studied at Yale 1762–1764, a Princeton graduate in 1766.

law suits; and there were no statutes prescribing forms until 1709, 1720 and 1731.

Under all these circumstances, the Bar developed even later than in Massachusetts. In 1667, the General Court prohibited "all persons from pleading as attorneys in behalf of any person that is charged or prosecuted for delinquency (except he speak directly to matter of law and with leave from the authority present)" under fine of ten shillings, or the stocks for one hour.

In 1708, an act was passed, regulating the admissions of attorneys to practise, and providing that:

"No person except in his own case, shall be admitted to make any plea at the Bar without being first approved of by the court before whom the plea is to be made, nor until he shall take in the said court the following oath, viz.: 'You shall do no falsehood, nor consent to any to be done in the court, and if you know of any to be done, you shall give knowledge thereof to the justices of the court, or some of them, that it may be reformed. You shall not wittingly and willingly promote, sue or procure to be sued, any false or unlawful suit, nor give aid or consent to the same. You shall delay no man for lucre or malice, but you shall use yourself in the office of an attorney within the court according to the best of your learning and discretion, and with all good fidelity, as well to the court as to the client. So help you God.'"[1]

This law required authority from the court in each particular case; and no statute providing for the general admission of attorneys existed until 1750.

In 1725, an act was passed, taxing all persons practising as attorneys in the Colony, "for their faculty," by which those who were "the least practitioners" were to be set in the list for fifty pounds, and others "according to their

[1] This form of oath is substantially the same as that in use in Massachusetts, and was derived from that in use in England in 1649.

practise." In 1730, the number of attorneys was limited as follows:

"Whereas many persons of late have taken upon themselves to be attorneys at the Bar so that quarrels and lawsuits are multiplied and the King's good subjects disturbed; to the end that said mischief may be prevented and only proper persons allowed to plead at the Bar, . . . be it enacted: that there shall be allowed in the Colony eleven attorneys and no more . . . which attorneys shall be nominated and appointed from time to time as there shall be occasion by the county courts."

And in actions to land titles involving ten pounds or less, each party was allowed one attorney to plead, and over ten pounds, two attorneys. The restriction of the number of attorneys, however, was abolished in 1731. In the statistics of the Connecticut Bar, prepared by the noted Judge Thomas Day, there appear the names of no lawyers practising in the Seventeenth Century.

Of Eighteenth Century lawyers before the Revolutionary War, there were comparatively few of distinction or legal training. One of the earliest was Thomas Fitch, born in 1699, a graduate of Yale in 1721, who codified the laws, became Chief Justice and later Governor; "probably the most learned lawyer who had ever been an inhabitant of the Colony," said the first President Dwight of Yale.

Jared Ingersoll, the elder, born in 1722, a Yale graduate of 1742, was a trained lawyer, and acted as the Colony's agent in England. Phineas Lyman, born in 1716, a Yale graduate of 1738, was also eminent about the middle of the Century.

Nothing illustrates the smallness of the Bar better than the fact that when the famous case of *Winthrop* v. *Lechmere*, 1724–1728, arose — the case of an appeal from the decisions of the Probate Judge and of the Superior Court, by a brother claiming the whole of the estate of an intestate, in conformity with the Common Law of England, and denying the validity of the Connecticut statute of descent, which was absolutely inconsistent with the English Common Law — no counsel were sent from Connecticut to argue the case before the King in Council in London; but both sides relied on English lawyers, Sir Philip Yorke, Attorney-General of England (later Lord Chancellor), appearing for the appellant; and for the appellee Sir John Willes (later Attorney-General and Chief Justice of Common Pleas), and a Mr. Booth (of whom nothing is known).[1]

One of the first American lawyers to argue before the King in Council was William Samuel Johnson, who appeared there in the famous Mohegan case, involving important landed interests in Connecticut. Born in 1727, a Yale graduate of 1744, and a Doctor of Civil Law at Oxford, he was one of the leaders of the Bar in the middle of the Century, and from 1766 to 1771 was Colonial Agent in London.

His influence was thus described in an obituary:

"His first appearance at the Bar forms an epoch in the legal history of his native state. The legal system of Connecticut was at that time exceedingly crude, and the irregular equity by which the courts were guided was rather perplexed than enlightened by occasional recurrence to a few of the old Common Law authorities which

[1] Nine years later, in 1737, when the similar Massachusetts case of *Phillips* v. *Savage* was argued before the King in Council, only one Colonial lawyer appeared in the case, Jonathan Belcher of Boston, with whom was Sir John Strange (later Master of the Rolls); Sir Dudley Ryder (later Lord Mansfield's predecessor as Lord Chief Justice) and John Brown (of whom nothing is known) appearing for the other side. See *Mass. Hist. Soc. Proc.*, Vol. V (1860).

*Mass. Hist. Soc. Proc.*, Vol. VIII, 2d Series (1893).

*The Talcott Papers, Conn. Hist. Soc. Coll.*, Vol. IV.

*Mass. Hist. Soc. Coll.*, 6th Series, Vol. V.

were respected without being understood. Dalton's *Sheriff and Justice of Peace* and one or two of the older books of Precedents formed the whole library of the Bar and the Bench. . . . Mr. Johnson rendered an important service to his countrymen by introducing to their knowledge the liberal decisions of Lord Mansfield and the doctrines of the civilians."

Two other lawyers were especially prominent before the Revolution. The first was Mathew Griswold, who was born in 1714, and quaintly described by President Stiles of Yale College in 1790 as follows:

"Fitted for college, settled a farmer, studied law *proprio Marte*, bo't him the first considerable Law library, took atty oath and began practice 1743 — a great reader of law,"

and who became Chief Justice in 1769, succeeding Jonathan Trumbull. The second was Roger Sherman, who was born in Massachusetts in 1721, admitted to practise in 1754, made a judge of the Court of Common Pleas in 1759, a member of the Council or Upper House in 1766 and also judge of the Superior Court, which latter position he held until 1789, the last four years being a colleague of Oliver Ellsworth. In 1783, he was appointed with Richard Law to digest the statutes. He was head and front of the Revolutionary movement and one of the Signers.

In 1779, Noah Webster, then just graduating from Yale, spoke of William Samuel Johnson, Oliver Ellsworth and Titus Hosmer as the "three mighties" of the Connecticut Bar. Contemporary with these were James A. Hillhouse,[1] Samuel Huntington,[2] Eliphalet Dyer,[3] Richard Law,[4] Amos

[1] Born in 1730, a Yale graduate of 1749.

[2] Born in 1731, judge of the Superior Court in 1774, Chief Justice in 1784, one of the Signers, of whom it is said "few lawyers enjoyed a more extensive practice."

[3] Born in 1721, a Yale graduate of 1740, Chief Justice 1789–1793.

[4] Born in 1733, a Yale graduate of 1751, Chief Justice 1786–1789.

Botsford, Samuel Holden Parsons,[1] Charles Chauncey[2] and Jesse Root.[3]

## New Hampshire

In New Hampshire no regular courts existed at all until 1641, when the Colony was united to Massachusetts, and came under its laws. When it was made a Royal Province in 1679, the President and Council acted as the court, with appeal to the General Assembly.

Richard Martyn, the first Chief Justice of the Superior Court of Judicature, in 1693, was a merchant without legal education.

In 1699, the Superior Court of Judicature was reorganized; but no one of its judges were lawyers—John Hinckes, Chief Justice, Peter Coffin, John Gerrish and John Plaisted. Inferior Courts of Common Pleas and Quarterly Courts of Sessions were also constituted in 1699. No practising attorney was appointed to the Bench until, in 1754, Theodore Atkinson, who had been a clerk of the Court of Common Pleas in Massachusetts and admitted to the Bar there in 1731, became the first Chief Justice with any legal training.[4] Prior to the Revolution, only two other judges were lawyers, — Leverett Hubbard, who had studied law in Rhode Island, appointed judge in 1763, and William Parker, appointed in 1771, "a well read and accurate lawyer" and the head of the Bar.[5]

From 1776 to 1782, the Chief Justice was Meschech Weare,

[1] Born in 1737, a student with Governor Mathew Griswold, the last royal Attorney-General.

[2] Born in 1747, judge of the Superior Court 1789–1793, "for forty years a lecturer on jurisprudence."

[3] Born in 1736, Princeton graduate of 1756, Chief Justice 1796–1807. author of *Root's Reports*.

[4] Born in 1697, Harvard graduate of 1716, Chief Justice 1754–1755.

[5] Born in 1703.

who had studied theology but did not preach;[1] Matthew Thornton, a physician, and John Wentworth, a lawyer of little distinction, being his associates. From 1782 to 1790, Samuel Livermore was Chief Justice. He was a trained lawyer, born in 1732, in Massachusetts, a graduate of Princeton in 1752, a student in the office of Judge Edmund Trowbridge, in 1769 King's Attorney in New Hampshire, Attorney-General of the State in 1776. He sat on the bench however with three associates who were not lawyers, and he himself was intolerant of legal precedent. It is said that in charging the jury he used to caution them "against paying too much attention to the niceties of the law to the prejudice of Justice;" and when reminded of previous rulings of his own contrary to his present ruling, he would reply that "every tub must stand on its own bottom."

Jeremiah Mason said in his Autobiography that law learning in 1791 was in a very low state in the New Hampshire courts, and that Benjamin West, "by far the best lawyer in this region of the country," told him this anecdote of Livermore, as illustrating the uselessness of citing precedents:

"Judge Livermore, having no law learning himself, did not like to be pestered with it at his courts. When West attempted to read law books in a law argument, the Chief Justice asked him why he read them; 'if he thought that he and his brethren did not know as much as those musty old worm-eaten books?' Mr. West answered, 'These books contain the wisdom of the ancient sages of the law.' The reply was, 'Well, do you think we do not understand the principles of justice as well as the old wigged lawyers of the dark ages did?'"

Josiah Bartlett, a physician, was Livermore's associate, of whom it was said, that "when the law was with the plaintiff, and equity seemed to him on the other side, he was sure to

[1] Born in 1713, Harvard graduate of 1735.

pronounce in favor of equity." John Dudley, the most prominent of the associate judges from 1785 to 1797, was a farmer and trader; and his style of charging the jury has been quoted as follows:

"Gentlemen of the jury, the lawyers have talked to you of law. It is not the law we want, but justice. They would govern us by the Common Law of England. Trust me, gentlemen, common sense is a much safer guide for us, the common sense of Raymond, Exeter and the other towns which have sent us here to try this case between two of our neighbors. It is our business to do justice between the parties not by any quirks of the law out of Coke or Blackstone — books that I never read and never will — but by common sense as between man and man."

In one case, in which Jeremiah Mason had filed a demurrer, Judge Dudley said that "demurrers were no doubt an invention of the Bar to prevent justice, a part of the Common Law procedure," but that he had always "thought them a cursed cheat." "Let me advise you, young man," he added, "not to come here with your new-fangled law — you must try your cases as others do, by the court and jury."

William Plumer thus describes the condition of the courts before the Revolution:

"Under the colonial government, causes of importance were carried up, for decision in the last resort, to the Governor and Council, with the right, in certain cases — a right seldom claimed — of appeal to the King in Council. As the executive functionaries were not generally lawyers, and the titular judges were often from other professions than the legal, they were not much influenced in their decisions by any known principles of established law. So much, indeed, was the result supposed to depend upon the favor or aversion of the court, that presents from suitors to the judges were not uncommon, nor, perhaps, unexpected. On one occasion, the Chief Justice, who was also a member of the council, is said to have inquired rather impatiently of his servant, what cattle those were that had waked him so unseasonably in the morning by their lowing under his window; and to have been somewhat mollified by the answer that they were a yoke of six-feet cattle, which Col. —— had sent as a present to His Honor. 'Has he?' said the Judge; 'I must look into his case — it has been in court long enough.'"

Under date of June 24, 1771, John Adams says:

"Mr. Lowell, who practised much in New Hampshire, gave me an account of many strange judgments of the Superior Court at Portsmouth. . . . During the Revolution, the same practice of going beyond the courts of law for redress was continued; and the form which it took, under the Constitution of 1784, was that of a special act of the Legislature, restoring the party to his law, as it was called, that is, giving him a new trial in the Superior Court, after his case had come to its final decision in the ordinary course of the law. . . . The supposed interest of lawyers in the multiplication of suits, the litigious spirit of parties, ever eager to grasp at new chances of success, and the love of power natural to legislative bodies, all combined to render this irregularity in the administration of justice not unacceptable to the public."

Belknap in his *History*, written in 1792, thus describes the legal conditions:

"In the administration of justice, frequent complaints were made of partiality. Parties were sometimes heard out of court, and the practice of watering the jury was familiarly known to those persons who had much business in the law."

While the rude decisions of the courts, based on common sense, were not wholly without value in their influence on the development of the law,[1] nevertheless, before a Bench

[1] As Judge Bell said, in *B. C. & M. R. R.* v. *State* (32 N. H. 231): "We regard the ignorance of the first colonists of the technicalities of the Common

so little addicted to legal methods there was small need or opportunity for trained lawyers; and the Bar of New Hampshire, during the whole of the Seventeenth and Eighteenth Centuries, was consequently few in number. In the former Century there was only one educated lawyer in the Province, John Pickering of Portsmouth, who was born in 1640 and died in 1721.

In the early Eighteenth Century, two may be especially mentioned, — Mathew Livermore, born in 1703, a Harvard graduate of 1722, who was regularly admitted to the Bar in Portsmouth in 1731; at which time, says John Adams, "there was no regularly educated lawyer in the town." He became Attorney-General in 1755 and died in 1776. Wiseman Claggett, one of the quaintest geniuses of the whole Colonial Bar, was born in 1721, arrived in Portsmouth in 1758, and was then admitted to the Bar of the Superior Court. He had been a barrister in the Inns of Court, and later a practising attorney in Antigua in the West Indies. Until the Revolution he divided the business of New Hampshire with Samuel Livermore (later the Chief Justice), Claggett receiving most of the criminal business, Livermore the civil.

In 1758, at the time of the chartering of Dartmouth College, there were only eight trained lawyers in New Hampshire; and none of them was of such ability as to be retained by President Wheelock, he engaging as his counsel William Smith and William Smith, Jr., of New York, and John Ledyard of Connecticut; the head of the Bar, William Parker, being legal adviser of Governor Wentworth.

There was no regular Bar Association until after the

Law as one of the most fortunate things in the history of the law, since, while the substance of the Common Law was preserved, we happily lost a great mass of antiquated and useless rubbish, and gained in its stead a course of practice of admirable simplicity."

Revolution. And to 1785, the Bar continued small, not exceeding twenty-nine in number, of whom the following lawyers were leaders, — John Prentice,[1] John Sullivan,[2] Benjamin West,[3] John Pickering,[4] and Joshua Atherton.[5]

The first legislation as to lawyers was in 1714, when an act was passed allowing parties to plead by attorney, providing an attorneys' oath and regulating fees.

## Maine

In Maine, Thomas Gorges, the head of the Colonial Government, was an English barrister, a practising lawyer and the only one in the Colony during the Seventeenth Century. The General Court at first tried all criminal and civil cases; later it established two inferior courts, which existed until 1692, when the Colony was incorporated into the Royal Province of Massachusetts, and came under its judicial system.

It was not until 1720 that there was a resident lawyer practising in the Maine courts — Noah Emery of Kittery, brought up as a cooper, but who later studied law.

As late as 1770, the only educated lawyers residing in Maine were David Sewall, Theophilus Bradbury, John Sullivan, James Sullivan, William Cushing and David Wyer.[6]

[1] Born in 1747, Harvard graduate of 1766, studied with S. Livermore, Attorney-General 1787–1793.

[2] Born in 1740, studied with S. Livermore, Attorney-General 1782–1785, U. S. District Judge 1789.

[3] Born in 1746, Harvard graduate of 1768, studied for the ministry, admitted to the Bar 1773.

[4] Born in 1737, Harvard graduate of 1759, Chief Justice 1790–1795, U. S. District Judge 1795–1801.

[5] Born in 1732, Harvard graduate of 1762.

[6] See *The Law, the Courts and Lawyers of Maine*, by William Willis (1863).

## Rhode Island

In Rhode Island, there was at first no distinction between the legislative and judicial branches of government. Under the early compact of 1638, a judge and three elders were chosen "who should govern according to the general rule of the word of God." The next year, a Governor and eight Assistants formed the General Court, having both judicial and administrative powers. When the charter of 1647 was granted, a President and four Assistants, one from each town, constituted a General Court of Trials. Under the Royal charter of 1662–1664 and until 1747–1749, the Governor, Deputy-Governor and ten elective Assistants exercised the judicial powers. It was not until 1747 that the judiciary was recognized by act of the General Assembly as a separate branch of the government. The Court then established consisted of a Chief Justice and four "judicious and skilful persons" chosen by the General Assembly, generally from among the ten Assistants (or magistrates).[1]

At no time was knowledge of the law considered essential to the members of the Court; and the judge, because of his ignorance, did not even charge the jury.[2]

In 1699, the Earl of Bellomont, in his report to the Lords of Trade, said:

"Thus courts of justice are held by the Governor and Assistants who sit as judges therein, more for constituting the court than for searching out the right of the causes coming before them or delivering their opinion on points of law (whereof it is said they know very little). They give no directions to the jury nor sum up the evidences to them, pointing unto the issue which they are to try. Their proceedings are very unmethodical, no wise agreeable to the

[1] *Judicial System in Rhode Island*, by Amasa M. Eaton, *Yale Law Journal*, Vol. XIV; *Early Rhode Island*, by William B. Weeden (1910).

[2] This custom remained unchanged in Rhode Island until 1833.

course and practice of the courts in England, and many times arbitrary and contrary to the laws of the place; as is affirmed by the attorneys at law that have sometimes practiced in their court."

The first Chief Justice of Rhode Island, Gideon Cowell, in 1747, was not a lawyer; the second, Joshua Babcock (a Yale graduate of 1724), was a physician. Stephen Hopkins, Chief Justice from 1751 to 1755, was a trained and able lawyer; but most of the judges during this Century were laymen, merchants or farmers.

As in Massachusetts and Connecticut, little deference was paid to the Common Law of England, and the lack of legal education in the judiciary rendered the citing of English precedents in the courts of little avail. A full code of law was adopted in 1647, embodying an elaborate classification of crimes, and providing that "in all other matters not forbidden by the code, all men may walk as their conscience persuades them." That alone was declared to be law which was made such by the Assembly. This meant the exclusion of English law, when unconfirmed by the Assembly.[1]

Of the early Bar, little or nothing is known. The earliest statutory reference to lawyers was in 1647, when it was provided that a man might "plead his own case . . . or make his attorney to plead for him, or may use the attorney that belongs to the court which may be then in town, to wit: discreet, honest and able men for understanding, chosen by the townsmen of the same town, and solemnly engaged by the head officer thereof not to use any manner of deceit to beguile either court or party." In 1668–1669, it was enacted that any person who was indicted might employ an attorney to plead in his behalf. In 1705, an act was passed requiring attorneys to take an oath.

[1] See *Colonial Records*, Vol. II, pp. 42, 147, 157.

In 1718, an act was passed limiting the number of lawyers to be permitted to argue in any case to two, one of them to be a freeholder of the Colony. In 1729, lawyers were forbidden to be deputies, their presence in the Assembly sitting as a Court of Appeal being "found to be of ill consequence." This act was repealed, however, in 1731.

The office of Attorney-General was created in 1650, by an act which quaintly declared that "because envy, the cut-throat of all prosperitie, will not fail to gallop with its full career, let the sayd attorney be faithfully engaged and authorized and encouraged." Henry Bull, who was born in 1689, and elected Attorney-General in 1721, tells an anecdote of himself, which seems to fairly illustrate the conditions of early law practise.

"When he made up his mind to practise law, he went into the garden to exercise his talents in addressing the court and jury. He selected five cabbages in one row for judges, and twelve in another row for jurors; after trying his hand thus awhile he went boldly into court and took upon himself the duties of an advocate, and a little observation and experience there convinced him that the same cabbages were in the court house which he thought he had left in the garden, — five in one row and twelve in another."

In 1745, the first meeting of the Bar was held, at which a compact regulating practise and fees was signed by Daniel Updike, James Honyman, Jr., John Aplin, John Walton, Mathew Robinson, David Richards, Jr., Thomas Ward and John Andrews. Two of the articles of this compact have a curious interest, as showing the solidarity of the "fraternity:"

"*VI.*—No Attorney to sign blank writs and disperse them about the colony, which practice it is conceived, would make the law cheap and hurt the business, without profiting anyone whatsoever.

"*VII.*—No Attorney shall take up any suit whatever against a practitioner who sues for his fees, except three or more brethren shall determine the demand unreasonable; and then, if he will not do justice, the whole fraternity shall rise up against him."

Few facts are known as to the personnel of the Bar in the Eighteenth Century, and almost the only lawyers with any legal training were the Attorneys-General, — Daniel Updike, in 1721; James Honeyman, in 1732; Augustus Johnson, in 1757;[1] Oliver Arnold, in 1766;[2] Henry Marchant, who, born in 1741, studied law with the learned Judge Trowbridge of Massachusetts, became Attorney-General in 1770, and United States District Judge in 1789; and William Channing, born in 1727, a graduate of Harvard in 1747, a leading lawyer at the time of the Revolution, and one of the signers of the Declaration of Independence, Attorney-General in 1777.

After the War, James M. Varnum, born in 1749, graduate of Brown in 1769, and a student of law in the office of Oliver Arnold, was one of the leaders of the Bar. He was the counsel for the defendant in *Trevett* v. *Weeden* in 1786, one of the first cases in which an American court of law assumed to pass upon the constitutionality of a legislative act.

The real Bar of Rhode Island, however, began with James Burrill[3] and Tristam Burges,[4] at the opening of the Nineteenth Century.

[1] Born about 1730. [2] Born in 1726.

[3] Born 1772, graduate of Brown College in 1788, studied in office of Theodore Foster and later that of David Howell (afterwards U. S. District Judge), admitted to practise in 1791, Chief Justice 1816–1817.

[4] Born 1770, studied at Brown College 1793–1797, admitted to the Bar in 1809, Chief Justice 1817–1818.

In his *Memoirs of Tristam Burges* (1835), Henry L. Bowen says, "Burrill has no superior in his native State, and few in any section of the Union."

Contemporary with Burrill and Burges were Ashur Robbins, William Hunter and Benjamin Hazard.

## NOTE

### To Connecticut Text

See, for authorities in general:

*Roger Ludlow*, by John M. Taylor (1900).
*History of the Judicial System of New England*, by Conrad Reno (1900).
*Oliver Ellsworth*, by William G. Brown (1905).
*Judicial and Civil History of Conn.*, by Dwight Loomis and J. G. Calhoun (1895).
Preface to *Kirby's Reports.*
Preface to *Root's Reports.*
*Lives of the Chief Justices of the U. S.*, by H. Flanders.
*Roger Sherman*, by Lewis Henry Boutelle (1896).
*Phineas Lyman*, in *Loyalists of the American Revolution*, by Lorenzo Sabine (1864).
*Roger Minott Sherman*, by William A. Beers (1882).
*Biography of the Signers of the Declaration of Independence*, by John Sanderson (1820–1827).
*Yale Men as Writers on Law and Government*, by S. E. Baldwin, *Yale Law Journal*, Vol. XI.
*Yale in its Relation to Law*, by Thomas Thacher, *Yale Law Journal*, Vol. XI.
*The Supreme Court of Connecticut*, by S. E. Baldwin, in *The Supreme Courts of the States and Provinces* (1897).
*Life of Jonathan Trumbull*, by J. W. Stuart (1859).

### To New Hampshire Text

*History of New Hampshire*, by Jeremy Belknap (1792).
*Judicial History of New Hampshire before the Revolution — Law Reporter*, Vol. XVIII, 301.
*Bench and Bar of New Hampshire*, by C. H. Bell (1894).
*Life of Jeremiah Mason*, by George S. Hillard (1873).
*Life of Jeremiah Smith*, by John H. Morison (1845).
*Review of Life of Jeremiah Smith — Law Reporter*, Vol. VIII.
*Life of Charles Marsh*, by James Barret (1871).
Address by David Cross, in *Southern New Hampshire, Bar Assoc. Proc.*, Vol. I.

*Samuel Livermore*, by Charles R. Corning, *Grafton & Coos Co. Bar Assoc. Proc.* (1888).
*Arthur Livermore*, by Ezra S. Stearns, *Grafton & Coos Co. Bar Assoc. Proc.* (1893).
*Life of William Plumer*, by William Plumer, Jr. (1856).
Parker, J., in 13 *New Hampshire Reports*, 536, 557, 558, 560.
*New Hampshire as a Royal Province — Col. Univ. Studies in History, Economics and Public Law*, Vol. XXIX (1908).
*Memoir of Wiseman Clagett*, in *N. H. Hist. Coll.*, Vol. III (1832).
*Sketch of Hon. S. Livermore*, in *N. H. Hist. Coll.*, Vol. V (1837).
*The Dartmouth College Cases*, by John M. Shirley (1879).

### To Rhode Island Text

*Gleanings from Judicial History of Rhode Island*, by Thomas Durgee, *R. I. Hist. Soc. Coll.*, No. 18.
*History of Rhode Island*, by Samuel G. Arnold (1859).
*Memoirs of the Rhode Island Bar*, by Wilkins Updike (1842).
Robert Lightfoot, in *Loyalists of American Revolution*, by Lorenzo Sabine.
*The Judicial System in Rhode Island*, by Amasa M. Eaton, *Yale Law Journal*, Vol. XIV.
*The Supreme Court of Rhode Island — Green Bag*, Vol. II.
*The Supreme Court of Rhode Island*, by W. P. Sheffield.
*State of Rhode Island and Providence Plantations at End of the Century*, edited by Edward Field (1902).

# CHAPTER VII

## THE LAW AND LAWYERS IN ENGLAND IN THE EIGHTEENTH CENTURY

THE Eighteenth Century in England was a period in which the law itself was being rapidly made, and great judges were making it.

In 1689, Sir John Holt was appointed Chief Justice of the Court of King's Bench; and in 1704 (a year before the birth of Lord Mansfield), he gave forth his epochal decision in *Coggs* v. *Barnard* (2 Lord Raym. 909). This was eight years before the first legally trained American lawyer took his place on the Massachusetts Bench, three years after the first lawyer sat on the Pennsylvania Bench, and five years before the first lawyers were formally licensed in New York.

In 1756, Sir William Murray, Lord Mansfield, became Lord Chief Justice of England. This was the year when John Adams began to study law, four years before Patrick Henry was admitted to the Bar, and while John Rutledge was studying in the Temple.

The *Leading Cases* (so called by the text-book writers of the Nineteenth Century) were, between 1700 and 1785, coming fresh from the printing press each year. Cases, now familiar to lawyers and law students as historical landmarks, were then of vivid interest to the practising lawyers of the American Colonies.

Thus in 1711 came the famous case on restraint of trade,

*Mitchell* v. *Reynolds* (1 P. Wms. 181); this was at the time when the whole Bar of Pennsylvania consisted of four lawyers. In 1719 came the case of *Cumber* v. *Wane* (1 Strange, 426), involving the doctrine of consideration. In 1722 came *Armory* v. *Delamire* (1 Strange, 504), the chimney sweep and the jeweller case; this was a year before the birth of William Livingston in New York, three years before the birth of George Wythe in Virginia and five years after the birth of the first great Pennsylvania lawyer, Benjamin Chew. In 1750 came *Penn.* v. *Lord Baltimore* (1 Ves. 444); this was two years after the foundation of the first Bar Association in New York. In 1773 came *Scott* v. *Shepard* (2 W. Bl. 892), the Squib case, as to actions of trespass; in 1789, *Pasley* v. *Freeman* (3 T. R. 51), establishing the law of deceit.

In these years, also, occurred the great State trials, like those of the Jacobites, Lord Kilmarnock, Lord Balmerino and Lord Lovat, for treason, before Lord Hardwicke in the House of Lords in 1746; the trial of John Wilkes for seditious libel, before Lord Camden in the Court of Common Pleas, in 1763; *Rex* v. *Woodfall*, in 1770, as to the publication of the Junius letters, the trial of Lord George Gordon in 1781; the famous legal battle on the law of libel, in the trial of the Dean of St. Asaphs, in 1783; the beginning of the impeachment trial of Warren Hastings, in 1787.

The status of Common Law in England, as it was when Lord Mansfield came on the bench, is thus described by Lord Campbell:

"This system was not at all badly adapted to the condition of England in the Norman and early Plantagenet reigns, when it sprang up, — land being then the only property worth considering, and the wants of society only requiring rules to be laid down by public authority for ascertaining the different rights and interests arising out of land, and determining how they should be enjoyed, alienated, and transmitted from one generation to another. In the reign of George II, England had grown into the greatest manufacturing and commercial country in the world, while her jurisprudence had by no means been expanded or developed in the same proportion. The legislature had literally done nothing to supply the insufficiency of feudal law to regulate the concerns of a trading population; and the Common Law judges had, generally speaking, been too unenlightened and too timorous to be of much service in improving our code by judicial decisions. Hence, when questions necessarily arose respecting the buying and selling of goods, — respecting the affreightment of ships, respecting marine insurances, — and respecting bills of exchange and promissory notes, no one knew how they were to be determined. Not a treatise had been published upon any of these subjects, and no cases respecting them were to be found in our books of reports, — which swarmed with decisions about lords and villeins, — about marshaling the champions upon the trial of a writ of right by battle, — and about the customs of manors, whereby an unchaste widow might save the forfeiture of her dower by riding on a black ram and in plain language confessing her offense. Lord Hardwicke had done much to improve and systematize Equity. . . but proceedings were still carried on in the courts of Common Law much in the same style as in the days of Sir Robert Tresilian and Sir William Gascoigne. Mercantile questions were so ignorantly treated when they came into Westminster Hall, that they were usually settled by private arbitration among the merchants themselves. If an action turning upon a mercantile question was brought in a court of law, the judge submitted it to the jury, who determined it according to their own notions of what was fair, and no general rule was laid down which could afterwards be referred to for the purpose of settling similar disputes." [1]

With the latter half of the Century, however, began the modern Common Law of business and personal relations, as distinguished from the old feudal Common Law, con-

[1] Campbell's *Lives of the Chief Justices*, Vol. III, p. 299.

fined as it was to questions of realty and pleading. The wide range of contract law began to be opened out. The doctrines of the laws of bills and notes, insurance and maritime commerce became fixed. The law of evidence, none of the present rules of which, except that excluding hearsay, were well established prior to 1688, was becoming well developed. On the other hand, the law of torts was hardly in existence before 1800; there were no negligence cases; the great contests of Erskine and Fox on the law of libel had not begun. The law of business corporations did not exist.

It was not until 1733, that Sir Peter King, Lord Chancellor, finally prevailed upon Parliament to provide that the English language should thenceforth be used in all law proceedings, although Lord Chief Justice Raymond and all other judges had opposed the change.

Coincident with the opinions on modern Common Law had been the advent of the first law reports of anything like modern accuracy — *Lord Raymond's Reports*, *Salkeld* and *Comyns* (of indifferent worth but covering Lord Holt's career); *Burrow's Reports* (1756–1772), *Cowper* (1774–1778) covering Lord Mansfield's decisions; and *Term Reports* and *Durnford and East* (1785–1800) covering the term of Chief Justice Kenyon.

Of Chancery reports, those of *Peere Williams* (1695–1735) were the chief source of study in the early part of the Century. *Atkyns*, *Vesey, Sr.* and *Ambler* included the decisions of the greatest of all the Chancellors, Philip Yorke (Lord Hardwicke) (1736–1756); and *Cox* and *Vesey, Jr.* reported the decisions of Charles Pratt (Earl Camden) and of Lord Thurlow.

Nevertheless, even as late as 1776, hardly more than one hundred and fifty volumes of reports were in existence in England; and probably not one-half of these had crossed the Atlantic; while hardly thirty were in familiar use in America.

Of law books of importance, the following were published during this Century: Bohun's *Institutio Legalis, or Introduction to the Study and Practise of the Laws of England,* appeared in 1708. Hale's *History and Analysis of the Common Law of England* was first published in 1713. In 1716 appeared Hawkins' *Pleas of the Crown,* and Foster's in 1762; Lilly's *Register* appeared in 1719; Wood's *Institutes* in 1722; and Francis' *Maxims in Equity* in 1728. Bacon's *Abridgment* was published in 1736; Jacob's *Law Dictionary* in 1729; Bohun's *Declarations* in 1733; Gilbert's *Ejectments* in 1734; Viner's *Digest* from 1742 to 1753; Comyns' *Digest* appeared between 1762 and 1767; Rutherforth's *Institutes of Natural Law* from 1754–1756; Fearne's *Contingent Remainders* in 1772; Reeves' *History of English Law to the Time of Elizabeth* in 1787. Of Blackstone's *Commentaries,* in 1765, mention will be made later. At the very end of the Century appeared Jones' *Bailments* in 1781; Wooddeson's *Elements of Jurisprudence* in 1783; Park's *Marine Insurance* in 1787; Powell's *Contracts* in 1790; Bayley's *Bills and Notes* in 1789; Chitty's *Bills and Notes,* and Tidd's *Practice* in 1799; and Fonblanque's *Equity* in 1797.[1]

This list, after all, is a scanty one; but in America few of these text-books were known, and fewer still were to be obtained.

The education of a law student in England during this Century was of the most meagre description. The old mootings and readings in the Inns of Courts had practically died out.

[1] Up to the publication of Joseph Story's books on *Equity,* Fonblanque's *Equity* was for one hundred years the best elementary book on equity in use in America. "It finally expired under the weight of its own notes," says J. C. Marvin in his *Legal Bibliography.*

Roger North wrote some years before his death (which occurred in 1733) a *Discourse on the Study of the Law,* in which he said:[1]

"Of all the professions in the world that pretend to book learning, none is so destitute of institution as that of the Common Law. Academick studies which take in that of the civil law, have tutors and professors to aid them, and the students are entertained in colleges under a discipline, in the midst of societies, that are, or should be, devoted to study; which encourages, as well as demonstrates, such methods in general as everyone may easily apply to his own particular use. But for the Common Law, however, there are societies which have the outward show or pretense of Collegiate Institution, yet in reality nothing of that sort is now to be found in them; and whereas in more ancient times there were exercises used in the Hall, they were more for probation than for institution; now even those are shrunk into mere form, and that preserved only for conformity to rules, that gentlemen by tale of appearances in exercises rather than by any sort of performances might be entitled to be called to the Bar."

And it has been recently said:

"There was really no legal education at the Inns of Court in the year 1800. In the days of Queen Elizabeth and James I regular courses of study were prescribed, attendance at moots and in hall was insisted on and discipline was vigorously maintained. But that had all fallen into misuse or lingered only in a few antiquated forms. There were still a few so called exercises. A student after dining in hall was provided with a printed form of questions. Armed with this he would tremblingly approach the dais and say to the first good-natured-looking bencher whose eyes he could catch, 'If I were seized in fee of Blackacre.' The bencher smiled and bowed. The student continuing the enunciation of the problem concluding boldly with

[1] This discourse was not published until 1824. See *Early History of Legal Studies in England,* by Joseph Walton, *Amer. Bar Ass. Proc.,* Vol. XXII (1899).

these words which were not on the paper, 'I maintain the widow shall have her dower.' The bencher bowed again and the student retired having 'kept his exercise.' Any student who had eaten the prescribed number of dinners and paid his fees was made a counsellor at law; the ceremony was conducted like the return of stolen goods 'without any questions being asked;' he need never have read a single page of any law book. Samuel Ireland in his historical account of the Inns of Court published in 1800 adverts to the 'ceremony of mootyng' as 'a custom long since in disuse except in New Inn for the benefit of students of the Middle Temple where about a year and a half since we are informed a mootyng took place to the no small diversion of the passers by.'

"The students had in fact to teach each other. There was in Tidd's office a society which met once a week exclusively for the discussion of legal questions. It was modelled upon the plan of the Court at Westminster, with a Chief Justice and counsel."[1]

Students of the Eighteenth Century gave their time largely to the pleasures of London. The *Spectator* of March 24, 1710, speaks of that

"numberless branch of peaceable lawyers — those young men who being placed in the Inns of Court in order to study the laws of their country frequent the playhouse more than Westminster Hall and are seen in all public assemblies except in a court of justice."

As stated above, no qualifications were required by the benchers of the Inns of those whom they were supposed to examine to be called as barristers, except the proof that they had kept twelve terms by eating the requisite number of dinners in the Inn.

Some few students, like Lord Thurlow about 1750, were placed in the office of a solicitor where they learned how actions were commenced and conducted, together with the practise of the courts.

[1] *A Century of Law Reform*, Chap. I, by W. B. Odgers (1901).

It was not, however, until the latter part of the Eighteenth Century that the regular practise began of studying in the office of some distinguished special pleader. This "pupilizing system" was introduced by the special pleaders, Thomas Warren and Mr. (later Mr. Justice) Buller; and in their offices and in those of George Wood, Tindal and Tidd were educated many of England's most famous judges; Erskine, Copley (Lord Lyndhurst), Cottenham, Campbell, Brougham, Parke (Lord Wenleysdale), Abbott (Lord Tenterden), and Denman.

The life of a student in such an office is well described by Lord Campbell in 1803:

"I got a letter from Mackintosh to Tidd the most eminent special pleader in England. With him I begin my studies in arte placitandi next week. He has six or a dozen pupils besides, dashing young fellows. . . . The terms of all special pleaders are the same, viz.: one hundred guineas for one year or two hundred guineas for three years. Tidd is by far the first man in this line. He has constantly from ten to fifteen pupils. . . . It is impossible for you to form any conception of the idleness of most of the nascent plea drawers. They drop into the office for half an hour on their way to Bond Street. For weeks and months they remain away altogether. When they are assembled the subjects discussed are not cases and precedents but the particulars of a new fashion in dress or the respective merits of the Young Chicken and Signora Crassini. . . . Nothing but the irresistible motives which spur me on could enable me to combat the disgust inspired by special pleading. It is founded upon reason but rude, rude is the superstructure. This however is now a necessary post in carrying on your professional advances. The four judges who preside in the Court of King's Bench all practised as special pleaders. . . . I continue to go regularly at eleven and stay till four. . . . In Tidd's office there was a society which met weekly for the discussion of juridical questions. This consisted of his pupils for the time being (among them Pepys) and any former pupils who chose to attend (among them Denman and Copley). . . . Special pleaders in general are not at the Bar. One or two who remain pleaders permanently are considered as something between attorneys and barristers but the common way is for a young man to plead a few years under the bar as they call it before being called. It is easier to get this kind of business than briefs in court and you thus gradually form and extend your connections. — Tidd is a man of very low origin. — He was clerk to an eminent man in this line and his master dying he set up for himself. — He published a *Practice of the Court of King's Bench* which has passed through several editions and gained him high celebrity. He makes between two thousand and three thousand pounds a year. . . . He takes very little pains with his pupils. He comes about one o'clock, saying 'How d'ye do' as he passes into his own room, remains there until four or five correcting what has been drawn, nods to any straggler who is still remaining and returns to Vauxhall for the day. His office however for a man really desirous and determined to improve himself is in my mind far the best in London. You see here such a quantity and such a variety of business that you may learn more in six months than by reading or hearing lectures for seven years."[1]

Of the course pursued by a student who could not enter a special pleader's office, Campbell's account of the student days of John Scott (Lord Eldon) gives the best idea:[2]

"The custom having been introduced for law students to become pupils of a special pleader or equity draughtsman, Mr. Scott would have been glad to have conformed to it if the state of his finances would have enabled him to pay the usual fee of a hundred guineas. . . . Mr. Duane, an eminent Catholic conveyancer agreed to let him have the run of his chambers for six months without a fee. (Conveyancing was chiefly in the hands of Roman Catholics, being prevented from being called to the Bar they prac-

[1] *Life of Lord Campbell*, Vol. I.

[2] Campbell's *Lives of the Lord Chancellors*, Vol. IX.

tised successfully in Chambers.) . . . To supply the deficiency arising from his not having been with a special pleader or equity draughtsman he copied all the MSS forms he could lay his hands upon.

"He went through a systematic course of reports and coming down to a Reporter of such low credit as Vernon he could tell the names of most of the cases reported with the volume and page where they could be found.

"We are not told that he ever dipped into the *Code*, the *Pandects*, or the *Institutes of Justinian;* or that he found any pleasure in *Puffendorf* or *Grotius* or that he ever formed the slightest acquaintance with *D'Agnesseau* or *Pothier*. Nor in any of his arguments at the Bar of judgments from the Bench does he as far as I am aware ever refer to the civil law or any foreign writer as authority or by way of illustration."

The course of reading advisable for a student either in his own or a special pleader's chambers was stated by Lord Chief Justice Reeves in 1787 as follows:

"Read Wood's *Institutes* cursorily and for explanation of the same, Jacob's *Dictionary*. Next strike out what lights you can from Bohun's *Institutio Legalis*, and Jacob's *Practising Attorney's Companion*, and the like, helping yourself by Indexes. Then read and consider Littleton's *Tenures* without notes and abridge it. Then venture on Coke's *Commentaries*. After reading it once, read it again, for it will require many readings. Abridge it. Commonplace it. Make it your own, applying to it the faculties of your mind. Then read Sergeant Hawkins to throw light on Lord Coke. Then read Wood again to throw light on Sergeant Hawkins. And then read the statutes at large to throw light on Mr. Wood."

In spite of this elaborate course for law students, the *Bibliotheca Legum Angliae* by John Worrall and Edward Brooke, published in 1788, mentions as the only books expressly intended for students; *Blackstone*, *Eunomus or Dialogues upon the Law and Constitution of England;* and the *Elements of Jurisprudence* by Dr. Wooddeson (Blackstone's successor as Vinerian Professor at Oxford). To these may be added Francis S. Sullivan's *Lectures on the Constitution and Laws of England*, published in 1776; and a little book, much used, Thomas Branch's *Principia Legis et Equitatis*.

Undoubtedly the real education gained by a law student in the Eighteenth Century was through attendance at the various courts.

Thus, it is said that Lord Mansfield's chief resource, in 1730 when studying at Lincoln's Inn, was in listening to the judgments of Lord Chief Justice Raymond in King's Bench. To such an extent was he influenced by this method of gaining a liberal knowledge of the law that later, when he became a judge himself, he was in the habit, in giving his judgments, of explaining the intricacies of the cases before him and the reasons of his judgments "for the sake of the students."[1] He even caused a box in the Court of King's Bench to be set apart for students to which students and barristers "flock by scores."

So too, it was said of John Scott (Lord Eldon), that "he diligently attended the courts in Westminster Hall (1775) with his note book in his hand. Lord Bathurst presiding in the Court of Chancery, from whom little was to be learned, he took his place in the students' box in the Court of King's Bench, where Lord Mansfield shone in the zenith of his fame."

Dr. Johnson said to Boswell: "You must take care to attend constantly in Westminster Hall, both to mind your business, as it is almost all learnt there (for nobody reads now), and to show that you want to have business."

[1] Campbell's *Lives of the Lord Chief Justices; Life of Lord Campbell.*

# CHAPTER VIII

## A COLONIAL LAWYER'S EDUCATION

ACQUISITION of the law is difficult without ready means of access to the books of the law and these were sadly lacking in the American Provinces.

Of the reports published in England by the time of the American Revolution (not over one hundred and fifty in number) hardly more than thirty were in familiar use on this side of the Atlantic; and the number of text-books accessible was even smaller. Practically all the law books used in the Colonies were imported from England.

Although printing had begun in the Colonies as early as 1638–1639, when Stephen Daye printed, at Cambridge, *The Oath of a Freeman*, the vast proportion of all books printed, from that date down to the American Revolution, was of a religious or historical nature. A careful examination of elaborate *American Bibliographies* discloses only thirty-three law books printed in America prior to 1776, including in this number at least eight repeated editions of the same book.[1]

Most of these books were manuals for use of justices of the peace, sheriffs and other petty officers, and treatises on the general rights of Englishmen, and especially of juries.

[1] See the monumental work of Charles Evans, *American Bibliography*, Volumes I, II, III (1893), and Isaiah Thomas, *History of Printing in America*, published in Vol. VI of *American Antiquarian Society Proceedings* (1874).

The first seven law books printed fairly illustrate the whole list.

1680 — *Reasons for Indictment of the Duke of York, Presented to the Grand Jury of Middlesex Saturday June* 26, 1680 (Boston).

1693 — *The Englishman's Right, A Dialogue between a Barrister at Law and a Juryman, plainly setting forth the antiquity, the excellent designed use and office and just privileges of juries by the law of England*, by Sir John Hawles (Boston).

1705 — *Lex Mercatoria Or the Just Rules of Commerce Declared. And Offences against the Rules of Justice in the Dealings of men with one another selected*, by Cotton Mather (Boston).

1710 — *The Constable's Pocket Book: Or a dialogue between an old Constable and a new, being a guide in their keeping the peace*, by Nicholas Boone (Boston).

1716 — *Lex Parliamentaria or a Treatise on the Law and Custom of the Parliaments of England*, by George Petyt (London, printed and reprinted in N. Y. and sold by William and Andrew Bradford in N. Y. and Phila.).

1720 — *The Security of Englishmen's Lives or the Trust, Power, and Duty of the Grand Jurys of England*, by John Somers.

1721 — *English liberties or the Freeborn Subjects' Inheritance, containing Magna Charta, Charta de Foresta, the Statute De Tallagio non Concedendo, the Habeas Corpus Act and several other statutes with comments on each of them.*

*Likewise the Proceedings in Appeals of Murder; of Ship Money; of Tonnage and Poundage; of Parliaments and the qualification and choice of members; of the three estates and of the settlement of the Crown by Parliament. Together with a short history of the succession not by any hereditary right; Also a declaration of the liberties of the subject; and of the oath of allegiance and supremacy. The Petition of Right with a short but impartial relation of the difference between King Charles I and the Long Parliament concerning the Prerogative of the King, the Liberties of the Subject and the rise of the Civil Wars. Of trials by Jury and of the qualifications of Jurors; their punishment for misbehaviour and of challenges to them. Lastly of Justices of the Peace, Coroners, Constables, Churchwardens,*

*Overseers of the Poor, Surveyors of the Highway, etc., with many law cases throughout the whole and Compiled first* by Henry Care and continued with large additions by W. N. of the Middle Temple Esq. The fifth edition.

The title of an early law book printed in Virginia, in 1736, also shows the kind of legal work chiefly in use and published in the Colonies.

*The Office and Authority of a Justice of the Peace.* And also *the Duty of Sheriffs, Constables, Coroners, Church Wardens, Surveiors of Highways, Constables & Officers of Militia. Together with Precedents of Warrants, Judgments, Executions and other legal Process, issuable by Magistrates within their respective Jurisdictions in Cases Civil or Criminal, and the Method of Judicial Proceedings before Justices of Peace in Matters within their Cognisance out of Sessions, Collected from the Common and Statute laws of England and Acts of Assembly now in force; and adapted to the Constitution and Practice of Virginia.* By George Webb, Gent. one of His Majesty's Justices of Peace of the County of New Kent, Williamsburg. Printed by William Parks.

There were also printed about thirty-five or forty books or pamphlets giving reports of famous cases, of which all but five or six were of criminal trials, murder, burglary and piracy. The first of these was the trial of Thomas Southerland for murder in West Jersey, printed in 1692; the next, the trial of Col. Nicholas Bayard in New York for high treason, published in 1702. A report of a case in Chancery in New York was printed in 1727. In 1736, John Peter Zenger printed a report of his famous trial for libel in New York in 1735. Two years later, another report of this trial was printed in Philadelphia, with comments by English barristers of the Barbadoes.

In 1753, a report of the case of *William Fletcher* v. *William Vassall* for defamation, tried in the Massachusetts Superior Court and pending on appeal to the King in

Council, was printed. A report of the trial of Admiral Byng by court martial in England was printed in 1757. A full account was printed in 1763 of the famous proceedings against John Wilkes in England, to which was appended *An Abstract of that Precious Jewel of an Englishman, the Habeas Corpus Act, also the North Briton No. 45 being the paper for which Mr. Wilkes was sent to the Tower — Addressed to All Lovers of Liberty.*

In 1770, a full report of the trial of the British soldiers in Boston for murder was published.

In 1774, was printed *Arguments against Slavery in the case of James Somerset, a negro, lately determined in the Court of King's Bench; wherein is attempted to demonstrate the unlawfulness of Domestic Slavery in England*, by Francis Hargrave.

No reprint was made in America, prior to 1776, of Coke, or of any standard English law writer, except Blackstone. There was no reprint of any English law reports.

It is not surprising therefore that scant references are found to English cases, or law reports in the Colonial court records; or that as a rule, the early cases contained citations of only the most elementary books, writers and principles.[1]

[1] Thus Wood's *Institutes* and Hale's *Analysis of the Law* seem to have been favorite citations of Chief Justice Sewall in the early part of the Eighteenth Century in Massachusetts. As early as 1730, in a printed argument in the Superior Court in Massachusetts, citations are found of 1 *Coke*, 2 *Coke Rep.*, 1 *Modern*, *Hobart* and *Chancery Cases*.

In *Harris and McHenry's Reports*, Vol. I, containing cases as early as 1658, the first English cases cited are in a brief of D. Dulany in *Gresham* v. *Gassoway* in 1718, the following authorities being cited: *Cro. Eliz.*, *Mod.*, *Sid.*, *Raym.*, *Keb.*, *Rolle Ab.*, *Co. Litt.*, *Poph.*, *Hutton*, *Winch*, *Bulst.*, *Sty.*, *Sal.*, *Saund.*, *Vent.*, *Vaugh.*

Some of the lawyers who came over from England brought with them their acquired knowledge of English cases. Thus in South Carolina in a trial of pirates in 1718 the Chief Justice Trott (an English barrister) quotes

The early Colonial lawyers were hampered not only by this scant supply of law books and reports, but their difficulties in studying and determining the statutory law of the Colonies were even more serious. While Massachusetts and Connecticut printed their statutes reasonably early, the other Colonies were late in doing so; thus the first collection of Colonial Laws of New York was published in 1710; the Acts and Laws of Rhode Island were first printed in 1730; those of New Jersey in 1732; those of Virginia in 1733; South Carolina in 1736; the first collection of Charters and other Public Acts relating to Pennsylvania in 1740, and all its laws in 1742; Bacon's *Compilation of Laws*, in Maryland in 1765.

So few copies were printed however that it was unusual for any lawyer to possess a full set of the local laws of his Colony.

"Even partial editions of Colonial laws (at least in Virginia) were extremely difficult to be obtained. Few gentlemen, even of the profession in this country, have ever been able to boast of possessing a complete collection of its laws," said St. George Tucker in 1803 in the preface to his edition of *Blackstone*.

The few law books and reports that existed in America were to be found almost entirely in the libraries of the richer lawyers,[1] and sometimes among the books of the local clergymen. "Fifty or one hundred volumes were considered a very considerable collection of books for a lawyer's library."[2] The following examples give some idea of the prevalent conditions. Even the largest library

*Spelman*, *Godolphin*, Coke's *First Institute*, Selden's *Notes on Fortescue*, *Laws of Oleron*, *Digests and Pandects of Justinian*.

[1] George Bliss in his address to the Bar of Hampshire County, Sept. 26, 1826, says John Worthington, Joseph Hawley and Jonathan Bliss had the only law libraries in all Western Massachusetts.

[2] *Biographical Sketches of Eminent Lawyers*, by S. L. Knapp (1821).

in the Colonies in the middle of the Eighteenth Century, that of William Byrd the younger, in Virginia, contained only 350 volumes of law and statutes out of a total of 3625.[1]

Judge Edmund Trowbridge of Massachusetts possessed what Theophilus Parsons called "not only the best but probably the only thoroughly good one (law library) then in New England, and even in America." It contained all the valuable books on English law then in existence.[2]

President Stiles of Yale writes, in 1790, of Governor Griswold, who was Chief Justice in 1769, that:

> "He bought him the first considerable law library in Connecticut, took Att. oath, and began practice in 1743 — a great reader of law. Has a fine library of well chosen books — about 550 volumes — now left in his study, besides a part of his library given to his son in Norwich — about two hundred Law Books, the rest history and divinity."[3]

The Philogrammatican Society of Connecticut, of which Jonathan Trumbull was Secretary, purchased for its library in 1735 ninety-four works of which the following were the only law books — Coke's *Institutes*, Lilly's *Abridgment*, *Coke's Reports*, Bohun's *Declarations and Pleadings*, Jacob's *Introduction to Common, Civil and Canon Law*.[4]

In the famous library of Rev. Thomas Prince of Boston, who died in 1758, out of about 1500 volumes, there were but five on the Common Law — *Britton* (1640), *English*

[1] *Old Virginia*, by John Fiske.

[2] For interesting account of Judge Trowbridge and his libraries see *Memoirs of Theophilus Parsons*, by T. Parsons, Jr.

[3] See MSS. *Itinerary of a Journey from New London to New Haven in 1790*.

[4] *Journal of American History*, Vol. I, No. 1. It is interesting to note that there were thirteen books on medicine, a half dozen or so on history, Milton's *Paradise Lost*, a few volumes of the *Spectator*, and all the rest of the library consisted of religious works.

*Liberties with Magna Charta, etc.* (1721), Cowell's *Institutes of English Law* (1664), *The Exact Constable, Church Warden, etc.* (1682), Spelman's *Archaeologus* (1626). There was also a copy of the *General Laws and Liberties* (1672), Bacon's *Novum Organum*, Grotius on *War and Peace* (1680), and five books on civil and canon law.[1]

The law library of Meschech Weare, a prominent lawyer and judge in New Hampshire, as inventoried in 1786, consisted of: Wood's *Institute, Raymond's Reports*, Jacob's *Law Dictionary*, Foster's *Crown Law, Privilege of Parliament, W. Salkeld's Reports, New Hampshire Law Books*, Dalton's *Country Justice, Magna Charta, Hugo Grotius*, and the *Journals of Congress*.[2]

John Adams wrote:

"I know not whether a set of the Statutes at large or of the State Trials was in the country. I was desirous of seeking the law as well as I could in its fountain, and I obtained as much knowledge as I could of *Bracton, Britton, Fleta* and *Glanville;* but I suffered very much for want of books which determined me to furnish myself at any sacrifice with a proper library, and accordingly, by degrees, I procured the best library of law in the State."[3]

Even the scanty supply of libraries which the Colonies possessed was depleted at the time of the Revolution by the flight of Tory lawyers, most of whom were wealthy and carried their books away with them.[4]

[1] See *Catalogue of Library of Rev. Thomas Prince* (1846).

[2] See *Mass. Hist. Soc. Proc.*, Vol. LXIII (1909).

[3] *John Adams' Works*, Vol. II, p. 50.

[4] Peter S. DuPonceau, who studied in Philadelphia in 1784 under William Lewis, writes in 1837 (*Penn. Hist. Soc. Proc.*, Vol. IV):

"I had gone through Blackstone's *Commentaries* and Wood's *Institutes* and was advised to enter upon the study of *Coke upon Littleton.* I wanted to have a copy of the work all to myself to read it at my ease; but it was not easy to be procured. After many fruitless applications I bethought myself of putting an advertisement in the papers in which I offered to give

Some of these law libraries of refugees were confiscated however, or were purchased for the judges and lawyers by legislative resolves. Thus a resolve of the Massachusetts Legislature, in 1779, authorized the sale to Hon. James Sullivan of the *Modern Entries*, *Pleas of the Crown*, *Foster*, and *Hawkins* and the *Reports* of *Strange*, *Keyling* and *Burrow* which had belonged to Benjamin Gridley who had become a royalist.[1]

The college libraries of the time contained practically no law books. In the first catalogue of the Harvard College Library (1723) works of Lord Bacon, Selden, Grotius and seven volumes of Common Law — Spelman's *Glossary*, Pulton's *Statutes*, Keble's *Statutes*, Coke's *First and Second Institutes* and two volumes of the *Year Books* were the only books on legal subjects. After the burning of the library in 1764, the following seven volumes, presented by Thomas Hollis, constituted for many years the sole law library of the College:[2] Bacon's *Historical Discourse* (1647); Burns' *Ecclesiastical Law* (1763); Carpenter D. P. *Glossarium etc.* (1766); Codex, *Theodosianus;* Glanvill R., *Tractatus de Legibus etc.* (1604); Horne's *Mirror* (1642); Prynne's *Sovereigne Power of Parliaments* (1643).

There were no public libraries in which books of law could be found.

And as there were in the Colonies no collegiate law lectures before 1780, and no law schools before 1784, the young man who aspired to be a lawyer had two courses open to him.

The first was, to pick up such scraps of knowledge of

a set of Valin's *Commentary on the French Marine Ordinances* in exchange. To my great astonishment and delight I received a note from Mr. Rawle, then unknown to me, accepting the offer."

[1] See *Life and Writings of James Sullivan*, by T. G. Amory.

[2] See Preface to the first official *Catalogue of Library of the Harvard Law School*, by Charles Sumner (1834); also edition of 1846.

practise, as he could, by serving as a copyist or assistant in the clerk's office of some inferior or higher court, and by reading such books, *Coke* chiefly, as he could borrow.

This was the exiguous training which many eminent lawyers received who could not afford the time or the money to adopt the second course. They are well described by Hugh Blair Grigsby in his picture of the venerable James Nimmo of the Norfolk (Virginia) Bar in 1802:

"He was of that substantial class of lawyers who, having received an elementary grounding in Latin and mathematics in the schools of the time, entered the clerk's office and served a term of duty within its precincts. He was thus well versed in the ordinary forms of the law and with the decision of the Courts in leading cases. With such men as a class there was no great intimacy with the law as a science. As long as the case lay in the old routine, this class of lawyers would get along very well; but novelties were unpleasant to them they hated the subtleties of special pleading, and they turned pale at a demurrer."[1]

Some few young men of pre-eminent native ability achieved distinction without training even in a clerk's office. Thus Patrick Henry was admitted to the Bar in September, 1760, at the age of twenty-four, after six weeks' solitary study of *Coke upon Littleton* and the Virginia statutes, although one of the three examiners, George Wythe, refused to sign his license, leaving it to Peyton and John Randolph to admit him. The latter said they "perceived him to be a young man of genius, very ignorant of law but did not doubt he would soon qualify himself." Wirt states, however, in his life of Henry,[2] that "in spite of his talents he never conquered his aversion to systematic study of

[1] *Discourse on Life and Character of Hon. Littleton Waller Tazewell*, by Hugh Blair Grigsby (1860).

[2] *Sketches of the Life and Character of Patrick Henry*, by William Wirt (1818).

the law and could rarely see the bearing of reported cases," this failing standing often in the way of success.

The second course open to a law student was the familiar one of entering the office of some leading member of the Bar, preferably one of the few who had good law libraries, and there absorbing, by study, observation, and occasionally by direct teaching from his senior, the principles of the law.

For the privilege of entering such an office a student was obliged to pay a sum of money, usually $100 to $200, sometimes as much as $500, if admission was desired to the office of some pre-eminent celebrity. An interesting illustration of the value set on these privileges is found in a promissory note (still extant) as follows:

"Phila. March 22, 1782. I promise to pay James Wilson Esq. or order on demand one hundred guineas, his fee for receiving my nephew Bushrod Washington as a student of law in his office. G. Washington."[1]

In the office, the student had access to all his senior's law books for study. He pored over the MSS. volumes of forms, and the abstracts, commonplace books, and MSS. notes of cases, which each lawyer of those days made for himself.[2] He was expected to copy out pleadings and other documents for his senior, and to draft briefs. In return the lawyer gave to his student such advice, information, or instruction as his time or his whim permitted.

As a rule, the lawyer was too busy a man to pay much attention to his students; and the chief advantage gained by them was in personal association with the able lawyers against whom he tried his cases, and in the general influence which great characters have on younger men who come in contact with them.

[1] See *Letters and Times of the Tylers*, by Lyon G. Tyler.

[2] For interesting description of a student's life, see *Life and Writings of James Sullivan*, by T. G. Amory.

Thus even so learned a lawyer as James Wilson was said to have been of slight advantage to his students, as an instructor:

"Mr. Wilson devoted little of his time to his students in his office (among whom were Judge Washington and Samuel Sitgreaves) and rarely entered it except for the purpose of consulting books. Hence his intercourse with them was rare, distant, and reserved. As an instructor he was almost useless to those who were under his direction. He would never engage with them in professional discussions; to a direct question he gave the shortest possible answer and a general request for information was always evaded."[1]

An interesting sidelight on this lack of sympathy in the relations between lawyer and student is found in an essay written by William Livingston,[2] while a student, in 1745, in the office of the great Scotch lawyer James Alexander, then the leading lawyer of New York, — an invective against the mode of studying law as then practised, and against the drudgery to which clerks were subjected.

The following extracts show the general feeling of the writer:

"There is perhaps no set of men that bear so ill a character in the estimation of the vulgar as the Gentlemen of the Long Robe: whether the disadvantageous idea they commonly entertain of their integrity, be founded upon solid reason, is not my design to enquire into; but if they deserve the imputation of injustice and dishonesty, it is in no instance more visible and notorious, than in their conduct towards their apprentices. That a young fellow should be bound to an attorney for 4, 6, or 7 years, to serve him part of the time for the consideration

[1] *Biography of the Signers*, by John Sanderson, (1820–1827).

[2] *Life of William Livingston*, by Theodore Sedgwick, Jr. (1833).

This essay appeared in print in Parker's *New York Weekly Post Boy* for August 19, 1745, signed "Tyro Philolegis." It is here reprinted from that newspaper.

that his master shall instruct in the mystery of the law the remainder of the term; and that notwithstanding this solemn compact (which is binding on either side, is reciprocally obligatory) the attorney shall either employ him in writing during the whole term of his apprenticeship or, if he allows him a small portion of the time for reading, shall leave him to pore on a book without any instruction to smooth and facilitate his progress in his study, or the least examination of what proficiency he makes in that perplexed science; is an outrage upon common honesty, a conduct scandalous, horrid, base, and infamous to the last degree!

"These gentlemen must either have no manner of concern for their clerk's future welfare and prosperity, or must imagine, that he will attain to a competent knowledge in the Law, by gazing on a number of books, which he has neither time nor opportunity to read; or that he is to be metamorphos'd into an attorney by virtue of Hocus Pocus. Is it the father's intention, when he puts his son to an attorney, and gives a large sum into the bargain, that he shall only learn to write a good hand? But whoever attentively considers how these apprentices are used, and forms a judgment from the treatment they meet with, would certainly imagine, that the youth was sent to the lawyer on purpose to write for him, because his father could find him no employment; and if his master, out of the exuberance of his humility, graciously condescends to instruct him, it 's only by the bye, in order to enable him to be a more profitable servant. . . . I averr, that 'tis a monstrous absurdity to suppose, that the law is to be learnt by a perpetual copying of precedents. These gentlemen may indeed plead custom, and in pleading that they admit my assertions. . . . It does not want any great measure of knowledge to see the ridicule of this monstrous practice; but what makes it the more astonishing, is its being practised by men of learning and unquestioned honesty. . . . It is therefore an affront to common sense to multiply arguments for the proof of a thing which none but a lawyer and a madman will pretend to deny. And if no logick can convince them of the injustice of such a practice I believe no reasonable person would blame an apprentice for discharging at them the argumentum basilinum, or what the English call Club-law, with full force and virtue. This is an argument of mighty energy, and was much in vogue in the Protector's time, when a man unable to convince his antagonist by syllogysm, knocked him down. And in no case can this coercive way of reasoning more justly be made use of, than in the case under consideration, as nothing whatsoever can be a greater provocation, or demand a more forcible kind of logick."

As an offset to the above, an interesting view of the more helpful relations between a lawyer and his student is found in John Quincy Adams' Diary, in his description of his senior, Theophilus Parsons:[1]

"Nov. 27, 1787. It is of great advantage to us to have Mr. Parsons in the office. He is in himself a law library, and a proficient in every useful branch of service; but his chief excellency is, that no student can be more fond of proposing questions than he is of solving them. He is never at a loss, and always gives a full and ample account, not only of the subject proposed, but of all matters which have any intimate connection with it. I am persuaded that the advantage of having such an instructor is very great, and I hope I shall not misimprove it as some of his pupils have done."

The best idea of the scanty sources of information, open to a student of those days, can be gained by a citation of the studies of a few of the prominent men of the time.

Thus Col. James Otis, father of the famous James Otis Jr., who studied law, prior to 1750, at Barnstable, Massachusetts, found as the only books obtainable, Coke's *Institutes*, Brownlow's *Entries*, and Plowden's *Commentaries* and *Reports*.[2]

Oliver Ellsworth, of Connecticut (later Chief Justice

[1] See *Mass. Hist. Soc. Proc.*, 2d Series, Vol. XVI (1902).

[2] *Address before the Bristol County Bar*, by Abraham Holmes.

of the United States Supreme Court), had as his only text-books, Bacon's *Abridgment* and Jacob's *Law Dictionary*.[1]

The following is the course of study recommended by William Smith, one of the early leaders of the Bar of New York, to a young friend of John Jay, about 1760:

"But now I bring our student home to the studies of his profession of the law and I would advise him to read these books in the following order:

"First, for the knowledge of the law in general,

"1. The treatise of law in Wood's *Institutes of the Civil Law*, or in *Domat*, which are both the same.

"2. *Puffendorf de officio Hominis et Civis*, or an English translation of it called *The Whole Duty of Man according to the Law of Nature, or the abridgment of Puffendorf* in two volumes by Spavin.

"And before entering further into the Law of Nature and Nations and the Civil Law, the writer advises a general study of the elements of the Common Law in the following order:

"Hale's *History of the Common Law.*

"Fortescue's *Practice of the Laws of England.*

"Sir Thomas Smith's *De Republica Anglorum.*

"First Book of *Doctor and Student, De Fundamentum Legum Angliae.*

"Second part of Bacon's *Elements.*

"Wood's *Institutes of the Common Law.*"

After recommending a further and more extensive reading of the Law of Nature and Nations and Civil Law, he remarks:

"Then to fill up and enlarge your ideas, you may read Bacon's *Abridgment of the Law* which it is presumed will all be soon published.

"In reading the *Abridgment*, which is contrived so as to be read pleasantly, I would advise that you constantly refer from the *Abridgment* to Wood, and from Wood to

[1] *Lives and Times of the Chief Justices*, by Henry Flanders (1881).

the *Abridgment* (1) because I would have these books the basis or foundation of all your studies."[1]

John Adams, at the age of twenty-five, records in his Diary a course of study which probably exceeds that of any other law student of the time, especially noticeable being his study of the Civil Law, of which he writes as early as 1758:

"Few of my contemporary beginners in the study of the law have the resolution to aim at much knowledge in the civil law. Let me therefore distinguish myself from them by the study of the civil law in its native languages. I shall gain the consideration and perhaps the favor of Mr. Gridley and Mr. Pratt by this means."

And in November, 1760, he records:

"I have read a multitude of law books — mastered but few — *Wood*, *Coke*, two volumes of Lillies' *Abridgement*, two volumes *Salkeld's Reports*, *Swinburne*, Hawkin's *Pleas of the Crown*, *Fortescue*, *Fitzgibbon*. Ten volumes in folio I read at Worcester quite through, besides octavos and lesser volumes, and many others, of all sizes, that I consulted occasionally without reading in course, as dictionaries, reporters, entries and abridgments. During the last two years Justinian's *Institutes* I have read through in Latin, with Vinnius' *Perpetual Notes*. Van Muyden's *Tractatio Institutionum Justiniani* I read through and translated mostly into English from the same language. Wood's *Institutes of the Civil Law* I read through. These on Civil Law. On the law of England I read Cowell's *Institute of the Laws of England*, and *Imitations of Justinian*, *Doctor and Student*, Finch's *Discourse of Law*, Hale's *History* and some reporters, *Cases in Chancery*, *Andrews*, etc., besides occasional searches for business; also a *General Treatise of Naval Trade and Commerce*, as founded on law and statutes. All this series of reading

[1] *Lives of the Chief Justices*, by George Van Santvord (1882). It will be noticed how closely this follows the course for study given in England by Chief Justice Reeves.

has left but faint impressions and a very imperfect system of law in my head. I must form a serious resolution of beginning and pursueing quite through the plans of my Lords Hale and Reeves. Wood's *Institutes of Common Law* I never read but once, and my Lord Coke's *Commentary on Littleton* I never read but once. These two authors I must get and read over and over again. And I will get them and break through, as Mr. Gridley expresses it, all obstructions.

"Besides, I am but a novice in natural law and civil law. There are multitudes of excellent authors on natural law that I have never read; and indeed I never read any part of the best authors *Puffendorf* and *Grotius*. In the civil law there are *Hoppius* and *Vinnius*, commentators on *Justinian*, *Domat*, etc., besides institutes of canon and feudal law that I have read. Much may be done in two years I have found already; and let it be my care that at the end of the next two years, I be better able to show that no time has been lost, than I ever have been yet."

Resources, however, such as Adams could have access to, in Boston, were not available for the country practitioner. And the office of the average country lawyer, even towards the end of the Eighteenth Century, contained little more than *Coke on Littleton*, Comyn's *Digest*, Bacon's *Abridgement*, Hale's or Hawkins' *Pleas of the Crown*, *Blackstone*, Lilly's *Entries*, *Saunders Reports* and some brief book on pleading and on practise.[1]

"Probably a copy of *Blackstone* was not to be found in Hampshire County before the year 1770. They had *Hale* and *Gilbert*, and, a short time before the Revolution, Bacon's *Abridgment*, but there was not in the county a copy of Comyn's *Abridgment*. They had *Coke* and *Littleton* as well as *Rastell*, *Fitzherbert*, *Bracton*, *Britton* and *Fleta*."[2]

[1] *Life of Charles Marsh*, by James Barret (1871).

[2] *Address of George Bliss to Hampshire County Bar*, September 26, 1826.

So said George Bliss in his address to the Hampshire Bar in 1826.

Partly because of the lack of books, partly because of the undeveloped state of the law of business and personal relations, a student spent most of his time on the subjects of real property and pleadings as found in the rigorous pages of *Coke on Littleton*, and often in the still more refractory volumes of *Bracton*, *Britton*, *Fleta* and *Glanville*.

John Adams says that when, as an applicant for admission to the Bar, he sought Gridley's aid:

"I have a few pieces of advice to give you, Mr. Adams, said Gridley. One is, to pursue the study of the law, rather than the gain of it; pursue the gain of it enough to keep out of it, enough to keep out of the briers, but give your main attention to the study of it. The next is, not to marry early; for an early marriage will obstruct your improvement; and, in the next place, it will involve you in expense. Another thing is, not to keep much company, for the application of a man who aims to be a lawyer must be incessant; his attention to his books must be constant, which is inconsistent with keeping much company. In the study of the law, the Common Law, be sure, deserves your first and last attention; and he has conquered all the difficulties of this law, who is master of the *Institutes*. You must conquer the *Institutes*. The road of science is much easier now than it was when I set out; I began with *Coke-Littleton* and broke through."[1]

It was on *Coke on Littleton* that Chief Justice Jay was brought up.[2] Littleton's *Tenures* were the main study of James Iredell, in 1770.[3]

[1] Adams' *Life and Letters*, Vol. II.

[2] *Lives of the Chief Justices*, by Henry Flanders.

[3] McRee, in his *Life of James Iredell*, gives the following account of his study; and the extracts from his diary show the difficulty with which the *Tenures* retained his attention.

"He was a diligent student, he copied Mr. Johnston's arguments and pleas in interesting cases. He read carefully and attentively the text books,

*Coke* and *Bracton* were the chief studies of Thomas Jefferson (1762–1767).

"When I was a student of the law after getting through *Coke Lyttleton* whose matter cannot be abridged, I was in the habit of abridging and commonplacing what I read meriting it, and of course sometimes making my own reflections on the subject.

"*Coke Lyttleton* was the universal elementary book of law students and a sounder Whig never wrote nor profounder learning in the orthodox doctrines of British liberties. Our lawyers were then all Whigs. But when his black letter text and uncouth but cunning learning got out of fashion, and the honeyed Mansfieldism of *Blackstone* became the student's horn-book, from that moment, that profession (the nursery of our Congress) began to slide into Toryism and nearly all the young brood of lawyers are now of that line. They suppose themselves indeed to be Whigs because they no longer know what whiggism or republicanism means."[1]

The older American lawyers agreed with Lord Eldon's views, who, in advising a young friend in 1800 to read *Coke* again and again, wrote:

"If it be toil and labour to you, and it will be so, think as I do when I am climbing up to Swyer or to Westhill,

referring to the authorities quoted, and collating and digesting kindred passages from all the writers within reach; he attended the courts, returned to his chamber and wrote out the arguments of his own applicable to the cases." . . . In his diary August 23, 1770, he writes: "I have not done as much as I ought to have done, read a little in Littleton's *Tenures* and stopt in the middle of his chapter on Rents, whereas, if I had gone through it, it would have been better and more agreeable than losing three or four games of billiards."

"August 24. — This morning pretty well employed; read a good deal in Littleton's *Tenures*, and afterwards a little in the *Edinburgh Magazine* for 1758.

"August 29. — Read a little in Littleton's *Tenures*, not much though, being interrupted."

[1] *Thomas Jefferson as a Lawyer — Green Bag*, Vol. XV.

that the world will be before you when the toil is over; for so the law world will be, if you make yourself complete master of that book. At present, lawyers are made good, cheap, by learning law from *Blackstone* and less elegant compilers. Depend upon it, men so bred will never be lawyers (though they may be barristers), whatever they call themselves. I read *Coke on Littleton* through, when I was the other day out of the office, and when I was a student I abridged it."[1]

Later Eighteenth Century lawyers, however, though still immersed in *Coke* by their instructors, did not share this profound admiration. Thus Mr. Justice Story wrote of his entry upon the study of law in 1798 as follows:

"I confess my heart sunk within me. . . . Then the student, after reading that most elegant of all commentaries, Mr. Justice Blackstone's work, was hurried at once into the intricate, crabbed, and obsolete learning of *Coke on Littleton*. . . . You may judge how I was surprised and startled on opening works where nothing was presented but dry and technical principles, the dark and mysterious elements of the feudal system, the subtle refinements

[1] *Life of Lord Eldon*, by Horace Twiss (1844).

Lord Campbell also writes in 1849 in his diary:

"I have taken to my old favorite *Co. Litt.* It certainly is very pleasant reading. I am more than ever struck by its unmethodical and rambling character, but one must admire the author's stupendous familiarity with all parts of the law of England; he is uniformly perspicuous, he gives amusing glimpses of history and manners and his etymologies and other quaint absurdities are as good for a laugh as *Joe Miller* or *Punch*. . . . No man can thoroughly understand the law as it is without knowing the changes it has undergone, and no man can be acquainted with its history without being familiar with the writings of Lord Coke. Nor is he by any means so dry and forbidding as is generally supposed. He is certainly unmethodical, but he is singularly perspicuous, he fixes the attention, his quaintness is often amusing and he excites our admiration by the inexhaustible stores of erudition which without any effort he seems spontaneously to pour forth. Thus were our genuine lawyers trained. Lord Eldon read *Coke upon Littleton*, once, twice and thrice and made an abstract of the whole work as a useful exercise."

and intricacies of the middle ages of the Common Law, and the repulsive and almost unintelligible forms of processes and pleadings. . . . Soon after Mr. Sewall's departure to Washington I took it (*Coke*) up, and after trying it day after day with very little success I set myself down and wept bitterly. . . . I went on and on and began at last to see daylight, ay, and to feel that I could comprehend and reason upon the text and the comments. When I had completed the reading of this most formidable work, I felt that I breathed a purer air and that I had acquired a new power. . . . I pressed on to the severe study of special pleadings and by repeated perusals of *Saunders Reports* acquired such a decided relish for this branch of my profession that it became for several years afterwards my favorite pursuit. . . . I also read through that deep and admirable work . . . *Fearne on Contingent Remainders and Executory Devises* and I made a MSS. abstract of all its principles."[1]

And Daniel Webster[2] who studied first in 1801 in the office of Thomas W. Thompson at Salisbury, New Hampshire, said:

"I was put to study in the old way, that is, the hardest books first, and lost much time. I read *Coke-Littleton* through without understanding a quarter part of it. . . .

"A boy of twenty, with no previous knowledge of such subjects, cannot understand *Coke*. It is folly to set him upon such an author. There are propositions in *Coke* so abstract, and distinctions so nice, and doctrines embracing so many distinctions and qualifications, that it required an effort not only of a mature mind, but of a mind both

[1] In a letter to his son W. W. Story, Feb. 9, 1841, Judge Story says, "It reminds me strongly of my own case when, escaping from the walls of college, I found myself in a lawyer's office, among the dusty rubbish of former ages; for at that time there were few elementary works to smooth the passage, and from reading the classical work of *Blackstone*, I had immediately to plunge into the dark page of *Coke upon Littleton*. I could say, with Spelman, that my heart sank within me."

[2] *Autobiography of Daniel Webster* (1829).

strong and mature, to understand him. Why disgust and discourage a young man by telling him he must break into his profession through such a wall as this? I really often despaired. I thought I never could make myself a lawyer and was almost going back to the business of school teaching."

John Quincy Adams records in his Diary:[1]

"March, 1788. I this day got through my folio of Lord Coke which has been hanging heavily upon me these ten weeks. It contains a vast mass of law learning, but heaped up in such an incoherent mass that I have derived very little benefit from it — indeed I think it a very improper book to put into the hands of a student just entering upon the acquisition of the profession. . . . The addition of Wood's *Institutes* and more especially of Blackstone's *Commentaries* has been an inestimable advantage to the late students in the profession."

It was the advent of Blackstone which opened the eyes of American scholars to the broader field of learning in the law. He taught them, for the first time, the continuity, the unity, and the reason of the Common Law — and just at a time when the need of a unified system both in law and politics was beginning to be felt in the Colonies.

Up to this time, wrote Blackstone, the student has been "expected to sequester himself from the world, and by a tedious, lonely process to extract the theory of law from a mass of undigested learning. How little therefore is it to be wondered at, that we hear of so frequent miscarriages, that so many gentlemen of bright inaugurations grow weary of so unpromising a search; and that so many persons of moderate capacity confuse themselves at first setting out and continue ever dark and puzzled during the remainder of their lives."[2]

[1] See *Mass. Hist. Soc. Proc.*, 2d series, Vol. XVI (1902).

[2] It was to Mansfield that the credit was due of discovering and turning to public usefulness the genius of Blackstone as a jurist. A vacancy occur-

The publication of Volume I of the *Commentaries* was made in England in 1765 and Volume IV in 1769; and as early as 1771–1772 an American edition of the full work was published in Philadelphia in four volumes at two dollars per volume, 1400 copies being ordered in advance. The list of subscribers was headed by four Governors and three Lieutenant-Governors: and the first name among private citizens was "John Adams, Barrister at law, Boston." The booksellers of Boston subscribed for 239 copies, of Charleston 89, of Philadelphia 84, of New York 60, of Norfolk, Williamsburgh and Winchester in Virginia 97. In addition there had previously been imported into the Colonies at least 1000 copies of the English edition, at ten pounds per set.[1]

The quaint wording of the advertisement inserted in the first volume of the American edition is of interest:[2]

"This volume can only be sold to those Gentlemen who are willing to subscribe for the whole of these celebrated *Commentaries*, by giving in their names as Encouragers. All independent gentlemen and scholars, as well as every Magistrate and officer and Lawyer, ought to possess this

ring in the Professorship of Civil Law at Oxford, Blackstone had been promised the appointment by the Duke of Newcastle; but the latter finding him unwilling to bestir himself for the Government in political agitation appointed another man. Mansfield then advised Blackstone to settle at Oxford and to read law lectures to such students as chose to attend.

These lectures in 1753 had attracted the attention of Charles Viner who had made a fortune from the proceeds of his *Abridgment* (published 1742 to 1753). And when Viner died, in 1756, he bequeathed a considerable sum for the maintenance of a professor at Oxford at a salary of 200 pounds — who should give a course of sixty lectures per year "On the Law of England in the English Language."

To fill this first professorship of law in any English speaking college William Blackstone, Esq., was appointed in 1758.

[1] See Preface to Hammond's *Blackstone's Commentaries.*

[2] See *Law Dictionaries — Amer. Law Review*, Vol. XXVIII (1894).

Splendid and Useful Work. Therefore, the Editor hopeth, Patriotism to encourage Native Fabrications, with the advantage of saving seven pounds on the purchase of ten pounds worth — the British edition being sold at Ten Pounds Pennsylvania Currency — together with that innate thirst for Knowledge, which is so admirably engrafted in the Contexture of the human mind, will nobly animate all whose Ideas are expanded in Search of Knowledge to encourage the American Edition."

Even prior to their publication in book form, Blackstone's lectures had been known in America; for in September, 1759, Jonathan Sewall wrote to John Adams: "Your account of Mr. Blackstone's lectures is entirely new to me. I am greatly pleased with it." Adams records in 1765 a conversation with Mr. Gridley on Blackstone; and the title page of a book entitled *Conductor Generalis*, published in 1764 in New Jersey — a manual for justices and petty officers — contains the following — "To which is added a treatise on the *Law of Descent in Fee Simple*, by William Blackstone, Esq., Barrister at Law, Vinerian Professor of the Law of England." [1]

The popularity of the *Commentaries* gave an impetus to

[1] James Iredell wrote from Edenton, North Carolina, July 31, 1771, to his father in London:

"Will you be so obliging as to procure Dr. Blackstone's *Commentaries on the Laws of England* for me, and send them by the first opportunity. I have indeed read them through by the favor of Mr. Johnston who lent them to me; but it is proper I should read them frequently and with great attention. They are books admirably calculated for a young student, and indeed may interest the most learned. The law there is not merely considered as a profession but as a science. The principles are deduced from their source, and we are not only taught in the clearest manner the general rules of law, but the reasons upon which they are founded. By this means we can more satisfactorily study, and more easily remember them, than when they are only laid down in a dictatorial, often an obscure manner.

"Pleasure and instruction go hand in hand."

See *Life and Letters of James Iredell*, by Griffith J. McRee (1857).

the importation of other law books; so that, by 1775, Edmund Burke said in the House of Commons:[1]

"In no country perhaps in the world is the law so general a study. The profession itself is numerous and powerful; and in most provinces it takes the lead. The greater number of the deputies sent to the Congress were lawyers. But all who read, and most do read, endeavour to obtain some smattering in that science. I have been told by an eminent bookseller, that in no branch of his business, after tracts of popular devotion, were so many books as those of the law exported to the plantations. The colonists have now fallen into the way of printing them for their own use. I hear that they have sold nearly as many of Blackstone's *Commentaries* in America as in England. General Gage marks out this disposition very particularly in a letter on your table. He states that all the people in his government are lawyers, or smatterers in law; and that in Boston they have been enabled, by successful chicane, wholly to evade many parts of one of your capital penal institutions. . . . This study renders men acute, inquisitive, dexterous, prompt in attack, ready in defence, full of resources. In other countries, the people, more simple, and of a less mercurial cast, judge of an ill principle in government only by an actual grievance; here they anticipate the evil, and judge of the pressure of the grievance by the badness of the principle. They augur misgovernment at a distance; and snuff the approach of tyranny in every tainted breeze."

Whether the change is to be attributed to the influence of Blackstone or to the increased facilities for obtaining books, or to the freer ideas brought about by the American Revolution, the broadening of the study of the law, after 1780, is a striking and remarkable feature in the history of law in this country.

The young lawyer was now expected to know something

[1] Speech on Moving Resolutions for Conciliation with the American Colonies, March 22, 1776.

of the general principles of public law and to approach jurisprudence in a spirit of scientific inquiry. He was taught general views in addition to particular rules.

Knowledge of technical details of feudal tenure, of obscure customs and bewildering pleadings, was no longer enough to qualify the best students.

A law course of reading prescribed in Judge Parker's office in Portsmouth, New Hampshire, and in Charles Chauncey's office in New Haven, Connecticut, for Ezra Stiles, Jr., was as follows:[1]

"Burlamaqui's *Principes de Droit Naturel;* Montesquieu's *l'Esprit des Lois;* Lord Kames' *History of Law; Blackstone;* Wood's *Maxims;* Wood's *Institutes; Co. Litt.;* Bacon's *Abr.;* Hawkins' *Pleas of the Crown;* Gilbert's *Evidence, Devises,* and *Tenures; Law of Bills of Exchange;* Molloy *De Jure Maritimo;* Hale's *Abridgment; Lex Testamentorum;* Sullivan's *Lectures;* Bohun's *Institutes and Declarations;* Boot on *Suits at Law; Offic. Cler. Pac.;* Burns' *Justice;* Dalrymple's *Institutions of the Laws of Scotland, etc.; Institutes of Tribonian* and part of the *Pandects; Puffendorf;* Poulton's *Crim. Law; Salkeld's Rep.;* 1 and 2 *Burrow;* part of *Lord Raymond's, Holt's* and *Shower's Reports,* Godolphin's *Legacy Orph.,* 40 volumes."

A similar course was assigned to John Quincy Adams who studied in the office of Theophilus Parsons in 1788, first, Robertson's *History of Charles V,* Vattel's *Law of Nature and Nations,* Gibbon's *Rome* and Hume's *England;* next, Sullivan's *Lectures,* Wright's *Tenures, Co. Litt.;* Wood's *Institutes;* Gilbert's *Evidence;* Foster's and Hawkins' *Pleas of the Crown;* Bacon's *Pleas and Pleadings;* Buller's *Nisi Prius;* Barrington's *Observations on the Statutes; Institutes of Justinian.*[2]

[1] *Literary Diary of Ezra Stiles,* Vol. II; *The Study of Elementary Law,* by S. E. Baldwin, *Yale Law Journal,* Vol. XIII.

[2] *Study of Elementary Law,* by S. E. Baldwin, *Yale Law Journal,* Vol. XIII; *Proc. Mass. Hist. Soc.,* Vol. XVI, 2d series.

The notebook of Israel Keith (Harv. 1771) contained the following entries as to advice for a law curriculum — Lord Chief Justice Hale's *Advice for study of Common Law;* Lord Chief Justice Reeves' *Advice to his nephew on the study of law;* a letter from Dr. Dickens, Regius Professor of Law at Cambridge, England, to Jeremiah Gridley on the books necessary to a knowledge of Civil Law, and a letter from Gridley to Judge Lightfoot of the Admiralty Court in Rhode Island on the study of admiralty law.[1]

So too the broader course of study in the latter part of the Eighteenth Century can be seen from Chancellor Kent's description of his legal education:[2]

"When the college (Yale) was broken up and dispersed in July 1779 by the British, I retired to a country village and finding Blackstone's *Commentaries* I read the fourth volume. Parts of the work struck my taste and the work inspired me at the age of sixteen with awe and I fondly determined to be a lawyer. In Nov. 1781, I was placed by my father with Mr. (now called Judge) Benson who was then attorney general, at Poughkeepsie. There I entered on law and was the most modest, steady, industrious student that such place ever saw. I read the following winter, *Grotius* and *Puffendorff* in large folios and made copious extracts. My fellowstudents who were gay and gallant thought me very odd and dull in my taste; but out of five of them four died in middle life drunkards. . . . In 1782, I read Smollett's *History of England*, and procured at a farmer's house where I boarded Rapin's *History* (a large folio) and read it through, and I found during the course of the last summer among my papers my MSS. abridgment of Rapin's *Dissertations on the Laws and Customs of the Anglo Saxons.* I abridged Hale's *History of the Common Law* and the old books of practice and read parts of *Blackstone* again and again. The same year I procured Hume's *History* and his

[1] *Quincy's Reports*, note, p. 178.

[2] *Memoirs and Letters of James Kent*, by William Kent (1898). See letter to Thomas Washington of Tennessee, written October 6, 1828.

profound reflections and admirable eloquence struck most deeply on my youthful mind. I extracted the most admired part, made several volumes of MSS."

A more old fashioned course of studies was pursued by Chief Justice Roger B. Taney who thus describes his legal education in his Memoirs:

"In spring of 1796, read law in office of Jeremiah Thurly Chase at Annapolis, Judge of General Court.

"From the character of the judges of the General Court, of the bar who attended it, and the business transacted in it, Annapolis was considered the place of all others in the State where a man should study law, if he expected to attain eminence in his profession.

"My reading in the office of a judge, instead of a practising lawyer, had some advantages; but upon the whole was I think a disadvantage to me. It is true, it gave me more time for uninterrupted study, but it gave me no instruction in the ordinary routine of practise, nor any information as to the forms and manner of pleading. In that day, strict and nice technical pleading was the pride of the bar and I might almost say of the court. And every disputed suit was a trial of skill in pleading between the counsel, and a victory achieved in that mode was much more valued than one obtained on the merits of the case. . . . Nor was it so easy in that day for an inexperienced young lawyer to satisfy himself upon a question of special pleading. *Chitty* had not made his appearance, and you were obliged to look for the rule in Comyn's *Digest* or Bacon's *Abridgment* or Viner's *Abridgment* and the cases to which they referred; and I have sometimes gone back to Lilly's *Entries* and *Doctrina Placitandi* in searching for a precedent. . . . We had no moot court. My preceptor, Mr. Chase, did not encourage them, and in this he agreed, I believe, with the leaders of the Bar in Annapolis in whose offices there were students. He thought that discussions of law questions by students was apt to give them the habit of speaking upon questions which they did not understand or of which they had but an imperfect and superficial knowledge — that its tendency therefore was to accustom them to loose arguments and to lay down principles without proper qualifications. He advised me to attend regularly the sittings of the General Court, to observe how the eminent men at that Bar examined the witnesses and brought out their cases, and raised and argued the questions of law, and afterwards to write a report of it for my own use. . . . All the lawyers of Maryland who had risen to eminence and leadership were trained in the manner described and advised by Mr. Chase."

A final and perhaps the best illustration of the average legal education is William Plumer, Jr.'s, account of his father, William Plumer, Sr., who was a contemporary of Jeremiah Mason, Jeremiah Smith, Daniel Webster, and Ichabod Bartlett in New Hampshire, and who studied law in 1784, in the office of Joshua Atherton:

"Atherton gave him *Coke upon Littleton*, as his first initiation into the mysteries of the law; and it is not strange that the ardor of the young aspirant was somewhat cooled by this selection of masters, so quaint, austere and forbidding. After digging for some three or four weeks, in the rugged soil of the feudal tenures, and beginning, as he thought, to get some glimpses of its hidden treasures, he was told by his instructor that he must suspend his legal studies and commence with the Latin Grammar. He must read *Virgil* and *Cicero* before he could understand *Coke* and *Littleton*. This was a new and, to him, most unwelcome labor. He, however, laid aside his law, and took up Lilly's *Latin Grammar*, probably the first grammar he had ever seen, certainly the first he had ever attempted to study. . . .

"In 1785, his new instructor, John Prentice, a graduate of Harvard College, though probably not a well-read lawyer, possessed a respectable standing at the Bar; and, like Atherton, was afterwards Attorney General. His law library consisted at this time of Blackstone's *Commentaries;* Wood's *Institutes of the Laws of England;* Hawkins' *Pleas of the Crown;* Jacob's *Law Dictionary; Salkeld; Raymond* and *Strange's Reports;* the *New Hampshire Statutes*, and a manuscript volume of pleas and declarations. . . . He read the whole of *Blackstone* rapidly through, in the first instance, to acquire, in this way, a general idea of its contents; and then went over it, more carefully, a second time, with a view to its more thorough comprehension. He devoted at least ten hours a day to this study, though he seldom read more than forty or fifty pages in that time. But these were carefully studied, or, if not fully understood, at least, examined with his best care and attention. His instructor was not much inclined, nor indeed always able, to answer the questions which he asked; and the few books within his reach often failed to furnish the desired information. Under these circumstances his practice was, after reading a portion of *Blackstone*, to trace the subject through other books; and then, taking a walk in some retired place, to review in his mind the substance of what he had read, examining the relations of one part with another, and of the whole with what he had learned before, till he felt himself master of the lesson, and prepared to go farther.

"On the important subject of pleas and pleading, Prentice had no books, except a manuscript volume of forms, said to have been collected by Theophilus Parsons. This the student copied, and added to it in the course of his practice, such other pleas and declarations as he thought worthy of preservation, whether drawn by himself, or derived from other sources. He, at the same time, took copious notes of his reading, and formed abstracts and digests of the law under separate heads, thus reducing his knowledge to a regular system."

Daniel Webster's own account of his course of study in the office of Christopher Gore, in 1804, is a typical example of the course followed in the early years of the Nineteenth Century.

Before coming to Boston, he had studied about two years in Salisbury, New Hampshire, the first works which he read being *Vattel*, *Burlamaqui* and *Montesquieu* on the Law of Nations: then *Blackstone* and *Coke;* and the histories of *Hume* and *Robertson;* and "happening to take up Espinasse's *Nisi Prius*," he wrote:

"I found I could understand it and arguing that the object of reading was to understand what was written, I laid down the venerable *Coke* et *alios similes reverendos* and kept company for a time with Mr. Espinasse and others, the most plain, easy and intelligent writers.

"Mr. Gore had just then returned from England, and renewed the practice of the law. He had rooms in Scollay's Building, and, as yet, had no clerk. A young man, as little known to Gore as myself, undertook to introduce me to him. In logic, this would have been bad. *Ignotum per ignotum.* Nevertheless, it succeeded here. We ventured into Mr. Gore's rooms, and my name was pronounced. I was shockingly embarrassed, but Mr. Gore's habitual courtesy of manner gave me courage to speak. . . . He talked to me pleasantly for a quarter of an hour; and, when I rose to depart, he said: 'My young friend, you look as though you might be trusted. You say you came to study, and not to waste time. I will take you at your word. You may as well hang up your hat at once; go into the other room; take your book and sit down to reading it, and write at your convenience to New Hampshire for your letters.' . . . It was a situation which offered to me the means of studying books and men and things. It was on the 20th day of July, 1804, that I first made myself known to Mr. Gore; and, although I remained in his office only till March following, and that with considerable intervening absences, I made, as I think, some respectable progress.

"In August the Supreme Court sat. I attended it constantly, and reported every one of its decisions. I did the same in the Circuit Court of the United States. I kept a little journal at that time, which still survives. It contains little besides a list of books read.

"In addition to books on the common and municipal law, I find I read *Vattel* for the third time in my life, as is stated in the journal, Ward's *Law of Nations*, Lord Bacon's *Elements*, Puffendorff's *Latin History of England*, Gifford's *Juvenal*, Boswell's *Tour to the Hebrides*, Moore's *Travels*, and many other miscellaneous things.

"But my main study was the common law, and especially the parts of it which relate to special pleading. Whatever was in *Viner*, *Bacon*, and other books then usually studied on that part of the science, I paid my respects to. Among other things I went through *Saunders' Reports*, the old folio edition, and abstracted, and put into English, out of Latin and Norman-French, the pleadings in all his *Reports*. It was an edifying work. From that day to this the forms and language of special pleas have been quite familiar with me. I believe I have my little abstract yet."

When all is said, however, as to the meagreness of a lawyer's education, one fact must be strongly emphasized — that this very meagreness was a source of strength. *Multum in parvo* was particularly applicable to the training for the Bar of that era.

There was truth in the reply of a great lawyer, when asked how the lawyers who formed the United States Constitution had such a mastery of legal principles, — "Why they had so few books."[1] "Many other students," wrote Webster, "read more than I did; but so much as I read, I made my own."

And Chancellor Kent's remark "that he owed his reputation to the fact that, when studying law during the war, he had but one book, Blackstone's *Commentaries*, but that one book he mastered,"[2] sums up very concisely the cause of the greatness of many an early American jurist.

[1] See *How Successful Lawyers were Educated*, by G. C. Macdonald (1896). Sir Edward Sugden in England once said, "I resolved, when beginning to read law, to make everything I acquired perfectly my own, and never to go to a second thing until I had entirely accomplished the first. Many of my competitors read as much in a day as I read in a week; but at the end of the twelve months, my knowledge was as fresh as on the day it was acquired, while theirs had glided away from their recollections."

[2] See *Magazine of American History*, Vol. XIII (1885).

## CHAPTER IX

### EARLY AMERICAN BARRISTERS, AND BAR ASSOCIATIONS

THE local law office does not account, however, for all the educated American lawyers of the Eighteenth Century.

A far greater number than is generally known, received their legal education in London in the Inns of Court; and the influence, on the American Bar, of these English-bred lawyers, especially in the more southerly Colonies, was most potent. The training which they received in the Inns, confined almost exclusively to the Common Law, based as it was on historical precedent and customary law, the habits which they formed there of solving all legal questions by the standards of English liberties and of rights of the English subject, proved of immense value to them when they became later (as so many did become) leaders of the American Revolution.

Probably from twenty-five to fifty American-born lawyers had been educated in England prior to 1760;[1] and it has been stated that 115 Americans were admitted to the Inns, from 1760 to the close of the Revolution;[2] from South Carolina 47, from Virginia 21, from Maryland 16, from Pennsylvania 11, from New York 5, and from each of the other Colonies 1 or 2.

Among the more distinguished may be named John

[1] *Life and Times of John Dickinson*, by Charles J. Stillé (1891).

[2] See Chapters I, II, III and IV, *supra*.

Rutledge, Edward Rutledge, Arthur Middleton, Charles Cotesworth Pinckney, Thomas Heyward, Thomas Lynch, John Julian Pringle, and John Laurens, from South Carolina; John Randolph, Peyton Randolph, Richard Henry Lee and Arthur Lee, from Virginia; Charles Carroll, from Maryland; Joseph Read, from New Jersey; and Thomas McKean, Edward Tilghman and William Tilghman, Jared Ingersoll, Benjamin Chew, William Rawle, Phineas Bond, and John Dickinson, from Pennsylvania, most of these being admitted to the Inner Temple and Middle Temple.[1]

An interesting record of the method of procedure in the English Inns is to be found in *The Black Books of Lincoln's Inn*, as follows:

"Called to the Bar, May 5, 1762: Joseph Reade, Jr., on his petition setting forth that he is desirous of being called to the Bar this term, having kept Commons, performed all his exercises, and conformed himself to the Rules of the Society, wanting two terms of his full standing; that he is a native of New Yorke in North America, and that it is necessary for him to go thither immediately, which he intends to do, and reside there. . . . He must pay five years' duties."

The breadth of education to be sought in England may be gathered from the following letter written, from Charleston, July 30, 1769, by John Rutledge to his brother in London:[2]

"The very first thing with which you should be thoroughly acquainted is the writing shorthand. . . . Be constant in attending the sittings in Chancery out of terms, and when there are no sittings at Nisi Prius in London or

[1] See *A Brief History of the Middle Temple*, by C. E. A. Bidwell (1909); *The Black Books of Lincoln's Inn; Masters of the Bench of the Inner Temple; Report of the Historical Manuscripts Commission*, Amer. Hist. Ass. (1896), pp. 573–689.

[2] See *American Jurist*, Vol. XIV.

Westminster; for I would prefer attending the King's Bench and Sittings of the Chief Justice of that Court at Nisi Prius when they are held. And remember what I hinted to you of attending alternately in the different courts by agreement between you and some of your intimate fellow students, and then of comparing and exchanging notes every evening. . . . But you must exert yourself to the utmost in being able by some means or other to attend the House of Commons constantly . . . I would not have this make you a dabbler in politics. What I intend by it is that you may have opportunities of seeing and hearing the best speakers, and of acquiring a good manner and proper address. . . . I believe Sheridan is the only lecturer in England upon oratory, and I think it would be advisable to attend him and mark well his observations. . . . And now in regard to particular law books — Coke's *Institutes* seem to be almost the foundation of our law. These you must read over and over with the greatest attention, and not quit him until you understand him thoroughly and have made your own everything in him which is worth taking out. A good deal of his law is now obsolete and altered by acts of Parliament; however, it is necessary to know what the law was before so altered. *Blackstone* I think useful.[1] The reports are too tedious to be all read through; at least whilst you are in England, I would give the preference to the most modern. . . . I look upon it that if you go through all the cases reported since the Revolution, when the Constitution seems to have been re-established upon its true and proper principles, and since which time by the alteration of the Judges' commission and their increasing independence, to what it is at this day, the law has been in its greatest perfection, and not encroaching either upon the people's liberties or the prerogative; I say, if you do this, you will have a collection of the very best cases. . . . I would read every case reported from that time to the present. Distinguish between your reading of law and equity, and don't confound the two matters. . . . They are kept very

[1] It is to be noted that this letter was written before *Blackstone* had been republished in the Colonies.

distinct in the Courts of England, though here blended together very often and very ridiculously. . . . I would have you also read the statute laws throughout. . . . Vast numbers of them you will find of no manner of use, except indeed as matter of history; but this thing I think in the main will be of vast service to you. . . . Stock yourself with a good collection of law maxims both Latin and English — they are of great use. . . . Make yourself thoroughly acquainted with all the terms of the law. . . . The little book called *Termes de la Ley*, will help you. *Doctor and Student* is a good book, though a little one, and good authority. *Bacon* you know is my favorite, and where authors seem to differ I think he will best reconcile them. Be well acquainted with Crown Law, Hale's, Hawkin's and Judge Foster's, and what other Crown Law books there are, read carefully."

In connection with study at the Inns of Court, the correspondence of Charles Carroll of Carrollton with his father is of singular interest. Carroll had chambers in the Inner Temple Inn for several years about 1760, being one of a group of young Maryland lawyers studying law in London — Edmund Key, Edmund Jenning, Lloyd Dulany, Alexander Lawson, William Paca and William Cooke.[1] In 1759, his father wrote to him:

"Many reasons ought to incline you to a close and serious study of ye law; it is a shame for a gentleman to be ignorant of ye laws of his country and to be dependent on every dirty pettifogger whose interest it may be to lead him by such a dependence into endless difficulties. On the other hand, how commendable is it for a gentleman of an independent fortune, not only not to stand in need of mercenary advisers, but to be able to advise and assist his friends, relatives and neighbors. What weight must such a one have on ye circle of his acquaintance! How endearing may he make himself to all by a benevolent

[1] See *Unpublished Letters of Charles Carroll of Carrollton and of His Father* (1902); *Life of Charles Carroll*, by Kate Mason Rowland (1898).

use of his knowledge! Suppose you should be called upon to act in any publick character, what an awkward figure would you make without ye knowledge of ye law, either as a legislator, judge, or even an arbitrator of differences among your neighbours and friends.

"The law in England is not only a road to riches, but to ye highest honours. It is true, as things now stand you are shut out from ye Bar; but you are not debarred from acting as a councellor. As I before observed, ye knowledge of it is absolutely necessary to every gentleman of fortune who has the least idea of being independent.

"I do not send you to ye Temple to spend (as many do) four or five years to no purpose. I send you to study and labour; it is what I expect from you — do not disappoint my hopes. . . . I understand that lately, in one of our Universities, there is a chair established for a Professor of ye Common Law; this has been long wished for. Whether ye Professor or his method answers ye expectation of ye publick, I know not; but it is certainly worth your while to enquire whether you may not reap some advantage from it, and to judge, yourself, you may in vacation time go to hear him.

"I approve your acquaintance with such of your school-fellows as are men of family and good morals; little tours at proper times to their country seats will be a relaxation and amusement. . . . You will meet several of your countrymen in London, with some of them in ye Temple or other Inns of Court. Treat them politely. If you should mention them in your letters, let it be to their advantage; but with them, as with all others, be reserved until you know them."

Again, on July 14, 1760, his father wrote:

"I think a student in ye Temple cannot apply himself properly to his studies and spend above 300 pounds a year; whether you spend 250 or 300 a year is to me immaterial, but to you it cannot be so, if by spending your money you misspend your time, which to you is more precious than money. . . .

"You vainly at present fancy you might study here;

— might not every gentleman in ye Temple say as much of his own home? The distractions and various occupations of a man once entered into ye world make such a scheme almost chimerical. A long series of years, research and experience, show that it was necessary to have particular places appointed for ye study of ye law; and that in such, a knowledge of it is soonest and best acquired."

Of Carroll's low opinion of the legal education to be obtained in the Temple, the following letters are an illustration. In 1762, he wrote to his father:

"No degree at law can be obtained without being called to the Bar. The being entered of the Temple is a necessary, previous and preparatory step to that ceremony, which, though a ceremony, is an opening to all preferments in the law; 't is attended with no other advantages, but many and great inconveniences; the chiefest is the frequenting loose and dissolute companions. For this reason I have resolved not to enter myself of the Temple; — to what? Why should I expose myself to danger and be at needless though small expense, without any view or hope of profit and advantage?"

And in 1763, he wrote:

"If I had known how to procure a person to instruct me in the law, or where such a person was to be found, I should not have neglected doing it; but indeed such a one is not easily to be met with. The best way to become a good lawyer is to be under an attorney; not as his clerk — that would not be so proper for a gentleman — but to be in his office on the footing of a gentleman by allowing him a handsome gratification. I should then have known the practical part of the law, by which knowledge many difficulties would be removed, which, for want of it, are now insurmountable. Most of our great lawyers have been brought up under attorneys. The great Lord Hardwicke is a recent instance of that method's being the best for forming a sound lawyer. Nothing can be more absurd than the usual manner of young gentlemen's studying the law. They come from the University, take chambers in the Temple, read *Coke Littleton* — whom they cannot possibly understand, — frequent the courts whose practise they are ignorant of. They are soon disgusted with the difficulties and dryness of the study, the law books are thrown aside, dissipation succeeds to study, immorality to virtue: one night plunges them into ruin, misery, and disease."

The facilities for legal study supplied by the Inns of Court were, however, the least of the opportunities open to young American barristers in London at this time; for these years, 1750 to 1775, formed a period of remarkable brilliance in English history. Students of law were not only studying at the Inns side by side with the future Chief Justices, Kenyon and Ellenborough, and the future Chancellors, Thurlow, Eldon and Erskine; but they were also listening to the luminous judgments of Lord Mansfield in King's Bench, to the commanding eloquence of Pitt (Lord Chatham), and the oratory of Charles Pratt (Lord Camden); they were elbowing, in the Inns themselves, the burly frame of Samuel Johnson the autocrat of literature; and they were witnessing David Garrick's "powers of acting vast and unconfined." [1]

In forming an idea of the Colonial lawyer's education, one further factor must be borne in mind, — the remarkable extent to which Eighteenth Century lawyers, especially those of New England, Virginia, and South Carolina, were college-bred men. Practically all the early lawyers in Massachusetts were Harvard graduates; and of the lawyers admitted to practise in Boston at the Suffolk Bar, in later years, from 1780 to 1817, 139 were Harvard grad-

[1] Of Jared Ingersoll who was in the Middle Temple in 1774, his son Charles J. Ingersoll wrote, that "Mansfield, Blackstone, Chatham and Garrick and other luminaries of that period were objects of his constant attention, and of his correspondence, and ever after among the pleasures of his memory." See *Life of Charles Jared Ingersoll*, by William M. Meigs (1897).

uates; 7 were from Brown, 6 from Dartmouth, 1 from Williams, 3 non-graduates.

In New Hampshire, in 1805, of the 106 members of the Bar, 77 were college graduates — from Harvard 35, Dartmouth 34, Yale 6, Brown 2.

In Maine, in 1770, of the six trained lawyers, four were Harvard graduates.

In Connecticut practically all the lawyers of distinction were Yale graduates.

In New Jersey, the prominent lawyers were almost exclusively college men, either from Yale, like David Ogden, or from Princeton, like Richard Stockton.

In Pennsylvania, as already noted, a large proportion of the Bar was educated in England or in the College of Philadelphia and the University of Pennsylvania.

The records of William and Mary College and of Princeton contained the names of many of Virginia's prominent lawyers.

In South Carolina, almost all of distinction at the Bar after the Revolution graduated from Princeton, Yale, or the College of South Carolina.

New York alone seems the exception in the matter of liberal training for her Bar; for in the early Eighteenth Century, men of education were rare in that Province. There were no college graduates on the Bench, except James Delancey, and none at the Bar, except William Smith. It seems that commerce engrossed the attention of the principal families, and their sons were sent from the writing school to the counting house, and thence to the West Indies.[1] In 1741, when William Livingston graduated from Yale, there were but six other lawyers in the Province who were college graduates, three of whom were his own brothers.

[1] *Life of William Livingston*, by Theodore Sedgwick, Jr. (1833).

And as the historian, William Smith, Jr. (born in 1728), writes of his own time:

"To the disgrace of our first planters, who beyond comparison surpassed their eastern neighbors in opulence, Mr. James Delancy, a graduate of the University of Cambridge, and Mr. Smith were for many years the only academics in the Province except such as were in holy orders — and, so late as 1746, the author did not recall above thirteen more."

In the later part of the Eighteenth Century, however, New York recruited her Bar very largely from graduates of King's College (Columbia).

After 1770, as the course of legal study became liberalized, and the Bar became more compact in its organization, and assured of its power, it gradually established very rigid rules, fixing requirements for office study by students desiring admission as lawyers. These rules paved the way for the establishment of regular law schools. They also tended to constitute lawyers as more and more of an educated guild.

Nothing gives a better view of the educational condition of the law student at the end of the Eighteenth Century than the *Bar Book Suffolk County 1770*, containing the records of its proceedings up to 1805.[1]

Mention has been made,[2] of the rule first adopted by the Essex Bar in 1768, and later generally by other Massachusetts County Bars that:

"It is agreed that we will not take any young gentleman to study with us, without previously having the consent of the Bar of this County; that we will not recommend any persons to be admitted to the Inferior Court as at-

[1] See *Mass. Hist. Soc. Proc.* (1882), and *Historical Sketch*, by George Dexter.

[2] Chapter III, *supra.*

torneys, who have not studied with some barrister three years at least, nor as attorneys to the Superior Court, who have not studied as aforesaid, and been admitted at the Inferior Court, two years at least; nor recommend them as barristers till they have been through the preceding degrees, and been attorneys at the Superior Court two years at the least — except those gentlemen who are already admitted in this County as attorneys at the Superior and Inferior Courts, and that these must be subject to this rule so far as is yet to come."

In 1800, the term of years was extended so that "students of college out of the State be not admissible to the Bar until they shall have studied one year longer than those educated at Harvard University;" and "gentlemen admitted to the Bar of other States who have practised thereat less than four years must have a term of study within this county of at least one year."

In 1771, the Suffolk Bar required that "consent of the Bar shall not be given to any young gentleman who has not had an education at college, or a liberal education equivalent in the judgment of the Bar." This at once established a very high educational standard for lawyers. In 1784, the standard was still further raised, by the provision, that any gentleman proposed who had not had a college education, should undergo an examination by a committee of the Bar, previous to admission as a student. The examination was apparently thorough, for, in August, 1784, it appears that:

"The report of the committee on the examination of Messrs. Gardiner and Hill was considered; and it appearing to the gentlemen present that, although those gentlemen were well versed in the Latin and English classics, yet that a course of study in the mathematics, in ethics, logic, and metaphysics was necessary previous to their admission as students of law; therefore *Voted* unanimously, That such admission be suspended."

Also, in 1793:

"The committee appointed for the examination of Mr. Joseph Rowe report that he received an academical education in the province of Canada; after which, at about seventeen years of age, he entered the office of the attorney-general for that province as a clerk and student of the law; that he diligently attended to the business of that office and a suitable course of study the term of two years; all which the committee conceive is equal to a collegiate education in that State. That he has resided more than three years in Boston as a clerk in the office of Mr. Tudor. The committee, having considered the qualifications of Mr. Rowe, are of opinion that he may be duly admitted to the Bar."

And in 1798:

"The Committee of Suffolk Bar, appointed to examine and ascertain the literary acquirements of Mr. Holder Slocum, Jr., now a student with Judge Minot, have attended that service, and report that they find Mr. Slocum has so far attended to the Latin language that a moderate degree of attention and practice will probably enable him to render it sufficiently familiar for the purposes of his intended profession. He has paid no attention to the Greek, and has not been sufficiently instructed in the opinion of your committee, in logic, metaphysics, and mathematics. He has read some approved writers in history, and has attended considerably to the French language.

"It is the opinion of the committee that on his remaining in an office three years from the present time, with an attention for part of the time, under the direction of his instructor, to history and metaphysics, and occasionally to the Latin language, it will be proper, at the expiration of that period, if he continues the assiduity and attention which he has hitherto manifested, to allow of his admission to the Bar."

Often, however, the rules were enforced liberally, owing to special circumstances. Thus, on July 21, 1778, it was voted that Mr. Christopher Gore (later Governor of Massachusetts and a noted lawyer) "be considered as having studied the law according to the rules of the Bar since the month of July, 1776, and that he be entitled to the privileges of such a student."

So, too, on December 3, 1779:

"Upon motion made by Mr. Tudor, that Mr. Fisher Ames might be considered as a student with him from April, 1778, although he had during that time pursued his studies at Dedham, after consideration and debate, *Voted*, That Mr. Ames be considered as a law student from the first day of January, 1779, only (this indulgence allowed from some particular circumstances in his favor), and that at the expiration of three years from that day, he continuing in Mr. Tudor's office for the future, he be recommended to be sworn only on condition that he submit to an examination by the Bar, particularly in the practical business of the profession."

It is interesting to note that the legal reputation of the Suffolk Bar was so high at this time that there were many applications from Southern law students — men who in pre-Revolutionary days would have gone to England to study in the Inns of the Inner or Middle Temple.

Thus, in October, 1783, it was voted:

"On motion of Mr. Hichborn, that Mr. Richard Brook Roberts be admitted as a student in his office with a deduction of one year from the usual term required by the rules for such students previous to their recommendation for the oath, *Voted*, That Mr. Roberts be admitted accordingly with the proposed allowance, provided he produces a certificate from a gentleman of the profession in Carolina that he has read law under such gentleman's direction for one year at least."

And, in July, 1784:

"On motion of Mr. Gardiner, to have his son, John Gardiner, admitted into his office as a student of law;

and on motion from Mr. Gore to have the liberty of taking into his office Mr. William Hill (a young gentleman from North Carolina), as a student of law, it appearing to the Bar that neither of these young gentlemen had received a college education, *Voted* unanimously, That a committee be appointed to examine the said young gentlemen with respect to their literary qualifications, and to report their opinion thereon to the Bar."

In 1780, it was voted by the Suffolk Bar, that "no gentleman take a student into his office for a less consideration than one hundred pounds sterling," and in 1783, that "no gentleman should in the future have more than three students in his office."

Of the standard of legal etiquette and morality, the vote of March 20, 1784, is significant:

"Voted unanimously that no gentleman of the Bar ought to go out of his office to put himself in the way of applications for drawing of writs nor to employ any other persons to do business for him out of his office."

Other States had similar restrictive provisions as to admission to practise, sometimes formulated by Bar Associations, and sometimes prescribed by rules of court or by statute. Thus, in New Hampshire, a State Bar Association, as early as 1788, and later in 1805, adopted elaborate *General Regulations for the Gentlemen of the Bar*, providing that:

"In case a candidate for admission as a student in an office has not had a degree in the arts he shall, excepting a knowledge of the Greek language, be duly qualified to be admitted to the first class of students of Dartmouth College."

College graduates were required to study in an office three years; non-graduates, five years. No member of the Bar could receive more than three students in his office; nor could he receive any student without the consent of the county Bar. No member of the Bar was allowed to receive less than $250 as a tuition fee for a student. No lawyer was to be admitted to the Bar of the Superior Court, until after two years' practise in the Court of Common Pleas.[1]

In Vermont, by statute of 1787, and by regulations of the Bar, the same conditions prevailed.

In Rhode Island, two years' study for college graduates, and three years' for non-graduates, were prescribed; and a candidate could not be proposed to the court until he had obtained the approbation and consent of his county Bar.

The same rule prevailed in Connecticut, as early as 1795, either by rule or custom, and after 1807 by rule of the Supreme Court; and the first Bar Association was formed in that State in 1783.

In New Jersey, a lawyer had to be recommended by the justices of the Supreme Court to the Governor for a license to practise, and to receive such recommendation, he must serve as a clerk three years if a college graduate, four years if a non-graduate. He must also pass an examination before a committee of three out of the twelve sergeants.

In New York, a Bar Association had existed from about 1745 to 1770; but little is known of it, and its records are not now extant. In the middle of the Century, the members of the Bar, to prevent inroads upon their practise, made an agreement not to receive into their offices, as clerks, any young men who intended to pursue the law as a profession. This rule did not long prevail; for it was

[1] *Rules of the Court*, by Joseph B. Walker, — *Southern New Hampshire Bar Ass. Proc.*, Vol. IV. See also *Proceedings of Grafton and Coos County Bar Ass.* (1891).

found that it would tend to cause young men to leave the Colony to study — as for instance, John Jay, whose father had decided to send him to England, but changed his mind when the Bar revoked its rule, and placed him in the office of Benjamin Kissam. In 1797, the Supreme Court of New York adopted rules, requiring a period of seven years' study, in the office of a practising attorney, before admission to practise; but a period not exceeding four years spent on classical studies might be credited on the seven years.[1] After four (changed to three in 1804) years' practise as attorney, or study under direction of a professor or counsellor, a person might be admitted as a counsellor to practise before the Supreme Court.

In Maryland, three years' study under inspection of some practising attorney or judge was required, and also an examination by two gentlemen of the Bar.

In Delaware, three years' study was prescribed.

In Pennsylvania, by rule of the Supreme Court in 1788, the requirements were, four years' study as a clerk and one year's practise in the Court of Common Pleas, or three years' clerkship and two years' practise and examination by two attorneys; or two years' clerkship after twenty-one years of age and two years' practise, and examination.

In Virginia, only one year's study was required.

In South Carolina, a candidate must pass an examination, unless he had served four years as attorney's clerk.

In Massachusetts, New York, and New Jersey, the old distinction between attorneys and counsellors existed. In the other States, there were no such separate classes of lawyers; but, in all of them, two years' practise before the inferior court was prescribed before admission was granted to practise in the higher court.

[1] For complete account, see *Admission to the Bar in New York — Yale Law Journal*, Vol. XVI (1906).

In two States, law clubs had existed for the promotion of social intercourse in the profession.

Thus, in Massachusetts, "The Sodality" was formed in 1765, with Otis, Gridley, Quincy, and Adams as its leading spirits, of which Otis said:

"Let us form our style upon the ancient and best English authorities. I hope, I expect to see at the Bar, in consequence of this Sodality, a purity, an eloquence, and a spirit surpassing anything that has ever appeared in America."

In New York, in 1770, "The Moot" was founded, as a club "to encourage a more profound and ample study of the civil law, historical and political jurisprudence, and the law of nature." Its most active member was William Livingston, and the "father of the Bar," Samuel Jones. Other veterans — Kissam, Smith, Scott, and Morris — used to attend, while the junior members of prominence were John Jay, Egbert Benson, Richard Morris Smith, Robert R. Livingston, Stephen DeLancey, and Lindley Murray. Many learned questions were seriously discussed; and it is said that a Chief Justice of the Superior Court once sent an issue of law to the Moot for its advice. Its last meeting was on January 6, 1775.[1]

One other feature in the practise of the profession in these early years, which disappeared later, had a marked influence on the lawyer's development — the close, personal relationship which the members of the Bar bore to each other.

This is well described in a letter from John Adams to his nephew William Cranch (the Supreme Court Reporter), of March 14, 1790.

"To the original of the Bar meetings I was a witness. . . . They introduced a candor and liberality in the practice

[1] See *The Republican Court*, by Rufus W. Griswold (1855).

of the Bar that was never before known in Mass. Mr. Pratt was so sensible of their utility that when we took leave of him at Dedham, his last words to us were, 'Brethren, forsake not the assembling of yourselves together. My advice to you and all the young gentlemen coming up, as well as to those now on the stage, is never to suffer such meetings to go into disuse, let who will clamor about them.' . . . What? is it unlawful for the gentlemen of the profession to spend an evening together once a week? to converse upon law and upon their practice; to bear complaints of unkind, unfair and ungentlemanlike practice; to compare difference; to agree that they will not introduce ignorant, illiterate, or ill bred, or unprincipled students or candidates; that they will not practice any kind of chicanery, or take unmanly disadvantages of one another, to the injury of clients, for accidental or inadvertent slips in pleading or otherwise?"

And again he wrote:

"Many of these meetings were the most delightful entertainments I ever enjoyed. The spirit that reigned was that of sense, generosity, honor, and integrity; and the consequences were most happy; for the courts and the Bar, instead of scenes of wrangling, chicanery, quibbling and ill manners, were soon converted into order, decency, truth and candor. Mr. Pratt was so delighted with these meetings and other effects, that when we all waited upon him to Dedham on his way to New York to take his seat as Chief Justice of that State, he said to us, Brethren, above all things forsake not the assembling of yourselves together."

The intimacy and gaiety of the intercourse between the Bar and the Bench, is shown in the account of the conditions surrounding James Sullivan's practise in Massachusetts and Maine in the latter part of the Eighteenth Century.[1]

"Professional habits were decidedly convivial, and gentlemen thrown together for several weeks, often under

[1] *Life and Writings of James Sullivan*, by R. G. Amory.

the same roof, were quite disposed to be amused. The manners of the judges were not only decorous, and the members of the Bar were courteous and well-bred; but in their familiar intercourse there was little formality or restraint and their festivities were seasons of wit and frolic, and often sufficiently uproarious. When the business of the term was nearly completed, it was customary for both Bench and Bar to assemble at the tavern for a social meeting. On these occasions, they constituted a court among themselves, appointing one of their number Chief Justice, for the trial of all breaches of good fellowship during the term. Judge Sewall describes one of these meetings at Biddeford, when the inferior court was sitting at Ladd's Tavern, there being no court-house in the place. John Lowell had arrived, late on Monday evening, to attend its sessions, and, finding the inn full, sought lodgings elsewhere, probably at his friend Sullivan's, where he was always a welcome guest. He left his horse tied at the inn door, expecting it would be properly cared for; but the landlord never gave it a thought. When, on Friday evening, a court was held for the hearing of all omissions and commissions which had occurred during the week, Ladd was called upon to answer for leaving the horse unattended to, and defended himself on the plea that he had received no orders to put him up. The case was tried with becoming gravity, and the judge, upon the evidence, sentenced Ladd to pay a single bowl of good punch for his neglect, and Lowell twice as much for not taking care of his own steed."

And the same conviviality existed in the other States, as Kennedy's description of the Virginia Circuits, during the early life of William Wirt, shows: [1]

"The riding of the Circuit, which always brought several into company, and the adventures of the wayside, gave to the Bar a sportive and lighthearted love of association which greatly fostered the opportunity and the inclination for convivial pleasure. A day spent upon the road on

[1] *Memoirs of the Life of William Wirt*, Vol. I, by John P. Kennedy (1849).

horseback, the customary visits made to friends upon the way, the jest and the song, the unchecked vivacity inspired by this grouping together of kindred spirits — all had their share in imparting brotherhood. Then the contests of the Bar which followed in the forum, the occasions they afforded for the display of wit and eloquence, and the congratulations of friends were so many additional provocatives to that indulgence which found free scope, when evening brought all together under one roof, to rehearse their pleasant adventures and to set flowing the currents of mirth and good humor, 'to make a night of it' as the phrase goes. The Bar yet retains some of these characteristics; but the present generation (1849) may but feebly conceive the pervading and careless joyousness with which in that early time the members of their mirthful craft pursued their business through a country side. . . . The present generation will bear witness to many an ancient green room joke of the circuit."

In fact, many older lawyers have been of the opinion that the largest and best part of the legal education of the past was this mingling of the whole Bar together in travelling from county to county, and from court to court, the enforced personal relations which were brought about, and the presence of the younger members of the Bar during the trials of cases by their seniors.

"An able Bar," said Hugh Blair Grigsby, of Virginia, in his eulogy of L. W. Tazewell, "is the best school of law; for of all lessons for a student, the contests of able men with each other in the practical game of life are the best."

Perhaps nowhere was this side of a lawyer's training better summed up than in the words by Senator George F. Hoar (writing, it is true, of a later period of practise (1845–1855, but of a period which had not entirely lost the old characteristics): [1]

[1] *Autobiography of Seventy Years*, by George F. Hoar, Vol. II.

"The judge and jurymen and the lawyers from out of town used to come into Worcester and stay at the old Sykes or Thomas Tavern.

"The court sat till six o'clock and often far into the evening and began at half past eight or nine — so there was no chance for country lawyers to go home at night. There was great fun at these old taverns in the evening and at meal time. . . . The whole Bar and the public seemed to take an interest in important trials. People came in from the country round about with their covered wagon, simply for the pleasure of attending court and seeing the champions contend with each other. The lawyers who were not engaged in the case were always ready to help those who were, with advice and suggestion. It used to be expected that members of the Bar would be in the court house hearing the trials, even if they were not engaged in them. . . . I cannot but think that the listening to the trial and argument of causes by skilful advocates was a better law school than any we have now and that our young men especially in the large cities fail to become good advocates and to learn the art of putting on a case and of examining and cross examining for want of a constant and faithful attendance on the courts."

A similar glimpse of the sociability of the judges and the lawyers, written of a later period, but descriptive of the earlier is to be found in the Diary of Richard Henry Dana, Jr.[1]

"March 10, 1853. Court at Dedham. We have very pleasant times here at the trials. The judge, the sheriff and the members of the Bar from out of town board together at the hotel; the judge sitting at the head of the table, and the sheriff at the foot, the lawyers seating themselves by a tacit understanding according to age and importance, and there is a good deal of pleasant conversation. At dinner there will often be a stray guest from Boston, who has come up to make a motion or look after his docket. Choate, Bartlett and Hallett dropped in on us

[1] *Richard Henry Dana*, by C. F. Adams, Vol. I (1891).

this week. Here, too, is the remnant of the old style in which the courts used to be received. The sheriff with a long white rod comes to the tavern and stands by the door and precedes the judge on his way to court and into his seat, and in the same way conducts him back at the adjournment each day."

# PART TWO

## FEDERAL BAR

# CHAPTER X

## PREJUDICES AGAINST LAW AND LAWYERS

The preceding chapters have shown how, at the time of the War of the Revolution, in each of the American Colonies a Bar had developed, composed of trained and able lawyers. The old antipathies towards the "attorneys," against whom so much legislation had been directed, in the earlier years had died away, for the character and talents of the men who undertook the practise of the profession had so distinctly changed.

The services rendered by the legal profession in the defence and maintenance of the people's rights and liberties, from the middle of the Eighteenth Century to the adoption of the Constitution, had been well recognized by the people in making a choice of their representatives; for of the fifty-six Signers of the Declaration of Independence, twenty-five were lawyers; and of the fifty-five members of the Federal Constitutional Convention, thirty-one were lawyers, of whom four had studied in the Inner Temple, and one at Oxford, under Blackstone.[1] In the First Congress, ten of the twenty-nine Senators and seventeen of the sixty-five Representatives were lawyers.

The rise of the real American Bar, however, was coincident with the birth of the Nation; and its history may be conveniently divided into three eras. The first begins

[1] *The Supreme Court of the United States*, by Hampton L. Carson. See also *Influence of the Bar in our State and Federal Government*, by J. H. Benton, Jr. (1894).

with the year 1789 and ends with the close of the War of 1812 — a period marked by the growth of the early Federal Bars composed chiefly of lawyers from Pennsylvania, Maryland and Virginia, by the initiation of law schools, and by the masterful work of the great jurists of the Bars in New York and in the New England States who laid so solidly the foundations of the real American Common Law. The second period comprises the years from 1815 to 1830 — the reign of Chief Justice Marshall — when the Federal Bar was composed of the legal giants from the Bars of all the States. The third period ends with the outbreak of the Civil War, covering roughly the years of ferment in the law, when the chief task before the legal profession was the great one of reformation, of adjusting the Common Law to meet the flood of changing conditions — social, economic and political — for which these years were notable.

While the American Bar developed great lawyers and great judges in the period from 1789 to 1815, there were three obstacles to its growth and to the study of law as a science. These obstructive factors were: first, the unpopularity of lawyers as a class; second, the bitter feeling against England and English Common Law; third, the lack of any distinct body of American law, arising from the non-existence of American law reports and law books.

Nothing in legal history is more curious than the sudden revival, after the War of the Revolution, of the old dislike and distrust of lawyers as a class. For a time, it seemed as if their great services had been forgotten and as if their presence was to be deemed an injury to the Nation. There were several contributing causes, however, which occasioned this outbreak of popular feeling.

In the first place, a large number of the most eminent and older members of the Bar, being Royalists, had either left the country,[1] or retired from practise. Thus, Maryland was deprived of two of her greatest advocates, Daniel Dulany and George Chalmers; Pennsylvania lost John Galloway; New York lost William Smith, Jr., Thomas Barclay and John Tabor Kempe; New Jersey lost Josiah Ogden. In Massachusetts, the losses to the Bar from this cause were especially heavy. The situation was graphically described in 1824 by William Sullivan, from his personal recollections.[2]

"Thirteen of the Bar, . . . were Royalists and left the country; and among them Jonathan Sewall, then Attorney-General, a man held in high esteem for professional talent; and Sampson Salter Blowers, who enjoyed an honorable reputation as a lawyer and the esteem of many affectionate friends; Samuel Quincy, Timothy Ruggles and James Putnam. Some who remained were neutral, so far as they could be, consistently with safety. The Royalists who departed, and those who remained, are not to be censured at this day, for conscientious adherence to the mother country. The former had little reason to rejoice in the course which they adopted. Few received such reward for loyalty as they expected. Some exchanged eminence in the Province for appointments, such as they were, in the Colonies; and some ease and comfort here, for insignificance and obscurity at home. Most of them deeply regretted their abandonment of their native land. Such effect had the Revolution on the members of the Bar, that the list of 1779 comprised only ten barristers and four attorneys, for the whole State, who were such before the Revolution."[3]

[1] See *Loyalists of the American Revolution*, by Lorenzo Sabine (1864).

It is to be remembered that in the American Colonies 25,000 Loyalists, at the least computation, took up arms for the King. Sabine gives sketches of the lives of at least 130 lawyers who left the country as Tories; and there were several hundred other lawyers whose lives were not of sufficient note to describe, but who also became refugees.

[2] *Address to Suffolk County Bar*, by William Sullivan (1825).

[3] Emory Washburn said that in 1775, when Levi Lincoln (Harvard 1772)

Of the lawyers who remained, many were either actively engaged in politics or in the army; while others had accepted positions on the bench.

This left the practise of the law very largely in the hands of lawyers of a lower grade and inferior ability.

Meanwhile, the social and financial conditions of the country after the Revolution tended to produce great unrest. Interruption of business by the war, and high prices, had brought about embarrassment in all classes, and an inability to meet their debts. Great Britain, in closing her ports by navigation laws and prohibitory duties, had deprived the American industries of employment. Public debts were enormous, necessitating ruinous taxation. The Federal Government owed to its soldiers large sums, and payment in the paper money of the time was farcical. The Tories whose estates had been confiscated were returning and making strenuous efforts to have their property restored. English creditors were trying to recover their claims, barred by various statutes of confiscation and sequestration.

The chief law business, therefore, was the collection of debts and the enforcement of contracts; and the jails were filled to overflowing with men imprisoned for debt under the rigorous laws of the times.[1]

Irritated by this excessive litigation, by the increase of suits on debts and mortgage foreclosures, and by the system of fees and court costs established by the Bar Associations,

settled in Worcester County, only two lawyers remained in the county, the rest having left the country.

See *Mass. Hist. Soc. Proc.*, Vol. XI (1869).

[1] In the little rural county of Worcester, Massachusetts, having a population of less than 5,000, there were at one time more than 2,000 actions on the docket of the Inferior Court of Common Pleas.

See for an excellent account of the condition of affairs at this time, from a lawyer's standpoint, the *Life of James Sullivan*, by T. G. Amory.

the people at large mistook effects for cause; and attributed all their evils to the existence of lawyers in the community. Thus, in the conservative little town of Braintree, close to Boston, the citizens in town meeting, in 1786, voted that:

"We humbly request that there may be such laws compiled as may crush or at least put a proper check or restraint on that order of Gentlemen denominated Lawyers, the completion of whose modern conduct appears to us to tend rather to the destruction than the preservation of the town." [1]

Another small town, Dedham, instructed its representatives in the Legislature as follows:

"We are not inattentive to the almost universally prevailing complaints against the practice of the order of lawyers; and many of us now sensibly feel the effects of their unreasonable and extravagant exactions; we think their practice pernicious and their mode unconstitutional. You will therefore endeavor that such regulations be introduced into our Courts of Law, and that such restraints be laid on the order of lawyers as that we may have recourse to the Laws and find our security and not our ruin in them. If upon a fair discussion and mature deliberation such a measure should appear impracticable, you are to endeavor that the order of Lawyers be totally abolished; an alternative preferable to their continuing in their present mode."

Other communities were more radical, and demanded the complete abolition of the legal profession.

Such was the popular discontent arising from all these conditions, that, in Massachusetts, an open rebellion broke out, in 1787 (the well-known Shays' Rebellion), directed

[1] *Three Episodes of Massachusetts History*, by Charles Francis Adams. See also Remarks of Charles Francis Adams, in *Proceedings of The American Antiquarian Society* (October, 1902).

largely against the courts and the lawyers, and requiring to be put down by military force.

As McMaster says:[1]

"The lawyers were overwhelmed with cases. The courts could not try half that came to them. For every man who had an old debt, a mortgage or a claim against a Tory or Refugee, hastened to have it adjusted. While, therefore, everyone else was idle, the lawyers were busy; and as they always exacted a retainer, and were sure to obtain their fees, grew rich fast. Every young man became an attorney, and every attorney did well. Such prosperity soon marked them as fit subjects for the discontented to vent their anger on. They were denounced as banditti, as blood-suckers, as pickpockets, as windbags, as smooth-tongued rogues. Those who having no cases had little cause to complain of the lawyers, murmured that it was a gross outrage to tax them to pay for the sittings of courts into which they had never brought and never would bring an action. . . . The mere sight of a lawyer . . . was enough to call forth an oath or a muttered curse from the louts who hung around the tavern."

McRee, in his Life of James Iredell, thus describes conditions in South Carolina:[2]

"The return of the Tories, and their strenuous efforts to procure the restoration of their property, the activity of the lawyers, stimulated by the opening of a lucrative career; the commencement of new, the revival of long dormant suits — all conspired to foster exasperation, cupidity, avarice, revenge. . . . A very violent prejudice, at this period, existed in narrow and vulgar minds against the legal profession. This antipathy was fermented by many persons of more talent and less principle as a means of destroying those whom they feared as rivals, and as an instrument by which they might effect their political ends. The lawyers of the State were generally conservatives;

[1] *History of the People of the United States*, by J. B. McMaster, Vol. I.

[2] *Life and Times of James Iredell*, by Griffith J. McRee.

hence it was that they excited, in addition to other causes, the animosity of the radicals; and in a signal degree the hatred of those who may be distinctively and exclusively characterized as demagogues, charlatans and political tricksters."

The *Letters of an American Farmer*, written in 1787, by H. St. John Crevecoeur, also express the sentiment of the time:

"Lawyers are plants that will grow in any soil that is cultivated by the hands of others, and when once they have taken root they will extinguish every vegetable that grows around them. The fortunes they daily acquire in every province from the misfortunes of their fellow citizens are surprising. The most ignorant, the most bungling member of that profession will, if placed in the most obscure part of the country, promote litigiousness and amass more wealth than the most opulent farmer with all his toil. . . . What a pity that our forefathers who happily extinguished so many fatal customs and expunged from their new government so many errors and abuses both religious and civil, did not also prevent the introduction of a set of men so dangerous. . . . The value of our laws and the spirit of freedom which often tends to make us litigious must necessarily throw the greatest part of the property of the Colonies into the hands of these gentlemen. In another century, the law will possess in the North what now the church possesses in Peru and Mexico."

Much the same conditions prevailed in all the States. In New Hampshire and in Vermont there were the same widespread outcries that the courts should be abolished, that the number of lawyers was too large, that the profession should be entirely suppressed, that their fees should be cut down, that the payment of debts and the foreclosure of mortgages should be postponed by "stay acts," until debtors could pay. There were numerous riots. The debtors of Vermont set fire to their court-houses; those of New Jersey nailed up their doors. Lawyers were mobbed in the streets, and judges threatened.

In Rhode Island, an act providing for payment of debts in paper money was held unconstitutional, in 1786, in the famous case of *Trevett* v. *Weeden;* whereupon the Legislature passed an act prohibiting lawyers from practising unless they took the test oath, agreeing to take paper money at par.

When the great debates were going on in the various State conventions, in 1787–1789, regarding the adoption of the Constitution, much of the opposition of the anti-Constitution men, or Anti-Federalists as they were later called, was due to the fact that the proposed Constitution "was the work of lawyers." [1]

For nearly thirty years after the Revolution, constant efforts were made in many States to mitigate the evil and the supposed monopoly of lawyers by abolishing the system of bar-call and fees established by courts or Bar Associations.

In Massachusetts, acts were passed, in 1785 and 1786, authorizing parties to a suit to argue their own causes in court and forbidding the employment of more than two lawyers by either party. Plans for law reform were urged even by prominent members of the Bar, such as John Gardiner [2] — to the disquiet, however, of most of their fellow members. Through Gardiner's influence, resolutions were introduced into the Legislature, in 1790, to in-

[1] See Elliot's *Debates on the Constitution.*

[2] John Gardiner was born in Boston in 1731, and removed to England, where he studied law and was called as a barrister at the Inner Temple. He became an intimate acquaintance of Lord Mansfield, appeared as junior counsel for the defendant in the famous John Wilkes case, and also for Beardmore and Meredith, two of the publishers indicted with Wilkes. He removed to the Island of Saint Christopher, where he became Attorney-General; thence he came to Boston in 1783.

vestigate "the present state of the law and its professors in the Commonwealth." A statute was enacted authorizing parties to empower under seal any person whom they chose, whether regular attorney or not, to manage their causes.

Perhaps the most powerful attacks on the "dangerous" and "pernicious" "order" of lawyers and their "malpractices, delays and extravagant fees" were the letters of Benjamin Austin, an able pamphleteer and Anti-Federalist politician of Boston, who wrote, in 1786, under the name of "Honestus," and whose letters had a widespread influence:

"The distresses of the people are now great, but if we examine particularly we shall find them owing in a great measure to the conduct of some practitioners of law. . . . Why this intervening order? The law and evidence are all the essentials required, and are not the judges with the jury competent for these purposes? . . .

"The question is whether we will have this order so far established in this Commonwealth as to rule over us. . . . The order is becoming continually more and more powerful. . . . There is danger of lawyers becoming formidable as a combined body. The people should be guarded against it as it might subvert every principle of law and establish a perfect aristocracy. . . . This order of men should be annihilated. . . . No lawyers should be admitted to speak in court, and the order be abolished as not only a useless but a dangerous body to the public."

The remedies he proposed were (*a*) an American code of law; (*b*) parties to appear in person or by any friend whether attorney or not; (*c*) referees, to take the place of courts; (*d*) a State Advocate-General, to appear for all persons indicted.[1]

[1] See *Observations on the Pernicious Practice of the Law by Honestus (Benjamin Austin) as Published occasionally in the Independent Chronicle in Boston in 1786* (1819).

The situation in Massachusetts was described by John Quincy Adams, when a senior in College, in 1787, as follows:[1]

"At a time when the profession of the law is laboring under the heavy weight of popular indignation; when it is upbraided as the original cause of all the evils with which the Commonwealth is distressed; when the Legislature have been publicly exhorted by a popular writer to abolish it entirely, and when the mere title of lawyer is sufficient to deprive a man of the public confidence, it should seem this profession would afford but a poor subject for panegyric; but its real ability is not to be determined by the short-lived frenzy of an inconsiderate multitude nor by the artful misrepresentations of an insidious writer."

And further in a letter to his mother, in December, 1787:

"The popular odium which has been excited against the practitioners in this Commonwealth prevails to so great a degree that the most innocent and irreproachable life cannot guard a lawyer against the hatred of his fellow citizens. The very despicable writings of Honestus were just calculated to kindle a flame which will subsist long after they are forgotten. . . . A thousand lies in addition to these published in the papers have been spread all over the country to prejudice the people against the 'order,' as it has invidiously been called; and as a free people will not descend to disguise their sentiments, the gentlemen of the profession have been treated with contemptuous neglect and with insulting abuse. Yet notwithstanding all this, the profession is rapidly increasing in numbers, and the little business to be done is divided into so many shares that they are in danger of starving one another; when I consider the disadvantages which are in a degree peculiar to the present time . . . I confess I am sometimes almost discouraged and ready to wish I had engaged in some other line of life."

[1] *Diary of John Quincy Adams — Mass. Hist. Soc. Proc.*, 2d Series, Vol. XVI (1902).

Even as late as 1803–1806, the public dissatisfaction, in Pennsylvania, against the legal profession and the judicial system generally, culminated in a series of statutes, which, in the language of an old lawyer of that State, "betray a more anxious than wise desire to make every man his own lawyer. . . . Then the Common Law was looked on with jealousy and the profession of the law regarded with distrust." [1]

These statutes provided an elaborate machinery by which a party having a claim or debt might file a statement in court, the other party might file an answer in informal shape, and thereupon the case should proceed to judgment without the intervention of counsel. Provisions were also made for decision of cases by arbitrators.

An interesting reference to the state of affairs is found in a letter of Charles Jared Ingersoll, of Philadelphia, in December, 1803: [2]

> "I am jogging on my professional path. My father nudges me along, and the Governor has given me a publick room adjoining the court, where I have established my desk and arm-chair. . . . Our State rulers threaten to lop away that excrescence on civilization, the Bar; and Counsellor Ingersoll declares he 'll go to New York. All the eminent lawyers have their eyes on one city or another, to remove to in case of extremes."

One of the most powerful attacks upon lawyers and the system of law administration, and an attack which represented the general popular attitude, was a pamphlet written by William Duane of Philadelphia entitled "*Sampson Against the Philistines or the Reformation of Lawsuits and Justice made cheap, speedy and brought home to every man's door agreeably to the Principles of the Ancient Trial by Jury*

[1] *Discourse before the Law Academy*, by R. McCall (1838).

[2] *Life of Charles Jared Ingersoll*, by William M. Meigs.

*before the same was innovated by Judges and Lawyers,"* published in 1804–1805. Duane was the editor of the Republican newspaper organ, the *Aurora;* and to his vigorous but rancorous pen Jefferson attributed in large part his election to the presidency. He had himself been tried for seditious riot in Philadelphia, in 1799, and acquitted — a case growing out of the unpopular Alien and Sedition Acts.

The following extracts illuminate clearly the popular sentiments regarding lawyers. It is interesting to note that Duane calls the profession "our national aristocracy," a phrase repeated thirty years later by De Tocqueville:

"The profession of the law assumes in every State a political consequence, which, considering the use which is made of it, has become truly a subject of the most serious concern; the loose principles of persons of that profession; their practice of defending right and wrong indifferently for reward; their open enmity to the principles of free government, because free government is irreconcilable to the abuses upon which they thrive; the tyranny which they display in the courts; and in too many cases the obvious understanding and collusion which prevails among the members of the bench, the bar, and the officers of the court, demand the most serious interference of the legislature and the jealousy of the people. . . .

"A privileged order or class, to whom the administration of justice is given as a support, first employ their art and influence to gain legislation; they then so manage legislation as never to injure themselves; and they so manage justice as to engross the general property to themselves through the medium of litigation; and the misfortune is, that to be able to effect this point, it is attended by loss of time, by delay, expense, ill blood, bad habits, lessons of fraud and temptation to villainy, crimes, punishments, loss of estate, character and soul, public burden, and even loss of national character."

Duane then compared the mystery with which the old

English clergy surrounded the Bible before it was printed in English to the "farrago of finesse and intricacy and abstruseness" to which the lawyers had brought the science of law.

His remedy was to promote speedy trials by confining the courts to local and county tribunals with scant and difficult right of appeal, and "if a lawyer should be thought necessary, let him be appointed and paid by government to assist to arrange and represent each party's cause to the jury." He also advocated a radical extension of a system of arbitration. He pointed out that when unbefogged by the sophistries of professionals, the law was not so mysterious and intricate as it seemed, and that if there were no lawyers, every man might acquire law for himself:

> "So long as justice can be demanded only by professional lawyers, so long will the knowledge of it be the exclusive property of the profession, and none will think it worth while to read what to him appears useless. If, on the contrary, it was not necessary to employ these professors to ask for justice, law would soon become a part of academic study, and no youth would leave college without reading Blackstone and Wilson; they would bring home their books of law, with their books of history, geography and ancient languages. By this means, and the practice every man would find in his private business, in helping his neighborhood to settle and adjust disputes, etc., society would be prodigiously advanced in knowledge and respectability of talents for legislators and statesmen."

In fact, one of the leading causes for this popular odium of the profession was the general feeling that the intricacies of special pleading which made the law so mysterious and unintelligible to laymen, the technicalities of the old Common Law, and the jargon of Latin, French and unfamiliar terms in which it was so often expressed were all tricks of the trade, designed and purposely kept in force by the Bar, in order to make acquisition of a knowledge of the law difficult to the public, and in order to constitute themselves a privileged class and monopoly.

As early as 1764, Governor Colden of New York had expressed this feeling in a letter to the Earl of Halifax:

"I have often thought that lawyers have introduced misteries and absurdities into their law forms that mankind in general who are not lawyers may not in such cases have the use of their own reason, in judging of them."

In a sketch of Chief Justice Parsons, written in 1821, the popular conception of the attitude of lawyers towards the community in 1774 is thus described:[1]

"When Parsons came to the Bar, in every case of importance, all was thought to depend on the learning, sagacity, cunning and eloquence of counsel. It would have been in vain for any one man to have attempted a reformation, for most practitioners at that period would have united against a change, from the mistaken idea that business depended on giving an air of mystery to the proceedings of the profession; forgetting that no science, however difficult to attain, has any mystery in its farthest researches or in its remotest principles. It can hardly be believed at this day, but it is a fact, that many old lawyers, who were in full practice when Blackstone's *Commentaries* first appeared in the country, were frequently heard to regret and complain that he should have so simplified and arranged his subject, and so clearly explained the principles of law, that the same amount of knowledge, which had cost them many years to collect, might be obtained in a short time."

Parallel with this animosity against lawyers as a class was the prejudice against the system of English Common Law on which the courts based their decisions — a prejudice

[1] *Biographical Sketches of Great Lawyers and Statesmen,* by Samuel L. Knapp (1821).

felt, not only by many intelligent as well as unintelligent laymen, but also by many American lawyers themselves.

After the Revolution, there had been much discussion in the courts as to the extent to which the Common Law of England was binding. Some States had expressly adopted, in their Constitutions, such parts of the Common Law as formed the law of the Colonies prior to 1775 or 1776 or to the date of the State Constitution — New York, New Jersey, Delaware, Maryland, Rhode Island, New Hampshire. In other States there had been much feeling of uneasiness until some authoritative declaration should be made.[1]

All parties, of course, agreed that English law, since the Revolution, had no binding force whatever; but many of the Anti-Federalists claimed that the English law prior to the Revolution had no force in the United States except and by virtue of these express Constitutions and statutes.

They sought to eliminate entirely English law from the United States; and their position is well stated in a letter of Jefferson to John Tyler, Judge of the United States District Court in Virginia, written in 1812:[2]

"I deride with you the ordinary doctrine that we brought with us from England the Common Law rights. This narrow notion was a favorite in the first moment of rallying to our rights against Great Britain. But it was that of men who felt their rights before they had thought of their explanation. The truth is that we brought with us the rights of men. On our arrival here, the question would at once arise, by what law will we govern ourselves. The resolution seems to have been, by that system with

[1] *The Adoption of the Common Law by the American Colonies* — *Amer. Law Register*, Vol. XXI (1882).

As to how far the Common Law has been adopted in the various States, see *Amer. and Eng. Encycl. of Law*, 2d ed., Vol. VI, p. 286, note 3.

[2] *Letters and Times of the Tylers*, by Lyon G. Tyler, Vol. I (1884).

which we are familiar, to be altered by ourselves occasionally and adapted to our new situation. . . . The state of the English law at the date of our emigration constituted the system adopted here. We may doubt, therefore, the propriety of quoting in our courts English authorities subsequent to that adoption, still more the admission of authorities posterior to the Declaration of Independence, or rather to the accession of that King whose reign *ab initio* was that every tissue of wrongs which rendered the Declaration at length necessary. . . . This relation to the beginning of his reign would add the advantage of getting us rid of all Mansfield's innovations."

Tyler himself, when Governor of Virginia, in a message to the Legislature, had spoken of

"the unfortunate practice of quoting lengthy and numerous British cases; the time of the court being taken up in reconciling absurd and contradictory opinions of foreign judges which certainly can be no part of an American judge's duty. . . . Shall we forever administer our free republican government on the principles of a rigid and high toned monarchy?"

And when he became a Federal judge, he used his utmost endeavor to eradicate the influence of English law, precedents and citations; and he held that:

"As soon as we had cut asunder the ligatures that bound us together as parent and children, the Common Law was done away until we saw fit to establish so much of it as did not contravene our republican system."

Francis Xavier Martin in the preface to his collection of the English statutes in force in North Carolina in 1792, said:

"It will at least disseminate the knowledge of a number of laws by which this people of this State are to be governed; until, substituting acts of their own legislature to those their forefathers brought over from Great Britain, they will shake off this last seeming badge and mortifying memento of their dependence on her."

At political dinners and meetings, toasts like the following were of frequent occurrence — "The Common Law of England: may wholesome statutes soon root out this engine of oppression from America."[1]

It was this same spirit which led the New Hampshire judges of the Supreme Court (1785–1800) to put to rout counsel arguing before them, by declining to listen to citations from "musty, old worm-eaten books," and by stating that "not Common Law — not the quirks of Coke and Blackstone but common sense" should control their decisions.

And as James Kent said of his early experience on the bench:

"We had but few American precedents. One judge was democratic, and my brother, Spencer, particularly of a bold, vigorous, dogmatic mind and overbearing manner. English authority did not stand very high in these early feverish times, and this led me a hundred times to bear down opposition or shame it by exhaustive research and overwhelming authority."

It was from this anti-English sentiment in New York that at least one lasting and invaluable addition to American law was made, in the introduction by Kent of civil law principles, of which he wrote:

"Between 1799 and 1804, I read *Valin* and *Emerigon*, and completely abridged the latter. . . . I made much use of the *Corpus Juris*, and as the judges (Livingston excepted) knew nothing of French or Civil law I had immense advantage over them. I could generally put my brethren to rout and carry my point by my mysterious

1 See account of the Fourth of July celebration in Cambridge in the *Columbian Centinel* (Boston, July 11, 1801).

wand of French and Civil law. The judges were Republicans and very kindly disposed to everything that was French and this enabled me without exciting any alarm or jealousy to make free use of such authorities and thereby enrich our commercial law."

Many lawyers as well as laymen felt that what was needed was a law wholly and strictly American. Thus wrote Benjamin Austin:

"Instead of the numerous codes of British law, we should adopt a concise system, calculated upon the plainest principles and agreeable to our Republican government. This would render useless hundreds of volumes which only serve to make practice mysterious. . . .

"One reason of the pernicious practice of the law and what gives great influence to the 'order' is that we have introduced the whole body of English laws into our courts. Why should these States be governed by British laws? Can the monarchical and aristocratical institutions of England be consistent with the republican principles of our Constitution? . . . We may as well adopt the laws of the Medes and Persians. . . . The numerous precedents brought from 'old English authorities' serve to embarrass all our judiciary causes and answer no other purpose than to increase the influence of lawyers."

Mingled with the antagonism to anything savoring of England and monarchy in our law was another factor, the influence of which was felt in the decisions of the United States courts for nearly seventy-five years of our early jurisprudence — namely, the jealousy of the individual States at any infringement by the National Government on their State jurisdiction. In the early cases brought before the Federal courts, the doctrine was upheld that these courts were bound by the Common Law of England as the national Common Law of this country.

In 1793, Judges Jay, Wilson, Iredell and District Judge Peters held all violations of treaties were indictable without a Federal statute; almost at the same time, before Judges Iredell, Wilson and Peters, an American was indicted at Common Law, for sending threatening letters to the British Minister.[1] In 1794, it was also laid down as law by Judge Iredell, in a charge to the Grand Jury, and by Chief Justice Jay in a case in Pennsylvania.

"Such was the state of the law when Judge Chase, in *U. S.* v. *Worrall* (2 Dall.), in 1798 (Chief Justice Jay, Judge Wilson and Judge Iredell being no longer on the Bench, and Chief Justice Ellsworth being abroad), without waiting to learn what had been decided by his predecessors, startled both his colleagues and the Bar by announcing that he would entertain no indictments at Common Law. No reports being then or for a long time afterwards published, of the prior rulings to the contrary, it is not to be wondered that the judges who came on the Bench after Judge Chase supposed that he stated the practice correctly."[2]

This decision, as stated above, caused an immense excitement among lawyers, and many protests were made against it by those of Federalist politics, who lamented this denial of Common Law jurisdiction. Their feeling

[1] See *Henfield's Case* in *Wharton's State Trials*, p. 49; *Wharton's State Trials*, p. 651; *Lives of the Chief Justices*, by G. Van Santvoord; *Constitutional Law*, by T. Sergeant (1822). See also *Federal Common Law* in *Virginia Law Register* (1904).

[2] See Wharton's *Criminal Law*, Vol. I, p. 168.

P. S. DuPonceau wrote in 1824 that: "This decision of Judge Chase made a great noise at the time and left vague but strong impressions, the more so as he was known to be a man of deep learning and considerable strength of mind, and more disposed to extend than to limit power."

See also *Review of DuPonceau's Dissertation on the Nature and Extent of the Jurisdiction of the Courts of the United States, April 22, 1824*, by Charles J. Davies, in *North Amer. Review*, Vol. XXI (1825), in which he says: "The opinion of Judge Chase seems to have been reverenced as a sort of perpetual edict."

was expressed, as late as 1820, by John Quincy Adams in his Diary, in his view of the life of Samuel Chase:[1]

"I considered Mr. Chase as one of the men whose life, conduct, and opinion had been of the most extensive influence upon the Constitution of this country. . . . He himself as a Judge had settled other (principles) of the highest importance — one of them in my opinion of very pernicious importance. He decided, as I think, directly in the face of an amendatory article of the Constitution of the United States (the seventh) that the Union in its federative capacity has no Common Law — a decision which has crippled the powers not only of the Judiciary but of all the Departments of the National Government. The reasons upon which he rested that decision are not sound, but, as they flattered the popular prejudices, it has remained unreversed to this day."

Equally strenuous, however, were the opponents of such Common Law jurisdiction; and Jefferson wrote to Edmund Randolph, August 18, 1799:[2]

"Of all the doctrines which have ever been broached by the Federal government the novel one, of the Common Law being in force and cognizable as an existing law in their courts, is to me the most formidable. All their other assumptions of un-given powers have been in the detail. The bank law, the treaty doctrine, the sedition act, the alien act, the undertaking to change the State laws of evidence in the State courts by certain parts of the stamp act, etc., etc., have been solitary, inconsequential, timid things in comparison with the audacious, barefaced and sweeping pretension to a system of law for the United States without the adoption of their Legislature, and so

[1] *Diary of John Quincy Adams*, Vol. V, Dec. 18, 1820. See also W. Rawle's *Constitution of the United States*, in which, as late as 1825, he strenuously sustained the doctrine that the United States courts possessed a Common Law criminal jurisdiction.

[2] See also letters of November, 1785, August 19, 1799, October 29, 1799, June 12, 1817, in *Writings of Thomas Jefferson*, Vols. IV, X (1892).

infinitely beyond their power to adopt. If this assumption be yielded to, the State courts may be shut up as there will then be nothing to hinder citizens of the same State suing each other in the Federal courts in every case, as on a bond for instance, because the Common Law obliges the payment of it and the Common Law they say is their law."

In January, 1800, the opposition took the form, in Virginia, of an instruction from the General Assembly to its Senators and Representatives in Congress,

"to use their best efforts to oppose the passing of any law founded on recognizing the principle lately advanced that the Common Law of England is in force under the Government of the United States.

"The General Assembly of Virginia would consider themselves unfaithful to the trust reposed in them were they to remain silent, whilst a doctrine has been publicly advanced, novel in its principles and tremendous in its consequences: That the Common Law of England is in force under the government of the United States. It is not at this time proposed to expose at large the monstrous pretensions resulting from the adoption of this principle. It ought never, however, to be forgotten, and can never be too often repeated, that it opens a new tribunal for the trial of crimes never contemplated by the federal compact. It opens a new code of sanguinary criminal law, both obsolete and unknown, and either wholly rejected or essentially modified in almost all its parts by State institutions. It arrests or supersedes State jurisdictions, and innovates upon State laws. It subjects the citizens to punishment, according to the judiciary will, when he is left in ignorance of what this law enjoins as a duty or prohibits as a crime. It assumes a range of jurisdiction for the Federal courts which defies limitation or definition. In short, it is believed that the advocates for the principle would themselves be last in an attempt to apply it to the existing institution of Federal and State courts, by separating with precision their judiciary rights, and thus preventing the constant and mischievous interference of rival jurisdictions."

Finally, the prejudices of the people crystallized in radical legislation. In 1799, the State of New Jersey actually passed a statute, forbidding the Bar to cite or read in court any decision, opinion, treatise, compilation or exposition of Common Law made or written in Great Britain since July 1, 1776, and prescribed heavy penalties.

In 1807, the State of Kentucky followed suit with a statute, providing that reports and books of decisions in Great Britain since July 4, 1776, "shall not be read or considered as authority in any of the courts." Under this statute, the court went so far as to stop Henry Clay from reading from 3 *East's Reports* 200 that portion of an opinion of Lord Ellenborough which stated the ancient law prior to 1776 (see *Hickman* v. *Boffman*, Hardin's Reports 356).

In Pennsylvania, the feeling against the Common Law took shape, in 1802–1805, in the impeachment trial of the Chief Justice and judges of the Supreme Court, Edward Shippen, Jasper Yeates and Thomas Smith, charged with a single "arbitrary and unconstitutional act," that of sentencing Thomas Passmore to jail for thirty days and imposing a $50 fine for a "supposed contempt," the ground of the impeachment being that punishment for contempt of court was a piece of English Common Law barbarism, unsuited to this country and illegal.[1]

[1] *The Courts from the Revolution to the Revision of the Civil Code*, by William H. Loyd, Jr., *Univ. of Penn. Law Review*, Vol. LVI (1908).

See also for a highly colored account of this case *Sampson against the Philistines*, by William Duane (1805).

In this trial, in which Caesar A. Rodney (later United States Attorney-General, appeared for the prosecution, and Alexander J. Dallas and Jared Ingersoll for the defendants, occurred one of the finest pleas in behalf of the Common Law, in the annals of American legal history.

The following extract from Dallas' argument, as reproduced in his

The result of the trial being the acquittal of the judges, public sentiment against the English law was still further inflamed in Pennsylvania; and in 1810, a statute was passed (and not repealed until 1836), forbidding the citation of any English decision made since July 4, 1776, except in cases involving the law of nations and maritime law.[1]

*Address to the Republicans of Pennsylvania, June, 1805*, is well worthy of preservation:

"In depicting the Common Law, they have ransacked the cells of monks; they have pillaged the lumber of colleges; they have revived the follies of a superstitious age; they have brandished the rigors of a military despotism; but in all this rage of research they have forgotten or concealed that such things enter not into the composition of the Common Law of Pennsylvania; for the Constitution tolerates only that portion of the Common Law which your ancestors brought voluntarily with them to the wilderness as a birthright. Let us not therefore be ensnared by prejudices nor be deceived by mere similitude of names. Every nation has its common law. The Common Law of Pennsylvania is the Common Law of England, as stripped of its feudal trappings, as originally suited to a colonial condition, as modified by acts of the General Assembly, and as purified by the principles of the Constitution. For the varying exigencies of social life, for the complicated interests of an enterprising nation, the positive acts of the Legislature can provide little, and, independent of the Common Law, rights would remain forever without remedies and wrongs without redress. The law of nations, the law of merchants, the customs and usages of trade, and even the law of every foreign country in relation to transitory contracts originating there but prosecuted here, are parts of the Common Law of Pennsylvania. It is the Common Law, generally speaking, not an Act of Assembly that assures the title and the possession of your farms and your houses, and protects your persons, your liberty, your reputation, from violence; that defines and punishes offences; that regulates the trial by jury; and that gives efficacy to the fundamental principles of the Constitution — simply because it originated in Europe cannot afford a better reason to abandon it, than to renounce the English or German languages, or to abolish the institutions of property and marriage, of education and religion, since they were too derived from the more ancient civilized nation of the world."

See *Life of Alexander J. Dallas*, by George M. Dallas (1871).

[1] Henry H. Brackenridge, then Judge of the Supreme Court of Pennsylvania, said in his *Law Miscellanies* (1814), that this act ought to be repealed, and he questioned its constitutionality, "as abridging the right of the judiciary to hear all reason on a question before them."

The question of the existence of a national Common Law in the criminal jurisdiction of the Federal courts was finally set at rest by the decision, in 1812, in the case of *U. S.* v. *Goodwin* (7 Cranch, 32), argued by Attorney-General Pinkney for the Government, Dana of Connecticut for the defendants declining to argue. Judge Johnson gave the opinion, holding that an indictment for libel on the President could not be sustained without a Federal statute on the subject, and stating that:

"Although this question is brought up now for the first time to be decided by this Court, we consider it as having long since been settled in public opinion — the general acquiescence of legal men shows the prevalence of opinion in favor of the negative of the proposition. . . . All exercise of criminal jurisdiction in Common Law cases is not within their implied powers."[1]

Even after this decision, a feeling of unrest at the weight given to the English Common Law by the courts cropped up through the country; and an excellent description of this condition was given by Peter S. DuPonceau, Provost of the Law Academy of Philadelphia, in an address to the students, as late as 1824:[2]

[1] See *U. S.* v. *Coolidge*, 1 Gallison 488, in 1813, in which Judge Story attempted to make a distinction between power to indict and power to punish. Judge John Davis dissenting, the case was taken to the Supreme Court on a division of opinion; but the Supreme Court refused (1 Wheaton, 415), in 1816, to hear an argument on the point.

[2] See *A Dissertation on the nature and extent of the Jurisdiction of the Courts of the United States, being a valedictory address to the students of the Law Academy of Philadelphia*, April 23, 1824, by Peter S. DuPonceau, Provost of the Academy.

Tucker's *Blackstone*, Vol. I, App. E; Kent's *Commentaries*, Vol. I, p. 311; *Rawle on the Constitution*, Chap. 30; *North American Review*, July, 1825; Speech of Bayard, in *Debates on the Judiciary*, in 1802, p. 372, Story's *Commentaries on the Constitution*, Vol. I, s. 158.

*Federal Common Law — Virginia Law Register*, Vol. X (1904); Wharton's *Criminal Law*, Vol. I.

"Various circumstances have concurred after the Revolution to create doubts in the public mind respecting the operation of the Common Law in this country as a national system, particularly in criminal cases. The bitter feeling of animosity against England which the Revolutionary War produced was not amongst the least of these causes. . . .

". . . I am well aware that this doctrine of the nationality of the Common Law will meet with many opponents. There is a spirit of hostility abroad against this system which cannot escape the eye of the most superficial observer. It began in Virginia, in the year 1799 or 1800, in consequence of an opposition to the alien and sedition acts; a committee of the legislative body made a report against these laws which was accepted by the House, in which it was broadly laid down that the Common Law is not the law of the United States. Not long afterwards, the flame caught in Pennsylvania; and it was for a time believed that the Legislature would abolish the Common Law altogether. Violent pamphlets were published to instigate them to that measure. The whole, however, ended in a law for determining all suits by arbitration in the first instance, at the will of either party, and another prohibiting the reading and quoting in courts of justice of British authorities of a date posterior to the Revolution.[1]

"It was not long before this inimical disposition towards the Common Law made its way into the State of Ohio. In the year 1819, a learned and elaborate work was published in that State[2] in which it was endeavored to prove not only that the Common Law was not the law of the United States, but that it had no authority in any of the States that had been formed out of the old Northwestern Territory. But few copies of his work have been printed; nevertheless, as it is learnedly and elaborately written, it cannot but have had a considerable degree of influence. In

[1] This spirit was considerably checked by a well-written pamphlet published at the time by Joseph Hopkinson, Esq., of Philadelphia, in which he demonstrated the absurdity of the project of abolishing the Common Law.

[2] *Historical sketches of the principles and maxims of American Jurisprudence, in contrast with the doctrines of the English common law on the subject of crimes and punishments*, by Milton Goodnow (Steubenvale, 1819).

other States, attacks upon the Common Law, more or less direct, have appeared from time to time. Its faults are laid hold of and exhibited in the most glaring light; its ancient abuses, its uncertainty, the immense number of volumes in which its doctrines are to be sought for, . . . and above all the supposed danger to our institutions from its being still the law of a monarchical country, the opinions of whose judges long habit has taught us to respect, which opinions are received from year to year and admitted in our courts of justice if not as rules, at least as guides for their decisions; these are the topics which are in general selected for animadversion."

It is probable that no one thing contributed more to enflame the public mind against the Common Law than did the insistence of the American courts on enforcing the harsh doctrines of the English law of criminal libel — that truth was no defence, and that the jury could pass only on the fact of publication and the application of the innuendo.

In Colonial times, there had been a long struggle between the Royal judges and the writers and printers for a wider freedom of the press; and trial after trial had been held, in which counsel had argued for the greater rights of the jury — notably *William Bradford's Case,* in Pennsylvania, in 1692; *Thomas Maule's,* in Massachusetts, in 1695; *John Chesley's,* in Massachusetts, in 1724 (in which the great John Read defended the printer); and *John Peter Zenger's,* in New York, in 1735 (in which Andrew Hamilton of Pennsylvania made one of the most famous arguments in American history). The narrow English doctrines had, however, prevailed until the Revolution.[1] When the

[1] See elaborate historical opinion in *Commonwealth* v. *Whitmarsh,* Thacher's Criminal Cases, p. 441 (1836); also interesting account of early cases in *Freedom of the Press in Massachusetts,* by C. A. Dunniway (1906).

The defence of truth was however allowed in an early Pennsylvania case, see *Proprietor* v. *George M. Keith et al.,* in 1692, referred to in *Constitutional Provisions guaranteeing Freedom of the Press in Pennsylvania — Amer. Law Register,* Vol. XLIII.

State Constitutions were being formed, the greatest care had been taken to insert ample clauses, guaranteeing freedom of speech and freedom of the press; and it was supposed that under these clauses the old law of libel could no longer flourish. It was a great shock, therefore, to the public, as well as to many members of the Bar, when Chief Justice Francis Dana held in the first case arising under the new Massachusetts Constitution, in 1791, — *Com.* v. *Freeman* — that the old Common Law of criminal libel had not been altered, and that with all its rigors it was still in force in that State. This decision excited much interest throughout the country. The obnoxious principle of the English law that truth was no defence was again applied in 1801, in the trial of another newspaper editor, Abijah Adams, the ardent Anti-Federalist publisher of the Boston *Independent Chronicle* — Chief Justice Dana, in his decision, terming the Common Law, "our cherished birthright."[1] The irony of this term, as voicing the real public sentiment, may be seen from an editorial printed in his paper on the day after Adams' release from prison: "Yesterday Mr. Abijah Adams was discharged from his imprisonment, after partaking of our adequate proportion of his birthright by a confinement of thirty days under the operation of the Common Law of England." Another editor, John S. Lillie, of the *Constitutional Telegraph*, in Boston, was indicted, in 1801, for libel in referring to Dana as "the Lord Chief Justice of England," "a tyrant judge," who administered "that execrable engine of tyrants the Common Law of England in criminal prosecutions."

Similar trials for libel were held throughout the United States during the era of Adams and Jefferson; and the

[1] See elaborate review of this trial and the principles involved, by George Blake, attorney for the defendant, in the *Independent Chronicle*, April 8–29, 1801.

decisions of the courts based on the English law became increasingly obnoxious to the public. Though, as Chief Justice Thomas McKean of Pennsylvania said, "libelling had become a kind of national crime," and though there seemed to be, at this time, no limit to the license in which political writers and speakers indulged, yet the people at large were not of a temper to have this license stopped by judicial decision. The judges were running counter to the spirit of the times. Everywhere, there was the demand that at least truth must be admitted as a defence, and that the English law must be discarded. Profound effect was produced by two pamphlets *On the Liberty of the Press*, issued in 1799 and 1803 by George Hay, an eminent lawyer of Virginia, in which he took the broad ground that every individual should have freedom to write or speak the truth about any other individual, provided no actual injury was intended or produced.

Finally, in 1804, Alexander Hamilton made the greatest forensic argument of his life, in vigorous opposition to the English doctrine of libel, in *People* v. *Croswell* (3 Johnson, 337) in which he laid down the principle that "the liberty of the press consists in the right to publish with impunity truth with good motives and for justifiable ends, whether it respects government, magistracy or individuals." The court and Chief Justice Kent adopted this to the extent of allowing truth to be published regarding public officers, if without malice. And so great was the impression made on the public that the New York Legislature, at its next session, in 1805, passed a declaratory act on the subject.

Three years later, the Massachusetts Supreme Court, by Chief Justice Parsons, took the first step towards breaking down the old law, in *Com.* v. *Clap* (4 Mass. 163), by practically adopting Hamilton's doctrine so far as it related to candidates for office and public officers.[1] Even this was only a partial step; the American law had not yet been brought into conformity with public opinion; and it was not until the decade from 1820 to 1830 that the States, by legislation largely, finally freed themselves from the bonds of the English law of libel.

The revolt against the Common Law in this one branch is merely an illustration of the general dissatisfaction of the American people and of their determination that their law should be progressive.

[1] See on this general subject two spicy pamphlets in 1823, *A Letter to Josiah Quincy by a Member of the Suffolk Bar*, by H. G. Otis; *Reflections on the Law of Libel, addressed to a Member of the Suffolk Bar*, by Edmund Kimball. See also *Com.* v. *Buckingham*, Thacher's Criminal Cases; and *Freedom of the Press in Massachusetts*, by C. A. Dunniway (1906).

## CHAPTER XI

### THE FEDERAL BAR AND LAW, 1789–1815

WITH the year 1789, American law as a national system began; and its early history falls, naturally, into two periods, the one closing in 1801, with the appointment of Chief Justice Marshall, the other with the end of the War of 1812, in 1815.

By far the most important work which greeted the first Congress when it met in 1789, was the establishment of a judicial system for the country. The honor of drafting the famous statute known as the Judiciary Act — one of the most remarkable and impregnable pieces of legislation ever framed — must be attributed chiefly to Oliver Ellsworth.

On April 7, 1789, the new Senate appointed Oliver Ellsworth of Connecticut, William Paterson of New Jersey, William Maclay of Pennsylvania, Caleb Strong of Massachusetts, Richard Henry Lee of Virginia, Richard Bassett of Delaware, William Few of Georgia and Paine Wingate of New Hampshire, "a committee to bring in a bill for organizing the judiciary of the United States." On June 12, the Committee, through Mr. Lee, reported a bill which was passed, July 17, by vote of fourteen to six, three of the Committee — Lee, Maclay and Bassett — opposing it. In the House of Representatives, there was bitter opposition led by Livermore of New Hampshire, to that part of the bill establishing the inferior courts. It was argued that a disastrous conflict of jurisdiction with the State courts would inevitably result; that the Federal courts would eventually "swallow up the State courts;" that the expense would be great; and, finally, that such Federal courts were entirely unnecessary, as the jurisdiction could as well be conferred on the various State courts with an appeal or writ of error in Federal cases to the United States Supreme Court.[1]

The bill was defended by Sedgwick, Ames and Gerry of Massachusetts, Benson of New York and Madison of Virginia; and after an amendment striking out the Circuit and District Courts had been rejected by a vote of thirty-one to eleven, the bill was passed.

Approved by the President, September 24, 1789, the Act provided for a Supreme Court with a Chief Justice and five Associate Justices; for thirteen District Courts, one for each State, and also for the Districts of Maine and Kentucky (not then States); and for a division of the country into three Circuits — the Eastern, the Middle, and the Southern, and for a Circuit Court for each, consisting of two Justices of the Supreme Court and the District Judge of the District where the Court was held.[2]

It is interesting to note that, though now regarded as a particularly wise and far-sighted measure, the Judiciary Act received bitter criticism in those early years. Thus, the great North Carolina lawyer, William R. Davie, wrote to Judge James Iredell, August 2, 1791:

"I sincerely hope something will be done at the next session of Congress with the Judiciary Act; it is so defective in point of arrangement, and so obscurely drawn or expressed that, in my opinion, it would disgrace the com-

[1] See *The New Court Bill — American Law Review*, Vol. X (1876).

[2] By the Act of 1792–1793, c. 22, the requirement that two Supreme Court judges must be present, was repealed.

position of the meanest Legislature of the States. The Attorney-General's Report is a type of it — an elegant piece of unmeaning obscurity."

And Samuel Dexter, in his argument in 1816, in *Martin* v. *Hunter's Lessee* (1 Wheat. p. 305) said:

"That great man, and those who advised him improvidently, assented to a law [the Judiciary Act] which is neither constitutionally nor politically adapted to enforce the power of the National Courts in an amicable and pacific manner."

On the day on which he signed the Act, September 24, 1789, President Washington sent to the Senate, as his nominees for the first United States Supreme Court, the names of John Jay of New York, as Chief Justice, and as Associate Justices, John Rutledge of South Carolina, James Wilson of Pennsylvania, William Cushing of Massachusetts (then Chief Justice of that State), Robert H. Harrison of Maryland and John Blair of Virginia. Harrison declining, in order to accept the position of Chancellor of Maryland, James Iredell of North Carolina took his place.

The Court was opened in New York, February 2, 1790; and the next day three lawyers were admitted to practise before it as counsellors, Elias Boudinot of New Jersey, Thomas Hartley of Pennsylvania and Richard Harrison of New York. By rule of court (amended in 1801) an attorney or counsellor who had practised as such in the Supreme Court of any State for three years, might be admitted to its Bar but he was required to make his election between the two degrees, and could not practise both as counsellor and as attorney.

It is interesting to note that in at least one of the United States Circuit Courts (the First), rules of court provided for four degrees at the Bar — attorneys, counsellors, barristers and sergeants. The latter degree was a distinct innovation in the United States, existing hitherto only in the Colony and State of New Jersey. To qualify as an attorney in the Circuit Court, an applicant must have been either a college graduate who had studied law in the office of an attorney or counsellor of the Court for three years (four years if a non-graduate), or admitted to practise in the State court for one year. After two years' practise in the Circuit Court as attorney, he was eligible for admittance as counsellor. Counsellors "of six years' standing in practise" might be "called by the court to the degree of Barrister, and after ten years' standing in practise to the degree of Sergeant at Law."

The conferring of these latter degrees was of rare occurrence, the most notable instance being the order made by Judge Story in 1812, as follows:

> "Whereas the court have a full knowledge of the learning, integrity and ability of the Hon. Jeremiah Smith and the Hon. Jeremiah Mason and upon the most entire confidence therein and being willing to express this opinion in the most public manner as well as a testimony to their merits as also a laudable example to the junior members of the Bar; and the court having taken the premises into their mature deliberation of their own mere motion and pleasure, have ordered and do hereby order that the honorable degree of sergeant-at-law be and hereby is conferred upon them. . . .
>
> "The court on mature deliberation do order that the degree of barrister at law be and hereby is conferred on the following gentlemen — Oliver Peabody, Daniel Humphreys, George Sullivan and Daniel Webster, Esquires, in testimony of the entire respect the court entertains for their learning, integrity and ability."

There being no business ready before the Supreme Court, its Judges entered at once upon their duties in the inferior courts, the first Circuit Court being held in the Eastern

Circuit, in New York, April 4, 1790, by Chief Jutsice Jay, Judge Cushing and District Judge Duane.

A contemporary account of the opening of the Circuit Court at New Haven, April 22, 1790, is given by President Stiles as follows:[1]

> "The federal circuit Supreme Court of the United States sat here for the first time since its institution by Congress. Present, 3 Judges, Hon. Ch. Just. Jay, late Ambassador to France, Judge Cushing, and Judge Law. The Ch. Justice sent the Marshall to me this morning to open the court with Prayer; but I was unable to go abroad and Dr. Dana prayed with the court. Then Mr. Jay made a speech to the Grand Jury: all the Attornies of two years' standing present were then admitted and Sworn Barristers, Attorneys and Counsellors of the Supreme Court."

As there continued to be few cases for the Supreme Court, only five being heard up to the February Term of 1793, the Circuit Court work remained for some time the chief occupation of the Judges — a very arduous work in those days, owing to the difficulties of interstate communication — "the life of a postboy" — so Iredell described it.[2] At first, the Judges were divided into pairs, and each assigned to one circuit permanently. As the Southern Circuit involved a journey of at least 1,900 miles from Philadelphia

[1] *Literary Diary of Ezra Stiles*, Vol. III.

[2] After the Circuits were annually changed, Judge Cushing's travels on Circuit are thus described:

"He travelled over the whole Union, holding courts in Virginia, the Carolinas and Georgia. His travelling equipage was a four-wheeled phaeton, drawn by a pair of horses which he drove. It was remarkable for its many ingenious arrangements (all of his contrivance), for carrying books, choice groceries and other comforts. Mrs. Cushing always accompanied him, and generally read aloud while riding. His faithful servant, Prince, a jet-black negro, whose parents had been slaves in the family, and who loved his master with unbounded affection, followed."

*Lives of the Chief Justices*, by Henry Flanders.

and return, to be covered twice a year, it is no wonder that Iredell, to whom it was assigned, should write to Jay, February 11, 1791, "I will venture to say, no Judge can conscientiously undertake to ride the Southern Circuit constantly and perform the other parts of his duty," — nor that Jay should reply, March 16, 1791, "The Circuits press hard upon us all; and your share of the task has hitherto been more than in due proportion." Later the Circuits were changed annually, the Judges taking them in turn.

As the Supreme Court sat in the City Hall in Philadelphia from 1791 to 1801, the chief practitioners appearing before it were naturally members of the Philadelphia Bar, then the ablest lawyers in the country. There were, in 1785, in Philadelphia, thirty-four counsellors at law, of whom William Lewis, the "Senior of the Bar,"[1] Edward Tilghman,[2] William Rawle,[3] Jared Ingersoll[4] and Alexander J. Dallas[5] argued most of the cases in the Federal Court. Other leading men of that Bar at this time were

[1] Born in 1748 and studied law in the offices of Nicholas Waln and George Ross; was admitted to the Bar in 1776, and became the great criminal lawyer of his day. He was the fearless counsel for John Fries in the case which led to the impeachment in 1805 of Judge Chase, of the United States Supreme Court.

[2] A grandson of Tench Francis, born in Maryland in 1750, studied in the Middle Temple, and was admitted to the Bar in 1774. He was the consummate Pennsylvania authority on all points connected with estates, tenures, uses and remainders.

[3] Born in 1759, studied law with Kemp in New York, and in the Middle Temple in 1781, and became United States District Attorney in 1791, being prosecutor in the whiskey Insurrection and in the famous John Fries case. "Between 1793 and 1813 his practice was as large as any lawyer at the bar."

[4] Born in 1749 in Connecticut, graduated at Yale in 1766, and educated in the Middle Temple, 1774–1778; admitted to the Bar in 1779.

[5] Born in Jamaica in 1759, studied in the Temple, and was admitted to the Bar in Philadelphia in 1785. He published the first volume of *Dallas' Reports*, in 1790.

William Tilghman,[1] William Bradford,[2] Jasper Yeates,[3] and Richard Peters.[4]

The Virginia Bar presented three lawyers of pre-eminent ability: John Marshall, who was born in 1755, attended the law lectures of Chancellor Wythe at William and Mary College in 1779, and was admitted to the Bar in 1780; Edmund Randolph, who was born in 1753, and was considered the head of the Southern Bar; and Charles Lee, who was born in 1758, and became United States Attorney-General in 1795.

Few lawyers appeared from other States — the chief ones being Samuel Dexter, from Massachusetts; James Reed and John Julian Pringle,[5] from South Carolina; Jeremiah B. Howell,[6] and Ashur Robbins,[7] from Rhode Island; James Hillhouse,[8] from Connecticut; Josiah Ogden Hoffman, from New York; John Thompson Mason,[9] from Maryland; and James A. Bayard,[10] from Delaware.

Such was the early Supreme Court Bar.

[1] Born in 1756, studied law with Kemp in New York, admitted to practise in 1783, and became Chief Justice of the State in 1806. He was a master of Equity Jurisprudence.

[2] Born in 1755, a Princeton graduate in 1772, was judge of the Pennsylvania Supreme Court in 1791 and the second Attorney-General of the United States, succeeding Edmund Randolph, of Virginia, in 1794.

[3] Born in 1745, graduate in 1761 of the College of Philadelphia, a student in the Temple, Judge of the Supreme Court in 1791.

[4] Born in 1744, graduate of College of Philadelphia in 1761, United States District Judge 1792.

[5] Born in 1753, College of Philadelphia, 1771.

[6] Born in 1772, Brown 1789, United States Senator 1811–1817.

[7] Born in 1757, Yale 1782, United States District Attorney 1795, United States Senator 1825–1839.

[8] Born in 1754, Yale 1773, United States Senator 1795–1810.

[9] Born in 1764, offered the position of United States Attorney-General by President Jefferson and by President Madison, but declined.

[10] Born in 1767, Princeton 1784, studied with Jared Ingersoll and Joseph Reed, United States Senator 1805–1813.

"During this period," says Kent, "the Federal Courts were chiefly occupied with questions concerning their admiralty jurisdiction, and with political and national questions arising out of the Revolutionary War, and the dangerous influence and action of the war of the French Revolution upon the neutrality and peace of our country — the principles of expatriation, of *ex post facto* laws, of constitutional taxes."

The first case on the docket of the Supreme Court was *Vanstophorst* v. *The State of Maryland* in the August term of 1791; but it was never argued.

During these first eleven years, the Court decided only fifty-five cases; but two of these, however, were of highest importance. The first, — *Chisholm* v. *Georgia* (2 Dallas, 419), — in 1793, in which the Court upheld the right of an individual to sue a State, emphasized the sovereignty of the new United States over one of its members, but at the same time nearly caused a disruption of the young Nation — owing to the outburst of resentment at the decision, coming from those who had opposed the Constitution as an infringement on States' Rights. It was argued by Edmund Randolph for the plaintiff, and a remonstrance was filed by Jared Ingersoll and Alexander J. Dallas of Pennsylvania for the State of Georgia, which declined to formally appear.[1] The other — *Ware* v. *Hylton* (3 Dallas, 199), the famous British Debts case — in 1796, involved a question of immense pecuniary importance; namely, whether the State laws, confiscating and sequestrating debts due to a hostile enemy, or allowing their payment in depreciated money, were valid against the provisions of the Treaty with England. In Virginia

[1] See *Life of Patrick Henry*, by William Wirt (1818); *Georgia as a Litigant — Georgia Bar Ass. Proc.*, Vol. XIII; *Letters and Times of the Tylers*, by Lyon G. Tyler.

alone, it is estimated that there were more than $2,000,000 of such debts: and on the decision of this case hung the fortunes of thousands of American citizens. The question had been originally argued, in 1791, in *Jones* v. *Walker* (2 Paine, 688), in the Federal Circuit Court in Virginia, before Judges Johnson and Blair of the Supreme Court, and District Judge Griffin, and again, in 1793, before Chief Justice Jay and Judge Iredell — Ronald, Baker, Starke and John Wickham, of the Virginia Bar appearing for the British creditors, and Patrick Henry, Alexander Campbell, and Attorney-General Innis of Virginia, for the debtors. Of these counsel, Judge Iredell in his opinion, said:

"The cause has been spoken to at the Bar, with a degree of ability equal to any occasion. However painfully I may reflect at any time on the inadequacy of my own talents, I shall, as long as I live, remember with pleasure and respect, the arguments which I have heard in this case. They have discovered an ingenuity, a depth of investigation, and a power of reasoning, fully equal to anything I have ever witnessed, and some of them have been adorned with a splendor of eloquence surpassing what I have ever felt before. Fatigue has given way under its influence and the heart has warmed, while the understanding has been instructed."

In the Supreme Court, the case was argued by Edward Tilghman and William Lewis, of Philadelphia for the creditors, and John Marshall and Campbell for the debtors, the latter losing their case, and the Court holding a treaty to be supreme over State law.

Of Marshall's argument — his only one in the Supreme Court — William Wirt who was present wrote: [1]

"Marshall spoke, as he always does, to the judgment merely, and for the simple purpose of convincing. Mar-

[1] See letter of W. Wirt to Gilmer, November 2, 1828, in *Memoir of the Life of William Wirt*, by John P. Kennedy (1849).

shall was justly pronounced one of the greatest men of the country. He was followed by crowds, looked upon and courted with every evidence of admiration and respect for the great powers of his mind. Campbell was neglected and slighted, and came home in disgust. Marshall's maxim seems always to have been, 'aim exclusively at strength.'"

Two other cases in the Supreme Court during this period deserve mention. One, *Hylton* v. *United States* (3 Dallas, 171), in 1796, which decided the meaning of the term "direct tax" in the Constitution, is noteworthy as being the only case ever argued before the United States Supreme Court by Alexander Hamilton. Associated with Hamilton was Charles Lee, United States Attorney-General, and opposed to him were Alexander Campbell, United States District-Attorney for Virginia, and Jared Ingersoll, Attorney-General of Pennsylvania.[1]

Of Hamilton's argument, Judge Iredell wrote, February 26, 1796:[2]

"The day before yesterday Mr. Hamilton spoke in our court attended by the most crowded audience I ever saw there, both Houses of Congress being almost deserted on the occasion. Though he was in very ill health he spoke with astonishing ability, and in a most pleasing manner, and was listened to with the profoundest attention. His speech lasted about three hours."

A contemporary newspaper account stated:[3]

"The whole of his argument was clear, impressive, and classical. The audience which was very numerous and

[1] In *Springer* v. *U. S.*, 102 U. S. 586 (1881), Chief Justice Chase said of the Hylton case: "It was one of great expectation, and a general interest was felt in its determination;" see also the history of the case given in Chase's opinion.

[2] *Life and Letters of James Iredell*, by Griffith J. McRee, Vol. II (1857).

[3] *Works of Alexander Hamilton*, by Henry Cabot Lodge, Vol. VII.

among whom were many foreigners of distinction and many of the members of Congress, testified the effect produced by the talents of this great orator and statesman."

Another case — *Georgia* v. *Brailsford* (3 Dallas, 1), in 1792, argued by Jared Ingersoll and Alexander J. Dallas, against William Bradford, Edward Tilghman and William Lewis is of interest as one of the very few cases in which a special trial by jury has ever been had in the United States Supreme Court.

In these eleven years, the Court suffered many changes. In 1791, Rutledge resigned to become Chancellor of South Carolina.[1] In 1795, Jay resigned, as Chief Justice, to become Governor of New York. Ellsworth, who was appointed Chief Justice, in 1796, resigned in 1800 because of ill health.[2]

[1] Rutledge was appointed Chief Justice on Jay's resignation, and presided over the Court during the August Term of 1795; but the Senate rejected his nomination.

William Cushing was appointed, but declined.

[2] Ellsworth, during his term as Chief Justice, served as Envoy Extraordinary and Minister Plenipotentiary to France, 1799–1800. At this time, he visited England, and was present at the trial of the famous case of *Rex* v. *Waddington*, 1 East, in which Mr. Law (Lord Ellenborough), Mr. Erskine, Mr. Garrow and Mr. Scott (Lord Eldon) were counsel. Wharton in his notes to *American State Trials* thus describes the scene in Westminster Hall:

"Notwithstanding Mr. Jay's previous appearance at the Court of St. James, and the contemporaneous appearance there of Mr. Rufus King, the fame of their accomplishments had not reached the King's Bench, whose precincts they had probably never invaded; and it was consequently with great curiosity that the elder lawyers, whose notions of America had been derived from the kidnapping cases which were the only precipitate cast on the reports of the Privy Council by the current of Colonial litigation, spied out the American Chief Justice. Mr. Ellsworth's simple but dignified carriage was in happy contrast to the awkwardness of the English Chief Justice (Kenyon); and as soon as it was discovered that, though his worn and marked features bore a stamp which had not then become familiar to the English eye, he was neither an Indian nor a Jacobin . . . he was surrounded by a knot of lawyers, curious to know how the Common Law stood transplanting."

Wilson died in 1798 and Iredell in 1799. Samuel Chase, of Maryland, became a Justice, in 1796, in place of John Blair (resigned), and William Paterson, of New Jersey, became a Justice, in 1793, in place of Thomas Johnson, who took Rutledge's place, in 1791; Alfred Moore, of North Carolina, became a Justice, in 1799; and Bushrod Washington, of Virginia, in 1798.

As late as 1800, Jay, in declining re-appointment, stated in a letter to President Adams that he

"left the bench, perfectly convinced that under a system so defective, it would not obtain the energy, weight and dignity, which were essential to its affording due support to the National Government; nor acquire the public confidence and respect which, as the last resort of the justice of the Nation, it should possess."

And the difficult situation in which the Court was placed in these early years was well depicted by Caleb Cushing, writing in 1824:[1]

"To say that the Supreme Court of the United States was forced to contend with all the prejudices and misconceptions which cast a cloud around the dawning of our national Constitution is far short of the reality; for its duties brought it directly in conflict with those prejudices and misconceptions in their worst and most aggravated shapes. As entrusted with the execution of the laws it was necessarily thrust forward to bear the brunt, in the first instance, of all the opposition levelled against the federal head; to enforce the collection of revenue; to punish riots which the pressure of odious taxes had excited; to quell disaffections maddened and inflamed into insurrection by popular clamor; to maintain the neutrality of the nation in spite of the usurpations of foreign armaments, consuls, ministers and directories; to compel obedience to commercial restrictions of which they on whom they

[1] Review of *Law Reports*, by Caleb Cushing, *North Amer. Rev.*, Vol. XVIII (1824).

fell most heavily, would not acknowledge the utility, efficiency or expediency; to withstand the pretensions of individual States to independent sovereignty; in short to guarantee the integrity of our Constitution wherever that instrument opposed the feelings or combatted the claims of constituent members of the Union."

John Adams, however, in the closing days of his administration, placed the Supreme Court at one stroke upon the pinnacle which it has ever since held, by his appointment of John Marshall, on January 31, 1801, Chief Justice — "a man born to be the Chief Justice of any country into which Providence should have cast him," said William Pinkney.[1]

A curious episode in the history of the Federal judiciary occurred soon after Marshall's appointment, in the passage of the Act of February 13, 1801, reducing the number of Associate Supreme Court Justices to four, relieving them of Circuit Court duty, and creating six new Circuits, each (with the exception of the Sixth Circuit in Kentucky and Tennessee) with a Chief Justice and two assistant judges. The appointment of these sixteen new judges on the very eve of President Adams' retirement from office gave rise to the derisive name of "Midnight Judges," and to an extremely bitter partisan attack by the Republicans. Notwithstanding that lawyers of the highest character had been appointed, such as William Tilghman of Pennsylvania, John Lowell of Massachusetts, Jeremiah Smith of New Hampshire, Egbert Benson of New York, Philip Barton Key of Maryland, and Thomas Bee of South Carolina, the Act was repealed, April 29, 1802, at President

[1] Edward C. Marshall, youngest son of the Chief Justice, writing of a visit to John Adams in 1825, said: "He gave me a most cordial reception, and, grasping my hand, told me that his gift of Mr. John Marshall to the people of the United States was the proudest act of his life."

Jefferson's behest; and the new Courts came to a sudden end.[1]

The prevalent fear of the multiplication of Federal Courts and the consequent infringement on the rights of the States is vividly shown in a series of articles by a prominent Boston Anti-Federalist, Benjamin Austin, published by the *Independent Chronicle* in 1801, in which he refers to these new Circuit Courts as follows:

> "This extensive machine, moving under the weight of a column of supernumerary judges, attended with the immense expense of their establishments, it is feared would ultimately reduce the people to the most abject state of servitude. Lawyers would generate in tenfold proportion to other professions, and in time the country would be as generally overrun by this 'order' as Egypt with Mamelukes."

The new Act of 1802, divided the country into six Circuits, restored the number of Supreme Court Associate Justices to five, and assigned each Judge of the Court permanently to one Circuit. The Federal judicial system, as thus finally established, continued without important change until 1869, the number of Associate Justices being

[1] The repealing act passed by a strict party vote of 16 to 15 in the Senate, and 56 to 30 in the House.

As the list of these unfortunate Federal judges who held office only fourteen months is rarely published, it may be of interest to insert it here:

First Circuit: John Lowell of Massachusetts, Chief Judge; Jeremiah Smith of New Hampshire, and Benjamin Bourne of Rhode Island. Second Circuit: Egbert Benson of New York, Chief Judge; Oliver Wolcott of Connecticut, and Samuel Hitchcock of Vermont. Third Circuit: William Tilghman of Pennsylvania, Chief Judge; Richard Bassett of Delaware, and William Griffith of New Jersey. Fourth Circuit: Philip Barton Key of Maryland, Chief Judge (vice Charles Lee declined); George Keith Taylor and Charles Magill of Virginia. Fifth Circuit: Thomas Bee of South Carolina, Chief Judge; John Sitgreaves of North Carolina and Joseph Clay, Jr., of Georgia. Sixth Circuit: William McClung of Kentucky.

increased to six in 1807 to provide one for a Western Circuit, and to eight in 1837.

With the installation of Marshall, the Supreme Court moved to Washington, and its first term held in the Capitol was in August, 1801. At that time the "Federal City," as it was known, was hardly more than a fever-stricken morass.

"The half finished White House stood in a naked field, overlooking the Potomac, with two awkward Department buildings near it, a single row of brick houses and a few isolated dwellings within sight and nothing more; until across a swamp, a mile and a half away, the shapeless, unfinished capitol was seen, two wings without a body. . . . Discontented men clustered together in eight or ten boarding houses, as near as possible to the capitol." [1]

As late as 1808, Sir James Jackson, the British Minister, described the city as "five miles long, the scattered houses intersected with woods, heaths and gravel pits. I put up a covey of partridges within three hundred yards of the house of Congress, yclept the capitol. It is more like Hampstead Heath than a city." Of the difficulties of a journey to the city, there are many contemporary descriptions. Edmund Quincy writes that his mother (wife of Josiah Quincy, President of Harvard College and previously Congressman) "used to describe the discomforts, and dangers even, of the journeys to Washington from Boston, as things to remember to the end of a long life." [2]

[1] *History of the United States*, by Henry Adams, Vol. I.

[2] *Life of Josiah Quincy*, by Edmund Quincy.

Hon. Elijah H. Mills, of Northampton, the leader of the Western Bar in Massachusetts, wrote to his wife from Washington in 1815. (See *Mass. Hist. Soc. Proc.*, Vol. XIX):

"My anticipations were almost infinitely short of the reality, and I can truly say that the first appearance of this seat of the National Government has produced in me nothing but absolute loathing and disgust. . . . From

Judge Story wrote to his wife, in 1812: "It will probably take me twelve days to reach home after I set out on the journey."

"Between Boston and New York was a tolerable highway, along which, thrice a week, light stage coaches carried passengers and mail, in three days. From New York, a stage coach started for Philadelphia every week day, consuming the greater part of two days, the road between Paulus Hook (now Jersey City) and Hackensack, being exceedingly bad. South of Philadelphia it was tolerable as far as Baltimore, but beyond Baltimore it meandered through forests. Four miles an hour was average speed everywhere. Beyond the Potomac, the roads were steadily worse; and south of Petersburg, even the mails were carried on horseback. Except for a stage coach which plied between Charleston and Savannah, no public conveyance of any kind was mentioned in the three Southernmost States. Of eight rivers in the one hundred miles between Monticello and Washington, Jefferson wrote, in 1801, "five have neither bridges nor boats." Six cents a mile was the usual stage fare. The cost of a journey from Baltimore to New York was about $21." [1]

The journey from Charleston, South Carolina, was even

Washington to Baltimore we went in the first day. There we took passage in a packet for French-Town, in the Chesapeake Bay, and were delayed by a dead calm, so that we were twenty-four hours performing a passage usually completed in six. On Wednesday, we left our packet and went overland to Newcastle. There we again took a packet, and arrived in Philadelphia late in the evening. On Thursday, we remained in that city, the stage being too full to receive us that day. . . . This morning we left it at two o'clock, and ought to have arrived in New York this evening. But the excessive badness of the roads has arrested our progress at a distance of about forty miles from it. I shall make no stay in New York, but shall press my journey with all the rapidity in my power, and shall be with you, my dear Harriette, I hope, by the Friday stage."

[1] *History of the United States*, by Henry Adams.

more of a task, requiring from ten days to three weeks, according to the lightness of the vehicle and swiftness of horse, the state of the rivers and swamps, or, if one went by Philadelphia packet, the fairness of the winds.[1]

For these reasons, the cases before the Supreme Court were, as a rule, argued by counsel who could make the journey thither with the least difficulty; consequently the Pennsylvania, Maryland, and Virginia Bars had a practical monopoly.

Peter S. DuPonceau, of Pennsylvania, thus describes the attendance of lawyers from that State:

> "The counsel engaged in those causes were in the habit of going together to Washington to argue their cases. These were Mr. Ingersoll, Mr. Dallas, Mr. Lewis, Mr. Edward Tilghman, Mr. Rawle and myself. We hired a stage to ourselves in which we proceeded by easy journies. The Court sat then in the month of February, so that we had to travel in the depth of winter through bad roads in no very comfortable way. Nevertheless, as soon as we were out of the city, and felt the flush of air, we were like school boys in the playground on a holiday.
>
> "Flashes of wit shot their corruscations on all sides; puns of the genuine Philadelphia stamp were handed about, old college stories were revived, songs were sung — in short it might have been taken for anything but the grave counsellors of the celebrated Bar of Philadelphia — except Mr. Ingersoll, who, sad, serious and composed, rode thinking of his causes and little inclined to mirth.
>
> "Our appearance at the Bar of the Supreme Court was always a scene of triumph. We entered the hall together, and Judge Washington was heard to say, 'This is my Bar.' Our causes had a preference over all others, in consideration of the distance we had to travel."[2]

[1] *Life of William Lowndes*, by Mrs. St. J. Ravenel.

[2] See *Letter of P. S. DuPonceau* in *Penn. Hist. Soc. Coll.*, Vol. IV.

Joseph Story gives the following lively description of the Pennsylvania Bar before the Supreme Court in 1808:[1]

"DuPonceau is a Frenchman by birth, and a very ingenious counsellor at Philadelphia.[2] He has the reputation of great subtilty and acuteness, and is excessively minute in the display of his learning. His manner is animated but not impressive, and he betrays at every turn the impatience and the casuistry of his nation. His countenance is striking, his figure rather awkward. A small, sparkling, black eye, and a thin face, satisfy you that he is not without quickness of mind; yet he seemed to me to exhaust himself in petty distinctions, and in a perpetual recurrence to doubtful, if not to inclusive arguments. His reasoning was rather sprightly and plausible, than logical and coercive; in short, he is a French advocate. Tilghman is quite an old man, of an unpromising appearance; his face indicates rather a simplicity and weakness of character. Indeed, when I first saw him, I could not persuade myself that he possessed any talent. I heard his argument, and it was strong, clear, pointed, and logical. Though his manner was bad, and his pronounciation not agreeable, every person listened with attention, and none were disappointed. Rawle is quite a plain but genteel man, and looks like a studious, ingenious, and able lawyer. He argues with a very pleasant voice, and has great neatness, perspicacity, and even elegance. He keeps his object steadily in view; he distinguishes with care, enforces with strength, and if he fail to convince he seldom spends his thoughts vainly. Ingersoll has rather a peculiar face, and yet in person or manner has nothing which interests in a high degree. He is more animated than Rawle, but has less precision; he is lèarned, laborious, and minute, not eloquent, not declamatory but diffuse. The Pennsylvanians consider him a perfect dragnet, that gathers everything in its course. Dallas is a book-man, ready, apt, and loquacious, but artificial. He is of a strong, robust figure, but his voice seems shrill and half obstructed. He grows warm by

[1] *Life and Letters of Joseph Story*, by W. W. Story (1851).

[2] Born in 1760.

method, and cools in the same manner. He wearies with frequent emphasis on subordinate points, but he cannot be considered as unscientific or wandering. Lee, of Virginia, is a thin, spare, short man; you cannot believe that he was Attorney General of the United States."

Maryland lawyers were especially distinguished for their knowledge of the science, and their skill in the practise, of special pleading; and the acknowledged head of the profession in that State was Luther Martin, Attorney-General of the State for many years, a lawyer of great force, of profound learning and memory.[1] Unfortunately he was often discursive, slipshod, and sometimes inaccurate. The rude vigor, pertinacity, and fearless courage of the man made him hated by those whom he opposed — "an unprincipled, impudent, Federal bull dog," so Jefferson called him.

No tribute has ever been paid to a lawyer in the United States so remarkable as the action taken by the Maryland Legislature, in 1822, in passing a resolve imposing a license tax on every practising attorney, of $5 annually, to be paid to trustees "for the use of Luther Martin," he being at the time broken in health and in fortune.[2]

Story gives this picture of Martin, before the Supreme Court in 1808:[3]

[1] Born in 1748, a Princeton graduate of 1766, admitted to the Bar in 1771, Attorney-General of Maryland 1778–1805, and again in 1818.

[2] This Resolve of the Legislature of Maryland passed in February, 1822, was as follows: "*Resolved* that each and every practitioner of law in this State shall be and he is hereby compelled . . . to obtain from the Clerk of the County Court in which he may practice, a license to authorize him so to practice, for which he shall pay annually . . . the sum of five dollars, which said sum is to be deposited . . . in the treasury . . . subject to the order of Thomas Hall and William H. Winder, Esquires, who are hereby appointed trustees for the application of the proceeds raised by virtue of this resolution to the use of Luther Martin . . . and provided that this resolution shall cease to be valid at the death of the said Luther Martin."

[3] *Life and Letters of Joseph Story*, by W. W. Story, Vol. I. See also

"Shall I turn you to Luther Martin, that singular compound of strange qualities? With a professional income of $10,000 a year, he is poor and needy; generous and humane, but negligent and profuse. He labors hard to acquire, and yet cannot preserve. Experience, however severe, never corrects a single habit. I have heard anecdotes of his improvidence and thoughtlessness which astonishes me. He is about the middle size, a little bald, with a common forehead, pointed nose, inexpressive eye, large mouth, and well formed chin. His dress is slovenly. You cannot believe him a great man. Nothing in his voice, his action, his language impresses. Of all men he is the most desultory, wandering, and inaccurate. Errors in grammar, and, indeed, an unexampled laxity of speech, mark him everywhere. . . . But everyone assures me that he is profoundly learned, and that though he shines not now with the lustre of his former days, yet he is at times very great. He never seems satisfied with a single grasp of his subject; he urges himself to successive efforts, until he moulds and fashions it to his purpose. You should hear of Luther Martin's fame from those who have known him long and intimately, but you should not see him."

After the argument of his first case in the Supreme Court in 1806, another Maryland lawyer, William Pinkney, stepped to the front, where he remained until his death in 1822 — the undisputed head of the American Bar.[1] So

*Luther Martin*, *American Law Review*, Vol. I; *Luther Martin*, by Henry P. Goddard, *Proc. Maryland Hist. Soc.* (1887); *Luther Martin as a Lawyer and Lover*, *Maryland Bar Ass.*, Vol. IV (1899).

[1] Born in 1764, studied with Judge Samuel Chase, admitted to practise in 1768, United States Attorney-General 1811–1814, United States Senator 1820. His first case in United States Supreme Court was *Manella* v. *Barry*, 3 Cranch, 415. See for his biography, *William Pinkney*, by Henry Flanders, *Proc. N. Y. State Bar Ass.* (1906); *Lives of the Chief Justices*, by Henry Flanders; *Life and Letters of Joseph Story*, by W. W. Story; *Miscellaneous Works*, by Joseph Story; *Life and Times of Roger B. Taney*, by Samuel Tyler; *Familiar Letters on Public Characters*, by William Sullivan — in which interesting anecdotes are told of Pinkney's appearance before the

great was his practise that in the eighth volume of *Cranch's Reports* he is found arguing in twenty-three out of forty-six cases. The comments of his contemporaries are interesting. "He appears to me," wrote Story when a Judge of the Court in 1812, "a man of consummate talents. He seizes his subject with the comprehension and vigor of a giant and he breaks forth with a lustre and a strength that keep the attention forever on the stretch." Chief Justice Marshall stated that he never knew his equal as a reasoner — so clear and luminous was his method of argumentation; and he further said: "Mr. Pinkney was the greatest man I have ever seen in a court of justice." "He had an oceanic mind," said William Wirt, "he was the most thoroughly equipped lawyer I ever met in the courts."

Chief Justice Taney wrote of Pinkney in 1854: "I have heard almost all the great advocates of the United States, both of the past and present generations, but I have never seen one equal to him."

Pinkney's preparation of his cases and arguments was elaborate to the uttermost degree. Though in manner, a fop, arrogant, vain and often boisterous, though laboring under the handicap of a harsh and feeble voice, "yet notwithstanding these defects," wrote Story, "such is his strong and cogent logic, his elegant and perspicuous language, his flowing graces, and rhetorical touches, his pointed and persevering arguments, that he enchants, interests, and almost irresistibly leads away the understanding."

The lawyer whose name appears in more cases than any

Massachusetts Supreme Court; *William Pinkney*, by Rev. William Pinkney (1853); *Life, Writings and Speeches of William Pinkney*, by Henry Wheaton (1826); Review of Wheaton's *Life of Pinkney*, *North Amer. Rev.*, Vol. XXIV (1826).

For a contemporaneous estimate of Pinkney's eloquence, see extract from *Charleston City Gazette*, quoted in *New York Evening Post*, February 25, 1820.

other member of the Bar between 1800 and 1815 also came from Maryland — Robert Goodloe Harper — able in mercantile cases, a thorough lawyer and a felicitous and graceful orator,[1] Philip Barton Key,[2] Francis Scott Key,[3] W. H. Winder,[4] and David Hoffman[5] were also prominent representatives of the Maryland Bar.

The Virginia Bar at this period was especially brilliant; and five men argued a large proportion of the cases in that State — John Wickham,[6] John Warden, Daniel Call,[7] Edmund Randolph, and William Wirt.[8]

Of the District of Columbia Bar, Walter Jones,[9] Charles Simms and Thomas Swann formed an eminent trio with an immense practise.

From the other States of the Union a mere handful of counsel appeared. Roger Griswold of Connecticut[10] argued in a case in 1801. James A. Bayard of Delaware appeared in 1803; John Quincy Adams of Massachusetts and William Hunter of Rhode Island[11] appeared in a noted case (*Head* v. *Providence Insurance Company*, 2 Cranch, 127) in 1804–1805. A Massachusetts case in the same volume (*Graves* v. *Boston Marine Insurance Company*) was argued by Richard Stockton of New Jersey and Luther Martin

[1] Born in 1765, Princeton 1785, admitted to the Bar in Charleston, South Carolina 1786, son-in-law of Charles Carroll of Carrollton, United States Senator 1815–1821.

[2] Born in 1757.

[3] Born in 1780, nephew of P. B. Key.

[4] Born in 1775.

[5] Born in 1784.

[6] Born in 1763.

[7] Born about 1765.

[8] Born in 1772, United States Attorney-General 1817–1829.

[9] Born in 1775, admitted to practise in 1796, United States District-Attorney 1802–1821.

[10] Born in 1762, Yale 1780, Judge of Supreme Court of Connecticut 1807.

[11] Born in 1774, Brown 1791, United States Senator 1811–1821.

of Maryland, against R. G. Harper and F. S. Key of Maryland and Jared Ingersoll of Pennsylvania. John Drayton [1] of South Carolina appeared in 1807 in *Rose* v. *Himely* (4 Cranch). Henry Clay [2] from Kentucky, made his appearance in 1808, in *Skillem's Executors* v. *May's Executors* (4 Cranch). In 1809, Horace Binney, destined to lead the Philadelphia Bar for nearly half a century, made his first argument before the Supreme Court in *Bank of the United States* v. *Deveaux;* [3] and in the same year he appeared in a case with John Quincy Adams and Ingersoll. Edward Livingston of New York and Louisiana appeared also in 1809.

In 7 and 8 Cranch (1812–1814), Samuel Dexter, Daniel Davis and Rufus G. Amory of Massachusetts, and Pitkin and Putnam of Rhode Island, appear in various prize cases. In 1814, the name of Daniel Webster appears, for the first time, he having been admitted to practise before the Supreme Court in the winter of 1813–1814. The next year, Clay, Charles A. Wickliffe,[4] and George M. Bibb [5] of Kentucky, argued; and for the first time prominent New York counsel appear, when Thomas Addis Emmet and J. Ogden Hoffman argued the famous case of *The Nereide* (9 Cranch, 388) against Dallas and Pinkney.

Such were the lawyers who built up the fabric of early American law; and, as has been justly remarked: "While no judge ever profited more from argument; it is not, perhaps, diverging into the circle of exaggeration to say, that no Bar was ever more capable of aiding the mind of the

[1] Born in 1766.

[2] Born in Virginia in 1777, admitted to the Bar in 1797.

[3] Born in 1780, a Harvard graduate of 1797, studied in office of Jared Ingersoll, admitted to the Bar in 1800.

[4] Born in 1788.

[5] Born in 1772, Princeton 1792, author of *Bibb's Reports*, 1808–1811, Chief Justice of Kentucky, United States Senator 1811–1814, 1829–1835.

Bench, than the Bar of the Supreme Court, in the time of Chief Justice Marshall."

The Attorneys-General of the United States during this period were Edmund Randolph of Virginia, appointed in 1789; William Bradford of Pennsylvania, in 1794; Charles Lee of Virginia, in 1795; Theophilus Parsons of Massachusetts, appointed in 1801, but who never served; Levi Lincoln of Massachusetts, in 1801; Robert Smith of Maryland, in 1805; John Breckenridge [1] of Kentucky, in 1805; Caesar A. Rodney,[2] of Delaware, in 1807; William Pinkney of Maryland, in 1811; Richard Rush [3] of Pennsylvania, in 1814.

In the above list of the Bar practising before the Supreme Court, the names of many notable lawyers who practised only in State courts are lacking, perhaps the most notable omission being that of Aaron Burr who, though a leader of the New York Bar, never argued a case before the United States Supreme Court. While the Bars of New Hampshire, New York and Massachusetts at this time were of peculiar lustre, their practise was largely local.

The part played by American lawyers in the development of American law can be best comprehended by a rapid survey of some of the noted cases in the United States Supreme Court during these years. And while the whole trend of political and economic history was fixed by the decisions of Chief Justice Marshall, a share in the tributes paid to the greatness of those decisions must be awarded to the great counsel who argued before the Court. In this connection, the views expressed by the Court and by contemporary writers as to these arguments and decisions will be found of interest.

[1] Born in 1760, United States Senator 1801–1805.

[2] Born in 1772, University of Pennsylvania 1789.

[3] Born in 1780, Princeton 1797.

Only five reported cases had been decided between the time when Marshall took his seat on the Bench and February 24, 1803, the date when he rendered the first of a long line of decisions which were to establish the United States Constitution irrevocably as the supreme law of the land, and the Supreme Court as the final arbiter of its construction and of the validity of State and Federal statutes. This was the case of *Marbury* v. *Madison* (1 Cranch, 137). It was argued by Charles Lee of Virginia, Ex-Attorney-General and by Levi Lincoln of Massachusetts, Attorney-General. Of its decision Rufus Choate said later:

"I do not know that I can point to one achievement in American statesmanship which can take rank for its consequences of good above that single decision of the Supreme Court which adjudged that an act of the legislature contrary to the Constitution is void and that the judicial department is clothed with the power to ascertain the repugnancy and pronounce the legal conclusion. That the framers of the Constitution intended this to be so is certain; but to have asserted it against Congress and the Executive, to have vindicated it by that easy yet adamantine demonstration than which the reasonings of mathematics show nothing surer, to have inscribed this vast truth of conservatism upon the public mind so that no demagogue not in the last stages of intoxication denies it — this is an achievement of statesmanship, of which a thousand years may not exhaust or reveal all the good." [1]

The decision was regarded far otherwise, however, by the contemporary political opponents of Marshall; and a prominent Anti-Federalist newspaper in Boston thus expressed its views:

"The efforts of Federalism to exalt the Judiciary over the Executive and Legislature, and to give that favorite

[1] *The Position and Functions of the American Bar as an Element of Conservation in the State*, by Rufus Choate, July 3, 1845.

department a political character and influence . . . will probably terminate in the degradation and disgrace of the judiciary. . . . The attempt of the Supreme Court of the United States by a mandamus to control the executive functions is a new experiment. It seems to be no less than a commencement of war between the constituted departments. The Court must be defeated and retreat from the attack; or march on till they incur an impeachment and removal from office."[1]

For many years, the authority, as law, of the doctrines announced by Marshall in this case were bitterly opposed by Jefferson and his adherents; and he wrote to George Hay during Burr's trial, in 1807:

"I observe that the case of *Marbury* v. *Madison* has been cited in the Burr case, and I think it material to stop at the threshold the citing that case as authority, and to have it denied to be law. . . . I have long wished for a proper occasion to have the gratuitous opinion in *Marbury* v. *Madison* brought before the public and denounced as not law; and I think the present a fortunate one because the case occupies such a place in the public attention. I shall be glad, therefore, if in noticing that case, you could take occasion to express the determination of the Executive that the doctrines of that case were given extra-judicially and against law, and that their reverse will be the rule of action with the Executive."[2]

[1] See *Independent Chronicle*, March 10, 1803.

[2] See *Writings of Thomas Jefferson*, Vol. IX.

This power to declare legislative acts void was asserted as early as 1780, by the Supreme Court of New Jersey, in *Holmes* v. *Walton*, a case referred to in *State* v. *Parkhurst* (4 Halstead, 444). The Virginia Court decided the same way, in *Com.* v. *Caton* (4 Call, 5), in 1782, and in the *Case of the Judges* (4 Call, 135), in 1788, and in *Kamper* v. *Hawkins* (1 Va. Cases, 20), in 1793. The Rhode Island Court held the same in *Trevett* v. *Weeden*, in 1786; North Carolina and Massachusetts followed with cases in 1788.

For interesting discussion of the subject, see *Origin and Scope of the American Doctrine of Constitutional Law*, by Prof. J. B. Thayer, *Harv. Law Rev.*, Vol. XII (1893); and J. W. Burrage, in *Political Science Quarterly*, Vol. X (1895); and *An Essay on Judicial Power over Unconstitutional*

The decision in this famous case was not rendered until over a year after its argument on December 4, 1801, owing to a very peculiar piece of political interference with the Court (the only instance of the kind in its history, except the action of Congress in 1866). It happened as follows: from 1789 until the passage of the Act of February 13, 1801, the terms of the Supreme Court were held in February and August; the Act of 1801 provided that they should be held in June and December. Accordingly, the Court sat in December, 1801, heard the argument in *Marbury* v. *Madison*, and adjourned, expecting to meet in June, 1802. In the meantime, however, Congress met, repealed all the judiciary legislation of the Adams administration, and reinstated the old August and February terms. Later, fearing that Marshall and his Court might hold the repealing statute unconstitutional, Congress abolished the August term and provided that the Court should have only a February term, thus, in effect, adjourning the Supreme Court by act of Congress, from December, 1801, to February, 1803. The Court, therefore, held no session at all in the year 1802.

It is interesting to note that just one week after the decision in *Marbury* v. *Madison*, the Court, though strongly Federalist, rendered a decision affirming Marshall's decision given in the lower court, upheld the constitution-

*Legislation*, by Brinton Coxe; *The Relation of the Judiciary to the Constitution*, by W. M. Meigs, *Amer. Law Rev.*, Vol. XIX; *The Supreme Court and Unconstitutional Acts of Congress*, by E. S. Corwin, *Michigan Law Rev.*, Vol. IV; *The Conflict over Judicial Powers in the United States to 1870*, by Charles G. Haines, *Columbia Univ. Studies in Hist. Econ. and Public Law.*

See also especially addresses of James T. Mitchell and Hampton L. Carson in *John Marshall, Life, Character and Judicial Services*, by John F. Dillon (1803); *Laws and Jurisprudence of England and America*, by John F. Dillon (1895); and elaborate note in *Marshall's Complete Constitutional Decisions Annotated*, by John F. Dillon, p. 39 (1903).

ality of Jefferson's repealing statute, and overthrew the Federalist Circuit Court power — *Stuart* v. *Laird* (1 Cranch, 308), decided March 2, 1803 — thus affording a shining illustration of non-political judicial action.[1]

Two years after the Marbury case, occurred one of the most famous of American State trials, and especially noted for the eminence of the counsel engaged. This was the impeachment of Samuel Chase, Judge of the United States Supreme Court, before the United States Senate, presided over by Vice-President Burr, in 1805.

The attempted impeachment failed disastrously, not only on the merits of the case, but also because of the overwhelming weight of legal ability on Chase's side — his counsel being Luther Martin, Robert G. Harper, Joseph Hopkinson, Philip B. Key and Charles Lee, while the case of the House of Representatives was presented by John Randolph, Cæsar A. Rodney, John Nicholson, Early and Nelson.[2]

A year and a half later, in May, 1807, came the trial of Aaron Burr for treason, held in the Circuit Court for the District of Virginia, before Chief Justice Marshall and District Judge Cyrus Griffin. No case of the day

[1] In William Rawle's *A View of the Constitution*, published in 1825, it is said: "The Supreme Court which affirmed a decision by which the validity of the repealing act was established, was at that time composed entirely of men politically adverse to that which, by a sudden revolution, had become the predominant party in the legislature. Yet the decision was unanimously given, one of the judges only being absent on account of ill health. . . . Party taint seldom contaminates judicial functions."

[2] It is stated that "several persons in the audience who had attended some portion of the trial of Warren Hastings avowed Burr presided with more dignity than the Lord Chancellor." See *Aaron Burr*, by Samuel L. Knapp (1835). It is to be noted that the Impeachment Trial of Warren Hastings had ended only ten years before, in 1795, having begun in 1788, and the same preponderance of able counsel had been on Hastings' side — Burke, Fox and Sheridan against Law (Lord Ellenborough), Sir Thomas Plumer and Dallas.

aroused more intense excitement or enlisted a more brilliant array of counsel. For Burr there appeared, first and foremost, Edmund Randolph, ex-Attorney-General of the United States, weighty in counsel, deep in knowledge, but ponderous in style; Charles Lee also ex-Attorney-General; John Wickham, the leader of the Virginia Bar, famed for his wit and versatility; Benjamin Botts of Virginia, a lawyer of much tact, local knowledge and common sense; Jack Baker, a local attorney and good fellow; and finally Luther Martin. Burr himself, with his keen and powerful intellect, originated and directed his whole defence. For the Government there appeared Cæsar A. Rodney, only recently appointed United States Attorney-General, who took part in the preliminaries of the trial; George Hay, United States District-Attorney, and son-in-law of James Monroe; William Wirt, then thirty-five years old, and practically at the beginning of his brilliant career, and Alexander McRae, Lieutenant-Governor of Virginia, a lawyer of courage and tenacity but lacking in tact. To these counsel, an interesting tribute was paid by the Chief Justice, who said in his opinion:

> "A degree of eloquence seldom displayed on any occasion has embellished a solidity of argument and a depth of research by which the Court has been greatly aided in forming the opinion it is about to deliver."[1]

[1] John Randolph was foreman of the Grand Jury. On May 22, the trial began, dragging on for five months. The first fight arose on Burr's move to have a subpoena duces tecum issued to President Jefferson, against whom Martin entered into a violent invective saying: "He has let slip the dogs of war, the hell hounds of persecution to hunt down my friend." On June 13, Judge Marshall gave a decision that the subpoena should issue. The President, however, never appeared, and for answer wrote to Hay, suggesting moving to commit Luther Martin as particeps criminis with Burr.

On June 24, the Grand Jury presented indictments against Burr for treason and misdemeanors. On August 17, the jury was impanelled; and

The definition of the law of treason laid down, with splendid freedom from political considerations, by Marshall saved Burr's life, but gave rise to bitter political attacks upon the Chief Justice, and renewed a popular demand for an elective judiciary or a limited term of office.

Jefferson wrote to James Wilkinson, September 20, 1807:[1]

"The scenes which have been enacted at Richmond are such as have never before been exhibited in any country where all regard to public character has not yet been thrown off. They are equivalent to a proclamation of impunity to every traitorous combination which may be formed to destroy the Union. . . . However, they will produce an amendment to the Constitution which keeping the judges independent of the Executive will not leave them so, of the Nation."

And again, on September 26, 1807, to William Thompson:

"The scenes which have been acting at Richmond are sufficient to fill us with alarm. We had supposed we possessed fixed laws to guard us equally against treason and oppression. But it now appears we have no law but the will of the judge. Never will chicanery have a more difficult task than has been now accomplished to warp the text of the law to the will of him who is to construe it."

In 1809, there occurred in the United States Supreme Court a case famous for its counsel — *Fletcher* v. *Peck*

on August 19, there began the long ten days of forensic argument, resulting in Marshall's decision that Burr could not be found guilty on the evidence.

Among the many lawyers who attended this trial were Andrew Jackson and Washington Irving.

*Trial of Aaron Burr*, by James A. Cabell, in *N. Y. State Bar Assn. Proc.*, Vol. XXIII; *Decisive Battles of the Times*, by Frederic Trevor Hill (1907).

[1] *Writings of Thomas Jefferson*, Vol. IX.

(6 Cranch, 87).[1] This case arose in the Massachusetts Circuit, and was first argued by Luther Martin, against John Quincy Adams and Robert G. Harper.

An entry in J. Q. Adams' Diary records that the case was thought by the Court to be a fictitious one — an interesting suggestion in view of the fact that the decision in the great *Dartmouth College Case*, ten years later, was based partly on this case:

"The Court met at the usual hour (11 A.M.) and sat until 12 M. Martin continued his argument until that time, and then adjourned until two. I went to the capitol and witnessed the inauguration of Mr. Madison as President of the United States. The House was very much crowded and its appearance very magnificent. . . . The Court had adjourned until two o'clock. I therefore returned to them at that hour. Mr. Martin closed the argument. March 7. In the case of *Fletcher and Peck*, he (the Chief Justice) mentioned to Mr. Cranch and Judge Livingston, and had done the same to me on Saturday night at the ball, the reluctance of the Court to decide the case at all, as it appeared manifestly made up for the purpose of getting the Court's judgment upon all the points. And although they have given some decisions in such cases, they appear not disposed to do so now."

[1] The case involved the famous Yazoo Frauds and the constitutionality of a statute of the State of Georgia of 1796, voiding certain grants of land made under a previous Act of 1795 on the ground that the passage of the Act of 1795 was obtained by fraud and corruption — see *The Yazoo Land Companies*, by Charles H. Haskins, *Amer. Hist. Ass. Papers*, Vol. V (1891); *James Wilson and the so-called Yazoo Frauds*, by M. C. Klingelsmith, *U. of P. Law Review*, Vol. LVI (1908); *Documents of Congress*, 1809; *Niles Register*, Vol. VI. See also *Brown* v. *Gilman*, 4 Wheaton, 255; *Brown* v. *Jackson*, 7 Wheaton, 218.

It is interesting to note that ten years previously the Massachusetts Supreme Court had held the Georgia statute unconstitutional, as impairing the obligation of contract — the very point on which the United States Supreme Court decided the case. See *Derby* v. *Blake*, cited, October 9, 1799, in the *Columbian Centinel*, a Boston newspaper.

The second argument [1] in 1810, was notable for the fact that Joseph Story, one year before his appointment as Supreme Court Judge, appeared as counsel on the winning side, in place of Adams (who had been appointed Minister to Russia). A complimentary comment on the counsel is to be found in Johnson's dissenting opinion:

"I have been very unwilling to proceed to the decision of this cause at all. It appears to me to bear strong evidence upon the face of it of being a mere feigned case. It is our duty to decide on the rights but not in a speculation of parties. My confidence however in the respectable gentlemen who have been engaged for the parties has induced me to abandon my scruples in the belief that they would never consent to impose a mere feigned case upon this court."

In 1811, occurred a case, interesting as one of the first involving the title to property under the Louisiana Purchase of 1803 — *Livingston* v. *Jefferson* (Federal Cases, No. 8411). This was an action known as the "Batture Case," brought by Edward Livingston against Thomas Jefferson for alleged trespass committed while President, in removing Livingston from property made by accretion of soil, known as the "batture," on the river front in New Orleans. A great controversy raged for years over this matter, in the courts, the newspapers and the law magazines. Its permanent effect on the jurisprudence of the country arose, however, from the political complexion of the case.

1 *Fletcher* v. *Peck*, at its first hearing went off on a point of jurisdiction; see the following entry in J. Q. Adams' Diary:

"March 11, 1809. This morning the Chief Justice read a written opinion on the case of *Fletcher and Peck*. The judgment in the Circuit Court is reversed for a defect in the pleadings. With regard to the merits of the case, the Chief Justice added verbally that circumstanced as the Court are, only five judges attending, there were difficulties which would have prevented them from giving any opinion at this term had the pleadings been correct."

While it was pending, William Cushing, Judge of the Supreme Court, died. The Court was Federalist in its politics; and Jefferson, whose personal fortune was at stake in the Livingston case, urged upon President Madison, with all the energy at his command, the extreme necessity for the appointment of a strong Republican to fill the vacant position. Jefferson's antipathy to Marshall and his distrust of his political motives led him to conceive that Marshall would take revenge by finding against him if the case came before him. Accordingly, he addressed urgent letters to Madison and to all his cabinet, of which the following may be cited.

Writing to Albert Gallatin, September 27, 1810, he said:[1]

"What the issue of the case ought to be, no unbiased man can doubt. What it will be, no one can tell. The Judge's inveteracy is profound and his mind of that gloomy malignity which will never let him forego the opportunity of satiating it on a victim.

"His decision, his instructions to a jury, his allowances and disallowances and garblings of evidence must all be subjects of appeal. I consider that as my only chance of saving my fortune from entire wreck. And to whom is my appeal? From the Judge in Burr's case to himself and his Associate Judges in the case of *Marbury* v. *Madison* — Not exactly however. I observe old Cushing is dead. At length then we have a chance of getting a Republican majority in the Supreme Judiciary. For ten years that branch braved the spirit and will of the Nation after the Nation has manifested its will by a complete reform in every branch depending on them. The event is a fortunate one and so timed as to be a Godsend to me. I am sure its importance to the Nation will be felt and the occasion employed to complete the great operation they have so long been executing by the appointment of a decided Republican with nothing equivocal about it.

[1] *Writings of Thomas Jefferson*, Vol. IX.

But who will it be? The misfortune of [Barnabas] Bidwell removes an able man from the competition. Can any other bring equal qualifications to those of [Levi] Lincoln?

"I know he was not deemed a profound common lawyer; but was there ever a profound common lawyer known in one of the Eastern States? There never was nor never can be one from these States. The basis of their law is neither common nor civil; it is an original, if any compound can be so called. Its foundation seems to have been laid in the spirit and principles of Jewish law, incorporated with some words and phrases of common law and an abundance of notions of their own. This makes an amalgam *sui generis;* and it is well known that a man first thoroughly initiated into the principles of one system of law can never become pure and sound in any other. Lord Mansfield was a splendid proof of this. Therefore I say there never was nor never can be a profound common lawyer from those States. [James] Sullivan had the reputation of pre-eminence as a common lawyer — but we have his history of Land Titles which gives us his measure. Mr. Lincoln is, I believe, considered as learned in their laws as any one they have. Federalists say that Parsons is better; but the criticalness of the present nomination puts him out of the question."

To Madison, he wrote, October 10, 1810:

"[George] Blake calls himself a republican but never was one at heart. His treachery to us under the embargo should put him by forever. [Joseph] Story and [Ezekiel] Bacon are exactly the men who deserted us on that measure and carried off the majority. The former unquestionably a tory and both are too young. I say nothing of professing federalists. Granger and Morton have both been interested in Yazooism. The former however has been clear of it."

All the lawyers mentioned in these letters were Republicans from Massachusetts (that being the State from which Cushing had been appointed).

Madison was evidently impressed with the appeals;

for, after offering the vacant judgeship to Levi Lincoln and to John Quincy Adams (both of whom declined), he finally appointed Joseph Story, then a young man of thirty-two, and a strong Republican. This appointment in its effect upon the future of American jurisprudence can be reckoned only second in importance to that of John Marshall. The appointment in its political aspect proved, however, a sore disappointment to Jefferson; for Story, soon after his accession to the Bench, became a staunch supporter of Marshall's strongly Federal doctrines.

When the "Batture Case" was finally argued in the United States District Court in 1811, the plaintiff's counsel was John Wickham, while George Hay, William Wirt and Littleton Waller Tazewell, appeared for Jefferson; District Judge John Tyler (father of President Tyler) and Chief Justice Marshall presided; and Tyler gave the opinion, finding for Jefferson on a point of jurisdiction.

The following extract throws a quaint light upon the lawyers of the day:

"While I freely acknowledge how much I was pleased with the ingenuity and eloquence of the plaintiff's counsel, I cannot do so much injustice to plain truth as to say that any conviction was wrought on my mind of the soundness of the arguments they exhibited, in a legal acceptation. It is the happy talent of some professional gentlemen, and particularly of the plaintiff's counsel, often to make the worse appear the better excuse. . . . These arguments and this eloquence, however, have been met by an Herculean strength of forensic ability which I take pride in saying sheds lustre over the Bar of Virginia."[1]

[1] See also *Livingston* v. *Dorgenois*, 7 Cranch, 577 (1813).

Livingston finally lost his case in the Louisiana Supreme Court, see *Morgan* v. *Livingston*, 6 Martin, 19 (1819).

And see Randall's *Life of Jefferson*, Vol. III; *Letters and Times of the Tylers*, by Lyon G. Tyler; *Opinions of DuPonceau, Rawle, Ingersoll, E. Tilghman and W. Lewis in behalf of Edward Livingston*, in Hall's *American Law*

Between 1789 and 1812, it may be said that the growth of American law was largely due to the lawyers and judges who moulded it. In 1812, there arose, however, a new factor to which may be attributed not only the rapid development of law, but also the far more important development of the legal profession. It is a singular fact that the War of 1812, while an event of slight influence on the political history of this country, had an incalculable effect upon American legal and economic history. To the economic conditions to which it gave rise, may be attributed the start of many of the branches of modern law and the consequent enhancement of the practise, importance and scope of the legal profession.

*Journal*, Vol. II (1809); *Proceedings of the United States Government in maintaining the Public Rights to the Beach of the Mississippi adjacent to New Orleans against the intrusion of Edward Livingston*, by Thomas Jefferson (1812), in Hall's *American Law Journal*, Vol. V (1816).

*An answer to Mr. Jefferson's Justification of his conduct in the case of the New Orleans Batture by Edward Livingston* (1813), in Hall's *American Law Journal*, Vol. V (1816).

On May 25, 1810, Jefferson wrote to Madison:

"In speaking of Livingston's suit I omitted to observe that it is a little doubted that his knowledge of Marshall's character has induced him to bring this action. His twistifications in the case of Marbury, in that of Burr and the late Yazoo case show how dexterously he can reconcile law to his personal biases; and nobody seems to doubt that he is prepared to decide that Livingston's right to the batture is unquestionable."

Marshall wrote to Story, July 13, 1821:

"For Mr. Jefferson's opinion as respects this department, it is not difficult to assign the cause. He is among the most ambitious and I suspect among the most unforgiving of men. That in a free country with a written Constitution any intelligent man could wish a dependent judiciary or should think that the Constitution is not a law for the Court as well as the Legislature would astonish me if I had not learnt from observation that with many men the judgment is completely controlled by the passions. The case of the mandamus (*Marbury* v. *Madison*) may be the cloak, but the batture is recollected with still more resentment."

See *Letters of Marshall in Mass. Hist. Soc. Proc.*, 2d series, Vol. XVI (1900–1901).

The impress of the War of 1812 on legal history is markedly seen in the following directions: first, in giving rise to a vast number of decisions on prize and admiralty law; second, in the growth of manufacturing corporations and the rise of the important branch of the law relating thereto; third, in turning commercial and industrial efforts from shipping and agriculture to manufactures and inventions, and consequently in establishing a system of patent law; fourth, in necessitating the development of internal means of communication — the coasting trade being ruined by the British blockade — and thus promoting the construction of canals, multiplying turnpikes, and preparing the people to demand the swifter means of transportation by steam railroads; fifth, in shutting off the country from its supply of English law reports and books, and thus throwing the lawyers and the courts upon strictly American resources in the solution of new legal problems.

The first great development in American law was naturally in that branch known as maritime, admiralty and prize law; and to the vast growth in this class of cases the American lawyer of the period owed most of his prosperity. The troubles with the French Directory, the Mediterranean pirates of Tripoli, the Berlin and Milan Decrees of Napoleon in 1806–1807; the retaliatory Orders in Council of the British Ministry, the Embargo and Non-Intercourse Acts of Thomas Jefferson, and finally, the War of 1812, — all had created conditions vital to the pockets of the wealthy merchants and shipowners of the United States.

"The Embargo had fallen like a withering curse upon New England. Under its desolating blight, her ships rotted at their wharves, her business stagnated, her industries were paralyzed, and her laboring population was thrown out of work. Ruin confronted her merchants;

poverty and starvation stared her workingmen in the face."[1]

At first, shipowners had looked to the courts for relief against the obnoxious laws. But in 1808, Judge John Davis had disappointed their hopes by his decision in the case of *U. S.* v. *Brigantine William*, in the United States District Court in Massachusetts, holding the Embargo Act constitutional, notwithstanding the fact that Samuel Dexter, the leader of the Massachusetts Bar, had argued to the contrary, and Theophilus Parsons, the great Chief Justice of Massachusetts had given an extra-judicial opinion as to the unconstitutionality of the obnoxious statute.[2]

Despairing of any remedy in the courts, the shipowners adjusted themselves to new conditions, and began to in-

[1] *Life and Times of George Cabot*, by Henry Cabot Lodge (1877).

[2] See report of the case in Hall's *American Law Journal*, Vol. II (1809). John Quincy Adams wrote:

"I wrote to Mr. Bacon that on the question of the embargo there was in Massachusetts a Judiciary of which he must think, what I could not say. It was with a repugnance, I could not express, that I saw a desperate party leader in the Chief Justice of the Commonwealth. It was from him alone that the pretence of the unconstitutionality of the embargo derived any countenance. Even Mr. Pickering had not ventured to start that idea. It was the stimulus to the people of forcible resistance against it. It was a gigantic stride towards a dissolution of the Union. Mr. Parsons not only broached the opinion, but very extra-judicially made no secret of it, upon the exchange and at insurance offices. Even the veneration entertained by the District Judge for his personal fame as a lawyer, was not exempted from the operation of its influence. Mr. Dexter argued against the constitutionality of the embargo, as a lawyer for his client. But there is one decisive proof that Mr. Dexter had no confidence in this argument. The District Judge to whom he addressed it and who decided against him was a Federalist. Four of the six Judges of the Supreme Court of the United States, Marshall, Cushing, Chase and Washington, were Federalists. Yet Mr. Dexter acquiesced in the decision of the District Judge and did not take an appeal to the Judge of the Circuit Court, Cushing."

See *Documents Relating to New England Federalism*, by Henry Adams (1870).

dulge in private warfare, disregarding all the various acts, orders in council and decrees; and privateering became a commercial business. "The merchant became marauder. From every port of the New England States, ships which had lain rotting and warping in the sun issued, new rigged as privateers, now returning with prizes, now captured by the enemy." [1]

The early State and Federal reports are flooded, therefore, with cases not only in the Federal admiralty courts, but also in the State courts, construing the policies of marine insurance companies, and adjusting the rights of captors, neutrals, belligerents, persons trading under licenses and privateering under letters of marque and reprisal or otherwise. From the large proportion of cases in the law reports involving these marine insurance companies, it would seem that the companies seldom paid a claim, without a contest at law.

The most successful and wealthiest lawyers at this time were those with a maritime practise; and as Horace Binney wrote of this period (1807–1817):

"The stoppings, seizures, takings, sequestrations, condemnations, all of a novel kind, unlike anything that had previously occurred in the history of maritime commerce — the consequence of new principles introduced offensively and defensively by the belligerent powers, gave an unparalleled harvest to the Bar of Philadelphia. No persons are bound to speak better of Bonaparte than the Bar of this city.

"He was, it is true, a great buccaneer and the British followed his example with spirit and fidelity; but what distinguished him and his imitators from the pirates of former days was the felicitous manner in which he first and they afterwards, resolved every piracy into some principle of the laws of nations. Had he stolen and called it a theft, not a single law suit could have grown out of

[1] *Life and Letters of Joseph Story*, by W. W. Story.

it. The underwriters must have paid. . . . But he stole from neutrals and called it lawful prize. . . . He always gave a reason, and kept the world of law inquiring how one of his acts and his reasons for it bore upon the policy of insurance."

To deal with this situation, a brand new body of law had to be formulated — and it was the good fortune of the United States that it possessed a judge, capable of performing this task, in Joseph Story, whose decisions practically made the prize and admiralty law for this country, just as the decisions of Sir William Scott [Lord Stowell] were contemporaneously establishing such law for Great Britain.

When Scott was appointed, in 1798, in England, there were no admiralty reports; and by 1811, *Robinson's Reports* of Stowell's decisions were practically the sole English authority, the old treatises of *Welwood*, *Malloy*, *Malynes* and *Marius* being imperfect and inaccurate. In the United States, all that Story had to go upon, were a few decisions in the first five volumes of *Cranch*, a small volume of *Bee's Reports* (So. Car.), *Mariott's Admiralty Forms*, and a small collection of precedents accompanying Hall's translation of *Clerke's Praxis;* hence cut off by the war from the benefit of Lord Stowell's contemporary decisions, Story construed admiralty law practically unaided and alone.

The first prize case of prime importance in the Supreme Court was *Rose* v. *Himely* (4 Cranch, 241), in 1808, in which ten counsel took part: Charles Lee, R. G. Harper, S. Chase, Jr., A. J. Dallas, W. Rawle, Ingersoll, and Drayton appearing against DuPonceau, E. Tilghman, and Luther Martin. Of this case, Story wrote, February 16, 1808 (before his appointment to the Bench):

"Here I am in the wilderness of Washington. . . . The scene of my greatest amusement as well as instruction in the Supreme Court. I daily spend several hours there. One cause only has been argued since I came here, and that was concluded to-day after occupying a space of nine days. Almost all the eminent counsel of the adjoining States were engaged in it."

Seven years later, in 1815, Judge Story delivered his celebrated opinion, in the Circuit Court, in *De Lovio* v. *Boit* (2 Gall. 398) — one of the most elaborate in the annals of the law, exploring and stating at length the history and extent of admiralty jurisdiction — a treatise in itself — an opinion which, in the words of its opponents, "sucked up jurisdiction like a sponge."

In the same year, the Supreme Court decided the famous case of *The Nereide* (9 Cranch, 388), in which Thomas Addis Emmet of New York [1] made his renowned argument, with J. Ogden Hoffman, against Alexander J. Dallas and William Pinkney. The latter, though unsuccessful, so dazzled the Court with his oratory that Marshall in his opinion felt obliged to advert to it:

"With a pencil dipped in the most vivid colors and guided by the hand of a master, a splendid portrait has been drawn exhibiting the vessel and her freighter, as forming a single figure, composed of the most discordant materials; and so exquisite was the skill of the artist, so dazzling the garb in which the figure was presented, that it required the exercise of the cold, investigating faculty which ought always to belong to those who sit on this bench, to discover its only imperfection — its want of resemblance."

[1] Thomas Addis Emmet, was at this time the leader of the New York Bar — born in 1765 in Ireland, a student in the Temple in London, he arrived in New York in 1804, and died in 1827.

See especially Story's description of Emmet in Story's *Life and Letters*, Vol. I.

See *Memoirs of Thomas Addis Emmet*, by Charles G. Haines (1829); and *Memoir*, in Story's *Miscellaneous Works*.

Judge Story (who dissented from Marshall's opinion) also wrote of this argument, February 22, 1815:[1]

"Mr. Pinkney and Mr. Emmet have measured swords in a late cause. I am satisfied that Mr. Pinkney towers above all his competitors. Mr. Emmet is the favorite counsellor of New York, but Pinkney's superiority to my mind was unquestionable. I was glad, however, to have his emulation excited by a new trial. It invigorated his exertion, and he poured upon us a torrent of splendid eloquence."

A most vivid contemporary picture of the Supreme Court judges of that day, sitting in their robes and powdered hair, and of the wonderful oratory of the great counsel practising before them, is given in two letters from George Ticknor in February, 1815, describing the argument of the case of *The Frances* (9 Cranch, 183) and of *The Nereide:*

"I passed the whole of this morning in the Supreme Court. The room in which the Judges are compelled temporarily to sit is, like everything else that is official, uncomfortable and unfit for the purposes for which it is used. They sat — I thought inconveniently — at the upper end; but, as they were all dressed in flowing black robes and were fully powdered, they looked dignified. Judge Marshall is such as I described him to you in Richmond; Judge Washington is a little, sharp-faced gentleman, with only one eye, and a profusion of snuff distributed over his face; and Judge Duval very like the late Vice-President. The Court was opened at half past eleven, and Judge Livingston and Judge Marshall read written opinions on two causes.

"After a few moments' pause, they proceeded to a case

[1] Feb. 27, 1829, Story wrote to W. Sampson:

"Mr. Emmet was a new and untried opponent and brought with him the ample honors gained at one of the most distinguished Bars in the Union. His speech was greatly admired for its force and fervor, its variety of research and its touching eloquence. It placed him at once by universal consent in the first rank of American advocates — but not before Mr. Pinkney."

in which Dexter, Pinkney, and Emmet were counsel. It was a high treat, I assure you, to hear these three lawyers in one cause. Pinkney opened it as junior counsel to Emmet; and it was some time before I was so far reconciled to his manner as to be able to attend properly to his argument. His person, dress, and style of speaking are so different from anything which I ever saw before, that I despair of being able to give you an idea of him by description or comparison.

"You must imagine, if you can, a man formed on nature's most liberal scale, who, at the age of fifty, is possessed with the ambition of being a pretty fellow, wears corsets to diminish his bulk, uses cosmetics, as he told Mrs. Gore, to smooth and soften a skin growing somewhat wrinkled and rigid with age, and dresses in a style which would be thought foppish in a much younger man. You must imagine such a man standing before the gravest tribunal in the land, and engaged in causes of the deepest moment; but still apparently thinking how he can declaim like a practised rhetorician in the London Cockpit, which he used to frequent. Yet you must, at the same time, imagine his declamation to be chaste and precise in its language, and cogent, logical and learned in its argument, free from the artifice and affectation of his manner, and, in short, opposite to what you might fairly have expected from his first appearance and tones. And when you have compounded these inconsistencies in your imagination, and united qualities which on common occasions nature seems to hold asunder, you will, perhaps, begin to form some idea of what Mr. Pinkney is.

"He spoke about an hour and was followed by Mr. Dexter, who, with that cold severity which seems peculiarly his own, alluded to the circumstances of his being left alone (his coadjutor not having come) to meet two such antagonists; then went on to admit all that Mr. Pinkney had said, and to show that it had nothing to do with the case in hand, and finally concluded by setting up an acute and, as I supposed it will prove, a successful defence.

"Mr. Emmet closed the cause in a style different from either of his predecessors. He is more advanced in life than they are; but he is yet older in sorrows than in years. There is an appearance of premature age in his person, and of a settled melancholy in his countenance, which may be an index to all that we know of himself and his family. At any rate, it wins your interest before he begins to speak.

"He was well possessed of his cause, and spoke with a heartiness which showed that he desired to serve his client rather than to display himself. He was more bold and free in his language, yet perhaps equally exact and perspicuous; and if Mr. Pinkney was more formally logical, and Mr. Dexter more coldly cogent, Mr. Emmet was more persuasive.

"When he had finished, I was surprised to find that he had interested me so much that, if he had not stopped, I should have lost my dinner."

"February 21, 1815.

"I was in Court all this morning. The session was opened by Judge Story and the Chief Justice, who read elaborate opinions. During this time Mr. Pinkney was very restless, frequently moved his seat, and, when sitting, showed by the convulsive twitches of his face how anxious he was to come to the conflict. At last the Judges ceased to read, and he sprang into the arena like a lion who had been loosed by his keepers on the gladiator that awaited him.

"The display was brilliant. Notwithstanding the pretension and vehemence of his manner, — though he treated Mr. Emmet, for whom I had been much interested yesterday, with somewhat coarse contempt, — in short, notwithstanding there was in his speech great proof of presumption and affectation; yet, by the force of eloquence, logic, and legal learning, by the display of naked talent, he made his way over my prejudices and good feelings to my admiration and, I had almost said, to my respect. He left his rival far behind him; he left behind him, it seemed to me at the moment, all the public speaking I had ever heard. . . . It is, however, in vain to compare him with anybody or everybody whom we have been in the habit of hearing, for he is unlike, and, I suspect, above them all.

"He spoke about three hours and a half, and when he sat down, Emmet rose very gravely. 'The gentleman,' said the grand Irishman, in a tone of repressed feeling which went to my heart, — 'the gentleman yesterday announced to the court his purpose to show that I was mistaken in every statement of facts and every conclusion of law which I had laid before it. Of his success to-day the court alone have a right to judge; but I must be permitted to say that, in my estimation, the manner of announcing his threat of yesterday, and of attempting to fulfil it to-day, was not very courteous to a stranger, an equal, and one who is so truly inclined to honor his talents and learning. It is a manner which I am persuaded he did not learn in the polite circles in Europe, to which he referred, and which I sincerely wish he had forgotten there, wherever he may have learnt it.'

"Mr. Pinkney replied in a few words of cold and inefficient explanation, which only made me think yet less well of him, and impelled me to feel almost sorry that I had been obliged so much to admire his high talents and success."

To meet the second set of conditions produced by the war — the rapid growth of business and manufacturing corporations — the law had few modern precedents or established rules.

The fundamental distinction between corporations, public and private, had been nowhere mentioned by Blackstone. Kyd's *Corporations*, in 1793, then practically the only book on the subject, related almost entirely to municipal corporations. In the United States, prior to 1800, there had been few cases involving corporations. *Kirby's Reports* (1789) contains only four such cases, one of an ecclesiastical society and three of municipal corporations; *Root's Reports* (1798), containing the earliest Connecticut cases, has one case of a church corporation. *Harris and McHenry's Reports* in Maryland (1809), containing the earliest American cases, have one church corporation case in 1796, and one private corporation case in 1799.

From 1790 to 1800, the Supreme Court of the United States had only a single corporation case before it — *Bank of North America* v. *Vardon* (2 Dallas, 78), in 1790. During the Colonial Governments before 1776, there were but six corporations of strictly American origin.[1] After the Revolution about two hundred charters were granted prior to 1800, mostly for banks, insurance, bridges and roads; but the only States to grant charters to any manufacturing corporations were Massachusetts which incorporated three; New York, three; Connecticut, Kentucky, and New Jersey, each one.[2]

[1] These were as follows: *The New York Company for Settling a Fishery in these parts* (1675); *The Free Society of Traders*, in Pennsylvania (1682); *The New London Society United for Trade and Commerce*, in Connecticut (1723); *The Union Wharf Company*, in New Haven (1760); *The Philadelphia Contributionship for the Insuring of Houses from Loss by Fire* (1768); *The Proprietors of Boston Pier of the Long Wharf in the Town of Boston in New England* (1772).

Pennsylvania also chartered in 1759 what was in effect a life insurance company, *The Corporation for the Relief of Poor and Distressed Presbyterian Ministers and of the Poor and Distressed Widows and Children of Presbyterian Ministers*. See *American Business Corporations before 1789*, by S. E. Baldwin, *Report of Amer. Hist. Ass.*, Vol. I (1902).

See also as to early associations in the nature of corporations, *Corporations in the Days of the Colony*, by A. McF. Davis, *Pub. of Colonial Soc. of Mass.* (1892-94).

[2] See *History of the Law of Business Corporations before* 1800, by Samuel Williston, *Harv. Law Rev.*, Vol. II (1888).

There had, however, been a considerable development of corporations formed for purposes other than manufacturing. As tabulated by Judge Simeon E. Baldwin, it appears that in the sixteen States, 5 corporations had been formed for aid of agriculture, 26 for banking, 36 bridge, 1 burying ground, 21 canal, 6 societies of trade and commerce, 1 aid of emigration, 1 fisheries, 25 insurance, 2 logging, 1 land, 1 mining, 26 improving navigation, 38 roads and turnpikes, 21 waterworks and aqueducts, and by the United States Government, 2 banks — a total of 213. Of these, Massachusetts had granted 88, or over a third; Connecticut, 37; New York, 21; and Virginia, 20.

See S. E. Baldwin in *Two Centuries Growth of American Law.*

The modern law of business corporations may be said to have been brought into being by Jefferson's Embargo Acts — statutes which produced also the insolvency acts which were soon to be the fruitful source of trouble in the courts and especially in interstate relations. Prior to the Embargo Acts [1] and the declaration of war in 1812, foreign commerce in New York and New England, and the production of food stuffs for export in the Southern States had been the great source of wealth. Both were prostrated by those acts. "The ships rotted in the docks, the crops in the fields and warehouses — a chain of suffering encircled the community." Under these conditions, attention was turned to the development of manufactures. Cotton, woolen, iron and glass factories sprang up, and with these industries arose the first large business corporations.

One of the first general incorporation acts was passed in New York in 1811, being limited to a few specified industries. Massachusetts however took the lead in number of corporations; and the scheme of law of business corporations in that State was largely developed on the lines of the charters, statutes, and court decisions relating to the other large corporations of the day — the turnpike corporations,[2] the "proprietors of bridges," the banking corporations, the "proprietors of mills," "the proprietors of locks and canals," and "the proprietors of log booms." The first case, however, in which a business corporation appeared as party in Massachusetts, was not decided until

[1] Judicially termed by Judge Sewall, in the first case arising under them in the Massachusetts State Courts in *Baylies* v. *Fettyplace*, 7 Mass. 325, 1811, "those extraordinary laws."

[2] The turnpike corporations had come largely into vogue between 1797 and 1810, and had been the source of much litigation, especially in the matter of assessment on stockholders, and payment of subscriptions to stock.

1813, when it was held that a foreign corporation might sue as plaintiff.[1]

In New York, the first case involving a business corporation (other than lock, bank, turnpike, or insurance) does not appear until 1816 — *Union Cotton Manufactory* v. *Lobdell* (13 John. 462 ).

In the Supreme Court of the United States, there had been but two cases involving corporation law between 1800 and 1815. Both, however, had a profound effect upon the development of the law — the one in restricting the growth of corporate liability, the other in emancipating corporate action from old Common Law bonds. In the first, in 1804, *Head* v. *Providence Ins. Co.* (2 Cranch, 600), Marshall laid down the doctrine that: "When the charter prescribes to them a mode of contracting, they must observe that mode, or the instrument no more creates a contract than if the body had never been incorporated."

In the other, *Bank of Columbia* v. *Patterson, Admr.* (7 Cranch, 299) in 1813, Mr. Justice Story held (largely on the authority of Massachusetts cases) that the old doctrine that a corporation could only act under seal was obsolete, and that "it could answer no salutary purpose, and would almost universally contravene the public convenience." [2] No greater impetus could have been given to business corporations than this decision, which thus

[1] See also early corporation cases. *Portsmouth Livery Co.* v. *Wilson*, 10 Mass. 91. *Medway Cotton Manufactory* v. *Adams*, 10 Mass. 360. *Salem Iron Factory* v. *Danvers*, 10 Mass. 514. *New York Slate Co.* v. *Osgood*, 11 Mass. 60. *Emerson* v. *Providence Hat Mfg. Co.*, 12 Mass. 237.

[2] As an illustration of the difficulties of law practise at this time, arising from the scarcity and infrequency of law reports the Court cites, in *Danforth* v. *Schoharie Turnpike Co.*, 12 John. 231, decided in May, 1815, this case of *Bank of Columbia* v. *Patterson, Admr.*, as authority; but the reporter adds in a note, "This case was cited and read to the Court from a gazette dated March 18, 1815," notwithstanding the case cited was decided in the United States Supreme Court, in 1813.

allowed them to make parol contracts by authorized agents; and the growths of modern corporation law may be dated from this case.

The rise of corporations was not viewed, however, with equanimity, even in those early days. And many lawyers, as well as laymen, echoed the sentiments of James Sullivan, Attorney-General of Massachusetts, who said in 1807 in his argument, in *Ellis* v. *Marshall* (2 Mass. 269), a case in which Theophilus Parsons and Samuel Dexter, also appeared:

"The great increase of corporations for almost every purpose is seriously alarming. . . . Interested and corrupt motives are growing daily more prevalent from this source. The independence and integrity of every branch of our government are attempted; and it is full time that a check be put to this spirit. And to an independent and enlightened judiciary can we alone look for its application."

With the development of manufacturing business, came the growth of insurance law. The first fire insurance corporation in the United States was *The Philadelphia Contributionship for Insuring Houses from Loss by Fire* incorporated on the mutual plan, in 1752. For many years, however, most of the fire insurance companies were unincorporated associations, existing principally in New York.

One of the earliest reported cases of fire insurance was *Stetson* v. *Mass. Mutual Ins. Co.* (4 Mass. 330), in 1808. There was no text book on the subject, however, prior to 1815. Marine insurance was an early and well developed part of the law, although carried on, until after the beginning of the Nineteenth Century, largely by private individuals unincorporated. Life insurance was, in 1815, hardly known, the earliest case being that of *Lord* v. *Dall* (12 Mass. 115), in 1809. Accident insurance was unknown.

The limited scope of the law of the times is perhaps best

illustrated by the fact that the law of torts which makes so large a part of the body of modern law, was, in 1815, practically confined to cases of trespass to person or property, assault, trover, replevin, and slander; actions of deceit and actions for negligence were very few. In *Kirby's Reports* in Connecticut, of two hundred and one cases from 1785 to 1788, fifty-two are actions of tort, of which one half are trespass, and one half actions of disseizin or ejectment. In *Harris and McHenry's Reports* in Maryland, published in 1809, covering the years 1658 to 1775, a large proportion of the cases are actions of ejectment or trespass.[1]

In New York, the first reported negligence case was not until 1810 (*Townsend* v. *Susquehannah Turnpike Road*, 6 John. 90); the first actions against a common carrier, in 1810 and 1813 (*Schiefflen* v. *Harvey*, 6 John. 170; *Elliott* v. *Russell*, 10 John. 1); the first negligence case involving a steam carrier, decided in the country, occurred in 1817 (*Foot* v. *Wiswall*, 13 John. 304), in which the conditions to which the law was to be applied were so novel, that the plaintiff argued seriously, that it was negligence, per se, to navigate a steamboat on a dark night.

In the year 1815, patent law in the United States was just beginning to come into existence. In 1790, there had been enacted the first general Patent Act; the first patent being issued "for making pot and pearl ashes." In 1792, thirty-three patents had been issued; in 1793, eleven; and in 1794, seventy-three, among which was Eli Whitney's cotton gin. In the whole first ten years, however, there were only two hundred and sixty-six patents.

[1] Sir Frederick Pollock, writing in 1886, says that the earliest and practically the only English text book on Torts which he could find "was a meagre, unthinking digest of *The Law of Actions on the Case for Torts and Wrongs*, published in 1720, remarkable chiefly for the depths of historical ignorance which it occasionally reveals."

The first book on patents was not written until 1803, when *Collier on Patents* was published in England. It was not until 1819, that cases of infringement of patents were brought under the equity jurisdiction of the United States Circuit Courts. In the Supreme Court prior to 1815, there had been only two patent cases — *Tyler* v. *Tuel* (6 Cranch, 324), in 1810, involving the right of an assignee of part of a patent to maintain an action on the case for infringement, and *Evans* v. *Jordan* (9 Cranch, 199), in 1815; the latter being the first of an interminable series of cases, involving an improved hopper boy for manufacturing flour and meal. In all the Federal Circuit Courts, there had only been thirteen patent cases, six of which had been decided by Judge Bushrod Washington, and five by Judge Story.

Perhaps one of the most important effects of the War of 1812 upon American law was the impetus which it gave to the publication of American law reports — first, through the increased spirit of nationality which it promoted; second, through the cutting off of the importation of English books.

It is to be remembered that in 1812, the first American law report was only twenty-three years old; in few of the States had law reports been published for more than six or eight years. In the great State of New York the first report had been published in 1801, and in Massachusetts in 1805.

Judges hitherto had not been in the habit of writing out their decisions; and had they done so, they had no reporter, and no way of making their decisions public, historical, or authoritative as precedent.[1]

[1] For interesting account of these legal conditions, see *Discourse on the Life, Character and Public Services of Ambrose Spencer, Chief Justice of New York*, by Daniel D. Barnard (1849).

With the beginning of printed reports, many of the cases were, therefore, so far as they were to be cited in the future, cases "of first impression." Hence, it was fortunate for the United States that, at the time when American decisions were beginning to be published and the cases so printed were to be used by future generations as establishing the law, there happened to be presiding over the courts of many of the States Chief Justices of pre-eminent ability as lawyers. In 1812, in Massachusetts, Theophilus Parsons was Chief Justice; in New Hampshire, Jeremiah Smith; in New York, James Kent (with whom were associated three great lawyers, Ambrose Spencer,[1] Brockholst Livingston and Smith Thompson;[2] in Pennsylvania, William Tilghman; in South Carolina, Henry W. De Saussure was Chancellor.[3]

It may also be noted as a fortunate chance that, for nearly twenty years (1804–1823) during this early crucial and formative period in the Federal law, a majority of members of the Supreme Court remained unchanged, and hence a steady policy could be adhered to by Marshall, Johnson, Livingston and Washington. The following changes took place in the personnel of the Court between 1800 and 1815: In 1804 William Johnson of South Carolina succeeded Alfred Moore on the latter's resignation; Brockholst Livingston succeeded William Paterson in 1806; Thomas Todd of Kentucky was appointed, in 1807, as the new Sixth Justice; Joseph Story succeeded William Cushing, in 1811; and Gabriel Duvall succeeded Samuel Chase, in 1811.

1 Born in 1765, Harvard 1783, Chief Justice 1819–1823.

2 Born in 1767, Chief Justice 1814–1819.

3 Born in 1763, Chancellor in 1808.

## CHAPTER XII

### EARLY STATE BARS OF NEW YORK AND NEW ENGLAND

OWING to the fact that few of the lawyers of New York and of the New England States appeared before the United States Supreme Court in its early years, it is due to the Bars of those States to give a separate description of the prevailing conditions.

### NEW YORK

The history of the courts and of the legal profession in the early years of the State of New York falls naturally into two periods — one covering the twenty years after the Revolution and ending with the death of Alexander Hamilton and the appointment of James Kent as Chief Justice, in 1804; the other covering the twenty years succeeding 1804 — the era of New York's great advocates, Emmet, Wells, Ogden and Van Vechten.

The first State Supreme Court in 1777 was composed of John Jay,[1] who served as Chief Justice until 1789, Robert Yates,[2] and John Sloss Hobart — the latter not having been bred to the profession of the law at all. Richard Morris became Chief Justice in 1789, succeeded in the next year by Robert Yates, who served until 1798, when

[1] Born in 1745, a Columbia graduate of 1764, admitted to the Bar in 1768, first Chief Justice of the Supreme Court of the United States in 1789.

[2] Born in 1738, studied with William Livingston.

John Lansing[1] took his place. In 1801, Morgan Lewis[2] succeeded Lansing.

James Kent, who at the age of thirty-five had been appointed on the Court in 1798, became Chief Justice in 1804. From 1794 to 1801, Egbert Benson,[3] Kent's instructor in law, sat on the bench with him as an associate judge. Robert R. Livingston[4] served as Chancellor from 1777 to 1801, being succeeded by John Lansing.

Judge Barnard, in his paper on the life of Ambrose Spencer, written in 1849, thus described the conditions of the Court prior to 1804:

"Up to Kent's time, the administration of the law had been conducted in a very inefficient and unsatisfactory way. The cases that came before the court were slightly examined both at the bar and on the bench. . . . The bench had not been without respectable talent and legal learning, but these had not been applied in that thorough, laborious and businesslike way so necessary to give strength and character to the court and to the law. It is a fact, however, that one of the number, Judge Hobart, who for twenty years had aided to give the decisions of the court such strength and character as they had, was not a lawyer — he had not been educated to the profession of the law. The judges did not write out their opinions — not even in the most important cases; and if they had done so, they had no reporter and no way of making their decisions public and historical. It was his (Kent's) practise, promptly begun, of bringing to the consultation of the judges, opinions in all important cases, carefully written out after the most laborious examination of the cases and of all the law applicable to them, to which the law is in-

[1] Born in 1754, studied with James Duane.

[2] Born in 1754, a Princeton graduate of 1773, studied with John Jay.

[3] Born in 1746, a Columbia graduate of 1765, Attorney-General 1777 to 1789.

[4] Born in 1746, a Columbia graduate of 1765, studied with William Smith and William Livingston.

debted for that entire change in the habits of all the judges. Still it must be observed that no attempt was made at regular reporting till 1803, and it was not till 1804, the year of the commencement of Judge Ambrose Spencer's judicial labors (and of Kent as Chief Justice), that the Legislature was induced to give authority to the Supreme Court to appoint a reporter. . . . I mention it as a fortunate circumstance that the business of reporting for the Supreme Court fell into the hands of that able and accomplished legal historiographer, William Johnson."

The first regular printed reports of decided cases were published in 1804, by George Caines, the Legislature constituting an official reporter also in that year. Of the evil effects of the lack of such reports, Caines said in the preface:

"The inconveniences resulting from the want of a connected system of judicial reports have been experienced and lamented by every member of that profession for whose use the following sheets are peculiarly designed. The determinations of the courts have been with difficulty extended beyond the circle of those immediately concerned in the suits in which they were pronounced; points adjudged have been often forgotten, and instances might be adduced where those solemnly established have, even by the bench, been treated as new. If this can happen to those before whom every subject of debate is necessarily agitated and determined, what must be the state of the lawyer whose sole information arises from his own practise or the hearsay of others? Formed on books the doctrine of which have in many respects been wisely overruled, he must have frequently counselled without advice and acted without a guide."

The Bar of New York increased vastly in weight during the twenty years after the Revolution. The important cases involving intricate questions of marine, insurance and mercantile law, crowded the courts; and the departure of many of the ablest lawyers who remained Loyalist during the war, opened a great opportunity to the younger members of the Bar.[1] Nevertheless, even as late as 1785, the New York City Bar numbered only forty.

An illuminating account of legal conditions and of the lawyers of this period after the Revolution was given by James Kent in his *Address to the Law Association of the City of New York*, in 1836.

"After the war had closed, by the peace of 1783, the landmarks of our ancient jurisprudence reappeared. They had, fortunately, not been obliterated or disturbed by the tempest. Almost the entire system of the English law recognized by our Constitution was put into operation. The profession was called into the most active business; and as the principles applicable to our Constitution were unsettled, and the rules of law unknown, except through the distant and dim vision of English reports, the claims of real property opened at once a large field of forensic litigation. Everything in the law seemed, at that day, to be new; we had no domestic precedents to guide us. English books of practice as well as English decisions were resorted to, and followed with the implicit obedience and reverence due to oracles. Our judges were not remarkable for law learning. Almost every point of practice had to be investigated and tested. Even Mr. Hamilton thought it necessary, at a circuit at which I was present, in 1784, to produce authorities to demonstrate and guide the power of the court in the familiar case of putting off a cause at a circuit. A few gentlemen of the colonial school resumed their ancient practice, but the bar was chiefly supplied by a number of ambitious and high spirited young men, who had returned from the field of arms with honorable distinction, and by extraordinary application,

[1] In 1779, the Legislature suspended all licenses to plead or practise law granted before April 21, 1777, subject to restoration provided that the lawyer should give satisfactory proof before a sheriff's jury that he had been true to the American cause. Many of those lawyers who had not become refugees were unable to take this oath.

they soon became qualified to commence their career at the bar with distinguished reputation.

"The whig lawyers, at the commencement of the war, were, most of them, afterwards called to fill important stations in public life, and they never resumed the practice of their profession. Among the members of the bar who took a leading share in business for some years after the close of the American war, we may very fairly select the names of Samuel Jones, Richard Harrison, Egbert Benson, Alexander Hamilton, John Lawrence, Aaron Burr, Henry Brockholst Livingston,[1] and Robert Troup.[2] Their minds were exercised, and acquired fervour and force, either in the great contest for independence, or in the equally interesting struggle for a national constitution. Colonel Burr was acute, quick, terse, polished, sententious, and sometimes sarcastic in his forensic discussions. He seemed to disdain illustration and expansion, and confined himself with stringency to the point in debate. Mr. Brockholst Livingston was copious, fluent, abounding in skilful criticism and beautiful reflections. His mind was familiar with the best classical productions in ancient and modern literature, and it was adorned with a cultivated and elegant taste. His forte lay in ingenious and sprightly illustration, and in popular and animated addresses to the jury. Colonel Troup united good sense with accurate practice; he was *par negotiis, neque supra.* By patient industry he came to the discussion at the bar a master of the law and learning of the case. He argued with simplicity, earnestness, and a winning candour, which commanded invariable attention and respect. Mr. Jones, the recorder of the city, and afterwards comptroller of the state was, in his day, the patriarch of the profession. No one surpassed him in clearness of intellect, and in moderation and extreme simplicity of character; no one equalled him in his accurate knowledge of the technical rules and doctrines of real property and in familiarity with the skilful and elaborate, but now obsolete and mysterious, black letter learning of the Common Law. Richard Harrison was a scholar of

[1] Born in 1757, a Columbia graduate of 1778, studied under W. Smith, Jr.

[2] Born in 1757, a Columbia graduate of 1774, studied under John Jay.

the first order, and after the age of seventy, he was studying the more obscure and minor Greek poets with the ardour of youth. He possessed very superior, and I think, unequalled attainments in all the complicated doctrines and refinements of equity jurisprudence, and he was deeply read in the learning of the civilians. In his calm, chaste, methodical and logical arguments at the bar, he was free from all loose and declamatory expansion, and his speeches were a steady flow of sound principles, supported by sound authority, and bearing strongly on the point in discussion. Nor will I permit myself to withhold the tribute of respect and gratitude due to the memory of my preceptor, the venerable Egbert Benson — he was perfectly instructed in the once vigorous, but now feeble and attenuated discipline of the old school of practice, and was, of course, a master of the old reports, and of the skill and logic of special pleading. He was possessed of neat and orderly business qualifications of the highest value, and he united great quickness and acuteness of mind, and was accustomed to carry his researches back to the recesses and grounds of the law, and to rest his opinion and argument on solid elementary principles. His candour and simplicity, his purity and integrity, his liberality and kindness, his great conversation powers, as well as the unquestionable ability and fidelity with which he discharged his public trusts, and especially that of attorney general of this state, for the first sixteen years of our independence, attracted general respect, as well as the warm personal attachment of his contemporaries of the last generation."

In addition to those named by Kent, there may be mentioned Richard Morris Smith, Richard Varick,[1] Josiah Ogden Hoffman, Gouverneur Morris,[2] Edward Livingston,[3] and Abraham Van Vechten[4] — the latter termed "the

[1] Born in 1750, Attorney-General 1789–1791.

[2] Born in 1752, a Columbia graduate of 1768, studied with W. Smith, Jr.

[3] Born in 1764, a Princeton graduate of 1781, admitted to the Bar in 1785, United States District Attorney 1801.

[4] Born in 1762, studied with John Lansing, Attorney-General 1810, 1813–1815.

father of the New York Bar," being the first lawyer admitted to practise under the State Constitution.[1]

The leadership of the Bar was generally assigned to Alexander Hamilton, who was born in 1757 and admitted to practise in 1782. From the date of his first great case of *Rutgers* v. *Waddington*, in 1784, until his appointment as Secretary of the Treasury in 1789, his legal fame was pre-eminent. Hamilton's chief competitor was Aaron Burr, who was born in 1756, graduated at Princeton in 1772, and was admitted to practise in the same year with Hamilton.

Three years later the famous James Kent was admitted to practise. Born in 1763, a Yale graduate of 1781, he studied in the office of Egbert Benson, the State Attorney-General, and practised at Poughkeepsie from 1786 to 1793. In 1797, he became Recorder of the City of New York; in 1798, Judge of the Supreme Court; in 1804, Chief Justice; and in 1814, Chancellor. Of Hamilton and Burr, Kent gave an interesting description in his *Address* in 1836, and also in his sketch of Hamilton in 1832, from which the following extracts are made:

"But among all his brethren Colonel Hamilton was indisputably pre-eminent. This was universally conceded. He rose at once to the loftiest heights of professional eminence by his profound penetration, his power of analysis, the comprehensive grasp and strength of his understanding, and the firmness, frankness and superiority of his character. . . .

"At that day everything in law seemed to be new. Our judges were not remarkable for law learning. We had no precedents of our own to guide us. . . . Nothing was settled in our courts. Every point of practice had to be

[1] A graphic summing up of a few of the leaders at the close of the Eighteenth Century is given in the *Discourse on the Life, Character and Public Services of Ambrose Spencer*, by Daniel D. Barnard (1849).

investigated, and its application to our courts and institutions questioned and tested.

"Mr. Hamilton thought it necessary to produce authorities to demonstrate and to guide the power of the court. . . . He never made any argument in court in any case without displaying his habits of thinking and resorting to some well founded principle of law. . . . Law was always treated by him as a science, founded on established principles. . . . There were no decisions of any of the courts published. There were none that contained any investigation. In the city of New York, Hamilton, Harrison, Burr, Cozine and perhaps John Lawrence and old Samuel Jones (then deemed and known as the oracle of the law) began to introduce the knowledge and cultivation of the law which was confined of course to Coke, Littleton, and the reporters down to Burrow.

"Hamilton brought a writ of right in a Waddell case in this city which made quite a sensation and created much puzzle in the court. The judges of the Supreme Court (Morris, Yates and Lansing) were very illiterate as lawyers. . . . The country circuit courts were chiefly occupied in plain ejectment suits and in trying criminals. In short, our jurisprudence was a blank when Hamilton and Harrison first began by their forensic discussions to introduce principles and to pour light and learning upon the science of law. . . .

"Mr. Hamilton returned to private life and to the practice of the law in New York in the spring of 1795. . . .

"Between the years 1795 and 1798 he took his station as the leading counsel at the Bar. He was employed in every important and especially in every commercial case. He was a very great favorite with the merchants of New York, and he most justly deserved to be, for he had uniformly shown himself to be one of the most enlightened, intrepid, and persevering friends to the commercial prosperity of this country. Insurance questions, both upon the law and the fact, constituted a large portion of the litigated business in the courts, and much of the intense study and discussion at the Bar. The business of insurance was carried on principally by private underwriters, and as the law had not been defined and settled in this country by a course of judicial decisions, and was open to numerous perplexed questions arising out of our neutral trade, and was left, under a complicated mixture of law and fact, very much at large to a jury, the litigation of that kind was immense. Mr. Hamilton had an overwhelming share of it, and though the New York Bar could at that time boast of the clear intellect, the candor, the simplicity, and black-letter learning of the elder Jones, the profound and richly varied learning of Harrison, the classical taste and elegant accomplishments of Brockholst Livingston, the solid and accurate, but unpretending, common law learning of Troup, the chivalrous feelings and dignified address of Pendleton, yet the mighty mind of Hamilton would at times bear down all opposition by its comprehensive grasp and the strength of his reasoning powers.

"He taught us all how to probe deeply into the hidden recesses of the science, or to follow up principles to their far distant sources. He was not content with the modern reports, abridgments or translations. He ransacked cases and precedents to their very foundations; and we learned from him to carry our inquiries into the commercial codes of the nations of the European continent, and in a special manner to illustrate the law of insurance by the severe judgment of Emerigon and the luminous commentaries of Valin. If I were to select any two cases in which his varied powers were most strikingly displayed, it would be the case of *Le Guen* v. *Gouverneur and Kemble*, argued before the Court of Errors in the winter of 1800, and the case of *Croswell* v. *The People*, argued before the Supreme Court in February term, 1804, and involving a libel on Thomas Jefferson."

During the years 1800 to 1824, the judges of the Supreme Court were men of more distinguished legal ability than in the previous period — Smith Thompson,[1] appointed in 1801, who succeeded Kent as Chief Justice in 1814;

[1] Born in 1768.

Ambrose Spencer,[1] appointed a judge in 1803 and Chief Justice in 1819; Daniel D. Tompkins,[2] a judge from 1804 to 1807; Brockholst Livingston, a judge from 1802 to 1807; William W. Van Ness, appointed judge in 1807, Joseph C. Yates, appointed in 1808; Jonas Platt, appointed in 1814; and John Woodworth, appointed in 1819. Of these, two became Judges of the United States Supreme Court — Livingston in 1807, and Thompson in 1824.

Chief Justice Kent succeeded Lansing as Chancellor in 1814.

During these years the Bar increased greatly in numbers, as appears from the following item in *Niles' Register*, June 27, 1818: ". . . Lawyers 'as plentiful as blackberries.' From a late census of the New York Bar, it appears that there are 1200 counsellors and attorneys at law that are fostered in the bosom of the State! 290 are practising in the city of New York."

Three lawyers stood forth pre-eminent above their fellows, and it would be difficult to decide between them for the leadership of the Bar — John Wells, Thomas Addis Emmet and David B. Ogden.[3]

[1] Born in 1765, a Harvard graduate of 1783.

[2] Born in 1774, a Columbia graduate of 1795, admitted to the Bar in 1797.

[3] Daniel Lord in his address before the New York Bar, December 14, 1847, on the death of Ex-Chancellor Kent, said of the Bar of the early Nineteenth Century:

"Let me bring up to your view Emmet whose enlarged and extensive learning was equalled by his childlike simplicity of heart. Colden, the polite scholar, the speculative philosopher, the able lawyer; also that model of all that is venerable in our memory, Van Vechten, whose teeming eloquence was Ciceronian and charmed every heart; the terse, the highly gifted Henry; the younger Jay full to abounding in every noble trait; and that union of scholar, lawyer, orator and gentleman, John Wells. Look, also, at the bench. The ingenious, polished Livingston; the sound and judicious Radcliff; Thompson, the honest, steady and stanch friend of all that was true and just; Van Ness, the accomplished man of genius; Platt, the sedate, the sober-minded; and last, him who in every trait and lineament, in every

Of these, the most eloquent advocate and the most interesting character was Thomas Addis Emmet. Born in Ireland in 1765, the brother of the famous Irish patriot, Robert Emmet, he had first studied medicine at Edinburgh, then read law in the Temple in London and had been admitted to practise in Dublin in 1791. He had actively engaged in the Irish rebellion against English rule, and being obliged to flee from the country, came to New York in 1804. As the rule of court prescribed a three years' study in the State for admission to practise in the Inferior Courts and six years in the Supreme Court, his application for a waiver of this rule met with great opposition from the Bar. The principal lawyers of New York were Federalists, and "the Federalist party hated France, hated Ireland in her revolutionary character, and hated Charles James Fox and his Whig party in England." A rebel against the English Tory Government was in their eyes a Jacobin, and the prejudice against Jacobins at the Bar was still extreme. Nevertheless, there was some strong Anti-Federalist lawyers, and the prevailing politicians were of that party. Governor George Clinton urged Emmet's case; and the Anti-Federalist judges, Ambrose Spencer, Daniel D. Tompkins and Smith Thompson were friendly to him. James Kent, then Chief Justice, being a rabid Hamiltonian Federalist, was hotly opposed to Emmet's admission, but the Court finally decided in Emmet's favor.

His reception at the New York Bar has been thus described by a contemporary lawyer:[1]

part and member was every way a giant, Ambrose Spencer. With these associates as competitors and coadjutors, did Judge Kent dispense justice. To whom of them all was he unequal?"

[1] *Memoir of Thomas Addis Emmet*, by Charles G. Haines (1829). See also *T. A. Emmet*, by Joseph Story; *The Emmet Family*, by Dr. T. A. Emmet (1898).

"The great men of the New York Bar were Federalists. They therefore turned their faces against Mr. Emmet. They formed a combination and agreed to decline all professional union and consultation with him. When Mr. Emmet ascertained the existence of the league he did not wait for an attack. He proved the assailant. Whenever he met any of the league at the Bar, he assumed the attitude of professional war, and he lost nothing by contact. If Mr. Emmet has any one extraordinary power, it is in the ready talent of successful and overawing reply.. The league was soon dissolved. Business flowed in and not long after his arrival his profession produced him $10,000 -$15,000 a year."

His remarkable eloquence at once carried him to the very head of the New York Bar; and in 1812, as an ardent friend of De Witt Clinton, he was made State Attorney-General.

John Wells was the exact opposite to Emmet in personal and professional characteristics. Emmet won his cases by his vehement and impassioned oratory as well as by his untiring study of the law. Wells convinced juries and judges by his unrivalled lucidity and the irresistible power of his logic. He was born in 1770, a graduate of Princeton in 1788, and admitted to practise as counsellor in 1795. Upon Hamilton's death, in 1804, he succeeded largely to his enormous business among the merchants of New York.[1]

David B. Ogden was born in 1769. For nearly twenty years after 1820 his practise before the United States Supreme Court exceeded that of any other New York lawyer, and, in fact, he argued more important cases before that tribunal than any other American lawyer save Daniel Webster and William Wirt. Of him, Chief Justice Mar-

[1] *Memorial of the Life and Character of John Wells, with Reminiscence of the Judiciary and Members of the New York Bar* (privately printed, 1874).

shall said that when he had stated his case, it was already argued.[1]

Contemporary with these three great lawyers, there were many of distinguished ability — Cadwallader D. Colden,[2] De Witt Clinton,[3] William Alexander Duer,[4] John V. Henry, Peter A. Jay,[5] Samuel A. Talcott, Daniel Cady,[6] John Anthon,[7] George Griffin,[8] Martin Van Buren,[9] Elisha Williams,[10] John Duer,[11] Henry Wheaton,[12] Hugh Maxwell,[13] and John C. Spencer.[14]

## Massachusetts

While the names of the lawyers of Pennsylvania, Maryland and the Southern States were known through the country, the Bar of New England remained, for at least twenty years after the Revolution, isolated and local in character and fame.

Nevertheless, the lawyers practising in this section of the country were men of ability quite equal to those of

[1] See *History of the Bench and Bar of New York City*, by Benjamin D. Silliman (1869). See also *Pleasantries about Courts and Lawyers of New York*, by Charles Edwards (1887); *Magazine of American History*, Vol. XIII (1885), article by Hon. C. P. Daly; see also *The Bench and Bar of New York*, by L. B. Proctor (1870).

[2] Born in 1769.

[3] Born in 1769, graduate of Columbia 1786, studied law under S. Jones, United States Senator 1802, Governor 1817–1828.

[4] Born in 1780, Judge Supreme Court 1822–1829.

[5] Born in 1776, graduate of Columbia 1794.

[6] Born in 1773, Judge Supreme Court 1847–1855.

[7] Born in 1784.

[8] Born in 1778, Yale 1797.

[9] Born in 1782.

[10] Born in 1773.

[11] Born in 1782, Chief Justice Superior Court 1857.

[12] Born in 1785.

[13] Born in 1787.

[14] Born in 1788.

the better known Bars. Several factors however contributed to this isolation. Previous to 1800, the difficulty of communication between the States was a serious obstacle. After that date, the extreme Federalism of their politics kept the New England lawyers out of touch with the Republican leaders of the Bar at Washington. The length of the journey necessary to attend the Supreme Court was also a serious obstacle.

The influence of the political situation was most marked on the Massachusetts Bar; and for that reason a description of some of its great leaders will throw light upon the legal conditions of the time.

Boston and the large towns of Massachusetts were Federal to the backbone. The clergy, the merchants, and most of the Bar, all united in that political belief. Party lines were rigidly and rancorously drawn, and nowhere more so than at the Bar; so that clients frequently retained counsel because of their political affiliations rather than their legal ability. "The democrat had no caste, he was not respectable," writes Henry Adams. "When, in 1793, the French nation seemed mad with the frenzy of its recovered liberties, New England looked upon the bloody and blasphemous work with such horror as religious citizens could but not feel. Thenceforward the mark of a wise and good man was that he abhorred the French Revolution and believed democracy to be its cause." [1]

In 1800, when the approaching victory of Jefferson was seen to be inevitable, the clergy and a large proportion of the educated citizens of New England began to feel towards the National Government the same distrust which they bore to democracy itself; and they agreed in general with George Cabot, the leader of the Federalists of Massachusetts and head of the so-called "Essex Junto," when he

[1] *History of the United States*, by Henry Adams, Vol. I.

said: "I hold democracy in its natural operation to be the government of the worst." [1] And when the Democratic (or Republican) electorate was beginning to increase in size and power even in Boston, Fisher Ames wrote to Christopher Gore in 1799:

"The Jacobins in the vicinity of Boston are as openly bitter as ever and on the whole the *rabies canina* of Jacobinism has gradually spread of late years from the cities where it was confined to the docks and mob, to the country . . . all that is base is of course Jacobin and all that is prejudice and jealousy and rancor."

To be an Anti-Federalist or "Jacobin," in Eastern Massachusetts, prior to 1800, meant social and business ostracism. "In my childhood," wrote Theophilus Parsons, the younger, "Federalists and Jacobins very seldom, I believe, met in society. I never saw one until I was ten years old, in 1807." [2] Of the Essex Bar in 1801, Joseph Story wrote:

"At the time of my admission, I was the only lawyer within its pale who was either openly or secretly a Democrat. Essex was at that time almost exclusively Federal, and party politics were inexpressibly violent — all the lawyers and all the judges in the county were Federalists."

This obstinate disbelief in the possibility of any good coming from the new, democratic, American spirit retarded the intellectual growth of Massachusetts in many directions; and the conservative, English, anti-American atmosphere greatly influenced the development of the Bar, tending to nurture lawyers steeped in the Common Law, but less in touch with the growing independence of thought characteristic of the Bars of such States as Pennsylvania, Maryland and Virginia.

[1] Cabot to T. Pickering, Feb. 14, 1804, quoted in *Life and Times of George Cabot*, by Henry Cabot Lodge.

[2] *Memoirs of Theophilus Parsons*, by T. Parsons (1859).

In February, 1781, the following rule had been made by the Superior Court of Judicature, — the first order relating to lawyers made by the Court after Massachusetts became a State:

"Whereas learning and literary accomplishments are necessary as well to promote the happiness as to preserve the freedom of the people, and the learning of the law when duly encouraged and rightly directed, being as well peculiarly subservient to the great and good purpose aforesaid, as promotive of public and private justice; and this court being at all times ready to bestow peculiar marks of approbation upon the gentlemen of the bar, who, by a close application to the study of the science they profess, by a mode of conduct which gives a conviction of the rectitude of their minds and a fairness of practice that does honor to the profession of the law, shall distinguish themselves as men of science, honour and integrity: Do order that no gentleman shall be called to the degree of Barrister until he shall merit the same, by his conspicuous learning, ability and honesty; and that the Court will, of their own mere motion call to the Bar such persons as shall render themselves worthy as aforesaid; and that the manner of calling barristers shall be as follows: The gentleman who shall be a candidate shall stand within the bar. The Chief Justice, or in his absence, the senior justice, shall, in the name of the Court, repeat to him the qualifications necessary for a Barrister of the Law; shall let him know that it is a conviction in the mind of the Court of his being possessed of these qualifications that induces them to confer this honour upon him; and shall solemnly charge him so to conduct himself as to be of singular service to his country by exerting his abilities for the defence of her constitutional freedom; and to demean himself as to do honour to the Court and Bar."

After 1784, no barristers were called by the Court; and in 1806 the Supreme Judicial Court adopted a rule substituting counsellors for barristers as follows:

"*Ordered* — First, no attorney shall do the business of a counsellor unless he shall have been made or admitted as such by the Court.

"Second, all attorneys of this Court who have been admitted three years before the sitting of this Court shall be and hereby are made counsellors and are entitled to all the rights and privileges of such.

"Third, no attorney or counsellor shall hereafter be admitted without a previous examination."

As late as 1800, the Boston Bar, though distinguished in quality, was small in number. It consisted of only thirty-three lawyers, of whom twenty were attorneys of the Supreme Court, eight attorneys of the Court of Common Pleas, and five barristers, James Sullivan, Theophilus Parsons, William Tudor, Perez Morton and Shearjashub Bourne. An interesting view of the Bar of that period is found in a letter from Fisher Ames to Christopher Gore, who was contemplating resuming practise in Boston, October 5, 1802:[1]

"Your share will be made up of insurance cases — questions which our bankrupt law is sowing for the harvest of 1804. . . . Mr. Parsons practises on this large scale, and, I will add, fees are infinitely better than they were in 1786. . . . Who are the rivals for this business with whom you must divide the booty? Parsons stands first, but he is growing older, less industrious, and wealth or the hypo may stop his practice. Otis is eager in the chase of fame and wealth, and with a great deal of eloquence is really a good lawyer and improving. Dexter is very able and will be an Ajax at the Bar as long as he stays. You know however that his aversion to reading and to practice is avowed. His head aches on reading a few hours, and if he did not love money very well he would not pursue the law. Sullivan, who seems immortal . . . will not be in our way. John Lowell's health is wretched. A number of eminent lawyers will be wanted in Boston; and though

[1] See *Life and Works of Fisher Ames* (1854).

the place is overstocked I think the prospect for 1804 not unhopeful. I know of no very dashing young men coming forward."

Of the members of the Bar thus mentioned, Fisher Ames was born in 1758, a Harvard graduate of 1774, and had studied law in the office of William Tudor. The Nestor of lawyers during the twenty years after the Revolution was James Sullivan, who shared with Theophilus Parsons the leadership of the Bar.[1] Born in 1744, he had fought as a general in the War, and served as Judge of the Superior and of the Probate Court for a few years. From 1790 to 1807 he was Attorney-General of the State, in spite of the fact that, unlike all his competitors at the Bar, he was strongly Anti-Federalist in politics. He was also the author of the first comprehensive American book on real estate law — *Land Titles*, in 1801. John Lowell was the son of the elder John Lowell who was the first United States District Judge in Massachusetts. He was born in 1769. After 1803 he retired from active practise, but became widely known as the keenest writer among the hot Federalists of New England. He was appointed the first professor of law at Harvard College in 1815, but declined.

With the exception of James Sullivan, Samuel Dexter had the largest practise of the Massachusetts lawyers of the early Nineteenth Century, and his name appears in most of the important cases in the early *Massachusetts Reports*.[2] He was born in 1761, graduated from Harvard in 1781, and studied law under Levi Lincoln (later Attorney-General of the United States). In 1799, he was United States Senator; in 1800, Secretary of State and Secretary of the Treasury under President Adams.

1 See *Life of James Sullivan*, by R. G. Amory.

2 For the best, though incomplete, sketch of Samuel Dexter, see *Reminiscences of Samuel Dexter*, by Lucius Manlius Sargent ("Sigma") (1857).

Of all Massachusetts lawyers, Dexter's services were most sought in argument of cases at Washington, in the early years of the United States Supreme Court. And it was into his place that Daniel Webster may be said to have stepped, on Dexter's death, in 1816. "For several years," said Joseph Story, "he passed his winters in Washington under engagement in many of the most important cases. Rarely did he speak without attracting an audience composed of the taste, the beauty, the wit and the learning that adorned the city." Just before his death in 1816, he argued for the State of Virginia, with St. George Tucker, the great case of *Martin* v. *Hunter's Lessee*, in which Judge Story settled, against Dexter's contention, the power of the Federal Supreme Court to review the decision of a State court on writ of error.

Like John Marshall, Dexter relied on his supreme power of reasoning rather than on precedents and citation of cases. So much was this his habit that William Plumer relates an argument used by him in a case against Parsons which might almost be thought the argument of one of the unlearned lawyers of the times. "The law in this case is as I have explained it," said Dexter, "and it lies, as your Honors see, in the compass of a nutshell. My brother Parsons has here a basket full of law books; and he will endeavor to show from them that it is all the other way. But one plain dictate of common sense, one clear maxim of the Common Law is worth a cartload of such rubbish."

"He had a disinclination," said Story, "to black-lettered law, which he sometimes censured as the scholastic refinements of monkish ages; and even for the common branches of technical science, the doctrines of special pleading, and the niceties of feudal tenure he professed to feel little of love or reverence. . . . In commercial causes, he shone with peculiar advantage. . . . Though he might be wrong upon authority and practise, he was rarely wrong upon the principles of international justice. No man was ever more exempt from fineness or cunning in addressing a jury. He disdained the little arts of sophistry or popular appeal. It was in his judgment something more degrading than the sight of Achilles playing with a lady's distaff."

Perhaps the best and liveliest description of his manner as a lawyer is found in Story's letter to his wife, March 10, 1814, describing the contests between William Pinkney of Maryland and Dexter, in a series of prize cases:

"I must, however, after all, give the preference to Mr. Pinkney's oratory. He is more vivacious, sparkling, and glowing; more select and exact in his language, more polished in his style, and more profound and earnest in his judicial learning. Mr. Dexter is calm, collected, and forcible, appealing to the judgment. Mr. Pinkney is vehement, rapid, and alternately delights the fancy and seizes on the understanding. He can be as close in his logic as Mr. Dexter when he chooses; but he can also step aside at will from the path, and strew flowers of rhetoric around him. Dexter is more uniform, and contents himself with keeping you where you are. Pinkney hurries you along with him, and persuades as well as convinces you. You hear Dexter without effort; he is always distinct and perspicuous, and allows you an opportunity to weigh as you proceed. Pinkney is no less luminous, but he keeps the mind on the stretch, and you must move rapidly or you lose the course of his argument."

Of all the lawyers in Massachusetts, the most profound in learning and weighty in argument, both at the Bar and on the Bench, was Theophilus Parsons.

Parsons was born in 1750 and graduated from Harvard in 1769.[1] He studied law at Portland, Maine (then Falmouth), under Theophilus Bradbury, and was admitted to practise in 1774. Portland being almost totally burned

[1] *Memoirs of Theophilus Parsons*, by T. Parsons.

by the British, in 1775 he removed to Newburyport, Massachusetts, and in 1800, to Boston.

His early success was as a master of prize and admiralty law, "of which," writes his son, "few lawyers then knew anything. In fact he had almost the monopoly of it and it was very profitable. The late Governor Sullivan, Judge Lowell, and my father were the only practising lawyers who had much knowledge of it. . . . My mother used to speak of the 'prize times' as the most profitable which she had ever known."

"He was the most learned lawyer of his time and was called the giant of the law. . . . He comprised in his professional attainments among other things a full and accurate knowledge of the common law, civil, martime and ecclesiastical law, the law merchant, the statute and common law of his own country, and the law of nations. From the methodical order of his mind, all he knew was ever familiarly at his command. His speeches to juries and judges were neither eloquent nor elegant in anything but pertinency and argument. They were never long. It is not remembered that he ever used a brief."

Thus wrote Chief Justice Isaac Parker, his successor.

In February, 1801, he was nominated as United States Attorney-General by President Adams, in place of Charles Lee, but though confirmed by the Senate, he declined the appointment.

In 1806, he was appointed Chief Justice of Massachusetts; and from that time until his death, in 1813, his judgments laid the foundations for a great portion of the law of Massachusetts.

"But few pages of the early reports can be read without finding illustrations of the fact that immemorial usage and early Colonial and Provincial statutes had upon a vast variety of subjects almost created a law of our own. Judge Parsons was precisely the man to learn, appreciate and apply this local jurisprudence; and his happiest efforts are those in which perhaps by way of reply to learned arguments of counsel founded upon the text of the English law he adduces unanswerable enactments and precedents to disprove its binding authority in the State of Massachusetts. In such cases we see the thoroughly practical man conversant with all sorts of things and familiar with all sorts of people; the man who, endowed by nature with extraordinary capacities which study and learning had indefinitely improved and developed, allowed none of the innumerable occasions to pass when he was brought into contact with the others without making some important addition to his stock of available knowledge."[1]

"Such was the veneration of the Bar for him as a lawyer that they exhibited an unusual awe in his presence. There was great neglect (then) in preparing papers for the court, and it was several years before it was properly attended to; and I have seen him non-suit our oldest counsellor for that cause very often. He had not much patience to hear an unsound argument nor to hear counsel advance an untenable point; and the lawyers were so poorly versed in legal lore they were not only willing but desirous that he should take the disposal of the whole case into his own hands. I have known him many times to do this."

So said one of his contemporaries.[2]

There is little doubt however that the slack methods of the Bar needed a strong hand to correct them; and probably Parsons' retort to the famous Samuel Dexter was well grounded. Dexter, being stopped in an argument by the Judge's remark that he was trying to persuade the jury of that for which there was no evidence, replied: "Your

[1] See *The Jurisprudence of Massachusetts*, *Central Law Journal*, Vol. I (1874); see also *American Jurist*, Vol. III (Jan., 1830).

See also *Parsons* in *Biographical Sketches of Eminent Lawyers*, by S. L. Knapp (1821).

[2] See Letter of Zachariah Eddy to Professor Emory Washburn, in 1851, in *Memoirs of Theophilus Parsons*, by T. Parsons.

Honor did not argue your own cases in the way you require us to." "Certainly not," was the reply, "but that was the judge's fault, not mine."

"No sooner had he taken his seat upon the bench than the whole air of the court room seemed charged with a terrible energy. No excuse was listened to; no delay was admitted. The dropsical dockets rapidly shrank, when gashed by the unsparing lancet of the new Chief. The lawyers at first grumbled; but suitors were better pleased, and the great improvement effected soon reconciled all persons to the new system."[1]

The name of Harrison Gray Otis stands well to the front of the brilliant Federalist lawyers and orators.[2] Born in 1765, graduating from Harvard in 1783, a classmate of the noted lawyers, Ambrose Spencer (later Chief Justice of New York), William Prescott, Artemas Ward, and William King Atkinson of New Hampshire, he studied in the office of Judge John Lowell, became United States District-Attorney in 1801 and United States Senator from 1817 to 1822. In the early *Massachusetts Reports* his name, with that of Charles Jackson, rivals even Dexter's in number of appearances. Unlike either Parsons or Dexter, it was on the charm of his manner and the eloquence of his speech that Otis depended for his success.

Besides the above, the following lawyers were distinguished at the Bar during the first quarter of the Nineteenth Century — William Prescott,[3] Christo-

[1] *The Bench and Bar*, by John T. Morse. *Memorial Hist. of Boston*, Vol. IV.

[2] See *Harrison Gray Otis* in *Memorial Biographies of N. E. Hist. Gen. Soc.*, Vol. I (1880).

[3] One of Parsons' "most valued friends," and a lawyer of great depth and soundness of learning and exclusive devotion to law was William Prescott of Salem. He was also the friend of young Joseph Story, the father of William H. Prescott the historian, and the father-in-law of Franklin Dexter. Born in 1762, a Harvard graduate in 1783, he was a favorite maritime and

pher Gore,[1] Charles Jackson,[2] Edward St. Loe Livermore,[3] William Sullivan,[4] Samuel Hoar,[5] Artemas Ward[6] and John Phillips,[7] all of whom were Federalists.

Of a younger generation, the most famous of all Massachusetts lawyers of the time was Joseph Story. He was born in 1779 in the seaport fishing town of Marblehead. To become, in later life, the great American judicial master of prize and admiralty law was, therefore, only his brithright. Graduating from Harvard College in 1798, he was admitted to the Essex Bar in 1801. "All the lawyers and all the judges in the County of Essex were Federalists," he wrote, "and I was the first who obtruded upon it as a

insurance lawyer. It was in his office, in 1815, that Theophilus Parsons the younger (later Professor in the Harvard Law School) studied. Of him, Story wrote in 1820, in his article on *Chancery Jurisdiction:* "His cautious, well instructed, modest and powerful mind would adorn an equity bench and create an equity bar for Massachusetts, equal to the Chancery Court of James Kent."

[1] Born in 1758, a Harvard graduate of 1776, a student of law in the office of John Lowell, United States District-Attorney in 1789, a Commissioner of the United States to London on the British Spoliation Claims in 1796, Governor of Massachusetts in 1809, United States Senator 1813–1816.

[2] Born in 1775, a Harvard graduate of 1793, a student of law in the office of Theophilus Parsons, Judge of the Massachusetts Supreme Court in 1813.

"Of all my pupils," said Parsons, "no one has left my office better fitted for his profession. He will prove himself the American Blackstone." See *Life of Charles Jackson* in *Law Reports*, Vol. XIII.

[3] Born in 1762 in Portsmouth, New Hampshire, a student of law in Theophilus Parsons' office, Judge of the New Hampshire Supreme Court in 1799, and afterwards practising law in Boston, especially in maritime cases.

[4] Born in 1774, a son of James Sullivan, Harvard graduate 1792, studied law with his father.

[5] Born in 1788, Harvard 1802, a student in the office of Artemas Ward, for many years the leader of the Middlesex County Bar.

[6] Born in 1762, Harvard 1783, brother-in-law of Samuel Dexter, Chief Justice of the Court of Common Pleas in 1821.

[7] Born in 1770, Harvard 1788, Judge of the Court of Common Pleas in 1809, first Mayor of Boston in 1822.

political heretic. I was not a little discouraged" as the only lawyer of Republican politics.

Such, however, was Story's evident ability, that even ardent Federalists like William Prescott, one of the leaders of the Bar, and Judge Sewall, in whose office Story studied, were forced to admit that political ostracism could not last long. "It is vain," said Sewall to Chief Justice Parsons, "to attempt to put down young Story. He will rise, and I defy the whole Bar and Bench to prevent it."

His earliest cases developed his remarkable knowledge of the law, and before he was thirty-two he had edited editions of four law books, which were among the earliest American productions of a legal nature: a work on *Pleading*, in 1805; *Chitty on Bills and Notes*, in 1809; *Abbott on Shipping*, in 1810; and *Lawes on Pleading in Assumpsit*, in 1811.

By the time he was twenty-six, Story was retained as counsel in cases in adjoining States, and especially in New Hampshire. He served in the Legislature with distinction from 1800 to 1808, and was elected to Congress in the latter year. Visits to New York and Washington in 1807–1808 enabled Story to see something of the Bar of other States. He visited the New York Supreme Court, sitting at City Hall, and was struck by Chief Justice Kent's celerity and acuteness. "He seems to be a good lawyer and despatches business with promptness. . . . On the whole, if he be not a very great man, I am satisfied he is not humble in his acquirements. He has the confidence of a great lawyer in all his actions, and is self poised on his own resources," he wrote; and he referred to the Bar of New York as "it is confessed not to be equal to what it has been. Its splendor has been obscured since Burr, Livingston and Hamilton have departed," and he is satisfied that "Massachusetts has legal talents and juridical learning equal to any of her sisters on this side of the Delaware. What lies beyond is now but speculation." In Baltimore, he met all the great lawyers, except Luther Martin. "They do not look like black-lettered scholars of the Inns of Court; but are pleasant and frank in their manners, and, as I understand, well versed in the general subjects of juridical consideration." With Robert Goodloe Harper he visited Judge Samuel Chase, whom he described: "In his person he is tall and not unlike Parsons. I suspect he is the American Thurlow — bold, impetuous, overbearing and decisive."

In 1810, Story argued the famous case of *Fletcher* v. *Peck* before the Supreme Court in Washington,[1] and he was re-elected to the Massachusetts Legislature. While serving as Speaker, he was appointed Justice of the United States Supreme Court to fill the vacancy caused by Judge Cushing's death, as described in a previous chapter.

The appointment of Story was not received with general enthusiasm. Among his political opponents it was ridiculed and condemned — "that Republican politician, Joe Story," as they called him. Others, by reason of his youth and active political course, augured a host of evil consequences. He was at this time only thirty-two years old — the youngest judge on the bench, and, with the exception

[1] The following letter from George Cabot to Timothy Pickering, Jan. 28, 1808, is interesting as coming from a vigorous political opponent. The "Georgia claimants" referred to in it were the parties involved in *Fletcher* v. *Peck*.

"Mr. Joseph Story of Salem goes to Washington as solicitor for the Georgia claimants. Though he is a man whom the Democrats support, I have seldom if ever met with one of sounder mind on the principal points of national policy. He is well worthy the civil attention of the most respectable Federalists; and I wish you to be so good as to say so to our friend Mr. Quincy and such other gentlemen as you think will be likely to pay him some attention."

See *Life and Times of George Cabot*, by Henry Cabot Lodge (1870).

of Mr. Justice Buller on the King's Bench in England, the youngest man then ever called to highest judicial station in either country.

Josiah Quincy, Jr., writes, in his *Figures of the Past:* "I remember my father's graphic account of the rage to the Federalists when 'Joe Story, that country pettifogger, aged thirty-two,' was made a judge of our highest court."

Among the few other Anti-Federalist lawyers, the most notable were Levi Lincoln,[1] Daniel Davis,[2] George Blake,[3] John Quincy Adams [4] and Perez Morton.[5]

Most of the lawyers above referred to practised in Boston; but in other parts of the State there were able Bars, among the leaders of which were Eli P. Ashmun, Elijah H. Mills, Samuel Howe, Caleb Strong, Benjamin Whitman, Timothy Bigelow, and Samuel Dana, Jr.; and the offices of these members of the Bar outside of Boston were, in fact, in most instances, miniature law schools, as students often came from the surrounding countryside to reside in the towns where these law offices were located.

Among the younger members of the Bar just coming into practise in 1815, were Lemuel Shaw,[6] Marcus Morton,[7]

[1] Born in 1749, a Harvard graduate 1772, United States Attorney-General 1801–1805.

[2] Born in 1762, a student under Shearjashub Bourne, Solicitor-General of Massachusetts 1800–1832.

[3] Born in 1769, Harvard 1789, a student under James Sullivan, United States District-Attorney 1801–1829.

[4] Born in 1767, Harvard 1787, a student under Theophilus Parsons.

[5] Born in 1751, Harvard 1771, Massachusetts Attorney-General 1810–1832.

[6] Born in 1781, a Harvard graduate of 1800, Chief Justice of Massachusetts 1830–1860.

[7] Born in 1784, a Brown graduate 1804, a student at Litchfield Law School, Judge of the Massachusetts Supreme Court in 1825, Governor in 1840.

Charles G. Loring,[1] Peleg Sprague,[2] William Minot[3] and Franklin Dexter.[4]

In 1816, Daniel Webster, then thirty-four years of age, came to Boston to practise law, having been admitted to the Suffolk Bar in 1805, and to practise before the United States Supreme Court in the winter of 1813–1814.

## New Hampshire

In New Hampshire, the close of the War of the Revolution marked an epoch in the history of the courts and the Bar.

With the appointments as Chief Justice of John Pickering, who sat from 1790 to 1795, and of Jeremiah Smith in 1802, the law as laid down by the courts became for the first time a science. "Chief Justice Smith found the law of New Hampshire in practise and administration, a chaos, and left it comparatively an organized and scientific system."[5]

With the year 1786, a new era for the Bar also began. Though still small, not exceeding twenty-nine in number, it contained a large proportion of exceedingly eminent lawyers.

In 1786, Jeremiah Smith began practise in New Hampshire. He was born in 1759; after having entered at Harvard in 1777, and remained for two years, he graduated from Queens (now Rutgers College), and studied law at Barnstable, Massachusetts, with Shearjashub Bourne. Jeremiah Mason, who, born in 1768, had graduated from Yale in 1788 and studied law in Judge Simeon Baldwin's office at New Haven, was admitted to practise in 1791,

[1] Born in 1794, Harvard 1812, a student at the Litchfield Law School and in the office of Charles Jackson.

[2] Born in 1793, Harvard 1812, student at Litchfield Law School.

[3] Born in 1783, Harvard 1802.

[4] Born in 1793, son of Samuel Dexter, Harvard 1812, a student in the office of Samuel Hubbard.

[5] See *Lisbon* v. *Lyman*, 49 N. H. 222.

and removed to Portsmouth in 1798. Nine years later, his only rival, Daniel Webster, arrived at Portsmouth. Webster was born in 1782, graduated at Dartmouth in 1801, studied in New Hampshire, and with Christopher Gore in Boston in 1804, and was admitted in 1805. With them may be mentioned Arthur Livermore,[1] George Sullivan,[2] Ichabod Bartlett,[3] William King Atkinson[4] and William Plumer.[5]

By the beginning of the Nineteenth Century, the Bar was one of great lustre, so that even Judge Story used to speak of its "vast law learning and prodigious intellectual power."[6] In 1805, it contained 106 lawyers, of whom 91

1 Born in 1776, studied with his brother Edward St. Loe Livermore, Judge of Superior Court 1798, Chief Justice in 1809.

2 Born in 1771, Harvard graduate of 1790, studied with his father Gen. John Sullivan.

3 Born in 1786, Dartmouth graduate of 1808, studied with Moses Eastman and Parker Noyes, admitted in 1812.

4 Born 1765, Harvard graduate of 1783, studied with John Pickering, Judge of Superior Court 1803, Attorney-General 1807.

5 Born 1759, studied with Joshua Atherton, admitted 1787.

6 "There were giants in the land in those days. It was customary for the advocates whose professional aid was in most request at that time to attend the courts from county to county through the State, as the leading barristers ride the circuit in England. Every important trial was a tournament in which these celebrated celebrities were matched against each other. . . . In the ratio of her population New Hampshire has contributed more mental and more moral strength to the Bar, to the Senate and to the Cabinet of the country than any other State in the Union. That was the season of her intellectual greatness. Ichabod Bartlett, the Randolph of the North, the brilliant flashes of whose wit, keen sarcasm and pungent irony gave life and spirit to the dry judicial discussions — Sullivan, the fascination of whose happy eloquence still lingers — Fletcher, whose legal acumen, clear, distinct and precise statement, closely reasoned argument and conscious mastery of his subject adorn no less the bench than formerly the bar. Jeremiah Mason, that counsellor of marvellous sagacity, unrivalled in his knowledge of human nature, and Daniel Webster. The collision of such minds invigorated and sharpened the faculties whose native temper was competent to sustain the shock. . . . It was in this school, that Judge Woodbury formed and fixed that habit which he ever afterwards

were admitted to practise in the Superior Court, and 77 of whom were college graduates — from Harvard 35, Dartmouth 34, Yale 6, Brown 2.

## Vermont

The settlers in the New Hampshire Grants (later the State of Vermont), were chiefly men who had come thither from Connecticut, Massachusetts and Rhode Island, for the purpose of enjoying greater religious freedom; and they had an instinctive prejudice against the institution of courts, which they conceived as controlled by the clerical and government interests in the Colonies from which they had emigrated. To such an extent was this feeling carried, that the Legislature of Vermont, in the first seven years of its existence, constituted itself a Court of Chancery; and passed frequent acts, vacating and commuting judgments of the courts, and forbidding prosecutions of real or possessory actions or actions on contracts; and while this was done to a less extent after the Constitution of 1786, it still kept up the practise of granting new trials, over the heads of the Courts.

It is not surprising that, under these conditions, neither great lawyers nor judges were produced in Vermont at this time, and that, as Mason says in his Autobiography:

"The courts of Vermont then were badly organized and usually filled with incompetent men. Most of the members of the Bar were poorly educated and some of vulgar manners and indifferent morals. Casting these circumstances over, I entertained serious thoughts of transferring

retained — which is the first need though the rarest accomplishment of an American statesman, to think continently."

*Eulogy on Justice Levi Woodbury*, by Robert Rantoul, Oct. 16, 1851, *Law Reporter*, Vol. XIV (1851).

my allegiance to the State of New Hampshire. The courts of the two States were nearly on an equality as to learning and talent, but those of New Hampshire had greatly the advantage in point of purity and integrity. The Bar of New Hampshire also were more orderly, better educated, and of better manners."

There were, however, in 1790, a few men of great ability at the Bar, like Charles Marsh,[1] Stephen R. Bradley,[2] Stephen Jacob, Royall Tyler (later Chief Justice)[3] and Elijah Paine (later United States District Judge).[4]

## Connecticut

In Connecticut, the Bar increased in numbers very greatly after the Revolution; and a Bar Association of thirty-two members was formed for the first time in 1783 in Hartford County. Noah Webster wrote in 1787: "Never was such a rage for the study of the law. From one end of the continent to the other, the students of this science are multiplying without number," and he stated that on the docket of Oliver Ellsworth, in whose office he studied, there were frequently from one thousand to fifteen hundred cases at a time. These cases were small, however, and brought in small fees; and Jeremiah Mason, who studied in the office of Simeon Baldwin at New Haven in 1789, wrote: "The time was a period of extreme depression and poverty throughout the country. . . . The profession of law felt this depression severely. The State of Connecticut was overstocked with lawyers. Most of them

[1] Born 1765, graduate of Dartmouth in 1786, student at Litchfield Law School, United States District-Attorney 1797.

[2] Born 1754, Yale graduate of 1775.

[3] Born 1757, studied with John Adams, 1794 Judge of Supreme Court, 1800 Chief Justice.

[4] Born 1757, Harvard graduate 1781, admitted to the Bar in 1784, Judge of Supreme Court 1791–1795, United States District Judge 1801–1845.

had but little business with fees and compensation miserably small. The professional income of Pierrepont Edwards, supposed to be the largest in the State, was said not to amount to $2000 a year. . . . Very few obtained half that sum." In 1798 there were about one hundred and twenty practising lawyers in the State. Among the more prominent were Noah Webster,[1] Zephaniah Swift,[2] Simeon Baldwin,[3] Oliver Wolcott,[4] Thomas S. Williams,[5] David Daggett,[6] Roger Griswold,[7] Chauncy Goodrich,[8] Pierrepont Edwards,[9] Thomas Day,[10] James Hillhouse,[11] James Gould,[12] and Uriah Tracy.[13]

The greatest Connecticut lawyer of the early Nineteenth Century was Roger Minott Sherman, who was born in 1773, graduated from Yale in 1792, studied in Judge Ellsworth's office and also attended lectures of Judge Reeve at his law school in Litchfield, admitted to the Bar in 1796.

1 Born in 1758, a Yale graduate of 1779, admitted to the Bar in 1781.

2 Born in 1759, Yale 1778, the author in 1795 of the *System of Laws of Connecticut*, and in 1822 of the *Digest of Laws of Connecticut*, which has the distinction of being the first comprehensive view of the English Common Law published in America, practically an American digest, Chief Justice in 1806–1819.

3 Born in 1761, a graduate of Yale in 1781, and Judge of the Superior Court in 1806.

4 Born in 1760, a graduate of Yale 1778.

5 Born in 1777, a graduate of Yale in 1794, Chief Justice in 1834.

6 Born in 1764, a Yale graduate of 1783, and United States Senator in 1813, Chief Justice 1832–1834.

7 Born in 1762, a Yale graduate of 1780.

8 Born in 1759, Yale graduate of 1776, and United States Senator in 1807–1813.

9 Born in 1750, a Princeton graduate of 1768.

10 Born in 1777, a Yale graduate of 1797.

11 Born in 1754, a Yale graduate of 1773, United States Senator 1796.

12 Born in 1770, a Yale graduate 1741, Judge of Superior Court 1816–1818.

13 Born in 1755, a Yale graduate of 1778, United States Senator 1796–1807.

## NOTE

### To New York Text

For authorities in general, see:

*A Political History of New York*, by A. S. Alexander (1906).
*American Law Review*, Vol. V, p. 445.
*Rufus King, Life and Correspondence*, by Charles R. King (1894).
*Address by George Shea* in *New York Bar Association Proc.*, Vol. II.
*New York Bar Ass. Proc.*, Vol. XII, p. 127.
*Address of James Kent before Law Association of City of New York*, Oct. 21, 1836.
*Memoir of Alexander Hamilton*, a letter by James Kent (1832).
*Life of James Kent*, by William Kent (1898).
*Aaron Burr*, by Samuel L. Knapp (1835).
*Aaron Burr, Life and Times*, by James Parton (1882).
*Diary and Letters of Gouverneur Morris*, by Anne Carey Morris (1888).
*Gouverneur Morris*, by Jared Sparks (1832).
*Alexander Hamilton*, by John T. Morse, Jr. (1876).
*Life of Edward Livingston*, by Charles H. Hunt (1864).
*Lives of the Governors of the State of New York*, by John S. Jenkins (1851).

### To New Hampshire Text

*History of New Hampshire*, by Jeremy Belknap (1792).
*Judicial History of New Hampshire before the Revolution*, *Law Reporter*, Vol. XVIII, 301.
*Bench and Bar of New Hampshire*, by C. H. Bell (1894).
*Life of Jeremiah Mason*, by George S. Hillard (1873).
*Life of Jeremiah Smith*, by John H. Morison (1845).
*Review of Life of Jeremiah Smith*, *Law Reporter*, Vol. VIII.
*Life of Charles Marsh*, by James Barret (1871).
Address by David Cross in *Southern New Hampshire, Bar Ass. Proc.*, Vol. I.

## CHAPTER XIII

### EARLY AMERICAN LAW BOOKS

IT has been seen in the preceding chapters how general was the feeling that the law in the United States should be emancipated from its dependence on English decisions. Conditions of life, of commerce, of real estate dealings, and of court practise were essentially different in the United States from those in England; and a distinct body of law was demanded for this country. To supply this demand there arose the body of American law reporters and law writers.

James Sullivan, of Massachusetts, well expressed this general sentiment of those who felt that the country should have a genuine American system of law based on American cases, in the preface to his work on *Land Titles*, in 1801:

"The want of accurate reports necessary to evince what statutes and principles of the English laws had been adopted, used, and practised upon before the Revolution is very discouraging in this work. . . . It would be well for us to have our own comments, and to reject those of other governments which have been issued since we became an independent nation. . . . We ought to have our own reporters, compilers and compositors. Everyone who will attempt something in this way ought to be encouraged by the public.

"There have been motions in some of the legislatures in the Union to prohibit the reading of English reports in our courts of justice. . . . The judges themselves in several of the States have with great propriety inclined to reject the reports of cases determined by England since the

American Revolution. These motions, however crude and undigested they may have been, no doubt had their origin in a strong love to our national independence. And the motive is therefore a laudable rather than a reprehensible one."

The same views were set forth in a letter from a Boston lawyer in the *Columbian Centinel*, in 1801:

"Too great inattention has hitherto prevailed as to the preservation of the decisions of our courts of law. We have neither authorized nor voluntary reporters. Hence we are compelled to the loose and interested recollections of counsel, or to depend wholly on British decisions."

And, as Cranch said in the preface to his Supreme Court *Reports*, in 1804:

"Much of that uncertainty of the law, which is so frequently and perhaps so justly the subject of complaint in this country, may be attributed to the want of American reports. Many of the causes, which are the subject of litigation in our Courts, arise upon circumstances peculiar to our situation and laws, and little information can be derived from English authorities to lead to a correct decision."

But before a body of American law could be established, there was need of some authoritative method of preserving the decisions of the courts, in order that the judges might have some means of knowing what the American precedents were.[1]

As a reviewer of one of the early volumes of American reports stated:[2]

"The United States have, until within a few years, trusted to traditions the reasons of their judicial decisions.

[1] For an excellent article on *American Reports and Reporters*, see *American Jurist*, Vol. XXII (1839).

[2] Review of Vol. I of *Tyng's Massachusetts Reports*, quoted in Hall's *American Law Journal*, Vol. I (1808).

But with wealth and commerce, and with more enlarged views of jurisprudence, it became obvious that the exposition of our statutes and the validity of our customs should rest upon a more secure basis than the memory of man or the silent influence of unquestioned usage."

An accurate view of the state of the law, resulting from the absence of recorded decisions, was given by John Duer, a contemporary of Kent, in describing the condition of New York courts before the era of law reports:[1]

"The decisions . . . were not the fruit of that careful and laborious investigations which is essential to the proper discharge of the judicial functions; and the authority they might otherwise have claimed was greatly impaired by these frequent differences of opinion that are the necessary result of imperfect examination and study. It was seldom that the opinions of the judges, even in the most important cases, were reduced to writing; and as no reports were then published, and no records preserved of the grounds on which their decisions were placed, the cases were numerous in which they had no rules to direct, no precedents to govern them. Of this state of things, the inevitable consequences were vacillation, contradictions, confusion, and uncertainty. . . . This defective administration of the law had a most unfavorable influence on the character and pursuits of the Bar; for when cases are slightly examined and rashly decided by the judges, the principal motives for a diligent preparation on the part of counsel cease to exist."

And as a writer in the *North American Review* said, in 1825:[2]

"The practice of reporting decisions with their grounds and reasons is indeed an insuperable barrier to the corruption of judges; and it is the strongest possible guard against

[1] *Discourse before the Bar of New York*, by John Duer (1848).

[2] Review of *Pickering's Reports*, Vol. I, by Willard Phillips, *North Amer. Rev.*, Vol. XX (1825).

negligent and inconsiderate decrees. . . . The publication of reports again affords the only means of informing the community of the laws by which their conduct is to be governed and their rights to be determined."

To the State of Connecticut is due the credit of making the first move towards the establishment of a record of American law, by the passage, through the efforts of two of its great lawyers, Roger Sherman and Richard Law, of a statute, in 1785, requiring the judges of the Supreme and Superior Courts to file written opinions, in disposing of cases on points of law, so that they might be properly reported, and "thereby a foundation laid for a more perfect and permanent system of Common Law in this State." This statute made possible the first regular printed law reports in America;[1] for in 1789, Ephraim Kirby, a country printer at Litchfield, formerly a student at Yale, and a soldier in the Continental Army, made the first collection of cases, and published the volume known as *Kirby's Reports*, in the preface to which he says:

"The uncertainty and contradiction attending the judicial decisions in this State have long been subjects

[1] While Kirby was the first American law reporter, in the legal use of the term, he was not the first person to publish reports of cases, for throughout the Eighteenth Century printed reports of famous criminal trials were to be found, and an occasional printed account of a civil action.

Neither does *Kirby's Reports* contain the earliest American cases; for *Harris and McHenry's Reports*, published in 1809, contains cases of a date as early as 1658; *Quincy's Reports* (Massachusetts), published in 1865, has cases from 1761–1772: and in 1829, there was published at Charlottesville, Virginia, a book by Thomas Jefferson entitled *Reports of cases determined in the General Court of Virginia from 1730 to 1740 and from 1768 to 1772*. (See *Forgotten Chapters in the Life of Jefferson*, in *Green Bag*, Vol. VIII.) *Bay's Reports*, in South Carolina, published in 1809, included cases dating from 1783; *Call's Reports*, in Virginia, published in 1801, includes cases dating from 1779; *Dallas' Reports*, in Pennsylvania, in 1790, included cases dating from 1754; and *Hughes' Reports*, in Kentucky, in 1803, included cases dating from 1785.

of complaint. The source of this complaint is easily discovered. When our ancestors emigrated here, they brought with them the notions of jurisprudence which prevailed in the country from whence they came. The riches, luxury, and extensive commerce of that country, contrasted with the equal distribution of property, simplicity of manners, and agricultural habits and employments of this, rendered a deviation from the English laws, in many instances, highly necessary. This was observed; and the intricate and prolix practice of the English courts was rejected, and a mode of practice more simple, and better accommodated to an easy and speedy administration of justice, adopted. Our courts were still in a state of embarrassment, sensible that the Common Law of England, 'though a highly improved system,' was not fully applicable to our situation; but no provision being made to preserve and publish proper histories of their adjudications, every attempt of the judges to run the line of distinction between what was applicable and what was not proved abortive, for the principles of their decisions were soon forgot, or misunderstood, or erroneously reported from memory. Hence arose a confusion in the determination of our courts. The rules of property became uncertain, and litigation proportionably increased.

"In this situation, some legislative exertion was found necessary; and in the year 1785 an act passed, requiring the judges of the Superior Court to render written reasons for their decisions in cases where the pleadings closed in an issue at law. This was a great advance towards improvement. Still it left the business of reformation but half performed; for the arguments of the judges, without a history of the whole case, would not always be intelligible, and they would become known to but few persons, and, being written on loose papers, were exposed to be mislaid, and soon sink into total oblivion.

"Hence it became obvious to everyone that should histories of important cases be carefully taken and published, in which the whole process should appear, showing the true grounds and principles of the decision, it would in time produce a permanent system of Common Law."

In this same year 1789, Francis Hopkinson of Pennsylvania, published a volume containing reports of four cases tried in Admiralty in 1785–1786.

Alexander J. Dallas followed Kirby, the next year 1790, with his first volume of decisions of Pennsylvania cases dating from 1754, of which Lord Mansfield wrote to Chief Justice McKean of Pennsylvania, in 1791: "They do credit to the Court, the Bar, and the Reporter; they show readiness in practice, liberality in principle, strong reason and legal learning." *Hopkinson's Admiralty Reports* were printed in 1792. *Chipman's Reports* came next in Vermont in 1793. Chancellor Wythe published his *Decisions of Cases in Virginia by the High Court of Chancery* in 1795 — a volume particularly interesting from the fact that Henry Clay, a lad of fifteen, then a poor assistant in the Clerk's office, was picked out by Wythe to write out and record his decisions for this work, and in the copies of these reports sent to Jefferson, John Adams, and Samuel Adams are notes in English and Greek written by Clay at Wythe's dictation.

*Martin's Reports* in North Carolina followed, in 1797; *Root's*, in Connecticut, and *Washington's*, in Virginia, in 1798; and *Haywood's*, in North Carolina, in 1799; *Addison's*, in Pennsylvania, in 1800; *Call's*, in Virginia, in 1801; *Taylor's*, in North Carolina, in 1802; *Hughes'*, in Kentucky, in 1803; *Pennington's*, in New Jersey, in 1808; *Hening and Munford's*, in Virginia, in 1808; *Bay's*, in South Carolina; *Harris and McHenry's*, in Maryland; *Binney's*, in Pennsylvania, and *Tyler's*, in Vermont, in 1809; *Hardin's*, in Kentucky, in 1810; *Martin's*, in Louisiana, in 1811; *Overton's*, in Tennessee, in 1813; *Bibb's*, in Kentucky, in 1815; *Coxe's*, in New Jersey, in 1816; and *New Hampshire Reports*, in 1819. It is a striking fact that printed law reports were published in all the Southern

States, before any were in existence in most of the Northern States. The first reports in New York were *Coleman's*, in 1801, and the first official reports were *Caines'* in 1804. It was Kent who introduced in New York the system of filing written opinions, as he writes:

"When I came to the bench (in 1798), there were no reports or State precedents. The opinions from the bench were delivered *ore tenus*. We had no law of our own and nobody knew what it was. I first introduced a thorough examination of cases and written opinions. In January 1799, the second case reported in I, Johnson's cases of *Ludlow* v. *Dale* is a sample of the earliest. The judges, when we met, all assumed that foreign sentences were only good *prima facie*. I presented and read my written opinion that they were conclusive, and they all gave up to me, and so I read it in court as it stands. . . .

"This was the commencement of a new plan and there was laid the first stone in the subsequently erected temple of our jurisprudence. . . . In 1814 I was appointed Chancellor. The office I took with considerable reluctance. . . . It is a curious fact that, for the nine years I was in that office, there was not a single decision, opinion or dictum of either of my two predecessors (Livingston or Lansing) from 1777 to 1814 cited to me or even suggested."

It was six years after Kent began his written opinions, before the Legislature provided (in 1804) for a regular Reporter on a salary — George Caines being the first to be appointed, and William Johnson being his successor.

In 1803, Massachusetts established the office of Reporter and initiated the publication of reports, intended at first as an experiment, for the statute was limited in its operation to three years. Ephraim Williams was made Reporter, and his first volume was published in 1805.

The first volume of United States Supreme Court reports was published by Dallas in 1798 (2 Dallas); and in 1804, Cranch began the publication of his reports, containing the first of Chief Justice Marshall's opinions. No provision was made for an official Reporter, by act of Congress, until 1817.

The American law text book, like the American law report, owed its origin largely to the demand for the creation of a native body of law, distinct from the English law.[1]

The need arose first in the department of pleading, and was well expressed in the preface to the first American collection of forms, published at Boston, in 1802, entitled *American Precedents of Declarations*.[2]

"The motives which induce this publication after the labored books of entries which, under the sanction of *Coke*, *Rastall*, *Lilly*, *Mallory* and *Raymond*, have received the approbation of the profession, become particularly necessary to be developed. The redundances of the English forms, however proper in their courts, where remuneration is proportionate to literal labour, have ever been the subjects of complaint among our own lawyers who have been obliged at a vast expense of time and money to purchase researches into ponderous volumes where the useful matter was buried amid heaps of antiquated learning and superfluous detail. This end has indeed been most severely

[1] The compilation of books described in these pages has been made largely from the comprehensive *Legal Bibliography*, published at Philadelphia in 1846, by James G. Marvin.

A practically complete list may also be found in the summaries of the law of the various States contained in the *Annual Law Register*, Vols. III and IV, published by William Griffiths, at Burlington, New Jersey, in 1822 — a most valuable source of information regarding legal conditions of the early part of the Nineteenth Century.

[2] Judge Iredell of the United States Supreme Court left unfinished at his death, in 1798, a legal treatise entitled *An Essay on Pleading in Suits at Common Law*, consisting of four volumes folio, 1229 pages of closely written manuscript — also 365 pages of *Doctrine of the Laws of England Concerning Real Property so far as it is in use or in force in the State of North Carolina;* also 12 chapters of 275 pages of an *Appendix to the Law of Evidence*, a work originally published by an anonymous writer in 1777.

See *Life and Letters of James Iredell*, by Griffith J. McRee, Vol. II (1857).

felt in New England, where juridical practice, though bottomed on the principles of the Common Law, from the character of the people and the peculiarity of the laws assumed a more compact and simple form. In addition to this, the structure of our government, so materially variant from European sovereignties, as well as domestic remedies of statutory appointment have created deficiencies and changes which no foreign works could meet and no personal industry supply. . . . They have been almost wholly transcribed from manuscript forms which have been preserved with veneration and collected with fidelity by the first ornaments of the bench and forum in our own and adjacent States. By the offers of celebrated living counsel, the work has been perfected in many valuable forms, which have either received judicial decisions or been approved by unquestionable authority."

In the same year, 1801, Thomas Harris published at Annapolis his *Modern Entries, adapted to the American Courts of Justice, being a complete system of approved precedents.*

Four years later, in 1805, Joseph Story, then only twenty-six years of age, published at Salem his *A Selection of Pleadings in Civil Cases*, of which J. G. Marvin, the author of *Legal Bibliography*, said, in 1847:

"The appearance of the volume was opportune and serviceable to the profession in this country, who had hitherto been obliged to resort to the voluminous books of *English Entries* for precedents. The notes and references show attainments in the service of special pleadings at the early age in which this his first attempt at legal authorship was published. The work gave a new impulse to study in this department of professional learning."

In 1806, Colinson Read of Philadelphia published *American Pleaders' Assistant.*

In 1810, John Anthon published, at New York, the second edition of *American Precedents of Declarations col-*

*lected chiefly from the manuscript of Chief Justice Parsons and other accomplished Pleaders in the State of Massachusetts.*

In 1811, W. W. Hening of Virginia published his *American Pleader*, in New York.

Although the early reports were largely filled with cases involving real property, the text books in use on that subject were mainly English.

In 1768, however, John Adams had written anonymously the first American book on this branch of the law, *An Essay on Feudal and Common Law*, first published in London, in 1768, but not until 1783 in this country, in Philadelphia.[1]

In 1794, William Wyche published in New York, *An Essay on the Theory and Practice of Fines;*[2] and in 1801, James Sullivan of Massachusetts published in Boston the first really comprehensive work on real estate law, entitled *Land Titles in Massachusetts.*

In 1808, John Kilty of Maryland published his *Landholders' Assistant and Land Office Guide.* In 1810, W. Graydon of Pennsylvania published *Forms of Conveyancing and Practise.* In 1816, Benjamin Lynde Oliver published his *Practical Conveyancing*, which long remained a standard work.

The important part which admiralty and maritime cases played in the courts in the thirty years, 1785–1815, is reflected in a remarkable degree in the number of trans-

[1] Its authorship was ascribed to Jeremiah Gridley, but a few persons knew its real author as the following letter from Rev. Dr. Chauncey to Rev. Dr. Stiles, Dec. 12, 1768, shows:

"He is but a young man not above 33 or 34 but of incomparable sense, a true son of liberty, and as well able to write or talk upon it as any one I am acquainted with. I esteem that piece one of the best that has been written. It has done honor to its author; and it is a pity but he should be known." See *Mass. Hist. Coll.*, 1st series, Vol. X, p. 187.

[2] See *Modern Law of Real Property*, — *Columbia Law Review*, Vol. I (1901).

lations made by American lawyers of the works of foreign writers on maritime, admiralty, civil, and international law. These translations displayed considerable legal scholarship, and proved the lawyers of this country to be largely in advance of their English brethren, who, in general, took little interest in anything outside of the Common Law of England. Thus in 1795, William Cobbett published in Philadelphia his translation of Martens' *Law of Nations.* A translation of *Burlamaqui* was published in 1792, in Boston. In 1802, Francis Xavier Martin published at Newbern, North Carolina, a translation of *Pothier on Contracts;* and in 1806, W. D. Evans published the same work, in Philadelphia.

In 1800, Montesquieu's *Esprit des Lois* was published in Boston; and in 1802, in Philadelphia. In 1805, *Vattel* was published, in Boston.

In 1806, *Azuni* was translated and published by William Johnson, in New York.

In 1808, John E. Hall published, at Baltimore, his translation of Clerke's *Praxis, with notes on American Admiralty Practice;* and in 1811, his translation of Emerigon's *Maritime Loans.*

In 1809, J. R. Ingersoll translated *Roccus.*

In 1810, P. S. DuPonceau, of Philadelphia, translated Bynkershoek's *Laws of War.* In 1812, Thomas Cooper published in Philadelphia a translation of Justinian's *Institutes.* In 1809, John E. Hall of Baltimore wrote a treatise on *Admiralty Practice;* and in the same year William J. Duane of Philadelphia wrote his *Law of Nations.* In 1815, Henry Wheaton wrote his able book on *Maritime Captures and Prizes.* In 1818, William Frick of Baltimore translated Jacobsen's *Laws of the Sea.*

Four general works on the Common Law, written in this period, showed genuine scientific thought and research; and have remained of more or less permanent value in American legal literature. In 1793, Nathaniel Chipman, Chief Justice of Vermont, published his *Dissertations.* In 1804, the lectures delivered before the students of the College of Philadelphia by James Wilson, Judge of the United States Supreme Court, were printed. In the year prior, St. George Tucker, Professor of Law, published his famous edition of *Blackstone*, in five volumes (following the 9th English edition of 1783), which work, under the title of *Tucker's Blackstone*, had widespread circulation, both as a text-book and otherwise, giving to him the sobriquet of the "American Blackstone," and containing the first legal commentaries on the Federal Constitution which appeared in the United States. In 1814, Judge H. N. Brackenridge, of Pennsylvania, wrote his *Law Miscellanies containing Introduction to the Study of the Law, Notes on Blackstone's Commentaries, Strictures on decisions of the Supreme Court of the United States with some law cases.* In 1795–1796, Zephaniah Swift published his *System of the Laws of Connecticut*, a keen, scientific work of much more than local interest.

There were a few scattered treatises on special subjects, but they were of little scientific or permanent value. Thus in 1794, William Wyche published a manual on New York Supreme Court practise, the earliest book of this kind; in 1797, John F. Grimke of South Carolina published his *Law of Executors;* in 1801, Thomas Cooper of Philadelphia published *The Bankrupt Law of America.* In 1803, Francis Xavier Martin published in North Carolina a short treatise on the *Powers and Duties of Executors and Administrators;* in the same year, Samuel Freeman at Boston, his *Probate Directory. A Treatise on Criminal Law* was published by H. Toulmin and James Blair, in 1804, at Frankfort, Kentucky. In 1808, James Bradly published in New York, a *Treatise on the Law of Distress.* In 1810, Zephaniah Swift, of Connecticut, published the first American *Digest of the Law of Evidence* and also a *Treatise on Bills of Exchange and Promissory Notes;* and Thomas G. Fessenden published *Essay on the Law of Patents.* In 1811, Samuel Livermore, of New Orleans, who at his death bequeathed his large law library to Harvard College, wrote the first American work on *Principal and Agent and Sales by Auction.*[1] In the same year, Thomas Sergeant, of Philadelphia, published a treatise on *Foreign Attachment.* In 1816, Judge Tapping Reeve, of the Litchfield Law School, published at New Haven, his work on the *Law of Baron and Femme, Parent and Child, Guardian and Ward, Master and Servant, and of the Powers of Courts of Chancery.*

The greater proportion, however, of the American law books consisted of mere manuals for town officers, justices of the peace, and petty officers — books of ephemeral value.[2]

For the most part, therefore, lawyers still continued to rely on important English text books and English editions of the law reports, although steps were also taken towards republishing and re-editing English works; and

[1] A new edition was published in two volumes in Baltimore in 1818.

[2] See James Parker's *Conductor Generalis* (N. Y. 1787); John F. Grimke's *Justices of the Peace* (S. C. 1796); Francis X. Martin's *Office of Justice of the Peace* (N. C. 1791), *Jurisdiction of Justices of the Peace in Civil Suits* (N. C. 1796), and *Powers and Duties of Sheriff* (N. C. 1806); Ewing's *Justice of Peace* (N. J. 1805); Samuel Freeman's *The Town Officer* (Boston, 1799, 1815), and the *Massachusetts Justice* (Boston, 1802, 1810); *Justices and Constables' Assistant*, by W. Graydon (Philadelphia, 1805); R. Bache's *Manual of Pennsylvania Justices of the Peace* (Philadelphia, 1810, 1814); C. Read's *Precedents in Office of Justice of Peace and Short system of Conveyancing* (Philadelphia, 1794, 1801); Samuel Whiting's *Connecticut Town Officer* (1814); *The Civil Officer* (Boston, 1809, 1814); John Tappan's *County and Town Officers of New York* (Kingston, N. Y. 1816); W. W. Hening's *The Virginia Justice* (Va. 1811); Rodolphus Dickinson's *Powers of Sheriff* (Mass. 1810); Jonathan Leavitt's *Poor Law of Massachusetts* (Mass. 1810); *Probate Directory* (Mass. 1812); *Overseers Guide* (Mass. 1815).

in this movement Joseph Story became a leader — editing *Chitty on Bills and Notes* in 1809; *Abbott on Shipping*, in 1810, and *Lawes on Assumpsit*, in 1811.[1]

Perhaps the best illustration of the condition of the times in this respect may be found in the fact that in the library of Theophilus Parsons the great Chief Justice of Massachusetts, which was sold at auction, June 2, 1814, the only American law books, out of the whole two hundred and eighty-two were the following: *Livermore on Agents and Factors* (Boston, 1811); *Lawes on Pleading with Joseph Story's Addition* (Boston, 1811); *Story's Pleading* (1805); *Laws of the United States* (10 vols.); *Laws of Massachusetts; Laws of New Hampshire; Cranch's Reports* (6 vols.); *Dallas' Reports* (4 vols.); *Day's Reports* (3 vols.); *Johnson's Reports* (8 vols.); *Journal of Congress* (13 vols.); and *Digest of Massachusetts Law* (1809).

In 1807, John E. Hall of Baltimore announced to the legal profession his intention to publish a legal periodical, in order to make the decided cases more quickly accessible to the Bar and more widely spread.[2] The first publication of this kind ever printed had been in existence only five years, since 1803, *The Law Journal*, edited in England by John Morgan and Thomas Walter Williams. And in January, 1808, appeared the first number of the *American*

[1] Among the more prominent English Text Books thus republished in America were *Jones on Bailments* (London, 1781; Boston, 1796); *Kyd on Bills and Notes* (London, 1795; Boston, 1798); *Park on Insurance* (Boston, 1800); *Burn on Marine Insurance* (N. Y. 1801); *Marshall on Insurance* (Boston, 1805; Philadelphia, 1810); *Sullivan's Lectures on the Feudal Law and the Constitution and Law of England* (London, 1776; Portland, Maine, 1805); *Runnington on Ejectment* (N. Y. 1806); *Ballantine on Law of Limitations* (London, 1810; N. Y. 1812, containing seventy-one decisions of American law); *Woodfall on Landlord and Tenant* (N. Y. 1816); *Lawes on Pleading* (Portsmouth, 1808).

[2] See *Digests of American Law Reports and American Law Periodicals — Amer. Jurist*, Vol. XXIII (1840).

*Law Journal and Miscellaneous Repository*, printed for Hall at Philadelphia. Six volumes were issued between 1808 to 1810 and 1813 to 1817. A review of its first volume in the *Boston Anthology* for June, 1809, says:

"We agree with the editor in his opinion of the importance of such a work as he has undertaken, and we believe the public voice approves the execution.

"Our country is composed of seventeen different communities, each enjoying independent Legislatures, each governed by laws, many of whose provisions, both statute and traditional, are very different. A publication like Mr. Hall's seems therefore absolutely necessary to afford information to an inhabitant of this State in the prosecution of his rights in New York, Maryland, or Carolina. It will also afford much assistance in producing uniformity in our decisions on commercial questions which would be so beneficial to the whole community . . . and must be considered by the politician as one of the surest bonds of the federal union."

Two volumes of a law magazine called the *North Carolina Law Repository* were published in 1813–1816.

The first distinct law library was founded by Philadelphia lawyers, who incorporated a Society for that purpose in March, 1802, described by John Samuel, in an address on the opening of the Law Library of the Law Association of Philadelphia, March 3, 1898, as follows:

"So far as I, after some research, have been able to discover, this was the first law library established in the United States, the Social Law Library of Boston, the next oldest, not being formed until two years later in 1804.[1] The oldest law library in New York is that of the New York State Library at Albany founded in 1818. A claim was set up to the establishment of the Kennebec Law Library in Augusta, Maine, as having been founded in 1800, but after inquiry

[1] The subscription paper for the formation of this Library is dated September 6, 1803.

I am convinced that no evidence can be adduced in support of this claim. In 1805 was published the first catalogue of the books of the Law Library Company of the City of Philadelphia. It was prepared by William Rawle, and, I believe, was the first printed catalogue of a law library published in the United States. It is a modest booklet of eleven duodecimo pages, containing 249 titles of 375 volumes, whose character is curiously suggestive. Nearly all the books are reports of cases; and of the small remainder, the large majority are books on practice — and treatises on commercial law and maritime insurance; but one digest, *Comyn's* and not over a dozen text books. Of the reports, all are English save three — *Dallas'* (Pennsylvania), *Caines'* (New York), and *Taylor's* (North Carolina) *Reports*."[1]

[1] In the *Life of Charles J. Ingersoll*, by W. M. Meigs (1897), reference is made to a movement for a law library in Washington, in a letter written by Ingersoll to R. Rush.

"Feb. 14, 1823. The Bar had a meeting to-day at which Mr. Wirt presided and Messrs. Clay, Harper and Winder were appointed a committee to devise means of procuring law library of which the want is deplorable here (Washington) and also of obtaining if practicable an establishment in which all the lawyers attending the Supreme Court may be accommodated with lodgings together which would be a convenience, I dare say."

## CHAPTER XIV

### EARLY LAW PROFESSORSHIPS AND SCHOOLS

WITH the close of the Revolutionary War, there began a new era in legal education.

The broadening of the field of general education and the development of American Nationality in all branches of arts and sciences, which then took place, were reflected in the plans which were made in various American colleges to introduce the study of the law into their curriculum. It seems to have escaped the attention of historians, however, that the first move in this direction was at Yale College — and by its President, Ezra Stiles, a man of singularly liberal learning and broad character.[1]

It appears from President Stiles' Diary that, at the time of his election in 1777, the Assembly or Legislature of Connecticut proposed to endow three professorships for the College — one of law, one of medicine, and one of

[1] See *Literary Diary of Ezra Stiles*, Vol. II, p. 209.

"Sept. 19, 1777. My election to the Presidency of Yale College is an unexpected and wonderful ordering of Divine Providence. Not but that it has been talked of for years past; but I knew such reasons in the breasts of the fellows and I tho't such were the sentiments of the Assembly and a plurality of the Pastors respecting my ideas of ecclesiastical polity and doctrinal system of divinity as that it was impossible I should be elected . . . I have no more resolved in my mind whether I am qualified for such an office than for that of a prime minister or a Sultan; or whether I should on the whole be desirous of it; considering the smallness of the salary, and the great and complicated difficulties and labours which attend it, and a hundred and fifty or 180 young gentlemen students is a bundle of wild fire not easily controlled and governed — and at best the diadem of a president is a crown of thorns."

oratory, provided the Assembly might have some voice in the appointment of professors and government of the College, and provided Stiles should be elected President.[1]

The plan was never consummated, as the Corporation of the College declined to yield any of its powers. Pending negotiations, however, President Stiles was actively interested in the project, as appears from his Diary, December 3, 1777:

"I drafted a plan of an University, particularly describing the Law and Medical Lectures, at the desire of the Corporation of Yale, to be by them laid before the Committee of the General Assembly of Connecticut, appointed to consider among other things whether it be expedient to found these two professorships."

Notwithstanding his failure to secure the adoption of his plan, President Stiles evidently retained his belief in the value of law as a part of an undergraduate education; for July 13, 1781, he notes in his Diary, "I gave an evening lecture on Law and Jurisprudence;" and on March 12, 1789, "This day I introduced for the first time Montesquieux Spirit of Laws as a Classical book into Yale College. The Senior Class began to recite the first volume this day. It never was used here before. But it has been recited in Jersey Coll (Princeton) ph. 3 or 4 years;" and on March 8, 1792, he noted that he gave a "Lect. on Law, 1. Law of Nature and Nations, 2. Jus Civile or antient Rom. Law, Pandects, Imperatorial Edicts and Eccl. or Canon

[1] See *Literary Diary of Ezra Stiles*, Vol. II, under dates of Sept. 27, 1777, Nov. 13, 1777, Nov. 14, 1777, Dec. 3, 1777, Feb. 12, 1778, Feb. 27, 1778.

A copy of President Stiles' plan for the law professorship from the original manuscript now in the Yale University Library, furnished to the author by the courtesy of Franklin B. Dexter, Assistant Librarian of Yale University, is given in full in the Appendix A.— See *infra*.

Law, 3. Law of Engl. Common Law, Statutes, Courts of Westminster Reports, 4. Laws of the United States."

Although the Bar of Virginia was by no means the most prominent of the Colonial Bars, the first American law professorship (and the second in any English speaking country) was founded at the College of William and Mary in 1779 — in the year after Blackstone had published the eighth and final edition of his lectures, and a year before his death.

It was to Thomas Jefferson that the science of law owed its first collegiate professor, eighty-seven years after the chartering of the College. In his Autobiography he says:

"On the first of June 1779, I was appointed Governor of the Commonwealth and retired from the Legislature. Being elected also one of the visitors of William and Mary College, a self electing body, I effected, during my residence in Williamsburg that year, a change in the organization of that institution, by abolishing the Grammar School and the two Professorships of Divinity and Oriental Languages, and substituting a Professorship of Law and Police, one of Anatomy Medicine and Chemistry and one of Modern Languages; and, the charter confining us to six Professors, we added the Law of Nature and Nations and the Fine Arts to the duties of the Moral Professor and Natural History to those of the Professor of Mathematics and Natural Philosophy."

The following regulation was then adopted:

"A student on paying annually 1000 pounds of tobacco shall be entitled to attend any two of the following professors, viz: of Law & Police; of Natural History and Mathematics; of Moral Philosophy, the Laws of Nature and of Nations, and of the Fine Arts."

Jefferson's old friend and teacher, George Wythe (then Judge in the Court of Chancery), was appointed law professor, instructions being given by lectures and moot courts. One of his first pupils, in 1779-1780, was John Marshall; but, the College exercises being interrupted by the occupation of the buildings successively by the British and French, in the summer before Yorktown, Marshall's law studies came to a rapid end, and he was admitted to the Bar, after slight preparation, in the same year, 1780.[1] Among other of Wythe's students, prior to 1800, who later became distinguished lawyers, were Spencer Roane, Marshall's rival at the Virginia Bar, Benjamin Watkins Leigh, John J. Crittenden, William A. Rives, Alexander Campbell, John Breckenridge, John Wickham, H. St. George Tucker, W. H. Cabell, L. W. Tazewell, William Munford, and George Nicholas.

"Wythe, above all early statesmen, was deeply learned in the law; had traced all its doctrines to their fountain heads, delighted in the year book, from doomsday down; had *Glanville*, *Bracton*, *Britton*, and *Fleta* bound in collects; had all the British Statutes at full length, and was writing elaborate decisions every day, in which, to the amazement of county court lawyers, *Horace and Aulus Gellius* were sometimes quoted as authorities."[2]

"He carried his love of antiquity rather too far, for he frequently subjected himself to the charge of pedantry; and his admiration of the gigantic writers of Queen Elizabeth's reign had unfortunately betrayed him into an imitation of their quaintness. . . . Yet, he was a man of great capacity, powerful in argument, elegantly keen and sarcastic in repartee — long the rival of Mr. Pendleton at the bar, whom he equalled as a common lawyer and greatly surpassed as a civilian . . . No man was ever more entirely destitute of art . . . This simplicity and integrity of character sometimes exposed him to the arts and sneers

[1] *American Historical Association Papers*, Vol. IV.

[2] *Discourse on Life and Character of Littleton Waller Tazewell*, by Hon. Hugh Blair Grigsby (1830).

of the less scrupulous . . . but he was not only pure, but above all suspicion."[1]

The quality of Judge Wythe's lectures may be estimated by the following opinion of Judge Roane, expressed regarding a manuscript copy of these lectures, in a letter from Governor John Tyler written to Jefferson, in 1810:

"Judge Roane has read them, or most of them, and is highly pleased with them, thinks they will be very valuable, there being so much of his sound reasoning upon great principles, and not a mere servile copy of Blackstone and other British Commentators . . . a good many of his own thoughts on our constitutions and the necessary changes they have begotten, with that spirit of freedom which always marked his opinions."[2]

1 *Sketches of the Life of Patrick Henry*, by William Wirt (1817).

John Randolph said of him, "He lived in the world without being of the world; that he was a mere incarnation of justice — that his judgments were all as between A and B; for he knew nobody; but went into court, as Astraea was supposed to come down from heaven, exempt from all human bias."

See especially *The Supreme Court of Appeals in Virginia*,— *Green Bag*, Vol. V.

2 The rest of the letter is of interest. It is not known if the lectures referred to are in existence now or not.

"Perhaps Mr. Ritchie before this time has informed you of his having possession of Mr. Wythe's MSS. lectures delivered at William and Mary College while he was professor of law and politics at that place. They are highly worthy of publication and but for the delicacy of sentiment and the remarkably modest and unassuming character of that valuable and virtuous citizen they would have made their way in the world before this. It is a pity they should be lost to society and such a monument of his memory be neglected. As you are entitled to it by his will (I am informed) as composing a part of his library, could you not find leisure time enough to examine it and supply some omissions which now and then are met with, I suppose from accident, or from not having time to correct and improve the whole as he intended.

"I do not see why an American Aristides should not be known to future ages. Mr. Wm. Crane gave it to Mr. Ritchie who I suppose got it from Mr. Duval who always had access to Mr. Wythe's library and was much in his confidence."

See *Letters and Times of the Tylers*, by Lyon G. Tyler, Vol. I.

The following interesting sidelight on this professorship of law is found in President Stiles' Diary, June 8, 1784:[1]

"His Excellency, Gov. Jefferson of Virginia visited me with a letter from Mr. (Roger) Sherman at Congress. . . . He was educated at and entered Wm. & Mary Coll. 1761, where he studied five years, and left in 1766. Then became a Lawyer. He was one of the 24 visitors of Wm. & Mary Coll. . . . The salaries of the professors were £80 in Tobacco, now worth £150 or £160, the price of tobacco has doubled. The Professors besides their salys. have about £8 in Tobacco, now £12 or £15, from each scholar per ann. for Instruction. There are Eighty Undergraduates Students at present. . . . The Professor is the Att.-Gen. of the State and he makes more by his Professorship than as Attorney. . . . The Gov. is a most ingenious Naturalist and Philosopher — a truly scientific and learned man — and every way excellent. . . . *Blackston* is the Basis of Law Lect. in Wm. & Mary Coll., Philosophy, Medicine and Law seem to be their object."

Wythe resigned his professorship in 1800, and the chair was filled by St. George Tucker, whose lectures became the basis of his famous edition of *Blackstone*, published in 1803, and containing his commentaries on the Federal Law and Constitution. It was not until 1824, however, that the College conferred any degree of LL.B.

Ten years after the foundation of this Virginia professorship, the College of Philadelphia, August 17, 1790, formally appointed as Professor of Law, James Wilson, then an Associate Justice of the United States Supreme

[1] See *Literary Diary of Ezra Stiles*, Vol. III, p. 124 (1901). Thomas Jefferson had been introduced to Stiles by Roger Sherman in the following letter dated Annapolis, May 11, 1784.

"I take the liberty to introduce to you the Honorable Thomas Jefferson, Esq. . . . He is a Gentleman of much philosophical as well as political knowledge — and I doubt not you will be very agreeably entertained with his conversation."

Court. The idea of this professorship probably originated in a request made to the trustees by Francis Hopkinson, in 1789, that a number of young lawyers, who had formed themselves into a society for their mutual improvement, might have permission to hold their meetings in a college room. A year later, in August, 1790, the Trustees appointed Edward Shippen, James Wilson and Charles J. Hare, a committee to consider the utility and propriety of a law professorship. Wilson reported a plan embracing "Constitutional and International Law, Origin and Rules of Common Law, Civil Law, Law Merchant and Maritime Law," designed "to furnish a rational and useful entertainment to gentlemen of all professions, and in particular to assist in forming the Legislator, the Merchant, and the Lawyer."[1]

Philadelphia, at this time, was the seat of the Federal Government; and the first of the twenty-four lectures which he was to deliver was given by Judge Wilson in the Hall of the Academy, in the presence of President Washington and his Cabinet, the Governor, Members of Congress and of the Legislature, Mrs. Washington and other ladies, "a polite assembly" as the papers of the day described it.[2] Although he had read law with John Dickinson, and had been one of the Signers of the Declaration of Independence, and one of the leaders of the Philadelphia Bar, "Mr. Wilson on the bench was not the equal of Mr. Wilson at the bar, nor did his law lectures entirely meet the expectations that had been formed," wrote William Rawle, who practised under him;[3] and another contemporary

[1] *Historical Sketch of the Law Department of the University of Pennsylvania*, by Hampton N. Carson (1882).

[2] As to these lectures of Judge Wilson, see *History of Law Schools*, *Amer. Bar Ass. Proc.*, Vol. XXIV. See also *American Law Schools*, by W. G. Hammond, *Southern Law Review*, Vol. VII.

[3] See *Address of Samuel Dickson,— Penn. Bar Ass. Proc.*, Vol. VI.

writer said: "These lectures (since included in his works, published in 1804), have not met with general approbation, nor is their excellence altogether undisputed." It seems that his violent criticisms of Blackstone, and his ultra-Federalist views as to the powers of the National Government, did not commend themselves to the lawyers or to the public.

Of this first lecture, Fisher Ames wrote from Philadelphia to Thomas Dwight, January 6, 1791:[1]

"I enclose Judge Wilson's introductory law lecture, addressed with a propriety which he says malice cannot question, to Mrs. Washington. . . . The great law learning and eminent station of the writer had raised great expectations of the performance. Whether there are not many parts that discretion and modesty . . . would have expunged you will be at liberty to judge. It will be a frolic for the London Reviewers to make the Judge's feathers fly. He has censured the English form of government and can expect no mercy."

The truth is, Wilson's temper and habits were those of an advocate, rather than of a judge. His style was diffusive; and the lectures, though scholarly and elegant essays on general jurisprudence, embellished with historical allusions, were not useful as practical instruction in Common Law.[2] Published in 1804, these lectures are now chiefly of interest for the complete exposition of Wilson's views of the principles of the Constitution and of the Federal Government.

The course was kept up through part of the second winter; but though requiring a third season for its com-

[1] *Life and Works of Fisher Ames.*

[2] See *The Study of the Common Law*, by W. D. Lewis, *Penn. Bar Ass. Proc.*, Vol. IV.

See also comments on these lectures by David Hoffman, in 1823, in his *Lecture introductory to a course of lectures now delivering in the University of Maryland.*

pletion, was discontinued, probably because of lack of general interest shown by the students. And although on the consolidation of the College of Philadelphia with the University of Pennsylvania, in 1792, a similar law professorship was founded, to which Wilson was appointed, he gave no lectures. He died in 1798. No step was taken to fill his place, until March 20, 1817, when Charles Willing Hare (who had been admitted to the Bar in 1799 with Charles Chauncey, John Sergeant, and John B. Wallace) was elected Professor.

From 1790 to 1824, it is stated that David Howell, a distinguished lawyer of Rhode Island, filled a chair of law at Brown College, being also Professor of Mathematics and Natural Philosophy; but little is known of his lectures.

There had been a professorship of natural law in King's College (Columbia) in New York, as early as 1773; but it does not appear from the records that anything like a system of education in Common Law, or in the preparation of young men for the Bar, was intended. The Professor probably taught political ethics, rather than law. At the disruption of the College, in 1776, when the British occupied New York, the professorship was discontinued. But in 1784, the College voted to establish an elaborate curriculum of sixteen professorships in the Faculty of Arts, eight in the Faculty of Medicine, three in the Faculty of Law and a Faculty of Divinity.[1] No further action was taken as to a Faculty of Law until December 2, 1793, when the trustees resolved to establish a professorship of law, with a salary of two hundred pounds per annum, to be paid out of the funds allowed to the College by the Legislature; and James Kent was elected to fill the chair.[2]

[1] *The College Curriculum in the United States*, by Louis F. Snow (1907).

[2] A pamphlet entitled *Present State of Learning in Columbia College*, says: "This Professorship is intended to comprise a brief review of the his-

A graduate of Yale in 1781, Kent had, at the time, a rather small practice in Poughkeepsie, but had "with an intensity of ardor embarked in Federal politics and quite gained an ascendant in the local proceedings and discussions."

". . . It was the character I had insensibly acquired as a scholar, and a Federalist, and a presumed (though it was not true) well read lawyer, that the very first year that I removed to New York, I was appointed a Professor of Law in Columbia College. The influence of Dr. S. Bard, of Judge Hobart (of the Supreme Court), of B. Livingston, Edward Livingston, and probably of Chief Justice Jay procured me the appointment."[1]

Kent wrote regarding his course of lectures which began in November, 1794, in the College Hall:

"I read that season twenty-six lectures (two a week), and was honored by the attendance, throughout the course, of seven students and thirty-six gentlemen, chiefly lawyers and law students who did not belong to the college. . . . They were very well received; but I have long since discovered them to have been slight and trashy productions. I wanted judicial labors to teach me precision. I soon became considerably involved in business, but was never fond of, nor much distinguished in, the contentions of the Bar."

tory, the nature, the several forms and just ends of civil government — a sketch of the origin, progress and final settlement of the government of the United States — a particular detail of the organization and duties of the several departments of the general government, together with an examination of such parts of the civil and criminal codes of the federal jurisprudence as shall be most susceptible of illustrations and most conducive to public utility. The constitutions of the several states and the connections they bear with the general government will then be considered and the more particular examination of the constitution of this state. The whole detail of our municipal law with relation to the rights of property and forms of administrating justice, both civil and criminal will be treated fully and at large."

[1] *Memoirs and Letters of James Kent*, by William Kent (1898).

One of his hearers, however, entertained a different view of the introductory lecture, and described the "views that it unfolds of the true nature and province of the law and of the advantages to be derived from its study" as "judicious, discriminating and comprehensive." This lecture was privately printed by the Trustees of the College in 1794; and, the next year, the first three lectures, or dissertations, on the *Theory, History and Duties of Civil Government*, the *History of the American Union*, and the *Law of Nations*, were published in book form by the author.

Of these lectures, John Adams wrote, in 1795, to his son: "I am much pleased with the Lecture and esteem the talents and character of the Professor." When he closed his course, in March, 1795, Kent wrote that his lectures had extended not only through the Constitution and jurisprudence of the Union, the Constitution of this and the other States, but our doctrine of real property.

"My first plan was to examine law of personal property, including the commercial branches and the system of our criminal code. But I found myself absolutely unable to complete the whole, and was obliged to leave this first course imperfect. It will be an easy thing to make these additions and review and improve the whole by next November."

As a matter of fact, Kent never did completely "make these additions," until his later lectures delivered in 1824, but the earlier lectures, together with the later, formed the nucleus of his famous *Commentaries*.

Of his second course, begun in November, 1795, Kent wrote:

"I read thirty-one lectures in my office, and had only two students, besides my clerks. The next season I attempted another course; but, no students offering to attend, I dismissed the business, and in May, 1797, sent a letter of resignation to the Trustees. This was not accepted; and, in the winter of 1797 and 1798, in my office, I read lectures to six or eight students; and, in April, 1798, I finally resigned the office."

In his letter of resignation to the Trustees he expressed the hope

"that the general principles of our Constitution and laws may still be academically taught, and that the institution which you have so liberally established may hereafter under abler professors, and in more auspicious times be crowned with happier success."

Though unsuccessful as a Professor, Kent's claims as a profound lawyer were recognized, in this same year, by his appointment as a Judge of the Supreme Court, by John Jay, Governor of New York. He was, at the time, just thirty-five years of age. It would be unjust, however, to Kent's fame as a jurist to attribute the failure of his law course to any lack of legal ability. Unquestionably, the heated political rancor of the time, the sharp division of parties, and the constant newspaper and pamphlet discussion of Federalist and Anti-Federalist principles caused the students of those days to regard these lectures as more political in their nature than legal. And while the lecturer's views on constitutional law were broad and scientific, they were essentially Federalist, — saturated with Alexander Hamilton, and presenting a view of the power of the courts which was not popular with the rising tide of Republican, anti-John-Adams lawyers and laymen.[1]

[1] The high conception of the place of a lawyer and of his duty to know the Constitution in a Republic, is shown in the following extracts from Kent's introductory lecture:

"The importance of a knowledge of our Constitutional principles as a part of the education of an American lawyer arises from the uncommon efficacy of our courts of justice in being authorized to bring the validity of a law to the test of the Constitution. . . . I consider them, the courts of

In the same year of Kent's resignation at Columbia, 1798, there was founded the first collegiate law professorship intended for other than undergraduates, which had any permanency. It is certainly striking that this event should have occurred in a little frontier town of about seventeen hundred inhabitants — at the University of Transylvania in Lexington, Kentucky. This institution was chartered in 1798, and in the next year the law department was organized, with George Nicholas as Professor of Law and Politics. On his death, the same year, he was succeeded by James Brown, who held the office until 1804. In that year, Henry Clay, a young man of twenty-seven, who had been at the Bar seven years, was appointed, and held the professorship until 1807. He was succeeded by John Monroe, in 1807. Then the office lapsed; but was revived in 1814, when John Pope held it until 1816, succeeded by Joseph Cabell Breckenridge, in 1817.

The University, though small and local, had, by 1802, acquired a library of 1,700 volumes and also a separate

justice, as the proper and intended guardians of our limited Constitution against the factions and encroachments of the legislative body.

". . . A lawyer in a free country . . . should be a person of irreproachable virtue and goodness. He should be well read in the whole circle of the arts and sciences. He should be fit for the administration of public affairs and to govern the Commonwealth by his councils, establish it by his laws and correct it by his example.

"The people of this country are under singular obligations from the nature of their government to place the study of the law at least on a level with the pursuits of classical learning. The art of maintaining social order and promoting social prosperity is not with us a mystery for only those who may be distinguished by the adventurous advantages of birth and fortune. . . . A wide field is open to all — all may be summoned into public employment. . . . Extensive legal and political knowledge is requisite to render men competent to administer the government. A general initiation into the elementary learning of our law has a tendency to guard against mischief and at the same time to promote a keen sense of right and warm love of Freedom."

law library. In 1814, out of a total attendance of 62, nine were law students; and, in 1818, the University had a total of 110 students, or fully half the number then in Harvard College.

Three years after Kent's resignation at Columbia, the Corporation of Yale College again took up the subject of legal education, and, as a part of President Dwight's efforts to broaden the scheme of studies, voted to establish a professorship of law:

"to furnish lectures on the leading principles of the Law of Nature and Nations, on the general principles of civil government, particularly of Republican representative government, on the Constitution of the United States and of the State of Connecticut . . . and on the various obligations and duties resulting from the social relations, especially those which arise from our own National and State Governments."

After that date, no lectures were given until 1826, when the Hon. Elizur Goodrich, of the Class of 1779, was appointed to the chair, and gave occasional lectures until 1810;[1] after which date, no regular lectures were given until 1826, when the Kent Professorship was founded

"for delivering lectures, or otherwise communicating instruction to the undergraduates in the academic department in natural, international, constitutional or municipal law, and civil polity, and such other subjects of jurisprudence as the Faculty or Corporation shall from time to time approve."

The Yale Law School, as a separate institution, did not confer degrees until 1843.[2]

[1] President Dwight, in his *Travels in New England*, published in 1821, says: "The Professor of Law at Yale is required to read 36 lectures only, to be completed in two years, on the Law of Nations, the American Constitution, and the Jurisprudence of Connecticut."

[2] See *Yale in its Relation to Law* in *Yale Law Journal*, Vol. XI (1901).

Princeton College offered instruction in law to undergraduates, 1795–1812, by its President Samuel S. Smith, whose lectures, as appears from the title page of vol. 2 of his *Moral and Political Philosophy* (1812), comprehended "those principles on the subjects of jurisprudence, politics and public law or the law of nature and nations, with which every man . . . in a free country ought to be acquainted." [1]

At Dartmouth College, as early as 1808, the Trustees, a large number of whom were eminent lawyers, planned to establish a law professorship, and accordingly passed the following vote January 7, 1818: [2]

"*Whereas*, An establishment of Professorships in different branches of education at universities facilitates improvement; and as a more general acquaintance with the important science of law would be greatly conducive to the welfare and prosperity of the citizens of our country; and as in promoting that end the establishment of a Professorship of Law at this university is highly desirable; Therefore,

"*Resolved*, Unanimously that this board will proceed to establish a Professorship of Law and appoint a suitable person to the office so soon as adequate means shall be furnished. And as all the present funds are necessarily applied to other objects of education the liberal and patriotic are earnestly solicited to favor and promote by their munificence the early accomplishment of this design.

"*Voted*, that the secretary be requested to cause a suitable number of subscription papers to be printed for the purpose of aiding the object contemplated in the foregoing resolution."

Owing to the factional troubles which prevailed among the governing officials of the College, and which finally

[1] See *Collegiate Study of Law*, by James F. Colby, *Amer. Bar Ass. Proc.*, Vol. XIX (1896).

[2] See *Legal and Political Studies in Dartmouth College*, by James F. Colby (1896).

culminated in the famous *Dartmouth College Case*, in 1817, no action was taken under this vote for many years.

In 1816, the Regents of the University of Maryland established a professorship of law, and appointed David Hoffman. He however gave no regular course of lectures; but, in his own words:

> "In America alone, a law student was left to his own insulated and unassisted efforts. In the hope of supplying what I deemed an important deficiency in the education of our country, I have since my appointment to the law chair devoted myself to performing a course of lectures, and sketched a plan, laid before the public in my *Syllabus* (April, 1821), embracing every title known to the great body of law, exceeding in variety and extent any scheme of lectures hitherto attempted. I prepared *A Course of Legal Study* — the first manual ever arranged for law students in England or this country (published in 1817)."[1]

Later, from 1821 to 1826, Hoffman conducted a struggling "Law Institute," a private affair of his own, to which he proposed to deliver his stupendous course of 301 lectures, combined with a most elaborate system of Moot Courts — his fee being $120. From lack of interest or the expense, the number of students was small, and the school gradually died out.

In 1816, Middlebury College in Vermont established a professorship of law, which attracted considerable attention, because of its incumbent, the noted Nathaniel Chipman, Chief Justice of Vermont.[2]

[1] *An Address to Students of Law in the United States*, by David Hoffman (July, 1824).

For further information as to Hoffman's work, see his *Syllabus* (April, 1821); his *First Lecture*, on *Law Books and Instruction*, published in Oct., 1823; his *Second Lecture*, published in 1825; his *Third Lecture* on *Moot Courts*, in 1826, and his *Ninth Lecture* on *Civil Law*, in 1832.

[2] See *Life of Nathaniel Chipman*, by Daniel Chipman (1846).

The system of study advocated was described by Chipman, in his introductory lecture:

"Let the student not content himself with merely learning to recollect or repeat the arguments or reasons which he has met with in reading as the arguments or reasons of others; but let him endeavor so to penetrate, understand and appropriate them that they may appear to his mind to be exclusively his own. The former is mere memory; the latter only is knowledge. . . . All this, the attentive student will find in the volumes of *Blackstone*, which as an elementary treatise, has not been surpassed in any science. The next step proper to be taken by the students is to proceed analytically; to begin with one branch and the minor divisions of that branch, to make himself fully master of it; and then and not till then, to proceed to another branch, until he shall have encompassed within his knowledge the whole system complete. In his course of reading it is indispensable for him if he wishes to make proficiency to turn to all the cases and authorities and to examine them for himself."

It will be readily seen that none of these professorships attempted to afford a complete or practical education for law students. Towards the end of the Eighteenth Century, however, several private law schools had been founded by individual lawyers, where such an education could be obtained.

Of these, the first and by far the most influential was that founded by Judge Tapping Reeve, and known as the Litchfield Law School. Oddly enough, this School, to which students came from all parts of the Union, grew up, not in any city or seat of learning, but in a little country town of Connecticut, a county seat, having hardly more than fifteen hundred inhabitants, the home of the distinguished Wolcott family, the birthplace of several Governors and Chief Justices of the Colony and of the State.

Here Judge Tapping Reeve began his own School for

law students, in 1784,[1] five years after Wythe was made professor of law at William and Mary, five years before the establishment of the United States Supreme Court, and five years before the publication (in Connecticut) of the first volume of American law reports. Judge Reeve was born in Long Island, New York, in 1744, a graduate of Princeton (then the College of New Jersey), in 1763, studied law with Jesse Root [2] at Hartford, and settled in Litchfield in 1772. Five years after he started his School, he was appointed Judge of the Superior Court, and he became later Chief Justice.

In 1798, one of his pupils, James Gould, then a practising lawyer in Litchfield, born in 1770, and a Yale graduate of 1795, became associated with him. Later Jabez W. Huntington [3] assisted Judge Gould as an instructor. Judge Reeve died in 1823, and Judge Gould had sole charge until 1833.

Prior to 1798, the School had, in all, about 210 students. From 1798 to its abandonment, in 1833, there were 805 students.

As proof of the national character of the School, it is interesting to note, that from 1798 down to the founding of the Harvard Law School in 1817, the students (other

[1] *Address of Prof. James Barr Ames*, at the dedication of the new building of the Law Department of the University of Pennsylvania (1900).

A writer in the *Albany Law Journal*, Vol. XX, in an article on the Litchfield Law School, says that it was established in 1782; and so it appears in the catalogue of the School, published in 1831. Professor Joel Parker, of the Harvard Law School, and other law writers, give the correct date, however, as being 1784. See *The Law School of Harvard College*, by Joel Parker (1871).

[2] Jesse Root was graduated at Princeton in 1756, became a preacher, was admitted to the Bar as a lawyer in 1763, and after serving as colonel in the war and a member of the Continental Congress, became a judge of the Superior Court.

[3] Jabez W. Huntington graduated at the School in 1808, was later United States Senator, and a judge of the Connecticut Supreme Court.

than those from Connecticut) hailed from the following localities: Massachusetts, 72; New York, 44; Georgia, 35; South Carolina, 27; Maryland, 25; New Hampshire, 15; Vermont and Delaware, 14 each; Rhode Island, 11; Kentucky, 9; Pennsylvania, 8; New Jersey and North Carolina, 7 each; Virginia, 6; Louisiana, 3; District of Columbia and Ohio, 2 each; Maine and Mississippi, 1 each.

Of its alumni — 16 became United States Senators; 50 Members of Congress; 40 Judges of higher State courts; 8 Chief Justices of State courts; 2 Justices of the United States Supreme Court; 10 Governors of States; 5 Members of the Cabinet. And as Professor Joel Parker of the Harvard Law School said in 1871:[1]

"Probably no law school has had — perhaps I may add never will have — so great a proportion of distinguished men on its catalogue, if for no other reason, because attendance upon a law school was then the rare exception, an advantage obtained in general only by very ambitious young men, and because there was then much less competition for the office and honors to which they aspired."

A contemporary opinion of the School is interesting. In 1813, it had fifty-four students, the largest in any one year of its history; and about that time, Timothy Dwight wrote:[2]

"It would not, it is believed, do discredit to any country. Law is here taught as a science, and not merely nor principally as a mechanical business; not as a collection of loose independent fragments, but as a regular well compacted system. At the same time, the students are taught the practice by being actually employed in it. A court

1 *Litchfield Hill*, by John D. Champlin, quoted in the Catalogue of 1900, prepared by George M. Woodruff and Archibald M. Howe.

*The Law School of Harvard College*, by Joel Parker (1871).

2 *Travels in New England*, by Timothy Dwight, Vol. IV. See also *Litchfield Law School — Albany Law Journal*, Vol. XX (1879).

is constituted, actions are brought and conducted through a regular process, questions are raised and the students become advocates in form. Students resort to this school from every part of the American Union. The number of them is usually about forty."

The catalogue of the Litchfield School gave the following detailed account of the schedule of its course and prices:

"According to the plan pursued by Judge Gould, the law is divided into forty-eight titles, which embrace all its important branches, and of which he treats in systematic detail. These titles are the result of thirty years' severe and close application. They comprehend the whole of his legal reading during that period, and continue moreover to be enlarged and improved by modern adjudications.

"The lectures, which are delivered every day, and which usually occupy an hour and a half, embrace every principle and rule falling under the several divisions of the different titles. These principles and rules are supported by numerous authorities, and generally accompanied with familiar illustrations. Whenever the opinions upon any point are contradictory, the authorities in support of either doctrine are cited, and the arguments, advanced by either side, are presented in a clear and concise manner, together with the lecturer's own views of the question. In fact, every ancient and modern opinion, whether overruled, doubted or in any way qualified, is here systematically digested.

"These lectures, thus classified, are taken down in full by the students, and after being compared with each other, are generally transcribed in a more neat and legible hand. The remainder of the day is occupied in examining the authorities cited in support of the several rules, and in reading the most approved authors upon those branches of the law, which are at the time the subject of the lectures.[1]

[1] Those interested in this early law school method may find a collection of notes of Judge Gould's lectures now in the Harvard Law School Library, complete in three manuscript volumes, presented by W. S. Andrews of Boston. See *Harv. Coll. Arch. Reports, Report of Law Librarian*, July 12, 1861.

"These notes, thus written out, when complete, are comprised in five large volumes, which constitute books of reference, the great advantages of which must be apparent to every one of the slightest acquaintance with the comprehensive and abstruse science of the law.

"The examinations, which are held every Saturday, upon the lectures of the preceding week, consist of a thorough investigation of the principles of each rule, and not merely of such questions as can be answered from memory without any exercise of the judgment. These examinations are held by Jabez W. Huntington, Esq., a distinguished gentleman of the Bar, whose practise enables him to introduce frequent and familiar illustrations, which create an interest, and serve to impress more strongly upon the mind the knowledge acquired during the week.

"There is also connected with this institution a Moot Court for the argument of law questions, at which Judge Gould presides. The questions that are discussed are prepared by him in the forms in which they generally arise. These courts are held once at least in each week, two students acting as counsellors, one on each side, and the arguments that are advanced, together with the opinion of the judge, are carefully recorded in a book kept for that purpose. For the preparation of these questions, access may at all times be had to an extensive library.[1]

"Besides these courts, there are societies established for improvement in forensic exercises, which are entirely under the control of the students.

"The whole course is completed in fourteen months, including two vacations of four weeks each, one in the spring, the other in the autumn. No student can enter for a shorter period than three months. The terms of instruction are $100 for the first year, and $50 for the second, payable either in advance or at the end of the year."

It remained, however, for Harvard College to establish the first public school of law which has remained permanently in existence since its founding.

[1] It is said that the law library of Judge Gould was then the largest and best in the United States.

In 1815, largely through the efforts of John Lowell, Jr., that College established a professorship of law for the benefit of College seniors and resident graduates; and to fill this place, Isaac Parker, Chief Justice of the Massachusetts Supreme Court, was appointed.

After lecturing for one year, Parker was convinced that attendance at lectures in this way did not furnish an adequate legal education for any young man desiring to enter upon the profession. He accordingly suggested that a separate school of law should be constituted; and in pursuance of his plan, the Harvard Law School was established May 14, 1817, and Asahel Stearns was appointed its Professor. For twelve years Stearns and Parker conducted the School. The system of education, as described in Professor Stearns' report of 1826, was as follows:

"1. *Recitations and Examinations* in several of the most important text books, such as *Blackstone's Commentaries*, *Cruise on Real Property*, *Saunders on Uses*, *Fearne on Remainders*, etc.

"In these exercises the points of difference between the law of England and of our own country are carefully distinguished and the grounds and occasions of the difference are fully explained to the students.

"2. *Written lectures* embracing a general course of legal instruction, in which those parts of our system of jurisprudence in which we do not adopt the law of England are particularly noticed, and the grounds of our departure from it are explained and illustrated by the decisions and practice of our own courts.

"3. *A Moot Court* in which questions are regularly argued (often at considerable length) before the Professor, who pronounces an opinion. In these fictitious actions the pleadings, bills of exceptions, demurrers to evidence, special verdicts and motions in arrest of judgment or for a new trial are drawn up in form by the students. — During the argument those students who are not of counsel are employed in taking minutes, with a view to the acquisition of facility and accuracy preparatory to practice. The cases to be argued are, of course, adapted to the progress of the respective students in their professional studies. But they are strongly urged to engage in them very soon after their commencement; it having been found by experience that no other exercise is so powerful an excitement to industry and emulation or so strongly interests the students in their professional pursuits.

"4. *Debating Clubs* including all the members of the Law School in which some question (generally in moral philosophy, political economy or civil polity) which admits an extended and free discussion, is debated once a week with a view to improvement in extempore elocution.

"5. *Written dissertations* by the student upon some title or branch of the law or the history of some department of legal or political science."

The number of scholars, however, was small, never exceeding twenty, and finally, in 1829, becoming reduced to one.

The legal profession had not yet fully accepted the idea that law could be learned in a law school as well as in a law office. Moreover, at this time, the difficulty of access to Cambridge, owing to the non-existence of railway communication, and the rise of other law schools, more convenient for attendance, were great obstacles to the success of the Harvard Law School.

Thus Peter S. DuPonceau, the noted Philadelphia lawyer, said in 1821:

"If that justly celebrated Seminary [Harvard Law School] were situated elsewhere than in one of the most remote parts of our Union, there would be no need perhaps of looking to this city for the completion of the object which we have in view. Their own sagacity would suggest to them the necessity of appointing additional professors for each important branch of our legal system and thus under their hand would gradually rise a noble temple dedicated to the study of our national jurisprudence. But their local situation and that alone precludes every such hope;

for otherwise the world well knows that they are neither; wanting in inclination or ability to pursue any great object that may redound to their fame and the benefit of their country."

The principal other competing law schools between 1820 and 1830 were as follows: at New Haven, Conn., a private law school kept by Seth R. Staples and Samuel J. Hitchcock was in thriving existence from about 1800 to 1824, at which latter date the noted Judge David Daggett became its head. In 1826, Judge Daggett was appointed to fill the vacant professorship of law in the academic department of Yale College (previously held by Elizur Goodrich, from 1801 to 1810).

In Philadelphia, a "Law Academy" was founded by Peter S. DuPonceau in 1821, which afforded an opportunity for students of law to attend lectures by the eminent practitioners of that city.

In Virginia, Dr. Thomas Cooper had been elected temporary Professor of Law in the University of Virginia, in 1817; and, after declinations by Francis W. Gilmer and his brother-in-law William Wirt, John Taylor Lomax had been appointed permanent Professor in 1826.[1]

The College of William and Mary continued to furnish an ample course of legal education. There were also in Virginia several local private law schools, the most noted being that founded by Judge Creed Taylor in 1821 at Needham, Va., the average attendance of students at which was twenty.[2]

In Massachusetts, the noted private school at Northampton founded by Judge Samuel Howe and Hon. Elijah H. Mills, assisted by John Hooker Ashmun, flourished from 1823 to 1829, with a yearly average attendance of ten stu-

[1] See *Jefferson, Cabell, and the University of Virginia*, by John S. Patton (1906).

[2] See *Journal of the Law School and of the Moot Courts attached to it at Needham in Virginia*, by Creed Taylor (1822).

dents. In October, 1828, the eminent Theron Metcalf (later Reporter of Decisions and Judge of the Massachusetts Supreme Court) opened a law school at Dedham.[1]

In June, 1829, a law school was opened at Amherst by Samuel F. Dickinson, referring to which the *American Jurist*, Vol. VIII (1829), said editorially: "We are glad to witness the efforts which are making to render law education in this country thorough and systematic."

In 1830, however, the Harvard Law School became a thriving institution at one bound, when by the munificence of Nathan Dane in establishing from the profit of his *Abridgment of American Law* a new professorship, Joseph Story, then Judge of the Supreme Court, was appointed to fill the position. Under the guidance of this great Judge and of his distinguished colleague, John Hooker Ashmun, and later the celebrated Simon Greenleaf, this institution became within a few years the leading law school in the land.[2]

[1] See *American Jurist*, Vol. VIII (1829); and *Theron Metcalf*, by George S. Hale, *Mass. Hist. Soc. Proc.* (1876).

[2] See *History of the Harvard Law School*, by Charles Warren (1908). In addition to the law schools mentioned in the text, the following were established between 1830 and 1860: Cincinnati College Law School, in 1833; Carlisle Law School, in 1836; Indiana University Law School at Bloomington, and Cumberland University Law School at Lebanon, Tennessee, in 1842; Louisville University Law School, in 1846; North Carolina University Law School at Chapel Hill, from 1846 to 1848 (reopened in 1875); Tulane University of Louisiana Law School, at New Orleans, in 1847; Washington and Lee University Law School at Lexington, Virginia, in 1849; Albany Law School, in 1851; University of Pennsylvania Law School, in 1852; Columbia College Law School, and the University of the City of New York Law School, in 1858; University of Georgia Law School at Athens, University of Michigan Law School at Ann Arbor, and University of Chicago Law Department (later, in 1873, the Union College of Law and since 1882 a department of the Northwestern University), in 1859. See list given in *Influence of the Bar in Our State and Federal Governments*, by J. H. Benton, Jr. (1894). See also *Report of the Commissioner of Education for the year 1890–91*, Vol. I (U. S. 1894), and *History of the Harvard Law School*, Vol. II, chap. XLVIII.

# CHAPTER XV

## THE FEDERAL BAR AND THE LAW, 1815–1830

THE years from 1815 to 1830 were an era of great cases and great lawyers.

At the beginning of this period it is to be noted that the Federal Bar was still almost entirely Eastern in its composition[1] — a fact well illustrated by an entry by John Quincy Adams in his Diary, October 30, 1817:

"The President said . . . he had written this morning Mr. Wirt of Richmond, Virginia, offering him the office

[1] Ten new States had been admitted into the Union prior to 1830.

*Kentucky* was admitted in 1792. Its first law reports were Hughes' Reports in 1803, the next, Hardin's in 1810.

*Tennessee* was admitted in 1796. Its first law reports were Overton's in 1813.

*Ohio* was admitted in 1802. Its first law reports were Hammond's in 1824.

*Louisiana* was admitted in 1812. Its first law reports were Martin's, published in 1811 for the Territorial decisions.

*Indiana* was admitted in 1816. Its first law reports were Isaac Blackford's in 1830.

*Mississippi* was admitted in 1817. Its first law reports were Robert J. Walker's in 1834.

*Illinois* was admitted in 1818. Its first law reports were Sidney Breese's in 1831.

*Alabama* was admitted in 1819. Its first law reports were Henry Minor's in 1829.

*Maine* was admitted in 1820. Its first law reports were Simon Greenleaf's in 1822.

*Missouri* was admitted in 1821. Its first law reports were Priestly H. McBride's in 1829.

Georgia's first law reports were Thomas U. P. Charlton's in 1824.

of Attorney-General; but it was very doubtful whether he would accept it. The President said that he should have been very desirous of having a western gentleman in the cabinet but he could not see his way clear. He had taken great pains to inform himself but he could not learn that there was any one lawyer in the western country suitably qualified for the office. He had particularly inquired of Judge Todd who had assured him there was no such suitably qualified person. Graham said that he had inquired this morning of Mr. Clay who told him also confidentially the same thing — that there was no lawyer in that country fit for the office of Attorney-General."

William Wirt succeeded Richard Rush as Attorney-General in 1817, accepting the position because it facilitated his private practise in the Supreme Court; and held the office until 1829.[1]

During this period, the Bar of the United States Supreme Court showed a marked change in composition; the lawyers of Pennsylvania and Maryland no longer held undivided sway; and the Bars of the other States contributed many eminent counsel, especially after 1825, when the city of Washington became easier of access, through the advent of steamboats in the West and East.

William Pinkney remained the undisputed head of the Bar, until his death, in 1822.[2] Thereafter, Daniel Webster

[1] Prior to the passage of the Act of 1814 requiring the Attorney-General to reside in Washington, such residence had not been necessary; and William Pinkney resigned the office in 1814, because of the injury to his immense private practise in Baltimore which would be caused by his compliance with the statute.

[2] Wirt wrote, May 9, 1822:

"Poor Pinkney! He died opportunely for his fame. It could not have risen higher. He was a great man. On a set occasion, the greatest, I think, at our Bar. I never heard Emmet nor Wells, and therefore I do not say the American Bar. He was an excellent lawyer; had very great force of mind, great compass, nice discrimination, strong and accurate judgment; and for copiousness and beauty of diction was unrivalled. He is a real

overshadowed all others in the importance of cases argued, and in the mastery of the great principles of constitutional law; although he had close rivals in Wirt, and Littleton Waller Tazewell, of Virginia, and in number of cases he was excelled by David B. Ogden of New York. In a letter of May 9, 1822, Wirt wrote to his brother-in-law:

"Tazewell and Webster have been reaping laurels in the Supreme Court, and I have been — sighing. North of the Potomac, I believe to a man, they yield the palm to Webster; South, to Tazewell. So, you see, there is section in everything. Time will set all these matters right."

The difficulties attendant on travelling to Washington in those ante-railroad days were reflected by the immense number of cases argued by eminent counsel residing in the District of Columbia. Probably from one-fifth to one-fourth of all the cases appearing in the volumes of the reporters, Henry Wheaton and Richard Peters, during this period, were argued by Francis Scott Key, John Law, Thomas Swann, Walter Jones or Richard S. Coxe — all local counsel residing in or about Washington. From Massachusetts, the chief counsel who argued before the Court were Webster, George Blake and George Sullivan; from Rhode Island, Ashur Robbins and William Hunter; none of the other New England States were represented by counsel in more than two or three cases. From New York, David B. Ogden [1] appeared in a large number of cases; Henry Wheaton [2] and Thomas Addis Emmet were almost

loss to the Bar. No man dared to grapple with him without the most perfect preparation and the full possession of all his strength."

See *Memoirs of William Wirt*, by John P. Kennedy, Vol. II.

[1] Born in 1769.

[2] Born in 1785, a Brown graduate 1802, Reporter of United States Supreme Court 1816–1827.

equally prominent; and Ogden Hoffman,[1] Samuel A. Foot,[2] T. J. Oakley,[3] J. Prescott Hall[4] and C. G. Haines[5] argued a few notable cases. From Pennsylvania, the names of John Sergeant, Joseph Hopkinson,[6] Joseph R. Ingersoll[7] and Charles J. Ingersoll[8] were the most prominent. Of the New Jersey Bar, George Wood[9] was the leading representative. The lawyers of Maryland naturally appeared in a large number of cases — William Pinkney, W. H. Winder, R. G. Harper, David Hoffman and (beginning about 1824-1825) Roger B. Taney;[10] Virginia sent L. W. Tazewell,[11] Edmund I. Lee, Benjamin Watkins Leigh[12] and Philip N. Nicholas.[13]

The unsettled condition of the finances, of real estate titles, and of the law in general, in a new frontier State, having somewhat crude courts, is shown in the undue proportion of cases coming from Kentucky and argued by

[1] Born in 1793, son of Josiah Ogden Hoffman, Columbia graduate of 1812. District Attorney of New York 1829-1835, for twenty-five years counsel in almost every notable criminal trial, 1840-1845 United States District Attorney, 1853-1855 Attorney-General of New York.

[2] Born in 1790, Union College 1811, Judge of Court of Appeals 1851.

[3] Born in 1783, Yale 1801, Attorney-General 1819, Judge of the Superior Court 1828, Chief Justice 1846-1857.

[4] Born in 1796, Yale 1817.

[5] Born in 1793, Middlebury College 1816.

[6] Born in 1770, University of Pennsylvania 1786, admitted 1791.

[7] Born in 1786, Princeton 1804.

[8] Born in 1782, Princeton 1799, United States District Attorney 1815-1829.

[9] Born in 1789, Princeton 1808, studied with Richard Stockton, admitted 1812, in 1837 removed to New York.

[10] Born in 1777, Dickinson College 1795, studied with Judge Samuel Chase, admitted 1799, brother-in-law of Frances Scott Key, United States Attorney-General 1831-1833, Chief Justice of United States Supreme Court 1837-1864.

[11] Born in 1774, William and Mary College, 1792, admitted 1796, United States Senator 1825-1833.

[12] Born in 1781, William and Mary College, 1802, United States Senator 1834-1837.

[13] Born in 1773, Attorney-General 1793, Judge of Court of Appeals 1823.

Kentucky lawyers, — Henry Clay, Benjamin Hardin,[1] Charles A. Wickliffe, George M. Bibb[2] and Isham Talbot.[3]

Of lawyers from other Southern and Western States — from Tennessee came John Overton,[4] Felix Grundy,[5] John Catron,[6] James K. Polk[7] and John H. Eaton;[8] from Missouri, Thomas H. Benton;[9] from Ohio, Charles Hammond[10] and Thomas Ewing;[11] from Georgia, John McPherson Berrien;[12] from South Carolina, Robert Y. Hayne[13] and Hugh S. Légaré;[14] and from North Carolina, William Gaston.[15]

This period was one of tremendous effect upon the future of American law, and especially of that branch known as

[1] Born in 1784, admitted in 1806.

[2] Born in 1772, Princeton 1792, United States Senator 1811–1814, 1829–1835, Secretary of Treasury 1844.

[3] Born in 1773, studied with George Nicholas, the first Attorney-General of Kentucky, United States Senator 1815–1819.

[4] Born in 1766.

[5] Born in 1777, United States Senator 1829–1838, United States Attorney-General 1838–1839.

[6] Born in 1778, Chief Justice of Tennessee 1830–1836, Judge of United States Supreme Court 1837.

[7] Born in 1795, University of North Carolina, studied with Felix Grundy.

[8] Born in 1790, United States Senator 1818–1829.

[9] Born in 1782, University of North Carolina, admitted in 1811 under patronage of Andrew Jackson, then Judge of Supreme Court of Tennessee, in 1815 went to Missouri.

[10] Born in 1779, admitted 1801, went from Maryland to Cincinnati in 1822, author of *Reports* 1821–1839.

[11] Born in 1789, admitted in 1816, United States Senator 1831–1837.

[12] Born in 1781, Princeton 1796, Judge United States District Court 1810–1821, United States Senator 1825–1829, 1840–1852, United States Attorney-General 1829–1831.

[13] Born in 1791, Attorney-General of South Carolina 1818–1822, United States Senator 1823–1832.

[14] Born in 1797, Attorney-General of South Carolina 1830–1832, United States Attorney-General 1841–1843.

[15] Born in 1778, Princeton graduate 1796, Chief Justice of North Carolina 1834–1844.

constitutional law — the distinctive creation of the great American judges and lawyers.

In 1816, the vital question of States' Rights was presented in *Martin* v. *Hunter's Lessee* (1 Wheaton, 305), by the refusal of the Virginia Court of Appeals to obey the mandate of the United States Supreme Court, issued in 1813 (*Fairfax* v. *Hunter*, 7 Cranch, 603) on the ground that the appellate power of the Supreme Court did not extend to revise a decision of the highest court of a State. In the State Court, the case (*Hunter v. Martin*, 4 Munford, 1) had been argued amid great excitement, for six days in April, 1814, by eminent counsel — Wirt and Leigh against Williams, Nicholas and Hay — and decision was not rendered until December, 1815. In the Supreme Court, it was argued by Walter Jones of Virginia against Samuel Dexter of Massachusetts and St. George Tucker of Virginia. The final decision upheld to their fullest extent the powers of the Supreme Court. Judge Story in his opinion showed his entire conversion to Marshall's constitutional views,[1] stating that upon the right decision of

1 "Mr. Justice Story was of the democratic party, and shared the general views of that party on questions of constitutional politics; but with a mind of too legal a cast to run into wild revolutionary extremes. Coming upon the bench with prepossessions of the character intimated, Mr. Justice Story rose immediately above the sphere of party; and with the ermine of office put on the sacred robe of the Constitution and the law. Henceforward it became his duty, his desire, his effort, neither to strain the Constitution, nor to travel round it, on the loose popular maxims which guide the partisans; but to interpret it with impartiality and administer it with firmness."

See review of Story's *Commentaries on the Constitution*, by Edward Everett, in *North Amer. Review*, Vol. XXXVIII (Jan. 1834).

The broad Federal powers in which Story had come to believe were stated by him in a letter to Henry Wheaton, Dec. 13, 1815:

"I was much pleased, on reading in a newspaper this morning, that you had published an essay on the necessity of a navigation act; most cordially do I subscribe to your opinion on this subject. I am truly rejoiced that there are found public spirited young men, who are willing to devote their time and talents to the establishment of a great national policy on all sub-

the questions involved "rest some of the most solid principles which have hitherto been supposed to sustain and protect the Constitution itself;" and he referred to the "difficulty of the task which has so unwelcomely fallen upon us" and to the "source of consolation that we have had the assistance of most able and learned arguments to aid our inquiries."

On December 9, 1818, Judge Story wrote: "The next term will probably be the most interesting ever known;" and this comment was certainly justified, for in the year 1819 the Court decided the three great cases of *Dartmouth College* v. *Woodward*, *Sturgis* v. *Crowninshield* and *McCulloch* v. *Maryland.*

The *Dartmouth College Case* was argued March 10–12, 1818, by Daniel Webster of Massachusetts and Joseph Hopkinson of Pennsylvania, against William Wirt of Maryland and John Holmes of Maine. It is graphically depicted in the following letters from Webster. On February 17, 1818, he wrote to William Sullivan:

"Brother [R. G.] Amory and I are all the brethren of the Boston Bar here — I forgot [George] Blake — Ogden and a Mr. Baldwin from New York; Hopkinson, Seargeant and C. J. Ingersoll, Philadelphia; Harper, Winder, Baltimore; Wickham, Leigh and Nicholas from Virginia; Berrien from Georgia, and the gentlemen of this District. Court meets at eleven, hears long speeches till four and adjourns."

jects. I hope you will follow up the blow by vindicating the necessity of establishing other great national institutions; the extension of the jurisdiction of the Courts of the United States over the whole extent contemplated in the Constitution; the appointment of national notaries, public and national justices of the peace; national port wardens and pilots for all the ports of the United States; a national bank and national bankrupt laws. I have meditated much on all these subjects, and have the details in a considerable degree arranged in my mind."

On March 13, he wrote to President Brown, of Dartmouth College:

"The argument in the cause of the College was finished yesterday. It occupied nearly three days. Mr. Holmes ventured to ask the Court whether it was probable a decision would be made at this term.

"The Chief Justice in answer said, that the Court would pay to the subject the consideration due to an act of the legislature of a State and a decision of a State court, and that it was hardly probable a judgment would be pronounced at this term. . . . Mr. Wirt said all that the case admitted. He was replied to in a manner very gratifying and satisfactory to me by Mr. Hopkinson. Mr. Hopkinson understood every part of our cause, and in his argument did it great justice. No new view was suggested on either side. I am informed that the Bar here are decidedly with us in opinion. On the whole, we have reason to keep up our courage."

On the same day, writing to Jeremiah Mason, he said:

"The case was opened on our side by me. Mr. Holmes followed. . . . Upon the whole he gave us three hours of the merest stuff that was ever uttered in a country court. Wirt followed. He is a good deal of a lawyer, and has very quick perceptions, and handsome power of argument, but he seemed to treat this case as if his side could furnish nothing but declamation. . . . Mr. Hopkinson made a most satisfactory reply keeping to the law, and not following Holmes and Wirt into the fields of declamation and fine speaking. . . . I may say that nearly or quite all the Bar are with us. How the Court will be I have no means of knowing."

On March 23, 1818, the *Boston Daily Advertiser* published a long letter from its Washington correspondent, dated March 14, thus describing the argument:

"Mr. Webster opened the cause in that clear, perspicuous, forcible and impressive manner for which he is so much distinguished; and for two or three hours enchained the Court and the audience with an argument which, for weight of authority, force of reasoning, and power of eloquence, has seldom been equalled in this or any court. Mr. Holmes opened the cause on the part of the University, and was followed by the Attorney-General, Mr. Wirt, in a very able and eloquent argument on the same side. Mr. Wirt's style is splendid, his manner vehement, and his action attended with much effort. Before he concluded he became so exhausted by his great efforts of voice and action, that he was obliged to request the Court to indulge him until the next day, expressing at the same time 'that he had not of the example of extreme coolness which had been set by the counsel associated with him.' Mr. Hopkinson closed the cause for the College with great ability, and in a manner which gave perfect satisfaction and delight to all who heard him. The cause stands continued for advisement. . . . In the meantime, there is no reason, I apprehend, for the friends of the College to be disheartened or to relax in their efforts."

Of Webster's great argument, many accounts have been given, but none more vivid than that of Rufus Choate in his eulogy in 1852 before the Bar of the United States Circuit Court, in Boston:

"Some scenes there are — some Alpine eminences rising above the high tableland of such a professional life, to which, in the briefest tribute we should love to follow him. We recall that day, for instance, when he first announced, with decisive display, what manner of man he was, to the Supreme Court of the Nation. It was in 1818, and it was in the argument of the case of Dartmouth College. William Pinkney was recruiting his great faculties and replenishing that reservoir of professional and elegant acquisition in Europe. Samuel Dexter, 'the honorable man and counsellor and the eloquent orator,' was in his grave. The boundless old school learning of Luther Martin; the silver voice and infinite analytical ingenuity and resource of Jones; the fervid genius of Emmet, pouring itself along *immenso ore;* the ripe and beautiful culture of Wirt and Hopkinson — the steel point unseen, not unfelt, beneath the foliage; Harper himself, statesman as well as lawyer — these and such as these were left of that noble Bar.

"That day, Mr. Webster opened the cause of Dartmouth College to a tribunal unsurpassed on earth in all that gives illustration to a bench of law.

"One would love to linger on the scene — when, after a masterly argument of the law, carrying, as we may now know, conviction to the general mind of the Court, and vindicating and settling for his life-time his place in that forum, he paused to enter, with an altered feeling, tone and manner, with these words on his peroration — 'I have conducted my alma mater to this presence, that if she must fall, she may fall in her robes, and with dignity,' and he broke forth in that strain of sublime and pathetic eloquence, of which we know not much more than that, in its progress, Marshall the intellectual — the self-controlled — the unemotional, announced visibly the presence of the unaccustomed enchantment."

The Judges being greatly divided in opinion, no decision was rendered at this term; and the defendants decided to retain William Pinkney and to ask for a re-argument. Hopkinson wrote to Webster, November 17, 1818:

"In my passage through Baltimore I fell in with Pinkney who told me he was engaged in the cause by the present University, and that he is desirous to argue it if the Court will let him. I suppose he expects to do something very extraordinary in it, as he says Mr. Wirt 'was not strong enough for it, has not back enough.' There is a wonderful degree of harmony and mutual respect among our opponents in this case. You may remember how Wirt and Holmes thought and spoke of each other. . . . I think if the Court consents to hear Mr. Pinkney it will be a great stretch of complaisance, and that we should not give our consent to any such proceedings."

No re-argument, however, took place, and the decision of the Supreme Court was rendered on the second day of the term, February 2, 1819. During the argument, the Court had held its session in "a mean apartment of moderate size," the Capitol not having been rebuilt after its destruction by the British troops in 1814.[1] In 1819, however, the Court met for the first time "in the splendid room provided for it in the Capitol," as *Niles' Register* states.[2] This room was a basement chamber, approached by a small hall, having an eastern door of entrance from the grounds of the Capitol.[3]

Of the decision, Hopkinson wrote Brown on the same day:

"Our triumph in the College cause has been complete. Five judges, only six attending, concur not only in a decision in our favor; but in placing it upon principles broad and deep, and which secure corporations of this description from legislative despotism and party violence for the future. The Court goes all lengths with us, and whatever trouble these gentlemen may give us in the future, in their great and pious zeal for the interests of learning, they cannot shake those principles which must and will restore Dartmouth College to its true and original owners. I would have an inscription over the door of your building, 'Founded by Eleazar Wheelock; Refounded by Daniel Webster.'"

In view of its immense effect upon the future jurisprudence and corporate growth in this country, it is interest-

[1] See description of Professor Chauncy A. Goodrich quoted in Curtis' *Life of Webster*, Vol. I.

[2] *Niles' Register*, Feb. 20, 1819.

[3] See *National Intelligencer*, Feb. 2, 1819: "We are highly pleased to find that the Court room in the Capitol is in a state fit for the reception of the Supreme Court. We shall not pretend to describe in the terms of art the structure and decoration of this apartment, though we will endeavor to prevail on some qualified person to do it for us. It is such as to have an effect on the beholder, considerably more agreeable than that which was produced on entering the same apartment previous to the remodification of it made necessary by the conflagration of the interior of the Capitol." See also *History of the United States Supreme Court*, by Hampton L. Carson.

ing to note that the importance of the case was little realized in the public press of the time. *Niles' Register*, the weekly periodical published at Baltimore, which gave a fairly complete summary of all political and legal occurrences, makes no mention of the decision. The New York newspapers contained very slight mention of the case, the *Evening Post* devoting only a few lines, February 5, and saying: "Judge Marshall delivered the opinion. It is pronounced by our correspondent as a most able and elaborate production." Even the Boston papers were scant in their accounts.

Nevertheless, within a year after the decision, the *North American Review* stated, in January, 1820: "Perhaps no judicial proceeding in this country ever involved more important consequences or excited a deeper interest in the public mind than the case of Dartmouth College."

Two weeks after the Dartmouth College decision, the Supreme Court decided the great case of *Sturgis* v. *Crowninshield* (4 Wheaton, 122), declaring the Insolvency Act of New York unconstitutional, though leaving unsettled the general power of the States to pass bankrupt laws, if confined to contracts made after the passage of the act. In view of the depressed condition of business affairs in the country, this decision was of immense importance.

The argument of the case, which occurred on February 8 and 9, 1819, was thus described in a letter written at the time:[1]

"The cause was very ably argued on both sides, and certainly there never was a question discussed in a court of justice where the court had the benefit of more instructive pleadings (evidently the result of laborious investigation).

"It was opened in a clear and perspicuous manner by

[1] See *New York Evening Post*, February, 1819.

Mr. David Daggett from Connecticut against the State laws. He was followed on the other side by Mr. William Hunter of Rhode Island in a very learned view of the history of bankrupt laws and a subtle examination of the import of the terms in the Constitution 'impairing the obligation of contracts,' on which the discussion mainly hinged. Mr. David B. Ogden of New York followed on the same side with a critical analysis. . . . He manifested strong logical powers and great learning in the investigation of the subject; and if any abilities could have saved the cause, I am sure it would have been saved. Mr. (Joseph) Hopkinson of Philadelphia closed the argument with his usual acumen and ingenuity. The decision . . . is no doubt to be lamented in regard to the temporary evils it must inflict.

"But certainly every intelligent and reflecting man must have anticipated the possibility of such a decision being ultimately pronounced by the highest tribunal of the country; and I know many of the best lawyers in it have confidently expected this would be the result."

The news of this decision on February 17 caused a great perturbation throughout the country; for it was at first supposed that the Court had decided that the States had no constitutional power to pass any bankrupt or insolvent laws whatsoever.

The *New York Evening Post* of February 23 said: "It causes a very considerable sensation in the city and we do not wonder at it."

The necessity for a national bankruptcy act seemed imperatively manifest. *Niles' Register* of February 27, in a long editorial upon the case, said:

"This opinion has given much alarm to many persons, it is highly interesting to every one. It will probably make some great revolutions in property and raise up many from penury whose 'eyes have been blinded by the dirt of the coach wheels of those who ruined them' and cause others to descend to the condition that becomes honest men by compelling a payment of their debts. . . . The decision powerfully shows the necessity of a general bankrupt law, and if it had taken place at an earlier period of the session of Congress, might have led to the passage of a bill on that subject, for it is exceedingly important whilst the present system of credits exists that either party to it may know what may be depended upon. The decision will afford a golden harvest to lawyers and sheriffs, we have heard of one gentleman who has ordered writs for the recovery of eighty thousand dollars due to him by persons that failed, but who are now able to pay."

Further study of the opinion made it clear, however, that it only affected statutes discharging debts incurred prior to the passage of the statute. The main question as to the general power of the States to pass bankruptcy laws was left undecided, and caused much business uncertainty for many years.

Within a few days after the decision of *Sturgis* v. *Crowninshield* the great case of *McCulloch* v. *Maryland*, involving the right of the State to tax the new Bank of the United States, was argued by William Pinkney, William Wirt and Daniel Webster for the Bank, and Luther Martin, Joseph Hopkinson and Walter Jones for the State of Maryland. The arguments began February 22, 1819, and lasted nine days. No such constellation of lawyers had ever appeared before the Court in a single case.

On February 25, 1819, the *National Intelligencer*, a newspaper published in Washington, said:

"The argument has involved some of the most important principles of constitutional law which have been discussed with an equal degree of learning and eloquence and have constantly attracted the attention of a numerous and intelligent auditor by whom the final decision of this most important question from the Supreme Tribunal is anxiously expected."

Of Pinkney's three days' speech, Judge Story wrote, March 3, 1819:

"Mr. Pinkney rose on Monday to conclude the argument; he spoke all that day and yesterday, and will probably conclude today. I never, in my whole life, heard a greater speech; it was worth a journey from Salem to hear it; his elocution was excessively vehement, but his eloquence was overwhelming. His language, his style, his figures, his arguments, were most brilliant and sparkling. He spoke like a great statesman and patriot, and a sound constitutional lawyer. All the cobwebs of sophistry and metaphysics about State rights and State sovereignty he brushed away with a mighty besom. We have had a crowded audience of ladies and gentlemen; the hall was full almost to suffocation, and many went away for want of room."

On March 6, 1819, only three days after the close of Pinkney's argument, Chief Justice Marshall rendered his renowned opinion, upholding to their fullest extent the rights of the National Government to charter the Bank as a Federal agency and to the exclusive control of such Federal agency, and holding the attempt on the part of the State of Maryland to tax it an interference with the Federal rights under the Federal Constitution (4 Wheaton, 316).

As soon as the decision was made known, the country at once was divided upon political lines in regard to it.

Judge Story wrote on Sunday, March 7:

"It excites great interest, and in a political view is of the deepest consequence to the nation. It goes to establish the Constitution upon its great original principle."

The *National Intelligencer* of March 13 said: "The Supreme Judicial authority of the nation has rarely, if ever, pronounced an opinion more interesting in its views or more important in its operation." The newspapers of the

Eastern and Northern States almost unanimously praised the decision.

On the other hand, the papers of the States upholding the theories of Jefferson and the strict States' Rights doctrines bitterly assailed it. *Niles' Register* of March 13 said:

"A deadly blow has been struck at the Sovereignty of the States, and from a quarter so far removed from the people as to be hardly accessible to public opinion. . . . We are awfully impressed with a conviction that the welfare of the Union has received a more dangerous wound than fifty Hartford Conventions, hateful as that assemblage was, could inflict . . . and which may be wielded to destroy the whole revenues and so do away with the Sovereignties of the States."

The *Richmond Enquirer* said: "If such a spirit as breathes on this opinion is forever to preside over the judiciary, then indeed it is high time for the State to tremble; that all their great rights may be swept away one by one, that those sovereign States may dwindle into paltry and contemptible corporations."

Chief Justice Marshall wrote to Judge Story, May 27, 1819:[1]

"This opinion in the Bank case continues to be denounced by the democracy in Virginia. An effort is certainly making to induce the Legislature which will meet in December, to take up the subject and to pass resolutions very like those which were called forth by the alien and sedition laws in 1799. . . . If the principles which have been advanced on this occasion were to prevail, the constitution would be converted into the old Confederation."

In this year, 1819, the United States Circuit Courts were busy with a branch of law which has now become almost

[1] *Mass. Hist. Soc. Proc.*, 2d series, Vol. XIV.

extinct — the law of piracy, incidentally involving illegal slave trade. For several years, the Government had been much embarrassed in its dealings with foreign nations, by the crowd of piratical privateers which sailed, largely from Southern ports of the United States, under flags of the infant, mushroom-like South American Republics. France and Spain had protested violently. Finally John Quincy Adams, as Secretary of State, adopted a vigorous policy, and prevailed on William Wirt, as Attorney-General, to prosecute the pirates. At first, the courts were inclined to rule the law in favor of the pirates. The following extracts from Adams' Diary are illuminating on the situation (allowing for his well-known bitter personal prejudices):

"May 26, 1817: I spoke to Wirt about the acquittal at Baltimore of the pirate Daniels. The case went off upon a legal quibble. Wirt says it is because the judges are too weak but very good old men who suffer themselves to be bullied and browbeaten by Pinkney.[1]

"August 21, 1817: Pinkney is the standing counsel for all pirates who, by browbeating and domineering over the courts and by paltry pettifogging law-quibbles, has

[1] See *Diary of John Quincy Adams*, Vol. IV, in which Adams continued with his extraordinary reflections on law as follows:

"I told him that I thought it was law logic — an artificial system of reasoning exclusively used in courts of justice, but good for nothing anywhere else. . . . The source of all this pettifogging is, that out of judicial courts the end of human reasoning is truth or justice, but in them it is law. 'Ita lex scripta est,' and there is no reply. Hence it is my firm belief that, if instead of the long robes of judges and the long speeches of lawyers, the suitors of every question debated in the courts between individuals were led blindfolded up to a lottery wheel and there bidden to draw, each of them one or two tickets, one marked Right and the other Wrong, and execution should issue according to the sentence of the whole, more substantial justice would be done than is now dispensed by courts of law. In criminal cases, by the humanity of the law, which is indeed its best and most amiable feature, the chances in favor of the culprit are multiplied; and when the subtilty and the passions of the judges combine in their favor, no criminal can be brought to justice and punishment."

saved all their necks from the richly merited halter. . . . Baltimore upon privateering and banking is rotten to the heart.

"March 29, 1819: The misfortune is not only that this abomination has spread over a large portion of the merchants and of the population of Baltimore, but that it has infected almost every officer of the United States in the place. . . . The District Judge Houston and the Circuit Judge Duval are both feeble, inefficient men, over whom William Pinkney, employed by all the pirates as their counsel, domineers like a slave driver over his negroes."

Finally, however, the conviction and sentence to death of about fifty persons were secured at Boston, Baltimore and Richmond.[1]

The law was settled in a series of nine piracy cases, decided in the United States Supreme Court by Judge Story (*U. S.* v. *Klintock* and *U. S.* v. *Smith*, 5 Wheaton), in 1820, against the strong arguments urged in behalf of the pirates by Daniel Webster, and by W. H. Winder of Maryland.

In 1821, the great question of State Sovereignty was again the important subject before the Court; and on March 3–5 Marshall rendered his opinion in *Cohens* v. *Virginia* (6 Wheaton, 264), reaffirming the supreme power of the Court to review decisions of the State courts in criminal as well as civil proceedings. Philip P. Barbour[2] and Alexander Smythe[3] appeared for the State of Virginia, and William Pinkney and David B. Ogden for the plaintiff.

The decision caused much excitement in the newspapers

[1] See *Diary of John Quincy Adams*, Vol. IV.

[2] Born in 1783, William and Mary College, offered Professorship of Law in University of Virginia in 1825, United States District Judge 1830, United States Supreme Court 1836.

[3] Born in 1765.

of the country, and was bitterly attacked by the upholders of States' Rights in letters and speeches.

*Niles' Register* said, March 17, 1821:

"The decision was exactly such as expected for we presumed that that high tribunal would act consistently — and on the termination of the case about the bank of the United States, *McCulloch* v. *Maryland*, we had no manner of doubt as to the result . . . and that the State Sovereignty would be taught to bow to the judiciary of the United States. So we go. It seems as if almost everything that occurs had for its tendency that which every reflecting man deprecates."

On July 7, 1821, *Niles' Register* said:

"The decision . . . still claims the attention of some of our ablest writers, and the correctness of it is contested with a fine display of talents and profound reasoning by 'Algernon Sidney' in the *Richmond Enquirer* and 'Hampden' in the *Washington City Gazette* — to which we refer those who are not already satisfied on the subject. For ourselves, though not exactly prepared to submit, it seems as if it were required that all who do not subscribe to their belief in the infallibility of that court are in danger of political excommunication."

Of the criticism on the case, Marshall wrote to Story, June 15, 1821:[1]

"The opinion of the Supreme Court in the lottery case has been assailed with a degree of virulence transcending what has appeared on former occasions . . . I think for coarseness and malignity of invention Algernon Sidney [Spencer Roane, Judge of the Virginia Court of Errors and Appeals] surpasses all party writers who have ever made pretensions to any decency of character."

Jefferson's views of the opinion were vigorously expressed by him two years later in a letter to Judge William Johnson, June 12, 1823:

[1] See *Mass. Hist. Soc. Proc.*, 2d Series, Vol. XIV (1900–1901).

"On the decision of *Cohens* v. *State of Virginia* in the Supreme Court of the United States in March, 1821, Judge Roane (presiding judge of the Court of Appeals of Virginia) under the signature of Algernon Sidney wrote for the *Enquirer* a series of papers on the law of that case. I considered these papers maturely as they came out, and confess that they appeared to me to pulverize every word that had been delivered by Judge Marshall of the extra-judicial part of his opinion, and all was extra-judicial, except the decision that the act of Congress had not purported to give to the corporation of Washington the authority claimed by their lottery of controlling the laws of the States within the States themselves.

"The practice of Judge Marshall of travelling out of his case to prescribe what the law would be in a moot case not before the court is very irregular and very censurable."

The most alarming effect of the opposition to the strong centralizing tendency of the Supreme Court opinions was the steady increase of propositions to limit the powers of that Court by legislation or constitutional amendment. Those who favored such measures pointed to the fact that between 1809 and 1822 the Court had exercised its power to declare unconstitutional, in whole or in part, nine statutes in eight States (Georgia, New Jersey, Virginia, New Hampshire, New York, Maryland, Louisiana and Pennsylvania).

Jefferson wrote, January 19, 1821:

"I am sensible of the inroads daily making by the Federal into the jurisdiction of its co-ordinate associates, the State governments. Its legislative and executive branches may sometimes err, but elections and dependence will bring them to rights. The judiciary branch is the instrument which, working like gravity, without intermission, is to press us at last into one consolidated mass."

On September 2, 1821, he wrote:

"To consider the judges as the ultimate arbiters of all constitutional questions, is very dangerous doctrine indeed and one which would place us under the despotism of an oligarchy. Our judges are as honest as other men, and not more so. They have, with others, the same passions for party, for power, and the privilege of their corps. Their maxim is '*boni judices est amplificare jurisdictionem*,' and their power the more dangerous, as they are in office for life and not responsible as the other functionaries are to the elective control. The Constitution has erected no such single tribunal, knowing that to whatever hands confided, with the corruptions of time and party, its members would become despots."

And again, on March 4, 1823, he wrote:

"There is no danger I apprehend so much as the consolidation of our government, by the noiseless and therefore unalarming instrumentality of the Supreme Court."[1]

Already in 1807–1808, soon after the Burr trial, attempts had been made in each branch of Congress to amend the Constitution so that all judges should hold office for a term of years and be removable by the President on address by two-thirds of both Houses. This proposition was supported by resolves of the Legislatures of Pennsylvania

[1] On December 25, 1820, Jefferson had written to Thomas Ritchie:

"The judiciary of the United States is the subtle corps of sappers and miners constantly working underground to undermine the foundations of our confederated fabric. They are construing our Constitution from a co-ordination of a general and special government to a general and supreme one alone. . . . Having found from experience that impeachment is an impracticable thing, a mere scare-crow, they consider themselves secure for life; they skulk from responsibility to public opinion, the only remaining hold on them, under a practice first introduced into England by Lord Mansfield. An opinion is huddled up in conclave, perhaps by a majority of one, delivered as if unanimous, and with the silent acquiescence of lazy or timid associates, by a crafty chief judge who sophisticates the law to his mind by the turn of his own reasoning.

A judiciary independent of a king or executive alone is a good thing; but independence of the will of the nation is a solecism, at least in a republican government."

See *Writings of Thomas Jefferson*, Vol. X, pp. 169, 184, 197, 246.

and Vermont, as well as by action of the House of Delegates in Virginia and one branch of the Legislature in Tennessee.

After the decision in the Cohens case, a Virginia member of Congress, in April, 1822, introduced a bill to repeal so much of the Judiciary Act as gave the Supreme Court power to revise final decisions of State courts; and a member from Kentucky proposed a Constitutional amendment giving appellate jurisdiction to the Senate in any case in which a State was a party. In December, 1823, Senator Johnson of Kentucky introduced a bill to change the Judiciary Act so as to require that no State law should be declared unconstitutional by the Court unless seven judges concurred; and in March, 1824, Senator Martin Van Buren from the Committee reported a bill. Representative Wickliffe, in January, 1824, offered a bill to repeal the entire twenty-fifth section of the Judiciary Act. The bills failed to pass, and another effort in 1825 met a similar fate.[1]

Of such attacks, Judge Story wrote to Jeremiah Mason, January 10, 1822:

"I am glad you write somewhat encouragingly respecting the Judiciary. My only hope is in the discordant views of the various interested factions and philosophists. Mr. Jefferson stands at the head of the enemies of the Judiciary, and I doubt not will leave behind him a numerous progeny bred in the same school. The truth is and cannot be disguised, even from vulgar observation, that the Judiciary in our country is essentially feeble, and must always be open to attack from all quarters. It will perpetually thwart the wishes and views of demagogues, and it can have no places to give and no patronage to draw around it close

[1] See *Senate Journal*, Dec. 10, 1823, pp. 40, 41; March 11, 1824, pp. 229, 232. See also *Annals of Congress*, 1823-1824, pp. 915, 916-921; *Annals of Congress*, 1824-1825, Jan. 25, pp. 365, 370.

defenders. Its only support is the wise and the good and the elevated in society; and these, as we all know, must ever remain in a discouraging minority in all Governments. If, indeed, the Judiciary is to be destroyed, I should be glad to have the decisive blow now struck, while I am young, and can return to the profession and earn an honest livelihood. If it comes in my old age, it may find me less able to bear the blow, though I hope not less firm to meet it. For the Judges of the Supreme Court there is but one course to pursue. That is, to do their duty firmly and honestly, according to their best judgments."

The spirit of the times with reference to the States' Rights issue in the courts is interestingly shown in a letter from Marshall to Story, September 26, 1823, referring to Judge William Johnson's recent decision in a South Carolina case (*Elkinson* v. *Deliesseline*, Fed. Cases, 4366):

"Our brother Johnson, I perceive, has hung himself on a democratic snag, in a hedge composed entirely of thorny State Rights in South Carolina, and will find some difficulty, I fear, in getting off into smooth, open ground.

"You have, I presume, seen his opinion in the *National Intelligencer*, and could scarcely have supposed that it would have excited so much irritation as it seems to have produced. The subject is one of much feeling in the South. Of this I was apprized, but did not think it would have shown itself in such strength as it has. The decision has been considered as another act of judicial usurpation; but the sentiment has been avowed that, if this be the constitution, it is better to break that instrument than submit to the principle. Reference has been made to the massacres of St. Domingo, and the people have been reminded that those massacres also originated 'in the theories of a distant government, insensible of and not participating in the dangers their systems produced.' It is suggested that the point will be brought before the Supreme Court, but the writer seems to despair of a more favorable decision from that tribunal, since they are deserted by the friend in whom their confidence was placed.

"Thus you see fuel is continually added to the fire at which the exaltées are about to roast the judicial department. You have, it is said, some laws in Massachusetts, not very unlike in principles to that which our brother has declared unconstitutional. We have its twin brother in Virginia; a case has been brought before me in which I might have considered its constitutionality had I chosen to do so; but it was not absolutely necessary, and as I am not fond of butting against a wall in sport, I escaped on the construction of the act." [1]

One of the most vivid contemporary views of the position of the Supreme Court and its relation to the subject of States' Rights is found in a letter of Attorney-General Wirt to President Monroe, May 5, 1823, relative to the filling of the vacancy caused by the death of Judge Brockholst Livingston:

"Can you make an appointment more acceptable to the nation than that of Judge Kent? I know that one of the factions in New York would take it in high dudgeon at first. Probably, too, some of the most heated republicans and interested radicals who seize every topic for cavil, might, in every quarter of the Union, harp a little for a time on the same string. But Kent holds so lofty a stand everywhere for almost matchless intellect and learning, as well as for spotless purity and high-minded honor and patriotism, that I firmly believe the nation at large would approve and applaud the appointment. . . . The appointment of a Judge of the Supreme Court is a national and not a local concern. The importance of that Court in the administration of the Federal Government begins to be generally understood and acknowledged. The local irritation at some of their decisions in particular quarters (as in Virginia and Kentucky for instance) are greatly overbalanced by the general approbation with which those same decisions have been received throughout the Union.

[1] Unpublished letter in the *Story Papers* in possession of the Massachusetts Historical Society.

If there are a few exasperated portions of our people who would be for narrowing the sphere of action of that Court and subduing its energies to gratify popular clamor, there is a far greater number of our countrymen who would wish to see it in the free and independent exercise of its constitutional powers, as the best means of preserving the Constitution itself. . . . It is now seen on every hand, that the functions to be performed by the Supreme Court of the United States are among the most difficult and perilous which are to be performed under the Constitution. They demand the loftiest range of talents and learning and a soul of Roman purity and firmness. The questions which come before them frequently involve the fate of the Constitution, the happiness of the whole Nation, and even its peace as it concerns other nations. . . .

"With regard to the great subject of State Rights, which has produced so much excitement in Virginia and Kentucky, it happens that, if he (Kent) has any learning, it is rather in favor of State Rights. This has been shown by his decisions in the steamboat cases, where he has uniformly upheld the State laws of New York against all the objections which could be raised of their repugnance to the Constitution and laws of the United States."

It is interesting to compare with this letter, a letter from George Bancroft, December 27, 1831, describing an interview with John Quincy Adams:

"Among other curious things, Mr. A. told me that in the year 1823 on the death of Judge Livingston he had named to Mr. Monroe, Van Buren as a candidate for the place on the bench of the Supreme Court. . . . Mr. Adams thinks that had Van Buren at that time been appointed, he would have followed in the tracks of Marshall and proved himself a sound interpreter of national principles."

Curious surmises may be made as to what would have been the future history of the law as laid down by the Supreme Court, had either Kent or Van Buren been in a position to succeed Marshall twelve years later; but neither of them was appointed, Smith Thompson of New York taking Livingston's place.[1]

The increasing power of the Supreme Court over the States was discussed by *Niles' Register*, December 18, 1824, as follows:

"There is one very important effect that results from conflicting cases between the Constitution and laws of the United States and of the several States. As yet, they have been decided and settled by the Supreme Court, but its decisions, though acquiesced in, have not always satisfied what may be called State pride. This, however, is not the worst of it; for in the progress of time, the exposition of the Constitution of the United States may more depend on the opinions of the Supreme Court than on its own very carefully defined powers. It is not in human affairs to hope for perfection; and it is impossible to draw up any instrument such as the Constitution, without leaving some points that will bear different and opposing constructions; but we think it safe that these constructions should in some degree be established by the people through the representatives of the State in the Senate than be made to depend on the opinions of a mere majority of the judges of the Supreme Court, who, however honorable and learned they may be, cannot be put down as infallible. It would appear essential to the public harmony that some plan should be adopted by which the decisions of the judges should be subjected to a solemn revision whenever they undertake to settle constitutional questions, and this revisionary power would perhaps be best confided to the Senate which has or is presumed to have many of the ablest and the best citizens of the different States among its members, who certainly would not dishonor the Supreme Court, if appointed to its bench."

In 1824, the constitutionality of a statute of one of the Northern States was involved in a case which has played a larger part in determining the economic, social and

[1] *Life and Letters of George Bancroft*, by M. A. DeW. Howe (1908).

political conditions of the country, than any case ever decided by the Supreme Court, — the great "Steamboat Case," *Gibbons* v. *Ogden* (9 Wheat. 1). For twenty-six years, Ex-Chancellor Robert R. Livingston and Robert Fulton and their assigns had enjoyed, under grant from the New York Legislature, an exclusive right to run steamboats in the waters of New York. Efforts in the courts to break this monopoly had been frequent but unavailing. A case in the United States Circuit Court, *Livingston* v. *Van Ingen*, in 1811, had been dismissed for want of jurisdiction. A case in the State Court of Appeals between the same parties had resulted in a decree upholding the power of the State to grant such exclusive rights. Pending this case, the State had passed a further statute authorizing the seizure of any steam vessel found in New York waters in violation of the Livingston grant, thus practically making it impossible for any person to try his rights in court, without first forfeiting his vessel. Retaliatory statutes were passed in New Jersey and Connecticut forbidding boats "operated by fire or steam" under the license granted by the New York Legislature from plying in the waters of New Jersey, or of Connecticut; and so bitter were the feelings aroused by the monopoly that, as William Wirt said in his final argument in the Supreme Court the three States "were almost on the eve of civil war." Finally, a test case was brought in New York by Ex-Governor Aaron Ogden, of New Jersey, who, having established a steamboat line between New York and Elizabethport in defiance of the monopoly, had been enjoined by John R. Livingston and had accepted a license from the latter. The defendant was Thomas Gibbons, of Georgia, a former partner of Ogden, but who had refused to act under the Livingston license, and had started an opposition line in 1818. A motion to dissolve the injunction issued was heard by

Chancellor Kent and denied in 1819; and the Court of Errors sustained Kent in 1820.[1] Thereupon an appeal was taken to the United States Supreme Court, an interesting reference to which is found in a letter of Judge Story, February 28, 1821:

"We are to take up, in a few days, another question, whether a State can give to any person an exclusive right to navigate its waters with steamboats, against the right of a patentee, claiming under the laws of the United States. The case comes from New York, and Mr. Emmet of New York, and Mr. Pinkney are on one side; and Mr. Webster, Mr. Ogden, of New York, and Mr. Wirt, the Attorney-General, on the other. The arguments will be very splendid."

The case was dismissed, however, on a point of practise. Meanwhile, other suits had been brought in the United States Circuit Court to test the question — one of which, *Sullivan* v. *Fulton Steamboat Company* (6 Wheaton, 450), in which Daniel Webster was counsel, reached the Supreme Court, but was dismissed for want of jurisdiction.

Before *Gibbons* v. *Ogden* came up in the Supreme Court again, William Pinkney, the leading counsel for Ogden, had died, February 23, 1822, and Thomas J. Oakley of New York was engaged in his place.

On February 4–7, 1824, the case was argued at Washington.

"To-morrow week," wrote William Wirt, "will come on the great steamboat question from New York. (T. A.) Emmet and (T. J.) Oakley on one side, Webster and myself on the other. Come down and hear it. Emmet's whole soul is in the case and he will stretch all his powers. Oakley is said to be one of the first logicians of the age;

[1] See *Livingston* v. *Van Ingen*, 1 Paine, 45 (1811); *Livingston* v. *Van Ingen*, 9 Johnson, 807 (1812); *Livingston* v. *Ogden and Gibbons*, 4 John. Ch. 150 (1819); *Gibbons* v. *Ogden*, 17 John. 488 (1820); *Steamboat Co.* v. *Livingston*, 3 Cowen, 741; 1 Wend. 560 (1824).

as much a Phocion as Emmet is a Themistocles, and Webster is as ambitious as Caesar. He will not be outdone by any man if it is within the compass of his power to avoid it. It will be a combat worth witnessing." [1]

The arguments excited the greatest interest, and the New York newspapers gave lengthy accounts of their brilliancy.

The opinion of the Court was read by Chief Justice Marshall, March 2, 1824, only three weeks after the argument, sustaining Webster's broad view of the Federal power over interstate commerce.[2] The decision was greeted with approval by most of the newspapers throughout the country, and the *New York Evening Post*, March 5, 1824, said of it:

[1] *Memoirs of the Life of William Wirt*, by John P. Kennedy (1849).

Daniel Lord, at the New York Bar meeting on the death of T. J. Oakley, said:

"Judge Oakley represented the mighty sovereignty of the State of New York. His associate was Thomas Addis Emmet, and by whom were they met? By Daniel Webster and William Wirt. These four men debated that question before Marshall, Story, Washington, Todd, and Thompson. This, I conceive, to have been the culmination of professional eminence. What court could have so great a question? What court could be so greatly constituted? What court had the power of bringing private men to sit in judgment upon sovereign States? What court could feel the capacity to arbitrate among arguments of such talent, power and learning?"

See *Law Reporter*, Vol. XX (1857).

In the *Passenger Cases*, 7 Howard, p. 437, in 1849, Mr. Justice Wayne said, "The case of *Gibbons* v. *Ogden* in the extent and variety of learning, and in the acuteness of distinction with which it was argued by counsel, is not surpassed by any other case in the reports of courts. The case will always be a high and honorable proof of the eminence of the American Bar of that day."

[2] Webster himself states Marshall's indebtedness in a letter to Edward Everett, October 30, 1851:

"I presume the argument in *Gibbons* v. *Ogden* was written by me and given to Mr. Wheaton. The argument is a pretty good one, and was on a new question. It has been often observed that the opinion of the court delivered by Chief Justice Marshall follows closely the track of the argument. He adopts the idea which I remember struck him at the time that by the Constitution, the commerce of the several States has become a unit."

"This morning Chief Justice Marshall delivered one of the most able and solemn opinions that has ever been delivered in any court on the Steamboat case. The court-room was crowded with people, and during more than an hour which was consumed in pronouncing the decision of the court, the most unbroken silence prevailed.

". . . This opinion drawn up by Chief Justice Marshall presents one of the most powerful efforts of the human mind that has ever been displayed from the bench of any court. Many passages indicated a profoundness and a forecast in relation to the destinies of our confederacy peculiar to the great man who acted as the organ of the court.

"The steamboat grant is at an end."

The immediate result of the decision was the destruction of the Livingston monopoly,[1] which otherwise would have lasted until 1838. Its secondary results were far-reaching.

It opened the Hudson River and Long Island Sound to the free passage of steamboats, thus tremendously increasing the freight and passenger traffic on those great waterways, and proving a potent factor in the building up of New York as a commercial centre. It promoted interstate communication by steam throughout the country, by removing the danger of similar grants of monopolies in other States.[2] It was of immense importance in developing the coal industry, then largely an experiment; for it produced a great demand for coal as a fuel on the

[1] For detailed account of *Gibbons* v. *Ogden*, presented with many interesting sidelights, see *The Federal Power over Carriers and Corporations*, by E. Parmelee Prentice (1907).

[2] New York had not been the only State to grant a steamboat monopoly; Pennsylvania, in 1813, and Georgia, in 1814, had granted such monopolies; Massachusetts, in 1815, had given an exclusive license to John L. Sullivan for steam tow-boats on the Connecticut River; and New Hampshire had granted a similar license in 1816. Louisiana, in 1811, had granted a monopoly, similar to that in New York, to Fulton and Livingston.

steamboats. It was largely responsible for the sudden growths of the New England manufacturing industries, by making possible the cheap transportation of coal to New England by water. It has been the great factor in the economic development of the whole country down to the present time.

A few weeks after the decision of the case, another States' Rights case was decided, after being argued twice with extraordinary ability. This was the famous *Osborn* v. *Bank of the United States* (9 Wheaton, 738). It arose out of attempt on the part of the State of Ohio to controvert the decision of the Supreme Court in the McCulloch case, and to defy an injunction issued by the Federal Circuit Court against the State Auditor restraining him from collecting a tax on the Bank.

It was argued in 1824 by Charles Hammond and John C. Wright [1] for the State of Ohio and by Henry Clay for the Bank, and re-argued by Ethan Allen Brown [2] and Wright of Ohio and Robert G. Harper of Maryland, against Clay,[3] Daniel Webster and John Sergeant [4] for the Bank. The Supreme Court again upheld the constitutionality of the bank charter and the sovereignty of the Federal law even over State officials.

The slavery question first came prominently before the Supreme Court, in 1825, in the great case of *The Antelope* (10 Wheaton, 66), argued by Key, Berrien, Charles J.

[1] Born in 1783, Judge of Supreme Court of Ohio 1831, author of *Ohio Reports* 1831–1834.

[2] Born in 1776, Judge of Supreme Court of Ohio 1810–1818, Governor 1818–1822, United States Senator 1822–1825.

[3] Judge Story wrote to Judge Todd, March 14, 1824: "Your friend Clay has argued before us with a good deal of ability; and if he were not a candidate for higher offices, I should think he might attain great eminence at the Bar. But he prefers the fame of popular talents to the steady fame of the Bar."

[4] Born in 1779, Princeton 1795, leader of the Philadelphia Bar.

Ingersoll and Wirt, in which Chief Justice Marshall held that the slave trade was not piracy or contrary to the law of nations, unless prohibited by statute law or treaty.

Another noted case involving the slave trade was decided by Judge Story, in 1826 — *The Marianna Flora* (11 Wheaton, 1) — John Knapp of Boston and T. A. Emmett of New York arguing against George Blake and Daniel Webster.

In 1829, another case involving a further phase of the slavery question arose, in *Boyce* v. *Anderson* (2 Peters, 150), in which Chief Justice Marshall was called upon to decide whether a steamboat company was liable for loss of slaves drowned in an accident — the question being whether slaves were passengers or merchandise freight, and the decision being that the Company was only to be fixed with a common carrier liability for passengers.

The year 1826 is to be noted for the prominent appearance of a future Chief Justice of the United States, Roger B. Taney, who had argued his first case in the Supreme Court, two years previously. Of the case in which he now appeared — *Etting* v. *Bank of the United States* (11 Wheaton, 59), involving the defalcation of the cashier, McCulloch, Judge Story wrote in March, 1826:

"The court has been engaged in its hard and dry duties with uninterrupted diligence. Hitherto we have had but little of that refreshing eloquence which makes the labors of the law light; but a case is just rising which bids fair to engage us all in the best manner. Webster, Wirt, Taney — a man of fine talents, whom you have probably not heard of — and Emmet are the combatants, and a bevy of ladies are the promised and brilliant distributors of the prizes."

Marshall, in his opinion on this case, also spoke of the "great efforts which have been bestowed upon the case" and the "elaborate arguments which have been made at the Bar."

In 1827, three cases of immense effect upon the future commercial development of the country were decided. In the first — *Brown* v. *Maryland* (12 Wheaton, 419) the Court announced for the first time the "original package" doctrine [1] and the phrase "police power" first appeared. Like most of the other cases of this period, it turned on the issue of States' Rights. It was argued by Attorney-General Wirt and W. M. Meredith [2] against Roger B. Taney and Reverdy Johnson and was decided March 12.

The constitutionality of State bankruptcy statutes was definitely settled by the decision, February 19, 1827, of *Ogden* v. *Saunders* (12 Wheaton, 213) — a case which had been twice argued by a remarkable array of counsel — first, March 3–5, 1824, by Henry Clay, David B. Ogden and Charles G. Haines for the debtor, and by Daniel Webster and Henry Wheaton for the creditor, and reargued in 1827 by William Wirt, Edward Livingston, David B. Ogden, Samuel Jones and William Sampson (the three latter from New York) against Webster and Wheaton. The final decision was given in favor of Webster's client, although the majority of the Court decided against his argument denying the power of the States to pass bankruptcy laws.[3] Marshall, Story and Duvall, however,

[1] The beginning of the "original package" rule may be traced to State statutes adopted under the Articles of Confederation, in Maryland and Pennsylvania.

See interesting historical discussion of this case in *The Federal Power over Carriers and Corporations*, by E. Parmalee Prentice (1907).

[2] Born in 1799, University of Pennsylvania 1812, Attorney-General of Pennsylvania 1861–1867.

[3] See *National Bankrupt Law* in *Amer. Jurist*, Vol. I (January, 1829). See also *Review of Dane's Abridgment*, Vol. IX, in *Amer. Jurist*, Vol. IV (July, 1830), in which it is said: "As long as Congress neglects to make a

dissented on the constitutional point; and the opinions rendered were so intricate that Webster wrote to Nicholas Biddle, February 20, 1827:

"You see what a fire the judges have made on the question of State bankrupt laws. No two of those who are for the validity of such laws agree in their reasons. Those who are against their validity concur entirely. Is there not an old saying — if there be not let it go for a new one — that truth is one; but error various."

In this same year, Judge Story gave a decision (Marshall dissenting), in *Bank of U. S.* v. *Dandridge* (12 Wheaton, 64), which settled for all time the doctrine, that approval of acts of its agents by a corporation may be shown by presumptive testimony, as well as by written record and vote. This case was a victory for Webster and Wirt arguing against L. W. Tazewell of Virginia.

Two letters from Webster to Nicholas Biddle, President of the Bank, relating to this case, are of extreme interest. In the first, March 21, 1826, he said:[1]

"Dandridge's case was not reached until almost the last day of the Court, and until the Court had intimated that they should not take up another long or important cause. It was ready for argument and printed cases are prepared for the use of the Court. In this case, according to your request, I engaged Mr. Wirt on the part of the Bank, as I have already advised you. I wish it to be understood in regard to this cause that I consider myself as

bankrupt law, this decision will certainly have a very satisfactory effect in leaving the States to supply this defect in national legislation."

[1] See *The Writings and Speeches of Daniel Webster*, Vol. XVI (1903).

In *American Jurist*, Vol. IV, p. 302 (October, 1830), it is said: "Chief Justice Marshall said he believed that his opinion, which had been declared in the court below, gave general surprise to the profession and was generally condemned; still he adhered to it. The case is now before the nation, and Judge Marshall, great as the authority of his opinion is, will have increasing cause to find that in this case he is disapproved."

only filling Mr. Sergeant's place temporarily. It he should be here at the next term he will conduct the case with Mr. Wirt."

On February 20, 1827, he wrote:

"As to Dandridge, we hear nothing from the Court yet. The Ch. Jus. I fear will die hard. Yet I hope, that as to this question, he is moribundus.

"In everything else, I cheerfully give him the Spanish Benediction, 'May he live a thousand years!' I feel a good deal of concern about this; first, because of the amount in this case; second, because of its bearing on other important questions, now pending or arising, as I have understood; and last, because I have some little spice of professional feeling in the case, having spoken somewhat more freely than usually befits the mouth of an humble attorney at law, like myself, of the 'manifest errors' in the opinion of the great Chief. I suppose we shall have a decision in a few days."

At the term of the Supreme Court in 1830, Marshall gave the last of his great constitutional decisions, *Craig* v. *Missouri* (4 Peters, 410). The case involved a State statute under which Missouri was held to be issuing bills of credit in contravention of the United States Constitution, and was one of the earliest in which Thomas H. Benton appeared before the Supreme Court.

The close of the Chief Justice's opinion gives a vivid idea of how urgently the vexed political question of States' Rights was pressed upon the courts of the period, and of the dignity with which the great Chief Justice dealt with it:

"In the arguments we have been reminded by one side of the dignity of a sovereign State; of the humiliation of her submitting herself to this tribunal; of the dangers which may result from inflicting a wound on that dignity; by the other, of the still superior dignity of the people of the United States who have spoken their will in terms which we cannot misunderstand.

"To these admonitions we can only answer, that if the exercise of that jurisdiction which has been imposed upon us by the Constitution and law of the United States shall be calculated to bring on these dangers which have been indicated; or if it shall be indispensable to the preservation of the Union, and consequently of the independence and liberty of these States, these are considerations which address themselves to those departments which may with perfect propriety be influenced by them. This department can listen only to the mandates of law, and can tread only that path which is marked out by duty."

During these years, 1815 to 1830, the changes in the United States Supreme Bench were few. In 1823, Brockholst Livingston, of New York, died, and a strong effort was made to secure the appointment of Chancellor James Kent in his place; but Kent's political Federalist views were too bitter to be acceptable to President Monroe, and Smith Thompson, one of Kent's associates when on the New York Supreme Court, was appointed. In 1826, Thomas Todd of Kentucky died, and was succeeded by Robert Trimble of Kentucky. In 1828, Trimble died, and John McLean of Ohio, took his place in 1829. In the latter year Bushrod Washington's death led to the appointment of Henry Baldwin of Pennsylvania in 1830.

The salary of the Judges was changed (under Act of February 20, 1819) from $4,000 to $5,000 for the Chief Justice, and from $3,500 to $4,000 for the Associate Justices.

During this period, however, the number, as well as the importance of the cases before the Court, had increased enormously.

From 1803 until 1827, the Court had met on the first Monday in February; and its sitting usually lasted six weeks. In 1825, however, when it adjourned, March 21, only 38 out of 164 cases on the docket had been argued, hardly more than one a day. In 1826, only 49 out of 190 cases were heard. It became necessary therefore to lengthen the term; consequently, beginning in 1827 (12 Wheaton) the Court met on the second Monday in January (under Act of May 4, 1826). In that year "after an arduous and important session, 80 cases, some of them of deep and delicate interest and of high consequence" were heard.[1]

These years constituted in American jurisprudence what may be justly characterized as the reign of Marshall; for in these fifteen years the great doctrines of American constitutional law were firmly established by him; and the supremacy of the power of the Federal Government forever secured against successful attack. "Marshall found the Constitution paper; and he made it power," said James A. Garfield. "He found a skeleton, and he clothed it with flesh and blood." "He was not the commentator upon American constitutional law; he was not the expounder of it; he was the author, the creator of it. . . . The field was absolutely untried. Never before had there been such a science in the world as the law of a written constitution of government. There were no precedents. . . . An original field of judicial exertion very rarely offers itself. To no other judge, has it ever been presented, except to Mansfield, in the establishment of the commercial law; unless perhaps the remark may be extended to the labors of Lord Stowell, in the department of English consistorial law, and to those of Lord Hardwicke in equity."[2]

[1] See *Niles' Register*, Vol. XXXII, p. 80; Vol. XXX, p. 83; Vol. XXVIII, p. 49.

[2] See address of Edward J. Phelps before the American Bar Association (1879).

In his five great cases — the Marbury case, the Cohens case, the McCulloch case, the Dartmouth College case and the Sturgis case — Marshall did not cite a single decision as authority. "His only light was the inward light of reason. He had 'no guides but the primal principles of truth and justice.'"[1] "The decisions of no other eminent judges have so few citations of authorities. It used to be said of him that, when he had formed his conclusions, he would say to one of his colleagues, 'There, Story, is the law. Now you must find the authorities.' Story himself said, 'When I examine a question, I go from headland to headland, from case to case; Marshall has a compass, puts out to sea, and goes directly to the result.'"[2]

In thirty years, Marshall had transformed the Supreme Court, from a weak and uncertain body, hesitating to measure its strength against the prevailing jealousy of the Federal power, into an acknowledged supreme authority.

As early as 1820, a writer in the *North American Review* (Vol. X), in a review of volume four of *Wheaton's Reports* spoke of the increasing weight of the decisions on constitutional questions:

"This part of the law of the land is daily becoming more interesting, and exerting a wider influence upon the affairs of our country, from the respect that is generally felt for judicial decisions from the intelligible forms in which principles are exhibited and from the gradual formation of a body of constitutional exposition which will furnish precedents and analogies to future times."

And a review of Kent's *Commentaries* by the able Massachusetts lawyer, Willard Phillips, in 1827, expresses the same view:[3]

[1] Address of Le Baron Colt before the Rhode Island State Bar Association, February 5, 1901.

[2] Professor Theophilus Parsons, in *American Law Review*, Vol. I.

[3] See *North American Review*, Vol. XXIV (1827).

"The decision in *Weymouth* v. *Southard* (10 Wheaton, 1) on one of the Kentucky 'stop laws' in relief of debtors,[1] and some other decisions of the Supreme Court have given great dissatisfaction to some of the people of Kentucky and provoked much virulent declamation against the court itself. During the late session of Congress, some member intimated that a judicial tyranny was secretly creeping in on us. . . . But notwithstanding all that has been said to the contrary, we verily believe that the citizens . . . feel their persons and rights almost as safe in the hands of the Supreme Court of the United States as in those of some of the States."

And in 1828, so staunch a Republican, States' Rights newspaper as *Niles' Register* said, January 19:

"Though the constitutional construction of this lofty tribunal is not wholly conformable to our humble opinion of right, we have often thought that no person could behold this venerable body without profound respect for the virtue and talents concentrated on its bench; and with a great degree of confidence that as there must be some power in every government having final effect, it could hardly be vested anywhere more safely than in the Supreme Court as at present filled."

Three decades later, Edward Everett paid to the Supreme Court of this earlier period the following eloquent tribute:[2]

"I do not know what others may think on the subject, but for myself, sir, I will say, 'that if all the labors, the sacrifices, and the waste of treasure and blood, from the

[1] This case involved the Kentucky statutes requiring judgment creditors to indorse on their executions that bank notes of the Bank of Kentucky or of the Bank of the Commonwealth of Kentucky, would be taken in payment. This law arose out of the antagonism to the Bank of the United States. Chief Justice Marshall held that the statute did not apply to executions issued in the Federal courts.

[2] See Address, February 26, 1851, in *Everett's Orations*, Vol. III.

first landing at Jamestown or Plymouth, were to give us nothing else than the Supreme Court of the United States, this revered tribunal for the settlement of international disputes (for such it may be called), I should say the sacrifice was well made. I have trodden with emotion the threshold of Westminster Hall and of the Palace of Justice in France; I thought with respect of a long line of illustrious chancellors and judges surrounded with the insignia of office, clothed in scarlet and ermine, who within these ancient halls have without fear or favor administered justice between powerful litigants. But it is with deeper emotions of reverence, it is with something like awe, that I have entered the Supreme Court at Washington. Not that I have there heard strains of forensic eloquence, rarely equalled, never surpassed, from the Wirts, the Pinkneys, and the Websters; but because I have seen a bright display of the moral sublime in human affairs. I have witnessed from the low dark bench, destitute of the emblems of power, from the lips of some grave and venerable magistrate, to whom years and gray hairs could add no new title to respect (I need write no name under that portrait), the voice of equity, and justice has gone forth to the most powerful State of the Union, administering the law between citizens of independent States, settling dangerous controversies, adjusting disputed boundaries, annulling unconstitutional laws, reversing erroneous decisions, and with a few mild words of judicial wisdom disposing of questions a hundred fold more important than those which, within the past year, from the plains of Holstein, have shaken the pillars of continental Europe, and all but brought a million of men into deadly conflict with one another."

It is curious to note, however, that in spite of the importance of the cases before the Court, the legal profession in general had not at that time begun to realize the necessity of a thorough knowledge of its decisions. The number of lawyers practising before the Court was comparatively small, and the sale of Supreme Court reports very slight. Daniel Webster wrote in 1818, reviewing volume three of *Wheaton's Reports*, "it is not very rapid. The number of law libraries which contain a complete set is comparatively small." [1]

And as late as 1830, Joseph Hopkinson, reviewing the *Condensed Reports of the United States Supreme Court by R. Peters*, wrote: [2]

"The editor goes on to inform us that the reports of the cases argued and determined in the Supreme Court are contained in 24 volumes which are so costly that there are found but few copies . . . in many large districts of our country in which there are Federal and State judicial tribunals. In some of those districts, not a single copy of the *Reports* is in the possession of anyone. . . . An important result of an extended circulation . . . will be found in the dissemination of the knowledge of the labours and usefulness of this tribunal, and a corresponding increase with the people of the United States of their attachment and veneration for this department of their government. Few of our citizens know what this Court has done for them."

## NOTE

In *Niles' Register* for April 10, 1830, some very interesting statistics are given, illustrating the influence of the decisions of the Supreme Court on the final status of our law, and the precarious reliance to be placed on the decisions of the inferior Federal Courts. A quotation is made from an article written by a correspondent in the *National Intelligencer*, giving the result of an examination of the reports of Dallas, Cranch, Wheaton, and volumes one and two of Peters, in showing the number of cases decided in the inferior Federal Courts in the forty years between 1789 and 1829 which were appealed to the Supreme Court, and the result of these cases in the Supreme Court, as follows:

[1] See *North American Review*, Vol. VIII (December, 1818).

[2] See *American Quarterly Review*, Vol. VII (March, 1830).

| Districts. | Affirmed. | Reversed. | Per cent affirmed. |
|---|---|---|---|
| N. H. . . . . . . . . . . . . | 3 | 1 | |
| Mass. . . . . . . . . . . . . | 28 | 18 | 57⅓ |
| R. I. . . . . . . . . . . . . | 16 | 16 | |
| Vermont . . . . . . . . . . . | 1 | 0 | |
| Conn. . . . . . . . . . . . . | 4 | 4 | 52⅔ |
| N. Y. . . . . . . . . . . . . | 15 | 14 | |
| N. J. . . . . . . . . . . . . | 4 | 0 | |
| Penn. . . . . . . . . . . . . | 21 | 12 | 67½ |
| Del. . . . . . . . . . . . . . | 4 | 0 | |
| Md. . . . . . . . . . . . . . | 39 | 39 | 52⅖ |
| D. of C. . . . . . . . . . . . | 137 | 97 | 58½ |
| Va. . . . . . . . . . . . . . | 15 | 10 | |
| N. Car. . . . . . . . . . . . | 5 | 3 | 60⅗ |
| So. Car. . . . . . . . . . . . | 13 | 11 | |
| Ga. . . . . . . . . . . . . . | 20 | 25 | 47½ |
| Ohio . . . . . . . . . . . . . | 13 | 12 | |
| Ky. . . . . . . . . . . . . . | 41 | 31 | 55½ |
| Tenn. . . . . . . . . . . . . | 20 | 17 | |
| Ill. . . . . . . . . . . . . . | 1 | 0 | 100 |
| Ind. . . . . . . . . . . . . . | 0 | 1 | |
| Ala. . . . . . . . . . . . . . | 3 | 3 | 50 |
| Miss. . . . . . . . . . . . . | 3 | 3 | 50 |
| Orleans . . . . . . . . . . . | 4 | 3 | 57 |
| La. . . . . . . . . . . . . . | 15 | 8 | 65⅖ |
| | 425 | 328 | 56⅓ |

## CHAPTER XVI

### THE FEDERAL BAR AND LAW, 1830–1860

THE Federal Bar in the years from 1830 to 1860 showed a marked change from that of the first thirty years of the Nineteenth Century.[1] Daniel Webster continued, until his death in 1853, the undisputed head; but the lawyers of Maryland, Pennsylvania and Virginia no longer monopolized the arguments. Massachusetts was brilliantly represented by noted lawyers like Franklin Dexter, Charles G. Loring, Sidney Bartlett, Caleb Cushing,[2] John H.

[1] Between 1830 and 1860 only nine new States were admitted into the Union in addition to the twenty-three composing the United States in 1830.

*Arkansas* was admitted in 1836. Its first law reports were Albert Pike's in 1840.

*Michigan* was admitted in 1837. Its first law reports were Samuel T. Douglass' in 1846.

*Florida* was admitted in 1845. Its first law reports were Joseph Branch's in 1847.

*Texas* was admitted in 1845. Its first law reports were Webb and Duval's in 1848, although James W. Dallam published a volume of decisions in 1845.

*Iowa* was admitted in 1846. Its first law reports were Eastin Morris' in 1847, covering Territorial court decisions, George Greene's in 1849, covering State court decisions.

*Wisconsin* was admitted in 1847. Its first law reports were Daniel H. Chandler's in 1850.

*California* was admitted in 1850. Its first law reports were Nathaniel Bennett's in 1851.

*Minnesota* was admitted in 1857. Its first law reports were Harvey Officer's in 1858.

*Oregon* was admitted in 1859. Its first law reports were in 1862.

[2] Born in 1800, a Harvard graduate of 1817, Judge of Massachusetts Supreme Court 1852, Attorney-General of the United States 1853–1857.

Clifford,[1] B. F. Hallett,[2] John Davis,[3] James T. Austin,[4] Richard Fletcher [5] and Willard Phillips. In 1840, Theophilus Parsons, Jr., argued *Peters* v. *Warren Ins. Co.* (14 Peters, 99) against Webster. In 1842, Richard H. Dana, Jr.,[6] argued the famous case of *Swift* v. *Tyson* (16 Peters, 1); and in the same year Rufus Choate [7] made his first appearance in *Prouty* v. *Ruggles.* In 1849, Benjamin R. Curtis [8] argued the noted case of *Peck* v. *Jenness* (7 Howard, 612).

New York sent a distinguished list of counsel, Ogden Hoffman,[9] John C. Spencer,[10] Benjamin F. Butler,[11] Charles O'Conor,[12] Samuel Beardsley,[13] George Wood, Daniel Lord,[14] William H. Seward,[15] Edward M. Dickerman, R. H. Gillet and William Curtis Noyes.

The District of Columbia lawyers, Key, Coxe, Simms,

[1] Born in 1809, Brown 1827, Attorney-General of Massachusetts 1849–1853, Governor 1853, Attorney-General 1854–1858.

[2] Born in 1797, Brown 1810, United States District Attorney 1853.

[3] Born in 1787, Yale 1812, United States Senator 1835–1841, Governor 1841, United States Senator 1845–1853.

[4] Born in 1784, Harvard 1802, son-in-law of Elbridge Gerry, Attorney-General of Massachusetts 1832–1843.

[5] Born in 1788, Dartmouth 1806, studied with Daniel Webster, Judge Massachusetts Supreme Court 1848.

[6] Born in 1815, Harvard 1837, United States District Attorney 1861–1866.

[7] Born in 1799, Dartmouth 1819, United States Senator 1841–1845, Massachusetts Attorney-General 1853–1854.

[8] Born in 1809, Harvard 1829, Judge United States Supreme Court 1851.

[9] Born in 1793, Columbia 1812.

[10] Born in 1788, son of Chief Justice Ambrose Spencer, Union College 1806.

[11] Born in 1795, United States Attorney-General 1833–1838.

[12] Born in 1804.

[13] Born in 1790, Judge New York Supreme Court 1844, Chief Justice 1847.

[14] Born in 1795, Yale 1814, studied at the Litchfield Law School.

[15] Born in 1801, Union College 1816–1819, studied with John Anthon, John Duer and Ogden Hoffman, Governor 1838–1842, United States Senator 1849–1861.

Mason and the veteran Thomas Swann (until his death in 1840) argued a vast number of cases. In the later years there appeared Henry May, Robert J. Brent and Joseph H. Bradley.

From Illinois, Abraham Lincoln [1] appeared, in 1850, in *Brabster* v. *Gibson* (9 Howard, 263); and other lawyers of distinction were Sidney Breese,[2] S. A. Douglas,[3] Charles Fox, Orville H. Browning,[4] James Shields,[5] Edward D. Baker and Lyman Trumbull.[6]

William Wirt of Maryland continued in constant and vigorous practise until his death in 1834, and his place at the Bar was taken by Reverdy Johnson,[7] who, for many years after Webster's death, was regarded as the leading American lawyer.

From Kentucky came Clay, Bibb, Wickliffe, John J. Crittenden [8] and James T. Morehead.[9] From Georgia came John McPherson Berrien [10] and William H. Crawford; [11]

[1] Born in 1809.

[2] Born in 1800, United States Senator 1843–1849, Judge Illinois Supreme Court 1841–1843, 1871–1872, Chief Justice 1873–1878.

[3] Born in 1813, United States Senator 1847–1861.

[4] Born in 1810, United States Senator 1861–1863.

[5] Born in 1812, Judge of Supreme Court 1843–1845, United States Senator 1849–1855.

[6] Born in 1813, Judge of Supreme Court 1848–1854, United States Senator 1855–1867.

[7] Born in 1796, St. Johns College, United States Attorney-General 1849–1850. An interesting article on *The Supreme Court in 1853–1854* in *American Law Register*, Vol. IV (1853–1854), says that "the largest practice before the Court is that of Reverdy Johnson."

[8] Born in 1787, William and Mary College 1807, 1809, Attorney-General of Territory of Illinois, 1817, 1829–1835, United States Senator from Kentucky, 1827.

[9] Born in 1797, United States Senator 1841–1847.

[10] Born in 1781, Princeton 1796, Judge United States District Court 1810–1821, United States Senator 1825–1829, 1840–1842, Attorney-General of United States 1829–1831.

[11] Born in 1772, United States Senator 1807–1813.

from Mississippi, Robert J. Walker,[1] Volney E. Howard, John Henderson[2] and Sergeant S. Prentiss.[3]

From Missouri came Thomas H. Benton,[4] who argued the great case of *Craig* v. *Missouri* (4 Peters, 410) in 1830, Hamilton R. Gamble,[5] and Henry S. Geyer.[6]

From Ohio there were Henry Stanberry,[7] and Salmon P. Chase[8] who first appeared in 1836, Noah H. Swayne,[9] Bellamy Storer, William Lawrence and George E. Pugh.[10]

From Rhode Island, there were Albert C. Greene,[11] Richard W. Greene, Thomas A. Jenckes and Samuel Ames.[12]

From Pennsylvania, the veteran John Sergeant headed the list of eminent lawyers, which also included Horace Binney,[13] Charles J. Ingersoll, Joseph R. Ingersoll, William M. Meredith, James Campbell,[14] Edwin M. Stanton,[15]

[1] Born in 1801, University of Pennsylvania 1819, United States Senator 1836-1845, Secretary of Treasury 1845-1849.

[2] Born in 1795, United States Senator 1849-1851.

[3] Born in 1808, Bowdoin College 1826.

[4] Born in 1782, United States Senator 1821-1851.

[5] Born in 1798, Judge Supreme Court 1851-1855.

[6] Born in 1790, United States Senator 1851-1857.

[7] Born in 1803, Washington College 1819, Attorney-General of Ohio 1846, United States Attorney-General 1866-1868.

[8] Born in 1808, Dartmouth 1826, studied with Wirt 1827, United States Senator 1849-1855, Governor 1855-1861, Chief Justice of the United States 1864-1873.

[9] Born in 1804, United States District Attorney 1831-1841, Judge United States Supreme Court 1862-1881.

[10] Born in 1822, United States Senator 1855-1861.

[11] Born in 1791, Attorney-General of Rhode Island 1825-1843, United States Senator 1845-1851.

[12] Born in 1806, Chief Justice of Rhode Island 1856-1865.

[13] Born in 1780, Harvard 1797, admitted 1800.

[14] Born in 1813, Attorney-General of Pennsylvania 1852.

[15] Born in 1814, Kenyon 1833, United States Attorney-General 1861.

Henry D. Gilpin,[1] George M. Dallas[2] and Job R. Tyson.[3]

From Michigan came William Woodbridge,[4] George E. Hand and Ezra C. Seaman.

From Alabama came John A. Campbell,[5] Leroy P. Walker and Alexander White.

South Carolina sent James L. Petigru.[6]

From Arkansas came William K. Sebastian,[7] and Albert Pike.

Louisiana sent a large corps of eminent lawyers: Alexander J. Porter,[8] Edward Douglas White,[9] George Eustis,[10] Pierre Soulé,[11] Charles M. Conrad,[12] Louis Janin, Judah P. Benjamin,[13] and William H. Hunt.[14]

From Indiana came Albert S. White,[15] Oliver H. Smith,[16] Richard W. Thompson,[17] Samuel Judah, and Thomas A. Hendricks.[18]

[1] Born in 1801, University of Pennsylvania 1819, studied with Joseph R. Ingersoll, United States District Attorney 1832, United States Attorney-General 1840–1841.

[2] Born in 1792, Princeton 1810, United States District Attorney 1829, United States Senator 1831–1833, Vice-President 1845–1849.

[3] Born in 1803.

[4] Born in 1780, Governor 1840–1841, United States Senator 1841–1847.

[5] Born in 1811, Judge United States Supreme Court 1853–1861.

[6] Born in 1789, Attorney-General 1822–1830.

[7] Born in 1814, United States Senator 1847–1861.

[8] Born in 1796, Judge of Supreme Court 1821–1833, United States Senator, 1834–1843.

[9] Born in 1795, Governor 1834–1838.

[10] Born in 1796, Harvard 1815, Chief Justice of Supreme Court, 1846–1852.

[11] Born in 1802, United States Senator, 1847–1853.

[12] Born in 1804, United States Senator 1842–1843.

[13] Born in 1811, United States Senator 1852–1861.

[14] Born in 1824, Attorney-General of Louisiana, 1876.

[15] Born in 1803, Union 1822, United States Senator 1839–1845.

[16] Born in 1794, United States Senator 1837–1848.

[17] Born in 1809.

[18] Born in 1819, United States Senator 1863–1869, Vice-President, 1885.

From New Jersey came William L. Dayton,[1] Samuel L. Southard,[2] and Joseph P. Bradley.[3]

From Maine came William Pitt Fessenden[4] and Charles G. Daveis.

From North Carolina came George E. Badger.[5]

The new States of Florida, Texas, Iowa, Wisconsin and California sent a few lawyers of distinction, but their Bars were more adequately represented at a later period.

Perhaps the most notable feature of the Federal Bar was the very great number of cases argued by members of the United States Senate. The mass of litigation from the Southern and Western States also marked this era.

The death of Webster in 1853, of Clay in 1852 and of Calhoun[6] in 1850, removed three of the greatest legal lights of this period.

The years 1831 and 1832 were notable in the field of Federal law, as well as in politics, for another determined attack on Federal sovereignty. January 28, 1831, Story wrote:

"A most important and alarming measure . . . to repeal the 25th section of the Judiciary Act. If it should prevail (of which I have not any expectation), it would deprive the Supreme Court of the power to revise the decisions of the State courts and State Legislature in all cases in which they were repugnant to the Constitution of the United States, so that all laws passed and all decisions made, however destructive to the National Government,

[1] Born in 1807, Princeton 1825, Judge of Supreme Court 1831–1842, United States Senator 1842–1856, Attorney-General, 1857–1861.

[2] Born in 1787, Judge of Supreme Court 1815–1820, United States Senator 1821–1823, 1833–1842, Attorney-General 1829–1832, Governor 1832.

[3] Born in 1813, Judge of United States Supreme Court 1870–1892.

[4] Born in 1806, Bowdoin 1823, United States Senator 1853–1865.

[5] Born in 1795, Yale 1813, United States Senator 1846–1855.

[6] Born in 1782, Yale 1806, Vice-President 1825–1832, United States Senator 1833–1843, 1845–1850.

would have no power of redress. The introduction of it shows the spirit of the times."

This bill was strongly urged by the upholders of the States' Rights doctrine, and was the result of the bitter feeling created by Judge Story's powerful opinion in *Martin* v. *Hunter* and Marshall's in *Cohens* v. *Virginia*, and in the long line of opinions in which the Supreme Court had now definitely established its right to review the decisions of State courts. The bill was defeated by a vote of 137 to 51; all but 6 of the 51 votes coming from Southern States.

In the same year occurred the case of the *Cherokee Nation* v. *Georgia* (5 Peters, 1) involving the constitutionality of a Georgia statute dealing with the Cherokee Indian lands, in countervention of a United States Treaty.

In this case, William Wirt and John Sergeant appeared for the Cherokee Chiefs and Horace Binney, James Kent, Ambrose Spencer and Daniel Webster were their advisers out of court, — a remarkable array of legal talent. The State of Georgia, declining to recognize the jurisdiction of the United States Supreme Court, refused to appear; the Court, however (Story and Thompson dissenting), decided the case on a technical point in favor of the State, although the Chief Justice stated in his opinion: "If courts were permitted to indulge their sympathies, a case better calculated to excite them can scarcely be imagined." "The great interest excited throughout the Union by this controversy," said the *North American Review* of that period, "was naturally to be expected from the novelty of the case, the dignity of the parties and the question, and the high importance of the principles involved." [1]

The rights of the State of Georgia were again involved

[1] See also review of *The Cherokee Case*, by Joseph Hopkinson, in *Amer. Quart. Review*, Vol. X (March, 1832).

in 1832 in *Worcester* v. *Georgia* (6 Peters, 515), another case involving the Cherokee Lands statute, in which the Court decided it unconstitutional, and issued a mandate ordering the release of persons imprisoned by virtue of the statute. Of this case Judge Story wrote to his wife, February 26, 1832:

"We have had from Mr. Wirt and Mr. Sergeant in the past week some fine arguments in the Cherokee case, brought before us in a new form. . . . Both of the speeches were very able, and Mr. Wirt's in particular was uncommonly eloquent, forcible and finished. . . . No person appeared for the State of Georgia."

And he wrote to Professor Ticknor, March 8:

"We have just decided the Cherokee case, and reversed the decisions of the State Court of Georgia, and declared her laws unconstitutional. The decision produced a very strong sensation in both houses; Georgia is full of anger and violence. . . . Probably she will resist the execution of our judgment, and if she does I do not believe the President will interfere. . . . The Court has done its duty. Let the Nation do theirs."

On March 4, he wrote to his wife:

"Yesterday morning the Chief Justice delivered the opinion of the court in the Cherokee case, in favor of the missionaries. It was a very able opinion in his best manner. Thanks be to God the Court can wash their hands clean of the iniquity of oppressing the Indians and disregarding their rights. . . .

"We shall adjourn about the sixteenth of the month, and I shall move towards Cambridge with all the rapidity with which steam and coaches can carry me."

Of the Supreme Court room at this period, Harriet Martineau gave her well known account in her *Retrospect of Western Travel:*

"I have watched the assemblage when the Chief Justice was delivering a judgment, the three judges on either hand gazing at him more like learners than associates; Webster standing firm as a rock, his large, deep-set eyes wide awake, his lips compressed, and his whole countenance in that intent stillness which easily fixes the eye of the stranger. Clay leaning against the desk in an attitude whose grace contrasts strangely with the slovenly make of his dress, his snuff box for the moment unopened in his hand, his small grey eye, and placid half-smile conveying an expression of pleasure, which redeems his face from its usual unaccountable commonness. The Attorney-General [Taney] his fingers playing among his papers, his quick black eye and thin tremulous lips for once fixed, his small face, pale with thought, contrasting remarkably with the other two; these men absorbed in what they are listening to, thinking neither of themselves nor of each other, while they are watched by the groups of idlers and listeners around them; the newspaper corps, the dark Cherokee chiefs, the stragglers from the far West, the gay ladies in their waving plumes, and the members of either House that have stepped in to listen; all these I have seen constitute one silent assemblage, while the mild voice of the aged Chief Justice sounded through the court. . . . How delighted we were to see Judge Story bring in the tall, majestic, bright-eyed, old man (the Chief Justice), old by chronology, by the lines on his composed face, and by his services to the republic; but so dignified, so fresh, so present to the time, that no feeling of compassionate consideration for age dared to mix with contemplation of him."

Another vivid contemporaneous description of Chief Justice Marshall at the time, is found in a letter of the instructor, George Bancroft, written December 23, 1832:

"We went to call upon Judge Story, and we found there Judge Baldwin and Chief Justice Marshall. I drew my chair up to the latter, nor can you readily conceive of the great suavity, or rather calmness of manner, by which he is distinguished. In conversation he makes no display, nor is he remarkable except for this venerable coolness of manner. There are about him no marks of genius; but in his entire collectedness, great precision and calm uniformity, you may discern the signs of an unerring judgment. He is by all acknowledged to stand foremost on the bench of the Supreme Court — a first rate man in the first class of greatness. He has travelled very little; has not been in New England since the War; has hardly seen New York, but has lived in the regular exercise of his judicial functions, unencumbered by any care other than that of giving character and respectability to the bench over which he presides." [1]

It is interesting to compare this picture with that portrayed by George Ticknor, seventeen years prior, who wrote on February 1, 1815, as follows:

"You will expect from me some account of the Chief Justice of the United States, the first lawyer — if not, indeed, the first *man* — in the country. You must, then, imagine before you a man who is tall to awkwardness, with a large head of hair, which looked as if it had not been lately tied or combed, and with dirty boots. You must imagine him, too, with a strangeness in his manners which arises neither from awkwardness nor formality, but seems to be a curious compound of both; and then, perhaps, you will have before you a figure something like that of the Chief Justice. His style and tones in conversation are uncommonly mild, gentle, and conciliatory; and before I had been with him half an hour, I had forgotten the carelessness of his dress and person, and observed only the quick intelligence of his eye and the open interest he discovered in the subjects on which he spoke, by the perpetual variations of his countenance." [2]

In view of the close connection between the decisions of the Supreme Court and the political question then most alive — State Sovereignty — it is interesting to note that

[1] *Life and Letters of George Bancroft*, by M. A. DeW. Howe (1908).

[2] *Life and Letters and Journals of George Ticknor* (1876).

in 1833 Judge Story published his *Commentaries on the Constitution of the United States* — the first adequate work on that great branch of law. Its especial value and appropriateness at the particular crisis in national politics — the Nullification Ordinance of South Carolina having been passed November 24, 1832, and President Jackson's strong Union proclamation issued in December — was noticed in a review by Edward Everett in the *North American Review*.[1]

"Its peculiar seasonableness at the present time gives Mr. Justice Story's work a value, which no work could have possessed under different circumstances. Constitutional law in our day, instead of being the calm occupation of the schools or the curious pursuit of the professional student, has become — as it were — an element of real life. The Constitution has been obliged to leave its temple and come down into the forum and traverse the streets."

The winter of 1833–1834 in Washington was marked in legal annals by the death of William Wirt, on February 18, 1834, and by the appointment of Roger B. Taney of Baltimore (Wirt's successor as Attorney-General of the United States under Jackson, and at that time Secretary of the Treasury) to the Supreme Bench, in place of Gabriel Duvall who had resigned. The appointment, however, was refused confirmation by the Senate.

A vivid glimpse of the Bar of the Supreme Court at this time is given in a letter from Charles Sumner to Professor Simon Greenleaf, March 3, 1834:

"Mr. Francis Scott Key is now speaking in the Supreme Court where I write these lines. The case before the Court is an important one, between Amos Binney and the Chesapeake Canal (8 Peters, 201) — Key, Walter Jones and Webster on one side, and Coxe and Swann on the other. Key has not prepared himself, and now speaks from his

[1] *North American Review* (January, 1837).

preparation on the trial below, relying upon a quickness and facility of language, rather than upon research. Walter Jones — a man of acknowledged powers in the law, unsurpassed, if not unequalled by any lawyers in the country — is in the same plight. He is now conning his papers and maturing his points — a labor which of course he should have gone through, before he entered the court room. And our Webster fills up the remiss triumvirate. He, like Jones, is doing the labor in court which should have been done out of court. In fact, politics has entirely swamped his whole time and talents. All here declare that he has neglected his cases this term in a remarkable manner. It is now whispered in the room that he has not looked at the present case, though the amount at stake is estimated at half a million of dollars.

"The insurance case (*Hazard* v. *N. E. Mar. Ins. Co.*, 8 Peters, 557, 1 Sumner, 218), argued by Selden of New York, at Boston last year before Judge Story, has been argued here, since my being in town, by Selden on one side and Charles G. Loring and Webster on the other side. It was Loring's first appearance in the Supreme Court, and he acquitted himself honorably . . . was very clear and full, delivering his arguments in a calm, undisturbed manner, which was a beautiful contrast to the rhetorical, excited, disturbed, tinselled manner of Selden, who spoke as if addressing his constituents at the Park or at Tammany Hall. . . . We expect a very interesting case — *Wheaton* v. *Peters* (8 Peters, 591) — an action brought by Wheaton (the old reporter) against Peters for publishing in his *Condensed Reports* the twelve volumes of *Wheaton*. . . . John Sergeant is Peters' counsel, and Webster, Wheaton's. Franklin Dexter made an argument here a few days before I came, which gained him a good reputation (*Carrington* v. *Merchants Ins. Co.*, 8 Peters, 495). . . . Judge Story has shown me immense kindness."

On July 6, 1835, Chief Justice Marshall died at the age of eighty, having seen during his lifetime the firm establishment of most of the fundamental doctrines of American constitutional and international law as applied by the courts of the country. Of Marshall's creative part, mention has already been made. How great was his physical share of the work may be judged from the following figures. Between 1790 and 1801, there had been only six constitutional questions involved in cases before the Supreme Court. Between 1801 and 1835 there were 62 decisions involving such questions, in 36 of which Marshall wrote the opinion. Of a total of 1,215 cases during that period, in 94 no opinions were filed; in 15, the decision was "by the court;" and in the remaining, 1,106 cases Marshall delivered the opinion in 519.[1]

In the same period, there were 195 cases involving questions of international law, or in some way affecting international relations. In 80 of these, the opinion was delivered by Marshall; in 37, by Story; 28, by Johnson; 19, by Washington; 14, by Livingston; 5, by Thompson; and 1 each by Baldwin, Cushing and Duvall; in 8, "by the court."[2]

The legal profession in general looked forward to the appointment of Judge Joseph Story as Marshall's successor. But "the school of Story and Kent," to use Jackson's phrase, could expect no favors at the hands of the President, for their political and constitutional views differed far too widely; and as Story wrote: "Whoever succeeds Marshall will have a most painful and discouraging duty. He will follow a man who cannot be equalled, and all the public will see or think they see the difference. . . . I take it for granted that all of us who are on the bench are *hors de combat.*"

[1] The *Development of the Constitution as Influenced by Chief Justice Marshall,* by Henry Hitchcock (1889).

[2] Address by John Bassett Moore before the Delaware State Bar Association, Feb. 5, 1901.

John Quincy Adams, in his Diary, July 10, 1835, thus described the situation from his peculiar standpoint:

"John Marshall died at Philadelphia last Monday. He was one of the most eminent men that this country has ever produced — a Federalist of the Washington School. The Associate Judges from the time of his appointment have generally been taken from the Democratic or Jeffersonian party. Not one of them, excepting Story, has been a man of great ability. Several of them have been men of strong prejudices, warm passions, and contracted minds; one of them occasionally insane. Marshall, by the ascendency of his genius, by the amenity of his deportment, and by the imperturbable command of his temper, has given a permanent and systematic character to the decisions of the Court, and settled many great constitutional questions favorably to the continuance of the Union. Marshall has cemented the Union which the crafty and quixotic democracy of Jefferson had a perpetual tendency to dissolve. Jefferson hated and dreaded him. It is much to be feared that a successor will be appointed of a very different character. The President of the United States now in office, has already appointed three Judges of the Supreme Court; with the next appointment he will have constituted the Chief Justice and a majority of of the Court. He has not yet made one good appointment. His Chief Justice will be no better than the rest."

President Jackson waited six months, and then, to the surprise of most of the Bar, appointed Roger B. Taney of Maryland as Marshall's successor, in December, 1835. The impression produced at the time by this appointment was well described by Ex-Judge Benjamin R. Curtis in his address on the death of Taney, before the Bar of the First Circuit Court of the United States, in Boston, October 17, 1864:

"I have been long enough at the Bar to remember Mr. Taney's appointment; and I believe it was then a general impression in this part of the country that he was neither a learned nor a profound lawyer. This was certainly a mistake. His mind was thoroughly imbued with the rules of the common law and of equity law; and when I first knew him, he was master of all that peculiar jurisprudence which it is the special province of the courts of the United States to administer and apply. His skill in applying it was of the highest order. His power of subtle analysis exceeded that of any man I ever knew . . . in his case balanced and checked by excellent common sense and by great experience in practical business, both public and private.

"It is certainly true, and I am happy to be able to bear direct testimony to it, that the surpassing ability of the Chief Justice, and all the great qualities of character and mind, were more fully and constantly exhibited in the consultation room, while presiding over and assisting the deliberation of his brethren than the public knew or can ever justly estimate. . . . There, his dignity, his love of order, his gentleness, his discrimination, were of incalculable importance. The real intrinsic character of the tribunal was greatly influenced by them, and always for the better."

After the accession of Chief Justice Taney to the Bench, in 1836, the decisions of the Supreme Court showed a decided reaction from the centralizing views of Marshall. This was first seen in three cases in 1837, in each of which a State statute alleged to be in violation of the Federal Constitution was upheld.

In *Mayor of the City of New York* v. *Miln* (11 Peters, 102), argued by D. B. Ogden against Walter Jones, a New York statute relative to the duty of masters of vessels to report all passengers arriving, was held constitutional, as not being a regulation of interstate commerce. In *Briscoe* v. *Bank of the Commonwealth of Kentucky* (11 Peters, 257), argued by White and Southard against Henry Clay and Benjamin Hardin, the Court reached a conclusion upholding a Kentucky statute, directly in conflict with Marshall's opinion in *Craig* v. *Missouri* (4 Peters, 410), decided in 1830.

In *Charles River Bridge* v. *Warren Bridge* (11 Peters, 420), a Massachusetts statute alleged to constitute an impairment of contract was held to be constitutional. This latter case had been argued for the first time as far back as 1831 by Daniel Webster and Warren Dutton against Walter Jones and William Wirt; and *Niles' Register*, March 26, 1831, had thus referred to it:

"It was a war of giants. It was Mr. Dutton's first essay in this court, and is spoken of in terms of high commendation — as impressive, logical, classical. Mr. Jones is well known to the public as one of the ablest advocates. Of Messrs. Webster and Wirt, it is needless to say a word except that they displayed the utmost of their mighty powers."

Owing to illness and absence of Judges and vacancies in the Court, the case had been continued from term to term; for, as Chief Justice Marshall stated in 1834: "The practice of this Court is not (except in cases of absolute necessity) to deliver any judgment in cases where constitutional questions are involved unless four Judges concur in opinion, thus making the decision that of a majority of the whole Court."

The second argument of the case, in 1837, by Webster and Dutton against Simon Greenleaf (who took Wirt's place after the latter's death) and John Davis of Massachusetts, is vividly described by Greenleaf in a letter to Charles Sumner, January 24, 1837:[1]

"For a week I have had scarcely a thought that was not upon Warren Bridge. The argument was begun Thursday by Mr. Dutton, who concluded Saturday morning. I

[1] See letter in the *Sumner Papers* in Harvard College Library.

spoke about two hours on Saturday and nearly three on Monday, and yet merely went straight over my brief, answering, by the way, a few objections on the other side. Mr. Davis followed me yesterday and concluded in three hours to-day, in a most cogent, close, clear and convincing argument. Peters the Supreme Court Reporter says the cause was not nearly as well argued before as now; and in proof of it says that his own opinion is changed by it and that he now goes for the Def'ts! Mr. Webster spoke about an hour this afternoon on general and miscellaneous topics in the cause, and will probably occupy all day to-morrow, as he said he should consume considerable time. He told us he should 'tear our arguments to pieces,' and abuse me. The former will puzzle him; the latter I doubt not he will do, as he was observed to be very uneasy and moody during the whole defense. Both Mr. Davis and I avoided everything 'peoplish' in our remarks, confining ourselves closely to legal views alone. But we expect a great effort from Mr. W. to-morrow.

"It causes me much uneasiness to be absent from the Law School so long; but I was delighted to learn from your letter to the Judge that things go on so well. They are capital fellows, and possess a large share of my affections.

"Present to them my hearty love and good will, and tell them I hope to see them all next week. . . . Had Judge Wayne been here at the opening of the Court, I should have been on my return as early within a day as I anticipated before I left home."

Judge Story wrote to Sumner, January 25, 1837:

"Every argument was very good, above and beyond expectation, and that is truly no slight praise, considering all circumstances. Our friend Greenleaf's argument was excellent — full of ability, point, learning, condensed thought, and strong illustration — delivered with great presence of mind, modestly, calmly, and resolutely. It was every way worthy of him and the cause. It has given him a high character with the Bench and with the Bar, and placed him in public opinion exactly where you and I could wish him to be, among the most honored of the profession.

He has given Dane College new *éclat,* sounding and resounding fame; I speak this unhesitatingly. But at the same time I do not say that he will win the cause. That is uncertain yet, will not probably be decided under weeks to come. I say so the more resolutely because on some points he did not convince me; but I felt the force of his argument. Governor Davis made a sound argument, exhibiting a great deal of acuteness and power of thinking. Dutton's argument was strong, clear, pointed, and replete with learning. Webster's closing reply was in his best manner, but with a little too much of *fierté* here and there. He had manifestly studied it with great care and sobriety of spirit. On the whole it was a glorious exhibition for old Massachusetts; four of her leading men brought out in the same cause, and none of them inferior to those who are accustomed to the lead here. The audience was very large, especially as the cause advanced; — a large circle of ladies, of the highest fashion, and taste, and intelligence, numerous lawyers, and gentlemen of both houses of Congress, and towards the close, the foreign ministers, or at least some two or three of them.

"The Judges go on quite harmoniously. The new Chief Justice conducts himself with great urbanity and propriety. Judge Barbour is a very conscientious and painstaking Judge, and I think will improve as he goes on. . . . Greenleaf departs to-morrow morning, but he leaves a high repute behind. I feel a sort of homesickness in parting with him, though I have seen less of him here than I should at home."

Chief Justice Taney delivered the opinion of the Court in favor of Greenleaf's client, and upholding the right of the State to incorporate a new bridge paralleling an old bridge, in spite of the latter's prior charter. The decision that "in the absence of express words in a charter giving exclusive privileges, no such grant can be inferred as against the State" was undoubtedly influenced by the economic condition of the times. It is to be recalled that railroads had been in existence for only half a dozen years, and the effect of a contrary decision upon these new projects might have been disastrous. For, as Taney pointed out:

"Let it once be understood that such charters carry with them these implied contracts, and give this unknown and undefined property in a line of travelling, and you will soon find the old turnpike corporations awakening from their sleep, and calling upon this Court to put down the improvements which have taken their place. The millions of property which have been invested in railroads and canals, upon lines of travel which had been before occupied by turnpike corporations, will be put in jeopardy. We shall be thrown back to the improvements of the last century, and obliged to stand still, until the claims of the old turnpike corporations shall be satisfied, and they shall consent to permit these States to avail themselves of the lights of modern science, and to partake of the benefit of those improvements which are now adding to the wealth and prosperity and the convenience and comfort of every other part of the civilized world."

The decision met with great disapproval in many quarters, and Ex-Chancellor James Kent wrote to Judge Story (who dissented), June 23, 1837:

"I have re-perused the Charles River Bridge case, and with increased disgust. It abandons, or overthrows, a great principle of constitutional morality, and I think goes to destroy the security and value of legislative franchises. It injures the moral sense of the community, and destroys the sanctity of contracts. If the Legislature can quibble away, or whittle away its contracts with impunity, the people will be sure to follow. *Quidquid delirant reges plectuntur Achivi.* I abhor the doctrine that the Legislature is not bound by every thing that is necessarily implied in a contract, in order to give it effect and value, and by nothing that is not expressed *in hæc verba*, that one rule of interpretation is to be applied to their engagements, and another rule to the contracts of individuals. . . . "

Judge Story, in his dissenting opinion, referred to the fact that Chief Justice Marshall, who had heard the first argument in each of these three cases, the Miln and the Briscoe cases in 1834 and the Charles River Bridge case in 1831, had agreed with him in believing all the statutes involved to be unconstitutional.

So great was Story's despondency over the new trend of the Court under Taney, that in a letter to Judge McLean, May 10, 1837, he said:

"The opinion delivered by the Chief Justice in the Bridge Case has not been deemed satisfactory; and, indeed, I think I may say that a great majority of our ablest lawyers are against the decision of the Court; and those who think otherwise are not content with the views taken by the Chief Justice.

"There will not, I fear, ever in our day, be any case in which a law of a State or of Congress will be declared unconstitutional; for the old constitutional doctrines are fast fading away, and a change has come over the public mind, from which I augur little good. Indeed, on my return home, I came to the conclusion to resign."

A writer in the *North American Review* in 1838, also uttered the same doleful forebodings in reviewing volume eleven of *Peters' Report:* [1]

"The volume is one of unusual and in certain respects even of singular interest. . . . It can hardly have failed to strike the dullest observation after a survey of the present volume, that some considerable change has come over the spirit of our Supreme National Judicature upon this great class of [constitutional] questions. . . . The prospect is charged, perhaps, to our too anxious apprehension, with shades which have not hitherto seemed to rest upon it . . . under the shape, not to say pretext, of internal regulations

[1] See *Constitutional Law, a Review of XI Peters,* in *North Amer. Rev.,* Vol. XLVI (January, 1838).

of police of the protective kind on the maritime side of commerical States. . . .

"Massachusetts also, we are sorry to say, furnished her contribution to swell the present volume. We say this with sorrow, because whatever may be thought of the merits of the question, it is undeniable that the tone and character of the decision chime in with doctrines which tend, or may be urged, deplorably, to the subversion of the principles of law and property.

"What was the law of the Court upon some important points remains so no longer. Within a brief space we have seen the highest judicial corps of the Union wheel about in almost solid column and retread some of its most important steps.

"It is quite obvious that old things are passing away. The authority of former decisions which had long been set as landmarks in the law is assailed and overthrown by a steady, destructive aim from the summit of that stronghold, within which they had been entrenched and established.

". . . It is very remarkable also that all the principles yielded by these decisions either have relation to the sovereign powers of the Union or to the very essence of social obligation. . . . We can hardly avoid the reluctant impression that it (the judiciary) has already capitulated to the spirit of the old confederation; and that we are fast returning, among other things, to an old continental currency, and to what were once denominated, moreover, anti-federal doctrines.

"Under the progressive genius of this new judicial administration we can see the whole fair system of the Constitution beginning to dissolve like the baseless fabric of a vision."

While the doctrine of State Sovereignty was upheld in these cases, succeeding cases soon dissipated the view that in Taney the States' Rights men would find a firm adherent. No Judge — not even Marshall himself — did more to place the Federal courts in a position of power and dignity than Taney, by his later decisions on the rights of corporations to sue and to be sued in Federal courts and to do business in States outside those of their incorporation, and by his decisions on the extent of the admiralty jurisdiction.

In 1838, the only notable case before the Supreme Court was *Rhode Island* v. *Massachusetts* (12 Peters, 657), argued by Daniel Webster and James T. Austin, Attorney-General of Massachusetts, against Hazard and Southard of Rhode Island. The Court held that it had jurisdiction over boundary disputes between States, thus again affirming the supremacy of the Federal jurisdiction.

The session of the Supreme Court in 1839 was marked by the decision of the great case of *Bank of Augusta* v. *Earle* (13 Peters, 519), which was argued by D. B. Ogden, Sergeant and Webster, against C. J. Ingersoll and Van de Graff, and which was the first case establishing the right of a corporation to do business outside the State of its incorporation.

The year 1840 was marked as the first year in which a railroad appeared before the Court as party in any suit. *The Philadelphia and Trenton Railroad Co.* v. *Simpson* (14 Peters, 448).

The year 1841 was notable for two celebrated cases. The first, *Groves* v. *Slaughter* (15 Peters, 449), involving the Mississippi statute prohibiting the introduction into the State of slaves as merchandise for sale, and affecting upwards of $3,000,000 of property, was argued by Henry D. Gilpin and Robert J. Walker, against Walter Jones, Henry Clay, and Daniel Webster. The second, *U. S.* v. *Amistad* (15 Peters, 518), in which Judge Story delivered one of his most celebrated opinions, was of peculiar interest, because of the appearance for the defendant of John Quincy Adams, then seventy-four years of age and whose last engagement as counsel before the Court had been in 1809, thirty-two years before, in *Hope Insurance Co.* v. *Boardman* (5 Cranch, 56).

The case involved the freedom of certain negroes who, while being brought to this country illegally by slave traders, had gained mastery of the vessel and murdered the officers. Having been taken together with the vessel into a United States port by a United States war vessel, they were claimed as slaves by their alleged Spanish owners. Much political feeling was aroused by this case, and Adams, in his Diary, thus describes his argument: [1]

"Feb. 24. The court room was full but not crowded, and there were not many ladies. I had been deeply distressed and agitated till the moment when I rose, and then my spirit did not sink within me. With grateful heart for aid from above, though in humiliation for the weakness incident to the limits of my powers, I spoke for 4¼ hours with sufficient method and order to witness little flagging of attention by the judges or the auditors. . . . The structure of my argument was perfectly simple and comprehensive, needing no artificial division into distinct points, but admitting the steady and undeviating pursuit of one fundamental principle, the ministration of justice. I then assigned my reason for inviting justice specially, aware that this was always the duty of the court, but because an immense array of power — the Executive Administration, instigated by the minister of a foreign nation — had been brought to bear in this case on the side of injustice. . . . I did not, I could not, answer public expectation; but I have not yet utterly failed. God speed me to the end."

Judge Story writing to his wife, February 28, 1841, described the old man as full of his accustomed virility and belligerency, and speaks of the "extraordinary" argument made by him — "extraordinary, I say, for its power, for

[1] Still more interesting is Adams' full account as to his retainer and of the progress of the case. See *Diary of John Quincy Adams*, Vol. X.

its bitter sarcasm, and its dealing with topics far beyond the record and points of discussion."

The January term of the Supreme Court in 1842 was notable for the rendering by Judge Story of two of his most famous opinions. In the case of *Prigg* v. *Pennsylvania* (16 Peters, 539), he held that the Federal Fugitive Slave Act of 1793 was constitutional; that Congress had exclusive power under the Constitution to legislate regarding fugitive slaves, and that the Fugitive Slave statute of Pennsylvania was unconstitutional.[1] This year marked the beginning of the Free Soil party; and by those upholding its views, the decision in the Prigg case was regarded as a direct surrender to the South and Southern principles. The attacks on Story were, however, entirely unwarranted; for no man was more sincere in his opposi-

[1] See *Com.* v. *Tracy*, 5 Metc. 1843, construing the opinions in this case.

John Quincy Adams wrote in his Diary under date of March 10, 1843:

"I spent much of this day in transiently reading the report of the trial in the Supreme Court of the United States of the case of *Edward Prigg, against the Commonwealth of Pennsylvania*, otherwise called the Fugitive Slave case — seven judges, every one of them dissenting from the reasoning of all the rest, and every one of them coming to the same conclusion — the transcendant omnipotence of slavery in these United States, riveted by a clause in the Constitution."

George Ticknor wrote to William Ellery Channing, April 20, 1842:

"On the subject of our relations with the South and its slavery, we must, — as I have always thought — do one of two things; either keep honestly the bargain of the Constitution as it shall be interpreted by the authorities — of which the Supreme Court of the United States is the chief and safest — or declare honestly that we can no longer in our conscience consent to keep it, and break it. I therefore rejoice at every legal decision which limits and restrains the curse of slavery; both because each such restriction is in itself so great a good, and because it makes it more easy to preserve the Union. I fear the recent decision in the case of Pennsylvania and Maryland works the other way, but hope it will not turn out so when we have it duly reported; and I fear, however the decisions may stand, that the question of a dissolution of the Union is soon to come up for angry discussion."

See *Life and Letters and Journals of George Ticknor*.

tion to slavery, and he believed most firmly that the legal doctrine which he had announced in the Prigg case would furnish the strongest bulwark to the National Government against the increase of the slave power in the States.

Another notable decision of Story at this term was that landmark in Federal law, *Swift* v. *Tyson* (16 Peters, 1), a case argued by W. P. Fessenden of Maine against Richard H. Dana, Jr., of Massachusetts.[1]

The chief case of importance in 1843 was *Bronson* v. *Kinzie* (1 Howard, 311), in which the doctrine of the Dartmouth College case received its first important extension in the twenty-four years since its decision. The Court held that a statute of Illinois, changing the mortgage law of that State, affected the rights and not merely the remedies of a mortgage, and therefore impaired the obligation of contracts.

The history of American law shows no more interesting feature than the manner in which the doctrines of the Dartmouth College case became so "imbedded in the jurisprudence of the United States as to make them to all intents and purposes a part of the Constitution itself." [2] Over forty-seven years after its decision, and twenty-three years after *Bronson* v. *Kinzie*, Judge Davis said in a case in 1866: "A departure from it now would involve dangers to society that cannot be foreseen, would shock the sense of justice of the country, unhinge business interests, and weaken, if not destroy, that respect which has always been felt for the Judicial Department of the Government." [3] The next year, Judge Swayne said: "Its principles are axiomatic in American jurisprudence." [4]

[1] See especially review in *Law Reporter*, June, 1842, Vol. V.

[2] Chief Justice Waite in *Stone* v. *Mississippi*, 101 U. S. 814 (1880).

[3] *Chenango Bridge* v. *Binghamton Bridge Co.*, 3 Wallace, 51 (1866).

[4] *U. S.* v. *Quincy*, 4 Wallace, 535 (1867).

And in 1872, Judge Swayne said that it contained "a principle of universal jurisprudence. It is necessary to the repose and welfare of all communities. A different rule would shake the social fabric to its foundations and let in a flood tide of intolerable evils. It would be 'contrary to the general principles of law and reason' and to one of the most vital ends of government." [1]

The spring of 1844 was notable in Washington for the argument of the famous case of *Vidal* v. *Philadelphia* (2 Howard, 127), involving the will of Stephen Girard.[2] The case had been first argued, in 1843, by Walter Jones against John Sergeant, but owing to the absence of three of the judges, it was re-argued in 1844 by Jones and Webster against Horace Binney and Sergeant.[3] As an example of the increase in legal facilities, it is to be noted that when a similar case was decided by Marshall in 1819 (*Baptist Association* v. *Hart's Executors*, 4 Wheaton, 1), the *Calendars*

[1] *Osborn* v. *Nicholson*, 13 Wallace, 654 (1872).

[2] See *The Will and Biography of Stephen Girard*—*American Quarterly Review*, Vol. XIII (1833).

[3] "When the case was carried up to the Supreme Court, Mr. Binney was joined with him at Mr. Sergeant's request, and went to England to make himself more familiar with the law of charitable cases. He returned fully prepared for the encounter. Mr. Binney was tall, large, well formed, always well dressed, and an Apollo in manly beauty. He spoke slowly and distinctly; his voice was full, musical and well modulated; his manners a blending of dignity, ease, suavity and high refinement. . . . He spoke three days, during which the court room was filled to its utmost capacity by beauty, talent and eminence; lawyers of eminent abilities were drawn from Richmond, Baltimore and New York, to listen. . . . Mr. Sergeant was a lawyer of no less ability, learning and eminence than Mr. Binney; but he has not his fine voice or imposing appearance. He spoke two days. . . . Mr. Webster, who made the closing argument in the case, had a Herculean task to perform. If any one could do it, he could; but it was beyond his power. He occupied the court for three days, the room the whole time being densely crowded."

See *Public Men and Events*, by Nathan Sargeant, Vol. II (1875); and see *Life of Horace Binney*, by Charles C. Binney.

*of the Proceedings in Chancery*, from which Binney in 1843 gleaned more than fifty precedents for his contention, were not even printed; and Marshall had positively stated that there was no trace whatever of any precedent.

Story thus described the argument, in a letter to his wife, February 7, 1844:

"We have been for several days engaged in Court in hearing arguments upon the great case of the Girard will, which involves seven millions of dollars; the heirs insisting that the main bequest for building a college for orphans is void. Mr. Jones, of this city, spoke on it nearly three days; Mr. Binney of Philadelphia, has been speaking on the opposite side (for the city) nearly three days, and has made a most masterly argument; Mr. Sergeant, of Philadelphia, is to follow on the same side, and the argument is to be concluded by Mr. Webster, for the heirs.

"February 10. Saturday evening. I was here again interrupted, and for the first time am now able to resume my pen. In the case of the Girard will, the arguments have been contested with increasing public interest, and Mr. Sergeant and Mr. Binney concluded their arguments yesterday. A vast concourse of ladies and gentlemen attended, with unabated zeal and earnest curiosity, through their speeches, which occupied four days. Mr. Webster began his reply to them to-day, and the Court-room was crowded, almost to suffocation, with ladies and gentlemen to hear him. Even the space behind the Judges, close home to their chairs, presented a dense mass of listeners. He will conclude on Monday. The curious part of the case is, that the whole discussion has assumed a semi-theological character. Mr. Girard excluded ministers of all sects from being admitted into his college as instructors or visitors; but he required the scholars to be taught the love of truth, morality, and benevolence to their fellow-men. Mr. Jones and Mr. Webster contended that these restrictions were anti-Christian, and illegal. Mr. Binney and Mr. Sergeant contended that they were valid, and Christian, founded upon the great difficulty of making ministers cease to be controversialists, and forbearing to teach the doctrines of their sect. I was not a little amused with the manner in which, on each side, the language of the Scriptures and the doctrines of Christianity were brought in to point the argument; and to find the Court engaged in hearing homilies of faith and expositions of Christianity, with almost the formality of lectures from the pulpit."

On February 13, 1844, John Quincy Adams notes in his Diary:

"To escape an hour or two of soporifics, left the Hall (of Representatives) and went into that where the Supreme Court were in session to see what had become of Stephen Girard's will and the scramble of lawyers and collaterals for the fragments of his colossal and misshapen endowment of an infidel charity school for orphan boys.

"Webster had just before closed his argument for which it is said, if he succeeds, he is to have fifty thousand dollars for his share of the plunder."

Story's decision upholding the will, and against Webster's argument, was generally supported by the profession and especially by Kent, to whom Story wrote August 31, 1844:

"I rejoice to know your opinion in the Girard case. The Court were unanimous, and not a single sentence was altered by my brothers, as I originally drew it. I confess, that I never doubted on the point; but it is a great, a sincere comfort to have your judgment, free, independent, learned, on it. Mr. Webster did his best for the other side, but it seemed to me, altogether, an address to the prejudice of the clergy."

The years 1845 and 1846 passed without any case of prime importance before the Supreme Court; and the chief event of legal note was Judge Joseph Story's resignation in 1845. As the only remaining Judge of the Bench as it was constituted in Marshall's day, he had for several years been out of touch with the tendencies of the decisions of the present Court; and on April 25, 1845, he wrote:

"Although my personal position and intercourse with my brethren on the Bench has always been pleasant, yet I have been long convinced that the doctrines and opinions of the 'old Court' were daily losing ground, and especially those on great constitutional questions. New men and new opinons have succeeded. The doctrines of the Constitution, so vital to the country, which in former times received the support of the whole Court, no longer maintain their ascendancy. I am the last member now living, of the old Court, and I cannot consent to remain where I can no longer hope to see those doctrines recognized and enforced. For the future I must be in a dead minority of the Court, with the painful alternative of either expressing an open dissent from the opinions of the Court, or, by my silence, seeming to acquiesce in them. The former course would lead the public, as well as my brethren, to believe that I was determined, as far as I might, to diminish the just influence of the Court, and might subject me to the imputation of being, from motives of mortified ambition, or political hostility, earnest to excite popular prejudices against the Court. The latter course would subject me to the opposite imputation, of having either abandoned my old principles, or of having, in sluggish indolence, ceased to care what doctrines prevailed. Either alternative is equally disagreeable to me, and utterly repugnant to my past habits of life, and to my present feelings. I am persuaded that by remaining on the Bench I could accomplish no good, either for myself or for my country."

In 1847, arose the celebrated *License Cases*, involving the constitutionality of the prohibitionist liquor legislation in Rhode Island, Massachusetts and New Hampshire — *Thurlow* v. *Massachusetts* (5 Howard, 504). In these cases, Webster, Rufus Choate and John Davis of Massachusetts and Samuel Ames[1] and Richard W. Greene of

[1] Born in 1806, Brown 1823, Chief Justice of Rhode Island 1856–1865.

Rhode Island appeared as counsel. In general, the State statutes were upheld, as not being an interference with interstate commerce. In this same year, the Court foreshadowed in *Waring* v. *Clarke* (5 Howard, 441) the extended admiralty jurisdiction which, four years later, it was to establish. This noted case was argued by Reverdy Johnson against John J. Crittenden; and a similar case was argued with it by Ames and Whipple of Rhode Island against Webster and R. W. Greene.

In the same year (1847), the famous case of *Jones* v. *Van Zandt* (5 Howard, 215) was decided, in which the slavery question had been argued at great length by William H. Seward and Salmon P. Chase [1] against Senator James T. Morehead of Kentucky.[2] It involved the constitutionality of a statute imposing a penalty for harboring a fugitive slave. In view of the fact that only ten years later, in 1857, in the Dred Scott case, the Court attempted to settle by judicial decision, the political question of slavery, it is curious to note that at this time — the year of the Mexican war, and three years before the passage of the Compromise and Fugitive Slave Act of 1850 — the Court refused to consider the political question involved, Judge Levi Woodbury, Story's successor, saying in his opinion:

"But before concluding, it may be expected by the defendant that some notice should be taken of the argument urging on us a disregard to this subject on account of the

[1] Salmon P. Chase, from this argument and from his appearance in numerous other slave cases at this time acquired the title of "the Attorney-General for runaway negroes."

See interesting account of this case in *Life of William H. Seward*, by Frederic Bancroft (1900), and *Life and Public Services of Salmon Portland Chase*, by J. W. Shuckers (1874).

[2] Born in 1797, Transylvania University 1818, Governor of Kentucky 1834, United States Senator 1841.

supposed inexpediency and invalidity of all laws recognizing slavery or any right of property in man. But that is a political question settled by each State for itself; and the Federal power over it is limited and regulated by the sacred compromises, and which we possess no authority as a judicial body to modify or overrule. . . . Whatever may be the theoretical opinion of any as to the expediency of some of those compromises or of the right of property in persons which they recognize, this Court has no alternative, while they exist, but to stand by the Constitution and laws with fidelity to their duties and their oaths. Their path is a straight and narrow one, to go where that Constitution and laws lead, and not to break both by travelling without or beyond this."

In 1849, the subject of the Dorr's Rebellion in Rhode Island arose in *Luther* v. *Borden* (7 Howard, 1) argued by B. F. Hallett and John H. Clifford of Massachusetts against Daniel Webster and Whipple of Rhode Island. In this case, Chief Justice Taney, in one of his finest legal opinions, held the question a political one, and declined to interfere.

The important cases known as the *Passenger Cases*, *Smith* v. *Turner* and *Norris* v. *Boston* (7 Howard, 283), were decided at this term. They involved the constitutionality of the passenger tax statutes of New York and Massachusetts, of which Webster wrote to his son, February 7, 1847: "It is strange to me how any Legislature of Massachusetts could pass such a law. In the days of Marshall and Story it could not have stood one moment. The present Judges I fear are quite too much inclined to find apologies for irregular and dangerous acts." He wrote again, February 3, 1849, just before the final decision: "In my poor judgment the decision will be more important to the country than any decision since that in the Steamboat cause." The Court itself was so gravely impressed with the question presented and so divided in opinion that the cases were argued six times — the New York case in December, 1845, by D. B. Ogden of New York and Webster against John Van Buren, then Attorney-General of New York, and Willis Hall, Ex-Attorney-General, again in December, 1847, and a third time in December, 1848; the Massachusetts case was argued first by Webster and Rufus Choate against John Davis of Massachusetts in December, 1846, again by Choate against Davis in December, 1847, and a third time by Webster, Rufus Choate, and J. Prescott Hall of New York against John Davis and George Ashmun of Massachusetts in December, 1848. The State laws were held unconstitutional.[1]

At the December term of 1850 the struggle for supremacy between the steamboats and the railroads came to the front, in the great case of *Pennsylvania* v. *Wheeling and Belmont Bridge Co.* (9 Howard, 647), argued by Edwin M. Stanton against Reverdy Johnson "with a degree of ability and learning worthy of the palmiest days of the old Bar of the Supreme Court." [2] It was held that the bridge was an obstruction to commerce, and also a nuisance as an infringement on the Common Law rights of the State of Pennsylvania.

In 1851, the question of the right of the States to legislate on matters affecting interstate commerce in the absence of Congressional legislation on the subject arose in *Cooley* v. *Port Wardens* (12 Howard, 299), a case involving the pilotage laws of Pennsylvania and argued by

[1] See letters of Webster to Fletcher Webster, Feb. 7, 1847, Dec. 7, 1847, January, 1848, June 10, 1849; to J. Prescott Hall, Feb. 10, 1849; and to S. Blatchford, Feb. 3, 1849, in *Writings, Letters and Speeches of Daniel Webster*, Vols. XVI and XVIII (1903). See *Law Reporter*, Vol. XI, p. 478.

[2] *History of the Supreme Court of the United States*, by H. G. Carson, Vol. II.

For interesting account of the important case see *Life and Public Services of Edwin M. Stanton*, by George C. Gorham (1899).

Phineas P. Morris and Job R. Tyson against James Campbell and George M. Dallas.

The case definitely settled the long struggle which had been going on since *Gibbons* v. *Ogden* in 1824 over the field of national control of commerce. The decision "separated the field over which Congress is given the power of regulation into two smaller fields — one consisting of matters of a general nature in which Federal jurisdiction, whether exercised or not, exclude all State action; the other field consisting of matters of a local nature in which the States may act until superseded by Congress."[1]

In this year came the decision in the *Genesee Chief* (12 Howard, 443), a case argued by Stanley P. Mathews of Ohio against William H. Seward of New York. Chief Justice Taney held that the old Common Law doctrine that admiralty jurisdiction was confined to the ebb and flow of the tide was unsuited to this country and that the admiralty courts extended to the Great Lakes and all navigable waters of the country. This decision was of extreme importance to American internal commerce, for it threw into the Federal courts a vast range of torts and contracts connected with shipping and maritime matters, thus giving a unity to this branch of the law extremely desirable in view of the development of the growing commerce in the new Western States.[2]

In 1852, the first railroad negligence case arose in this Court, *Philadelphia & Reading R. R.* v. *Derby* (14 Howard, 468), in which the Court referred to the "new, power-

[1] See *The Right to engage in Interstate Commerce*, by E. P. Prentice, *Harv. Law Rev.*, Vol. XVII (1903); and see comments in *Crandall* v. *Nevada*, 6 Wall. 62; and *Mobile* v. *Kimball*, 102 U. S. 702.

[2] See article in *American Law Register*, Vol. I (1852).

"As questions of collisions and on the law of carriers are daily arising, especially in our western waters, our readers will see the very important character of this decision."

ful but dangerous agency of steam" and to the detriment to the public safety that would come from any relaxation of a stringent policy.

In 1853, the case of *Smith* v. *Swormstedt* (16 Howard, 288) involving the division of the great Methodist Episcopal Church into two organizations one for the slave holding States and one for the other States, argued by Stanberry against Badger and Ewing, throws a light on the manner in which the slavery question entered even into religion. In 1856, this question presented itself in its most dangerous form in the case of *Dred Scott* v. *Sanford*, argued by Montgomery Blair of Maryland [1] and George Ticknor Curtis of Massachusetts [2] for the slave Scott and Reverdy Johnson and H. S. Geyer of Missouri [3] for the owner. It was reargued in 1856, and the opinion was given March 6, 1857, two days after the inauguration of President Buchanan (19 Howard, 393).

No more fatal legal or political delusion ever appeared in any judicial decision than in the following words of Mr. Justice Wayne:

> "The case involves private rights of value and constitutional questions of the highest importance about which there had become such a difference of opinion that the peace and harmony of the country required the settlement of them by judicial decision."

Few other cases of prime importance were decided prior to 1860, except that of *Ableman* v. *Booth* (21 Howard, 506) in 1859 in which the constitutionality of the Fugitive Slave Act of 1850 was upheld, and the judgment of the Supreme Court of Wisconsin declaring it unconstitutional was reversed.

[1] Born in 1813.

[2] Born in 1812, Harvard 1832.

[3] Born in 1790, United States Senator 1851–1857.

With the outbreak of the Civil War, the early history of the American Bar and law comes to an end. The cases which arose after that era were, in large part, of a distinctly different character; and the lawyers of the fifty years since have been grappling with questions of which their predecessors knew nothing, — the political, social and economic problems growing out of the Thirteenth, Fourteenth and Fifteenth Amendments; the development of the great modern corporations; the intricacies of modern finance, with its mass of new law relating to shares of stock, bonds, mortgages, stockholders and receivers; and the vast increase in novel and revolutionary economic legislation.

The American Bar of the years 1860–1910 presented, therefore, an entirely different type, — the modern corporation or business lawyer, whose history is not within the scope of this book.

As, however, the Bar of the period from 1830 to 1860 differed in many respects, as greatly from its predecessors of the earliest years of the Nation, as the modern lawyer does from the ante-bellum lawyer, the three following chapters of this book will be devoted to a description of the conditions under which the Bar of the middle of the Nineteenth Century flourished, and of the problems which faced it for solution. That Bar may fairly be termed a reformatory Bar. The times were alive with new ideas, with the spirit of change; and the great lawyers must be men of vision. And though the times were also filled with the ferment of new business and corporate methods, the Bar was not so largely engrossed with that side of the law, as to forget that it was the prophet of humanity as well.

During the twenty years between 1830 and 1850, the cases before the Supreme Court multiplied so greatly, with the growth of the country and the rise and increase of railroads making access to Washington so much easier, that in 1845 the sessions of the Court, which since 1827 had begun in January (under Act of May 4, 1826), were now lengthened one month, beginning in December of one year and continuing through March of the next year (under Act of June 7, 1844). The number of Associate Judges was increased from six to eight by the Act of March 3, 1837. The changes in the personnel of the Court during these years were many. Senator George F. Hoar in his autobiography says that, when his brother E. Rockwood Hoar visited Washington in 1836, "Webster received him with great kindness, showed him about the capital and took him to the Supreme Court where he argued a case. Mr. Webster began by alluding very impressively to the great change which had taken place in that Tribunal since he first appeared as counsel before them. He said: 'No one of the Judges who was here then, remains. It has been my duty to pass upon the question of the confirmation of every member of the Bench; and I may say that I treated your honors with entire impartiality, for I voted against every one of you.'"

In 1834, William Johnson of South Carolina died and James M. Wayne of Georgia took his place in 1835. Philip P. Barbour of Viriginia was appointed, in 1836, in place of Gabriel Duvall (resigned). Taney succeeded Marshall as Chief Justice, March 15, 1836. In 1837, John Catron of Tennessee and John McKinley of Alabama were appointed as the two new Associate Judges.

In 1841, Peter L. Daniel of Virginia succeeded Barbour on the latter's death. In 1845, Samuel Nelson of New York took the place of Smith Thompson, who died in 1843. In the same year, Levi Woodbury succeeded Story; and was himself succeeded on his death, in 1851, by Benjamin R. Curtis of Massachusetts. In 1844, Robert C.

Grier of Pennsylvania succeeded Henry Baldwin. In 1853, John A. Campbell of Alabama succeeded McKinley. In 1858, Nathan Clifford of Maine took Benjamin R. Curtis' place on the latter's resignation. There were in the seventy-one years between 1789 and 1860 just thirty-six Justices, including five Chief Justices.

The Attorneys-General were Roger B. Taney of Maryland (1831–1833), Benjamin F. Butler of New York (1833–1838), Felix Grundy of Tennessee (1838–1839), Henry D. Gilpin of Pennsylvania (1840–1841), John J. Crittenden of Kentucky (1841), Hugh S. Legaré of South Carolina (1841–1843), John Nelson of Maryland (1843–1845), Nathan Clifford of Maine (1846–1848), Reverdy Johnson of Maryland (1849–1850), John J. Crittenden of Kentucky (1850–1853), Caleb Cushing of Massachusetts (1853–1857), Jeremiah S. Black of Pennsylvania (1857–1860) and Edwin M. Stanton (1860–1861).

## NOTE

Though not within the scope of this book, which is not intended to encroach on the modern era of the law which began with the Civil War, it may be of interest, in order to complete the view of the Federal Courts, to note the following changes which have occurred in the legislation as to them.

By Act of March 3, 1863, a ninth Associate Justice was added to the Supreme Court. In 1866, because of the fear that President Johnson might appoint to the Court men imbued with his political views, the precedent set by Congress in President John Adams' day was revived, and by Act of July 23, 1866, it was provided that no further appointments should be made to the Court until the number of Associate Justices was reduced to six, and that, thereafter, the Court should remain at that number. This statute was repealed by Act of April 10, 1869, and since that Act the Court has consisted of a Chief Justice and eight Associate Justices, as it did from 1837 to 1863.

The term of the sitting of the Court, which, since 1844, had begun on the second Monday in December, was changed by Act of July 23, 1866, to the second Monday in October. The salaries of the Judges were increased, March 3, 1871, from $6,500 to $8,500 for the Chief Justice, and from $6,000 to $8,000 for the Associate Justices; and were further increased, March 3, 1873, to $10,500 and $10,000.

By Act of February 24, 1855, the United States Court of Claims was established, consisting of a Chief Justice and four associate judges.

By Act of April 10, 1869, the Circuit Courts of the United States were re-organized with separate Circuit Court judges. By Act of March 3, 1891, the Circuit Court of Appeals was established. Recent years have witnessed the creation of two further Federal Courts of inferior jurisdiction — the United States Court of Customs Appeal by Act of August 5, 1909, and the Commerce Court by Act of June 18, 1910.

## CHAPTER XVII

### THE PROGRESS OF THE LAW, 1830–1860

THE years 1830 to 1860 constitute a period of legal development in State and Federal law greater than any period in the legal history of the country. During these years, students and practitioners of law were witnessing the slow up-building of many a legal structure now complete.

Two things were especially characteristic of this era — the first being the increasing recognition and protection of individual rights under the law[1] — the emancipation of married women; the safeguards thrown around infants, insane and criminals; prison reform; milder forms of criminal punishment; abolition of imprisonment for debt; the treatment of bankruptcy as a misfortune and not a crime; the removal of the bars against the testimony of witnesses and parties in civil and criminal cases; the recognition of labor unions; and the simplification of the law by codes and statutory revisions, for the benefit of laymen as well as lawyers.

These radical changes in personal status brought about by statutes and judicial decisions were undoubtedly due in considerable degree to a political change, the influence of which has never received adequate attention — the gradual abolition, from 1820–1840, of property qualifica-

[1] See *Jurisprudence — Its Development during the Past Century*, by Joseph H. Beale, Jr., *Congress of Arts and Sciences*, Vol. VII (1906).

tions for voting and for holding office. Such property qualifications had existed in Connecticut, until 1818; in Massachusetts and New York, until 1821; in Virginia and Tennessee, until 1830; and in some other States for ten or fifteen years later. Their abolition, however, changed the character of the electorate, democratized it, altered the constituent parts of the Legislatures, and thus produced entirely new tendencies in legislation. This broadened spirit of the statutes after 1820 is very noticeable; and as the courts of the United States are generally responsive to their surroundings, the trend of judicial decisions shows the influence of the democratic popular voice. The abolition of property qualifications, therefore, while responsible, in politics, for the birth of the new Democratic party and the election of President Jackson and his successors, was also unquestionably a factor in the liberal and progressive, sometimes radical, decisions for which the courts (especially in Massachusetts, New York, and Pennsylvania) were noted during this era.

The second characteristic of the era was the remarkable modernization of old legal doctrines. The inventions that so thronged it were a severe test of the malleability of the old Common Law, and of its capability of adaptation to fit the new economic, commercial and social conditions. It was to the everlasting credit of the great judges and of the great lawyers of the times that the Common Law was proved fully adequate to meet the strain.

Of the Chief Justices who have left a marked impress upon the course of legal development, there may be mentioned especially John Bannister Gibson, in Pennsylvania, from 1827 to 1851; Isaac N. Blackford, in Indiana, from 1817 to 1853; Henry W. Green, in New Jersey, from 1846 to 1860; William M. Richardson, from 1812 to 1838, and Joel Parker from 1838 to 1847, in New Hampshire; and Thomas Scott Williams, in Connecticut, from 1834 to 1847.

One jurist stood out above all others in his ability to shape the Common Law to modern needs — Lemuel Shaw, the great Chief Justice of Massachusetts, whose term of service on the bench covered exactly these thirty years (1830–1860).

In the words of the address presented to him upon his retirement, in 1860, by the Bar of Massachusetts:

> "It was the task of those who went before you, to show that the principles of the common and the commercial law were available to the wants of communities which were far more recent than the origin of those systems. It was for you to adapt those systems to still newer and greater exigencies; to extend them to the solution of questions, which it required a profound sagacity to foresee, and for which an intimate knowledge of the law often enables you to provide, before they had even fully arisen for judgment. Thus it has been, that in your hands the law has met the demands of a period of unexampled activity and enterprise; while over all its varied and conflicting interests you have held the strong, conservative sway of a judge, who moulds the rule for the present and the future out of the principles and precedents of the past. Thus too, it has been, that every tribunal in this country has felt the weight of your judgments, and jurists at home and abroad took to you as one of the great expositors of the law. . . ."

With the advent of railroads and the body of law which arose out of their relations to the public and to their employees came the development of the law of torts in the branch with which modern courts are chiefly concerned with it — accident law.

As is well known, the common employment or employer's non-liability doctrine was established in this country in 1842 — five years later than in England[1] — by Chief Justice Shaw in the noted case of *Farwell* v. *Boston and Worcester R. R.* (4 Metc. 49), the decision in this case being largely influenced by economic conditions and the need of favoring the young and struggling institution of railroads, even if such action placed a burden on a class less able to bear it.

The lateness of the development of the branches of accident law which now fill the law reports may be realized in noting that the first accident case brought in a manufacturing State like Massachusetts by an employee against a manufacturing corporation was in 1850;[2] and in *Redfield on Railways*, published as late as 1858, only five pages are devoted to the law relating to accidents caused by negligence of fellow servants or use of machinery and appliances. The first accident case for defect in a sidewalk brought in Massachusetts against a city or town was in 1849.[3]

Actions for death caused by negligence arose in England after the passage of Lord Campbell's Act (9 & 10 Vict. c. 93), in 1846. New York followed in this country, by giving similar cause of action, through a statute passed in 1847; and Ohio, Pennsylvania, and Indiana, in 1851.

The question of the right of recovery at Common Law in such cases had arisen for the first time in a case in Massachusetts in 1848, in which the court denied the right, saying: "These actions raise a new question in our jurisprudence. . . . If such a law would be expedient for us, it is for the Legislature to make it."[4]

1 *Priestley* v. *Fowler*, 3 Meeson and Welsby, was decided in England, in 1837.

2 *Albro* v. *Agawam Canal Co.*, 6 Cush. 75 (1850).

3 *Bacon* v. *Boston*, 3 Cush. 174 (1849).

4 *Carey* v. *Berkshire R. R. Co.*, 1 Cush. 475 (1848).

In a note relative to this case in *United States Law Magazine* for January, 1851, it is said: "The question, entirely new in our jurisprudence, was here

The slight part which torts played in the law of the day may be seen from the fact that the first American law book on the subject did not appear until 1859 — Francis Hilliard's *The Law of Torts and Private Wrongs* of which the *Law Reporter* (Vol. XXII) said in a review:

"This work is a well conducted attempt to do for the law of private wrongs what has been so often and so elaborately done for simple contracts, to collect in one book the principles and cases applicable to all the various departments of the general subject: An attempt, as the author justly says, never made before either in England or America excepting in a very general way as, for example, in Blackstone's *Commentaries*."

The law of torts was of course much developed through the introduction of the many new inventions for which this period was especially noted, changing so greatly the economic, social and commercial conditions of the times.

The electric telegraph was first put in successful operation in 1844, and with that year began a new body of law relating to this invention. In 1849, the first statute in Massachusetts relating to telegraph companies was enacted, and one of the early cases in the United States involving the new invention was a case of injury to a traveller on the highway from a telegraph pole established under this statute — *Young* v. *Yarmouth* (9 Gray, 386), in 1857.[1]

The first reported telegraph case arose in 1851, in one of the inferior courts of Pennsylvania, involving a statute forbidding disclosure of a message.[2]

In the next nine years through the year 1860, only fifteen cases arose, relating to telegraph companies. Most of

raised concerning the legal right to complain in a civil court for the death of a human being as an injury. At the argument, no case was cited in which a like action had been the subject of adjudication, or even of discussion."

[1] See also *Byron* v. *N. Y. State Printing Tel. Co.*, 26 Barb. 39 (1859).

[2] See *Telegraph Cases*, by Charles Allen (1873).

these cases involved the question of the liability of the companies for mistakes in transmission or delivery of messages, whether the company was to be subject to the liability of insurer as a common carrier, and regardless of negligence. By 1860, the law was well settled against such liability [1] — another instance of the tendency of the courts to construe the Common Law in aid of the promotion of a new industry.

The first telegraph case in the United States Supreme Court was decided in 1858, *Western Tel. Co.* v. *Magnetic Tel. Co.* (21 Howard, 456), in which it was held that where there was no infringement of patent, no company had a monopoly of the right to telegraph between two places. "It must be expected that great competition will exist in the transmission of intelligence, when telegraphic lines have been established throughout the country."

No case was reported in Massachusetts until 1866 when it was held that telegraph companies were not subject to the liability of common carriers — *Ellis* v. *Amer. Tel. Co.* (13 Allen, 226), Chief Justice Bigelow (Shaw's successor) saying:

"It appears to have been taken for granted at the trial of this case, as it certainly was in the arguments of learned counsel at the bar of this court that the rights of the parties were to be determined solely by having recourse to the rules and principles of the Common Law. This we think an error. We entertain no doubt that these would have been found fully adequate to the satisfactory solution of the various questions to which the pursuit of this novel branch of human skill and industry will in the course of time necessarily give rise. But the Legislature of this Commonwealth have not deemed it wise or expedient to leave to the slow progress of judicial determination the regulation

[1] See the famous "two hundred bouquets" case of *N. Y. and Washington Printing Tel. Co.* v. *Dryburg*, 35 Pa. St. 298 (1860).

of a business on which so many of the daily transactions of life involving the most important rights and interests are made to depend."

Another economic improvement in this era introduced a new line of cases and a new topic in the law — the liability of gas corporations.

The first negligence case in the United States against a gas company was in 1850 — *Brown* v. *N. Y. Gaslight Co.* (Anthon's N. P. Cases, 351). The first case in Massachusetts was for negligence in allowing leaks — *Holly* v. *Boston Gas Light Co.* (8 Gray, 123), in 1857.

Similar cases for injuries due to escaping gas arose in many instances in Connecticut, New York and Pennsylvania from 1850 to 1860.[1]

In 1852, the first successful street railway was started in New York. In 1853, the Cambridge Street Railway Company and the Metropolitan Street Railway Company were chartered in Massachusetts, and began running in 1856. The first comprehensive case, dealing with the respective rights of street cars and other travellers on the highway was decided in 1860 — *Commonwealth* v. *Temple* (14 Gray, 69). The opinion in this case was one of the greatest as well as one of the last of Chief Justice Shaw's opinions, and displayed his wonderful ability to adapt the Common Law to new conditions:

"Since horse railroads are becoming frequent in and about Boston and are likely to become common in other parts of the Commonwealth, it is very important that the rights and duties of all persons in the community, having any relations with them, should be distinctly known, and understood, in order to accomplish all the benefits, and as far as practicable avoid the inconveniences, arising from their use. . . . These railroads being of recent origin, few cases have arisen to require judicial consideration,

[1] *Digest of Gas Cases*, by Charles P. Greenough (1883).

and no series of adjudicated cases can be resorted to as precedents to solve the various new questions to which they may give rise.

"But it is the great merit of the Common Law that it is founded upon a comparatively few broad, general principles of justice, fitness, and expediency, the correctness of which is generally acknowledged, and which at first are few and simple; but which, carried out in their practical details and adapted to extremely complicated cases of fact, give rise to many and often perplexing questions. Yet these original principles remain fixed and are generally comprehensive enough to adapt themselves to new institutions and conditions of society, modes of commerce, new usages and practices, as the progress of society in the advancement of civilization may require."

The first accident case against a street railway in Massachusetts was decided in 1862 — *Wright* v. *Malden and Melrose Street Ry.* (4 Allen, 283).

In the decade 1850–1860, economic conditions in Europe and in the United States were laying the foundations for a new branch of law relating to the cultivation and storage of grain. The year 1854 marked the culmination of bad crops and political troubles in Europe.[1] Immigration to

[1] George Ticknor wrote to King John of Saxony, Nov. 20, 1855. See *Life, Letters and Journals of George Ticknor*, Vol. II.

"Your short crops in Europe are filling the great valley of the Mississippi with population and wealth. The wheat which it costs the great farmers in Ohio, Illinois and Michigan — whose population in 1850 was above three millions and is now above four — the wheat which costs $40 to those great farmers to raise, they can sell at their own doors for above $100 and it is sold in London and Paris for nearly $300. Indeed, your European wars are not only making the States in the valley of the Mississippi the preponderating powers in the American nation but you are making them the granary of the world, more than ever Egypt and Sicily were to Rome. So interchangeably are the different parts of Christendom connected, and so certainly are the fates and fortunes of each in one way or another dependent on the condition of the whole. The war in the Crimea raises the price of land in Ohio. . . . The prolétaires of Paris enrich the farmers in Illinois of whose existence they never heard."

the United States was at its highest, having grown from 114,371 in 1845 to 427,833. These immigrants, and the emigrants from New England sent out under the auspices of the New England Emigrant Aid Company to save Kansas from slavery, were about to develop the great Western farm lands.

In this year 1854, the great case of *Seymour* v. *McCormick* (16 Howard, 480), sustaining the validity of the McCormick reaping machine patent was decided in the United States Supreme Court. By 1855, grain elevator and warehouse law began to come into prominence in the law reports in Ohio, Iowa and Wisconsin;[1] and by 1867, it was said in a Massachusetts case — *Cushing* v. *Breed* (14 Allen, 376): "The use of elevators for the storage of grain has introduced some new methods of dealing; but the rights of parties who adopt these methods must be by the principles of the Common Law."[2]

In the early years of this period, 1830-1860, the only form of insurance which received any great development was marine insurance, and the law reports are strikingly filled with cases on this subject. In the making of this law, as well as in that of patents and copyrights, Judge Joseph Story stood at the head of all judges.

Arnould in the preface to his book on *Marine Insurance* published in London in 1848, says:

"I have resorted generally to the decisions of the American tribunals on the many novel and interesting points in the law of marine insurance which in a commerce of vast activity and a seacoast of unrivalled extent seem to be continually arising for their adjudication. In the present state of legal knowledge, no work professing to treat with any tolerable degree of completeness the sub-

[1] See especially *Chase* v. *Washburn*, 1 Ohio St. 244.

[2] See also articles by Oliver Wendell Holmes, Jr., on *Grain Elevator Cases* in *Amer. Law Review*, Vol. VI.

ject could avoid frequent reference to the jurisprudence of the United States. The names of Chancellor Kent and Mr. Joseph Story have indeed an European celebrity which would make apology ridiculous for the citation of their authority."

Gradually, however, the subject of fire insurance attained importance, as the incorporation of mutual fire insurance companies became general. Yet as late as 1837, a report of a Commission in Massachusetts stated:

"It is not too much to affirm that the whole law of insurance as far as it has been ascertained and established by judicial decisions and otherwise may now be stated in a text not exceeding thirty pages of the ordinary size."

And even in 1852, Chief Justice Shaw said in *Fogg* v. *Middlesex Fire Ins. Co.* (6 Cush. 337):

"Fire insurance as a branch of legal knowledge is, comparatively speaking, in its rudiments. The cases on marine insurance throw little, if any, light on the present question. . . . The question of loss by lightning is very summarily disposed of in the older authorities by treating electricity as fire from heaven. But the progress of knowledge has led to juster notions of the nature of lightning and of course to different conclusions touching its legal relations."

And in the same year, he said in *Scripture* v. *Lowell Mutual Fire Ins. Co.* (10 Cush. 356):

"Fire insurance has become so important in the business of the community that it is much to be regretted that the practical management of the business is not conducted with more care and skill in its details so as better to secure the rights of the parties as they are to be established by the contract when rightly made and rightly understood."

The advent of steamboats and railroads, making life more hazardous, was contemporaneous with a great growth of life and accident insurance companies and the rise of an entirely new body of law.

The earliest and one of the most noted life insurance companies was chartered in Massachusetts in 1818 — the Massachusetts Hospital Life Insurance Company. Kent in his *Commentaries* as late as 1844 (5th edition) said:

"The practice in Europe of life insurance is in a great degree confined to England, and it has been introduced into the United States. It is now slowly but gradually attracting the public attention and confidence in our principal cities."

The only case cited by him on the subject was *Lord* v. *Dall*, decided in Massachusetts, in 1810.

Prior to 1850, five cases only had been reported as decided by the State and Federal courts on the subject; and "in some cases of the States no case has as yet been reported," said a writer in 1872.[1]

The first question litigated was that of insurable interest — on which twelve cases were decided prior to 1860, the first case in Massachusetts arising in 1852 — *Morrell* v. *Trenton Ins. Co.* (10 Cush. 282), and the leading case on the subject being decided by Chief Justice Shaw in 1856 "on the rules and principles of the Common Law" in *Loomis* v. *Eagle Life and Health Ins. Co.* (6 Gray, 396).

On the important questions of false representation and warranty — a subject so much litigated later, the leading case arose in 1850 in Massachusetts — *Vose* v. *Eagle Life and Health Ins. Co.* (6 Cush. 42). In this case it was said:

"Insurance on life was formerly held to be unlawful, and was forbidden in some foreign countries by particular enactments as being repugnant to good morals and opening

[1] *Digest of Life and Accident Insurance Cases*, by John R. Sharpstein (1872).

a door to abuses. But a very different view of the subject is taken at the present time. Life insurance has now become a very common and a very extensive business and is regarded as highly beneficial to the community."

As late as 1873, James Schouler in his book on *Personal Property* wrote:

"Like the historian of some American State in the far West, the text writer on life insurance finds his materials fresh, and modern methods at work in shaping them. The lawyer discarding his Coke, Blackstone and Kent might lay his hand on a few volumes, perhaps exactly three which are hardly yet dry from the press, and say that he had the whole jurisprudence of life insurance as a special subject so far as the English and American Courts had laid it open. Far different will it be twenty years hence."

Between 1810 and 1830, the Supreme Court gave decisions in only five patent cases; and the Circuit Courts in only thirteen, most of which were decided by Judge Story, in the First Circuit. The real history of patent law in the United States dates from the year 1836, in which year, the building of the Patent Office, then a branch of the Department of State, was burned, destroying the models and records of the old system, under which only 10,020 patents had been issued. In that year also, a complete revision of the patent laws was enacted by Congress and the United States Patent Office (which, in 1849, became a branch of the Department of the Interior) was established.

As illustrative of the increase of patent litigation, it is to be noted that the list of adjudicated patents contains 18 patents issued between 1776 and 1815; 57 between 1816 and 1835; 395 between 1836 and 1859 inclusive.[1]

Between 1835 and 1845, a very large proportion of the

[1] *Adjudicated Patents*, by Lineas D. Underwood (1907).

patent cases in the country were tried before Judge Joseph Story in the United States Circuit Court in Boston — Benjamin R. Curtis, Franklin Dexter, Charles G. Loring, Benjamin Rand and Willard Phillips appearing as the principal counsel.

It was not until after 1845, however, that patent cases began to come before the United States Supreme Court in any number.

One of the early famous cases was decided in 1842 — *Prouty* v. *Ruggles* (16 Peters, 336), in which Rufus Choate argued against Franklin Dexter. In 1846, the Woodsworth planing machine patent of 1828 was involved in *Wilson* v. *Rousseau* (4 Howard, 646) and other cases, one being argued by William H. Seward, John H. B. Latrobe [1] and Daniel Webster against Thaddeus Stevens; another being argued by Henry D. Gilpin against John B. Henderson and Reverdy Johnson.

Stimpson's grooved railroad rail patent of 1831 was involved in the case of *Stimpson* v. *Baltimore and Susquehannah R. R. Co.*, in 1850, in which Brantz Mayer argued against James Campbell.

Tatham's lead pipe patent of 1846 was adjudicated in 1852 and, in 1859, in *Leroy* v. *Tatham* (14 Howard, 156; 22 Howard, 132).

In 1852, one of the most noted cases in all patent litigation involving one of the most bitterly fought patents — Goodyear's India rubber patent of 1844, was decided by Judge Grier in the United States Circuit Court in *Goodyear* v. *Day* (2 Wall. Jr. 283), the patent being upheld. In this case Daniel Webster made his last great legal argument, Rufus Choate being the opposing counsel.

In 1853, the head note to a case (15 Howard, 62) announced the decision in a matter of immense import to the develop-

[1] Born in 1803.

ment, commercial, political and legal, of this country — the case of *O'Reilly* v. *Morse*. "Morse was the first and original inventor of the electro magnetic telegraph for which a patent was issued to him in 1840 and re-issued in 1848. His invention was prior to that of Steinhiel of Munich or Wheatstone or Davy of England."

The counsel were James Campbell and George Harding of Philadelphia and Archer Gifford of New Jersey for Morse, and Ransom H. Gillet of New York and Salmon P. Chase of Ohio for O'Reilly. The practicability of this great invention had been proved nine years before, in 1844, by a line put in operation between Baltimore and Washington, under an appropriation from Congress.[1]

The next year, 1854, was marked by the decision in the case of *Seymour* v. *McCormick* (16 Howard, 480), upholding the McCormick reaper patents of 1834, 1845 and 1847. The counsel were Thaddeus Stevens of Pennsylvania and Reverdy Johnson of Maryland for McCormick and Ransom H. Gillet, and Henry R. Selden of New York for Seymour. In the same year as the Dred Scott decision (1857), another case involving this important patent was decided — *Seymour* v. *McCormick* (19 Howard, 96) in which Edward M. Dickerman and Reverdy Johnson appeared for McCormick and H. R. Selden, P. H. Watson and Edwin M. Stanton for Seymour.[2]

[1] John Quincy Adams says in his Diary, May 27, 1844, "This was the day on which the two Democratic conventions to nominate candidates for the offices of President and Vice President . . . were held at Bailtmore. . . . By the new invention of the electro magnetic telegraph of Professor Morse the proceedings of those bodies . . . were made known here at the capital and announced as soon as received."

For an interesting account of this early telegraph — see *Public Men and Events*, by Nathan Sargent, Vol. II (1875).

[2] For an interesting account see *Lincoln as a Lawyer*, by Frederic Trevor Hill.

It is interesting to note that Abraham Lincoln acted as counsel for Mc-

To the decade of 1850–1860 belong also the great inventions of the breech loading fire arm, Elias Howe's sewing machine, the steam fire engine and the fire alarm telegraph.

The leading American law book on the subject of patents was published in 1837 by Willard Phillips.

Between 1815 and 1830 only five copyright cases had been decided in the United States Circuit Courts and only three in the State courts. It was not until 1819 that the Circuit Courts obtained jurisdiction in equity in copyright matters; and as late as 1827, Kent wrote in his *Commentaries* (Vol. II): "There are no decisions in print on the subject and we must recur for instruction to principles settled by the English decisions under the statute of Anne and which are no doubt essentially applicable to the rights of authors under the acts of Congress."

Charles J. Ingersoll, the noted Philadelphia lawyer, wrote in 1823:[1]

> "It is to be regretted that literary property here is held by an imperfect tenure, there being no other protection for it than the provisions of an inefficient act of Congress, the impotent offspring of an obsolete English statute. The inducement to take copyrights is therefore inadequate, and a large proportion of the most valuable American books are published without any legal title. Yet there were 135 copyrights purchased from January, 1822, to April, 1823."[2]

Cormick, with Reverdy Johnson and Edwin M. Dickerman, against Edwin M. Stanton and George Harding in the United States Circuit Court in *McCormick* v. *Manny* (6 McLean, 529) in 1856.

[1] See Review of *A Discourse concerning the Influence of America on the Mind, Oct. 18, 1823, by C. J. Ingersoll,* by Jared Sparks, *No. Amer. Rev.*, Vol. XVII (1824).

[2] The condition of the law of copyright fairly illustrates the general conditions of literature in the United States at the time. Thus, prior to 1830, the only works of American literature of any considerable fame that had

The law of copyright was practically formulated by Judge Joseph Story in his Circuit Court decisions 1830–1845,[1] and by the United States Supreme Court in the great case of *Wheaton* v. *Peters* (8 Peters, 591), in 1834, in which Elijah Paine and Daniel Webster appeared for Henry Wheaton (the former Supreme Court Reporter) and Charles J. Ingersoll and John Sergeant for Richard Peters (the then Reporter).

Few cases came before the Supreme Court on this subject — the most important being *Stevens* v. *Gladding*, in 1854 (17 Howard, 447).

Another branch of the law which practically originated in the years 1830–1860 was that of trademarks.

been published were: *Webster's Dictionary*, in 1806, Washington Irving's *Knickerbocker History of New York*, in 1809, his *Sketch Book* in 1819, his *Life of Columbus*, in 1820, and his *Conquest of Granada* in 1829. In 1817, Bryant's *Thanatopsis* had appeared, and in the same year Wirt's *Life of Patrick Henry*. In 1821, Fenimore Cooper wrote *The Spy*, and in 1826, *The Last of the Mohicans*. In 1827, Poe's *Tamerlane* and Goodrich's *Peter Parley's Tales* were published. In 1828, came Hawthorne's first book, *Fanshawe*.

It may be noted that coincident with the rise of copyright law came the great development of American literature and American journalism. The years 1835–1860 witnessed the production of the works of Emerson, Hawthorne, Lowell, Longfellow, Prescott, Motley, Bancroft, Hildreth and Whittier.

The *North American Review*, founded in 1815, was still in existence. The *American Quarterly Review* was published from 1827 to 1837; the *Knickerbocker Magazine* from 1833 to 1858. Of the great newspapers the *New York Herald* was first published in 1835, yet by 1846 it had a circulation of only 15,000. The *New York Tribune* started in 1841; the *New York Evening Post* in 1842 with a circulation of 2,500; the *Springfield Daily Republican* in 1844.

In 1841, *Graham's Magazine* was first published; in 1842, the *Southern Quarterly Review;* and in 1845, the *American Review*.

In 1850, *Harper's Monthly Magazine* was established; in 1853, *Putnam's Monthly Magazine;* in 1836, *Harper's Weekly;* and in 1857, the *Atlantic Monthly*.

[1] See *Gray* v. *Russell*, 1 Story, 16; *Folsom* v. *Marsh*, 2 Story, 113 (1841); *Emerson* v. *Davies*, 3 Story, 779.

The first of the trademark cases in the history of the country (*Snowden* v. *Noah*), a motion in the New York Court of Chancery by the owner of a newspaper called *The National Advocate*, for an injunction against the owner of *The New York National Advocate*, was tried before Chancellor Sandford, in January, 1825.

In 1837, the leading case of *Thomson* v. *Winchester* was decided in Massachusetts (19 Pick. 214) in which Theophilus Parsons and Charles Sumner were counsel for the defendant. Chief Justice Shaw held that it was a fraud to make and sell medicines as and for medicines made and prepared by the plaintiff — this decision being the foundation of the law of unfair trade in this country. In 1840, in *Bell* v. *Locke* in New York (8 Paige, 75) the court was asked to enjoin the use of a trade name. In 1844, Judge Story in the United States Circuit Court in *Taylor* v. *Carpenter* (3 Story, 458) granted the first injunction ever issued in this country restraining the infringement of a real trademark. From that year, the law may be said to have been definitely established. The first act for the protection of trademarks was passed in Massachusetts in 1852, c. 197.[1]

The list of trademark and trade name cases between 1845 and 1860 numbers only 36, of which 28 were decided in inferior courts of New York, 5 in United States Circuit Courts, 2 in Rhode Island and 1 in Pennsylvania.[2]

The law as to trade names was practically fixed by the noted decision of *Marsh* v. *Billings* in Massachusetts in 1851 (7 Cush. 322). This was an action of trespass on the case alleging injuries from the use by the defendant of the words "Revere House" in transporting passengers and baggage. The court said:

[1] See *Ames* v. *King*, 2 Gray, 382 (1854).

[2] *Trademark Cases*, by Rowland Cox (1892).

"The principle involved is one of much importance to the plaintiffs and to the public. But the principle is by no means novel in its demands . . . substantially the same which has been repeatedly recognized and acted on by courts in regard to fraudulent use of trademarks and regarded as of much importance in a mercantile community."

As before stated, this era was especially characterized by the increasing recognition paid to individual rights and the protective safeguards thrown about the weaker classes.

No portion of the community was more favored by the development of the law between 1830 and 1860 than the debtor class.

In the argument of David Daggett in *Sturgis* v. *Crowninshield*, in 1819, it is said that, "no acts, properly called bankrupt laws, have been passed in more than four or five States. Rhode Island had an act . . . (adopted in 1756) by which the debtor might, on application to the Legislature, be discharged from his debts. In New York, a law of the same character has been in operation since the year 1755, and also in Maryland for a long period (since 1774). In Pennsylvania, a bankrupt law operating in the city and county of Philadelphia existed for two or three years; and in Connecticut, the Legislature has often granted a special act of bankruptcy on application of individuals. But in all the other States, these laws on this subject have been framed with reference to the exemption of the body from imprisonment, and not to the discharge of the contract."

The first general insolvent law in the United States discharging the debts as well as the person of the debtor was that of New York in 1784, and later more progressive statutes had been passed in 1801, 1811, 1813, 1817 and 1823. So undecided, however, was public opinion as to the value of such laws that, as late as 1819, Chancellor

Kent and the judges of the New York Supreme Court in a report to the Legislature said:[1]

"Judging from their former experience and from observation in the course of their judicial duties, they were of opinion that the insolvent law was the source of a great deal of fraud and perjury. They were apprehensive that the evil was incurable and arose principally from the infirmity inherent in every such system which . . . had a powerful tendency to render him (the debtor) heedless in the creation of debt and careless as to payment . . . and probably ever must be, from the very nature of it, productive of incalculable abuse, fraud, and perjury, and greatly injurious to public morals."

Nevertheless, the commercial distresses due to the financial crises after the close of the War of 1812, and during the depreciated currency period of 1815 to 1825, caused constant pressure for relief to the debtor class. The uncertainty whether or how far the United States Supreme Court would sustain the constitutionality of State insolvent laws produced great confusion and hesitation in legislation until the final decision of the question in *Ogden* v. *Saunders*, in 1827. As Kent wrote, in that year: "The laws of the individual States . . . have hitherto been unstable and fluctuating, but they will probably be redigested and become more stable, since the decisions of the Supreme Court have at last defined and fixed the line around the narrow inclosure of State jurisdiction."[2]

So progressive a State as Massachusetts, however, had no insolvency law until as late as 1838; but an antique and complicated system of assignments for benefit of creditors had prevailed for many years, which in its workings had proved most unjust and productive of fraud.[3]

[1] *Kent's Commentaries*, Vol. II, p. 324, note b (1st ed. 1827).

[2] *Kent's Commentaries*, Vol. II, p. 326, note a (1st ed. 1827).

[3] See for graphic description of actual conditions, *Law Reporter*, Vol. II (1839).

Creditors raced for the property of their debtor; a general assignment protected only those creditors who assented to it; and fraudulent assignments intended to benefit the debtor rather than to protect his creditors were the rule.

In 1831, Charles Jackson, Samuel Hubbard and John B. Davis were appointed Commissioners to consider the subject of an insolvent law and they prepared a draft. For seven years, however, the Legislature failed to take any favorable action. After the great financial panic of 1837, the general distress among debtors was so great that the State enacted this law, which proved so excellent and so liberal that it served as a model for similar acts in other States and for future United States bankruptcy statutes.

By 1845, most of the States had enacted insolvent laws; but there was great diversity in the extent to which these laws were operative. Thus in Maine, New Hampshire, Virginia and Kentucky, they were confined to debtors charged on execution. In New Jersey, Delaware, Maryland, Tennessee, North Carolina, South Carolina, Georgia, Alabama, Mississippi and Illinois, they extended only to debtors in prison on mesne or final process. In New York, Massachusetts, Connecticut, Rhode Island, Pennsylvania, Ohio, Indiana, Missouri and Louisiana, they extended generally to debtors in or out of prison.

In some of these States, like New Jersey, Connecticut, Ohio and others, the laws were insolvent laws in the old technical meaning of the term, i. e. laws discharging the debtor from imprisonment only. In other States, like Massachusetts, New York and others, these laws though termed insolvent were really bankrupt laws, in that they discharged the debt itself.[1]

Kent thus described the confused condition as late as 1840:

[1] See *Kent's Commentaries*, Vol. II, p. 394 (5th ed., 1844).

"The Commissioners appointed to revise the civil code in Pennsylvania, in their Report in January, 1835, complained in strong terms of the existing state of things. Congress will not exert their constitutional power and pass a bankrupt law, and no State can pass a bankrupt or insolvent law except so far as regards its own citizens; and even then, only in relation to contracts made after the passage of the law. Foreign creditors and creditors in other States cannot be barred, while State creditors may be. The former preserve a perpetual lien on after-acquired property except so far as the statutes of limitations interpose. State bankrupt and insolvent laws cannot be cherished under such inequalities."

It was to remedy this condition of affairs that, after a thirty years' struggle, Congress finally enacted the National Bankruptcy Law in 1841, which went into effect February 1, 1842, and was repealed in 1843. It was however much more extended in its provisions than the earlier National Bankruptcy Law of 1800 and than the English bankruptcy acts, as it was not confined to "traders" and also included cases of voluntary application.[1]

The enactment of this law was largely due to the great distress following the panic of 1837 and President Tyler's veto of the Bank Act. There had been tremendous expansion of credit and speculation by private individuals as well as by the States themselves, especially in the South and West. The rage for railroad building, 1830–1840, and the numerous subscriptions by means of State stock and bond issues made by the States to induce railroad construction had piled up State debts to such an extent that many States had repudiated their obligations.[2]

[1] See *Griswold* v. *Pratt*, 9 Metc. 16 (1845), for a good description of the history of bankruptcy and insolvency legislation and the reasons for and against it in the United States and in Massachusetts.

[2] The first instance of the use of the term "repudiation" was in an official message of the Governor of Mississippi advising this course. In 1853,

In this period, the position of the debtor class was still further alleviated by the gradual adoption of statutes abolishing the old harsh system of imprisonment for debt.[1] Such imprisonment had already been abolished outright by Kentucky in 1821 and by New York in 1831. Four States, Maine, New Hampshire, Massachusetts and South Carolina, soon abolished imprisonment for debts of sums less than $5 to $30. Statutes practically abolishing imprisonment for debt were passed in Vermont, Ohio and Michigan in 1838, in Alabama in 1839, in New Hampshire and Tennessee in 1840, in Pennsylvania and Connecticut in 1842. By the year 1857, when Massachusetts by statute provided that, "imprisonment for debt except in cases of fraud is hereby abolished forever," practically all the States had enacted this relief to debtors.[2]

by decision of the Supreme Court of the State, Mississippi was forced to pay its repudiated bonds. See *Law Reporter*, Vol. XVI.

See also *Repudiation*, by Benjamin R. Curtis, *North Amer. Rev.*, January, 1844.

As George Ticknor wrote May 30, 1842:

"Large portions of the country are suffering. At the South and Southwest where individuals and States borrowed rashly and unwisely there is great distress. To individuals the Bankrupt Law is bringing appropriate relief. But to States the process must be more slow. Some of them like Illinois and Indiana never will pay. They have not the means and cannot get the means. They are honest and hopeless bankrupts and will do what they can. Others like Mississippi which repudiate its obligations so shamelessly will be compelled to pay by the force of public opinion. . . . The lesson will have been an useful one."

[1] Kent wrote in his *Commentaries*, in 1827: "The power of imprisonment for debt in cases free from fraud, seems to be fast going into annihilation in this country, and is considered as repugnant to humanity, policy and justice."

The constitutionality of State laws abolishing imprisonment for debt was upheld in *Mason* v. *Haile*, 12 Wheat. 370, in 1827.

[2] See McMaster's *History of the United States*, Vol. VI.

See *Imprisonment for Debt*, by Asa Kinne (1842).

*Kent's Commentaries*, Vol. II (5th ed., 1844).

Another step in advance for the protection of debtors was the enactment of homestead laws exempting from execution a homestead for the shelter and protection of the family occupying it. The first of these liberal statutes was passed by the Republic of Texas in 1836; the next in Vermont in 1849. Most of the other States soon enacted such laws.[1]

But it was not only by statutes that the law showed its tender side towards debtors. The trend of judicial decision was distinctly favorable to them.

Thus Kent in 1844 said:[2]

"In noting the vacillating and contradictory decisions on the point of the validity of voluntary gifts and conveyances of property by persons indebted at the time, it is painful to perceive, in so many instances, the tendency to a lax doctrine on the subject. The relaxation goes to destroy conservative principles and to commit the sound, wholesome and stern rules of law to the popular disposal and unstable judgment of jurors."

Another instance of the tenderness of the new law towards the interests of debtors is to be seen in the growth of the doctrine of implied warranties on sales of personal property — a development which Kent said,[3] "trenched deeply upon the plain maxim of the common law, *caveat emptor;* and I cannot but think that the old rule and the old decisions were the safest and wisest guides; and that the new doctrine . . . will lead to much difficulty and vexatious litigation in mercantile business."

In still another form, the debtor was protected through the relaxation, by the courts of Massachusetts and of several other States, of the old English law that a sale of

[1] *Law of Homestead*, by Seymour D. Thompson.

[2] *Kent's Commentaries*, Vol. II, p. 442, note (5th ed., 1844).

[3] *Kent's Commentaries*, Vol. II, p. 479, note (5th ed., 1844).

chattels without delivery was conclusive evidence of fraud upon creditors.

"This tendency," said Kent, "is greatly to be regretted. . . . Since the remedy against the property of the debtor is now almost entirely deprived of the auxiliary coercion intended by the arrest and imprisonment of his person, the creditor's naked claim against the property ought to receive the most effective support and every rule calculated to prevent the debtor from secreting or masking it to be sustained with fortitude and vigor."

The bare rudiments of legal protection to a class which had hitherto received little protection from the law — the laboring class — developed in this era, although even by 1860 very slight recognition to the rights of the laborer had been shown by the courts.

Three early cases in inferior courts in New York and Pennsylvania [1] had held that associations of workingmen to raise prices or wages were illegal in themselves; but this stringent Common Law doctrine was overturned in Pennsylvania as early as 1821 in *Com.* v. *Carlisle* (Brightley's Reports, 36); and in the great leading case of *Com.* v. *Hunt* in Massachusetts, in 1842 (4 Metc. 111). This case involved the legality of the acts of the labor organization of the Journeymen Bootmakers Society, and was argued by Attorney-General James T. Austin against Robert Rantoul, Jr. Chief Justice Shaw delivered one of his greatest opinions, upholding the right of laborers to combine for proper purposes without being liable to indictment for criminal conspiracy. A case in New York, in 1835, arising

[1] *Boot and Shoemakers of Philadelphia.* See Pamphlet Report in 1806.
*People* v. *Melvin,* 2 Wheeler's Criminal Cases, 262 (N. Y.), in 1824.
*Journeymen Cordwainers of Pittsburg.* See Pamphlet Report in 1811.
*Journeymen Cordwainers of New York,* in 1810. See *Sampson's Discourse,* by Pishey Thompson (1826).

under a special statute had been decided to the contrary — *People* v. *Fisher* (14 Wendell 1).[1]

An earlier labor case in Massachusetts, in 1827, — *Boston Glass Manufacturing Co.* v. *Binney* (4 Pick. 425), argued by William Sullivan and Samuel Hubbard against Lemuel Shaw had involved the question of liability for enticing workmen from the plaintiff's employ.

These cases and those cited in the notes were practically all the labor cases in the country which occurred prior to 1867.[2]

The change in the attitude of the law during this period towards the status and rights of married women was very remarkable.

The first liberal step in breaking down the harsh Common Law doctrine as to the legal identity of husband and wife was in Mississippi, in 1839, by the passage of a statute allowing to a wife separate ownership of property. Massachusetts followed, in 1845, by an act authorizing a married woman to hold property to her separate use by express ante-nuptial agreement;[3] and by statutes in 1855 and 1857 in that State, the rights of married women were extended so as to give them unrestricted authority to hold property, to contract, to convey and otherwise to act like a *feme sole.*

Between 1844 and 1860, twenty-one States had enacted similar legislation, although few of them had granted as great freedom to the wife as had Massachusetts.[4] The

[1] See also *Journeymen Tailors of Philadelphia.* See Pamphlet Report (1827).

*Hartford Carpet Weavers.* See Pamphlet Report (1836).

[2] See *Bowen* v. *Matheson* (14 Allen, 499) in Massachusetts, in 1867; and *Stevedores' Association* v. *Walsh* (2 Daly, 1) in New York, in 1867.

[3] See *Beal* v. *Warren*, 2 Gray, 457 (1854).

[4] For a history of the spread of legislation of this nature, see Bishop's *Law of Married Women*, Vol. II (1875); *Willard* v. *Eastham*, 15 Gray (1860); and *Lord* v. *Parker*, 3 Allen, 129 (1861).

first American law book on the subject, since Judge Tapping Reeve's book on *Domestic Relations*, appeared in 1861 — William H. Cord's *Treatise on Legal and Equitable Rights of Married Women.* As late as 1873, Joel P. Bishop's *Law of Married Women* says: "No first class text book has ever been written upon the subject." [1]

The chief advances in criminal law during this period were in the abolition of the death penalty for many crimes; the reform and amelioration in the sentences and in the methods of treatment in prisons and reformatories; and the change in the law of evidence giving the defendant the right to testify.

Among the new doctrines of criminal law established by the courts, the one of chief importance was the settlement of the law as to insanity as a defense — in England by *McNaughten's Case* in the House of Lords in 1843 [2] — in the United States by two famous cases; one in Massachusetts in 1844, *Com.* v. *Rogers* (7 Metc. 500). G. T. Bigelow and G. Bemis being counsel and Chief Justice Shaw delivering one of his most notable opinions; the other in New York in 1847, *People* v. *Freeman*

[1] The only books other than the above written previous to 1871 on the subject were as follows — all English:

*Baron and Feme* (1700).

*Law of Marriage and other Family Settlements*, by Edward G. Atherley (1813).

*Essay on Equitable Rights of Married Women*, by James Claney (1819).

*Law of Property arising from Relation of Husband and Wife*, by R. S. Donniston Roper (1820).

*Rights and Liabilities of Husband and Wife at Law and in Equity*, by John F. MacQueen (1849).

*Law of Property as arising from the Relation of Husband and Wife*, by S. S. Bell (1849).

[2] Even as late as 1827 Lord Tenterden had said in *Brown* v. *Godrall* (3 Carr. & Payne, 30), that "no person can be suffered to set up his own lunacy as a defense" in a civil action.

See also article on *Insanity*, in *Western Jurist*, Vol. IV.

(4 Denio, 29), in which William H. Seward established his legal reputation by his brilliant defense of the insane negro defendant.

Perhaps one of the most necessary revolutions in the old Common Law doctrines brought about in this period was the great reform in the law of evidence — especially in the removal of the rules which barred a witness from testifying because of interest, and because of being a party.

The old Common Law bar of interest had become absurd in its application to modern trials. It resulted in many instances in the complete exclusion of the truth as to the facts of a case. In other instances, it was a direct inducement to fraud, as persons desired as witnesses, and likely to be excluded on grounds of interest, made releases of their interest before the trial, only to receive a re-grant of the interest so released, after the trial was over. In many directions the Legislature had removed the bar, quite illogically, as to certain classes of witnesses.

The reform in this direction had started in England in 1843 in Lord Denman's Act, which abrogated the disability of a witness for interest or infamy. This Act was spoken of by the *Law Reporter* in 1844 (Vol. VI) "as justly regarded as the greatest innovation of the day," and termed by Brougham "the greatest measure under the head of judicial procedure since the Statute of Frauds." New York followed this with an act, in 1846, removing the bar of religious incapacity from witnesses, and, in 1848, the bar of interest. Michigan adopted the English statute in 1846; and Connecticut passed a similar act in 1848.

One further step remained to be taken — the removal of the unreasonable disqualification, as witnesses, of parties to the suit. This reform was bitterly antagonized by the Bar for many years, chiefly on the ground that it would be a tremendous inducement to perjury. England again led the way by the passage of Lord Brougham's Act in 1850.[1]

By a statute in 1851 known as the Practise Act (substantially a Code of Civil Procedure), Massachusetts allowed the filing of interrogatories to parties to a suit, and abolished the bar of interest and infamy. In 1853, Ohio adopted in full the provisions of Lord Brougham's Act. Connecticut had already anticipated the English statute by an act passed in 1848. Massachusetts and Maine followed in 1856; New York, in 1857; and Congress passed an act for the Federal courts in 1864.

In 1864, Maine became a leader in this department of the law by allowing defendants in criminal cases to testify. Massachusetts passed a similar statute in 1866, and New York in 1867. Gradually this reform became general over the United States, defendants in criminal cases in the Federal courts being allowed to testify by an act in 1878.[2]

It would be interesting to trace the effect on the doctrines of substantive law, of this exclusion from the witness stand of parties who had the chief and the best knowledge of the facts in conflict. That the substantive law was considerably moulded by the conditions imposed by this rule

[1] See article on *Law of Evidence* in *Southern Law Review*, N. S. (1875). *Disqualification of Parties as Witnesses* in *American Law Register*, Vol. V (1856–1857) saying,

"We rejoice to see the spirit of reform is at work."

See a brilliant and interesting series of articles in *American Jurist*, Vols. I to XIII (1829–1835), advocating these changes in the law of evidence. See also article in 1851 in the *Law Reporter*, Vol. XIV; and also articles in the same volume explaining the workings of the new English Act of 1850.

[2] See *A Chapter of Legal History*, by James B. Thayer, *Harvard Law Review*, Vol. IX (1895).

of evidence, there can be no question. The subject may be a fruitful one for some writer of legal history.[1]

[1] A minor illustration may be given of the results of this rule of evidence as applied to the development of modern economic conditions. In 1846, when railroad law was being formulated every day in the courts, as a new branch of law, a plaintiff failed to recover against a railroad company for loss of his baggage due to the railroad's negligence, simply on the ground that he alone knew what was in his trunk, and yet he was barred from testifying, because a party. The court said:

"The question whether the plaintiff was a competent witness is of much practical importance to the community, as in consequence of the facilities for travelling, the passenger travel is constantly on the increase and railroad companies being carriers of passengers and baggage are liable by the rules of common law for losses. . . . But the law of evidence is not of a fleeting character."

To counteract this decision (*Snow* v. *Eastern R. R. Co.*, 12 Metc. 44), the Legislature of Massachusetts was compelled by public opinion to pass an act (St. 1851, c. 147) allowing a passenger to put in evidence his own schedule or written descriptive contents of his trunk. [See *Harlow* v. *Fitchburg R. R.*, 8 Gray, 237 (1857).] Similar acts were passed in other States. See *Mad. River, etc., R. R.* v. *Fulton*, 20 Ohio St. 319 (1853); and *Livingston's Monthly Law Magazine*, January, 1853.

## CHAPTER XVIII

### THE RISE OF RAILROAD AND CORPORATION LAW

It is a commonplace to remark that the effect of railroads upon the history of the United States has been profound. As Judge John F. Dillon has well said: "Marshall's judgments and our lines of railways and telegraph have done more than any other visible agencies in making and keeping us one united nation." It is, however, because of the notably marked influence which railroads and the doctrines of law growing out of the problems presented by them, have had upon the development of the American Bar and upon the legal history of the country, that a separate chapter may properly be devoted to this distinctive feature of the middle of the Nineteenth Century.

The years 1830 to 1860 witnessed the creation and practical establishment of the law of railroads.

The great Middlesex Canal Corporation, chartered in 1793, had been in successful operation in Massachusetts for many years. In 1825 came the completion of the Erie Canal in New York and the beginning of the Delaware and Hudson Canal in New Jersey. In the same year, 1825, however, Governor Levi Lincoln of Massachusetts in his message approving a canal from Boston to the Connecticut River suggested that he had "been assured that another mode, by railways, had been approved of in England," and, he added, "how far they would be affected by our severe frosts cannot be conjectured yet." He also stated that whether they were better than canals remained to be determined.

For twenty years before the actual operation of railroads, clear-visioned men had prophesied the certain success of this form of the application of steam power.

As early as 1812, Oliver Evans, who in 1804 had actually operated in Pennsylvania a combination scow and wagon by steam, said:[1]

"I verily believe that the time will come when carriages propelled by steam will be in general use, as well for the transportation of passengers as goods, travelling at the rate of fifteen miles an hour or 300 miles per day."

In 1822, *Niles' Register* had said:[2]

"Distance — What is it?

"In noticing the progress of improvement, we have many times asked this question. New York and Norfolk are now brought within forty-eight hours' journey of each other, by means of a steam tug that plies with passengers and freight between them.

"We shall soon have Oliver Evans' ideas of steam wagons realized, when a trip to Pittsburg will be only a little excursion — the mighty ridges of the Alleghanies being sunk by the pressure of scientific power. Over the water and over the earth — when shall we travel in the air as we will it? — By steam? — we know not, but dare not say what is impossible in respect to it."

In 1828, *Niles' Register* said:[3]

"Prophecy almost fulfilled. Oliver Evans 40 years ago said that the child was born who would travel from Phila-

[1] See *Niles' Register*, Add. to Vol. III, p. 5; and *Niles' Register*, Vol. XXXV, p. 72.

[2] *Niles' Register*, Vol. XXIII, p. 130.

[3] *Niles' Register*, Vol. XXXV, p. 19.

delphia to Boston in one day — 24 hours. The journey may now be made in about twenty-nine hours! The use of steam coaches, with some little further improvement in steamboats, may in less than five years fulfil what was thought the mad prophecy of Oliver Evans; for then the journey was one of serious moment and with severe travelling occupied five or six days."

The first railroad operated in this country, the Granite Railway Company, was chartered in Massachusetts in 1826 and constructed to transport, by horse power, granite for the new Bunker Hill Monument.[1]

In the same year, New York chartered the Mohawk and Hudson Railroad Company.

The next year, 1827, Massachusetts became a pioneer in the railway agitation by appointing a Board of Commissioners of Internal Improvements to survey a route for a railway from Boston to the Rhode Island boundary, and also to the New York boundary. It made a report to the Legislature, urging that the roads when built should be operated by horse power;[2] and this was the power for which all the early railroads were designed.

But in October, 1826, George Stephenson had demonstrated in England the success of his steam locomotive,

[1] *The Journal of Law* (Phil. 1831), Vol. I, contains an article on the *Law Relating to Masters of Ships and Common Carriers* which makes no mention of railroads, but notes the "increasing importance of carriers by canal boats."

[2] A contemporary view of this project is given by J. T. Buckingham in his *Personal Memoirs*. "It was in the summer of 1827 that the railroad mania began to manifest itself. The idea of a railroad from Boston to Albany or even to Springfield was met with ridicule in the Legislature as a project too absurd to be discussed with gravity.

"An editorial in the *Boston Courier* in June says, 'a project which every one knows, who knows the simplest rules in arithmetic, to be impracticable but at an expense little less than the market value of the whole territory of Massachusetts, and which if practicable every person of common sense knows would be as useless as a railroad from Boston to the Moon.' "

the "Rocket;"[1] and the introduction of steam power in the United States soon followed.

July 4, 1828, the Baltimore and Ohio Railroad was begun, fourteen miles being opened for traffic by horse power in 1830, and sixty-one miles by steam in 1831. English locomotives drew trains on the Delaware and Hudson Canal Railroad in 1829, and in 1830, the first American steam locomotive was used on the South Carolina Railroad.[2] Between 1825 and 1830, thirty-six miles of railroad had been built in South Carolina, New Jersey and Maryland. In Massachusetts, though a number of railroads were incorporated, construction was not begun for several years, owing to the discouraging effect produced upon investors of capital by the decision in the famous case of *Charles River Bridge* v. *Warren Bridge* (7 Pick. 344), in 1828. This case, holding that the grant of a toll bridge charter by the Legislature did not preclude a later Legislature from chartering a free bridge, located so close to the former bridge as to deprive it of all profits, and that a legislative charter did not grant exclusive rights by implication, proved an obstacle in the path of railroad promoters for almost nine years, i. e. until the question was finally settled

[1] A full descripion of this trial trip appeared in the *Boston Daily Advertiser*, November 23, 1826, and on November 25, that newspaper stated that: "These experiments constitute a new era in the history of railroads. They prove conclusively that they are adapted in the most perfect manner for rapid travelling, whatever power may be used."

[2] An article on *Internal Improvements* in *American Quarterly Review*, Vol. VIII, in December, 1830, said:

"So far then as animal power is concerned, railroads are not more than half as advantageous for transportation as canals. The search at the present moment is therefore for such friction-saving apparatus as will place railroads on a level with canals. . . . Upon the success of some such friction-saving apparatus must depend the great question whether railroads can compete with canals. . . . Railroads, however, are about to derive new advantages from the application of steam to locomotion."

on appeal by the Supreme Court of the United States in 1837.[1]

The advent of canals and railroads sounded the death knell of the turnpike companies. In fact, the increasing wealth of the towns and the consequent building of town highways had already affected the prosperity of turnpikes; and in 1827, Massachusetts had passed an act allowing turnpikes to be laid out as public highways, by the town authorities.[2] In turn, however, the ruin of the canal com-

[1] A brief résumé of the progress of railroad building during these years is of interest.

Twelve miles from Albany to Schenectady, on the Mohawk and Hudson R. R., were opened in 1831. The Camden and Amboy R. R. (chartered in New Jersey in 1830) was completed in 1834 as a through route from New York to Philadelphia. In Massachusetts, the State in which the greatest railroad development occurred, the Boston and Worcester R. R. (chartered in 1831) opened nine miles for travel in the summer of 1833; the Boston and Providence R. R. (chartered in 1831) was opened in June, 1834; the Boston and Lowell R. R. (chartered in 1830) was opened in 1835.

From 1830 to 1848, there was a total of 5,205 miles of railroad in the whole United States; but the year 1849 marked the beginning of the great railroad extensions, and by 1860, 30,135 miles had been built.

By 1840, however, it was possible to go from New York by various connecting railroads as far South as Roanoke, No. Car., and as early as 1836, as far West as Utica, N. Y. In 1842, the first long single through route was completed, that from Boston to Albany. In 1850, the Erie R. R. was opened through to Lake Erie; and in 1853 came the first important railroad consolidation, when eleven lines between Albany and Buffalo became the N. Y. Central R. R. By 1854, the Chicago and Rock Island R. R. reached the Mississippi River, and by 1859, the Hannibal and St. Joseph had penetrated to the Missouri River. In 1850, Chicago had only one short railroad. In 1852, it received railroad connection with the East by the completion of the Michigan Central R. R. and the Michigan Southern R. R.; in 1851, the Pennsylvania R. R. extended its system to Chicago; and by 1860, that city had become a railroad centre.

[2] St. 1827, c. 77; see *Andover and Medford Turnpike Corp.* v. *County Com.*, 18 Pick. 486 (1836).

Another contributing factor to the lapse of turnpikes was the decision of Chief Justice Shaw in 1836, that turnpike corporations were liable for injuries caused even by latent defects in their roads, and irrespective of negligence. See *Yale* v. *Hampden and Berkshire Turnpike Corp.*, 18 Pick. 357.

panies was brought about by the growth of the railroads, and most of them either failed or were bought up by the railroads or dragged out a feeble existence with no profits.[1]

To Chief Justice Shaw of Massachusetts chiefly belongs the glory of laying down the broad principles on which the law of railroads was framed by judicial decision, although the courts of New York also took a large part in its making. As Judge Thomas strikingly said:[2]

"The first puff of the engine on the iron road announced a revolution in the law of bailments and of common carriers. How much Shaw's wisdom and foresight and that clear comprehension of the principles of the Common Law, which enabled him to separate the rule from its old embodiments and to mould it to new exigencies, contributed to build up this law, to give it system and harmony, and a subtraction of solid sense, is well known to the profession."

No more superb statement of the manner in which the principles of the Common Law are to be adapted to new conditions of modern life has ever been made than by Shaw, in 1854, in a case involving the liability of railroads as warehousemen; and a quotation from his opinion is worthy of reproduction at length:[3]

"The liability of carriers of goods by railroads, the grounds and precise extent and limits of their responsibility, are coming to be subjects of great interest and importance to the community. It is a new mode of transportation, in some respects like the transportation of ships, lighters and canal boats on water, and in others like that by wagons on land; but in some respects it differs from both. Though the practice is new, the law, by which the rights and obli-

[1] See *Forward* v. *Hampshire and Hampden Canal Co.*, 22 Pick. 465 (1839); *Chase* v. *Sutton Mfg. Co.*, 4 Cush. 152 (1839), for interesting comments on the downfall of the canals.

[2] *Memoir of Chief Justice Shaw*, by Benjamin F. Thomas, *Mass. Hist. Soc. Proc.*, Vol. X (1867–1869).

[3] *Norway Plains Co.* v. *B. & M. R. R.*, 1 Gray 263 (1854).

gations of owners, consignees and of the carriers themselves, are to be governed, is old and well established. It is one of the great merits and advantages of the Common Law, that, instead of a series of detailed practical rules, established by positive provisions, and adapted to the precise circumstances of particular cases, which would become obsolete and fail, when the practice and course of business, to which they apply, should cease or change, the Common Law consists of a few broad and comprehensive principles, founded on reason, natural justice and enlightened public policy, modified and adapted to the circumstances of all the particular cases which fall within it. These general principles of equity and policy are rendered precise, specific and adapted to practical use, by usage, which is the proof of their general fitness and common convenience, but still more by judicial exposition. . . . The effect of this expansive character of the Common Law is, that when new practices spring up, new combinations of facts arise, and cases are presented for which there is no precedent in judicial decision, they must be governed by the general principle, applicable to cases most nearly analogous, but modified and adapted to new circumstances, by considerations of fitness and propriety, of reason and justice which grow out of those circumstances."

The original conception of a railroad was that of an immovable structure graded for the use of vehicles moving on rails provided for the purpose, on which everyone who could procure the proper carriage and apparatus would have the right to travel, on paying a proper toll for the use of the road and conforming to any reasonable regulations.

It was regarded as a better kind of turnpike. Companies chartered to build were primarily construction companies building a road for the use of others; and on these principles the early cases in the courts were decided.[1] With

[1] See *Lake Superior and Miss. R. R.* v. *U. S.*, 93 U. S. 401, pp. 446, 450. "It is undoubtedly familiar to most of those whose recollection goes back to that period that railroads were generally expected to be public high-

this in view, the early railroad charters were framed practically on the form of the old turnpike corporation charters, and the Revised Statutes of Massachusetts in 1836 included them all together in a chapter headed "Of Turnpikes, Railroads and Canals." It was not until later that this theory was changed by legislation.

Chief Justice Shaw thus stated the early theory:[1]

"The railroad contemplated by our earliest legislation upon the subject was but an iron turnpike, the use of which was to be paid for by tolls collected of persons travelling upon it. It apparently was not anticipated that the railroad companies were to become themselves the carriers of goods and passengers.

"But this idea or policy as to the mode in which railroads were to be used was abandoned before any of our railroads were fully constructed and put into operation. In the act incorporating the Boston and Worcester Railroad Company (St. 1831, c. 72), powers were given to the corporation for the transportation of persons and goods, and for the purchase of engines and cars for the purpose. These provisions were inserted, it is understood, under the advice of a distinguished member of our profession deeply

ways, on which every man who could procure the proper carriages and apparatus would have the right to travel. This was the understanding in England where they originated. . . . Most of the early railroad charters in this country were framed upon the same idea. — Thus the charter of the Mohawk and Hudson R. R. Co. (New York, 1826); and in subsequent charters granted in 1828 and succeeding years, the intent is still more plainly expressed. . . . So, in the early charters granted by Massachusetts and Maine, as late as 1837, New Hampshire as late as 1844. See also the charter of the Camden and Amboy R. R. Co. in New Jersey in 1830, and that of the New Jersey R. R. in 1832, the Philadelphia and Trenton R. R. Co. in Pennsylvania in 1832. . . . In Massachusetts, the right of the public to use them was expressly abrogated by the Act of 1845. . . . The general course of legislation demonstrates the fact that in the early history of railroads it was quite generally supposed that they could be public highways in fact as well as in name. The railroads constructed under the early charters are, theoretically at least, public highways to-day."

[1] *Com.* v. *Fitchburg R. R.*, 12 Gray, p. 187 (1858).

interested in works of internal improvement. All the subsequent legislation of the Commonwealth has assumed and proceeded upon the ground that railroad companies were to be the carriers of passengers and merchandise upon their respective roads."

And in another case, he said:[1]

"It was ascertained very early after railroads were brought into use, that it would not only be attended with great inconvenience, but also with imminent hazard and danger to the public, to allow different and independent railroad companies to run their cars on the same track; and that it was indispensable to the public safety that every car carried upon a railroad should be under the control and direction of the particular company by which it was owned. Accordingly it was provided, that no locomotive engine or other motive power should be allowed to run upon any railroad constructed under authority of this commonwealth, except such as should belong to and be controlled by the corporation owning and managing such road, unless by their consent; and also that every railroad corporation owning a railroad in actual use should be required, at reasonable times and for a reasonable compensation, to draw over their road the passengers, merchandise and cars of any other railroad corporation which had been duly authorized to enter upon or unite their road with it. St. 1845, c. 191, ss. 1, 2. After the enactment of this statute, the only right of the proprietors of other railroads to enter or run their cars upon it was under the special provisions contained in it."

As an illustration of the recent date of railroad law, it may be noted that the first railroad case decided in the courts was in New York in 1835 — *Camden and Amboy R. R. and Transportation Co.* v. *Burke* (13 Wend. 611) — in which David Graham, Jr., was counsel against William Anthon. The case involved the question whether the company "as proprietor of a line of steamboats and of a

[1] *Fitchburg R. R. Co.* v. *Gage*, 12 Gray, p. 396 (1859).

railroad and carriages between New York and Philadelphia" was liable as a common carrier for loss of "wardrobe, music and musical instruments of the plaintiff's minor son, Master Burke, a stage player."

The earliest cases in Connecticut and Pennsylvania were in 1838, in Maine in 1842, in Vermont in 1847, and in New Hampshire in 1850.

The railroads at first attempted to escape from the rigid Common Law carrier's liability by issuing general notices to restrict their obligations for loss; and the early cases were much concerned with litigation on this subject. It was decided in New York as early as 1838, that such restriction was invalid — *Hollister* v. *Nowlen* (19 Wend. 234), and the United States Supreme Court rendered a like decision in 1848, in *New Jersey Steam Navigation Co.* v. *Merchants' Bank* (6 How. 344), in a case involving a steamboat and an expressman.[1] Later, special notice, brought home to the shipper or passenger, was held to exempt the railroad.

Another much mooted question in the earliest railroad and steamboat cases was whether these new kinds of common carriers were obliged to make delivery of freight at the actual residence or place of business of the consignee. It was to the action of the courts in recognizing usage and convenience as decisive in restricting the railroad's obligations in this respect that the business of expressman owes its origin, about 1838.[2]

Incidentally it is to be noted that the express business constituted another new form of common carrier; and as the *Law Reporter* said, in 1849, in a review of *Angell on*

[1] See *Law of Carriers' Notices* in *Law Reporter*, Vol. XV (1852).

[2] See interesting article on *Power of Usage and Custom to alter the Common Law* by John F. Dillon — *Southern Law Review*, Vol. VII (1881–1882). See also *Law Reporter*, Vol. XIV, p. 134 (1851).

*Carriers*, "the rights and liberties of expressmen have become most important subjects. At one time they deranged our whole postal system; and they have yet to be accurately defined."

No case arose in the United States Supreme Court in which a railroad was a party until 1845 — *Maryland* v. *Baltimore and Ohio R. R.* (3 How. 534), a case involving a stock subscription; not until 1852 was the first railroad accident case argued in that Court — *Philadelphia and Reading R. R.* v. *Derby* (14 How. 468).

As the number of railroad cases decided in Massachusetts practically equalled that of all the other States combined; and as the principles laid down by Chief Justice Shaw practically established the railroad law for the country, the gradual growth of that law from year to year may be substantially traced in the court decisions of that State.

The first mention of the term "railroad" in the Massachusetts reports was *In re Wellington* (16 Pick. 87) in 1834 — "railroads, a recent form of public works." In 1835 came the first case in which a railroad was a party — *Boston Water Power Co.* v. *Boston and Worcester R. R. Corp.* (16 Pick. 512; 23 Pick. 360). In this case, the right of a railroad to exercise the power of eminent domain was considered.

The first tort case against a railroad was not decided until 1839 — *Lowell* v. *Boston and Lowell R. R.* (23 Pick. 24). The first ruling that a railroad was a public work and that its property was intended for public use was in *Worcester* v. *Western R. R.* (4 Metc. 564) in 1842.

In this same year, 1842, came the epoch-making decision of Chief Justice Shaw exempting employers from liability to their employees for negligence of fellow employees—*Farwell* v. *Boston and Worcester R.R.* (4 Metc. 49.)

The most noteworthy fact relative to this case is the extent to which public policy and convenience, formed the grounds of the decision. As Shaw said:

"This is an action of new impression in our courts and involves a principle of great importance. . . . It is an argument against such an action, though certainly not a decisive one that no such action has before been maintained. . . . If we look from considerations of justice to those of policy they will strongly lead to the same conclusions. In considering the rights and obligations arising out of particular relations it is competent for courts of justice to regard considerations of policy and public convenience and to draw from them such rules as will in their practical application best promote the safety and security of all parties concerned."

It is to be recalled that at this date the oldest railroads had been constructed hardly ten years, and they were by no means an assured financial success.[1] Undoubtedly, the fact that a contrary decision would have imposed a great burden on these struggling institutions had a great effect in influencing the decision reached in this case.

The rule of law laid down in this case having been founded on public policy, it is only natural that, at the present time, when public policy tends quite in the opposite direction, the Legislatures should be reversing very generally, by statutory action, the worn-out doctrine. As long

[1] So great were the financial obstacles in the way of railroad promoters, that in most States of the Union, the early railroads were assisted by legislative and municipal grants. It was the lavish expenditure of State money and issue of State bonds in behalf of railroads, which hastened the great commercial panic of 1837, and the subsequent repudiation of the State debts by various States — Maryland, Pennsylvania, Illinois.

In Massachusetts, the Western R. R. which was chartered in 1833 to connect Boston with the West through Albany, did not succeed in raising its capital of $2,000,000 until 1835, and was obliged to obtain assistance from the State of Massachusetts in 1838 through a State subscription to stock.

ago as 1883, a shrewd law-writer pointed out the basis of the doctrine, and thereby foreshadowed its probable future overturn:

"He must be a bold man who would undertake to tell where the doctrine of common employment ends and that of the master's duty to be present begins in any State in the Union. Much of the trouble has arisen from the fact that judges have often failed to perceive that the rule first laid down in Farwell's case was established by a great and wise legislator as a species of protective tariff for the encouragement of infant railway industries. It was a harsh but a plain and simple rule. Pressed by considerations of humanity and public policy the courts began step by step to relax the rule and chaos reigns."[1]

Of the financial difficulties under which railroad promoters worked, Chief Justice Shaw said later:

"Of course, neither the government nor the undertakers had any experience, and could not form any accurate or even approximate estimates of the cost of the work, or the profits to be derived from it. . . . With this want of experience, and with an earnest desire on the part of the public to make an experiment of this new and extraordinary public improvement it would be natural for the government to offer such terms, as would be likely to encourage capitalists to invest their money in public improvements; and after the experience of capitalists, in respect of the turnpikes and canals of the Commonwealth, which had been authorized by the public, but built by the application of private capital, but which as investments had proved in most cases to be ruinous, it was probably no easy matter

[1] See *Future of our Profession* by John M. Shirley, *Amer. Law Review*, Vol. XVII (1883).

In *Stevens* v. *Little Miami R. R. Co.* in the Hamilton Court of Common Pleas in Ohio in 1850, the court states that "it has no respect for *Priestley* v. *Fowler* nor the *Farwell Case*. . . . Sound public policy not in favor."

to awaken anew the confidence of moneyed men in these enterprises." [1]

In 1844, it was decided that, as an incident of its power as a common carrier, a railroad had power to make regulations as to the use of its road and depots — *Com.* v. *Power* (7 Metc. 596), Shaw saying:

"They are in this respect on the footing of owners of steamboats. Both are modern modes of conveyance, but the rules of the common law are applicable to them as they take the place of other modes of carrying passengers."

In 1845, the liability of a railroad for freight stored in its depots and warehouses was decided in *Thomas* v. *Boston and Providence R. R.* (10 Metc. 472), in which Shaw said:

"This is an important question to our community from the magnitude and variety of the interests concerned in it. . . . The proprietors of these novel and important modes of travel and transportation which have received so much public favor have become the carriers of great amounts of merchandise. They advertise for freight . . . and as a legal consequence of such acts they have become common carriers."

In 1847 came the first case of damage from engine sparks, arising under the statute of 1840 (c. 85) imposing a liability for such damage — *Hart* v. *Western R. R.* (13 Metc. 99). Cases of this nature and also cases of injuries caused to cattle straying on the tracks, and to trespassers walking on the tracks constituted the most frequent causes of litigation in these early days of railroad law.

In 1848, the first case involving liability of a railroad for death of a person not a passenger arose in *Carey* v. *Berkshire R. R.* (1 Cush. 475). The decision in this case holding the railroad not liable for death was the first on this

[1] *Boston and Lowell R. R.* v. *Salem and Lowell R. R.*, 2 Gray 1 (1854).

subject in the country, and brought about a series of acts in the various States changing the Common Law rule. The Legislature of Massachusetts had previously acted on the subject in 1840 (c. 80) by imposing a liability to indictment upon a railroad causing death of a passenger.

In 1849, it was decided that a railroad was liable for loss of personal baggage — *Jordan* v. *Fall River R. R.* (5 Cush. 72), the court saying:

"It is now well settled, and it is a matter of great and general convenience and accommodation in this age of general and perpetual travelling, that passenger carriers are responsible for the baggage of a passenger and that the reward for conveying the baggage is included in the passenger's fare. . . . Some persons, and in this particular, the wisest, perhaps take little or nothing with them in travelling, while others take many things and large quantities. . . . Money bona fide taken for travelling expenses and personal use may properly be regarded as forming a part of the traveller's baggage. The time has been in our country when the character and credit of the local currency were such that it was expedient and needful for persons travelling through different States to provide themselves with an amount which could not conveniently be carried about the person to defray travelling expenses."

In the same year, 1849, the first accident case brought by a passenger was decided — *McElroy* v. *Nashua and Lowell R. R.* (4 Cush. 400).

In 1854, the question of the liability of a railroad for loss or damage occurring beyond its own line on freight shipped to a point on another railroad was decided in *Nutting* v. *Conn. River R. R.* (1 Gray 502).

In 1855, the first railway mortgage case — *Shaw* v. *Norfolk County R. R.* (5 Gray 162) — was argued by the two leaders of the Massachusetts Bar, Sidney Bartlett against Rufus Choate.

In 1858, the much mooted question of the liability of landowners to fence their lands to prevent cattle from straying on the railroad tracks was decided in Massachusetts in *Browne* v. *Providence, etc. R. R.* (12 Gray 59), in which the court said:

"In view of the recent origin of railroads and of the dangers that attend their operations by means of steam which was never used on highways as a motive power, we cannot think that the law (statute) by which these defendants were bound to make all needful fences and cattle guards by the sides of their road was intended to hold them only to the Common Law duty and liability of adjoining lands, under the old order of things; but we are of opinion that it was intended to be applied to the 'new circumstances and conditions of things arising out of the general introduction and use of railroads in the country.'"

The question had arisen in New York as early as 1848.[1]

Such was the general course of development of railroad law in Massachusetts; and with slight variations it was typical of the progress of the law in other States.

The first law book which treated of railroads was published in 1849 — *Angell on Carriers* — which included railroad law as a part of the general law of carriers.[2] In its preface it is said:

[1] See *Tonawanda R. R.* v. *Munga*, 5 Denio 225; 4 Comstock 255; *Clark* v. *Syracuse and Utica R. R.*, 11 Barbour 112; *Jackson* v. *Rutland and Burlington R. R.*, 25 Vermont, 150 (1853).

[2] "In the review of this book in the *Law Reporter*, in 1849, Vol. XII, it is said:

"The law of carriers especially in this country has acquired a peculiar importance. The extent of the American confederacy, that perfect system of free trade which is kept up within its limits and the increased facilities of travelling and transportation contribute to this result. Under these circumstances, it is remarkable that we have not had hitherto any work devoted exclusively to this subject except two English treatises, one by Jer-

"Since the commencement of the present century, and more especially since American inventive genius has rendered the accelerative and reliable agency of steam subservient to the transportation of commodities and of travellers, the legal duties, liabilities and rights of public carriers of both things and persons have become subjects of vastly more interest and greater moment than before this era was realized or even generally anticipated. . . . So instrumental have railroads proved, in combination with the employment of the agency just mentioned, in cementing in this connection and dependence sections of the country far removed from each other, that the interest of the mercantile and travelling public, and more especially of the legal profession, in the direction of the subject of the following work has attained its acme."

Six years later, in 1855, was published Judge Milo L. Bennett's edition of an English work Shelford's *Law of Railways* — "the best treatise we have on the subject," said the *American Law Register* (Vol. III).

In 1857 came the first American text-book devoted entirely to the subject — Edward L. Pierce's *Review of American Railroad Law* — "the first book of the kind upon a subject of increasing interest" said the *Law Reporter* (Vol. XX).

In 1858 appeared Judge Isaac F. Redfield's book on *Railways*, in the preface to which the author speaks of this

emy published in 1815, one by Jones (George Frederic), published in 1827. The only other sources to which we can recur for an exposition of this branch of the law are the leading case of *Coggs* v. *Bernard* (2 Lord Raym.) 909, by which Lord Chief Justice Holt incorporated the whole of the civil law on the subject of bailments into the common law of England, and the two treatises, English and American, on the *Law of Bailments*, the first by Sir William Jones and the latter by the late Mr. Justice Story.

". . . In Lord Holt's decision, however, and in each of the treatises we have named, the law of carriers is considered in its place only as a part of the comprehensive law of bailments. Besides, so great have been the changes in the mode of travelling within the past few years that even the recent work of Mr. Justice Story may require some modification."

"law appropriate to a department of enterprise which combines the grandest material energies of the age and unfolds views of national greatness which patriotism delights to contemplate." [1]

Probably no economic institution was more affected in its growth, and no branch of law received greater impetus, between the years 1830 and 1860, through judicial decisions, than that of corporations; and the great increase in number and influence of corporations was largely affected by the doctrines laid down by the courts.

In the earlier years, the corporations were much restricted in their growth by statutory provisions imposing on stockholders the liability of partners. Notwithstanding these restrictions, as early as 1826, Kent in his *Commentaries* [2] referred to "the propensity in modern times to multiply civil corporations, especially in the United States, where they have increased in a rapid manner and to a most astonishing extent. The various acts of incorpora-

[1] In a review of this book, the *Law Reporter* (Vol. XX) said:

"To many of the profession the time has been since they began to practise that a book with such a title would have been a matter of new and curious speculation. . . . As a single illustration in the first three volumes of the U. S. Digest bringing down the decided cases to near 1847 there were only two cases to be found under the head of Railroad.

"The next two volumes contain only about 50 of these cases. So rapidly had they multiplied, however, that the volume for the single year 1855, containing the cases in 48 volumes of reports, embraces as many under the head of Railroad within some two or three as are found in the digests of the whole 650 volumes just mentioned.

"No better or more striking illustration of the flexibility and expansion of the common law to new circumstances can be offered than the readiness and ease with which it supplies the rules and elements of jurisprudence by which the multifarious interests and relations upon the subject of railways are regulated. And what, moreover, ought to increase our confidence in and respect for the common law is the general uniformity which prevails in the decision of these questions as they have arisen from time to time in the courts of some thirty different and independent States."

[2] *Kent's Commentaries*, Vol. II, pp. 219–220 (1st ed., 1827).

tion . . . constitute a mighty mass of charters which occupy a large part of the volumes of the statute law. The demands for acts of incorporation is continually increasing and the propensity is the more striking as it appears to be incurable; and we seem to have no moral means to resist it, as was done at Rome by the unshaken determination of the Emperor Trojan."

Of the policy up to 1826, Kent wrote:[1]

"There has been a disposition in some of the States to change in an essential degree the character of incorporated companies, by making the members personally responsible in certain events and to a qualified extent for the debts of the company. This is intended as a check to improvident conduct and abuse and to add to the general security of creditors; and the policy has been pursued to a moderate and reasonable degree only in Rhode Island, New York, Maryland and South Carolina. . . . The tendency of legislation and of judicial decisions in the several States is to increase the personal responsibility of stockholders, . . . and to give them more and more the character of partnerships with some of the power and privileges of corporations."

Legislation of this character had been the standing policy of Massachusetts — the State of the greatest number of manufacturing corporations — from 1809 to 1827.[2]

1 *Kent's Commentaries*, Vol. II, p. 273, note b (5th ed., 1844).

2 See Remarks of Chief Justice Parker in *Marcy* v. *Clark*, 17 Mass. 335, in 1821:

"The legislature have thought fit and we think wisely to subject the property of all members of these corporations to a liability for the debts of the company. By this, in fact, they only continue the principle of copartnership in operation; and considering the multitude of corporations which the increasing spirit of manufacturing gives rise to, regard to the interest of the community seems to require that the individuals whose property thus put into a common mass enables them to obtain credit universally, should not shelter themselves from a responsibility to which they would be liable as members of a private association.

"Since this statute was enacted all who deal with such companies look for their security to the individual members rather than to this joint stock."

But in his message to the Legislature, June 2, 1825, Governor Levi Lincoln recommended a relaxation of this policy, saying:

"As the law now exists, it is to be feared that no inconsiderable portion of advantage which would result from the employment of capital in a profitable business and from the encouragement of an industrious population is lost to the Commonwealth.

"In this age of great undertakings and of strenuous competition for pre-eminence in local advantages and influence, it is surely wise to regard with care the permanent resources of the Commonwealth. These will be found especially to consist in the profitable investment at home of the monied capital of our wealthy citizens, and in the encouragement of employment thereby of an ingenious, industrious and virtuous population."

And in his message of May 31, 1826, he said:

"The number of corporations already created and the immense amount of capital employed in their operation must prevent the possibility hereafter of a successful competition with them in business by individual means, and presents the single inquiry whether these public establishments can advantageously be multiplied and encouraged. The period has long since passed in which the manufacturing interest could be regarded as unfavorable to commerce or inconsistent with the prosperity of an agricultural people."

"The effect has been to drive millions of capital into other States for investment." — "The unreasonable severity of the present laws is a subject of general complaint." said writers in the *American Jurist*, in 1829 and 1830.[1]

[1] See *Manufacturing Corporations; Constitutionality of Corporators Liability Laws*, by Charles G. Loring in *American Jurist*, Vol. II (1829); Vol. IV (1830); Vol. V (1832).

See also, St. 1808, c. 65; St. 1817, c. 183; St. 1821, c. 38; St. 1822, c. 638; St. 1826, c. 137; St. 1829, c. 53; and *Child* v. *Coffin*, 17 Mass. 64 (1820).

By an act passed in 1830, however, Massachusetts began to adopt a more liberal policy towards stockholders. At the same time, nevertheless, and even in those early days of corporate activity, there was generally prevalent a fear of the increase of corporations, an example of which may be found in the *American Jurist*, in October, 1830:

"In our republics, they are still more numerous; and it is difficult to set bounds to the general desire to increase them. . . . Unless restrained by legislative enactment, judicial construction or the good sense and discretion of the stockholders, they will absorb the greatest part of the substance of the Commonwealth. The extent of the wealth and power of corporations among us demands that plain and clear laws should be declared for their regular restraint; for without a salutary and strict control over them everyone may be compelled to adopt the fears of the Roman Emperor who when requested to institute a fire company of 150 men on an assurance that they should not exceed their powers beyond the objects of the association, refused the grant, observing that associations had greatly disturbed the peace of cities and whatever name he gave them they would not fail to be mischievous (2 Kent, 217).

"The doctrine of corporations in this country, on account of their extent as well as the defective state of their existence and operation, presents a most interesting field of inquiry to American jurists, and demands that their best energies should be applied to the subject and that corporations may be protected and wisely directed in effecting the great public good of which they are capable and restrained from inflicting the public and private evils within their powers and to which they are often tempted by their own views of interest. . . . The courts of Massachusetts have made many decisions from which it must be inferred that they favor the doctrine and are inclined to adopt it that corporations have no powers but such as are plainly granted in their charters or are clearly necessary to effect the useful purposes for which they were created.

Such rules of construction can hardly be considered yet as established anywhere in their full extent.

"In the courts above referred to [N. Y., U. S., Mass.] the Common Law incidents to corporations are sometimes cited with approbation, and in other State courts they are generally referred to without qualification. The evident utility of the new construction will probably soon recommend it to general adoption.

"When such becomes the declared law of the States, and when it shall become the law that corporations are generally liable for the acts of their authorized agents; for contracts by implication; for all wrongs and injuries that they are capable of inflicting; and for all injurious omissions to perform their duties, there will be no longer need of statutes of mortmain and wills; or constitutional impediments or restraints to the multiplication of corporate charters. It might still, however, be wise for legislatures to reserve more direct control over corporations of future creation than they are accustomed to do in most of the States. . . .

"When these doctrines shall become fully established and legislatures grow careful to reserve visitorial powers in granting charters for civil corporations, the fear and apprehension of corporations now existing and too justly forced by experience into the public mind, will probably subside. Such fears have induced the legislatures in some States to adopt measures which should and to a great extent do deter the public from encountering the perils resulting from the ownership of corporate stocks."[1]

[1] Governor Lincoln himself, in vetoing a bill to authorize the incorporation of the Mozart Association in Salem, with power to hold real estate to the value of $10,000, said February 16, 1827:

"The course of legislation for several of the last years has a tendency to absorb individual property in the capital of corporations and thereby to destroy its future divisibility and voluntary disposition to an extent I believe which is hardly apprehended by the community. It may well deserve regard to what consequences an unrestricted indulgence in this policy may lead. . . . The worst evils of a monopoly of wealth and possessions in corporations on the one hand, and of consequent poverty and dependence in individuals on the other, will commence and be aggravated, until by the

After 1827, the more liberal legislation limiting stockholders' liability promoted the turning of partnerships into trading and manufacturing corporations. The protective tariffs and the increasing production of coal were a great factor in the growth of these corporations. The expiration of the charter of the United States Bank in 1836 caused large numbers of State and private banks to be incorporated. Life insurance corporations were just coming into existence. Fire insurance corporations were being much more extensively developed. The era of railroad corporations began in 1830.

By 1832, the body of corporation law had become so large as to demand a text-book, and in that year appeared the first American and the first modern book on the subject — *Angell and Ames on Corporations.* In the preface, the authors stated:

"The inconvenience experienced from the want of a work of reference upon the legal rights and obligations which grow out of the relations between a body corporate and the public and between a body corporate and its members has in this country long been a subject of complaint."

And they cite a comment by Judge Roger in *Bushel* v. *Commonwealth Ins. Co.* (15 Serg. & Rawle, 176):

"With the multiplication of corporations which has and is taking place to an almost indefinite extent, there has been a corresponding change in the law respecting them. . . . This change of law has arisen from that silent legislation by the people themselves which is continually

intervention of statutes of mortmain and other violent legal enactments, or by popular excitement and revolution, the grievous and intolerable pressure of corporate power over individual possession shall be removed and property again be restored to those who by the laws of nature had the original right to its enjoyment."

going on in a country such as ours, the more wholesome because it is gradual and wisely adapted to the peculiar situation, wants and habits of our citizens." [1]

It is to be noted that, at this time, most of these corporations were created by special charters; for general incorporation acts existed in but few States.[2] The first general statute had been enacted in Pennsylvania in 1791, authorizing incorporation generally of literary, charitable and religious associations. In New York, a general act for public libraries was passed in 1796, and for business corporations in 1811; but by the Constitution of 1821, the people of the State, alarmed at the tremendous increase of corporations, provided that no charter should be granted except by a two-thirds vote of each branch of the Legislature. Georgia enacted general manufacturing corporation acts in 1843 and 1845. New York enacted the broadest general corporation act in the country in 1848; and in 1849, Pennsylvania enacted a general business corporation act. Massachusetts had no general manufacturing or banking corporation acts until as late as 1851. As the *Law Reporter* stated in that year (Vol. XIV):

"In Massachusetts, similar provision existed before in regard to parishes and religious societies, wharves and some other real estate ownerships, lyceums and cemeteries, and some other specified cases; but it was taken for granted

[1] Chief Justice Shaw in *Tisdale* v. *Harris* (20 Pick. 9) in 1838 holding stock certificates within the Statute of Frauds said:

"These companies have become so numerous, so large an amount of the property of the community is invested in them, and as the ordinary indicia of property arising from delivery and possession cannot take place, there seems to be peculiar reasons for extending the provisions of the statute to them."

[2] See *Address of Henry Hitchcock* in *Amer. Bar Ass. Proc.*, Vol. X.

In 1784 in New York, and in 1787 in Delaware, general statutes were enacted for incorporation of religious societies.

that such provision could not be safely applied, as it had been done in other States, to corporations generally, and especially those of a trading or business nature. The Legislature has overstepped this line in the case of manufacturing companies and banks, and we think wisely. We believe . . . we shall see laws passed hereafter to meet the analogous cases of insurance and railroad corporations."[1]

A general insurance act was not passed in Massachusetts until 1872; a general railroad act, until 1872; and a street railway act, until 1874.

The influence of the decision in the *Dartmouth College Case* on corporation law during this period was very pronounced. That case, deciding that a corporate charter was a contract and within the protection of the United States Constitution, gave a great impetus to the creation of corporations; and so many valuable rights were irrevocably granted away in corporate charters by the State Legislatures, that a movement began to change this condition of affairs. Acting on a precedent adopted on the suggestion of Chief Justice Parsons, as early as 1809, in an act incorporating manufacturing companies, the Legislature of Massachusetts in 1830 passed a general statute relating to all corporations, and making every charter thereafter granted subject to the right of the Legislature to alter, amend or repeal. New York had already inserted a similar clause in its Constitution of 1826. Connecticut and other States had been accustomed for several years to append such clauses to all special corporate charters. Wisconsin followed Massachusetts in 1848, and California in 1849. Many States, however, still hesitated, especially

[1] The number of special charters to manufacturing corporations in Massachusetts is stated in the *Law Reporter*, Vol. XXII, in 1859, as follows: between 1780 and 1809, 9; 1800–1817, 100; 1780–1835, 500; 1835–1859, about 30 per annum.

those that were undeveloped and had the greatest need for corporations.[1]

In 1838, a question of corporate law arose, the decision of which was likely to affect the course of commercial dealings in the United States to a greater degree than any decision since that in the great steamboat case of *Gibbons* v. *Ogden*, in 1824.

In the United States Circuit Court in Alabama, a railroad company incorporated in Louisiana had brought suit

[1] *Rise and Probable Decline of Private Corporations*, by Andrew Allison, *Amer. Bar Ass. Proc.*, Vol. IV (1881).

It is interesting to note that the fear of corporations continued extremely prevalent. It was well stated by a Massachusetts lawyer of prominence, Robert Rantoul, Jr., in an argument, made in 1835 in the Massachusetts Legislature, in protest against a special charter to an iron and steel company with a capital as large as $500,000:

"The evil of incorporation had become so great that the justice of the opinions expressed in Gov. Lincoln's message (vetoing the incorporation of the Mozart Society) was immediately acknowledged by the Legislature. This evil has increased; it is infinitely greater now than it was in 1827; and by and by the subject will become the first in the eye of the people. The people will stand up against corporations. They will say, 'we will see whether the citizens of the Commonwealth are to govern themselves or are to be governed by corporations.' . . . A great party will grow up against them, and then corporations must look to themselves. . . . Agrarianism, levelling, Jacobinism, war of the poor against the rich — these are the cries against me. This is stale trash. . . . In all the earliest manufacturing corporations the stockholders were mostly leading federalists, and the whole power of the corporation was federal power."

Two years later, in 1837, the same apprehension as to monopolies and wealthy corporations appeared judicially in the opinion given by Judge Marcus Morton of the Massachusetts Supreme Court in *Alger* v. *Thatcher* (19 Pick. 51). This was the first well considered case on restraint of trade decided in the United States and Judge Morton said:

"The law . . . is found on great principles of public policy and carries out our constitutional prohibition of monopolies and exclusive privileges. . . . Such contracts . . . prevent competition and enhance prices. They expose the public to all the evils of monopoly. And this especially is applicable to wealthy companies and large corporations who have the means unless restrained by law to exclude rivalry, monopolize business and engross the market."

on a bill of exchange made and discounted by it in Alabama. The question had thus been presented of the power of a corporation to make and sue on a contract, signed outside the State in which it was chartered. To the surprise and consternation of the business interests of the country, Mr. Justice McKinley of the United States Supreme Court, sitting in the Circuit Court, decided that a corporation had no power to do business in a State other than that in which it was incorporated. The effect produced by this decision is graphically described by Judge Story in a letter to Charles Sumner, June 17, 1838:[1]

"My brother McKinley has recently made a most sweeping decision in the Circuit Court in Alabama which has frightened half the lawyers and all the corporations of the country out of their proprieties. He has held that a corporation created in one State has no power to contract (or, it would seem, even to act) in any other State either directly or by an agent. So banks, insurance companies, manufacturing companies, etc., have no capacity to take or discount notes in another State or to underwrite policies or to buy or sell goods. The cases in which he has made these decisions have gone to the Supreme Court. What say you to all this? So we go!"

As the Bank of the United States and other moneyed corporations had, for many years, been in the habit of discounting bills in States throughout the country, this decision opened the door to widespread repudiation of their obligations by debtors whose contracts were made in States other than the chartering State. These debtors at once took advantage of the defense thus offered to them. Manufacturing and trading corporations hesitated to continue to do business in outside States. The business of the fire and life insurance companies which were just being organ-

[1] Unpublished letter in *Sumner Papers* in Harv. Coll. Library.

ized for the first time to any great extent, was curtailed. General commercial confusion ensued. The disastrous result of this decision was also enhanced by its being rendered at a time when the effects of the great financial panic of 1837 were still being severely felt.

Ex-Chancellor Kent and other eminent lawyers, being consulted, gave their opinions against the doctrine laid down by Judge McKinley.[1] Steps were at once taken to carry the case to the United States Supreme Court. Accordingly, in 1839, the great case of *Bank of Augusta* v. *Earle* (13 Peters, 519) was argued before that Court by David B. Ogden of New York, Daniel Webster of Massachusetts and John Sergeant of Pennsylvania, against Charles J. Ingersoll of Pennsylvania and William H. Crawford of Georgia.[2]

The arguments were largely based on considerations of public policy and economics, the counsel for the plaintiffs arguing with great ardor the inconvenience, mischief, injustice and injury which would result to commerce and trade, if the decision of the Circuit Court should be upheld.

Thus David B. Ogden argued:

"A deeper wound will be inflicted on the commercial business of the United States than it has ever sustained. The principal means by which the commercial dealings between the States of the United States and Alabama is conducted will be at an end; and there will be no longer the facilities for intercourse for the purposes of traffic by which alone it is prosperous and beneficial. . . . The purchases of bills of exchange in that State are extensively made by the agents of corporations of other States; thus by the competition which is produced, the rates of ex-

[1] See opinion of Kent, printed in full in *Law Reporter*, Vol. I, July, 1838.

[2] There were three cases consolidated for argument — *New Orleans and Carrollton R. R. Co.* v. *Earle*, *Bank of the United States* v. *Earle*, and *Bank of Augusta* v. *Earle*.

change are kept in due proportion to those of other States. The large productions of cotton in that State are thus enabled to realize to the planter a proper and an equal price to that obtained by the planter in the neighboring States. The proposition in the Circuit Court . . . is that a corporation of one State can do no commercial business, can make no contract and can do nothing in any State of the Union but in that in which it has been created. The proposition is the more injurious as in the United States associated capital is essentially necessary to the operations of commerce and the creation and improvement of the facilities of intercourse which can only be accomplished by large means. . . . One of the most important objects and interests for the preservation of the Union is the establishment of railroads. Cannot the railroad corporations of New York, Pennsylvania or Maryland make a contract out of the State for materials for the construction of a railroad? Cannot these companies procure machinery to use on their railroads, in another State?"

And Daniel Webster said:

"A learned gentleman on the other side said the other day that he thought he might regard himself in this cause as having the country for his client. . . . I agree with the learned gentleman, and I go indeed far beyond him in my estimate of the importance of this case to the country. . . . For myself, I see neither limit nor end to the calamitous consequences of such a decision. I do not know where it would not reach, what interests it would not disturb, or how any part of the commercial system of the country would be free from its influence, direct or remote."

On the other side, Charles J. Ingersoll pointed out the danger of increasing the power of corporations in this country, and insisted that a State ought not to be forced, by any doctrine of comity or otherwise, to allow a corporation of another State to do business within its borders:

"It is true that in order to keep pace with the flood of these associations, the Common Law with its characteristic adaptation to exigencies has counteracted their intolerable privilege by holding them to personal liability. . . . Power to pronounce it (the Common Law) impolitic, to break in upon or discard it, if it exists in any court should be sparingly exercised. . . . These United States as such can have no private corporation; and if upon false notions of commercial intimacy they are to be consolidated by traders, corporations and professional dogmas, contrary to the true spirit of our political institutions, not only the rights of all the States but the Federal Constitution itself will be at an end. . . . It is confidently submitted to the Court that it will best fulfil its duties by holding the States united by sovereign ties; by the State remaining sovereign and the corporations subject; not by sovereign corporations and subject States. . . . If courts are bound by Common Law to restrict corporations to the specific purposes of their creation, they are bound by the same Common Law to prevent their wandering out of place as much as out of purpose. . . . This is perhaps a question rather of politics than of jurisprudence."

The Court, in an opinion rendered by Chief Justice Taney, overruled the Circuit Court and denied the doctrine of the confinement of a corporation to business within the State of its charter. From the decision of this case, therefore, the great development of interstate corporate business may be said to date.

The following interesting comment is made by William M. Meigs in his *Life of Charles J. Ingersoll:*

"This was a very important case — rather one of politics or public law than of mere private right between suitors. Mr. Ingersoll . . . entered into the case with intense interest . . . and was evidently disappointed at losing, and wrote to Mr. (Henry D.) Gilpin to that effect, but was told in reply that he should not be worried at his inability to defeat a corporation when the whole country had to bear them, as Sinbad had his burden. . . . The prevailing view today probably is that the decision was both right and desirable; but such questions were then far more open to doubt in the public mind than now; and the thoughtful observer may well question in view of the unrest now so prevalent (1897) and the so general feeling that organized capital has too much power, whether our country might not have been more sound at the core if some of the most important decisions had gone the other way."

One other decision of the United States Supreme Court during this period had immense effect on the growth of modern corporate commerce.

From 1809 to 1844, it had been held by that Court, ever since the decision of Chief Justice Marshall in *Bank of the United States* v. *Deveaux* (5 Cranch, 61), that the Federal Courts had no jurisdiction on the ground of diverse citizenship, in a case where a corporation was a party, unless all the individual stockholders of the corporation were citizens of a State other than that of the other party to the suit. Such a doctrine of course greatly restricted the rights of a corporation to sue in a Federal Court, and made such suit almost impossible.

In 1844, however, in *Louisville R. R.* v. *Letson* (2 Howard, 497) Chief Justice Taney delivered an opinion, taking the broad ground that a corporation, although an artificial person, was to be deemed an inhabitant of the State of its incorporation, and to be treated as a citizen of that State for purposes of suit. Of this case, Judge Story, wrote to Ex-Chancellor Kent, August 31, 1844:

"I equally rejoice, that the Supreme Court has at last come to the conclusion, that a corporation is a citizen, an artificial citizen, I agree, but still a citizen. It gets rid of a great anomaly in our jurisprudence. This was always Judge Washington's opinion. I have held the same opinion for very many years, and Mr. Chief Justice Marshall had, before his death, arrived at the conclusion, that our early decisions were wrong."

In 1853, in *Marshall* v. *Baltimore and Ohio R. R.* (16 Howard, 314) it was held that there was a conclusive presumption of law that all the shareholders were citizens of the State of incorporation; and this was further strengthened by a decision in 1857, in *Covington Drawbridge Co.* v. *Shepherd* (20 Howard, 227) that parties were to be held estopped from denying such citizenship.[1]

These decisions not only opened the door wide to interstate commerce by corporations, but they were of vast importance in breaking down the barriers sought to be erected by the political supporters of the narrow States' Rights doctrines, and in increasing the strength of the Federal power.

In one direction, the great growth of corporations made necessary the development of a branch of corporate law to which little attention had hitherto been paid — the limits of the scope of corporate action and the doctrine of *ultra vires*. As stated in the preface to the first book on this subject, *Brice on Ultra Vires* published in 1874, it is said:

"The doctrine of ultra virés is of modern growth. Its appearance as a distinct fact and as a guiding and rather misleading principle in the legal system of this country dates from about 1845, being first prominently mentioned in the cases, in equity of *Colman* v. *Eastern Counties Ry. Co.* (10 Beavan, 1) in 1846, and at law of *East Anglian Ry. Co.* v. *Eastern Counties Ry. Co.* (11 C. B. 775) in 1851."

In the United States Supreme Court, however, in 1858, it was referred to as "not a new principle in the jurisprudence of this Court." [2]

[1] For interesting articles on this subject see *A Legal Fiction with its Wings Clipped*, by S. E. Baldwin, in *Amer. Law Review*, Vol. XLI (1907). *Abrogation of Federal Jurisdiction*, by Alfred Russell, *Harv. Law Review*, Vol. VII (1892). *Corporate Citizenship a Legal Fiction*, by R. M. Benjamin, *Albany Law Journal*, Vol. LXIX (1907).

[2] *Pearce* v. *Railroad Co.*, 21 Howard, 441.

This period, 1830–1860, also witnessed the beginning of the formation of the law as to the financial management of corporations — questions relating to the status of shares of stock, overissues, fully paid stock, coupon bonds and the like, the law as to which, however, was not finally put in satisfactory shape until after 1860. The rudimentary conditions of the law as to the financing of corporations may be gathered from the following statements in *Redfield on Railways*, published in 1858:

"But few questions in regard to the subject of railway investments have been definitely settled in this country. . . . There have been some expedients resorted to for purpose of enabling companies to complete their works without the requisite capital bona fide subscribed paid, which, as they do not seem to have come much under discussion in the judicial tribunals of the country, we could do little more than allude to, but which have so serious a bearing upon the safety and permanent value of railway investments that we could not perhaps with perfect propriety altogether pass over them. . . .

"There is very little law as yet in this country as to the power of a railway corporation to mortgage the property and franchise without statutory authority."

# CHAPTER XIX

## THE ERA OF CODES, 1820–1860

THE years 1820–1850 were a period not only of adjustment of the Common Law to fit modern conditions, but also of a widespread movement towards the codification of the law.

So many new subjects of legislation had arisen, so many changes from the old Common Law had been made necessary by the new economic and social conditions, that the statute books of most of the older States contained an accumulation of resolves and statutes, contradictory, illogical, unnecessary, partly repealed, and partly obsolete.

The popular trend towards codification was the result of five intermingling factors: first, the old, underlying antagonism of the American public towards the Common Law, as being of English origin; second, the ever-active jealousy, entertained by laymen in a democracy, towards lawyers, as a privileged class and a monopoly, and the consequent desire to make the law a layman's law; third, the increase in the number of law reports deemed, even then, to be "vast and unwieldy;" fourth, the success of the *Code Napoléon* in Europe; fifth, the influence of Jeremy Bentham.

Of the existence, as late as 1820, of the popular prejudices against the Common Law because it was English, description has already been given. A conservative expression of this feeling was given by Charles J. Ingersoll, an eminent lawyer of Philadelphia, in an address made by him in 1823, as follows:[1]

"The number of the Bar has been lately computed at 6,000, which is probably an under estimate. American lawyers and judges adhere with professional tenacity to the laws of the Mother Country. The absolute authority of recent English adjudications is disclaimed; but they are received with a respect, too much bordering on submission. British Commercial Law, in many respects inferior to that of the continent of Europe, is becoming the law of America. The prize law of Great Britain was made that of the United States by judicial legislation during flagrant war between the two countries. . . . Our professional bigotry has been counteracted by penal laws in some States against the quotation of recent British precedents, as it was once a capital offence in Spain to cite the Civil Law, and as the English Common Law has always repelled that excellent code from its tribunals. . . .

". . . I deplore the colonial acquiescence in which they (the late English law books) are adopted, too often without probation or fitness. The use and respect of American Jurisprudence in Great Britain will begin, only when we cease to prefer their adjudications to our own. By the sáme means, we shall be relieved from disadvantageous restrictions on our own use of British wisdom; and our system will acquire that level to which it is entitled by the education, learning and purity of those by whose administration it is formed.

". . . The brutal, ferocious and inhuman law of the feudists, as they were termed by the civilians (I use their own phrase), the arbitrary rescripts of the Civil Law, and the harsh doctrines of the Common Law have all been melted down by the genial mildness of American institutions. Most of the feudal distinctions between real and personal property, complicated tenures, and primogeniture, the

[1] *A Discourse concerning the Influence of America on the Mind*, by Charles J. Ingersoll (1823).

salique exclusion of females, the unnatural rejection of the half-blood, and ante-nuptial offspring, forfeitures for crimes, the penalties of alienage, and other vices of European jurisprudence, which nothing but their existence can defend, and reason must condemn are either abolished or in a course of abrogation here. Cognisance of marriage, divorce and posthumous administration, taken from ecclesiastical, has been conferred on the civil, tribunals. Voluminous conveyancing and intricate special pleading, among the costliest systems of professional learning in Great Britain, have given place to the plain cheap substitutes of the old Common Law. . . . Sanguinary and corporal punishments are yielding to the interesting experiment of penitential confinement."

A natural result of this trend of thought was to inculcate the belief that a brand new body of strictly American law could and should be constructed and formulated in codes, which would render the United States independent of English law.

The second factor — the jealousy of lawyers because of their supposed special privileges — a deeply rooted feeling which had existed in the United States for almost two centuries, was the influence which especially led to the statutory revision of the old Common Law system of pleading; for the intricate science of special pleading and the technicalities of the Common Law were supposed to be the means adopted by the lawyers, as a class, to disable the uninitiated from maintaining or defending their causes in courts. The Bar Associations and the Bar rules were also supposed to protect lawyers in their attempt to monopolize a knowledge of the law. It was to render this monopoly less possible that the laymen were anxious by legislation to make law so plain, that every man might be his own lawyer.

In 1786, as already described, the prejudice against

lawyers resulted in violent outbreaks against them as "an undemocratic order;" and many plans had been promulgated for a total reform in the system of Bar rules and Bar Associations in the New England States and elsewhere. Nearly fifty years later, in 1832, a layman of Essex County in Massachusetts, whose right to appear as attorney in a court case had been questioned by Rufus Choate, published an open letter to Choate in which the alleged attitude of the legal profession was thus complained of: [1]

"But you have other arts still more effectual to secure your privileged order a monopoly in the practice of the law. By adopting the Common Law of Great Britain, the customs of the most barbarous ages, and of a nation whose principles of government are totally abhorrent to our own, customs contained in a thousand different books so intricate, so ambiguous, so contradictory that no man ever yet understood them — and by involving the practice of the law in inexplicable obscurity and formality, by the adoption of all the cumbrous learning of special feeling, by motions for non-suits, for discontinuances, for nolle prosequi, for retraxit, for injunctions, for continuance; by imparlance, by whole defence, by half defence, by oyers, by proferts, by vouchers, by aid prayers, by tenders, by protestandoes, by estoppels, by averments, by giving color, by demurring for duplicity, for departure, for repugnance, for negative pregnants, for surplusage, for prolixity, for verification; by pleading generally, by pleading specially, by pleading double, bypleading in abatement, by replication, by rejoinders, by surrejoinders, by rebutters, by surrebutters, by joining issue; by hard words in the Saxon, in the Norman, in the French, in the Latin; and by having the judges also members of your fraternity and interested in your monopoly — you have heretofore contrived to exclude everyone who would not submit to your offensive exactions,

[1] *A Letter to the Hon. Rufus Choate containing a brief exposure of Law Craft and some of the encroachments of the Bar upon the Rights and Liberties of the People*, by Frederic Robinson (1832).

to all your unconstitutional rules, and regulations, from the important right of doing business in our public courts. It seems to have been the whole study of your brotherhood in this way to involve the laws and the practice of the laws in such a dark maze of uncertainty as to render it impossible for anyone to practise law, without a previous understanding with every other practitioner."

In fact, this popular feeling against lawyers as a priviledge body almost warranted De Tocqueville's well known description (written in 1835) of the American lawyers, as "the American aristocracy:"

"The special information which lawyers derive from their studies ensures them a separate station in society; and they constitute a sort of privileged body in the scale of intelligence. . . . Lawyers are attached to public order beyond every other consideration and the best security of public order is authority. . . . In the mind of an English or an American lawyer, a taste and reverence for what is old is almost always united to a love of regular and lawful proceedings. . . . In America there are no nobles or literary men, and the people are apt to mistrust the wealthy; lawyers consequently form the highest political class and the most cultivated circle of society. They have therefore nothing to gain by innovation, which adds a conservative interest to their natural taste for public order. If I were asked where I place the American Aristocracy, I should reply without hesitation, that it is not composed of the rich, who are united by no common tie, but that it occupies the judicial bench and the bar."

The third factor in the movement towards codification in the United States was the success in Europe of the various Codes known as the *Code Napoléon*. These Codes, being published in this country about the time of the War of 1812, when the anti-English feeling was at its height, naturally met with favorable consideration.[1]

[1] See *Review of The Code Napoléon*, by Edward Everett — *North American Review*, Vol. XX (1825).

The most important factor, however, in the crusade for the codification of the law was the influence of the works of Jeremy Bentham and his followers. It was Bentham who first impressed the subject upon the public mind of England. He was the inventor of the words, "codify," and "codification." In fact, the word "code," in its modern significance, does not appear to have been in common use, prior to 1797 — forty-nine years after his birth; though several of the old English law books have been designated as codes, by writers who apply the word wrongly to any unofficial compilation of the law — such as the *Miroir des Justices* (written in 1307 and first printed in 1642).[1] The true meaning of the word, however, is the official declaration of the body of the law or of sections of law by legislative or executive act, and it was to obtain a code of this kind that Bentham devoted his lifelong labors. The first movement towards such a code in England was taken by Francis Bacon, who, when only thirty-one years old, proposed in the House of Commons, in 1592, a plan to amend and consolidate the whole body of English law. About fifty years later, in Cromwell's time, a Commission was appointed to take into consideration "what inconveniences there are in the law and how the mischiefs that grow from the delay, the changeableness, and the irregularities in law proceedings may be prevented and the speediest way to reform the same." And in 1653, Sir Matthew Hale, as

See also *The Historical Development of Code Pleading*, by Charles M. Hepburn (1897).

The *Code Civile* was reported in 1801, by the Commission appointed to draft it, and it was published in France in 1805; the *Code de Procédure Civile* was published in France in 1806; the *Code de Commerce* and the *Code Pénale* were published in France, in 1817 and 1810, respectively, and by Peter S. DuPonceau, in the United States in the *American Review* (Vol. II), in 1811 (the former being also republished in the *United States Law Journal*, in 1823); the *Code d'Instruction Criminelle* was published in France, in 1808.

[1] See *Early English Codes*, in *Law Mag. and Rev.*, Vol. XXX (1870–1871).

chairman of a Commission, of which Cromwell himself, Sir Algernon Sydney, and Sir Anthony Ashley Cooper were also members, drew up a plan for law reform. It failed of adoption, however. "The lawyers were opposed," said Cromwell. "These sons of Zeruiah are yet too strong for us; and we cannot mention the reformation of the law but they presently cry out we design to destroy propriety."

That grave need of at least a statutory revision was felt even in those days, may be seen from the following entry in *Pepys Diary*, April 25, 1666:

"Mr. Prin, till company came did discourse with me a good while about the laws of England, telling me the main faults in them; and amongst others their obscurity through multitude of long statutes, which he is about to abstract out of all of a sort, and as he lives and Parliament, get them put into laws and the other statutes repealed, and then it will be short work to know the law, which appears a very good noble thing."

Parliaments came and went, however, for one hundred and sixty years after Mr. Prin's discourse; but neither he, nor anyone else, succeeded in "abstracting" the laws of England. It remained for Jeremy Bentham to make it the mission of his life to endeavor to bring about such legislation that it might be "a short work to know the law, which appears a very good noble thing."

Jeremy Bentham was born in 1748, ten years before John Adams was admitted to the Bar; he graduated at Oxford in 1763, two years after James Otis argued the Writs of Assistance. He wrote his *Fragment on Government, a Criticism of Blackstone*, in 1776, the year of American Independence.

In 1802, one year after John Marshall became Chief Justice of the United States Supreme Court, he published, in Paris, his *Legislation, Civil and Criminal.* In 1817, the year of the *Dartmouth College Case*, appeared his *Codification.* His great work on *Judicial Evidence* appeared, in Paris, in 1823; and, in England, in 1825. He died in 1832, three years before the death of Chief Justice Marshall.[1]

His cardinal doctrine was thus expressed by him: "That which we have need of is a body of law, from the respective parts of which we may each of us, by reading them or hearing them read, learn, and on each occasion know, what are his rights and his duties." The code, in his plan, was to make every man his own lawyer.

Of Bentham's influence upon this history of the law, it has been said that it is difficult to speak in too exaggerated terms. His bold and insistent attacks on the absurdities and injustice of the Common Law of evidence and of the English system of criminal law were the fountain head of all the law reform of the Nineteenth Century; and various legal writers have said of him:

"Bentham's theories upon legal subjects have had a degree of practical influence upon the legislation of his own and various other countries comparable only to those of Adam Smith and his successors upon commerce."[2]

"He it was who made first the mighty step of trying the whole provisions of our jurisprudence by the test of expediency, fearlessly examining how far each part was connected with the rest, and with a yet more undaunted courage inquiring how for even its most consistent and symmetrical arrangements were framed according to the principles which should pervade a code of laws, their adaptation to

[1] *Bentham and his School of Jurisprudence*, by John F. Dillon, *Ohio Bar Association Proc.*, Vol. XI (1890).

*Mirabeau*, by T. B. Macaulay (1832); *Bentham and the Codifiers*, by Charles M. Gregory, *Harvard Law Review*, Vol. XIII (1899).

[2] *History of Criminal Law of England*, by Sir James Fitz James Stephen, Vol. II (1883).

the circumstances of society, to the wants of men and to the promotion of human happiness."[1]

"I do not know a single law reform effected since Bentham's day which cannot be traced to his influence."[2]

"The results which Bentham produced, and the changes in the law which he effected, however, were not the product of his direct personal efforts; and, in fact, he did not live to see most of these changes brought about. But these results and these changes were the work of more judicious men, over whose minds Bentham had had a controlling power and influence."[3]

As John Stuart Mill said:[4]

"Bentham is one of the great seminal minds in England of his age. . . . He is the teacher of teachers. . . . It is by the influence of the modes of thought with which his writings inoculated a considerable number of thinking men that the yoke of authority has been broken, and innumerable opinions, formerly received on tradition as incontestible, are put upon their defence. Who, before Bentham, dared to speak disrespectfully in express terms of the British Constitution or the English law? Bentham broke the spell. It was not Bentham by his own writings; it was Bentham through the minds and pens which those writings fed."

Judge John F. Dillon repeats the story that the remark having been made to Talleyrand: "Of all modern writers, Bentham is the one from whom most has been stolen and stolen without acknowledgment." — "True," replied Talleyrand, "*et pillé de tout le monde, il est toujours riche.*"

The acknowledged English disciples of many of Bentham's views on law reform were, first and foremost the great lawyer Sir Samuel Romilly, John Mill, John Stuart

[1] *Lord Brougham's Speeches*, Vol. II (Black's edition, 1838).

[2] *Early History of Institutions*, by Sir Henry Maine.

[3] See *History of Law*, by Emlin McClain, *Reports of the Congress of Arts and Sciences*, Vol. II (1906).

[4] *Essay on Bentham*, in *Dissertations and Discussions*, Vol. I.

Mill, Henry Bickersteth (Lord Langdale), Henry Brougham, and Sir James Mackintosh.

In the United States the influence of Bentham was felt earlier than in England, through the works of Edward Livingston. Livingston had left New York in 1804, to make his home in New Orleans; and at that time he received, so he wrote later to Bentham, his first impulse "to the preparation of an original comprehensive and complete system of penal legislation," from the great work of Bentham on *Legislation Civil and Criminal* which had first appeared in print in Paris, in 1802.

"The perusal of your works first gave method to my ideas, and taught me to consider legislation as a science, governed by certain principles applicable to all in different branches, instead of an occasional exercise of its powers, called forth only on particular occasions, without relation to or connection with each other. . . . Hereafter no one can, in criminal jurisprudence, propose any favorable change that you have not recommended, or make any wise improvement that your superior sagacity has not suggested."[1]

As a result of this impulse, Livingston drafted a Code of Procedure which became the first real code in America, being adopted by the Legislature of Louisiana in 1805, in an act of 20 sections of about 25 printed pages.

In 1820, Livingston, at the request of the Louisiana Legislature, began to prepare a complete Code of Crimes and Punishments, Criminal Procedure, Evidence, and Prison Discipline. He made a report to Louisiana, in 1822; and the entire work was finished in 1824, although not printed in full until 1833.[2]

[1] See *Life of Edward Livingston*, by Charles H. Hunt (1864). *Edward Livingston and the Louisiana Codes*, in *Columbia Law Review*, Vol. II.

[2] Part of the work was published in England in 1824, and in France in 1825.

Although never enacted into law as a complete whole, it proved, as George Bancroft said, "an unfailing fountain of reforms;"[1] and Chancellor Kent declared that Livingston had "done more in giving precision, specification, accuracy, and moderation to the system of crimes and punishments than any other legislator of the age;" while Bentham himself urged Parliament to print the whole work for the use of the English Nation.[2]

Meanwhile Bentham had been turning his attention towards the United States as affording a more promising field for his efforts than England, where the conservative Bar was almost completely dominated by the rigid views of Lord Eldon.

Between 1811 and 1817 he addressed a series of letters to President Madison, to the various State Governors, and to the "Citizens of the several American United States," offering to construct a complete code for the United States,[3] and advising them "to shut our ports against the Common Law, as we would against the plague."

Among those who fell under his influence was a brilliant Irish lawyer of New York, William Sampson, who began,

[1] A review of *Livingston's Penal Code of Louisiana*, by Caleb Cushing, in *North Amer. Review*, Vol. XVII (1823), said, "Mr. Livingston's code will sensibly contribute, we doubt not, to the diffusion of an unexceptionally liberal system of criminal law throughout the United States."

[2] See on the whole subject, an interesting note in Lecture XII of *Laws and Jurisprudence of England and America*, by John F. Dillon.

See also *Livingston's Penal Codes*, *Amer. Jurist*, Vol. XVIII, Vol. XXII.

[3] *Letters of Jeremy Bentham an Englishman to the Citizens of the several American United States on the Codification of the Law*, in *Bentham's Works*, Vol. IV.

President Madison in declining Bentham's proposals, in 1816, wrote these prophetic words: "Although we cannot avail ourselves of them in the mode best in itself, I do not overlook the prospect that the fruits of your labor may in some other, not be lost to us."

in 1823, a fiery and radical series of addresses and letters in denunciation of the English Common Law.[1]

These publications aroused a widespread discussion of the subject throughout the United States. Many prominent jurists, notably Judge Thomas Cooper, President of Columbia College, South Carolina, agreed with Sampson's strictures on the Common Law; and the question of codification was actively and fiercely debated during the years 1820 to 1830. Nothing shows the extent to which the subject occupied men's minds better than the number of references to codification, in magazine articles ostensibly written on other subjects. The Bar was sharply divided on the subject, and the attitude of both factions may be seen from a few quotations from the reviews of the day. Thus in 1818, Theron Metcalf (later Reporter and Judge of the Massachusetts Supreme Court) said in the *North American Review:* [2]

"About thirty years ago, the Russian code of laws was reprinted in this country in the compass of a common spelling book. Many visionary men at that time exclaimed with wonder at the comparatively massy bulk of our own statutes, and seriously talked of simplifying our jurisprudence and reducing all our laws into a narrow, elementary compend. Reformers sprang up like locusts, in the time of Shays' Insurrection and our statute book now bears witness to their folly. These crude notions had their day and disappeared. . . . But the fog in which the boastful reformers of Shays' time were bewildered has recently confused the vision of less factious malcontents."

In the same year, Daniel Webster, in a review of the third volume of *Wheaton's Reports*, said: [3]

[1] See *Sampson's Discourse on the Origin, Antiquities, Curiosities and Nature of the Common Law; and Correspondence with various learned Jurists upon the History of the Law*, by Pishey Thompson (1826).

[2] See *North American Review*, Vol. VII (July, 1818).

[3] See *North American Review*, Vol. VIII (December, 1818).

"Those who have embraced the notion of the practicability and utility of a written code of laws extending to all possible cases which arise in the intercourse of men, and who look upon the influence of the unwritten or Common Law as our oppressive domination, will naturally lament the appearance of every new volume of reports of legal decisions. To them, it can only seem another rivet to their fetters. . . . We do not belong, however, to this fraternity. . . . Feeling no disposition to estimate lightly the usefulness of legislation, it yet appears to us to be among the idlest of and weakest theories of the age that it is possible to provide beforehand by positive enactment and in such manner as to avoid doubts and ambiguities for all questions to which the immense variety of human concerns give rise. An opinion of this sort becomes so important as to deserve refutation, only in consequence of the apparent gravity with which some distinguished men in the learned world have treated it."

Quite different views from the above were held by many lawyers who viewed with alarm the increase of the number of law reports, and who were profoundly impressed with the success of the *Code Napoléon*. To the lawyer of today, who finds that the law reports issued in the United States number about eight thousand five hundred, the fear of the paltry two hundred in existence in 1825 seems ridiculous; but the lawyers of those days felt otherwise. Thus Joseph Story in his *Address to the Suffolk Bar*, in 1821, said:

"The mass of the law is, to be sure, accumulating with an almost incredible rapidity. . . . It is impossible to look without some discouragement upon the ponderous volumes which the next half century will add to the groaning shelves of our jurists."

David Hoffman, a Professor of Law in Maryland, wrote in his *Syllabus*, in 1821:

"The American books of reports (from 1789 to 1804) did not exceed 8 volumes, whereas they amount at this time to about 170! . . . The last ten years have been prolific of law works beyond former example. . . . Scarcely a week passed in England without ushering to light a new treatise of law. The reports, too, are becoming alarmingly numerous."

Caleb Cushing (later Judge of the Massachusetts Supreme Court, and Attorney-General of the United States) wrote in 1824:[1]

"The vast and increasing multiplication of reports as well as law treatises is a very remarkable fact in our legal history. . . . This, we are aware, has been a standing subject of complaint these many years. . . . Previous to the year 1804, but eight volumes of indigenous reported cases had been printed in America, and the lapse of only one-fifth of a century has added to the number 190 volumes exclusive of many valuable reports of single cases. . . . Whither is this rapid increase of reports to lead us?"

Willard Phillips, a prominent lawyer of Boston, wrote, in 1825:[2]

"The men of the law seem to have suffered under more than their just share of this general and ancient calamity if we may believe their lamentations over the ration of their number of books to that of their clients. On this ground, we hear loud calls from many quarters for codes and abridgments."

P. S. DuPonceau in his address to the Law Academy, in Philadelphia, February 21, 1821, referred to

"The immense increase of bulky reports which has lately taken place and will at last drive the student in despair to compilation and the works of private jurists

[1] See *North American Review*, Vol. XVIII (1824).

[2] Review of *Pickering's Reports*, Vol. I, by Willard Phillips — *North Amer. Rev.*, Vol. XX (1825); and in a *Review of Greenleaf's Cases*, by G. Mellen — *North Amer. Rev.*, Vol. XXII (1826), it is said: "Our age is not peculiar in its complaint of the increase of law books."

and thus will most probably be subverted the ancient basis of the jurisprudence of England."

James Kent wrote in volume four of his *Commentaries* that "the multiplication of books is becoming, or rather has become, an evil that is intolerable."

Henry D. Sedgwick, an eminent lawyer of New York, one of the strongest adherents of codification, wrote in 1824:[1]

"We would then suggest the propriety that at least some of the larger and more wealthy States of the Union should cause their laws to pass under general revision and to be formed into written codes. . . . The multiplication of reports, emanating from the numerous collateral sources of jurisdiction, is becoming an evil alarming and impossible long to be borne. It has of late increased enormously, in every mode of increase; the establishment of new tribunals; the increased habit of reporting; and the prolix methods adopted by the reporters."

And again in 1825:

"Your old-fashioned folks in Boston are all out in thinking that codification will not take. Is not this the great State and Mr. Clinton its great man and will not our Legislature follow his lead? This is going like most other great improvements — the craft generally opposed; few lawyers now living above forty will assent to it. Scarcely any below twenty-five will oppose it. The cause cannot be in better hands than those of Livingston in New Orleans and Duer and Butler here."

The conflicting views on codification as a remedy are well seen in the following letters to Jared Sparks, then an editor of the *North American Review*. George Ticknor wrote, January 31, 1825:

"I pray you, however, to beware of an article in favor of general codification. Mr. Jefferson, Mr. Madison, Mr.

[1] Review of *Sampson's Discourse*, by H. D. Sedgwick, *North Amer. Rev.*, Vol. XIX.

Webster, Mr. Hopkinson, Mr. Binney and not only all the old fellows but — all the little dogs will be after you at once. . . . What are you going to say about the *Code Napoléon?* Mr. DuPonceau says if you defend that and come out for codification he shall give you up. All this shows how much influence you have."

In 1825, Edward Everett wrote:[1]

"The word 'codification' has grown into use, we believe has been coined, within a few years, in the progress of the lucubrations of an individual, whose reputation and character we consider too enigmatical to be rashly pronounced upon. We mean of course Mr. Bentham.

"When the question is stated, it is plain that it is a question not as to the expediency of codifying, but as to the mode of doing it, and the probability that it would be done for us by a visionary foreign philosopher as much distinguished, at least, for his zeal in party politics as for his learning in jurisprudence. . . .

"It is sometimes intimated that the friends of codification expect to destroy litigation by making the law on all points so clear that no question could arise. — If this were the proposed and expected advantage to result from codification it would certainly be a work to be left to the jurists of Laputa."

Joseph Story wrote to Everett, January 4, 1825:

"I do not believe quite so much in the infallibility of the Common Law as my brethren; and notwithstanding all that is said to the contrary, I am a decided friend to codification, so as to fix in a text the law as it is, and ought to be, as far as it has gone, and leave new cases to furnish new doctrines as they arise, and reduce these again, at distant intervals, into the text."

Meanwhile the State of New York had taken the first step towards codification, in the limited sense of the term —

[1] Review of *The Code Napoléon*, by E. Everett — *North Amer. Rev.*, Vol. XX (1825).

the revision of the statutes, taken in connection with the cases decided in the courts on the subjects involved.

The first revision of the statutes in New York had occurred in 1683; her Colonial laws were first collected and published in 1710; in 1762, the Colonial laws then in force were "collected, revised and published under the authority of the General Assembly" by William Smith, Jr., and William Livingston; and another authoritative revision took place in 1774. The first collection and revision of the laws of the State of New York was published in 1789 by Samuel Jones and Richard Varick; and another revision was made by direction of the Legislature in 1801, when Chief Justice James Kent and Judge Jacob Radcliff of the Supreme Court were appointed to publish the laws then in force. In 1813, similar authority was given to William P. Van Ness and John Woodworth. On the adoption of the new State Constitution, in 1824, Erastus Root, James Kent and Benjamin F. Butler were appointed Commissioners to revise the laws. The first two resigning, Henry Wheaton and John Duer took their places; and later John C. Spencer was appointed in Wheaton's place. This Commission made its report, March 14, 1826, presenting a bill, containing a radical and sweeping reformation of the law in many of its features — a bill which may properly be termed the first modern American code.

In their report, the Commissioners said:

"The practicability and advantages of reducing the common law of England to a written code have recently been maintained in that country by several able writers. In this country also similar opinions have been advanced by some of our ablest jurists; and we think those opinions are gradually gaining ground in both countries. On the other hand, a majority of the legal profession in each is adverse to the schemes."

This report was referred to by William H. Gardiner, a Massachusetts lawyer, in the *North American Review* (Vol. XXIV), in 1827, as follows:[1]

"There are few questions of internal improvement upon which sound and liberal minds are more divided among us than upon the expediency and practicability of substituting a general code for the whole mass of common and statute law. . . . The sense of the profession in this country, we think, is against this great scheme of legal reform. . . . But learned and eminent counsellors are ranged on both sides of the controversy. . . .

"We believe the final completion of this great work will constitute a new era of legislation in New York, the benefits of which will be experienced ere long by the necessary force of example in her sister States."

In 1828, the State of New York enacted this remarkable statute, which entirely reconstructed the law of real property; and as has been said:

"It struck at the vital part of the huge fabric that the English real property lawyers and judges had been building for three centuries, until the whole toppled and fell. Even Chancellor Kent, himself a reformer, stood aghast at the extent of the demolition. They remodelled the law of descent, simplified the creation and division of estates . . . remodelled real actions, abolishing fictitious suits, changed the whole law of perpetuities and limitations and wills, . . . reconstructed the entire law of executor and administrator, simplified uses and trusts."[2]

This work, while not a true code, was, nevertheless, a great step in advance towards a scientific statement of the law; and it became the foundation and model for most of the revised and collected statutes adopted in other States in later years, especially for the *Revised Statutes*

[1] See also *Projected Revision of the Laws of New York*, by Caleb Cushing, *North American Rev.*, Vol. XXI (1825).

[2] *The Common Law*, by Charles P. Daly (1896).

of Massachusetts of 1836 (which, however, contained many improvements over its model).

About this same time, Henry Brougham moved in the House of Commons in England, in 1828, for a Commission, "to inquire into the defects, occasioned by time and otherwise in the laws of the realm, and into the means necessary for reducing the same." That the United States, however, was far in advance of England in the state of its law was noticed in a review of Brougham's speech, in the *American Jurist*, in 1829 (Vol. I):

"No American can read this work without being surprised to find how many of the evils of which it complains have been remedied in this country. . . . The greatest change in this country outside of real property and criminal law are in the machinery of justice, rules of pleading and evidence and modes of trial."

Many other English legal writers were agitating for reform in the legal system of England.[1]

Parliament accordingly appointed a series of Commissions to inquire into the law of procedure and other subjects; and a report in 1831 on Common Law practise and

[1] See *Observations on the Actual State of the English Law of Real Property with outlines for systematic reform*, by James Humphreys (2d ed., 1827); *Contre projet to the Humphreysian code*, by Prof. J. J. Park (1828).

*A letter to James Humphreys on his proposal to repeal the laws of real property and substitute a new code*, by E. Sugden (3d ed., 1827).

Tracts by Hayes, Beaumont, Long, Dixon, Christie, Barnes, Swinburne, Boileau, Jacob Phillips; attacks on the Chancery Courts in *Edinburgh Review; A Brief Account of some of the Important Proceedings in Parliament on the Court of Chancery*, by C. P. Cooper (1828); *A letter to the Lord Chancellor of Great Britain on the expediency of a new civil code for England*, by John Reddie (1828).

*A Letter to the Lord Chancellor on the practicability of forming a code of the laws of England*, by Crofton Uniacke (1827).

*Juridical Letters* by "Eunomus" (Prof. J. J. Park) (1830).

And see especially *Amer. Jurist*, Vol. VII (July, 1832).

procedure led to the adoption of certain moderate reforms known as the *New Rules of the Hilary Term of 1834*.

This movement in England and the successful passage of the New York act spurred the opponents of codification in the United States to renewed efforts; and they singled out Bentham himself for vigorous attack. Thus, George Bancroft, writing in the *American Quarterly Review* in 1827, said:[1]

"The success of the Napoleon Code has set all Europe codifying. In Italy, Germany, Russia, Switzerland and the Netherlands, the code makers are at work. . . . England has caught the rabies, and her writers, at the head of whom is the celebrated Jeremy Bentham, are exercising their pens on the subject of this mode of legislation — God preserve us from the extreme remedy of general codification!"

Anthony Laussat, a Philadelphia lawyer, wrote in 1829:[2]

"Mr. Jeremy Bentham, with the usual adventurousness of those who have no practical knowledge of their subject was the first to broach the subject of reform . . . a complete revision of the Common Law. The speculations of Mr. Bentham on the subject are such as might be expected from a closet philosopher; and though certainly beautiful in theory are about as fit to be applied to the practical operations of the law as some of his political schemes are to the actual government of mankind."

Mr. Laussat recognized, nevertheless, that, both in England and in the United States, there was a real demand for reform in legal conditions:

"It is evident to all those who have diligently watched the signs and motions of the times, that a great era is now

[1] Review of *Kent's Commentaries*, by George Bancroft, *Amer. Quarterly Review*, Vol. I (1827).

[2] *Codification*, by A. Laussat, *Amer. Quarterly Rev.*, Vol. VI (1829).

approaching in jurisprudence. There is a spirit abroad which never can be appeased until the sacrifice is consummated of everything that is pernicious. Its progress in England may be marked not only in the writings of jurists and speeches of legislators but in the deep agitation pervading all classes from the meanest suitor to the chancellor on his woolsack. Their eyes are now turned to the legal profession of this country as those who were the first to advance into the great field of philosophic jurisprudence."

Two years after the New York revision of the statutes, Pennsylvania took up the subject; and a Commission, composed of William Rawle, Thomas J. Wharton and Joel Jones, was appointed to revise the civil code, under a resolve of March 23, 1830. This Commission made its first report, January 31, 1832, recommending many revisions of the statutes, and stating that no revision had taken place since 1700; five other reports were made, 1832–1835, and the statutes enacted between 1834 and 1836, based on these reports, formed its *Revised Code*.[1]

The next State, after Pennsylvania, to take the step towards codification in its limited sense, viz., the complete revision of its statutes in connection with the decided cases, was Massachusetts. Previous compilations of the statutes had already been made in that State — in 1800 by a Committee composed of Nathan Dane, George R. Minot and John Davis; in 1812 (the *Colonial and Provincial Laws*) by a Commission composed of such brilliant lawyers as Nathan Dane, William Prescott and Joseph Story; in 1823, by Asahel Stearns (then Professor in the Harvard Law School), and Lemuel Shaw (later Chief

[1] See *Revised Code of Pennsylvania — Amer. Quarterly Review*, Vol. XIII (March, 1833), and Vol. XIX (June, 1836); *Amer. Jurist*, Vol. XIII (1835).

Justice);[1] but as most of the lawyers in the State were opposed to codification,[2] no further action was taken until 1832. In that year by resolve of the Legislature, Asabel Stearns, John Hooker Ashmun (succeeded by John Pickering in 1833) and Charles Jackson were appointed a commission to codify existing statutes.[3]

This Commission made a report in 1834, and on November 4, 1835, the *Revised Statutes* of Massachusetts were enacted, to take effect April 1, 1836. "They have ever since served as the model on which many similar works have been formed in other States," said the *Law Reporter*, in 1859 (Vol. XXI); another and contemporary view of this important statutory work is to be seen in a review in the *American Jurist*, in 1835 (Vol. XIII):

"New York has the distinction of taking the lead in codification in the United States. It is a glorious preeminence. And the men who propelled that State forward to the attempt deserve on this ground alone, a high place in history. . . . A few years ago, codification had a direful import to the conservative party in jurisprudence; and not wholly without reason; since some of its early cham-

[1] See Review of *The General Laws of Massachusetts, by A. Stearns and L. Shaw*, by Caleb Cushing, *North Amer. Rev.*, Vol. XVII (1823). "The necessity of a new revised edition of our statutes has been very sensibly felt."

[2] Theron Metcalf, in a *Review of Greenleaf's Reports* in *North Amer. Rev.*, Vol. XV (1822), said: "It has been thought that certainty in statute law might be promoted by reducing all that has been enacted upon one subject, though at distant intervals, into one chapter. We trust the ill success of such attempts will prevent their repetition. The present Probate Law of Massachusetts is a standing monitory memento on this subject.

[3] See *Revision of the Laws of Massachusetts — Amer. Jurist*, Vol. XIII; *Codification of the Common Law in Massachusetts*, *Amer. Jurist*, Vol. XV; see also articles on codification and law reform, *Amer. Jurist*, Vol. VII, p. 226, note; *Written and Unwritten Systems of Law*, *Amer. Jurist*, Vol. V, Vol. IX; *Legal Reform*, Vol. IX; *Codification and Reform of the Law*, *Amer. Jurist*, Vols. XIV, XV, XVI, XXI, XXIII, XXIV.

pions were sturdy radicals in legal reform. In this view codification was another name for juridical revolution. . . . But the alarm has subdued. . . . The substitution of the terms revision and consolidation of statutes for that of codification has contributed in no small degree to the change of thinking on the subject. . . . Here, the plan pursued has been to incorporate into the code the former decisions on the construction of the statutes revised. The formation of a code is a magnificent enterprise worthy of a State, success in which is one of the most glorious events in the annals of any community, however brilliant may be its history in other respects. Every part of the report teems with useful improvements; and its completion and adoption, in the spirit in which the court has been thus far conducted, in the able hands to which it has been committed will make a great epoch in the jurisprudence of the State."

In 1836, Massachusetts at the initiative of Governor Edward Everett,[1] and of radical Democrats like Robert Rantoul, Jr., took a still further step in advance, by appointing Joseph Story, and Simon Greenleaf, Theron Metcalf, Charles E. Forbes and Luther S. Cushing as a Commission, "to take into consideration the practicability and expediency of reducing in a written and systematic code the Common Law of Massachusetts or any part thereof."

This Commission made a report to the Legislature in 1837, favoring the codification of that part of the law relating to civil rights and duties of persons in relation to other persons, rights and titles to real and personal property, rights, duties and claims arising from acts and implied contracts — also the Common Law as to crimes and evidence, the latter as the first object for the deliberation of the Legislature.[2]

[1] See Message to Legislature, January 15, 1836.

[2] See *American Jurist*, Vol. XVI (1837).

The recommendations of this report, however, were not carried out; although, in 1837, a Commission composed of Charles Jackson, Willard Phillips, John Gray Rogers, Luther S. Cushing and Samuel B. Walcott was appointed to codify the law of crimes — James C. Alvord later taking Jackson's place.

This Commission reported in 1839, recommending the subject to the Legislature for careful examination, and submitting a sample of a codification of the law of murder.[1] Nothing further was done by the Legislature.

Meanwhile in Ohio, Samuel Portland Chase, the future Chief Justice of the United States, then a youth of twenty-five, had completed, in 1833–1834, his *Revision of the Statutes of Ohio*, "a work of great magnitude, which gave him an immediate and solid claim to distinction and at present placed him in the foremost rank among the lawyers of his State if not of the nation." [2]

In 1839, David Dudley Field of New York began his agitation for more radical code reform.[3]

As early as 1842, a bill was submitted in the New York Legislature, to provide more simple and speedy administration of justice in civil cases in courts of Common Law;

[1] See *American Jurist*, Vol. XXI (1839).

[2] See *Life and Public Services of Samuel Portland Chase*, by J. W. Shuckers (1874).

James Kent wrote to Chase, July 1, 1835: "Your edition of the statutes of Ohio is a great work."

Judge Story wrote to Chase, March 1, 1834:

"It does equal honor to your enterprise, your industry and your talents. I wish with all my heart that other States would imitate this example, for in most of them there is a sad neglect of the old repealed laws; and it is difficult to trace out the history and progress of their legislation. I shall feel honored by the privilege of having a copy in my library.

See also *Ohio Legislation* in *Amer. Jurist*, Vol. XI (January, 1834).

[3] *David Dudley Field and His Work*, in *New York Bar Ass. Proc.*, Vol. XVIII.

another bill was introduced, for courts of Equity; and a third, to simplify indictments. These were forerunners of, and in some parts identical with, the radical code adopted six years later.[1]

In 1846, a wave of democracy and reform was sweeping over the world. In England, it took shape in the Chartist agitation; and in Europe, in the revolutions which, in 1848, convulsed almost every country.[2] In the United States, the jealousy of privilege focused itself in an attack on the Bar Associations, the lawyers and the judges. A new Constitution in New York, adopted after a political convulsion, swept away all the old existing courts and judges, established elective judges with a limited tenure, and provided that, "any male citizen of twenty-one years, of good moral character, and who possesses the requisite qualifications of learning and ability shall be entitled to admission to practise in all the courts of the State." [3]

It further provided that the Legislature should appoint a Commission, "to reduce into a written and systematic code the whole body of the law of the State or so much and such parts thereof as to the said Commissioners shall seem practicable and expedient." Under this, a Commission composed of David Dudley Field, William Curtis Noyes

[1] *Law Reform in the United States and its Influence Abroad*, by D. D. Field, in *Amer. Law Rev.*, Vol. XXV (1891).

[2] See *A Century of Judge Made Law*, by W. B. Hornblower in *Columbia Law Review*, Vol. VII (1907).

[3] Of this new constitution Timothy Walker said in the *Western Law Journal*, Vol IV. (May, 1847):

"We have always been earnest advocates of law reform; but the New York experiment goes far beyond anything we had dreamed of. It is in fact a revolution, and not the less so because a blooded one. We hope that the people of that State will never see cause to regret what they have done; but we predict that, before many years, another convention will be called, to reform some of the late reform. There is a deep-seated veneration for ancient landmarks which can ill brook to see them all swept away at once."

and Alexander Bradford in 1857, reported in 1865 a Civil Code, containing sweeping changes in substantive law.

This was the first real code in the broad and correct sense of the term, prepared in this country. The opposition which it encountered from the legal profession, however, was too strong, and it failed of adoption by the Legislature of New York.[1]

But in spite of the unsuccessful culmination of the movement for this radical form of codification, a more limited form, — the reform by statute of the old systems of pleading and practise — made decided progress at this time.

For two hundred years, skill in special pleading had been the proudest boast of the Common Law lawyer. In no branch of the science had the great leaders of the American Bar been more adept; but to no part of the Common Law had there been more valid ground for objection, or more justifiable cause for the popular prejudices. The early volumes of American reports, like the English reports before Mansfield's time, were filled with cases lost, not on their merits, but on technical points of pleading. There were American "Baron Surrebutters," before the time of the English Mr. Justice Parke, who took their greatest pleasure in deciding a case on a defective declaration or a mistaken plea.

1 Other States later were less conservative; and in 1865, this Field Code, prepared for New York, was adopted by the Territory of Dakota, and in a modified form was still later adopted by the States of North Dakota, South Dakota, Montana and Idaho. In 1873, California adopted the New York Code, revised and amended.

In 1858, Georgia appointed a Commission to prepare a code to embrace the Common as well as the statute law of the State; and in 1860, that State enacted a Revision of the Statutes, Part II of which was entitled "*The Civil Code — which treats of rights, wrongs and remedies*," to take effect January 1, 1862.

As the *American Jurist* said in 1833:

"Take the whole number of reported decisions, both in England and America on the subject of contracts; and we venture to affirm that a majority, yes, a large majority, have gone off on questions of form. This is a stupendous evil. No wonder that the law suffers under the imputation of uncertainty, and of a tendency to encourage quibbling and chicanery. The suitor who is turned out of court on a point of form, when he knows that he has right on his side, has good reason to consider himself oppressed. . . . No wonder if with such impressions, he imbibes a hatred both of the law and its ministers.[1] On the other hand, while the laymen were insistent upon a decided change in the methods of pleading, the Bar still retained its belief in special pleading, agreeing with Judge Joseph Story in his Address to the Suffolk Bar when he said that: 'Special pleading contains the quintessence of the law; and no man ever mastered it who was not by that means made a profound lawyer.'"

The leader in law reform in this direction was the State of Massachusetts which passed a statute in 1836 (c. 273), dispensing with all pleas in bar, abolishing special demurrers, and constituting the general issue as the only form of defense.

As with the other reforms in the law, this action was passed in response to a popular demand, and in face of opposition by the legal profession.

The *American Jurist* (Vol. XVI), in a vigorous attack upon the new law, said in 1836, that legislative action had been hurried forward without careful examination, the profession not being asked to state their opinions or given opportunity to do so, and the courts not being consulted:

"Not a judge on the bench, not an eminent lawyer in whom the public are in the habit of confiding would probably

[1] See *Legal Reform — Amer. Jurist*, Vol. IX.

have advised this measure;" — and it complained that "the use of no other form of defence than the general issue tends to produce surprise, uncertainty and want of exactness, thereby defeating the ends of justice, and brings before the jury mixed questions of law and fact without having the law settled by the court, except in the necessarily hurried mode of charging at nisi prius."

Twelve years after this Massachusetts Act of 1836, came the New York *Code of Civil Procedure*, adopted pursuant to the New York Constitution of 1846. That Constitution, in addition to a provision for a Commission to codify the substantive law, had further provided for the appointment of a Commission "to revise, reform, simplify and abridge the rules of practice, pleadings, forms and proceedings of this State." This Commission was appointed in April, 1847; and the Legislature instructed it, "to provide for abolition of the present forms of action and pleadings in cases at common law; for a uniform course of proceedings in all cases whether of legal or equitable cognizance, and for the abandonment of all Latin and other foreign tongues so far as the same shall by them be deemed practicable, and any form and proceedings not necessary to ascertain and preserve the rights of the parties."

The Commission, composed of David Dudley Field, David Graham and Arphaxed Loomis, reported, on February 29, 1848, a *Code of Civil Procedure*, the enactment of which by the Legislature, April 12, 1848, startled the legal profession throughout the country.[1]

The *Law Reporter*, severely critical, said that this Code "was undoubtedly the greatest innovation upon the Common Law which was ever effected by a single statute. In one section it struck out of existence all of that law which

[1] *The New York System of Procedure*, by Joseph S. Auerbach (1877).
*The Historical Development of Code Pleading*, by Charles M. Hepburn (1897).

was inconsistent with the doctrines of equity, and in another obliterated the whole of the two systems of pleading at law and in equity, replacing both by a single and homogeneous body of rules. So radical a change amazed, and for a while confounded the entire legal profession. They were unprepared for it, and unwilling to believe even that it had been accomplished. . . .

"The early reports of decisions under the Code testify abundantly to the dire confusion which it created, and the bitter opposition which it met among both judges and lawyers. For some years it was judicially repealed in a large part of the State, so far as its two main features, before mentioned, were concerned."[1]

In 1849, a feeling of restlessness again prevailed in Massachusetts over the cumbrous system of court procedure, which was well voiced in an article in the *Law Reporter*, calling for the abolition of all diversities of civil remedies, and the removal of the absurd Common Law bar against interested witnesses:[2]

"A movement towards a radical change in the practice of law courts in a neighboring State has recently startled the Bar of New England. The powerful hand of progress has been seen prying under the pedestal of the most time honored institution of law. . . . The time seems to us to have come when progress ought to venture within the precincts of Bench and Bar. . . . As the increasing and concentrated light of civilization illuminates the various departments of legal practice, many ancient styles of attaining equity, sometimes perverted to deception and fraud, often to injustice, should be essentially modified or altogether removed. . . . The character and wants of the people are changing; and upon this character and wants the modes of the law, as well as the law itself are dependent. Some years since in obedience to this necessity, Massachu-

[1] See *Law Reporter*, Vol. XI (1847); Vol. XIII (1850); Vol. XVIII (1855); Vol. XXV (1862).

[2] *Law Reform Practice*, in *Law Reporter*, Vol. XII (1849).

setts ordered that the rules of special pleading, hoary with antiquity, should no longer manacle the equities of judicial proceedings, and lay upon the necks of innocent clients the penalties for the faults of an uneducated attorney.

"In obedience to the same necessity, they have suspended the rule of incompetency for interest from witnesses who may be members of political corporations and of incorporated mutual fire and marine insurance companies, parties to the suit. Yet not one element of logic is found to distinguish in principle between incorporated mutual companies and incorporated stock companies. And we may add, between them and copartnerships, and these last and individual parties."

A Commission was appointed in 1849 to frame a new code of procedure, composed of Reuben A. Chapman, N. J. Lord and Benjamin R. Curtis, Chairman. Their report was adopted by the Legislature in 1851 — the same year in which Curtis was made judge of the United States Supreme Court; and the *Law Reporter* said of this action: [1]

"The desire for legal reform has now become so strong among all classes in this country that it cannot be checked. It is idle to contend against it especially when all admit that there are so many sound reasons which warrant such a feeling. It therefore eminently becomes the profession to allow the movement to go on."

By this Practise Act of 1851 the forms of action were reduced to three, — tort, contract and replevin; pro-

[1] See *Law Reporter*, Vol. XIII (1851).

A year later the Common Law Procedure Act of 1852 went into effect in England, framed by a Royal Commission, appointed in 1850, composed of Sir John Jervis (later Chief Justice of Common Pleas), Sir Alexander Cockburn (later Lord Chief Justice of England), Sir Samuel Martin (later Baron of Exchequer), Sir James Willes (Justice of Common Pleas), William Bramwell (later Lord Bramwell).

See *English Law Reform* in *Law Reporter*, Vol. XVIII (1855).

visions were made for the verification of pleadings by oath or affirmation at every stage, speedy settlement of actions, and the right of both parties to fill interrogatories. The bar of exclusion of witnesses for interest or infamy was abolished.

This act, which was largely copied by Alabama (1852), Maryland (1856), and Tennessee (1858), was opposed for many years by the more conservative members of the Bar; [1] it was judicially condemned by Chief Justice Shaw in several decisions; and, in 1859, in the United States Supreme Court, Judge Grier said, referring to these statutes changing Common Law procedure: [2]

"This system matured by the wisdom of ages, founded on principles of truth and sound reason, has been ruthlessly abolished in many of our States, who have rashly substituted in its place the suggestions of sciolists who invent new codes and systems of pleadings to order. . . . The result of these experiments, so far as they have come to our knowledge, has been to destroy the certainty and simplicity of all pleadings and introduce on the record an endless wrangle in writing, perplexing to the court, delaying and impeding the administration of justice."

The reforms introduced in the Practise Acts of New York and Massachusetts have, however, amply justified

[1] "The simplification attempted by the Practice Act has not been productive of the results hoped. On the whole the practice has become looser but not really easier. It is not a fit season to consider whether a recurrence to some of the essential features of the system of special pleading is not advisable," said the *American Law Review*, Vol. XI (1876–1877).

[2] *McFaul* v. *Ramsey*, 20 Howard, 525.

In *Farin* v. *Tesson*, 1 Black, 315 (1861), Judge Grier said:

"It is no wrong or hardship to suitors who come to the courts for a remedy, to be required to do it in the mode established by the law. State legislatures may substitute by codes, the whims of sciolists and inventors for the experience and wisdom of the ages; but the success of these experiments is not such as to allure the court to follow their example."

themselves in practical working, and they remain to-day (1911) substantially unchanged.[1]

1 Within five years after 1848, Civil Procedure Codes based on that of New York had been adopted in seven States; in Missouri, in 1849; in California, in 1850; in Iowa, Kentucky and Minnesota, in 1851; in Indiana, in 1852; and in Ohio, in 1853.

Charles M. Hepburn says that the New York Code has been enacted in substance and often in letter in sixteen other States and Territories: Oregon and Washington, in 1854; Nebraska, in 1855; Wisconsin, in 1856; Kansas, in 1859; Nevada, in 1861; Dakota, in 1862; Arizona and Idaho, in 1864; Montana, in 1865; North Carolina and Arkansas, in 1868; Wyoming, in 1869; South Carolina, Florida and Utah, in 1870.

See also the Colorado Code of 1877, the Connecticut Practise Act of 1879 and the Codes of Oklahoma of 1890 and 1893.

## CHAPTER XX

### AMERICAN LAW BOOKS, 1815–1910

From 1815 until 1830, when the fourth volume of Kent's *Commentaries* was published, American legal literature made slight advance. A review of Dane's *Abridgment* in the *American Jurist* (Vol. IV) in 1830 described conditions at that time as follows:

"The original treatises and compilations, as well as the numerous volumes of reports of domestic production that have made their appearance in our libraries of late years are evident indications of our juridical progress; but our ready access to England for laws adapted to our institutions and habits, while it was a great advantage, was at the same time a weighty discouragement to the undertaking of any original works. . . . At length we began to make compilations of precedents and forms, and, after a time here and there a bold spirit would venture upon something in the shape of a treatise; but still with an apologizing and fearful tone, doubting his strength to heave off the ponderous weight of British authority, and stem the mighty current of British competition. Our emancipation from this oppression . . . of foreign juridical authority has since been accomplished."

David Hoffman's *Course of Legal Study*, which for many years was the standard manual for law students, appeared in 1817.

In 1823, Nathan Dane published the first volume of his *Abridgment of American Law*, the profits from which were to be the means of the re-creation of the Harvard Law School.

In 1821, Caleb Cushing edited the first American translation of Pothier's *Maritime Contracts.*[1]

In 1822, came a second edition of the first book on patent law, Fessenden's *Law of Patents for New Inventions;* in 1823, the first American book on insurance law, by Willard Phillips.

In 1824, came *Angell on Watercourses,* in the preface to which is found the following interesting comment, showing the book to have really been the first American Case Book:

"The plan of putting adjudged cases into an appendix . . . was recommended, by one whose distinguished talents and profound knowledge of the law have made him an ornament and blessing to his country — Mr. Justice Story."

The book contained 96 pages of text and 246 pages of cases.

In the years 1822 and 1825, a new department of legal literature was opened by the publication in Philadelphia of Thomas Sergeant's *Constitutional Law* and William Rawle's *A View of the Constitution of the United States;* and

[1] See also *Digests of American Reports and American Law Periodicals — Amer. Jurist,* Vol. XXIII (1840).

*Kent's Commentaries,* Vol. III, p. 201, note (1st ed.):

"The translation of Pothier's *Treatise on Maritime Contracts* by Mr. C. Cushing and published at Boston in 1821 is neat and accurate and the notes which are added to this volume are highly creditable to the industry and learning of the author. . . . It would contribute greatly to the circulation and cultivation of maritime law in this country if some other treatise of Pothier and also the commentaries of Valin could appear in an English dress."

In the third edition, Kent said: "Mr. L. S. Cushing has published at Boston a translation of Pothier's *Treatise on the Contract of Sale;* and if duly encouraged, as we hope and trust he will be, he promises a translation of the other excellent treatises of Pothier on the various commercial contracts."

in 1823 John Taylor published in Philadelphia his *New Views of the Constitution of the United States*.

In the same years, another subject was treated for the first time in the United States — that of contracts — in Daniel Chipman's *Essay on the Law of Contracts for Payment of Specific Articles* (Middlebury, 1822),[1] and in Gulian C. Verplanck's *Essay on Doctrine of Contracts; being an Inquiry how Contracts are affected in Law and Morals by Concealment, Error, or Inadequate Price* (New York, 1825).

In a review of this latter work by Joseph Hopkinson, a noted lawyer of Philadelphia, the state of American legal writing is thus depicted in 1827:[2]

"The learning and industry of the American lawyer have been repeatedly exercised in the republication of professional works, with such additions as were proper to render them more useful to the American student; but an original treatise on the science of jurisprudence is a rare occurrence with us."

In 1824, Asahel Stearns published his *Summary of the Laws and Practice of Real Actions*, in the preface of which he states that the treatise is the "substance of his course of lectures at the Law Department in the University."

The year 1826 was a landmark in American legal literature for in the spring of that year Chancellor Kent, at the age of sixty-three, undertook the task of embodying in a book, the mass of American Common Law, using as a basis his lectures given in 1823 and 1824 at Columbia College;[3] and in the fall, Volume I of his *Commentaries* was

[1] See Review by Nathan Dane in *North American Review*, Vol. XVII (1823).

[2] See Review in *American Quarterly Review*, Vol. I (March, 1827).

[3] See letter of Kent to Story, Dec. 18, 1824, *Mass. Hist. Soc. Proc.*, 2d series, Vol. XVI (1902).

"I sent a day or two ago by the mail, the summary of the first twenty lectures of my present or 2nd course. I know you are so kind as to take some

published. In April, 1830, Volume IV was published; and the work meeting with instant and enthusiastic success, a second edition was printed as early as 1832.

In a review of this work, George Bancroft said in 1827:[1]

"Now we know what American Law is; we know it is a science which indeed has not reached its utmost degree of perfection, but is fast advancing towards it. We know it is a science which in the course of another fifty years will by its own force, *vi propria*, expel from our shelves the ponderous mass of foreign lore by which they are still encumbered, and perhaps (the idea is not at all wild or extravagant) and perhaps, we venture to say, make the works of our writers on jurisprudence the ornament of the libraries of foreign jurists."

In the same year, Chief Justice Isaac Parker referred to it in one of his judicial opinions, as "a recently published book which I trust from the eminence of its author and the merits of the work will soon become of common reference in our courts."[2]

In 1828, Charles Jackson, Judge of the Supreme Court of Massachusetts, published his well known, much needed, and much used *Treatise on the Pleadings and Practice in Real Actions*, in the preface of which he refers to Professor Stearns' book as composed on a different plan, saying, "an inconvenience has attended the use of real actions in this country from the want of some digest of this branch

interest in my pursuits, and this emboldened me to trouble you with such an uninteresting paper. . . . You need not be apprehensive that the topics I am discussing will lead to commence a crusading war on your judicial opinions. . . . I almost uniformly agree with you and in every case in which due opportunity offers I speak of you and of your court as you desire in the height of your ambition. I shall find some fault with the Steamboat Case, but most decorously."

[1] See *Kent on American Law*, by George Bancroft, in *American Quarterly Review*, Vol. I (March, 1827).

[2] *Dean* v. *Richmond*, 5 Pick. 466.

of the law and of a manual of pleadings adapted to our jurisprudence and modes of proceeding."

An interesting sidelight on the learning of the American lawyer of this period is found in Kent's comments, in 1829, on Jackson's book:

> "I think it must somewhat startle and surprise the learned sergeants at Westminster Hall if they should perchance look into the above treatise of Judge Jackson on *Pleadings and Practice in Real Actions* or into the work of Professor Stearns on the *Law and Practice of Real Actions* to find American lawyers much more accurate and familiar than, judging from some of the late reports, they themselves appear to be with the learning of the Year Books, Fitzherbert, Rastel and Coke on the doctrine and pleadings in real actions. Until the late work of Mr. Roscoe on *Law of Actions relating to Real Property* which was subsequent to that of Professor Stearns . . . there was no modern work in England on Real Actions to be compared with those I have mentioned. Those abstruse subjects are digested and handled by Judge Jackson with a research, judgment, precision and perspicacity that reflect lustre on the profession in this country."

The scope of the American law books above enumerated, however, shows the limited field of the law of this period.[1]

The period from 1830 to 1860 was one of great activity and of splendid accomplishment by the American law writers. Chief, of course, of all legal works were the great series of commentaries on the law written by Judge Joseph Story and which appeared as follows: *Bailments* (1832);

[1] In addition to the books given above, the following are the only law works of importance written by Americans at this period:

*Angell on Adverse Possession*, in 1827, and *Angell on Assignments*, in 1825; John Anthon's *Law of Nisi Prius*, in 1820; Blake's *New York Chancery Practice*, in 1818; Dunlap's *New York Supreme Court Practice*, in 1821; Daniel Davis' *Justices of the Peace*, in 1828; Reeve's *Law of Descent*, in 1825.

*Constitutional Law* (1833);[1] *Conflict of Laws* (1834); *Equity Jurisprudence* (1836); *Equity Pleading* (1838); *Agency* (1839); *Partnership* (1841); *Bills of Exchange* (1843). Of his *Commentaries on the Conflict of Laws* it is not too much to say that its publication constituted an epoch in the law; for it became at once the standard and almost the sole authority. It was reprinted almost immediately in England, France and Germany, and received the honor of being practically the first American law book to be cited as authority in English Courts.[2]

[1] Two other books on constitutional law attracted attention at this critical period — W. A. Duer's *Outlines of the Constitutional Jurisprudence of the United States*, and P. DuPonceau's *Brief View of the Constitution of the United States*.

[2] Sir N. C. Tindal, Chief Justice of Common Pleas, in *Huber* v. *Steiner*, 2 Bing. New Cases, 211, said: "It would be unjust to mention it without at the same time paying a tribute to the learning, acuteness and sagacity of its author."

And Daniel Webster in his argument before the Supreme Court in *New Jersey Steam Navigation Company* v. *Merchants Bank*, 6 Howard, 92 (1848), paid this splendid tribute:

"It is a great truth that England has never produced any eminent writer on national or general public law — no elementary writer who has made the subject his own, who has breathed his own breath into it and made it live. In English judicature Sir William Scott has, it is true, done much to enlighten the public mind on the subject of prize causes, and in our day Mackintosh has written a paper of some merit. But where is your English Grotius? Where is your English Barbeyrac? Has England produced one? Not one. The English mind has never been turned to the discussion of general public law. We must go to the continent for the display of genius in this department of human knowledge. What have the Courts of Westminster Hall done to illustrate the principles of public law? With the exception of a tract by Mansfield, of considerable merit, more great principles of public law have been discussed and settled by this Court within the last twenty years, than in all the Common Law Courts of England for the last hundred years. Nay, more important subjects of law have been examined and passed upon by this bench in a series of twenty years, than in all Europe for a century past. And I cannot forbear to add, that one in the midst of you has favored the world with a treatise on public law, fit to stand by the side of Grotius, to be the companion of the Institutes,

In 1832, Joseph K. Angell and Samuel Ames published their *Law of Private Corporations*, the first book on the subject; and Judge James Gould of the Litchfield Law School published his famous book on *Pleading*.

In 1837, Timothy Walker published his *Introduction to American Law*, which for many years was used as a text-book for American law students. In 1836 appeared Henry Wheaton's *Elements of International Law*.

In 1838, Francis Hilliard published his *Real Property* which largely replaced Cruise's *Digest* with American lawyers.

In 1839, appeared John Bouvier's noted *Law Dictionary*.

In 1842, came the first volume of *Greenleaf on Evidence*.

In 1847, Theodore Sedgwick, Jr. published his *Elements of Damages* — the first book on the subject then written, excepting only a "slender and shadowy book of Sayers (London, 1770)."[1]

In 1849, appeared *Angell on Carriers*, the first book to treat of the subject of railroads.

In 1853, Professor Theophilus Parsons of the Harvard Law School issued his famous work on *Contracts;* and in 1856, his *Elements of Mercantile Law*, and in 1859, his *Maritime Law*. In 1856, came Joel P. Bishop's *Criminal Law*.

In 1857, came the first book devoted to railway law, Edward L. Pierce's *American Railway Law* — "the first book of the kind on a subject of increasing interest," said

a work that is now regarded by the judicature of the world, as the great book of the age— Story's *Conflict of Laws*."

[1] See review in *Law Reporter*, Vol. IX.

An article in *American Law Register*, Vol. II, in 1853-1854, on the case of *Hadley* v. *Baxendale*, treats the law of damages as a new branch of law, saying:

"Among the interesting questions which are daily arising in our courts of law we may certainly rank those which relate to the measure of damages awarded to the successful party in an action."

the *Law Reporter* (Vol. XX); and in the next year, 1858, came Judge Isaac F. Redfield's valuable book on *Railways*.[1]

In 1857, Causten Browne's *Statute of Frauds* was published — the first book on the subject since Roberts' in England, fifty years before.

A group of three law books of great importance in their time was devoted to a legal topic, now happily obsolete — the law of slavery: *A Practical Treatise on the Law of Slavery* by Jacob D. Wheeler, issued in 1837; *Law of Freedom and Bondage in the United States*, by John C. Hurd, and *Law of Negro Slavery in the United States*, by T. R. R. Cobb, the two latter books appearing in 1858, only four years before, by the emancipation of the slaves, all books of law on the subject became unnecessary.

During the period from 1820 to 1860, several law journals of eminence were published.

In 1822-1823 there appeared William Griffith's valuable *Annual Law Register*.

Between 1822 and 1826, the *United States Law Journal*, edited by members of the Connecticut and New York Bars, had been published; in 1829, the *United States Law Intelligencer and Review* had been started at Providence, but lasted only three years; and in the same year the noted *American Jurist*, in Boston, which lasted until 1842 and to which Story, Charles Sumner, Asahel Stearns, Charles G. Loring, Luther S. Cushing, George S. Hillard, and many of the ablest lawyers of Massachusetts were contributors.[2] The *Law Reporter* was published at Boston from 1838 to 1866; the *Western Law Journal*, at Cincinnati, from 1843 to 1853; the *American Law Register*, at Philadelphia, from 1852 to 1861 (old series); and the

[1] In 1851, a collection of *The Railroad Laws and Charters of the United States* had been issued — see review in *Law Reporter*, Vol. XIV.

[2] See article on *American Law Journals*, in *Law Reporter*, Vol. VII.

*American Law Magazine*, at Philadelphia, from 1843 to 1845. The *American Law Review* began in 1867.

While it is not within the scope of this book to describe the Federal Bar or the legal conditions of a date later than 1860, the following rapid survey of legal literature since that year to the present time, may serve to throw a side-light on the development of the modern American lawyer.

The period from 1860 to 1885 was one of splendid achievement in American legal literature. No attempt is here made to give a complete list; but some of the works of importance in the development of the law, or of interest in denoting changing economic conditions, are mentioned in order to illustrate the influences under which the modern lawyer has worked.

In 1860–1862 appeared Emory Washburn's *American Law of Real Property*, the first comprehensive native book on this subject; in 1863, Washburn's work on *Easements;* in 1865, Theophilus Parsons' on *Promissory Notes and Bills of Exchange;* and in 1867, his book on *Partnership.* These were the work of two professors at the Harvard Law School, whose "distinguished jurists have done so much to illustrate and adorn American jurisprudence," said the *Law Reporter* (Vol. XXIII).

In 1867 appeared one of the early books on a new branch of the law which had developed within fifteen years, — Gregory Yale's *Legal Titles to Mining Claims*, etc., of which the *American Law Review* (Vol. II) said:

"In the Mississippi Valley, and, above all, on the Pacific Ocean, States have sprung into existence and reached a full growth in the midst of the intelligence of the Nineteenth Century. Nowhere else can we so well learn the origin of customs and the ripening of customs into law. The growth of these communities has been so rapid as to outstrip all legislation, and the people have had to become a law unto themselves. The topic of the present work is perhaps the best illustration. The feudal law of real property has had to give way to the exigencies of the case, and the miners of California have had to establish for themselves a set of rules which is now declared, or rather recognized by the courts and the legislature, as the common law of the land."

The great development of railroad and street railway law within ten years was marked by a third edition of *Redfield on Railways* in 1867, of which the *Law Review* (Vol. II) said:

"In the nine years which have elapsed since the second edition was published, few departments of the law have received so much additional light from litigation as that concerning the powers and liabilities of railway corporations. . . . A valuable feature of this treatise is a discussion of the numerous vexed questions concerning horse-railways. We do not know that this has been done before; but it certainly is high time that it should be done. The horse-railway system grew up with probably as little consideration of the legal aspects of the question that were certain to arise, as was possible in such a community as ours."

In 1868, John Norton Pomeroy published the first substantial book on *Constitutional Law* since Judge Story's in 1833; and in the same year appeared Thomas M. Cooley's *Constitutional Limitations*.

The first treatise on the *Law of Telegraphs* by William L. Scott and Milton P. Jarnagin appeared also in 1868, which the *American Law Review* (Vol. II) described as:

"the best which can now be written, considering the newness of the subject discussed and the contrariety of the judicial mind with regard to the duties and responsibilities of those who engage in the transmission of messages by the electric telegraph."

The tremendous increase during the last forty years in the part which the subject of negligence plays in the practise of the law is illustrated by the fact that the first law book on that special subject was published as late as 1869 by Thomas G. Shearman and Amasa A. Redfield — *Treatise on the Law of Negligence,* — of which the *Law Review* (Vols. IV, V) stated:

"Negligence has now for the first time been treated of as a special subject. The volume is, as its authors claim, 'a pioneer in its peculiar field.' . . . The authors were philosophical in their first step when they planted themselves upon a legal conception instead of a branch of trade, as is too often the case nowadays. Negligence is a better subject for a law book than telegraphs."

The year 1870 is to be especially noted for the appearance of a landmark in legal education, Christopher C. Langdell's *A Selection of Cases on the Law of Contracts.* This was the work which introduced the teaching of what is known as the "case system" in American law schools — a revolution in former methods of legal instruction. The legal profession received this new method with much conflict of opinion, and with a decided preponderance of hostility. The following articles show the varying views. The *American Law Review* (Vol. XIV), as late as 1879, paid an enthusiastic tribute to Langdell in a review of the second edition of his *Contracts:*

"It is hard to know where to begin in dealing with this extraordinary production, equally extraordinary in its merits and its limitations. No man competent to judge can read a page without at once recognizing the hand of a great master, and every line is compact of ingenious and original thought. Decisions are reconciled, which those who made them meant to be opposed, and drawn together by subtle lines which were never dreamed of before Mr. Langdell wrote. It may be said without exaggeration that there cannot be found in the legal literature of this country such a *tour de force* of patient and profound intellect working out original theory through a mass of detail, and evolving consistency out of what seemed a chaos of conflicting actions."

On the other hand, in this same year (1879), the *Southern Law Review* said:

"We never could clearly appreciate why this collection (now for the first time issued in two volumes), and Professor Langdell's corresponding collection of *Cases on Sales* were published. He appears to have had a hobby, and this hobby that the law ought to be taught exclusively by means of cases in some form. . . . We suppose we must accept a reappearance of the second edition of this work without much change as an evidence that Professor Langdell's original views are still persisted in. There is just as much sense in endeavoring to instruct students in the principles of law by the exclusive reading of cases as there would be in endeavoring to instruct the students of the West Point Military Academy in the art of war by compelling them to read the official reports of all the leading battles which have been fought in the world's history. . . . In our judgment, the chief value of the present work consists in the Summary which Professor Langdell has appended to the second volume. We cannot doubt that it is a valuable review of the matter presented in the cases. At a glance we can see that it performs one important office: it points out which of them are overruled!"

The year 1872 was remarkable for a group of law books of prime importance, chief of which was a legal classic, in the writing of which Judge John F. Dillon had spent nine years, his *Municipal Corporations*, the first American book entirely devoted to this branch of law. In the same year, Jairus W. Perry published his *Law of Trusts and Trustees;* Francis Wharton, his *Conflict of Laws* (the first on this subject since Story's in 1834); Melville M. Bigelow, his *Law of Estoppel*, "a treatise on a new subject — a new branch of law, estoppel by matter *in pais*," as the *Law Review* (Vol. VI) termed it; Orlando F. Bump, his *Conveyances made by Debtors to Defraud Creditors*, "a work of novel impression."

In the next two years came three books of value: James Schouler's on *Personal Property* (1873); James L. High's on *Injunctions* (1874); A. C. Freeman's on *Judgments* (1873), — the first on this topic, of which the *Law Review* (Vol. VII) said: "Modern growths of civilization necessarily develop new topics in the law; but here is one of the oldest subjects which has been overlooked, though its importance is second to almost none."

The year 1876 was fruitful in important works, chief of which were John W. Daniels' *Negotiable Instruments;* Cooley's *Taxation* — "a substantially new subject in law," said the *Law Review* (Vol. X); High's *Receivers*, — "the first effort to present the entire body of English and American laws on the subject." Of this latter book, it may be noted that the great fires in Boston and Chicago, and the financial troubles of the country, of that period, made its appearance extremely timely. A book published in the next year, 1877, illustrated the growth of a body of law, due also to disastrous conditions of railroad and municipal finances, — G. C. Clemens' *Law of Corporate Securities as Decided in the Federal Courts*. The *Law Review* (Vol. XIII) speaking of the "magnitude of the proportions of railroad litigation," in a review of Leonard A. Jones' *Law of Railroad and Other Corporate Securities*, in 1879, said: "The disasters to railroad enterprises, and the extraordinary and prolonged depression of business within the last seven years, have placed extraordinary temptations before municipalities, groaning under the burdens arising from extravagance, to seek to evade the payment of their contracts for the aid of railroads. The result has been an unexampled number of suits."

Other books reflecting the financial conditions were Jones' work on *Mortgages* in 1878, of which the *Law Review* (Vol. XIV) said: "An essentially clear field . . . during the last half dozen years has come more directly home to what Lord Dufferin aptly describes as the '*pectora et negotia*' of the community, than any subject treated of during that period;" and Dillon's *Removal of Causes from State Courts to Federal Courts*, in 1877, and a third edition in 1881 of the latter, of which the *Law Review* (Vol. XV) said: "The expansion of the monograph from 105 pages in 1877 to 168 pages in 1881 illustrates the appalling growth of case law in this country, — the strong tendency of the Federal judiciary to assert vigorously their own jurisdiction."

In 1877 appeared Melville M. Bigelow's *Fraud;* in 1879, Philemon Bliss' *Code Pleading*, illustrating the spread of Davis Dudley Field's propaganda in behalf of civil codes of procedure; and in 1879, Henry E. Mills' *Eminent Domain*, another work of novel impression.

The immense modern growth of private corporation law made necessary new work on special topics, like Seymour D. Thompson's *Law of Stockholders in Corporations* in 1879, and *The Liability of Directors and Other Officers and Agents of Corporations*, in 1880; and the modern view of corporations was expressed in Victor Morawetz's work on *Private Corporations*, in 1882, of which the *Law Review* (Vol. XVI) said:

"The book is an illustration of the transition through which the law is passing from the view that a corporation is a unit, a personality, to the view that it is a legal institution which is merely the source of rights belonging to various classes of persons, which rights, like many other rights, can ordinarily be affected only through the action or neglect of those to whom they belong."

The twenty years from 1880 to 1900 were less fruitful of great works. In 1880 appeared Cooley's *Constitutional Law.* In 1881 appeared Oliver Wendell Holmes, Jr.'s, remarkable work of juristic research and originality *The Common Law;* and Pomeroy's *Equity Jurisprudence* (the first complete work of the kind since Story's in 1836). Henry N. Sheldon's *Subrogation,* in 1882, and John D. Lawson's *Law of Usages and Customs,* in 1881, filled real lacks in legal literature. In 1883 appeared one of the few American legal works of absolute authority, John C. Gray's *Restraints on the Alienation of Property.* Frederic J. Stimson's *American Statute Law,* in 1886, William W. Cook's *Stock and Stockholders,* in 1887, and Floyd R. Mechem's *Agency* in 1889 may be noticed. In 1890, Roger Foster's *Federal Practice,* bore witness to the greatly increased importance of the Federal courts; B. F. Dos Passos' work on *Collateral Succession and Inheritance Taxes* introduced a knowledge of a form of taxation in comparatively little use at that period; and William C. Robinson published the most comprehensive work on *Patents* written up to that time.

Seymour D. Thompson's *Law of Electricity,* in 1891, was thus spoken of in the *Harvard Law Review* (Vol. V): "The growing popularity of the electric current as a means of facilitating travel and communication of all kinds has necessarily brought with it an endless flow of litigation of an entirely novel character;" and it was followed by Edward R. Keasbey's *Laws of Electric Wire on Streets and Highways,* in 1892, the preface to which said: "It is always interesting to observe the manner in which the courts deal with new inventions and apply old principles of law to new conditions."

In 1892 came one of the first books on a topic which has played a very leading part in legal and economic history since, — William Draper Lewis' *The Federal Power over Commerce*, — the Interstate Commerce Act having been passed in 1887. Judge John M. Vanfleet's *Law of Collateral Attack in Judicial Proceeding*, in 1892, was "the first work in a new and stony field."

The first book involving the law as applied to labor and trust questions, — Charles A. Ray's *Contractual Limitations Including Trade Strikes and Conspiracies, and Corporate Trusts and Combinations*, appeared in 1892; and in 1894 appeared (at the time of the Pullman strike) Thomas S. Cogley's *Strikes and Boycotts*. An important book on a novel branch of law was William A. Keener's *Quasi Contracts*, in 1893. The law of the Employers' Liability Acts, which had existed in England only since 1880, in Alabama since 1885, in Massachusetts since 1887, and in Colorado and Indiana since 1893, was treated in Conrad Reno's *Employers' Liability Acts*, in 1896.

Thompson's *Commentaries on the Law of Private Corporations* was a notable publication in 1895; and an important contribution to legal learning, in 1898, was James B. Thayer's *A Preliminary Treatise on Evidence at the Common Law*. In 1898, the growing importance of trust questions was shown by Charles F. Beach's *Monopolies and Industrial Trusts*, and *The Commerce Clause of the Federal Constitution*, by E. P. Prentice and John G. Egan.

The centennial anniversary of John Marshall's installation as Chief Justice was celebrated on February 4, 1901, throughout the country, the proceedings on which day were fitly recorded in Dillon's *John Marshall — Life, Character, and Judicial Service*.

In 1904-1905, there was published what the *Harvard Law Review* termed "unquestionably one of the most important treatises on a legal subject published during the last generation," — John H. Wigmore's monumental work *A Treatise on the System of Evidence in Trials at Common Law*. *American Railroad Rates*, by Walter C. Noyes, in 1905, marked the rise of the regulation of railroad rates as a legal problem; and his *Law of Intercorporate Relations*, in 1902, also illustrated the extent to which complicated corporation financial questions filled the courts. *The Law of Railroad Rate Regulation*, by Joseph H. Beale and Bruce Wyman, was published in 1906.

Possibly the most novel and remarkable development in legal literature in the last forty years has been the writing of Case Books for the teaching of law on the system founded by Professor C. C. Langdell at the Harvard Law School in 1871. After much opposition on the part of lawyers and law professors, this system made such progress that, in 1902, the following summing-up was made by Professor Ernest W. Huffcut, of Cornell, in an address before the American Bar Association.[1] Of the 98 law schools reporting to him, he stated, 12 had unequivocally adopted the Case System; 34 had unequivocally adopted the text-book system or the text-book and lecture system; 33 employed a combination of the Case System with use of text-books and lectures; 15 announced the use of text-books and cases for regular study and discussion.

The extent of the practical endorsement that has been given by the professors of law may be seen from the fact that 83 Case Books were advertised in the *Harvard Law Review* in June, 1908, of which only 27 had been prepared by professors of the Harvard Law School, the others being the work of professors in the Law Schools of Columbia, Cornell, University of Michigan, Boston University,

[1] *A Decade of Progress in Legal Education*, by E. W. Huffcut, *American Bar Assn. Proc.*, Vol. XXV (1902).

University of Indiana, University of Missouri, University of Minnesota, University of Pennsylvania, University of Chicago, George Washington University, Northwestern University, University of Nebraska, New York Law School, University of the City of New York. In addition, a series of over 30 volumes "covering the fundamentals of the law for the purpose of class room instruction," known as the *American Case Book Series* is being issued.[1]

In the last one hundred years the accumulation of law reports has, as is well known, been vast. In 1810, there had been only 18 American reports published; 452 by 1836; about 800 by 1848; 2,944 by 1822;[2] 3,798 by 1885;[3] and in 1910 there were in existence 8,208 volumes of American law reports (exclusive of about 2,000 volumes of reprinted collections of cases).[4]

Such an increase made necessary the publication of the various great synopses of the law — the *American and English Encyclopædia of Law* in 1887–1896, and its second edition in 1896–1905; the *Cyclopædia of Law and Procedure* in 1901–1911; and the *American Digest, Century Edition*, in 1897–1904.

The most comprehensive view of the historical progress of American law is to be found in *Two Centuries Growth of*

[1] In this connection it may be of interest to refer to an article by Professor Albert Martin Kales entitled *The Next Step in the Evolution of the Case Book*, in *Harvard Law Review*, Vol. XXI (1907); and to an article by Henry W. Ballantine on *Adapting the Case Book to the Needs of Professional Training*, in *Amer. Law School Review*, Vol. II (1908).

See also the Report of the United States Commissioner of Education in 1890–1891, for a full bibliography on the subject of Legal Education.

[2] See *What Shall Be Done with the Reports? — Amer. Law Review*, Vol. XVI (1882).

[3] See *Laws and Jurisprudence of England and America*, by John F. Dillon (1895).

[4] See valuable list of reports given in *Where to Look for the Law* (Lawyers' Co-op. Publishing Co. [1910]).

*American Law*, published in 1901 by members of the Yale Law Faculty.

The principal tools of his trade furnished to the modern American lawyer during the past fifty years have now been enumerated; and the list, though comprising a mass of dry details, throws an interesting light on his progress in the one hundred and twenty-two years since 1789.

The attempt has been made in this book to present in historical series some of the conditions affecting the Bar and the Bench of this country. The law cannot rightly be regarded as something aside and apart from the lawyers and the judges who make it. As a writer in the *American Law Review* said, in 1882:[1] "To study law without understanding the character and habits of the race with which it has grown up, is studying history without geography. . . . It was not by devoting themselves to the niceties of the law that Mansfield and Marshall became great magistrates. Their studies had been such as qualified them for statesmen as well."

In studying a case and the meaning of its decision, the lawyer must, if he would fully grasp its import, know something of the judges who rendered the decision, the influences surrounding them, and the ability of the counsel who argued before them. That a case was argued by Pinkney, Webster, Jeremiah Mason, Rufus Choate, Reverdy Johnson, William Wirt, or John Sergeant, means of itself that every possible assistance was given to the court. Thus, Mr. Justice Miller spoke in one of his decisions of a case in volume ten of *Peters' Reports*, as one "argued at much length by Mr. Webster, Mr. Sergeant and Mr. Clayton, whose names are a sufficient guarantee that the matter

[1] See, *Three Kinds of Law Books — American Law Review*, Vol. XVI (1882).

was well considered." And Professor Simon Greenleaf, in addressing his law students in 1838, pointed particularly to this need of a knowledge of the law from its personal and historical side:

"Judges and lawyers, like other classes of men, become interested in the absorbing topics of the day, and subjected to their magnetic influences; and some passages in the history of the times, or some glimpses of their temper and fashion may be seen in the most dispassionate legal judgments. . . . The manner of the decision, the reasons on which it is professedly founded, and even the decision itself, may receive some coloring and impress from the position of the judges, and their political principles, their habits of life, their physical temperament, their intellectual, moral and religious character. . . . Thus we should hardly expect to find any gratuitous presumption in favor of innocence or any leanings *in mitiori sensu* in the bloodthirsty and infamous Jeffries; nor could we, while reading and considering their legal opinions, forget either the low breeding and meanness of Saunders, the ardent temperament of Buller, the dissolute habits, ferocity and profaneness of Thurlow; or the intellectual greatness and integrity of Hobart, the sublimated piety and enlightened conscience of Hale, the originality and genius of Holt, the elegant manners and varied learning of Mansfield, or the conservative principles, the lofty tone of morals, and vast comprehension of Marshall.

"Neither should we expect a decision leaning in favor of the liberty of the subject from the Star Chamber; nor against the King's prerogative among the judges in the reigns of the Tudors or of James the First; nor should we, on this side of the water, resort to the decisions in Westminster Hall to learn the true extent of the Admiralty jurisdiction which the English Common Law Courts have been always disposed to curtail and in many points to deny; while it is so clearly expounded in the masterly judgments of Lord Stowell, and of his no less distinguished and yet living American contemporary (Story)."

And that a knowledge of contemporary history, and economic, political and social conditions is necessary, both in the decision and in the study of cases, has been well pointed out by Judge Simeon E. Baldwin in an article in *History of the Common Law:*

"The judge cannot shut his eye to the history and spirit of the day and time in which and for which he speaks. The history of the Anglo-American Common Law is very far from being a mere history of judicial precedent. It is rather a history of public custom. No collection of precedents could ever be answerable to the wants of a civilized community. The only collection to satisfy them must be one of the principles of justice and incidents of history from which those precedents were derived."

And, as Oliver Wendell Holmes, Jr., said in *The Common Law:*

"The life of the law has not been logic; it has been experience. The felt necessities of the times, the prevalent moral and political theories, intuitions of public policy, avowed or unconscious — even the prejudices which judges share with their fellow-men, have had a good deal more to do than the syllogism in determining the rules by which men should be governed. The law embodies the story of a nation's development through many centuries. . . . In order to know what it is, we must know what it has been, and what it tends to become. We must alternately consult history and existing theories of legislation. . . . The substance of the law at any given time pretty nearly corresponds, so far as it goes, with what is then understood to be convenient. . . . The very considerations which judges most rarely mention, and always with an apology, are the secret root from which the law draws all the juices of life. I mean, of course, considerations of what is expedient for the community concerned. Every important principle which is developed by litigation is in fact and at bottom the result of more or less definitely understood views of public policy; most generally, to be sure, under our practices and traditions, the unconscious result of instinctive preferences and inarticulate convictions, but none the less traceable to views of public policy in the last analysis."

In reviewing the history of the development of the American Bar, one cannot fail to be impressed with the fact that the lawyers and the judges who have left their mark on the law have been those who were sensitive to the progressive thought of their time, and keenly perceptive of the trend of economic and social conditions. "Reasons of public benefit and convenience weigh greatly with me," said Lord Hardwicke, in *Lawton v. Lawton* (3 Atkins, 16) in 1743; "In considering the rights and obligations arising out of particular relations, it is competent for courts of justice to regard considerations of policy and public convenience, and to draw from them such rules as will in their practical application best promote the safety and security of all parties concerned," said Chief Justice Shaw, in *Farwell v. Boston and Worcester R. R.* (4 Metcalf, 49), in 1842.

On the other hand, nothing can tend more to destroy the influence of the ministers of justice than argument or decision in which principle is subordinated to demands of policy or popular whim. The impressive words of Lord Chief Justice Scroggs in an address to the jury, in 1679 (16 Howell's State Trials, 242) are still full of warning: "If once our courts of justice come to be awed or swayed by vulgar noise, and if judges and juries should manage themselves so as would best comply with the humor of the times, it is falsely said that men are tried for their lives or for times; they live by chance, and enjoy what they have, as the wind blows, and with the same certainty." "Public policy is a very unruly horse, and when once you get astride it you never know where it will carry you," said Judge Burrough, in 1824, in *Richardson v. Mellish* (2 Bingham, 252).

The great lawyer and the great judge — so history will show — is he who is progressively sympathetic with the public needs, but not submissive to the popular demands.

This book, therefore, has been written with the design of illustrating a few of the factors which have produced the American law of to-day, and which have made its history a glorious one. Hence, it is fitting that the last fact to be recorded should be the foundation of the American Bar Association, in 1878, the work and influence of which has done much to place the American lawyer of to-day in the position where, using the words of old Cotton Mather, written two hundred years ago: "You may, Gentlemen, if you please, be a Vast Accession to the Felicity of your Countreys."

## APPENDIX

The following is the earliest plan ever drafted for an American professorship of law. It is the work of President Ezra Stiles, of Yale College, in 1777, and is here reproduced from the original manuscript now in the Yale University Library:

"The Professorship of Law is equally important with that of Medicine; not indeed towards educating Lawyers or Barristers, but for forming *Civilians*. Fewer than a quarter perhaps of the young gentlemen educated at College, enter into either of the learned professions of Divinity, Law or Physic: The greater part of them after finishing the academic Course return home, mix in with the body of the public, and enter upon *Commerce* or the *cultivation of their Estates*. And yet perhaps the most of them in the Course of their Lifes are called forth by their Country into some or other of the various Branches of civil Inprovement & the public offices in the State. Most certainly it is worthy of great attention, the Discipline and Education of these in that knowledge which shall qualify them to become useful Members of Society, as Selectmen, Justices of Peace, Members of the Legislature, Judges of Courts, & Delegates in Congress. How happy for a community to abound with men well instituted in the knowledge of their Rights & Liberties? This Knowledge is catching, & insinuates [among those] not of liberal Education — to fit them for public service. It is greatly owing to the Seats of Learning among us that the arduous Conflict of the present day has found America abundantly furnished with Men adequate to the great and momentous Work of constructing new Policies or forms of Government and conducting the public arrangements in the military, naval & political Departments & the whole public administration of the *Republic of the United States*, with that Wisdom & Magnanimity which already astonishes Europe and will honor us to late Posterity. We are enlarging into still greater Systems, in which we may transplant the Wisdom of all Countries & Ages. It is in this view chiefly, & principally for this end, that the several States may see the Expediency of endowing Professorships of Law in the Colleges. It is scarce possible to enslave a Republic of Civilians, well instructed in their Laws, Rights & Liberties. The Lectures of a Professorship of Law may be resolved into four series.

I. The *civil Law.* It will be necessary to exhibit an idea of the antient Roman Law in its purest State under the Senate, before the period of the Cæsars, & previous to the mutations which the Jus civile received by the imperatorial Edicts: then to take a view of the imperatorial Law down to the Times of Justinian. Then instead of attending to the mutations it assumed by being blended with the local Laws of the Roman Conquests, the Provinces — instead of considering how much of it is still preserved in the Jurisprudence of Poland, Germany, Holland, France, Spain or Italy — go directly to England and consider how much of the Jus civile entered into the Jurisprudence of England, for the greatest part of the Jurisprudence of America has been adopted from England. Three Streams of the imperial Law entered England & obtaines there with Efficacy to this day. The first is the canon or ecclesiastical Law, which it is hoped will never enter America; the second testamentary law; the third the maritime Law in Admiralty Courts. This last is of great importance, for the Laws of Rhodes & Oleron. The whole system of Maritime Law will probably be adopted by these States, under the Improvement of a Jury for Trials in maritime Courts. This is all of the Civil Law which will be ever necessary for Americans to study.

II. The second series of Lectures may be upon the *Common Law* of England. For although neither this nor any other foreign Law will ever be in force in America by any Authority or Jurisdiction on the other side the Atlantic, it will however prevail by derivative use, Custom & Adoption. It will be of particular Utility to exhibit a Lecture of Negatives, *i. e.*, a number of capital Things of the common Law of England which never could be, nor ever was introduced here — & so to draw the Line — leaving all the rest as the common Law System of these States. Connected with this may be a summary

Representation of the Statute Law, both those designedly made by Parliament for the Colonies which are henceforth forever abolished, & those adopted by the American Legislatures: and tho' many of these will be repealed, yet the greater part may remain in the Jurisprudence of the United States. As Justinian's Institutes may be the Textual Book for the Civil: so Hale's Analysis &c may be for the common Law.

III. The Subject of the third Series will be the Codes of the thirteen States. The Professor will exhibit the Spirit & Governing Principles of each Code. Connected with this will be a particular Representation of the Jurisprudence of Connecticut, the Courts & their Jurisdictions, and as much of the Course of Practice as is founded in principle, and not merely officinal, for this is best learned at the Bar & by living with a Lawyer. Degrees to be taken.

IV. The last Series may consist of Lectures exhibiting the Policies and Forms of Government of all the Kingdoms, Empires & Republics in the World, especially those of Europe & that of China — which last is perhaps the best formed Policy on Earth, as it alone combines one-third of the whole human race. The Nature & Wisdom of such a Policy is worthy the peculiar Attention of the infant Empire in America, growing into a future Greatness & Glory surpassing perhaps what have ever appeared. And as we shall transplant all the Improvement in Knowledge, Manufactures & Commerce from all Countries, so by a thorough Knowledge of the fundamental Principles of their respective public Politics, we may learn how to distinguish & avoid Precedents dangerous to Liberty. Summary Representations of the Spirit of the Laws & Jurisprudence of each & all the Kingdoms & States will shew us what, having endured the Trial of Ages, will be worthy of Adoption by the American Legislatures. All this will lay a Foundation for the accurate Knowledge of the *Laws of Nations* — Laws of mutual Intercourse & political Transactions between separate Sovereignties & Independent States, a Branch of Knowledge necessary to regulate the Intercourse between these States, as well as the negotiations with European & other foreign Powers. This will enable such a multitude of Gentlemen among the body of people at large to judge on political matters, as shall owe those into Fidelity whom the States may entrust with public & important negotiations. This political Knowledge diffused through a State, will establish its Liberty, Security & Aggrandizement too firmly to be overturned by either a military power or those insidious Arts & Corrupt measures, which in conjunction with Arms have at length in all countries prostrated the Rights of mankind, in a general ruin. The cultivation of this political Knowledge & Wisdom will tranfuse a spirit among the body of the people in America [which] will be the only security of their Liberty under Providence, & tend to effect that public Virtue & produce those wise Institutions which may advance the United States to the Summit of political Perfection & Honor."

# INDEX

[Note. Law cases and titles (in condensed form) of law books are printed in italics.]

## A


*Ableman* v. *Booth*, 441.
Accident Law, 449–450.
Adams, John, 83; on Hutchinson, 77; as to law profession, 79–80; on admission to Bar, 82, 84; on study of law, 79, 83; on barristers, 87; as to scarcity of law books, 163; course of law study, 171–173; description of Bar meetings, 203; opinion of Marshall, 252 note; *Feudal and Common Law*, 334.
Adams, John Quincy, 318; views of Coke, 177; legal education of, 181; on prejudices against lawyers, 220; as to Judge Chase, 230; in early Supreme Court, 261, 262; argues *Fletcher* v. *Peck*, 270; opinion of legality of embargo act, 277 note; as to Federal Bar in 1817, 366; opinion of Pinkney, 382; on law logic, 328 note; opinion of Marshall, 421; argues *U. S.* v. *Amistad*, 429–430; views of *Prigg* case, 431 note.
Adams, Samuel, 82.
Addington, Isaac, 75.
*Addison's Reports*, 330.
Admiralty Law, early English books on, 34 note; in United States, 279.
Alabama, first law reports, 366; Federal bar of, 412.
Alexander, James, 95.
Allen, William, 104.
Alvord, James O., 531.
Ambler, John, 46.
American Bar Association, founded, 562.
*American Digest, Century Edition*, 557.
*American and English Encyclopædia of Law*, 557.
*American Jurist*, 547.
*American Law Journal*, 339.
*American Law Magazine*, 548.
*American Law Register*, 547.
*American Law Review*, 548.
American Literature before 1830, 461 note.
American Magazines, between 1815 and 1860, 461 note.
*American Precedents of Declarations*, 332, 333.
Ames, Fisher, 109; letter as to Boston Bar, 308.
Ames, Samuel, 411, 436, 437; *Corporations*, 546.
Amory, Rufus G., 262.
Andrews, John, 142.
Angell, Joseph K., *Watercourses*, 541; *Corporation*, 546; *Carriers*, 547.
*Annual Law Register*, 547.
Anthon, John, 304; *American Precedents*, 333.
Aplin, John, 142.
Arkansas, first law reports, 408; Federal bar of, 412.
*Armory* v. *Delamire*, 147.
Arnold, Oliver, 143.

Ashmun, Eli P., 318.
Ashmun, George, 439.
Ashmun, John H., 529.
Ássheton, Robert, 107.
Assheton, William, 108.
Atkinson, Theodore, 134.
Atkinson, William K., 320.
Attorneys-General of United States, 263, 367, 444.
Attorneys, see LAWYERS.
Atwood, William, 92.
Auchmuty, Robert, 76, 78.
Austin, Benjamin, attack on lawyers by, 219, 228.
Austin, James T., 409, 429, 469.
Avery, William, 123.
*Azuni*, 335.

B

Babcock, Joshua, 141.
Bacon, Francis, Common Law, 34; plans a code, 513.
B..on, Matthew, *Abridgment*, 150.
Badger, George E., 413.
Baker, Edward D., 410.
Baldwin, Abraham, 126.
Baldwin, Henry, 401, 444.
Baldwin, Simeon, 323.
Bancroft, George, description of Marshall, 416.
*Bank of Augusta* v. *Earle*, 429; description of, 500–505.
*Bank of Columbia* v. *Patterson Admr.*, 287.
*Bank of North America* v. *Vardon*. 285.
*Bank of U. S.* v. *Dandridge*, account of, 399–400.
*Bank of U. S.* v. *Deveaux*, 505.
Bankruptcy, law of, 463–466; Supreme Court decisions as to, 377–379, 398.
Bar, genial relations of, 84–85, 203–207; rules for admission to, 201–203; Suffolk County records of, 83–85, 88, 196–200. See also FEDERAL BAR and LAWYERS.
Bar Associations, in Massachusetts, 83, 88; in New York, 98, 201; in New Jersey, 113; in New Hampshire, 138–139; in Rhode Island, 142; Suffolk County records, 196–200; New Hampshire regulations, 200; Connecticut, 201; first in Connecticut, 322; prejudices against, 510–511.
Barbour, Philip P., 383, 443.
Barker, Thomas, 123.
Barradale, Edward, 46.
Barristers, in England, 28–30; in Massachusetts, 85–88; in New Jersey, 113; American lawyers as, 188–189; appointments of in U. S. Circuit Court, 243; last in Massachusetts, 307.
Bartlett, Ichabod, 320.
Bartlett, Josiah, 135.
Bartlett, Sidney, 408.
Batture Case, 271–274.
Bayard, James A., 246, 261.
*Bay's Reports*, 330.
Bayley, John, *Bills and Notes*, 150.
Beach, Charles F., *Monopolies*, 555.
Beale, Joseph H., *Railroad Rate Regulation*, 556.
Beardsley, Samuel, 409.
*Bell* v. *Locke*, 462.
Bellingham, Richard, 59.
Bemis, George, 471.
Benjamin, Judah P., 412.
Benson, Egbert, 293, 297.
Bentham, Jeremy, description of his life and works, 513–518; *Legislation Civil and Criminal*, 514; *Judicial Evidence*, 515; *Codification*, 515.
Benton, Thomas H., 370, 411.
Berrien, John M., 370, 396, 410.
Bibb, George M., 262, 410.
*Bibb's Reports*, 330.
Bigelow, George T., 451, 471.
Bigelow, Melville M., *Estoppel*, 551; *Fraud*, 553.
Bigelow, Timothy, 318.
Binney, Horace, 262; description of effect of embargo on lawyers, 278, 410, 414; in *Vidal* v. *Phil*, 433–435.

*Binney's Reports*, 330.
Bishop, Joel P., *Married Women*, 471; *Criminal Law*, 546.
Black, Jeremiah S., 444.
Blackford, Isaac N., 447.
*Blackstone's Commentaries*, 150, 177–179.
Blackstone, William, 150, 177 note.
Blair, John, 47, 242, 251.
Blair, Montgomery, 441.
Blake, George, 318, 368.
Bliss, Philemon, *Codes*, 553.
Blowers, Sampson S., 83.
*Body of Liberties*, 64–65.
Bohun, William, *Institutio*, 150; *Declarations*, 150.
Bollan, William, 82.
Booth, A., *Examen*, 34.
Bordley, Stephen, 54.
Bordley, Thomas, 54.
*Boston Glass Mfg. Co.* v. *Binney*, 470.
Botsford, Amos, 134.
Botts, Benjamin, 268.
Bouvier, John, *Law Dictionary*, 546.
*Boyce* v. *Anderson*, 397.
Brackenridge, Henry N., *Law Miscellanies*, 336.
Bracton, Henry, *Laws of England*, 32.
Bradbury, Theophilus, 83, 139.
Bradford, Alexander, 533.
Bradford, William, 246, 250.
*Bradford's Case*, 236.
Bradley, Joseph H., 410.
Bradley, Joseph P., 413.
Bradley, Stephen R., 322.
Bradley, James, *Distress*, 337.
Bradstreet, Simon, 59.
Branch, Thomas, *Principia*, 156.
Breese, Sidney, 410.
Brent, Mrs. Margaret, 52.
Brent, Robert J., 410.
Bridges, John, 92.
*Briscoe* v. *Bank*, 422.
Britton, John, *Abridgment*, 32.
*Bronson* v. *Kinzie*, 432.
Brooke, Sir Robert, *Abridgment*, 33.
*Brown* v. *Maryland*, 398.
*Brown* v. *N. Y. Gaslight Co.*, 452
Brown College, law professorship, 349.
Browne, Causten, *Statute of Frauds*, 547.
Browning, Orville H., 410.
Brownlow, Richard, *Declarations*, 34.
Bull, Henry, 142.
Bullivant, Benjamin, 72.
Bump, Orlando F., *Fraudulent Conveyances*, 552.
Burges, Tristam, 143.
Burke, Aedanus, 122.
Burke, Edmund, views of American knowledge of law, 180.
Burr, Aaron, 298; description of by Kent, 296; trial of, 267–269.
Burrill, James, 143.
Butler, Benjamin F., 409, 444, 524.
*Bynkershoek's Laws of War*, 335.
Byrd, William, 45; law library of, 162.

## C

Cady, Daniel, 304.
Caines, George, 294, 331.
*Caines' Reports*, 331.
Calhoun, John C., 413.
California, first law reports, 408.
Call, Daniel, 261.
*Call's Reports*, 330.
*Calye's Case*, 19.
Campbell, Alexander, 248.
Campbell, James, 411, 440, 458, 459.
Campbell, John A., 412, 444.
Campbell, Lord, on legal education, 153–155; on common law in 18th century, 147–148; opinion of Coke, 175 note.
Care, Henry, *English Liberties*, 34.
Carr, Dabney, 47.
Carrington, Paul, 47.
Carroll, Charles, 54; letters as to Inns of Court Education, 191–194.
Carroll, Charles, of Carrollton, 56.
*Case Books*, 556–557.
Catron, John, 370, 443.
Cauther, James, 51.
Chalmers, George, 56.

Chancery Reports, in England, 17th century, 36–38; 18th century, 149.
Channing, William, 143.
Chapman, Reuben A., 537.
*Charles River Bridge* v. *Warren Bridge*, account of, 423–426, 478.
Charlton, John, 123.
Chase, Salmon P., 411, 437, 459; *Revision of Ohio Statutes*, 531.
Chase, Samuel, 56; decision on Federal common law, 229–230; impeachment trial, 267, 291.
Chauncey, Charles, 134.
Checkley, Anthony, 73, 74.
*Cherokee Nation* v. *Georgia*, account of, 414.
*Chesley's Case*, 236.
Chew, Benjamin, 104, 110.
Chief Justice, in States who develveloped the common law, 447–448; in Colonies, see separate Colonies, courts in.
Chipman, Daniel, *Contracts*, 542.
Chipman, Nathaniel, *Dissertations*, 336; as law professor, 356.
*Chipman's Reports*, 330.
*Chisholm* v. *Georgia*, 247.
Chitty, Joseph, *Bills and Notes*, 150.
Choate, Rufus, 409; description of *Marbury* v. *Madison*, 264; description of *Dartmouth College* case, 374, 436, 439; in *Goodyear* case, 458.
Circuit Courts of United States, 241, 244–245; under 1801 statute, 252–253; under 1802 statute, 253; under 1869 statute, 445.
Circuit Court of Appeals, 445.
Civil Law Books, early American translations of, 335.
Claggett, Wiseman, 138.
Clark, Thomas, 107.
Clay, Henry, 262; as law professor, 353, 370; in *Bank* case, 396; in *Ogden* v. *Saunders*, 398, 410, 422, 429; death, 413.
Clayton, John, 45.
Clemens, G. C., *Corporate Securities*, 552.
*Clerke's Praxis*, 335.
Clifford, John H., 409, 438.
Clifford, Nathan, 444.
Clinton, De Witt, 304.
Clinton, George, 98.
Cobb, Thomas R. R., *Slavery*, 547.
Codes, in New York, 524–525; in England, 526; in Pennsylvania, 528; in Massachusetts, 528–531, 534, 536–538; in New York, 531–533, 535–536; in other States, 539 note.
Code Napoléon, 508, 512, 513, 520, 527.
Codification, agitation for in United States, 517–528.
Coffin, Peter, 134.
*Coggs* v. *Barnard*, 146.
Cogley, Thomas S., *Strikes*, 555.
*Cohens* v. *Virginia*, 383–385.
Coke, Sir Edward, advice as to study of law, 31; *Institutes;* Eldon's opinion of, 174–175; Campbell's opinion, 175 note; study of, by American lawyers, 171–178.
Colden, C. D., 304.
*Coleman's Reports*, 331.
Colleges, education of colonial lawyers in, 18, 194–195.
College of Philadelphia, law professorship, 346–349.
Colonial statutes, publication of, 161.
Columbia College, law professorship, 349–352.
Commerce Court, 445.
Common law, in Colonies, 10–15; in Virginia, 39; in Maryland, 49–50; in Massachusetts, 60–66; in New York, 90–91; in Pennsylvania, 102–103; in South Carolina, 120; in Connecticut, 12–13; in Rhode Island, 13, 140–141; in England in 18th century, 147–148; binding in new States, 225; prejudices against, 225–239, 508–512; in Federal Courts, 228–231; development of American, 446–448.
*Com.* v. *Carlisle*, 469.

*Com.* v. *Clap*, 238.
*Com.* v. *Freeman*, 237.
*Com.* v. *Hunt*, 469.
*Com.* v. *Rogers*, 471.
*Com.* v. *Temple*, 452.
Comyns, John, *Digest*, 150.
Conflict of Laws, first books on, 545, 551.
Connecticut, colonial bar in, 130–134; courts in, 129; rules for admission of lawyers, 201; early State bar, 322–323; first bar association in, 322; first law reports in, 328–329.
Conrad, Charles M., 412.
Conspiracy, first statute in England as to lawyers, 24.
Contracts, early American books on, 542.
Cook, William W., *Stockholders*, 554.
Cooley, Thomas M., *Constitutional Limitations*, 554.
*Cooley* v. *Port Wardens*, 439.
Cooper, Thomas, *Bankrupt Law*, 336; as law professor, 364.
Copyright, law of, 460–461.
Cord, William H., *Married Women*, 471.
Corporations, first book on, in England, 34; early law in United States, 284–288; development after 1815 of law of, 492–507.
Cotton, John, 63.
*Covington Drawbridge Co.* v. *Shepherd*, 506.
Cowell, John, *Institutes*, *Interpreter*, *Dictionary*, 33.
Cowell, Gideon, 140.
Coxe, Richard S., 368, 409.
*Coxe's Reports*, 330.
*Craig* v. *Missouri*, 400, 423.
Cranch, William, 331.
Crawford, William H., 410, 502.
Criminal Law, insanity in, 471.
Crittenden, John J., 410, 437, 444.
*Cumber* v. *Wane*, 147.
Cummings, William, 123.
Curtis, Benjamin, R. 409; opinion of Taney, 421–422; 443, 444, 537.
Curtis, George T., 441.
Curwin, Jonathan, 74.
Cushing, Caleb, 408; views of early Supreme Court, 251; 444; his *Pothier*, 541.
Cushing, Luther S., 530, 531.
Cushing, William, 75, 83, 139, 242, 244 note, 272.
*Cyclopedia of Law and Procedure*, 557.

D

Daggett, David, 323; as law professor, 364, 378, 463.
Dallas, Alexander J., 245, 247, 250, 256, 257, 279, 280; defence of common law, 233 note; his *Reports*, 330.
Dallas, George M., 411, 440.
Dalton, Michael, *Justice*, 33.
Damages, first book on, 546.
Dana, Francis, 83, 237.
Dana, Richard, 82.
Dana, Richard H., Jr., 409, 432; description of legal practice in Massachusetts, 207.
Dana, Samuel, Jr., 318.
Dane, Nathan, 528; *Abridgment*, 540.
Daniel, Peter L., 443.
Daniels, John W., *Negotiable Instruments*, 552.
Dartmouth College, law professorship, 355.
*Dartmouth College* v. *Woodward*, account of, 372–377; place in American jurisprudence, 432–433; influence of on legislation, 499.
Davie, William R., 125; opinion of judiciary act, 241.
Daveis, Charles G., 413.
Davis, Daniel, 318, 262.
Davis, John, 409, 423, 424, 436, 439, 528.
Dawson, John, 123.
Day, Thomas, 323.
Dayton, William L., 413.
Death, liability statutes for, 449.
Debtors, increasing protection to, by law from 1830 to 1860, 463–469.

Delaware, rules for admission of lawyers, 202; Federal bar of, 246.
De Lancey, James, 92.
*De Lovio* v. *Boit*, 280.
De Peyster, Abraham, 92.
De Saussure, Henry W., 291.
De Tocqueville, Alexis, on lawyers, 222, 512.
Dexter, Franklin, 319, 408, 419, 458.
Dexter, Samuel, 246, 262, 277; description by Ticknor, 282–283; sketch of, 309–311, 371.
Dickerman, Edward M., 409, 459.
Dickinson, John, 110.
Dickinson, Samuel F., law school of, 365.
Dillon, John F., *Municipal Corporations*, 551; *Removal of Causes*, 553.
District of Columbia, bar of, 368, 409.
District Courts of United States, 241.
*Diversity of the Courts*, 32.
Doddridge, John, *Lawyer*, 34.
Dos Passos, B. F., *Collateral Inheritance*, 554.
Douglas, Stephen A., 410.
Downing, Emanuel, 59.
Drayton, John, 262, 279.
Drayton, William H., 122.
Duane, James, 98.
Duane, William, attacks on lawyers by, 221–223.
Duane, William J., *Law of Nations*, 335.
Dudley, John, 136.
Dudley, Joseph, 92.
Dudley, Paul, 75, 78.
Dudley, Thomas, 59.
Duer, John, 304; describes legal conditions in New York, 327, 524.
Duer, William A., 304; *Constitution*, 545 note.
Dugdale, William, *Origines*, 34.
Dulany, Daniel, Jr., 55.
Dulany, Daniel, Sr., 50, 51, 54.
*Dumpor's Case*, 19.
Dunce's Parliament, 25, 70.
Duponceau, Peter, 257; describes Pennsylvania bar before early Supreme Court, 256; 279; describes prejudice against common law, 235; Law Academy founded by, 364; *Constitution*, 545 note.
Dutton, Warren, 423.
Duvall, Gabriel, 291, 418.
Dyer, Eliphalet, 133.

E

Eaton, John H., 360.
Edwards, Pierrepont, 323.
Eldon, Lord, education of, 154–156; opinion of Coke, 174–175.
Ellsworth, Oliver, 129; legal education of,170; drafts judiciary act, 240; in England, 250 note.
Elmsly, Alexander, 123.
*Elkinson* v. *Deliesseline*, 388.
*Ellis* v. *Amer. Tel. Co.*, 451.
Embargo, 276–277.
*Emerigon*, 335.
Emery, Noah, 139.
Emmet, Thomas Addis, 262; argues *The Nereide*, 280–284; sketch of, 302–303; 368; in steamboat case, 393, 397.
English language, law books in, 22, 33, 149.
Estoppel, first book on, 552.
Eustis, George, 412.
Everett, Edward, description of status of Supreme Court, 404–405; review of Story's *Constitution*, 418; views as to codes, 523, 530.
Evidence, change in law of, 472–474.
Ewing, Thomas, 370, 441.

F

*Fairfax* v. *Hunter*, 371.
*Farwell* v. *Boston & Worcester R. R.*, 449, 485, 561.
Fearne, Charles, *Remainders*, 150.
Federal Bar, first lawyers admitted, 242; early Supreme Court, 245–246, 256–262; between 1815 and

1830, 366–370; between 1830 and 1860, 408–413; description by Sumner in 1834, 418–419.
Fenwick, Cuthbert, 51.
Fessenden, Thomas G., *Patents*, 337, 541.
Fessenden, William P., 413, 432.
Field, David Dudley, 532, 535.
Finch, Henry, *Common Law*, 33.
Fire Insurance, early law of, 288; later law of, 455–456.
Fitch, Thomas, 131.
Fitzherbert, Anthony, *Abridgment*, 32.
Fitzhugh, William, 45.
*Fleta*, 33.
Fletcher, Richard, 409.
*Fletcher* v. *Peck*, 269–271, 317.
Florida, first law reports, 408.
*Fogg* v. *Middlesex Fire Ins. Co.*, 455.
Fonblanque, John, *Equity*, 150.
Foot, Samuel A., 369.
Forbes, Charles E., 530.
Foster, Michael, *Crown Pleas*, 150.
Foster, Roger, *Federal Practice*, 554.
Fox, Charles, 410.
Francis, Richard, *Maxims*, 150.
Francis, Tench, 109.
Freeman, Abraham C., *Judgments*, 552.
Freeman, Samuel, *Probate Directory*, 336.
Fulbeck, William, *Study of Law*, 31.
*Fundamental Orders*, 128.

G

Gaillard, Theodore, 122.
Gamble, Hamilton R., 411.
Gardiner, John, plans for law reform of, 218.
Gas, law of accidents from, 452.
Gaston, William, 370.
*Georgia* v. *Brailsford*, 250.
*Genesee Chief*, 440.
Georgia, colonial bar and courts in, 125–126; first law reports, 366; Federal bar of, 370.
Gerrish, John, 134.
Geyer, Henry S., 411, 441.
Gibbes, William H., 122.
*Gibbons* v. *Ogden*, account of, 392–396.
Gibson, John B., 447
Gifford, Archer, 459.
Gilbert, Geoffrey, *Ejectments*, 150.
Gillet, Ransom H., 409, 459.
Gilpin, Henry D., 412, 429, 444, 458.
Glanville, Ramulf de, *Laws of England*, 32.
*Goodyear* v. *Day*, 458.
Goodrich, Chauncy, 323.
Goodrich, Elizur, as law professor, 354.
Gordon, Charles, 56.
Gordon, Thomas, 112.
Gore, Christopher, 315.
Georges, Thomas, 139.
Gould, James, 323; as law professor, 358–361; *Pleading*, 546.
Governors, Royal, antagonism of lawyers to, 8; in Maryland, 55; in New York, 98–101.
Gray, John C., *Restraints on Alienation*, 554.
Graham, David, 535.
Graham, John, 95.
Grain elevators, law of, 454.
Green, Henry W., 447.
Greene, Albert C., 411.
Greene, Richard W., 411, 436, 437.
Greenleaf, Simon, in *Charles River Bridge* case, 423–425; 530; his *Evidence*, 546.
Gridley, Jeremiah, 81; advice to Adams on study of law, 83, 171–173.
Grier, Robert C., 444.
Griffiths, William, *Annual Law Register*, 547.
Griffin, George, 304.
Grimke, John F., 122; *Executors*, 336.
Griswold, Mathew, 133; law library of, 162.
Griswold, Roger, 261, 323.
*Groves* v. *Slaughter*, 429.

Growdon, John, 104.
Grundy, Felix, 370, 444.
Guest, John, 104.

H

Haines, Charles G., 369, 398.
Hall, Sir Matthew, work of law reform, 21, 514; *Pleas*, 34; *Common Law*, 150.
Hall, John E., *Admiralty*, 335.
Hall, J. Prescott, 369, 439.
Hall, Willis, 439.
Hallett, Benjamin F., 438.
Hamilton, Alexander, 298; argues *People* v. *Croswell*, 238; only appearance in Supreme Court, 249.
Hamilton, Andrew, 108, 236.
Hammond, Charles, 370, 396.
Hammond, John, 56.
Harrison, Benjamin, 45.
Hand, George E., 412.
Hardin, Benjamin, 370, 422.
*Hardin's Reports*, 330.
Harding, George, 459.
Hare, Charles W., 349.
Harper, Robert Goodloe, 261, 262, 267, 270, 279, 369, 396.
*Harris and McHenry's Reports*, 330.
Harris, Thomas, *Modern Entries*, 333.
Harrison, Richard, 296.
Harvard College Library, law books in, 164.
Harvard Law School, 361–364.
Hastings, Warren, trial of, 47, 267 note.
Hawle, John, *Englishman's Right*, 34.
Hawkins, William, *Crown Pleas*, 150.
Hawley, Joseph, 82.
Hay, George, pamphlets on libel, 238; letter from Jefferson, 265; at Burr trial, 268; in *Batture Case*, 274; in *Hunter* v. *Martin*, 371.
Hayne, Robert Y., 370.
Haynes, John, 128.
Haywood, John, 125.
*Haywood's Reports*, 330.
*Head* v. *Provident Ins. Co.*, 261, 287.
Hearne, Joseph, 79.
Henderson, John, 411.
Henderson, John B., 458.
Hendricks, Thomas A., 412.
Hengham, Ralph de, *Register*, 33.
Hening, William W., *American Pleader*, 334.
*Hening and Mumford's Reports*, 330.
Henry, John V., 304.
Henry, Patrick, 47; legal education of, 165, 248.
Heyward, Thomas, 122.
Hicks, Whitehead, 97.
High, James L., *Injunctions; Receivers*, 552.
Hillhouse, James, 246, 323.
Hillhouse, James A., 133.
Hilliard, Francis, *Real Property*, 546.
Hinckes, John, 134.
Hoar, George F., description of legal practice in Massachusetts, 206.
Hoar, Samuel, 315.
Hobart, John Sloss, 292.
Hoffman, David, 261; law school of, 356; 369.
Hoffman, Josiah Ogden, 246, 262, 280, 297.
Hoffman, Ogden, 369, 409.
*Hollister* v. *Nowlen*, 484.
Holloway, John, 46.
*Holly* v. *Boston Gaslight Co.*, 452.
Holmes, Oliver W., Jr., *Common Law*, 554.
Homestead Laws, 468.
Honyman, James, Jr., 142, 143.
Hooper, William, 125.
Hopkinson, Francis, 110; *Reports*, 330.
Hopkinson, Joseph, 267, 369; in *College* case, 372–374; in *Sturgis* case, 378; in *McCulloch* case, 379.
Hopkins, William, 46.
Horne, Andrew, *Miroir des Justices*, 33.
Horsmanden, Daniel, 93.
Hosmer, Titus, 133.

Harvard, Volney E., 411.
Howe, Samuel, 318; law school of, 364.
Howell, David, as law professor, 349.
Howell, Jeremiah B., 246.
Hubbard, Samuel, 465, 470.
Hubbard, Leverett, 134.
*Hughes' Reports*, 330.
Humphreys, John, 59.
Hunt, William M., 412.
Hunter, William, 261, 368.
*Hunter* v. *Martin*, 371.
Huntingdon, Jabez W., 358.
Huntingdon, Samuel, 133.
Hurd, John C., *Slavery*, 547.
Hutchinson, Thomas, 75-77.
Hutson, Richard, 122.
*Hylton* v. *U. S.*, 249.

## I

Illinois, first law reports, 366; Federal bar of, 410.
Imprisonment for debt, law of, 467.
Indiana, first law reports, 366; Federal bar of, 412.
Ingersoll, Charles J., 369; on prejudices against lawyers, 221, 396, 411, 461, 502; on prejudices against common law, 509–510.
Ingersoll, Jared, Sr., 131.
Ingersoll, Jared, Jr., 245, 247, 249, 250, 256, 257, 262, 279; as to inns of court education, 194 note.
Ingersoll, Joseph R., 369, 411.
Inns of Chancery, 28, 67 note.
Inns of Court, history of, 27–30; in 18th century, 150–156; in Shakespeare, 68 note; American lawyers at, 188–194.
Insanity, as a defence, 471.
Insolvency, law of, 463–466.
Iowa, first law reports, 408.
Iredell, James, 124; legal education of, 173; a judge, 242; opinion of counsel in British debts case, 248; opinion of Hamilton's argument, 249; death, 251.

## J

Jackson, Charles, 315, 465, 531; *Real Actions*, 543.
Jacob, Stephen, 322.
Jacobs, Giles, *Dictionary*, 150.
*Jacobsen's Laws of the Sea*, 335.
Jamieson, David, 95, 112.
Janin, Louis, 412.
Jarnagin, Milton P., *Telegraphs*, 549.
Jay, John, 98, 292; views of Supreme Court, 251.
Jay, Peter A., 304.
Jefferson, Thomas, 47; legal education of, 171; views as to common law, 230; views on *Marbury* v. *Madison*, 265, 272; views of Burr trial, 269; interest in the *Batture* case, 271–274; opinion of Levi Lincoln, James Sullivan and Joseph Story, 273; opinion of Marshall, 272, 275 note; founds first collegiate law professorship, 343; opinion of Marshall, and *Cohens* case, 384–385.
Jenckes, Thomas A., 411.
Johnson, Augustus, 143.
Johnson, George, 47.
Johnson, Reverdy, 410; in *Brown* v. *Maryland*, 398; 437, 439, 441, 444, 458, 459.
Johnson, Dr. Samuel, advice on law study, 156.
Johnson, Thomas, 56.
Johnson, William, 291, 331, 398, 443.
Johnson, William S., 132, 133.
Jones, George, 54.
Jones, Joel, 528.
Jones, Leonard A., *Railroad Securities*, 552; *Mortgages*, 553.
Jones, Samuel, 97, 296, 524.
Jones, Thomas, 123.
Jones, Walter, 261, 368, 371, 379, 422, 423, 429, 433.
Jones, William, *Bailments*, 150.
*Jones* v. *Walker*, 248.
*Jones* v. *Van Zandt*, 437.
Jowles, Henry, 54.

Judah, Samuel, 412.
Judges, Ignorance of Colonial, 8, 9; in England in 17th century, 20, 22, 74; in Virginia, 44–45; in New York, 92; in South Carolina, 120; in Pennsylvania, 104; in New Jersey, 112; in Connecticut, 129; in New Hampshire, 134–136; in Rhode Island, 141.
Judges of United States Supreme Court, first, 242; changes in early years, 251; additional, 254; picture of, in 1815, 281; changes in, 401; salary of, 401; additional, 443–444; salary, 445. See SUPREME COURT OF THE UNITED STATES.
Judiciary Act, 240–241; attempts to change 25th section, 385–387, 413.
*Justinian's Institutes*, 335.

K

Keasbey, Edward R., *Electric Wires*, 554.
Keener, William A., *Quasi-Contracts*, 555.
Kempe, John T., 97.
Kent, Benjamin, 82.
Kent, James, 293; description of 17th century New York bar, 97; legal education of, 182, 187; views of early Supreme Court, 247; description of early New York State bar and Hamilton, 295–300; sketch of, 298; as law professor, 349–352; his *Commentaries*, 351, 542–543; considered as Supreme Court judge, 389, 401; adviser of Cherokees, 414, 524; sketch of, by Story, 316.
Kentucky, statute forbidding English citations, 232; bar of in early Supreme Court, 262; first law reports, 330, 366; Federal bar of, 370, 410.
Key, Francis S., 261, 262, 368, 396, 409.
Key, Philip B., 261, 267.
Kilty, John, *Landholders' Assistant*, 334.
Kinsey, John, 104.
Kirby, Ephraim, 328; his *Reports*, 328–329.
Kitchen, John, *Courts*, 33.
Kyd, Stewart, *Corporations*, 284.

L

Labor, law of, 469–470; first law book on, 555.
*Lampleigh* v. *Braithwait*, 19.
Langdell, Christopher C., *Contracts*, 550–551.
Langhorne, Josiah, 104.
Lansing, John, 293.
Latrobe, John H. B., 458.
Laurens, John, 122.
Law, John, 368.
Law, Richard, 133.
Law Books, in England in 17th century, 32–34; in Massachusetts in 17th century, 71; in England in 18th century, 150; earliest printed in Colonies, 157–160; early American, 325–338; between 1815 and and 1910, 540–558.
Law Journals, in the United States, 338–340.
Law Libraries, in colonies, 161–164; first in United States, 339–340.
Law Professorships, 341-365.
*Law Reporter*, 547.
Law Reports, in England 17th century, 34–38; in colonial Pennsylvania, 105; in England 18th century, 149; earliest printed in colonies, 159–160; early American, 290, 328–332; views as to increase of from 1800 to 1825, 520–522; statistics of, 557.
Law Schools, early American, 341–365; between 1830 and 1860, 365 note.
Lawrence, William, 411.
Lawson, John D., *Usages*, 554.
Lawyers, reputation in England

in 17th century, 6; history of rise of in England, 23–27; in Virginia colonial, 41, 45–49; in Massachusetts colonial, 68–88; in New York colonial, 94–101; in Pennsylvania colonial, 107–110; in New Jersey colonial, 112–114; in South Carolina colonial, 120–122; in North Carolina colonial, 123–125; in Connecticut colonial, 130–134; in New Hampshire colonial, 138–139; in Maine colonial, 139; in Rhode Island colonial, 141–143; methods of education of colonial, 157–187; education in England in 18th century, 150–156; educated in Inns of Courts, 188; rules for admission of in the various states, 196–202; as signers of the declaration, members of Federal Convention and first Congress, 211; as Loyalists, 213; 1785–1800 prejudices against, 214–224; first before Supreme Court, 242; early Supreme Court bar, 245, 246, 256–262; later bars, 366–370, 408–413. See FEDERAL BAR.

Leading Cases, in 17th century, 19; in 18th century, 146–147.

Lechford, Thomas, 62, 68–69.

Lee, Charles, 246, 249, 258, 264, 267, 268, 279.

Lee, Edmund I., 369.

Lee, Richard H., 47.

Legal Education, in England in 17th century, 30–38; in colonial Virginia, 45–46; in Massachusetts, 74–77; in New York, 92; in Pennsylvania, 110; in England in 18th century, 150–156; in the Colonies in general, 157–187; in Inns of Court and colleges 188–195; in law schools, 341–365; by case-books, 556.

Légaré, Hugh S., 370, 444.

Leigh, Benjamin W., 369, 371.

Leonard, Daniel, 83.

*Leroy* v. *Tatham*, 458.

Lewger, John, 51.

Lewis, John, 47.

Lewis, Morgan, 293.

Lewis, William, 245, 248, 250.

Lewis, William D., *Interstate Commerce*, 555.

Libel, Early American law of, 236–239.

Life Insurance, law of, 456–457.

Lilly, John, *Register*, 150.

Lincoln, Abraham, 410.

Lincoln, Levi, 318, 264; Jefferson's opinion of, 273.

Litchfield Law School, 357–361.

*Littleton's Tenures*, 32.

Livermore, Arthur, 320.

Livermore, Edward St. Loe, 315.

Livermore, Mathew, 138.

Livermore, Samuel, 135, 138.

Livermore, Samuel, *Agency*, 337.

Livingston, Brockholst, 291, 296, 301, 401.

Livingston, Edward, 262; his *Batture* Case, 271–274, 297; in *Ogden* v. *Saunders*, 398; his code, 517.

Livingston, Robert R., 293.

Livingston, William, 97; letter as to law students, 167, 524.

*Livingston* v. *Jefferson*, 271.

*Livingston* v. *Van Ingen*, 392.

Lloyd, David, 104, 107, 108.

*Locke's Constitutions*, 118, 120, 122.

Logan, James, 104.

Lombard, William, *Archaiomea*, *Eisenachia*, 33.

Loomis, Arphaxed, 535.

*Loomis* v. *Eagle Life etc. Ins. Co.*, 456.

*Lopus* v. *Chandelor*, 19.

Lord, Daniel, 409; description of argument of early New York bars, 301 note; description of *Gibbons* v. *Ogden*, 394 note.

Lord, N. J., 537.

*Lord* v. *Dall*, 288, 456.

Lord Brougham's Act, 473.

Lord Campbell's Act, 449.

Lord Denman's Act, 472.

Loring, Charles G., 319, 408, 419.

Louisiana, first law reports, 366; Federal bar of, 412.
*Louisville R. R. Co.* v. *Letson*, 505.
Lowell, John, 309.
Lowther, G., 107.
Loyalists, lawyers who became, 114 note, 213.
Ludlow, Roger, 128.
*Luther* v. *Borden*, 438.
Lyman, Phineas, 131.
Lynch, Thomas, Jr., 122.
Lynde, Benjamin, 73, 75.
Lynde, Benjamin, Jr., 75.
Lynde, Samuel, 72.
Lyons, Peter, 47.

M

Magazines, American, 461 note.
Maine, colonial bar and courts, 139; first law reports, 408; Federal bar of, 413.
*Manby* v. *Scott*, 19.
Manigault, Peter, 121.
Manwood, John, *Forest Law*, 33.
*Marbury* v. *Madison*, 264–266.
March, John, *Slander*, 34.
Marchant, Henry, 143.
Marine Insurance, law of, 454.
Married Women, law of, 470–471.
Marsh, Charles, 322.
*Marsh* v. *Billings*, 462.
Marshall, John, 246; appointment as Chief Justice, 252; Pinkney's opinion of, 252; Adams' opinion of, 252 note; opinion in *Marbury* v. *Madison*, 264–266; at Burr trial, 267–269; opinion of Jefferson, 275 note; opinion of Pinkney in *The Nereide*, 280; opinion in *McCulloch* case, 380; opinion in *Steamboat* case, 394–395; view on States' rights, 400; influence on position of Supreme Court, 402–405; description of, by George Bancroft, 416; by George Ticknor, 417; death, 419; J. Q. Adams' opinion of, 420; number of opinions, 421.
*Marshall* v. *B. & O. R. R.*, 506.
*Marten's Law of Nations*, 335.
Martin, Francis X., opinion as to common law, 226; *Reports*, 330; *Pothier on Contracts*, 335; *Executors*, 336.
Martin, Luther, 258–259, 261, 267, 268, 270, 279, 379.
*Martin's Reports*, 330.
*Martin* v. *Hunter's Lessee*, 371.
Martineau, Harriet, description of Supreme Court, and Marshall in 1834, 416.
Martyn, Richard, 134.
Maryland, colonial bar in, 50–56; colonial courts in, 50; rules for admission of lawyers, 202; bar in early Supreme Court, 258–261; first law reports, 330; Federal bar of, 369, 410; description of lawyers by Story, 317.
Maryland, University of, law professorship, 356.
*Maryland* v. *B. & O. R. R.*, 485.
Mason, George, 47.
Mason, Jeremiah, 135, 243, 319.
Mason, John Thompson, 246, 410.
Massachusetts, 17th century bar in, 59; 18th century bar in, 79–88; courts in, 61, 72–74; law books in, 71; rules for admission of lawyers, 196–200; legislation as to attorneys in 1785–1790, 218; barristers and counsellors in early State, 307–308; early State bar, 304–319; first law reports, 331; Federal bar of, 368, 408; railroad law in, 485–490; corporations in, 493–500; codes in, 528–530, 534, 536–538.
Masters, Giles, 73.
Mathews, Stanley P., 440.
*Maule's Case*, 236.
Maxwell, Hugh, 304.
May, Henry, 410.
Mayer, Brantz, 458.
McClaine, Archibald, 125.
McCulloch, Henry E., 123.
*McCulloch* v. *Maryland*, account of, 379–381.

McKean, Thomas, 110.
McKinley, John, 443, 444, 501.
McLean, John, 401.
McRae, Alexander, 268.
Mechem, Floyd R., *Agency*, 554.
Mercenary Attorneys Acts, in Virginia, 41–42.
Meredith, William M., 398, 411.
Metcalf, Theron, law school of, 365; views of codes, 519, 530.
Michigan, first law reports, 408; Federal bar of, 412.
Middlebury College, law professorship, 356.
Middleton, Arthur, 122.
Midnight Judges, 252.
Mills, Elijah H., 318; law school of, 364.
Mills, Henry E., *Eminent Domain*, 553.
Minnesota, first law reports, 408.
Minot, George R., 528.
Mississippi, first law reports, 366; Federal bar of, 411.
Missouri, first law reports, 366; Federal bar of, 370, 411.
*Mitchell* v. *Reynolds*, 146.
Moland, John, 108.
Mompesson, Robert, 76, 92, 104, 112.
*Montesquieu's Esprit des Lois*, 335.
Moore, Alfred, 125, 251, 291.
Moore, A. Maurice, 125.
Moot, The, 203.
Morawetz, Victor, *Corporations*, 553.
More, Nicholas, 104.
Morecraft, John, 52.
Morehead, James T., 410, 437.
*Morrell* v. *Trenton Ins. Co.*, 456.
Morris, Gouverneur, 297.
Morris, Lewis, 92.
Morris, Phineas P., 440.
Morris, Richard, 292.
Morris, Robert H., 112.
Morton, Marcus, 318.
Morton, Perez, 318.
Morton, Thomas, 67.
Municipal Corporations, first book on, 551.

## N

Negligence, early American law of, 289; first book on, 550.
Nelson, John, 444.
Nelson, Samuel, 443.
New Hampshire, colonial bar in, 138-139; courts in, 134–138; rules for admission of lawyers, 200; early state bar, 319–321; first law reports, 330.
New Jersey, colonial bar in, 112–114; courts in, 111–112; rules for admission of lawyers, 201; statute forbidding English citations, 232; first law reports, 330; Federal bar of, 369, 413.
*New Jersey Steam Nav. Co.* v. *Merchants Bank*, 484.
Newton, Thomas, 79.
New York, colonial bar in, 94–101; courts in, 91–93; rules for admission of lawyers, 201; bar of in early Supreme Court, 262; early state bar, 292–304; first law reports, 294, 331; Federal bar of, 369, 409; codes in, 525, 532, 535–536.
*New York* v. *Miln*, 422.
Nicholas, George, as law professor, 353.
Nicholas, Philip N., 369, 371.
Nicholas, Robert C., 47.
Nicoll, Benjamin, 98.
*Norris* v. *Boston*, account of, 438–439.
North Carolina, colonial bar in, 123–125; courts in, 123; first law reports, 330; Federal bar of, 370, 413.
*North Carolina Law Repository*, 339.
North, Roger, on legal education, 151.
*Nova Statuta*, 32.
*Novae Narrationes*, 32.
Noyes, William C., 409, 532.

## O

Oakley, Thomas J., 369, 393.
Oath of Attorney, in England, 26;

in Virginia, 43; in Maryland, 53; in Massachusetts, 72, 77; in New Jersey, 113; in South Carolina, 121; in North Carolina, 123; in Georgia, 126; in Connecticut, 130; in New Hampshire, 139; in Rhode Island, 141.
O'Conor, Charles, 409.
Ogden, David, 114.
Ogden, David, B., 303; in *Sturgis* case, 378; 383; in *Ogden* v. *Saunders*, 398; in *N. Y.* v. *Miln*, 422; in *Passenger* cases, 439; 502.
*Ogden* v. *Saunders*, account of, 398–399.
Ohio, first law reports, 366; Federal bar of, 411; revised statutes of, 531.
*Old Natura Brevium*, 32.
*Old Tenures*, 32.
Oliver, Benjamin L., *Practical Conveyancing*, 334.
Oliver, Peter, 75.
*O'Reilly* v. *Morse*, 459.
Oregon, first law reports, 408.
Original Package, first use of, 398.
*Osborn* v. *Bank of the United States*, account of, 396.
Otis, Harrison Gray, 314.
Otis, James, Sr., 82; legal education of, 160.
Otis, James, Jr., 82.
Overton, John, 370.
*Overton's Reports*, 330.

P

Paca, William, 56.
Paine, Elijah, 322, 461.
Paine, Robert Treat, 82.
Palmer, John, 95.
Park, James A., *Marine Insurance*, 150.
Parker, Isaac, as law professor, 362.
Parker, Joel, 448.
Parker, William, 134, 138.
Parsons, Samuel H., 134.
Parsons, Theophilus, his law office, 169; course of law study, 181; decision on law of libel, 238; sketch of, 311–314; his library, 338.
Parsons, Theophilus, Jr., 409, 462; *Contracts*; *Mercantile Law*; *Maritime Law*, 546; *Notes and Bills*, 548.
*Parsons' Case*, 47.
*Pasley* v. *Freeman*, 147.
Patent Law, early, 289–290; from 1815 to 1860, 457–460.
Pelham, Henry, 59.
Pendleton, Edmund, 46.
Penn, John, 125.
Penn, William, trial of, 20; views on common law, 101–103.
*Penn* v. *Lord Baltimore*, 147.
*Pennington's Reports*, 330.
Pennsylvania, colonial bar in, 107–110; courts in, 103–107; rules for admission of lawyers, 202; prejudices and legislation against lawyers, 221; against common law, 232–233; bar before early Supreme Court, 245, 256–258; first law reports, 330; Federal bar of, 369, 411.
*Pennsylvania* v. *Wheeling etc. Bridge Co.*, 439.
*People* v. *Croswell*, 238.
*People* v. *Fisher*, 470.
*People* v. *Freeman*, 471.
Perkins, John, *Conveyancing*, 33.
Perry, Jairus W., *Trusts*, 551.
Peters, Richard, 246.
Petigru, James L., 412.
Phaer, Thomas, *Precedents*, 32.
*Phil. & Reading R. R.* v. *Derby*, 440, 485.
*Phil. & Trenton R. R.* v. *Simpson*, 429.
Phillips, John, 315.
Phillips, Willard, 409, 531; *Patents*, 546.
Phillips, William, *Legalis Ratio*, 31.
*Phillips* v. *Savage*, 132 note.
Pickering, John, 138, 139.
Pierce, Edward L., *Railways*, 546.
Pike, Albert, 412.

Pinckney, Charles C., 122.
Pinckney, Thomas, 122.
Pinkney, William, opinion of Marshall, 252; description of, 259–260; argues *The Nereide*, 280–284; head of bar, 367, 369; in *College* case, 375; in *McCulloch* case, 379–380; in pirate cases, 382; in *Cohens* case, 383; death, 393.
Pirate cases, 382–383.
Plaisted, John, 134.
Platt, Jonas, 301.
Plumer, William, 136; legal education of, 184, 320.
Plymouth Bay Colony, lawyers and courts in, 59–60.
Police Power, first use of phrase, 398.
Polk, James K., 370.
Pomeroy, John N., *Constitutional Law*, 549; *Equity Jurisprudence*, 554.
Porter, Alexander J., 412.
Powell, John J., *Contracts*, 150.
Pratt, Benjamin, 82, 92, 93, 204.
Prentice, E. P., *Commerce Clause*, 555.
Prentice, John, 139.
Prentiss, Sergeant S., 411.
Prescott, William, 314, 528.
Princeton College, law professorship, 355.
Prince Library, law books in, 162.
Pringle, John J., 122, 246.
Property Qualifications for voting, influence on the law, 446–447.
*Prouty* v. *Ruggles*, 458.
Pugh, George E., 411.
Pulton, Ferdinando, *Penal Statutes*, 33.

Q

Quincy, Josiah, Jr., 83.

R

Radcliff, Jacob, 524.
Railroads, history of, 475–479; development of law of, 480–492; first law books on, 490–491.
Randolph, Edmund, 246, 247, 261, 268.
Randolph, John, 46.
Randolph, John, 267, 268.
Randolph, Sir John, 46.
Randolph, Peyton, 46.
Rantoul, Robert, Jr., 469, 530.
Rastell, John, *Laws of England*, 32.
Rastell, William, *Register*, 32.
Rawle, William, 245, 256, 257, 279, 528; *Constitution*, 541.
Ray, Charles A., *Strikes*, 555.
Read, Colinson, *American Pleaders*, 333.
Read, George, 110.
Read, Joseph, 80; admission to Lincoln Inn, 189.
Receivers, first book on, 552.
Redfield, Amasa A., *Negligence*, 550.
Redfield, Isaac N., *Railways*, 547, 549.
Reed, James, 246.
Reeves, John, *History*, 150; course of reading for legal study, 155.
Reeve, Tapping, 358; *Baron and Femme*, 337; as law professor, 357.
Reno, Conrad, *Employers' Liability*, 555.
Reports, see LAW REPORTS.
*Returna Brevium*, 32.
*Rex* v. *Woodfall*, 147.
Rhode Island, colonial bar in, 141–143; courts in, 140–141; rules for admission of lawyers, 201; Federal bar of, 368, 411.
*Rhode Island* v. *Massachusetts*, 429.
Richards, David, Jr., 142.
Richardson, John, 72.
Richardson, William M., 447.
Ridgely, Robert, 54.
Robbins, Ashur, 246, 368.
Robinson, Mathew, 142.
Rodney, Caesar A., 267.
*Roccus*, 335.
Rogers, John G., 531.
Rolle, Henry, *Abridgment*, 34; advice as to study of law, 30.
Root, Erastus, 524.

Root, Jesse, 129, 134.
*Root's Reports*, 330.
*Rose* v. *Himely*, 279.
Rudyard, Thomas, 95.
Ruggles, Timothy, 82.
Russell, Chambers, 75.
Rutherforth, Thomas, *Institutes*, 150.
Rutledge, Edward, 122, 189.
Rutledge, Hugh, 122.
Rutledge, John, 121; letter as to inns of court education, 189.

## S

Saltonstall, Nathaniel, 74.
*Sampson against the Philistines*, 221.
*Scaccario*, 32.
Schouler, James, *Personal Property*, 552.
Scott, John M., 97.
Scott, William L., *Telegraphs*, 549.
*Scott* v. *Sandford*, 441.
*Scott* v. *Shepard*, 147.
*Scripture* v. *Lowell Mut. Fire Ins. Co.*, 455.
Seaman, Ezra C., 412.
Sebastian, William K., 412.
Sedgwick, Henry, view as to codes, 522.
Sedgwick, Theodore, 83.
Sedgwick, Theodore, Jr., *Damages*, 546.
Selden, H. R., 459.
*Semayne's Case*, 19.
Sergeant, John, 369, 396, 411, 414, 433, 461, 502.
Sergeant, Peter, 74.
Sergeant, Thomas, *Foreign Attachment*, 337; *Constitutional Law*, 541.
Serjeants, in England, 23; in New Jersey, 113.
Sewall, David, 139.
Sewall, Jonathan, 82.
Sewall, Samuel, 74, 75.
Sewall, Stephen, 75.
Seward, William H., 409, 437, 440, 458, 472.
*Seymour* v. *McCormick*, 454, 459.
Shaw, Lemuel, 318; moulder of common law, 448, 452; influence on railroad law, 455; 456, 462, 469, 470, 471, 480–483, 529.
Shearman, Thomas G., *Negligence*, 550.
Sheldon, Henry N., *Subrogation*, 554.
*Shelley's Case*, 19.
Sheppard, William, *Common Law*, 34; *Touchstone*, 34; *Corporations*, 34.
Sherman, Roger, 133.
Sherman, Roger Minott, 323.
Shields, James, 410.
Shippen, Edward, 110, 232.
Shirley, William, 82.
Simms, Charles, 261, 409.
*Slade's Case*, 19.
Slavery, cases involving, 396–397; law books on, 547.
Smith, Jeremiah, 319.
Smith, Oliver H., 412.
Smith, Richard Morris, 297.
Smith, Robert, 123.
Smith, William, 92.
Smith, William, 95; course of legal study advised by, 170.
Smith, William, Jr., 97, 524.
*Smith* v. *Swormstadt*, 441.
*Smith* v. *Turner*, account of, 438–439.
Smythe, Alexander, 383.
*Snowden* v. *Noah*, 462.
Sodality, The, 203.
Soulé, Pierre, 412.
South Carolina, colonial bar in, 120–122; courts in, 119–120; rules for admission of lawyers, 202; first law reports, 330; Federal bar of, 370, 412.
Southard, Samuel L., 413, 422.
Spelman, Henry, *Glossary*, 33; views on law, 6.
Spencer, Ambrose, 291, 301, 414.
Spencer, John C., 304, 409, 524.
*Spencer's Case*, 19.
Sprague, Peleg, 319.
St. Germain, Christopher, *Doctor and Student*, 32.
Stanberry, Henry, 411, 441.

Stanton, Edwin M., 411, 439, 444, 459.
Staples, Seth R., law school of, 364.
State Trials, in England, 20–21, 147.
States' Rights, 371, 381, 384–391, 400, 413, 414, 418, 438–439.
Statham, Nicholas, *Abridgment*, 32.
Statutes, publication of colonial, 161; codification of, see CODES. See UNCONSTITUTIONAL STATUTES.
Staunford, William, *Pleas*, 33.
Stearns, Asahel, as law professor, 362, 528, 529; *Real Actions*, 542.
*Stetson* v. *Mass. Mutual Ins. Co.*, 288.
Stevens, Thaddeus, 458, 459.
*Stevens* v. *Gladding*, 461.
Stiles, Ezra, on common law, 14; as to library of M. Griswold, 163; describes U. S. Circuit Court, 244; plans law professorship, 341–342, and Appendix I; his views on William and Mary Professorship, 346; as to Jefferson, 346 note.
Stiles, Ezra, Jr., legal education of, 181.
*Stimpson* v. *Baltimore etc. R. R.*, 458.
Stimson, Frederic C., *Statute Law*, 554.
Stockton, Richard, 114, 261.
Stone, Thomas, 56.
Storer, Bellamy, 411.
Story, Joseph, views on Coke, 175; appoints barristers in Circuit Court, 243; description of early Supreme Court bar, 257–258; describes Luther Martin, 259; argues *Fletcher* v. *Peck*, 271, 317; Jefferson's opinion of, 273; appointment on Supreme Court, 274; founder of admiralty law, 279, 280; sketch of, 315–318; his *Pleadings*, 333; opinion in *Martin* v. *Hunter*, 371; on attacks on Supreme Court, 387; letter as to *Steamboat* case, 393; opinion of Taney as a young lawyer, 397; views of *Cherokee* case, 415; his *Constitution*, 418; international law opinions, 420; views on *Charles River Bridge* case, 424–427; description of J. Q. Adams, 430; decision in *Prigg* case, 431; describes *Vidal* case, 434; resignation and views, 435–436; marine insurance law, 454, 457; copyright law, 461; views of codes, 523, 528, 530; *Bailments*, 544; *Constitutional Law*, 545; *Conflict of Laws*, 5; *Equity Pleading*, *Equity Jurisprudence*, *Agency*, *Partnership*, *Bills of Exchange*, 545.
Stoughton, William, 72, 74, 75.
Street Railways, law of, 452–453.
Strong, Caleb, 83, 318.
*Stuart* v. *Laird*, 267.
*Sturgis* v. *Crowninshield*, account of, 377–379.
Suffolk County Bar, early records of, 83–85, 88, 196–200.
Sullivan, Francis S., *Lectures*, 156.
Sullivan, George, 320, 368.
Sullivan, James, 139; law books sold to, 164; condition of Bar in his practise, 204–205; Jefferson's opinion of, 273; sketch of, 309; *Land Titles*, 325, 334.
Sullivan, John, 139.
Sullivan, William, 315, 470.
Sumner, Charles, 412; describes Federal Bar in 1834, 418; 462.
Supreme Court of United States, first, 242; changes in early years, 251; additional judges, 254; power to decide statutes unconstitutional, 264–266; picture of, in 1815, 281; first reporter, 331–332; legislative attacks on, 385–388, 413; changes in judges, 401; terms of, 402; status of court under Marshall, 403–406; sale of reports of, 405; Federal bar of, 366–371, 408–412; description of, in 1834, by H. Martineau, 416; practise in constitutional cases, 423; change in policy, 427–428; additional judges, 443–444; change in personnel, 1830–1860, 443; patent

law cases in, 458–460; corporation cases in, 501–506.
*Sutton Hospital Case*, 19.
Swann, Thomas, 261, 368, 410.
Swayne, Noah H., 411.
Swift, Zephaniah, 323; *System of Laws*, 336; *Evidence*, 337.
*Swift* v. *Tyson*, 409, 432.
Swinburne, Henry, *Wills*, 33.

T

Talcott, Samuel A., 304.
Taney, Roger B., 369; legal education of, 183; opinion of Pinkney, 260; first case in Supreme Court, 397; in *Etting* case, 397; in *Brown* v. *Maryland*, 398; as Chief Justice, 418, 421; Curtis' opinion of, 422; decision in *Charles River Bridge* case, 425–426; decision in *Luther* v. *Borden*, 438; decision in *Genesee Chief*, 440; Attorney-General, 444; opinion in *Bank of Augusta* case, 504.
Taylor, Creed, law school of, 364.
Taylor, John, *Constitution*, 542.
*Taylor* v. *Carpenter*, 462.
*Taylor's Reports*, 330.
Tazewell, L. W., 274, 368, 369, 399.
Telegraph, law of, 450–452.
Tennessee, first law reports, 366; Federal bar of, 370.
Texas, first law reports, 408.
Thacher, Oxenbridge, 82.
Thayer, James B., *Evidence*, 555.
*The Antelope*, 396.
*The Marianna Flora*, 397.
*The Nereide*, 262, 280.
Theloal, Simon, *Writs*, 33.
Thomas, Nathaniel, 73.
Thompson, Richard W., 412.
Thompson, Seymour D., *Stockholders, Directors*, 553; *Electricity*, 554; *Corporations*, 555.
Thompson, Smith, 291, 401, 443.
Thomson, Stevens, 46.
*Thomson* v. *Winchester*, 462.
Thornton, Matthew, 135.
*Thorogood's Case*, 19.
Thoroughgood, Cyprian, 51.
*Thurlow* v. *Massachusetts*, 436.
Ticknor, George, description of Supreme Court in 1815 by, 281; description of Marshall, 417; views as to codes, 522; views of slavery, 431 note.
Tidd, William, *Practice*, 150.
Tilghman, Edward, 245, 248, 250, 256, 257, 279.
Tilghman, William, 246.
Todd, Thomas, 401.
Tompkins, Daniel D., 301.
Torts, early law of, 289; law of, 449–450.
Toulmin, H., *Criminal Law*, 336.
Tracy, Uriah, 323.
Trademarks, law of, 462.
Transylvania University, law professorship, 353.
*Trevett* v. *Weeden*, 143, 218.
Trimble, Robert, 401.
Troup, Robert, 296.
Trowbridge, Edmund, 75, 81; library of, 162.
Trumbull, John, 129.
Trumbull, Lyman, 410.
Tucker, St. George, account of Virginia bar, 48; his *Blackstone*, 336; as law professor, 346, 371.
Tudor, John, 95.
*Twyne's Case*, 19.
Tyler, John, 47; opinion of common law, 225–226; opinion on *Batture* case, 274.
Tyler, Royall, 322.
*Tyler's Reports*, 330.
Tyson, Job R., 412, 440.

U

*Ultra Vires*, 506.
Unconstitutional Statutes, power of Supreme Court to decide, 265–266 note; 385–387.
*United States Law Journal*, 547.
*U. S.* v. *Amistad*, 429–430.
*U. S.* v. *Brigantine William*, 277.

*U. S.* v. *Klintock*, 383.
Updike, Daniel, 142, 143.

V

Van Buren, John, 439.
Van Buren, Martin, 304; as to possible appointment as judge of Supreme Court, 390.
Van Cortlandt, Stephen, 92.
Vanfleet, John M., *Collateral Attack*, 555.
Van Ness, William W., 301.
Van Ness, William P., 524.
Van Schaack, Peter, 97.
*Vanstophorst* v. *Maryland*, 247.
Van Vechten, Abraham, 297.
Varick, Richard, 297, 524.
Varnum, James M., 143.
*Vattel*, 335.
*Vaux* v. *Newman*, 19.
Vermont, rules for admission of lawyers, 202; early State bar, 321–322; first law reports, 330.
Verplanck, Gulian C., *Contracts*, 542.
*Vetera Statuta*, 33.
*Vidal* v. *Philadelphia*, account of, 433–435.
Viner, Charles, *Digest*, 150.
Virginia, colonial bar in, 41, 45–49; colonial courts in 40, 44; rules for admission of lawyers, 202; resolutions as to common law in Federal courts, 231; bar before early Supreme Court, 246, 261; Judge Tyler's opinion of, 274; first law reports, 330; Federal bar of, 369.
Virginia, University of, law professorship, 364.
*Vose* v. *Eagle Life etc. Ins. Co.*, 456.

W

Walcott, Samuel B., 531.
Walker, Leroy P., 412.
Walker, Robert J., 411, 429.
Walker, Timothy, *American Law*, 546.
Walton, George, 126.
Walton, John, 142.
War of 1812, effect on American law, 275–286.
Ward, Artemas, 315.
Ward, Nathaniel, 64.
Ward, Thomas, 142.
Warden, John, 261.
*Ware* v. *Hylton*, 247.
*Waring* v. *Clarke*, 437.
Washburn, Emory, *Real Property*, *Easements*, 548.
Washington, Bushrod, 251, 291, 401.
Washington, City of, in early days, 254–256.
*Washington's Reports*, 330.
Watson, John, 73.
Watson, P. H., 459.
Wayne, James M., 443.
Weare, Meschech, 134; library of, 163.
Webster, Daniel, views on Coke, 176; legal education of, 185–187; head of bar, 367–368; in *College* case, 372–377; in *McCulloch* case, 379; in *Steamboat* case, 393–395; in *Bank* case, 396; in *Ogden* v. *Saunders*, 398; letters as to *Dandridge* case, 399–400; in *Cherokee* case, 414, 419; in *Charles River Bridge* case, 423–426, 429; argues *Vidal* case, 433–435, 436, 437, 438; account of *Passenger* cases, 438–439; account of changes in Supreme Court, 443; in *Goodyear* case, 458; in *Wheaton* case, 461; view of codes, 519; death, 413.
Webster, Noah, 133, 323.
Wells, John, 303.
Wentworth, John, 135.
West, William, *Symboleography*, 33.
West, Benjamin, 139.
*Western Law Journal*, 547.
*Western Tel. Co.* v. *Magnetic Tel Co.*, 451.
Wharton, Francis, *Conflict of Law*, 551.
Wharton, Thomas J., 528.
Wheaton, Henry, 304, 368, 398;

*Maritime Captures*, 335; 524; *International Law*, 546.
*Wheaton* v. *Peters*, 419, 461.
Wheeler, Jacob D., *Slavery*, 547.
White, Albert S., 412.
White, Alexander, 412.
White, Edward D., 412.
Whitman, Benjamin, 318.
Wickham, John, 248, 261, 268, 274.
Wickliffe, Charles A., 262, 410.
Wigmore, John H., *Evidence*, 556.
William and Mary College, law professorship, 343–345.
Williams, Elisha, 304.
Williams, Ephraim, 331.
Williams, Thomas S., 323, 448.
Wilson, James, his law students, 167; 242, 251; his lectures, 336; as law professor, 346–349.
*Wilson* v. *Rousseau*, 458.
Winder, William H., 261, 369.
Wingate, Edmund, *Common Law*, 34.
Winthrop, John, 59, 63.
Winthrop, John, Jr., 128.
Winthrop, Wait, 74, 75.
*Winthrop* v. *Lechmere*, 131.
Wirt, William, 261; opinion of Marshall's argument, 248; opinion of Pinkney, 260; at Burr trial, 268; in *Batture* case, 274; attorney-general, 366–367, 371; in *College* case, 372–375; in *McCulloch* case, 379; letter as to Kent, 389; argues *Steamboat* case, 393–394; in *Antelope* case, 396; in *Brown* v. *Maryland*, 398; in *Ogden* v. *Saunders*, 398; in *Dandridge* case, 399; in *Cherokee* case, 414; in *Charles River Bridge* case, 423; death, 410.
Wisconsin, first law reports, 408.
Wolcott, Oliver, 323.
Wolcott, Roger, 129.
Women, as lawyers, in England, 26; in Maryland, 52.
Wood, George, 369, 409.
Wood, Thomas, *Institutes*, 150.
Woodbridge, William, 412.
Woodbury, Levi, 443.
Wooddeson, Richard, *Jurisprudence*, 150.
Woodworth, John, 301, 524.
*Worcester* v. *Georgia*, account of, 415.
Worrall, John, *Bibliotheca*, 155.
Worthington, John, 82.
Wragg, William, 121.
Wright, John C., 396.
*Wright* v. *Malden etc. Ry.*, 453.
Wyche, William, *Fines*, 334; *Supreme Court Practise*, 336.
Wyer, David, 139.
Wyman, Bruce, *Railroad Rate Regulation*, 556.
Wythe, George, 47; as first law professor, 343–345.
*Wythe's Reports*, 330.

## Y

Yale, Gregory, *Mining*, 548.
Yale College, law professorship, 354.
Yale Law School, 354.
Yates, Joseph C., 301.
Yates, Robert, 98, 292.
Yazoo Frauds, 270 note.
*Year Books*, 34.
Yeates, Jasper, 246.

## Z

*Zenger's Case*, 236.